Windows® 2000 Active Directory

Black Book

Adam Wood

President and CEO
Keith Weiskamp

Publisher
Steve Sayre

Acquisitions Editor
Charlotte Carpentier

Development Editor
Michelle Stroup

Marketing Specialist
Tracy Schofield

Project Editor
Greg Balas

Technical Reviewer
Rob Mcfarlane

Production Coordinator
Laura Wellander

Cover Designer
Jody Winkler

Layout Designer
April Nielsen

Windows® 2000 Active Directory Black Book

The Coriolis Group, LLC
14455 N. Hayden Road
Suite 220
Scottsdale, Arizona 85260

(480) 483-0192
FAX (480) 483-0193
www.coriolis.com

Library of Congress Cataloging-in-Publication Data
Wood, Adam, 1978-
    Windows 2000 active directory black book / Adam Wood.
      p. cm.
    Includes index.
    ISBN 1-57610-256-4
    1. Microsoft Windows (Computer file) 2. Operating systems (Computers) 3. Directory services
(Computer network technology) I. Title.
QA76.76.O63 W6553 2000
004.4'769--dc21   00-058994
                                            CIP

Printed in the United States of America
10 9 8 7 6 5 4 3 2 1

CORIOLIS™

The Coriolis Group, LLC • 14455 North Hayden Road, Suite 220 • Scottsdale, Arizona 85260

Dear Reader:

Coriolis Technology Press was founded to create a very elite group of books: the ones you keep closest to your machine. Sure, everyone would like to have the Library of Congress at arm's reach, but in the real world, you have to choose the books you rely on every day *very* carefully.

To win a place for our books on that coveted shelf beside your PC, we guarantee several important qualities in every book we publish. These qualities are:

- *Technical accuracy*—It's no good if it doesn't work. Every Coriolis Technology Press book is reviewed by technical experts in the topic field, and is sent through several editing and proofreading passes in order to create the piece of work you now hold in your hands.

- *Innovative editorial design*—We've put years of research and refinement into the ways we present information in our books. Our books' editorial approach is uniquely designed to reflect the way people learn new technologies and search for solutions to technology problems.

- *Practical focus*—We put only pertinent information into our books and avoid any fluff. Every fact included between these two covers must serve the mission of the book as a whole.

- *Accessibility*—The information in a book is worthless unless you can find it quickly when you need it. We put a lot of effort into our indexes, and heavily cross-reference our chapters, to make it easy for you to move right to the information you need.

Here at The Coriolis Group we have been publishing and packaging books, technical journals, and training materials since 1989. We're programmers and authors ourselves, and we take an ongoing active role in defining what we publish and how we publish it. We have put a lot of thought into our books; please write to us at **ctp@coriolis.com** and let us know what you think. We hope that you're happy with the book in your hands, and that in the future, when you reach for software development and networking information, you'll turn to one of our books first.

Keith Weiskamp
President and CEO

Jeff Duntemann
VP and Editorial Director

Look for these related books from The Coriolis Group:

Windows 2000 System Administration Black Book
by Stu Sjourwerman, Barry Shilmover, and James Michael Stewart

Windows 2000 TCP/IP Black Book
by Ian McLean

Windows 2000 Systems Programming Black Book
by Al Williams

Windows 2000 Registry Little Black Book
by Nathan Wallace

Windows 2000 Security Little Black Book
by Ian McLean

Windows 2000 Reducing TCO Little Black Book
by Robert E. Simanski

Windows 2000 Mac Support Little Black Book
by Gene Steinberg and Pieter Paulson

Windows 2000 Professional Upgrade Little Black Book
by Nathan Wallace

Windows 2000 Professional Advanced Configuration and Implementation
by Morten Strunge Nielsen

Also recently published by Coriolis Technology Press:

Exchange 2000 Server Black Book
by Marcus Goncalves

XHTML Black Book
by Steven Holzner

For Jo....

About the Author

Adam Wood is an independent computer consultant who has been living, breathing, and working with computers for the vast majority of his life, and has been working with what is now called Windows 2000 since late 1998. His varied experience in the computer industry includes metadirectory development, and systems and database support in the City of London. He now works as an independent consultant and trainer specializing in Windows 2000 and Active Directory.

Adam is a Microsoft Certified Trainer (MCT), Microsoft Certified Systems Engineer (MCSE), and Microsoft Most Valuable Professional (MVP) for Windows 2000. He holds a Batchelor of Arts degree in Mathematics from Cambridge University, and lives in Cambridge, England. His personal Web site is **www.adamwood.com**, and you can contact him by email at **adam@adamwood.com**.

Acknowledgments

Even though there's only one name on the cover—and one person to blame for errors and omissions—there is a dedicated team behind this book, without whom, an author would be free to agonize over so much more than just the writing.

Among the many people behind the scenes, I would especially like to thank Acquisitions Editor Charlotte Carpentier at The Coriolis Group for offering me the chance to write this book, Rob Mcfarlane for tech reviewing the book and for keeping me honest by demanding awkward details, and most of all Greg Balas the Project Editor at The Coriolis Group for bringing the whole thing together. I'm sure readers will also join me in thanking Michelle Stroup the Development Editor at The Coriolis Group for her cheerful efforts in developmental editing the book, and Bonnie Smith for copyediting the book and keeping the chapters readable. In addition, I would like to thank Laura Wellander, the Production Coordinator, April Nielsen, the Layout Designer, and Jody Winkler, the Cover Designer at The Coriolis Group, and James Vincent for typesetting the book. Also, thanks to Jill Greeson for proofreading, and Tim Griffin for indexing.

In addition, I would also like to thank Andrej Budja, David Rowbory, and my brother, Rupert, for all their support and helpful comments during the writing of this book. Also, I must thank my mother, Molly, for her support and belief in me.

Finally though, my greatest debt of thanks must go to my girlfriend, Jo, without whose support I wouldn't have finished this book with my health intact, and without whose willingness to learn too much Active Directory, this book wouldn't have been nearly so readable and accessible.

Contents at a Glance

Table of Contents

Chapter 3
Domain Name Systems (DNS) 67

Chapter 12
Understanding Group Policy 293

Introduction

Thanks for buying the *Windows 2000 Active Directory Black Book*. Active Directory is probably the most central, complex, and important new feature introduced in Windows 2000. It is Microsoft's first full-service directory service and provides a central repository for user, computer, and group information on your network.

Windows 2000 is itself a complex subject—some say there's too much to fit in one person's head—and Active Directory is the most important new feature introduced by Windows 2000. It is also the new feature that causes the greatest shift in mindset as to how you design, manage, and troubleshoot a network.

Active Directory is central to the operations of a Windows 2000 network, it provides authorization, security services, management capabilities, the ability to delegate administrative tasks, and understanding use of other services such as DNS, is vital to making your network run efficiently. For these reasons, if you buy and thoroughly read only one book on Windows 2000, make sure it's a book on Active Directory (and make sure it's this one)!

Is This Book for You?

The *Windows 2000 Active Directory Black Book* was written with the intermediate or advanced user in mind. Among the topics that are covered are the following:

- Fundamental Active Directory Concepts
- Managing Active Directory domains and domain controllers, including by ADSI Scripting
- Group Policy for user and computer settings management
- Migrating to Windows 2000 Active Directory

How to Use This Book

Experience has taught me that people rarely pick up technical books and read them cover-to-cover in one go. In particular, books such as this one in the Black Book series are designed so they are accessible in a non-linear manner, with dipping into and out of chapters as necessary.

That said, however, there is a basic level of understanding necessary to become *au fait* with the operation of Active Directory. Because of this, my advice is to read the "In Depth" sections of first nine chapters of the book in order, before dipping into and out of the rest.

In fact, the book is divided into three main areas:

- *Chapters 1 to 9*—Cover the basic concepts underlying Active Directory, and how to install Active Directory, and implement core service.

- *Chapters 10 to 17*—Cover Active Directory operations such as the maintenance of domain controllers, and the creation of users and groups.

- *Chapters 18 to 22*—Cover more advanced topics including design issues, and interoperability with other directory services.

Because Active Directory is a large, new subject, you should not rush into deploying it in a live environment. Although the fourth chapter of this book deals with installing Active Directory, you should read at least the first nine chapters before creating a test environment, and ideally, the whole book before contemplating a live deployment.

This is for the simple reason that mistakes are easiest dealt with by not making them in the first place, and many of the common errors that I've seen in Windows 2000 networks come about from an administrator simply not knowing about a piece of functionality.

The *Black Book* Philosophy

Written by experienced professionals, Coriolis *Black Books* provide immediate solutions to global programming and administrative challenges, helping you complete specific tasks, especially critical ones that are not well documented in other books. The *Black Book*'s unique two-part chapter format—thorough technical overviews followed by practical immediate solutions—is structured to help you use your knowledge, solve problems, and quickly master complex technical issues to become an expert. By breaking down complex topics into easily manageable components, our format helps you quickly find what you're looking for, with the code you need to make it happen.

I welcome your feedback on this book. You can either email The Coriolis Group at **ctp@coriolis.com**, or email me directly at **adam@adamwood.com**. Errata, updates, and more are available at **www.adamwood.com** and **www.coriolis.com**.

Chapter 1

Introduction to Active Directory

In Depth

The Active Directory is the most important part of any Windows 2000 network. It's a centralized store of information about your network and its resources, such as users, computers, and printers, which allows administrators to manage these resources and users to find information.

Windows 2000 (formerly known as Windows NT 5) introduces many new or improved technologies that simplify network management and common tasks that either rely on, or are enhanced by, Active Directory. For example, Group Policy is a replacement for Windows NT system policy used to implement client settings, such as desktop appearance, on a networkwide basis. Group Policy allows multiple levels of settings to be defined that are applied based upon a user's location in Active Directory. To maximize the benefit of these technologies and to keep your network running smoothly, it's important to fully understand Active Directory and what it can do for you.

This chapter will introduce you to the concepts underlying Active Directory and direct you to some of the key administrative tools. The tools and topics introduced here are covered in greater detail in subsequent chapters.

What Is a Directory Service?

Directory services are not a new concept in computing. In fact, directory services aren't even new to Windows NT-based operating systems with the release of Windows 2000. The Windows NT 4 directory service is responsible for replicating account information from the primary domain controller (PDC) to backup domain controllers (BDCs).

Before we consider exactly what Active Directory is, it's important to understand what directory services are and what they can do. Directories are all around us in our everyday lives. One striking example of a directory service is the phone book, otherwise known as the telephone directory.

Fundamentally, a directory service is a mechanism that stores information and makes it available, so the book itself is the store of information in a telephone directory, and the alphabetical indexing allows you to search the directory. Within the analogy, other features are found from computer-based directory services. When you look up a number in the phone book or talk to the operator, a security mechanism is in place that prevents you from seeing unlisted numbers, or perform a reverse lookup by searching for the owner of a particular number.

Also, the phone company stores more information about each user than just a name, number, and address. Another attribute associated with each user is information such as bank details and account balance. Though one could tell the local phone company to change the bank account from which it takes one's payments, it's unlikely to respond to polite requests to change one's outstanding bill down to zero. Thus, the attributes of a person's account have varying levels of security from world-readable on someone's name and number, to some items that are modifiable by the individual, and to others that can't change directly, or perhaps to some that the customers don't even know about.

On computer networks, full-service directory services are thus intended as central stores for all useful information about the objects that comprise the network. These objects could represent user accounts, computers, groups of users, printers, or virtually any other item you could wish to address.

What Is Active Directory?

Active Directory is Microsoft's implementation of a full-service directory service in Windows 2000. It provides a single location to efficiently manage resources on a network. The term *Active Directory domain* is also used to describe a Windows 2000 domain.

The directory stores information about objects, such as users, printers, groups, and computers, on your network. These objects are organized into containers, such as Organizational Units, which allow you to break down the long lists often associated with Windows NT 4's management tools. They also let you devolve power within your network by granting specific rights to users and groups over objects, based upon where the objects reside within your Organizational Unit structure.

A common complaint about Windows NT 4 is the reliance on a small group of all-powerful accounts that are members of the Administrators' group. Active Directory allows you to implement a better security policy with, hopefully, fewer people having full administrative privileges, and with a greater level of delegation to junior administrators or to help desk staff.

Users and groups of users can be assigned rights to see and modify portions of the directory, similar to the telephone directory example. For example, you could let everyone see all the information stored about themselves, all details of other employees, except their pay details, and you could give them the right to modify all information about themselves, except payroll. In addition, the accounts department may have rights to view and modify payroll data.

Payroll is just an example—by default, the Active Directory doesn't have fields defined for pay information, but it's possible to extend what is known as the *schema*, which defines what data can be stored about objects within Active Directory. Other examples include adding a photograph field to user objects or even creating new objects to represent other components of your network or organization, such as the routers on your local area network (LAN).

Benefits

Active Directory is also responsible for making the information available via searches and to applications. Users could quickly find a color duplex laser printer or the home address of a coworker from the Search option on the Start menu.

Active Directory servers are also the LDAP servers. Support for LDAP standard versions 2 and 3 means the Active Directory can field queries from any LDAP-enabled application. Many mail clients, such as Outlook Express and Netscape Mail, support searching LDAP servers for user email addresses. Also, support for LDAP enhances interoperability between Active Directory and the many other LDAP-compliant servers available.

The basic unit of partition within Active Directory is the domain. Active Directory domains correspond in many ways to Windows NT 4 domains. The data for the domain is stored on domain controllers, and clients connect to these domain controllers for authentication to log into the network. This single signon mechanism is then used to allow access to a variety of resources within the domain and access to any trusting domains, without the need for users to keep entering and reentering passwords.

Improvements for Administration

Active Directory offers many improvements over the administrative features of Windows NT 4 and enables other benefits, as listed here:

- *Single point of administrations to all users, groups, computers, and printers on your network*—Active Directory allows you to manage desktop settings for users and even deploy software, including applications and service packs, to subsets of users or computers.

- *Single signon*—This means that users should only have to log on once to be able to use resources that accept Active Directory credentials. Support for a single signon in this way is a requirement for applications displaying the Windows 2000 logo.

- *Group Policy*—This replaces NT 4's system policy and allows for flexible, delegated management of users' desktop environments. By combining a number of policy settings into a group, known as a Group Policy Object

(GPO), and assigning these GPOs to specific portions of the directory, you can configure settings, such as software deployment, application settings, and background wallpaper, for users within the directory.

- *Scalability*—Active Directory has been demonstrated supporting 100 million objects. This contrasts with perhaps 40,000 user objects, causing unacceptable performance degradation in Windows NT 4 domains. Enhanced scalability means enterprises will need fewer domains, which makes management easier.

- *Standards support*—Support, including LDAP versions 2 and 3, means that Active Directory can interoperate with other directory services.

- *Security enhancements over Windows NT 4*—These enhancements, including the use of Kerberos version 5 as an authentication protocol and organizationwide recovery for Windows 2000's encrypting file system support. In addition, the Active Directory itself is protected with access control lists at the attribute level.

- *Extensibility*—By defining new properties and objects within the schema that defines Active Directory, you can expand the scope of the data stored to include anything required by custom or third-party applications.

Improvements for Users

Users will also benefit from networks running Active Directory and Windows 2000. Publishing objects in a single directory for the entire enterprise makes it easier for users to find email address or telephone numbers of coworkers or external contacts.

When information changes, such as an employee marrying and changing her surname, having a centralized information store means that the change only has to be made in one place. If applications use the Active Directory, then, because they don't duplicate the information themselves, they'll see the updates as soon as Active Directory is updated, and there won't be any need to manually make the same change five or 10 times.

Not all applications that maintain databases support Active Directory, and your current versions of applications never will. It is, however, possible to keep information synchronized between disparate sources, such as Active Directory, a legacy payroll application, and a human resources application, with what is known as a *metadirectory*.

Literally, a metadirectory is a second-order directory, and the term is used to mean a directory of directories that brings together information from multiple sources and uses it to synchronize them, so for example, changing a user's surname in the payroll application could automatically change it in the associated Active Directory user account. We'll explore metadirectories in the final chapter, Chapter 22.

Of course, the real driver behind any new technology, such as Active Directory, is the desire to reduce waste. By making administration quicker, processes more efficient, and users more productive, Active Directory is designed to save businesses money.

To maximize that cost saving and make it as easy as possible to administer, it's important to fully understand the capabilities and the limitations of Active Directory. Before we introduce the makeup of the directory itself, we must first see where Active Directory fits into the network.

The Role of DNS

The *Domain Naming System (DNS)* has an important part to play in Active Directory. One basic requirement for any truly useful global directory infrastructure that allows information to be shared between organizations is the unique naming of these directories.

Directory services, such as X.500, employ a global name registration system whereby companies centrally register their X.500 directory name before implementing an X.500 directory, and Microsoft could have gone a similar route with Active Directory. However, such a system would be expensive to run and would lead to debates and arguments over who gets the best directory name, similar to those we have seen over the registration of DNS names and "domain squatting," whereby people speculatively register the names of large companies to make a quick profit by selling them later on.

With the emergence of Transmission Control Protocol/Internet Protocol (TCP/IP) as the global networking standard, principally because of the Internet, and the ubiquity of organizations having unique DNS names, such as **microsoft.com**, the design decision to name Active Directory domains in the DNS style seems an inspired one.

DNS as a Locator Service

Not only does Active Directory use the existing unique DNS namespace that allows easy location of directories by name, but it also uses DNS internally to locate resources by registering several special service location and alias records. These can then be resolved into the IP address of the "best" domain controller in a given circumstance, which usually means the closest.

The Windows 2000-style logon using DNS to locate nearby domain controllers is more efficient than the Windows NT 4-style Network Basic Input/Output System (NetBIOS) broadcasts or WINS queries used to find a domain controller; it's a little like asking the barman to point out the stranger you're meeting for a drink rather than walking into the bar and loudly announcing your presence to one and all. DNS hasn't, however, replaced NetBIOS completely because Windows 2000 obviously maintains support for all existing client operating systems. To this end, Windows 2000 domains also have a NetBIOS or downlevel domain name equivalent to a Windows NT 4 domain name.

TIP: *The term downlevel is widely used by Microsoft when talking about Windows 2000 and, depending on context, it refers to some form of an earlier version. For example a downlevel domain controller is a domain controller running Windows NT 4 (or earlier), and a downlevel domain is one with an NT 4 or earlier Primary Domain Controller (PDC). A downlevel client is anything other than a Windows 2000 (or later) computer, and downlevel computer/domain names are NetBIOS names.*

The Structure of Active Directory

To work effectively with Active Directory, you must understand both its logical and physical structures. The logical structure allows you to arrange objects in hierarchies and within domains, primarily for administrative reasons. The main components of logical structure are domains, which can be arranged into trees and forests. Within domains, objects can be grouped within Organizational Units. Logical structure is considered in greater detail in Chapters 5 and 6.

When working with Active Directory, you should also consider the physical structure of your network. To help processes run smoothly and efficiently, mechanisms exist to allow you to store information about the physical composition of your network. Having such information published in a central place allows software to optimize network flow, for example by clients, authenticating against nearby domain controllers.

The fundamental unit of the Active Directory is the domain, which is similar in scope to a Windows NT 4 domain.

Domains

When you install Active Directory on the first server in your network or upgrade a Windows NT 4 PDC to Windows 2000, you create an Active Directory domain.

The *domain* itself is physically hosted in database files on a number of Windows 2000 domain controllers. You're able to make changes to the information in the domain database on any of these domain controllers, and these changes are then replicated to other domain controllers within the same domain.

The replication topology used by Windows 2000 is known as *multi-master repli-cation*, because all Windows 2000 domain controllers are able to commit changes to the information within the directory. This contrasts with the single master scheme employed within the Windows NT 4 Security Accounts Manager (SAM), where one domain controller is designated as primary, and only the PDC is able to commit changes to the database.

Although the multi-master model provides greater fault tolerance and removes the reliance on a single point of failure, it introduces questions of consistency. The details of replication are in Chapter 8, but it's important to realize that, in general, domain controllers in the same domain won't have exactly the same Active Directory data at any given moment, although if you leave the network for long enough without making changes, then the information on all domain controllers will converge. For a single building and default settings, this convergence time will most likely be on the order of 15 minutes.

Active Directory domains can contain downlevel domain controllers in addition to those running Windows 2000. However, Windows NT domain controllers don't support Active Directory, so objects, such as users and groups, must be replicated in a compatible manner. Specifically, this means that you're restricted to running Windows 2000 in a compatibility mode known as *mixed mode*.

While in mixed mode, certain new features, such as the nesting of security groups, aren't available, and though downlevel BDCs still exist on the network, you must still consider the performance limitations of the SAM that restrict you to perhaps 40,000 users per domain. If no downlevel domain controllers are in a domain, it can easily be converted to a native mode domain, which then enables support for the new features, such as nested groups, that are incomprehensible to the storage mechanisms used on Windows NT domain controllers.

Besides domain controllers, Active Directory domains can contain information about any resource you choose to add (and if no built-in support exists for the type of object you wish to add, you can extend the Active Directory schema to let you do so). Some of the most common items on your network about which you'll want to store information include users, computers, and groups of users.

Objects

In Active Directory, all data is stored within *objects*. Some simple examples of objects are Organizational Units, user accounts, and computer accounts. Each object in the directory is an instance of a particular class of object, and the class of an object determines what information can be stored in its properties.

For example, a user account that allows a worker to access the network is of class User and has a wide variety of properties where you store information such as account name, password, full name, address, and telephone number.

By defining new properties or creating new classes of objects, you're able to extend the schema and increase the scope of information stored within Active Directory. A variety of vendors produce software that extends the schema. For example, Cisco has an application to allow you to add your routers to Active Directory, and Microsoft Exchange 2000 extends the schema and uses Active Directory as its directory service.

Objects in the directory actually store the information within their properties. The properties available depend on what's known as the *class* or *type* of the object. All objects must have at least a name, which allows them to be addressed uniquely within the directory.

One key property of an object is whether or not it's a container, which is to say whether or not it can contain child objects. The most basic class of container objects is simply known as *Container* (a capital *C* will distinguish the specific object class from the general concept of containers). By using containers, you can create a logical structure with Active Directory to gather together objects for administrative purposes.

When you first install Active Directory, a number of Containers are created to hold built-in users and groups, as well as computer accounts. These Containers are required as a default location for users, groups, and computer accounts added with Windows NT 4's User Manager for Domains, and other tools, that don't recognize the logical structure within Active Directory. Probably the most useful container object is the Organizational Unit.

Organizational Units

Organizational Units (OUs) are descendents from the Container class that add a powerful collection of properties. They allow the assignment of Group Policy and delegation of administrative control to junior administrators.

In practice, Organizational Units are always used in preference to Containers because OUs can do everything that Containers can and more. Because placing objects under Organizational Units is required to realize some of the major benefits of Active Directory, creating an OU structure is one of the first tasks to perform after creating a Windows 2000 domain.

You'll find a sample Organizational Unit structure in Figure 1.1, with two departments and one divided into subdepartments to allow for finer-grained control of resources to be specified.

Many factors can influence the design of the OU structure within your domain, and detailed explanations of reasons to modify your designs in certain ways are contained later in this book. Because Group Policy is applied and administrative control is delegated primarily at the OU level, your OU design will have a great

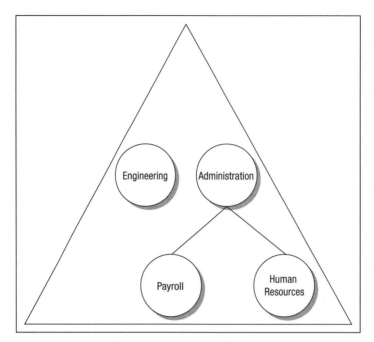

Figure 1.1   Possible OU structure within **example.com**.

impact on the simplicity (or otherwise) of performing these functions in your network, so it really does pay to get the design right from the outset.

For this reason, it's important to carefully plan OU designs before going ahead and deploying Windows 2000. The overriding aim of such a design should be to use the natural inheritance of Group Policy and delegated control to increase simplicity and avoid duplication of settings. Though it's possible to modify the default inheritance of settings from parent to child OUs, this should be minimized (not least because it makes troubleshooting more difficult).

User Accounts

By using centralized user accounts stored in Active Directory, users are able to log on once and access all resources on the network. In fact, user accounts store not just logon information but extra details about an individual that can be published in the directory, searched by coworkers, or made available to applications.

For accountability, it's always best to have only one user log in with each user object, because if you give multiple people the password for one account, then you're unable to tell which of them did what in the event of a security breach. There are even occasions where it's beneficial to create two user accounts for someone—a low-privilege account for day-to-day operations and a high-privilege account for administrative purposes.

TIP: *The secondary logon service that allows you to start applications as a different user is a new feature in Windows 2000. For example, you could be logged on as an ordinary user and be launching the administration tools as an administrator account by either using runas.exe or Shift + right-clicking a shortcut. This makes using two accounts easier, because you no longer have to log off and back on again, saving open documents and closing email clients as you do so.*

User accounts are best arranged into Organizational Units and have certain management functions that can be delegated at the OU level and inherited by lower levels. For example, you could group most user accounts into OUs beneath an Ordinary Users OU and assign members of the Help Desk group the right to change user passwords in the Ordinary Users OU and its children. In this way, you can give members of the Help Desk the ability to manage a subset of user account passwords without letting them change the passwords of accounts kept outside the Ordinary Users OU. Specifically, you wouldn't want to put full administrative accounts into this hierarchy, because if you did, help desk staff could reset a full administrator's password and gain additional privileges.

Groups

Groups allow you to combine user or computer accounts to assign permissions or even to just send email to sets of people. For example, if all of the managers within your organization require access to a secure directory of important files, you would create a group called Managers, add the individual user accounts of each manager to that group, then assign permissions to that group.

Even if you only need to assign permissions to one person, it's still better to use groups because if at some future point someone else takes over that role, then instead of having to manually re-create the security settings, you can simply add them to the existing group.

In Windows 2000, Microsoft has introduced the concept of *group type*. Two possible types of groups exist: security or distribution. Security Groups are the equivalent of Windows NT 4 groups and can have a range of permissions assigned to them.

Distribution Groups are a new feature of Windows 2000 and essentially just allow you to send messages to a collection of users if you have the correct software, such as Microsoft Exchange 2000. Distribution Groups have a lighter overhead than Security Groups; they require marginally less space in the directory and don't impact logon performance, because they don't make a difference to your rights on the network. Hence, Distribution Groups are perfect if you just want to send email to a group of individuals. They can also be converted to Security Groups if necessary.

A second important property of a group is its scope. Three scopes of group are available:

- *Domain Local Groups*—Can contain users and Global/Universal Groups from any trusted domain but can only be assigned permissions within their domain.

- *Global Groups*—Can contain users and Global Groups from their domain and can be granted rights and permissions in any trusting domain.

- *Universal Groups*—Combine features of both Domain Local and Global Groups. They can contain users, Global Groups and Universal Groups from any trusted domain and be assigned permissions or added to Local or Universal Groups in any trusting domain.

NOTE: Universal Security Groups and Global Group nesting are only available once a domain has been converted to native mode, because downlevel domain controllers don't support these features.

When assigning permissions, the best practice is to add user accounts to Global Groups and add these Global Groups to Domain Local Groups. The permissions themselves are assigned to the Domain Local Groups. Using this scheme, you should create Domain Local Groups based on the resource to which they have access, such as a single Domain Local Group for a set of personnel file shares.

Global Groups should be created by function, so for example, you may create a Global Group for all managers in your domain and one for the human resources department. These Global Groups could then be added to the Personnel Domain Local Group to grant permissions.

In this way, you can reuse the Global Groups if only the managers or only the human resources departments need access to other specific items on the network, such as confidential company strategy documents. This system is simpler and easier to manage than creating a single Personnel Files Global Group, then also having to create a separate Managers Global Group to grant access to the strategy documents.

Another new feature of groups in Active Directory worthy of further comment is the nesting of Global (and Universal) Groups. This makes it possible to place Global Groups inside other Global Groups or Universal Groups, as well as Universal Groups within Universal Groups, once a domain has been converted to native mode.

A possible use for nested groups arises if you have a department that's split geographically. For example, if the IT department is based half in London and half in Edinburgh, then you may create a Global Group called London IT, one called Edinburgh IT, and one simply called IT.

Using this scheme, you would add users based in Edinburgh to Edinburgh IT, users based in London to London IT, and just add the London IT and Edinburgh IT groups to the IT group. Permission could then be granted either to IT or to the geographical groups based on need in order to finely control security. Another unexpected advantage of this is that you can easily send email just to people in your building and department, so people several hundred miles away needn't be troubled by invitations to come to the pub in half an hour.

By granting permission to add users to a group, it's possible to enable the management of groups by people other than members of the built-in administrator groups.

In addition to groups stored in the directory, a number of calculated groups are in Windows 2000. The membership of these groups can't be set and is, instead, based on specific factors:

- *Everyone*—The Everyone Group contains absolutely everyone, whether they're logged into the network or unauthenticated.

- *Authenticated Users*—The Authenticated Users Group contains anyone who has logged onto the network.

- *Interactive*—The Interactive Group specifies anyone who is logged on locally to a computer.

- *Network*—As the name suggests, the Network Group applies to any user connecting via the network.

- *Terminal Server User*—With Windows 2000, Terminal Services can be installed on any server and allow users to use a client application to display a desktop that runs on the terminal server. As the name suggests, the Terminal Server User Group applies to any user logged on via Terminal Services.

Computer Accounts

To be able to log into the domain, machines running any version of Windows NT or Windows 2000 (and subsequent releases) require their own computer account objects within Active Directory. Machines running Windows 98, 95, or earlier don't.

Creating computer account objects requires sufficient privileges in the domain. They're used for authentication, so users in the domain can be granted permissions to resources, such as printers and file shares, on machines other than domain controllers.

In addition, computer accounts are used in Windows 2000 to allow Group Policy to be applied to specific machines. With Group Policy, you can specify settings applied to computers regardless of who logs on to them (or even whether anyone logs on), such as deploying software or securing the desktop.

Domain Controllers

Domain controllers have their own special objects within the directory, which are, by default, created in the Domain Controllers OU. Numerous special properties of domain controllers, such as replication configuration, are stored within domain controller objects or as child objects.

Printers

When a printer is shared from a Windows 2000 computer that's a member of a Windows 2000 domain, it's published in Active Directory by default. By specifying properties and locations for the printers in your organization, users are able to search for them from the Start menu to find local printers; printers with special features, such as duplex support; or even printers in far-flung parts of the company, so that they can send hard-copy documents to colleagues.

Also, having printer objects in the directory allows you to group them within Organizational Units and delegate control of management functions. Printers shared from non-Windows 2000 computers can also be manually added to the directory.

Other Objects

In addition to those discussed above, numerous other objects are included in the schema by default and limitless possibilities exist to create your own beyond these. For example, a contact object exists that can contain similar information to a user object without the security permissions. By publishing contacts in the directory, you facilitate central storage of information about clients and suppliers, with the benefit of there being a single place to find and alter such data.

Trees

It's possible that you need multiple domains within a single organization, and one solution is to create new domains as children beneath existing domains. In doing so, you organize the domains into what is known as a *tree*. Incidentally, if you only have one domain, it's still a tree (just a small and uninteresting one).

Instead of specifying a full, new DNS name for the child domain, you simply have to give an additional component, which is added to the beginning of the DNS name of the parent. For example, if you were to create a domain representing Europe beneath the existing **example.com** hierarchy, the full DNS name of the child domain would be **europe.example.com.** The relationship is illustrated in Figure 1.2.

NOTE: *Although geographic names are used for the above domains, don't assume that this means you should create domains on this basis. See Chapter 6 for more information about when to use multiple domains.*

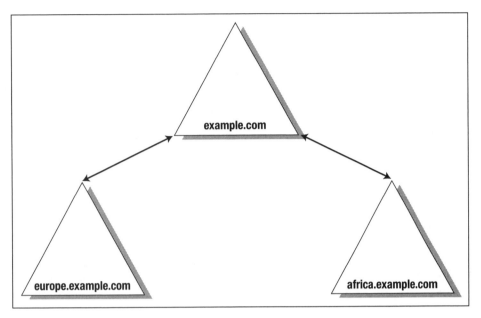

Figure 1.2   Sample **example.com** domain tree with children for Europe and Africa.

Observe from the diagram that the convention used here is to illustrate Windows 2000 domains by triangles. This makes for a good contrast with downlevel domains, which are drawn as circles.

Windows 2000 domains are more scalable and offer a greater degree of flexibility than Windows NT 4 domains. Consequently, you'll find that fewer Windows 2000 domains are needed within a large organization than with NT 4 domains.

One of the greatest headaches in multiple domain Windows NT 4 environments is that of trust relationships. A *trust relationship* between two domains allows resources, such as printers, from the trusting domain to be used by users in the trusted domain. In Windows NT 4, all trusts are one-way, and manual trust relationships must be created for every domain that you wish to trust.

Though not a problem with only one or two domains, the amount of work required to manage a complete trust model grows quickly with the number of domains. For example, adding a fifth domain to a complete trust model requires eight trusts to be configured—one in each direction with the four existing domains. Adding a sixth would require 10 more trusts and so on.

When you add a child domain in a Windows 2000 domain tree, a *two-way transitive trust* is created between it and the parent domain. This means no configuration work has to be done for a domain to trust its parent and vice versa; it will automatically trust every other domain in the tree.

This is because a transitive relationship is one that carries through. For example, "is taller than" is a transitive relationship because if Alice is taller than Bob and if Bob is taller than Charlie, then Alice is also taller than Charlie. Another example of a transitive relationship is equality, whereas inequality is intransitive, because if Alice is not the same height as Bob, and if Bob is not the same height as Charlie, we know nothing about the relative heights of Alice and Charlie.

Going back to the diagram above, because both europe.example.com and africa.example.com share two-way transitive trusts, with example.com, there's implicit trust between them. Trusts with Windows NT 4 domains and trusts between forests are always intransitive.

Forests

Instead of adding a new domain within your organization as a child to an existing domain, it's possible to create a domain with a distinct DNS name that still trusts your existing tree. In doing so, you create a new tree within your organization's forest, so a forest is defined as containing one or more trees.

The root of each new tree in a forest has a two-way, transitive trust relationship with the first domain created in the forest. Hence, a path of trust exists between all domains in a forest, allowing resources to be shared. The addition of a new tree called **coriolis.local** to the existing **example.com** domain structure is illustrated in Figure 1.3.

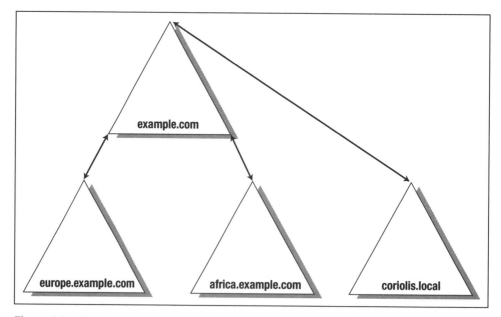

Figure 1.3   A multiple tree forest.

Note that the root of the new tree is drawn in line with the first-level children of the example.com. This is because **example.com**, the first domain created within the forest, has a number of special properties. For one thing, you can see that if more trees are added to the forest, any path of trust between trees will pass through **example.com.**

The first domain in any forest is called the *forest root*, and in addition to being central to trust evaluation, it also contains a number of special groups, including the all-powerful Enterprise Admins. Although every domain in a forest contains a Domain Admins group similar to NT 4, there's only one Enterprise Admins Group per forest, which is the only Group, by default, to have permission to perform a number of special tasks, such as adding new domains to the forest.

In addition to trusting each other by default, all domains in a single forest share two other important items: a Global Catalog and a common schema. At a technical level, all Windows 2000 domain controllers store three partitions. A directory partition is a subtree of the directory that forms a unit of replication. The partitions stored on every domain controller are the following:

- *Domain partition*—Named after the Active Directory domain, this contains the actual objects that make up the domain, such as user and computer accounts. It is replicated to all other domain controllers in the domain only.

- *Configuration partition*—Named after the configuration object with the forest root domain, the configuration schema stores information about the domains, domain controllers, and replication topology for the current forest. The configuration partition is every domain controller within a forest.

- *Schema partition*—Named after the schema object within the configuration partition, the schema partition contains the rules that define what types of objects and attributes can be stored in the directory. The schema partition is replicated to every domain controller within a forest, thus all domains in a forest share a common schema.

In addition, Global Catalog servers carry domain partitions for all domains in the forest, each containing only a subset of objects.

The Global Catalog

Though the objects within each domain in a forest are stored fully on only the domain controllers of that domain, some domain controllers on your network can be designated Global Catalog servers.

These *Global Catalog* servers store a read-only subset of information about every object in the forest. Servers designated Global Catalog servers contain a partial, read-only copy of every domain partition in the forest, not just their own domain's partition. Besides being needed for authentication in multiple domain environments, the information about objects stored in the Global Catalog is typically what you might want to search.

For example, by having the telephone numbers of your users stored in the Global Catalog, you can quickly find the right number for anyone in your organization, regardless of which domain their user account is in, without the search having to be referred over wide area network (WAN) links to multiple domains around the world.

The Schema

In common with any other database, a set of rules specifies exactly what values can be stored within the Active Directory database. These rules make up what is known as the *schema*. A single schema is used for every domain in the forest. This allows a single Global Catalog to exist and objects to be moved between domains.

Specifically, the schema comprises a list of attributes and a list of object classes. Attributes represent properties of objects, such as user logon names, computer names, or telephone numbers. Attributes are of a certain type, such as string value or binary data, just as fields in a database can be and may be designated single or multivalued.

Multivalued attributes, such as other telephone numbers, allow several values to be stored in one field representing several pieces of information in a list. Directory operations, such as replication, work at the attribute level. In the case of multivalued attributes, if one value changes then the entire list must be replicated. This isn't usually a problem for a couple of keywords, but in the case of lists with several thousand entries, this becomes more of a burden because it increases replication traffic.

Every object in the directory is an instance of a class. *Object classes*, such as users or groups, bring together a number of properties from the schema that can be either mandatory or optional and actually define what you can add to the directory. It's possible to both extend existing object classes and add entirely new classes, including creating subclasses that build upon classes already in the directory.

From a storage point of view, it's worth noting that the Active Directory database only allocates the space it needs for the properties that you use in each instance of an object. The amount of space consumed by a user object is not fixed and is, instead, the minimum needed for the attributes that you fill in.

Every object in the directory is an instance of a particular object class. For one thing, this makes it currently impossible to delete an object class from the directory, because consistency issues arise if you delete the class of an object that still exists. Similarly, you can't delete an attribute. The best you can do is to disable them and prevent new instances from being created. Full details of the schema are given in Chapter 9.

Multiple Forests

The final possibility when creating a second domain is to create it within its own forest. This isn't recommended within an organization's production network, because two-way transitive trusts can't exist between forests, so administrative benefits are lost.

Also, because forests can have different schemas, no possibility of a single Global Catalog exists, which means that users will have to search multiple locations for each object they wish to find. This will lead to the duplication and inefficiencies that Active Directory is designed to avoid.

Though it can't be emphasized enough, multiple forests in a production network are generally a very bad thing and should only be used to solve very peculiar problems. However, this isn't to say you should never create a second forest.

As we'll see in Chapter 9, changes to the Active Directory schema are, to a large extent, irreversible. It's essential, then, that when considering changing the schema of your production network, you create a separate forest to test and evaluate the schema modifications before deploying them in a live environment.

The Components of Active Directory

In addition to the logical components of Active Directory that we've so far reviewed, you'll need to understand issues relating to the directory controllers themselves. Also, the directory keeps information about its physical layout to optimize processes, such as replication and logon traffic.

Domain Controllers

The Active Directory itself is stored in a database file on *domain controllers*, which are Windows 2000 Server computers that have been promoted to be domain controllers. Each domain controller belongs to exactly one of the domains within your forest, and all objects within a single domain are replicated to all domain controllers within the domain.

It is possible to have a mixture of Windows NT BDCs and Windows 2000 DCs in a domain, but it's not possible for Windows 2000 to act as a domain controller in a domain that has a Windows NT PDC.

Windows 2000 domain controllers are (basically) all equal—there are no concepts of primary and backup domain controllers in Windows 2000 domains and, consequentially, no such single point of failure.

The truth, as ever, is slightly more complicated than the simple statement that all domain controllers are equal. Although objects and their properties stored within Active Directory are multi-mastered and can thus be updated on any domain controller, there are several functions that can't be transferred to a multi-master environment or that don't make sense to do so.

This leads to a number of flexible single master operations roles (FSMOs). Two operations master roles exist on a per-forest basis; these are as follows:

- *Schema Master*—The forestwide schema is a relatively static entity, and when changes are made, it's essential that they don't conflict with changes made elsewhere in the forest, because having two properties with the same name but different data types is a hard problem to resolve without losing information. For these reasons, as well as for security, only one computer in the forest at a time can have write access to the schema. This is known as the Schema Master.

- *Domain Naming Master*—System administrators should avoid having two new domains with the same domain name added to the forest at the same time. To prevent this from happening, all additions (and deletions) of child domains must be processed on the Domain Naming Master. Also, the Domain Naming Master is the only domain controller that can create cross-referenced objects to refer requests to external directories or to other parts of the forest.

Further, three operations master roles exist on a per-domain basis. These are as follows:

- *PDC Emulator*—Many applications written for downlevel clients, such as Windows NT 4's User Manager for Domains, try to connect to a primary domain controller (PDC) of a domain. For compatibility purposes, exactly one domain controller in each Windows 2000 domain must answer such requests. In addition, the PDC Emulator role receives preferential updates of password changes and is checked against before domain controllers refuse an invalid password, in case they have changed recently.

- *RID Master*—Relative Identifiers, or RIDs, form part of the unique *security identifier (SID)* used to uniquely distinguish each user, group, or computer in the domain for security purposes, such as the assignment of permissions. Because every domain controller in the domain can create new objects, every domain controller must be able to distribute unique RIDs. Domain controllers are assigned pools of RIDs that they alone can issue, and the RID master assigns those unique pools to other domain controllers.

- *Infrastructure Master*—The infrastructure master is responsible for updating references in the directory to objects from other domains in the forest when they are renamed or deleted.

These roles are called *flexible* because they can easily be transferred between domain controllers using the administration tools or seized in the event of failure.

By default, operation master roles are given to the first possible server, so the first domain controller in the forest root domain becomes Schema Master Domain Naming for the domain, as well as PDC Emulator, Infrastructure Master, and RID Master for the forest root domain. The first domain controller in subsequent domains becomes PDC Emulator, Infrastructure Master, and RID Master for its domain.

To install Active Directory on a Windows 2000 computer, that machine must be running one of the Windows 2000 Server family operating systems, but it doesn't matter which of Server, Advanced Server, or Datacenter Server is in use. The additional features in the more expensive Advanced and Datacenter Servers focus around increased support for multiple processors and larger quantities of RAM, as well as clustering and load balancing services. As we'll later see, these services aren't used to cluster or load balance domain controllers; other methods of doing so are available. Hence, exactly which Server product is installed on a particular domain controller isn't relevant and, of course, you can mix the various versions of Windows 2000 Server within the same domain and forest.

For the remainder of this book, assume that Windows 2000 Server will be used to refer to any of the Server family of products, unless otherwise stated explicitly.

Sites

In addition to storing details about logical objects contained within the network, information about the physical network is stored on a per-forest basis. *Sites* in Active Directory should be defined to group together computers that share reliable, high-bandwidth connections.

The idea is that this information is used to optimize processes, such as Active Directory database replication, or any site-aware application. For replication purposes, it's assumed that domain controllers within the same site have plenty of network bandwidth, so changes are sent frequently and uncompressed. Between sites, you're able to define a schedule for replication and, in addition, replication data is compressed.

The *Knowledge Consistency Checker (KCC)* is an automated process that, among other things, is responsible for automatically managing the replication topology. It uses sites to ensure that WAN link usage is minimized by having a small number of replication connections between sites as compared to within sites, so that there's a single "bridgehead" server communicating at each side of each site link.

Another important process that uses sites is the Windows 2000 logon process. When a user at a Windows 2000 Professional client enters her username and password to log into the domain, site information is used to contact a local domain controller.

Just in case the seasoned NT 4 administrator in you is wondering, at this point, about the implication that you can reliably run Windows 2000 domains across WAN links, it's because you can. One of the greatest improvements of Active Directory replication over Windows NT 4 SAM replication is how well it copes with low bandwidths.

Technically, to define a site, you must specify a range or several ranges of IP addresses that make up that site. You do this with one or more subnet objects.

Subnets

An Active Directory site is a group of one or more subnet objects. The intention is that within a large network, routers separate areas of high connectivity, so by defining objects representing the IP subnets within your network, you can specify sites.

Better than this, subnet objects don't even have to match the subnet masks of clients, so you specify an even finer granularity of range of IP addresses to comprise sites.

To illustrate this with an example, imagine you're the administrator of a company with a head office in London and smaller offices in Paris and Frankfurt, and you use the address ranges 10.1.1.10, 10.1.1.20 and 10.1.1.30 with subnet masks of 255.255.255.0, respectively, at the offices. In this case, you would define three subnet objects and three sites and associate each address range with its geographical site.

Site Links

The connections between the sites in your network are recorded within the directory by site link objects. *Site links* can be assigned an arbitrary cost based on the available bandwidth for replication between the sites that they connect.

These costs are then used to further optimize the replication topology by taking into account the relative connectivity between sites. In the above example, if London and Paris were connected by a 256Kbps link, if London and Frankfurt were connected by a 512Kbps link, and if Paris–Frankfurt had a 128Kbps link, you might assign a cost of 50 to the London–Frankfurt link, 100 to the London–Paris link, and 200 to the Paris–Frankfurt link. This would cause the replication topology to be less likely to replicate directly from Paris to Frankfurt.

Site Link Bridge

A *site link bridge* is a set of site links that are considered transitive. By default, no site link bridges exist in the directory, and all site links are considered transitive. To enable site link bridges, you must first disable the bridge and all site links options.

Recall from trust relationships that if something is transitive, then it carries through. In the case of site links, transitivity means that if site A is linked to site B, and site B is linked to site C, then direct replication is possible from site A to site C.

Going back to the previous example, if we assume WAN links are available only from London to Paris and London to Frankfurt, and then we have the hub-and-spoke topology illustrated in Figure 1.4.

In this case, you may wish to prevent direct replication between domain controllers in Paris and Frankfurt. To achieve this, you would turn off transitivity of the site link bridges, and then place the two site links in separate site link bridges.

Object Naming

Every object within the directory database must be addressable uniquely for it to be useful. In practice, objects within the directory have many different names stored as properties of them. These names have varying degrees of uniqueness and are used for different purposes either by Active Directory itself or by other applications.

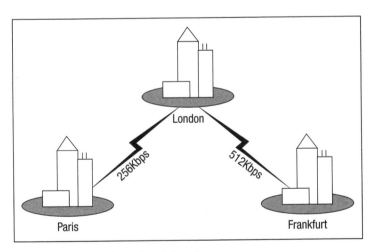

Figure 1.4   Sample network topology.

Distinguished Names

Primarily, unique object naming is achieved through what is known as the distinguished name of the object, or DN. A typical DN is the following:

```
cn=James Smith,ou=Engineering,dc=example, dc=com
```

The above refers to an object called James Smith in the Engineering Organizational Unit of the example.com domain. The DN is made up of a number of components separated by commas.

Each component is of the form **prefix=object name**. In Active Directory, only three valid prefixes exist:

- *dc*—This prefix stands for domain component and is used to represent portions of DNS domain names. Domain names are simply split at the dots, and each portion is prefixed by **dc=** to derive the DN, so for example, the DN of Microsoft.com is:

```
dc=microsoft,dc=com
```

- *ou*—This prefix stands for Organizational Unit and is used to prefix the names of Organizational Units in distinguished names.

- *cn*—This prefix stands for common name and is used for all other types of objects, including users, groups, computer accounts, and built-in containers in the directory such as the Users container.

In other directories' service implementations, other prefix codes can be used, such as **c** for country, **o** for organization, and **l** for locality. Such prefixes aren't used in Active Directory, and all domains must have DNS-style names. The relative distinguished name (RDN) of an object is the initial and least significant component of its DN. The RDN of James Smith's user object is simply:

```
cn=James Smith
```

Fortunately, distinguished names are mainly only used for administrative purposes, and users are insulated from having to know the DNs of their user accounts.

Globally Unique Identifiers

Because the unique name of an object can, and often does, change over time, another property stored with objects in the directory is a *Globally Unique Identifier (GUID)*.

A GUID is a 128-bit number that's generated when an object is created in the directory by a process that guarantees it to be unique, and this number will never change during the lifetime of an object, nor be reused when an object is deleted.

Security Identifiers

Certain objects within the directory are designated as security principals, and such objects have an additional unique number—a *security identifier* or *SID*.

Examples of security principals include pretty much any object you can assign security permissions to, so user objects, group objects, and computer objects are all included. Technically, a SID is comprised of a hierarchy of fields; for example, a user's SID would comprise a revision number, an issuing authority, an identifier for the domain, and, finally, a portion unique within that domain known as the relative identifier (RID).

When permissions for accounts are stored either for directory objects or files, they're stored by SID, so that it's possible to rename accounts and move them around within domains and maintain access control configuration settings.

Of course, SIDs are never reused, so if you delete an account, then its SID is lost for good, so all security permissions assigned to it can't be replaced simply by creating a new object with the same name.

Unlike GUIDs, the SID of an object can change. If you move a user account between domains, then its old SID that's based on the SID of its old domain is no longer useful, so a new SID is generated. Fortunately, Active Directory stores a list of former SIDs of an object in what is known as the SID history. By evaluating the SID history, as well as the current SID of an object, security permissions are maintained as an object is moved between domains.

You may be wondering why SIDs are used at all when GUIDs are guaranteed to never change and to be globally unique. The answer is: for backward compatibility. Because Windows 2000 must interoperate with Windows NT 4, you can assign permissions to Windows 2000 user accounts on NT 4 file servers, and because NT 4 uniquely identifies users by their SIDs, Windows 2000 must do so as well.

Some Other Unique Names

In addition to those discussed above, the properties of Active Directory objects can hold a great variety of names for objects. Two of the most important are discussed below.

User Principal Names

The *User Principal Name (UPN)* of a user object is a new property of user accounts in Active Directory. In essence, it's an email address-style name unique within the forest.

The UPN can, in fact, be arbitrary, but because UPNs can be used as logon names, it makes sense for them to correspond with email addresses, so all users can simply use their email addresses to log on anywhere in the forest.

NetBIOS Names

Because Windows 2000 domains support Windows NT 4.BDCs, as well as any client operating system that can access NT 4 domains, it's essential for Windows 2000 users and group and computer accounts to have NetBIOS names that are used by these systems.

Thus domains must have a NetBIOS name unique within the enterprise, and user, group, and computer accounts must have NetBIOS names unique within the domain.

The Importance of Planning

Installing, upgrading to, or migrating to Active Directory isn't something to be taken lightly. Certainly you shouldn't amble over to the PDC and install on the off chance that you might like it, as one network manager tried to do (fortunately in this story, an NT administrator stopped her before she started the install process).

You should fully understand how Active Directory works and how it can benefit your environment before making any changes. Take time to read this book and plan carefully. Probably the most important part of planning is developing an exit strategy if something goes wrong. This and other aspects of upgrades are covered in Chapter 20.

The chapters of background material are also vital for administrators, because they should understand how Active Directory functions and what the impact of any changes they make is.

You should, however, create a test Windows 2000 network to experiment with the procedures covered in this book. Such a network should be isolated from any existing production network, especially DNS servers.

TIP: *If you're short on test computers, the excellent program called VMware from **www.vmware.com** will allow you to run multiple copies of Windows 2000 as virtual machines on one computer. You can create a rich environment with multiple domain controllers and clients to be able to experiment properly with features, such as replication. Be warned: it's RAM and CPU hungry, though.*

In this chapter's "Immediate Solutions" section, you'll learn how to prepare the installation of Windows 2000 Server or Advanced Server and how to open the most important Active Directory administration tools.

NOTE: *Active Directory can only be added after you've installed Windows 2000 and, unlike Windows NT 4 and earlier, it's not an option during installation. One added benefit of this is that you can later remove Active Directory from a Windows 2000 server. Installing Active Directory is covered in Chapter 4.*

Immediate Solutions

Installing Windows 2000 Server

This isn't intended as a step-by-step guide to installing Windows 2000 Server, but merely to highlight the most important parts of the process from the point of view of later configuring the computer as a domain controller.

Prerequisites

Four versions of Windows 2000 are available: Professional, Server, Advanced Server, and Datacenter Server. Collectively, the latter three are referred to as the Windows 2000 Server Family.

The minimum and recommended requirements for installing Windows 2000 Server are shown below.

Of course, it has long since been very difficult to buy new processors as slow as 133MHz, but perhaps the most important number up there is the RAM. Although it's possible to run Active Directory and Windows 2000 on as little as 64MB for testing purposes, more is required in production networks. A good, general rule when specifying servers is to buy a slightly slower processor and spend the money saved on additional RAM.

In addition to the minimum 1GB to install Windows 2000, 40MB is required to install Active Directory. In typical live environments with 10,000 users, Active Directory databases require on the order of 100MB of disk space. Even with log files and allowing for a safety cushion, the disk space demands of Active Directory aren't excessive. The exact figure depends, of course, on how much information you store about each object in the directory—it will be considerably higher if you store a JPEG photo of each and every user. Active Directory database sizing will be covered in detail in Chapter 5.

Table 1.1   Windows 2000 Server hardware requirements.

Item	Requirement
CPU	Pentium-compatible running at 133MHz or higher
RAM	256MB recommended (128MB minimum supported)
Hard Disk	1GB minimum free space

The Windows 2000 installation process is divided into two halves: text mode and graphical mode.

Text Mode

To start the Windows 2000 installation process, you must either boot from the CD, use boot floppies, or install via the network.

TIP: *To create the four Windows 2000 boot floppy disks, use MAKEBOOT.EXE or MAKEBT32.EXE from the \BOOTDISK folder on the Windows 2000 Server CD-ROM.*

The two main points to note during this portion of setup are:

- *NTFS*—Active Directory requires at least one partition formatted with NT File System (NTFS) to store shared files.

- *1MB Unallocated Space*—To use Windows 2000's Dynamic Disk facilities, you should leave 1MB of unallocated space on each physical disk.

In general, you should only create the partition(s) you need to install onto during setup, and use the administration tools within Windows 2000 to configure additional partitions.

Graphical Mode

After the server reboots, a minimal version of Windows 2000 loads to allow you to complete the setup wizard. The key points to note here are:

- Windows 2000 Domain Controllers must be assigned a fixed IP address, so don't accept the default TCP/IP configuration.

- Correctly configured DNS is essential for a correctly working Active Directory, so if this isn't the first domain controller in the forest, specify the appropriate DNS server.

- Although in practice it makes little difference, you may prefer to join the server to another domain in the forest so you can log on as a member of Enterprise Admins, even if you intend to create a new domain with this server.

The option to become a domain controller isn't available during setup, and Active Directory can't be installed until the system has rebooted after setup completes. Installing Active Directory is covered in Chapter 4.

Related solution:	Found on page:
Installing Active Directory	118

Working with Active Directory Administration Tools

With the introduction of Active Directory, administering a Windows 2000 network becomes synonymous with administering the Active Directory. Once you install Active Directory onto a Windows 2000 Server by promoting it to be a domain controller, shortcuts to the three main administrative tools are added.

These are Active Directory Users and Computers, Active Directory Domains and Trusts, and Active Directory Sites and Services. The tools themselves are covered in greater detail in Chapter 2, but because their use is referred to throughout the book, I'll introduce how to start them here.

Active Directory Users and Computers

You'll use Active Directory Users and Computers to manage the objects within your domain. This includes some of the most common tasks, such as creating user accounts, groups, Organizational Units, and delegating control.

Here's how to open the Active Directory Users and Computers administrative tool:

1. Click Start|Programs|Administrative Tools.
2. Select Active Directory Users and Computers.

TIP: *If you're at a domain controller and Active Directory Users and Computers isn't visible, you may be experiencing Windows 2000's Personalized Menus that hide infrequently used menu items. To reveal all shortcuts, click the double arrow at the bottom of the list of options. To disable personalized menus, clear the appropriate checkbox from the Start|Settings|Taskbar & Start menu dialog box.*

Active Directory Domains and Trusts

You'll use Active Directory Domains and Trusts to manage the trust relationships between Windows 2000 and NT domains.

Here's how to open the Active Directory Domains and Trusts administrative tool:

1. Click Start|Programs|Administrative Tools.
2. Select Active Directory Domains and Trusts.

Active Directory Sites and Services

You'll use Active Directory Sites and Services to manage physical aspects of Active Directory. This includes creating and managing sites and the subnet objects that comprise them, as well as managing aspects of the domain controllers within those sites, such as configuring and forcing replication.

Here's how to open the Active Directory Sites and Services administrative tool:

1. Click Start|Programs|Administrative Tools.

2. Select Active Directory Sites and Services.

Chapter 2

Management Tools

In Depth

Before we look at Active Directory in detail, it's important to understand the technologies used to configure, administer, maintain, and troubleshoot Active Directory.

This chapter is broken down into three main areas:

- *Microsoft Management Console*—This is an application that acts as a place-holder for the many Snap-ins used to perform management tasks. For example, you can add Domain Name System (DNS) and Dynamic Host Configuration Protocol (DHCP) Snap-ins to a single console to enable you to manage both services from one application.

- *Other Utilities*—The Other Utilities section will cover anything not installed by default with Windows 2000, ranging from the Support Tools found on the CD to the Windows 2000 Server Resource Kit and downloadable tools.

- *Scripting*—Increasingly, scripting is becoming an essential weapon in the accomplished system administrator's arsenal and this book presents scripting solution alongside how to accomplish tasks by more normal means. In some cases, such as modifying the Active Directory schema, however, scripting is one of the preferred methods, because it limits the possibility of typing errors.

Microsoft Management Console

The *Microsoft Management Console (MMC)* is a framework that allows multiple Snap-ins to be added to a common administrative application. Snap-ins replace the familiar Windows NT 4 administration tools such as Server Manager and User Manager For Domains and aren't full-blown applications themselves but, instead, are run through the MMC.

In fact, the three Active Directory administration tools presented at the end of Chapter 1 are MMC Snap-ins, as are almost all entries in the Administrative Tools menu.

Basic Concepts

The MMC is a shell for various Snap-ins provided by Microsoft or third parties. It provides a common, explorerlike user interface with a left-hand tree pane and usually a list of objects on the right. In Windows 2000, most administration tasks are performed by right-clicking objects in the right-hand pane, then using the properties Dialog box to change settings.

For example, with Active Directory Users and Computers, the left pane shows the organizational unit structure of your directory and the right pane shows the objects within the selected Organizational Unit (OU). Right-clicking on an object allows you to administer it via the Properties dialog box.

An important concept is that of focus. Most Snap-ins can be focused either on the local computer or on remote computers. For example, you can use the Computer Management Snap-in to start and stop services, view network connections, and even repartition the hard disks on remote machines. Certain Active Directory Snap-ins can be focused on a particular domain/forest or a particular domain controller. If you choose only to connect to a particular domain, then you will, in fact, connect to a nearby domain controller.

The key flexibility of the MMC comes from the fact that you can add multiple Snap-ins to your console, and these consoles can be saved for later use. For example, you can build consoles to perform certain tasks, such as an Active Directory management console containing all of the Active Directory Snap-ins, or a network management console containing multiple Computer Management Snap-ins, one focused on each machine on your local network.

It's even possible to create limited, task-based views of management consoles known as taskpads, which present a simplified interface and are ideal for members of staff with limited administrative rights and responsibility. Common users of taskpads are help desk staff whose only account management responsibility may be to reset passwords.

Snap-in Types

Two types of Snap-ins are available: stand-alone and extension. Extension Snap-ins are added to stand-alone Snap-ins to extend functionality. For example, a Terminal Services extension Snap-in can be used to manage properties of users that relate to connecting to terminal servers. This extension Snap-in simply extends the Properties dialog box for user accounts in the directory with Active Directory Users and Computers.

Some Snap-ins function both as extensions to other Snap-ins and stand-alone Snap-ins in their own right. For example, the Group Policy Snap-in for managing Group Policy Objects (GPOs) is available as an extension of Active Directory Users and Computers so that you can click on an organizational unit and edit the group policies applied to it, as well as a stand-alone Snap-in for editing Local Group Policy.

The MMC Interface

An empty Microsoft Management Console has the explorer style interface shown in Figure 2.1.

Consoles have two panes—a left-hand tree and the right-hand details pane. By default, the tree starts at "Console Root", to which you can add consoles beneath. It's also possible to create locked-down consoles limited to a specific console or subset of a console, but usually, you'll see "Console Root" as the first entry here.

Snap-ins can be added from the Console menu. It's possible to add the same Snap-in many times, perhaps focusing them in different places. For instance, you can add the Active Directory Users and Computers Snap-in once for each domain controller on your network and use them to display the current state of the objects in each copy of the directory on the network.

Once you've added and configured Snap-ins as required, you can save the current configuration to disk. This creates an .msc file, which can be distributed to other administrators or used again later.

Within the console, a number of menus depend on the Snap-in in use and the context. A common option in the View menu is Advanced Features, which toggles

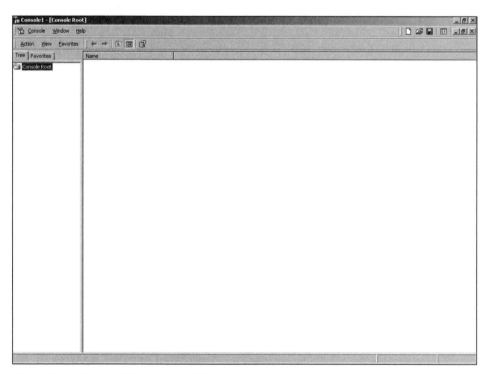

Figure 2.1   Microsoft Management Console without any Snap-ins.

the display of infrequently used, "behind the scenes" details, such as cached queries in DNS and certain special objects within Active Directory Users and Computers. However, some objects in the directory are totally hidden in the usual administration tools that are only visible with specialist utilities, such as the Active Directory Administration Tool (ldp.exe).

Taskpads

It's possible to simplify parts of the management console interface by creating *taskpads*. A taskpad is a customized view of a particular part of the directory, which typically has limited functionality, such as being fixed on a certain organizational unit and only having the option of changing user passwords.

Creating such a taskpad for help desk staff, who only have the privileges to reset account passwords and no other account management functions, makes training the help desk cheaper. Also, it means they can concentrate on their job without receiving lots of "permission denied" messages when they try to change details they aren't supposed to. An example taskpad is shown in Figure 2.2.

Favorites

In the same way that it's possible to bookmark Web pages in your browser, it's possible to make a list of favorites in the management console. Unlike Web

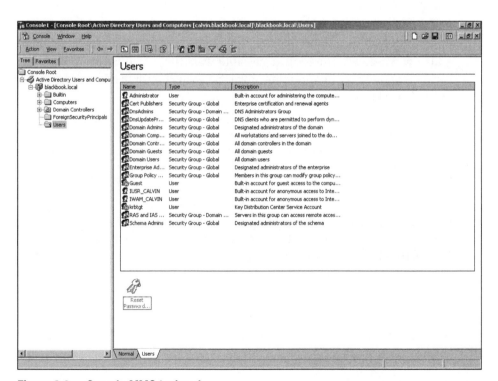

Figure 2.2   Sample MMC taskpad.

bookmarks, these are stored on a per-console basis, because it would be strange to bookmark a Snap-in that isn't currently loaded.

These favorites simply change the active right-hand pane to the bookmarked container in the left-hand tree. A separate menu in the MMC allows you to add, organize, and launch favorites and they can also be added as commands on taskpads.

Console Modes

Management Consoles (.msc files) run in one of four modes:

- *Author mode*—All new consoles begin life in Author mode. This gives full control over the contents of the console and allows you to use all of the features of MMC to customize the console. In Author mode, you can add/remove Snap-ins and create custom views known as taskpads.

- *User mode—full access*—This provides access to all the features of the Snap-ins but not the facility to add/remove Snap-ins or change settings. If you make changes when running a console in any of the User modes, you won't be prompted to save changes.

- *User mode—limited access, multiple windows*—This is a more restrictive type of User mode that hides the MMC menu bar and leaves only the Snap-in menu available.

- *User mode—limited access, single window*—This is the most restrictive view and presents a fixed user interface with no options or the possibility to add new windows. The tools accessible from the Administrative Tools menu are, in fact, consoles containing single Snap-ins configured in User mode—limited access, single window.

TIP: *It's possible to open any console in Author mode by using the **/a** command line switch on mmc.exe or right-clicking on .msc files and selecting Author. Opening in Author mode applies to only a single, so if you want to change the mode, you must do so explicitly.*

Because any console can be opened in Author mode, using limited access User mode consoles isn't a valid way of securing your network. Junior or departmental administrators with restricted responsibility must be given equally restricted permissions to the network to prevent them from using their own .msc files or third-party utilities for administration. The various modes and features of management consoles are intended to make people more productive by hiding unnecessary features from view.

The mode of a console can be changed from the Options dialog box from the Console menu of MMC.

Snap-ins in Windows 2000 Server

Many Snap-ins are shipped with Windows for managing both core and optional components. By and large, Snap-ins used to manage core functions, such as the Computer Management and Event viewer Snap-ins, are installed by default, whereas those for optional components aren't. For example, the DNS Snap-in is only installed if the Domain Name System (DNS) Server service is installed on the computer. To add a complete set of Snap-ins, see "Installing All Bundled MMC Snap-ins on Windows 2000" in this chapter.

The included Snap-ins are the following:

- Active Directory Domains and Trusts
- Active Directory Schema
- Active Directory Sites and Services
- Active Directory Users and Computers
- Certificates
- Certification Authority
- Component Services
- Computer Management
- Device Manager
- Dynamic Host Configuration Protocol (DHCP)
- Disk Defragmenter
- Disk Management
- Distributed File System
- Domain Name System (DNS)
- Event Viewer
- Fax Service
- Group Policy
- Indexing Service
- Internet Authentication Service
- Internet Information Services
- IP Security Policies
- Local Users and Groups
- Performance Logs and Alerts
- Quality of Service (QoS) Admission Control

- Remote Storage

- Removable Storage

- Routing and Remote Access

- Security Configuration and Analysis

- Security Templates

- Services

- Shared Folders

- System Information

- Telephony

- Windows Internet Name Service (WINS)

- Windows Management Instrumentation (WMI) Control

Some of the Snap-ins are added to the Administrative Tools menu as preconfigured consoles, and others are only available as extensions of Snap-ins or by explicitly adding them to your own, customized console.

In addition, it's possible to add folders to group Snap-ins within your console and hyperlinks to Web documents. In fact, you could add every available Snap-in to one console and administer the entire network from one application.

Other Management Tools

In addition to the MMC Snap-ins provided as part of the default installation of Windows 2000 Server, many other useful tools are available from both Microsoft and third parties.

Command Line

Although one of the strengths of Windows 2000 is the intuitive and user-friendly set of graphical user interfaces for administration, Microsoft recognizes that there is a place for command-line administration. Moreover, they try to ensure all tasks can be performed from the command line.

The Windows 2000 Command Prompt (cmd.exe)—which is often incorrectly referred to as the DOS prompt—can be launched from the Accessories menu. By default, the command prompt opens at the root of the drive that Windows 2000 is installed on.

TIP: *Use the cmdhere.inf from the Resource Kit to add "Command Prompt Here" to the context menu in Explorer. This allows you to right-click a folder in Explorer and start a command prompt with the path of the selected folder.*

The most important command-line utility for Active Directory administration is **ntdsutil.exe**. Internally, in registry settings and so forth, Active Directory is often called NTDS for NT Directory Service, so any mention of NTDS could be thought of as an Active Directory. Other command-line utilities useful for Active Directory administration can be installed as part of the Support Tools and Resource Kit Tools.

NTDSUTIL

ntdsutil.exe is an invaluable command-line Windows 2000 tool for administering Active Directory. In fact, it has its own quirky interface and command set shown in Figure 2.3.

The key uses of **ntdsutil** are in restoring deleted objects from Active Directory and seizing operations master roles, such as PDC emulator, when their current holder fails. Details of **ntdsutil** are covered in Chapter 16.

Recovery Console

As an optional installation, Windows 2000 includes a command-line-based recovery console that allows you to enable and disable services, reformat drives, and read/write to disks (including those formatted NTFS). The recovery console can also be started by booting from the Windows 2000 CD-ROM.

To use the recovery console on a member server or Windows 2000 Professional computer, you need to authenticate with administrative access. On domain controllers, a special password separate from the domain administrator is used for both the recovery console and what is known as Directory Services Restore mode.

Directory services restore mode is a startup option in which the Active Directory service isn't started, so various operations, such as moving the database

```
Command Prompt - ntdsutil                                          _|□|×|
C:\>ntdsutil
ntdsutil: help

?                             - Print this help information
Authoritative restore         - Authoritatively restore the DIT database
Domain management             - Prepare for new domain creation
Files                         - Manage NTDS database files
Help                          - Print this help information
IPDeny List                   - Manage LDAP IP Deny List
LDAP policies                 - Manage LDAP protocol policies
Metadata cleanup              - Clean up objects of decommissioned servers
Popups %s                     - (en/dis)able popups with "on" or "off"
Quit                          - Quit the utility
Roles                         - Manage NTDS role owner tokens
Security account management   - Manage Security Account Database - Duplicate SID Cleanup
Semantic database analysis    - Semantic Checker

ntdsutil:
```

Figure 2.3   **ntdsutil.exe** command help.

files or restoring Active Directory, can be performed. It's covered in detail in Chapter 16.

NetSh

NetSh.exe is an extensible command-line utility for managing network-related configuration of Windows 2000. For example, it can be used to configure DHCP, WINS, and routing. It also provides its own interactive console or can be scripted with a simple text file of **netsh** command. You can even dump the current configuration to a script file to duplicate settings or in case of error.

Support Tools

A number of utilities are included on the Windows 2000 Server CD-ROM but aren't installed with the operating system. These are known as the Support Tools and are found in the \support\tools directory of the CD-ROM.

Active Directory Tools

Some of the most important Support Tools relate to Active Directory management. These are the following:

- *ACL Diagnostics (acldiag.exe)*—The access control list diagnostics tool allows you to output the permissions set on directory objects. Access control lists (ACLs) list the security protection applied to objects, either in the directory or on NTFS volumes. The diagnostic, **acldiag.exe**, also allows you to view the effective permission on a directory object for a specified user or group, so it's useful for troubleshooting permission problems.

- *Active Directory Administration Tool (ldp.exe)*—This tool is, in effect, a general Lightweight Directory Access Protocol (LDAP) client, which can be used to search any LDAP-compliant directory, including Active Directory servers.

- *Active Directory Diagnostic Tool (dsastat.exe)*—The command-line utility, **dsastat.exe**, is used to compare the copies of directory data on two domain controllers or Global Catalog servers. It can be used to check whether or not they're up-to-date with each other and report the differences at a fine-grained level.

- *Active Directory Object Manager (movetree.exe)*—This command-line tool allows administrators to move objects between domains within a forest. For example, if your organization has two domains representing your operations in different continents, then **movetree.exe** is the tool to use if a worker transfers to the other continent. It can only be used to transfer objects within a forest—**ClonePrincipal** provides similar functionality to move or copy objects between forests.

- *Active Directory Replication Monitor (replmon.exe)*—The replication monitor is a graphical tool, which provides rich functionality for monitoring replication within your forest. It can record the replication of Active Directory data, report on the current state of replication, and even draw a picture of the replication topology of your network. It's covered in detail in Chapter 8.

- *Active Directory Search Tool (search.vbs)*—This is a sample VBScript that allows administrators to perform command-line searches of LDAP directories.

- *ADSI Edit*—ADSI Edit is to Active Directory what regedit is to the Windows 2000 registry. It is a MMC Snap-in that allows you to add, delete, and move objects within the Active Directory, as well as view and edit all properties of objects. It works on a lower level than management tools, such as Active Directory Users and Computers, and lets you see many objects and containers that are hidden by other management tools. ADSI Edit is shown in Figure 2.4.

WARNING! ASDI Edit is a powerful tool. In a similar way to the Windows 2000 registry editors, it allows administrators to destroy some very important information within your system and break the Active Directory, so it should be used with care.

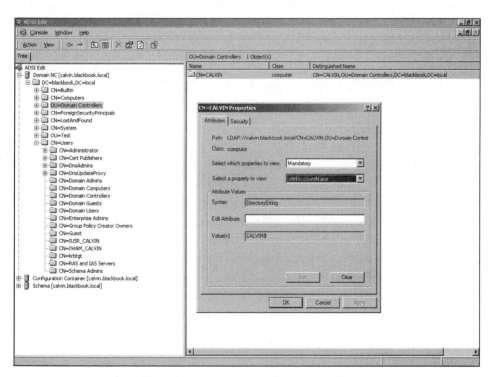

Figure 2.4   Properties of a domain controller object in ADSI Edit.

- *ClonePrincipal (clonepr.dll)*—**ClonePrincipal** is a scriptable component object model (COM) object that enables objects, such as users and groups, to be copied or moved between Windows 2000 forests or between a Windows NT 4 domain and a Windows 2000 forest.

- *Domain Controller Diagnostic Tool (dcdiag.exe)*—This is a command-line tool that allows a number of tests, such as checking the availability of operations masters and the integrity of the replication topology.

- *DsAcls (dsacls.exe)*—This command-line tool allows you to view and modify access control lists of the directory service. It's the Active Directory equivalent of cacls.exe, which allows you to view and modify the access control lists of files on NTFS volume.

- *Replication Diagnostics Tool (repadmin.exe)*—**repadmin.exe** is a command-line tool, which can be used to manage and troubleshoot replication. It can report similar information to the Replication Monitor tool and perform tasks available from the Active Directory Sites and Services Snap-in, such as adding replication connections and manually forcing replication to happen.

- *Windows 2000 Domain Manager (netdom.exe)*—The **netdom.exe** utility is a tool that enables domain related administration tasks to be performed at the command line. For example, it can be used to add computers to domains, as well as manage trust relationships between domains.

Perhaps the most important tools are the Active Directory Administration Tool, Active Directory Replication monitor, and ADSI Edit. These are covered in Chapters 5, 8, and 17 respectively.

Other Useful Tools

Utilities in the Support Tools are useful for Active Directory administrators but don't relate directly to Active Directory. Two important examples are the following:

- *DNS Server Troubleshooting Tool (dnscmd.exe)*—This grandly titled tool is, in effect, a command-line method of managing Windows 2000 DNS servers. As well as allowing you to view information about DNS servers locally or remotely, you're also able to add, delete, and modify resource records or zones via **dnscmd.exe**.

- *Registry Console Tool (reg.exe)*—The registry console tool allows you to make changes to the local or to a remote registry from the command line or in a batch file.

Deployment Tools

In addition to the above, a small number of deployment tools are found in the \support\tools directory of your Windows 2000 Server CD but aren't installed with the other support tools. These tools are contained in **deploy.cab** and include the System Preparation tool (**sysprep.exe**) and the Setup Manager wizard (**setupmgr.exe**).

Sysprep is used to prepare Windows 2000 computers for cloning, because it removes the unique security identifier and causes a new one to be generated when the computer reboots. Setup Manager is used to create "answer files" that can be used to automate the installation of Windows 2000 by replacing the need to manually enter details during setup. The use of Setup Manager with a new method of deploying Windows 2000 Professional known as Remote Installation Services (RIS, pronounced "rizz") is discussed in Chapter 14.

*TIP: Any updated versions of the support tools will be available for download from **www.microsoft.com/windows2000**.*

Resource Kit

Besides having well over 7,000 pages of reference material, the Windows 2000 Server Resource Kit contains a CD with many useful utilities. If you have a subscription to TechNet or MSDN Professional or Universal, you'll also have the Windows 2000 Server Resource Kit on CD-ROM, including an electronic form of the books and all of the tools.

*TIP: Some, but not all, of the Windows 2000 Server Resource Kit Tools can be downloaded from **ftp.microsoft.com/ reskit/win2000**.*

Active Directory Tools

The majority of Microsoft-provided, Active Directory-related tools ship to all users in the Support Tools on the Windows 2000 Server CD. However, some helpful tools are in the resource kit. These are as follows:

- *Group Policy Migration (gpolmig.exe)*—This is used to help migrate Windows NT 4 System Policies to their Windows 2000 replacements, Group Policy objects.

- *Group Policy Verification Tool (gptool.exe)*—This command-line tool allows you to display under-the-hood information about Group Policy objects, beyond what is available in the graphical interface.

- *Group Policy Results (gpresult.exe)*—As will be discussed in Chapter 12, Group Policy can be applied at many levels but has the potential to become complicated due to inheritance and filtering options. The **gpresult.exe** tool shows information about the Group Policy currently applied, as well as useful diagnostic information about the current user, site, and authenticating domain controller.

- *Kerberos List (klist.exe)*—The Kerberos authentication protocol is used for authentication in Windows 2000, and this command-line tool allows you to view details of the Kerberos authentication "tickets" issued to the current user.

- *Kerberos Tray (kerbtray.exe)*—This is a graphical user interface (GUI) tool similar to Kerberos List that displays Kerberos information. For more information on Kerberos see Chapters 5 and 6.

- *Move Users (moveuser.exe)*—This changes the security on a user's profile so it's useful when moving a user between domains or renaming an account when roaming profiles are in use.

- *OID Generator (OIDGen.exe)*—X.500 object identifiers (OIDs) are required as additional unique identifiers for classes and attributes in the Active Directory schema. This tool allows you to generate your own unique base OIDs to use with your custom schema modifications.

- *RPC Ping (rpingc.exe, rpings.exe)*—This is a client-server pair application used to test RPC connectivity in a similar way to **ping.exe** being used to test TCP/IP connectivity. Active Directory replication uses RPC for intrasite replication and can use RPC for intersite replication, so RPC Ping is a useful diagnosis tool if network problems are a suspected cause of replication failure.

Other Useful Tools

Also, a number of the more general tools are useful for system administration. Two that stand out are:

- *User Manager for Domains (usrmgr.exe)*—This is the Windows 2000 version of the NT 4 administration tool that allows you to remotely manage users and groups on Windows NT 4 domains and computers.

- *File Locator (where.exe)*—Where.exe is a useful little command-line tool that allows you to find the location of files on your computer or network drives.

Many other helpful utilities are in the resource kit, and I would recommend browsing the Windows 2000 Resource Kit Tools help file to familiarize yourself with them.

Downloadable Tools

From time to time, Microsoft makes additional or updated tools available for download. In the case of Microsoft, some tools weren't finalized when Windows 2000 released, so they've been made available for download from the Web.

Microsoft's Windows 2000 downloads Web site at **www.microsoft.com/windows2000/downloads** includes a number of important security updates, as well as a section on management and deployment tools. The tools of interest for Active Directory administration are:

- *Windows 2000 Active Directory Migration Tool (ADMT)*—This tool helps migrate domains to Windows 2000 Active Directory and includes functionality to diagnose problems before making the change, and it supports the migration of users from Windows NT 4 to Windows 2000 domains. It's discussed further in Chapter 20.

- *Windows 2000 Active Directory Sizer Tool*—The Active Directory Sizer is designed to help you assess how large your Active Directory database will be and what hardware you'll need. It uses a series of wizards to gather details of the proposed domains and sites within your organization. It's discussed in Chapter 5.

Scripting

A third approach to managing your Active Directory that we'll consider in this book is *scripting*. If you ask a smart aleck how to solve any tricky system administration problem, the answer "script it" invariably comes back. More often than not, this off-the-cuff reply is made without thinking whether or not he knows how to write the script or even whether it's possible to script it.

Knowledge of scripting isn't essential to understanding or managing the Active Directory, but it's definitely useful. If the thought of anything similar to programming fills you with dread, by all means, skip this section and the example scripts found later in the book on a first reading, but do consider coming back to them, because it isn't as hard as it looks (honestly!).

The main aims of the scripting coverage in this book are to ensure that you know how to write scripts to manage Active Directory and also to provide a practical introduction to scripting for administrators who either want to, or feel they should, learn a little more about the subject.

Although scripting has its place in system administration, it's only one possible way of solving a problem. Surprisingly, many people can sit down and write a script without realizing that it would be quicker just to use the administration tools to do the same job. Of course, there are occasions, such as performing the same task a great many times, when scripting is the best solution, and it's in these situations where it's most useful.

First, let's diffuse some of the (initially) impenetrable acronyms that shroud the subject in mystery.

WSH

The *Windows Scripting Host (WSH)* is a language-independent framework, which allows you to run scripts. This means that you can use any scripting language you like within reason ("reason" meaning that a WSH engine is available in this instance).

Microsoft supplies WSH engines for Visual Basic Scripting Edition (VBScript) and their equivalent of Java Script (JScript); engines are also available for languages such as Perl or Python.

For the purposes of this book, I'll use VBScript (no-one calls it Visual Basic Scripting Edition for very long), because it's the easiest to learn of the two languages shipped by Microsoft.

Scripts are essentially text files with special extensions that depend on the language they were written in, such as .vbs for VBScript. When you run these scripts using either of the interpreters—**cscript.exe** or **wscript.exe**—the Windows Scripting Host parses the text file, performs specified actions, and outputs the results either on the command line or in graphical windows. This method of execution differs from compiled programs created in language, such as C++, where the source code is first passed through a compiler, which in turn produces an .exe file that can be distributed and run on any computer.

The interpreted nature of these script files, whereby they are run via **cscript.exe** or **wscript.exe**, means that they can only function on computers that have the Windows Scripting Host installed. It installs by default on Windows 2000 and Windows 98 and can be downloaded from **msdn.microsoft.com/scripting** for Windows NT 4 and Windows 95 machines.

Scripting languages tend to be very flexible in what their built-in functions can do. This is for security, because, for example, it prevents them from being used to access your hard drive when they're embedded in Web pages. Instead, they rely on using a number of external objects to provide functionality. These objects provide a number of functions to scripts, such as outputting text or connecting to an Active Directory. Some objects are provided with WSH and others can be added, such as objects for manipulating Active Directory.

COM

The *Common Object Model (COM)* is a specification for writing objects that can be used to build up programs. For the purposes of this book, the COM objects we encounter will be provided by Microsoft, but it's also possible to write your own in your favorite programming language, then use these COM objects within your script. In fact, you can even write COM objects in VBScript.

The principle behind objects is that systems can be divided into parts, and each part need know nothing about the internals of any other part—instead, the parts provide a consistent interface and can be swapped easily. For example, when you get into a model of rental car that you've never driven before, you're able to accelerate and brake, because the gas and brake pedals are in the same place as in other cars. This consistent interface means you don't have to learn to drive again each time you get into a new car.

Similarly, the use of objects to build programs means that programs can be changed piece by piece without ill effect. Because of the COM specification, it also means that you can script easily and script them with VBScript or other WSH-capable language.

ADSI

The most important set of COM interfaces for Active Directory administration is the *Active Directory Service Interface (ADSI)*. ADSI is installed by default on Windows 2000, and no additional software is needed.

ADSI is an interface to a number of directories. Not only can you use it to administer Active Directory, or indeed any LDAP compliant directory, but it also can be used with Windows NT 4 systems.

It provides functionality to perform system administration tasks, such as enumerating objects in the directory, adding users, adding members to groups, starting and stopping services, and managing resources, such as printers, file shares, and system configuration.

WMI

Windows Management Instrumentation (WMI) is Microsoft's implementation of an industrywide initiative known as Web-Based Enterprise Management (WBEM). By providing a consistent way to obtain management data from a variety of hardware and software devices, WBEM aims to lower the cost of ownership by saving the need for proprietary methods to obtain the same data from different equipment.

WMI is very cool technology, and it allows simple scripts to obtain and report detailed information about systems anywhere in your network. Don't worry about the details, but Listing 2.1 is five simple lines that prints a list of processes running on the local computer:

Listing 2.1   ADBB-02-01-WMIDemo.vbs.

```
Set WMI = GetObject("WinMgmts:")

Set objs = WMI.InstancesOf("Win32_Process")
```

```
For Each obj In objs
    WScript.Echo obj.Description
Next
```

Introduction to VBScript

The example scripts given later in this book are all almost "ready to run," requiring only minor modifications to suit your environment. This section is intended to do no more than introduce you to the basics of VBScript so that you can follow how the examples work.

Hello, World!

The traditional way to introduce a programming language is by getting it to output "Hello, World!" to the reader. As you would expect from a simple scripting language, this can be achieved very easily and is, in fact, the single-line program shown as Listing 2.2.

Listing 2.2   ADBB-02-02-HelloWorld.vbs.

```
Wscript.Echo "Hello, World!"
```

NOTE: *The convention used to name scripts in this book is ADBB-Chapter Number-Script Number-Description.vbs. All of the listings can be found in the \script directory of the companion CD-ROM.*

Listing 2.2 is an example of using the **Echo** method of the built-in **wscript** object to print the string between the double quotes. If it were run using **cscript.exe** from a Windows 2000 command prompt, you would see the following:

```
C:\Scripts>cscript ADBB-02-02-HelloWorld.vbs
Microsoft (R) Windows Script Host Version 5.1 for Windows
Copyright (C) Microsoft Corporation 1996-1999. All rights reserved.

Hello, World!
```

Alternatively, if you double-click on the file or launch using **wscript.exe**, you see the message box shown in Figure 2.5.

Figure 2.5   "Hello, World!" output.

One point to note is that, when using **wscript.exe** to run script that contains multiple **Wscript.Echo** commands, execution will pause until you OK or close each message box.

Variables

When writing programs more complicated than the "Hello, World!" example above, you will likely encounter variables. Put simply, a variable can be thought of as a bucket in which you store information for use later in the script. A slight modification of Listing 2.2 to include a variable is shown in Listing 2.3.

Listing 2.3   ADBB-02-03-HelloWorldVar.vbs.

```
TheMessage = "Hello, World!"
Wscript.Echo TheMessage
```

This will produce exactly the same results as the original "Hello, World!" script but does so by using a variable called **TheMessage**, which is assigned the string of the message itself. Passing this variable as an argument to **Wscript.Echo** outputs its contents.

Many programming languages require you to declare variables before you use them, but by default, VBScript will automatically declare variables on their first use. This can both be a *Bad Thing* and a *Good Thing*. It's good because it allows you to quickly write scripts without regard to declaring each variable that you need—it's often the case when programming that I decide to add a new variable in the middle of a program and forget to go back and append it to the list of declarations. With VBScript's automatic declaration on first use, you're saved from tiresome error messages (and an urge to shout at the computer).

However, it can also be bad. Consider the script in Listing 2.4.

Listing 2.4   ADBB-02-04-HelloWorldBad.vbs.

```
TheMessage = "Hello, World!"
Wscript.Echo TheMassage
```

If you run this script, you get no output, because a typographical error is in one of the variable names. Though **TheMessage** contains the string we wish to display, the variable that we're passing to **Wscript.Echo** to display is, unfortunately, **TheMassage**. Although this isn't a major problem in a two-line script, because you could quickly spot what was wrong, in a longer, more useful script this sort of error leads to unexpected behavior, which is time-consuming to pin down.

A solution is at hand in the form of the directive **option explicit** that, when included as the first executable statement of a script, requires that all variables be declared. All of the example scripts found in later chapters use **option explicit.**

To declare a variable, you use the **Dim** command. Multiple variables can be declared on the same line if commas separate them, for example, see the following:

```
Dim TheMessage, AnotherMessage
```

All variables in VBScript are of the same type, known as variant. No ability exists to declare a variable as a string, as a number, or as whatever. Instead, you can hold any type of data in any variable. The internals of VBScript accommodate the conversion between types as necessary.

Variable Naming

An important part of making a script maintainable is using meaningful variable names. If you just go through calling them **a**, **b**, **c**, and so on, you'll find it difficult to come back to the script in six months time to make a minor modification to solve a new problem.

The practice of prefixing variable names with an identifier representing their type is known as *Hungarian notation*, partly after the Hungarian programmer Charles Simonyi, who was an early proponent of the system, and partly after the fact that using it makes variables look like words in a foreign language. Some common prefixes are shown in Table 2.1.

Hungarian notation is one subject likely to flare up heated debate between programmers, with some being violently in favor and others violently against. Regardless of personal feelings, Microsoft uses Hungarian notation in all of its example code, so it will be used throughout this book.

Commenting Code

In addition to clear variable names, an important way to make scripts readable and maintainable is by using comments. Comments are simple parts of a script

Table 2.1   VBScript variable naming conventions.

Type	Prefix	Example
Boolean (Yes/No)	bln	blnAccountDisabled
Date/Time	dtm	dtmLastLogin
Integer	int	intMinimumPasswordLength
Object	obj	objUserAccount
String	str	strDomainName

that are ignored by the scripting engine. In VBScript, a single quote (') marks the rest of the line as a comment. For an example, see the following:

```
'This is a comment
a = 1
b = 2 'This is also a comment
'c = 3
```

In the code snippet above, we assign the values 1 to **a** and 2 to **b**. No value is assigned to the variable **c** because that final line of code is commented out.

It's good practice to begin each script with a block of comments explaining the purpose of the script and any assumptions that it makes. In addition, any complicated statements should be commented to explain their purpose.

Objects

VBScript is a partially object-orientated language. Scripts use a variety of objects that are each an instance of a particular class. *Objects* have methods and properties associated with them, and it's these methods and properties that allow you to manipulate the objects.

A method is a procedure or function associated with an object and allows you to perform an action. For example, the **Wscript** object has the **Echo** method that we encountered in the "Hello, World!" script. This method outputs its parameter.

Properties store information about an object. They can be read-only, such as the **Version** property of **Wscript** that reports the version of WSH in use, or read/write such as properties representing details of user accounts in Active Directory. It's also possible for properties to invoke procedures when they're changed. For example, an exchange rate object with **Dollar** and **Pounds** properties might recalculate the **Dollar** property in response to a script changing the value of **Pounds**.

Operators

In programming and scripting languages, operators are used to assign, combine, and compare variables. Some common operators in VBScript are shown in Table 2.2.

NOTE: *In VBScript, the equal symbol, =, is used both to assign values to variables and as a comparison operator. This contrasts with languages, such as Perl, where two equal symbols, ==, are used for comparison and one equal symbol, =, for assignment.*

Table 2.2   Important VBScript operators.

Operators	Example	Meaning
=	**a = b**	Assignment. Makes **a** equal to **b.**
&	**strA & strB**	String concatenation. Results in the contents of **strA** followed by **strB**.
+	**intA + intB**	Addition. Adds **intA** and **intB**.
-	**intA − intB**	Subtraction. Subtracts **intB** from **intA**.
*	**intA * intB**	Multiplication. Results in the product of **intA** and **intB**.
/	**intA / intB**	Division. Results in **intA** divided by **intB**.
<, <=, >, >=	**intA < intB**	Comparison operators. Result in either **True** or **False**.

Conditional Statements

Scripts execute line-by-line, in sequence, in the order they're in within the file. If you wish to amend the order of execution or leave out statements in certain cases, then some form of flow control is necessary. The simplest form of flow control is the **If** conditional statement.

The simplest use of **If** is the following:

```
If condition Then statement
```

Here *condition* is a VBScript statement that is evaluated first. If the result is **True** or non-zero then *statement* is executed. Otherwise *statement* is skipped and the script continues. Here is a simple example:

```
a = 1
If a = 1 Then WScript.Echo "a equals one"
```

The script above would output "a equals one" because the condition, **a** equals 1, is **True**. Conditional statements can become more complicated by having multiple-line *statements* or having **Else** clauses, which are executed if the *condition* is **False** or zero. For example:

```
a = 2

If a = 1 Then
  WScript.Echo "a equals one"
Else
  WScript.Echo "a does not equals one"
End If
```

It's also possible to have several different conditions and one, all-encompassing **Else** by using an **ElseIf** statement, as depicted in the following:

```
a = 2

If a = 1 Then
  WScript.Echo "a equals one"
ElseIf a = 2 Then
  WScript.Echo "a equals two"
Else
  WScript.Echo "a does not equals one or two"
End If
```

Loops

Often when scripting, you might want to perform the same action or test on a number of items, such as a list of user accounts from the directory. To do so, some form of loop construction is required in your script.

The following shows an example of the simplest and probably most common type of loop available, the **Do While** loop, the syntax of which is:

```
Do While condition
  statement
  .
Loop
```

Similarly to the **If Then** statement, *condition* is evaluated, and if it's **True**, the following *statements* are executed as normal; otherwise, they're skipped. However, once this is complete, the **Loop** means that VBScript goes back and starts processing from the corresponding **Do While** line again. Obviously, this means that the condition is reevaluated, and the statements may be executed over and over again.

TIP: *It's a very good idea to ensure that the statements alter the condition so the script doesn't execute indefinitely.*

Another form of loop available is **Loop While**, which is similar to **Do While**, but the condition is tested after each execution of the *statement* block, so the *statement* block is guaranteed to happen at least once. The syntax is:

```
Do
  Statement
  .
Loop While condition
```

A final, important form of loop is the **For** loop. This is most useful when processing a collection of variables, such as the results returned by an ADSI or WMI function. An example can be seen in the WMI example.

Writing Readable Code

This section could alternatively be entitled, "Reading Well-Written Code", and it consists of four important points of style that make scripts easy to read and write.

The first is the use of indentation and spacing. Spaces at the beginnings of lines make no difference as to how VBScript scripts are interpreted, so they should be used to make the code more readable. Consider Listings 2.5 and 2.6:

Listing 2.5 ADBB-02-05-BadIndentation.vbs.

```
intA=1
intBeta=2
If intA=1 Then
If intBeta=2 Then
Wscript.Echo "Result 1"
Else
Wscript.Echo "Result 2"
End If
End If
```

Listing 2.6 ADBB-02-06-GoodIndentation.vbs.

```
intA    = 1
intBeta = 2

If intA = 1 Then
  If intBeta = 2 Then
    Wscript.Echo "Result 1"
  Else
    Wscript.Echo "Result 2"
  End If
End If
```

Both of these scripts produce exactly the same result, but the second is more readable, because each level of flow control is indented by two spaces, and the equal signs are lined up for variable assignment. Aligning equal signs makes it easier to see clearly the values assigned to each variable. Indenting flow control makes it easy to see the scope of each **If** statement, and the script becomes easier to read and to follow through for other script authors who see it for the first time.

The second point of style and maintainability is keeping "magic numbers" out of the main body of the script and, instead, declaring variables for them at the beginning of the script. For example, imagine script for adding users to an Active Directory domain that uses the name of the domain in several different places.

If you wished to use the script against a different domain (or were cribbing it from a book) you would have to hunt through and change every occurrence of the domain name to match your new domain, but if the domain name only occurred once at the start of the script then amending the script would be an easier task (and you're less likely to change only half of them and end up with an unholy mess).

Third, VBScript isn't a case-sensitive language, so the mixture of upper- and lowercase that you use only affects how easy to read your scripts are. A sensible use of capitalization is:

- Use capital letters only for the first letter of keywords such as **If, Then,** and **Else.**
- Use capital letters to delimit words in variable names but not for naming prefixes, such as *str* or *int*, or elsewhere in variable names.

Finally, in VBScript, the underscore, _, is used as a line continuation character. This is necessary, because unlike languages, such as C and Perl, VBScript has no explicit line termination character and relies, instead, on carriage returns.
This is fine except when you want to use a very long line of code and have it all fit on the screen (or on the page of a book). To bypass this problem, the line continuation character or underscore, _, is interpreted as "consider the next line as an extension of this one". For example

```
pi = 3.1415
```

is processed in exactly the same way by VBScript as:

```
pi = _
3.1415
```

Immediate Solutions

Creating a Customized Console

The first step before using a customized console is creating it. To illustrate this we'll create a console containing some useful Active Directory Snap-ins.

Obtaining a Blank Console

Initially, we need a completely empty console to which we can add Snap-ins. To start the management console with no Snap-ins loaded:

1. Click the Start menu button, then select the **Run** command.

2. Type "mmc".

This launches the Microsoft Management Console with no Snap-ins loaded. Alternatively, if you're already running a console in Author mode:

1. Go to the Console menu and select New (Ctrl+N).

2. If required, save changes to the current console.

Adding Snap-Ins

To add a Snap-in to a console in Author mode:

1. Go to the Console menu and select Add/Remove Snap-in (Crtl+M).

2. Click Add to bring up a list of available standalone Snap-ins.

3. In turn, select each Snap-in that you wish to have in the console, and click Add.

4. Close the Add Standalone Snap-in dialog box when done.

Additionally, it's possible to create a hierarchy of Snap-ins within the console by selecting the Snap-in or folder to use as a parent in the Add/Remove Snap-in dialog.

Configuring Extension Snap-ins

On the second tab of the Add/Remove Snap-in dialog, you can configure which extension Snap-ins are available. Some extension Snap-ins are added by default, and others may be made available by third parties. By default, all extension Snap-ins are enabled.

Under some circumstances, such as when creating a limited functionality console, it may be desirable to limit the extension Snap-ins available to reduce clutter in the interface. To configure extensions:

1. Go to the Console menu, and select Add/Remove Snap-in (Crtl+M).

2. Switch to the Extensions tab.

3. Select Snap-ins to configure from the drop-down list and use the Add all extensions and individual extension checkboxes to make Snap-ins available or unavailable.

Removing Snap-ins from the Microsoft Management Console

To remove a Snap-in from a console while in Author mode:

1. Go to the Console menu, and select Add/Remove Snap-in (Crtl+M).

2. Select the Snap-in(s) you wish to remove.

3. Click Remove to delete them. You aren't prompted for confirmation, so be careful.

Changing the Mode of a Console

If you intend to distribute a customized console, or if you simply want to preserve its current state, you can change the mode of a console while in Author mode. To do so:

1. Go to the Console menu, and select Options.

2. Choose the mode from the Console mode drop-down list as required.

3. If you have selected one of the three types of User mode, you can prevent the context menus obtained by right-clicking being accessed, changes being saved, and console views being customized with checkboxes.

4. Click OK when done to accept changes. The console remains in Author mode until you close and reopen it.

Creating Taskpads

Microsoft Management Console Taskpads are, in effect, just different ways of viewing information with the Snap-in. They allow you to streamline the administration process by creating one-click buttons for common tasks. They also allow commands for nonmenu items, such as script execution, to be added as buttons.

To Create a New Taskpad

The process of creating a new taskpad is relatively straightforward and the same for any Snap-in.

1. Open the Snap-in of your choice, and select the container in the left-hand tree pane that you wish to create the Taskpad for.

2. Go to the Action menu and select New Taskpad View.

3. The New Taskpad View Wizard starts. Click Next to continue.

4. The Taskpad Display step of the wizard shown in Figure 2.6 allows you to select a preferred arrangement for the items in the view. Make a selection, and click Next to continue.

5. Select whether you wish this taskpad to apply to the current item only or to all items of its class.

6. The final information to give is a Name to appear on the tabs from which the taskpad can be selected and a description to be shown at the top of the taskpad when it's visible.

At this point, the outline of the taskpad is configured, and it only remains to add commands to provide functionality.

Adding Tasks to Taskpads

To make a taskpad useful, you must add one or more tasks to it. These can either be menu commands, links to views of other parts of the Snap-in, or even short-cuts to external programs or scripts.

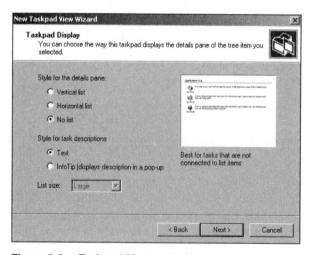

Figure 2.6   Taskpad Display choices.

Tasks are added using the New Task Wizard, which can be launched after creating a taskpad or from the property dialog box of a taskpad, which is accessed from the Action|Edit Taskpad View menu command. To add a task to an existing taskpad:

1. Open the console containing the taskpad in Author mode and display the taskpad.
2. Choose the Edit Taskpad View command from the Action menu.
3. Change to the Tasks tab of the resultant Properties dialog box.
4. Click New to start the New Task Wizard.

From within the New Task Wizard:

1. Select the type of command to add. The choice is between:
   - *Menu command*—This option allows you to add a button representing any menu command available in the current Snap-in.
   - *Shell command*—This allows you to add a button that starts any application or script of your choice. You also have the option to specify command-line parameters, including properties of the selected directory object, so that it's possible to create a custom script to make several changes to an object with a single click.
   - *Navigation*—This adds a shortcut to one of your favorites in the current console to the taskpad.
2. After specifying the options for your chosen command, you're prompted for a name and description. The name is used as a caption for the task's icon, and the description is the icon's tool tip.
3. Finally, you're offered a choice of icons for the task.

Tasks can be deleted and reordered from the Taskpad property dialog box. Once you've finished customizing your console, use the Console|Save menu command (Ctrl+S) to commit changes to disk.

Editing Consoles Saved in User Mode

Once you've customized a console and saved it to an .msc file in one of the three User modes for use by other administrators, or to prevent you from being prompted to save changes, you may wish to edit it again. To do so, you must start the console in Author mode as follows:

1. Right-click on the .msc file you wish to modify, either in Explorer on the desktop or from the Start menu. A context menu similar to Figure 2.7 will appear.

Figure 2.7   Explorer context menu for an .msc file.

2. Select Author from the list of options. The console will open in Author mode, and you're able to make and save changes.

Alternatively, you can start the console in Author mode from the command-line switch, **/a**. For example, any of the following will launch **myconsole.msc** from the root of the C: drive in Author mode:

```
C:\>myconsole.msc /a
```

```
C:\>mmc myconsole.msc /a
```

```
C:\>start myconsole.msc /a
```

Running Consoles as a Different User

Good security practice dictates that administrators should normally log on using accounts with normal, user-level privileges to prevent malicious Web pages or email viruses being unleashed with administrative access to the network; administrators should only use their administrative accounts when necessary. Windows 2000 includes the ability to launch processes as a different user. This solution can be applied to most Windows 2000 files and applications and isn't limited to just .msc files.

This functionality is known as *Run As* and can be achieved either via the command line or through the GUI. It supersedes the Substitute User (su) utility from the resource kit, which implements a similar feature found in Unix operating systems. To use the Run As facility graphically:

1. Right-click on the .msc file you wish to open, and select Run As from the context menu. If you're launching an application or other file type, you may need to shift + right-click to see the Run As option.

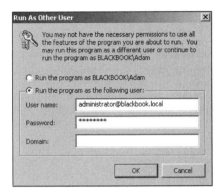

Figure 2.8   Explorer context menu for an .msc file.

2. Enter the details of the account you wish to run the console as into the dialog box, similar to Figure 2.8. You can specify either a User Principal Name (UPN) with the domain box blank or a downlevel account and domain name.

Installing All Bundled MMC Snap-ins on Windows 2000

The Microsoft Management Console Snap-ins used to administer server services are only installed as the services are. If you wish to administer them remotely—such as from your Windows 2000 Professional desktop computer—you must separately install the Windows 2000 Administration Tools. To install the Windows 2000 Administration Tools:

1. Run **adminpak.msi** from %SystemRoot%\system32 on a Windows 2000 Server machine or from the \i386 directory of a Windows 2000 Server CD-ROM.

TIP: .msi files are installation files that use Microsoft Installation Services. You'll notice that many Microsoft applications tools are now distributed as .msi files. The benefits of Microsoft Installer technology, such as self-repairing applications, are discussed in Chapter 14.

2. Click Next to allow the tools to install, and select Finish when installation is complete. The tools are added to the Administrative Tools menu.

Related solution:	Found on page:
Registering the Active Directory Schema Snap-In	231

Installing the Recovery Console

The Windows 2000 Recovery Console can be installed to aid in-system recovery or repair in the event of partial failure, such as unstable services or bad drivers. To install it perform the following:

1. Insert the Windows 2000 Server CD-ROM or connect to a network share containing it.

2. Start a Command Prompt, change to the i386 directory, and issue the following command:

```
D:\i386>winnt32 /cmdcons
```

This adds the recovery console as an advanced option accessible via F8 on system startup. Selecting it will let you choose a particular installation of Windows 2000 (on dual boot machines only) then prompt for logon credentials before presenting you with a command-line interface.

Installing the Support Tools

The Windows 2000 Support Tools are found on the Windows 2000 Server CD-ROM but aren't installed as part of the setup process. To add them after you've installed Windows 2000:

1. Insert the Windows 2000 Server CD-ROM or connect to a network share containing it.

2. Change to the \support\tools directory.

3. Launch the file 2000rkst.msi and follow the prompts.

In addition, some deployment tools are included with the Support Tools but must be installed separately. To do so:

1. Start Explorer either from the Accessories menu or using the Windows Key + E shortcut.

2. Insert the Windows 2000 Server CD-ROM or connect to a network share containing it, and navigate to the Support\Tools directory.

3. The Deployment Support Tools are contained within the compressed deploy.cab file. Double-click this file to explore its contents.

NOTE: *Software, such as WinZip, may have associated itself with .cab files, so you may find double-clicking on deploy.cab launches such an application. If this is the case for you, follow the intention but not the detail of the remainder of the solution.*

---

4. Use Edit|Select All (Ctrl+A) to select the contents of the cabinet file.

5. Double-click one of the selected files.

Installing the Windows 2000 Server Resource Kit Utilities

The Windows 2000 Server Resource Kit Utilities, available from either the companion CD-ROM or as part of a TechNet or MSDN subscription, can be installed as follows:

1. Insert the Windows 2000 Server Resource Kit CD-ROM. If the autorun facility is disabled on your computer, start the autorun.exe from the root of the CD.

2. Select "Install Resource Kit".

3. Follow the prompts. A "Typical" installation will install all options.

Creating Windows Scripting Host Scripts

Script files, such as VBScript or JScript files, simply contain text and, as such, can be created with your favorite text editor, such as Notepad. With one major caveat, the steps to create or edit a script file are straightforward:

1. Open Notepad from the Accessories menu or by launching notepad.exe.

2. Type in a new script, or open and edit an existing script as required.

3. Save the script using File|Save and enter a filename that ends with .vbs.

NOTE: *In previous versions of Notepad, including those in betas of Windows 2000, you have to change the "Save as type" to All Files to prevent .txt being appended to your filename. With Windows 2000 you don't need to do this for common extensions such as .vbs, .ini, and .bat.*

Running Windows Scripting Host Scripts

Two executables can be used to run WSH scripts, such as those written in VBS. These are **cscript.exe** and **wscript.exe**, and the difference between them is command-line or graphical execution. The preferred host for administrative scripts is generally **cscript.exe**, because it allows a number of status messages to be displayed without requiring user intervention.

When executing script files using **start.exe**, executing a script from within Explorer, or using the **Run** command from the Start menu, the default host will be used. To manually specify which host will execute a script, you must use one of the commands at the Run dialog box or from the command line:

```
WScript script.vbs
CScript script.vbs
```

When running scripts from the command line, it's possible to use one of several options to modify processing and also specify parameters that can be used as values for variables within the script. The two most important options to know for the moment are **//B**, which runs in batch mode, suppressing all errors and prompts, and **//T:**nn, which specifies a time-out after nn seconds. Options are specified before arguments, and all are separated by spaces. For example, to run script.vbs in batch mode with two arguments that have values **argument1** and **argument2** you would type in the following:

```
CScript script.vbs //B argument1 argument2
```

Setting the Default Host

When a WSH script, such as a .vbs file, is executed by double-clicking and selecting Open from the context menu or by using the **start.exe** command-line launcher, only one of the two WSH hosts can process it. Initially, the default host is **wscript.exe** and you can change it to **cscript.exe** as follows from a command prompt:

```
C:\>cscript //h:CScript
```

Similarly, to change it back to **wscript.exe**:

```
C:\>cscript //h:WScript
```

What this command actually does is change a number of values in the **HKEY_CLASSES_ROOT** hive of the registry to point to **cscript.exe** instead of **wscript.exe**.

Setting the Default Script Action

By default, when a script file is double-clicked in Windows 2000, it's executed by the default host. This can be useful for users, although it's unfortunate when mischievously named scripts are, in fact, email worms, and unwitting users spread them by running the script.

When developing scripts, it's useful to have the default action associated with a VBScript as Edit. Changing this setting doesn't affect the processing of logon scripts that use .vbs files, and you're still able to execute scripts easily by right-clicking and selecting Open. To make the change in a two-line script, use the code in Listing 2.7:

Listing 2.7   ADBB-02-07-VBSActionToEdit.vbs.

```
Set objWShell = createobject("Wscript.Shell")
ObjWShell.RegWrite "HKCR\VBSFile\Shell\", "Edit", "REG_SZ"
```

The key line in the script is highlighted. It changes the default value of specified registry key –**HKEY_CLASSES_ROOT\VBSFile\Shell**—to Edit. Replacing the "Edit" with "Open" will reset the default action to Open. See Listing 2.8.

Listing 2.8   ADBB-02-08-VBSActionToOpen.vbs.

```
Set objWShell = createobject("Wscript.Shell")
ObjWShell.regWrite "HKCR\VBSFile\Shell\", "Open", "REG_SZ"
```

NOTE: *An alternative default action for .vbs files is Print, although there's little use of setting it as such (except, maybe, to confuse people who try to start scripts).*

Chapter 3

Domain Name Systems (DNS)

(continued)

In Depth

The Domain Name System (DNS) is the mechanism used on the Internet to translate hostnames into IP addresses and vice versa. Active Directory mechanisms, such as logon and replication, use DNS as a locator service to find domain controllers, and for this reason, both DNS and the TCP/IP protocol are essential for Active Directory.

DNS is essential to Active Directory because service (SRV) resource records are required to locate domain controllers. This replaces the NetBIOS broadcasts or WINS lookups used to locate domain controllers by downlevel clients. In fact, Windows 2000 domains don't need Network Basic Input/Output System (NetBIOS) at all, so WINS isn't required. Instead, the primary name resolution service is DNS and dynamic DNS, known as DDNS, is used to register IP addresses obtained from Dynamic Host Configuration Protocol (DHCP).

DNS Overview

DNS is, in fact, a good example of a global directory service, albeit one with a limited and well-defined scope. DNS uses a distributed database, with small portions being stored on many servers around the world, allowing for local administration of records.

The DNS protocol is defined in a series of standards documents known as RFCs. Don't be fooled by the fact that RFC stands for *Request for Comments*, because these are the approved standards documents of the Internet; they aren't merely inviting feedback on whether you think they're a good idea.

The IETF, RFCs, and Internet-Drafts

The Internet Engineering Task Force (IETF) is an open organization that sets the standards of the Internet. These standards documents are the deceptively titled Request for Comments (RFCs), which are usually referred to by number. Proposed standards are known as Internet-Drafts.

More about RFCs, Internet-Drafts, and the IETF can all be found at **www.ietf.org**. RFC documents do not all define standards, and may also be merely informational or even experimental.

Namespace

For host and domain names, DNS uses a hierarchical naming structure, which comprises a number of components separated by periods. An example DNS name is the following:

www.microsoft.com

In the DNS namespace, a trailing period represents the root from which all names are derived. When configuring DNS servers with text files, it's often necessary to add this trailing period to indicate that a name is fully qualified. Failure to do so may result in the default domain being appended to the name you specify, and you end up registering something like **www.microsoft.com.microsoft.com** by mistake. This isn't a problem with the Windows 2000 DNS Microsoft Management Console (MMC) Snap-in.

One of the key intentions of DNS is that all systems reside in a common namespace, so that every DNS server should be able to resolve every other DNS server. In practice, this isn't always the case, because firewalls and disconnected networks prevent it, but good design should take into account the possibility of future connections. So even if you don't currently have a permanent connection to the Internet, you should use a DNS design compatible with this—either an already registered domain name or a private **.local** address that doesn't conflict with outside domains.

The most restrictive specification for DNS domain names limits names to include alphabetic, numeric, and dash ('-') characters only. Windows 2000 will automatically convert underscores in hostnames to dashes when computers are upgraded. However, the implementation of DNS in Windows 2000 supports UTF-8 (Universal Text Format-8), a standard for multibyte characters in domain and hostnames and actually uses underscores in certain, special resource records.

Zones

The DNS namespace is divided into administrative portions known as *zones*. Zones are named after their root, for example the zone named corp beneath **microsoft.com** is called **corp.microsoft.com**. They can contain information for all hosts whose DNS names end with their root. It's also possible to delegate control of subdomains of a zone to different zones.

For example, the root in the DNS namespace is called '.' and beneath this, the subdomains com, net, org, edu, mil, gov, and the various country codes are delegated to separate zones. When you register a name with a DNS registrar, you're then delegated a zone beneath one of these top-level domains (or beneath a second-level domain in countries where the namespace is further divided by organization type, such as the UK). That zone is then under your control, and you are free to delegate zones beneath it.

DNS servers can host multiple zones, and the data for each is considered a separate entity on the server. Traditionally, each zone on a server is either primary or secondary. Primary zones are the single, central, authoritative copy of the zone and can be both read and written to. Secondary copies of zone data are replicated to the hosting servers from the primary or other secondary servers for that zone and are read-only.

Active Directory-Integrated Zones

With Windows 2000, Microsoft has introduced the concept of *Active Directory-integrated zones*. These are primary zones for which the data is stored as objects in the Active Directory itself, and is, thus, replicated to all domain controllers in the hosting domain. This allows DNS data to be written on multiple servers instead of just one, integrates zone replication with Active Directory replication, and allows integration with Windows 2000 security.

Not all domain controllers in the domain have to run the DNS server service for you to use Active Directory-integrated zones, although the data is replicated to all domain controllers. If you do install DNS on any domain controller in a domain with one or more Active Directory-integrated zones, these are added automatically to the list of zones hosted.

In some sense, an Active Directory-integrated zone makes all of the domain controllers hosting it that run DNS look like primary servers for that zone. Thus, it's possible to configure other DNS servers to host secondary copies of the zone in the normal way.

Along with the introduction of Active Directory-integrated zones, Microsoft has renamed the "old"- style zone types to standard secondary and standard primary, and it's perfectly possible to use standard zones—hosted on Windows 2000 DNS or any other suitable server—to support Active Directory.

Resource Records

Within DNS zones, data is stored in terms of resource records (RRs). A *resource record* is one of a variety of possible types, according to purpose, and has a number of properties available as a result of being this type. Common examples of resource records include: A records that map hostnames to IP addresses, PTR records that map IP addresses to hostnames, and NS records that identify DNS name servers. To understand how Active Directory uses DNS you must first understand the mechanics of some key RRs.

The resource records discussed below are only those that are necessary to understand to implement Active Directory. These are by no means complete, because many more RRs are defined in the standards documents and implemented by popular DNS servers. See RFCs 1035 and 2181 for more information on RRs not discussed here.

A

A records are used to map hostnames to single IP addresses. When you type a Web address, such as **www.coriolis.com**, into your browser, an A record will be returned, so that your browser can contact the Web server by its IP address. When specified in a text file, an A record will look something like:

```
calvin 600 IN A 10.0.87.1
```

In this text representation, the first item is the name of the record, which is relative to the zone name. The second value, **600**, is the time-to-live (TTL) that specifies, in seconds, how long the record can be cached for. The **IN** indicates this is an Internet record, as all those in this book are. Some representations omit the **IN**, because it will be assumed if absent.

The fourth piece of data—the A—is the record type, and what follows that is the data field. In this case, it's a single IP address. Hosts with multiple IP addresses are assigned them through multiple A records. When clients query to resolve that hostname to an IP address, the records are all returned, but in *round-robin* fashion. That is to say, the order that the possible IP addresses are returned rotates so as to share the load between each IP address. For example, imagine the following four A records present in a DNS server:

```
calvin 600 IN A 10.0.87.1
calvin 600 IN A 10.0.87.2
calvin 600 IN A 10.0.87.3
calvin 600 IN A 10.0.87.4
```

The results of successive queries for the IP address of a host called **calvin** would be:

```
10.0.87.1, 10.0.87.2, 10.0.87.3, 10.0.87.4
10.0.87.2, 10.0.87.3, 10.0.87.4, 10.0.87.1
10.0.87.3, 10.0.87.4, 10.0.87.1, 10.0.87.2
10.0.87.4, 10.0.87.1, 10.0.87.2, 10.0.87.3
10.0.87.1, 10.0.87.2, 10.0.87.3, 10.0.87.4
```

You can think of this system returning a queue each time, with IP addresses being advanced in the queue after each request and the first address being sent to the back.

CNAME

CNAME, or canonical name, records are aliases for hostnames. If a hostname is resolved and a **CNAME** record is found, then DNS will resolve the host specified by the data of that **CNAME** record until an A record is found.

Thus, **CNAME** records can be used to specify additional names for a host. For example, if you knew your Web and FTP servers would always reside on the same computer, you would specify the following two records:

```
www 600 IN A      192.168.0.1
ftp 600 IN CNAME www.example.com.
```

Note that **CNAME**s use the fully qualified DNS name of the server for which they are an alias, including the trailing '.'. That represents the root of the DNS namespace. The benefit of using a **CNAME** record for **ftp.example.com** is that if the IP address of the server ever changed, you would only have to update one record. However, if you think you'll eventually separate the two services onto different computers, you would use multiple A records so they can be updated independently, as follows:

```
www 600 IN A      192.168.0.1
ftp 600 IN A      192.168.0.1
```

CNAME records are registered for the Globally Unique Identifiers of Active Directory domain controllers, referencing the hostname of the domain controller. These **CNAME** records are used for Active Directory replication. Additionally, this will allow Microsoft to add the facility to rename domain controllers (although this isn't possible with the release version of Windows 2000).

NS

NS, or name server, records are used to specify a list of DNS servers authoritative for a zone. The name of the record is the zone name, and one NS resource record should exist per name server. Each record specifies just the fully qualified DNS name of a DNS server hosting the zone server. For example:

```
example.com. CNAME calvin.example.com.
```

Because a DNS server need not be contained in a zone it hosts, it may be necessary to add so-called *glue records* , which reference other domain controllers in the zone to enable out-of-zone servers to be resolved.

PTR

PTR, or pointer, resource records are used for reverse lookups and map IP addresses to names. They're contained in what are known as Reverse Lookup zones, which are named after the IP address ranges that they contain. As the order of octets is reversed and a special suffix—**in-addr.arpa**—appended, a series of domains is created, which corresponds to ranges of IP addresses.

The common confusion with reverse lookups is the fact that you have to reverse the range of the IP address when forming the reverse lookup record name. The reason for this is clear when you understand that reverse lookup zones can be delegated as illustrated in Figure 3.1.

Here the layers of the diagram show how the reverse lookup zones for the octets of the 10.0.0.0/24 private address could be delegated. Each octet of eight bits of IP address comprises one of the four decimal numbers that makes up the IP address, and they're created as zones beneath the preceding octet. For example, the zone pictured at the bottom right represents the 10.0.87.x address space. To work out the domain name of this zone, as with any other DNS domain name, you walk the tree backwards and find that it is **87.0.10.in-addr.arpa**.

The resource records within these zones that are named after IP addresses and have host names as data are the PTR resource records. For example, to map

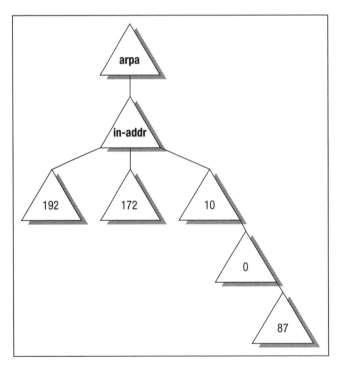

Figure 3.1   Reverse lookup namespace.

10.0.87.1 to **calvin.example.com** in the **87.0.10.in-addr.arpa**. zone file, the PTR resource record would be as follows:

```
1 1200 IN PTR calvin.example.com.
```

SOA

The *SOA*, or start of authority, resource record of a zone is used to specify the primary name server for the zone and additional information. This record is used to locate a writable copy of the zone file for processes that wish to update DNS information.

In text format, an example of an SOA record looks like:

```
@  3600 IN SOA calvin.example. adam.example.com. (
                    5  ; serial number
                  900  ; refresh
                  600  ; retry
                86400  ; expire
                 3600) ; minimum TTL
```

In text representations of resource records, such as zone files, semicolons indicate comments and brackets denote multiple-line resource records. The meanings of the components are as follows:

- *Name*—The **@** indicates that the value is the same as the parent, which, in this case, is the zone itself (**example.com**).

- *TTL*—The time-to-live, in seconds, of this record.

- *Class*—As with all records discussed here, the class is **IN** for Internet.

- *Record Type*—This has the value **SOA** because this is a start of authority resource record.

- *Server*—The domain name of the primary server for the zone.

- *Administrative mailbox*—An email address for the administrator of the zone with the **@** symbol replaced by a period so the email address specified is in fact **adam@example.com**.

- *Serial number*—A 32-bit version number for the zone file, which is incremented when changes are made. It's not altered by zone transfers, and is, hence, used by secondary servers to determine whether or not their zone data is up-to-date.

- *Refresh*—The time, in seconds, that secondary servers should wait before testing for a more up-to-date copy of the zone data.

- *Retry*—If a refresh fails, the secondary server will wait for the number of seconds specified by Retry before attempting another refresh.

3. Domain Name Systems (DNS)

- *Expire*—The length of time, in seconds, which can elapse before a secondary should consider the zone data redundant. If no refresh is completed within this time period, a secondary server will consider the zone data as out-of-date and no longer authoritative. 86,400 seconds is one day.

- *Minimum TTL*—The lowest value that can be returned for the time-to-live of a resource record in the current zone. If a lower TTL is specified for a RR, the zone minimum will be returned instead.

SRV

For Active Directory, the most important resource record type is the *SRV*, or service, resource record. SRV resource records allow you to specify the names of computers that provide a particular service on your network. Multiple SRV resource records can be added for the same service, and mechanisms exist that allow you to set parameters defining the relative importance of each provider. A typical SRV RR for a Windows 2000 domain controller is the following:

```
_ldap._tcp.example.com. 600 IN SRV 0 100 389 calvin.example.com.
```

Read in turn, what the components of the above record specify:

- *Name*—The DNS name queried to find the service. Here the service is **_ldap._tcp.example.com**, which specifies a Lightweight Directory Access Protocol (LDAP) server accepting TCP requests in the **example.com** domain. The underscores in the service identifiers are used to avoid clashes with any existing domains you have, for example called **tcp.example.com**.

- *TTL*—The time to cache the entry in seconds. Here 600 seconds represents 10 minutes, the default timeout for Windows 2000 domain controller **SRV** RRs.

- *Class*—As with all records discussed here, the class is **IN** for Internet.

- *Record Type*—This has the value **SRV**, because this is an **SRV** resource record.

- *Priority*—The importance of this host's provision of the service. When several computers have identically named **SRV** RRs, the priority field can be used to specify the order in which they are contacted. Priorities can be in the range 0 to 65535, and the lowest numbered priority host is tried first. Where several hosts have the same priority, the host to be contacted is chosen randomly for each query based on their weight. The default priority for Windows 2000 domain controllers is 0.

- *Weight*—When several hosts have the same priority for a service, the weight parameter is a load-balancing mechanism, which sets their relative likelihood of the host being chosen for a given request. The chance of being chosen is proportional to the value of the weight, which can lie in the range of 1 to 65535. The default value of Windows 2000 domain controllers is 100.

- *Port*—This is the port number that the service is offered on. Here the value of 389 is the default LDAP port.

- *Target*—The domain name of the host that provides this service.

As an example of how weight and priority interact, consider the following four **SRV** resource records for the same service:

```
_ldap._tcp.example.com. 600 IN SRV  0  80 389 server1.example.com.
_ldap._tcp.example.com. 600 IN SRV  0  80 389 server2.example.com.
_ldap._tcp.example.com. 600 IN SRV  0  40 389 server3.example.com.
_ldap._tcp.example.com. 600 IN SRV 10 100 389 server4.example.com.
```

When a request for **_ldap._tcp.example.com** is received, all four matching SRV resource records are returned to the client. The client will first consider the three records with the best—the lowest—priorities. Three of these records exist, and the chance each is called first will be proportional to the weight assigned.

The total weights between these three servers is 200, so server1 will be contacted first 80 in 200 times, server2 will be contacted first 80 in 200 times, and server3 will be contacted first 40 in 200 times.

NOTE: *Out of the box, Windows 2000 implements SRV resource records according to a draft of RFC 2052. After Windows 2000 was finalized, RFC 2782 was released and made RFC 2052 obsolete.*

WINS

To enable DNS to handle DNS lookups for computers listed on *Windows Internet Name Service (WINS)* servers, a WINS resource record can be added to a zone. When a zone configured with a WINS record receives a query for a host that doesn't exist, the WINS servers specified in the WINS resource record will be queried, in turn, to try and find an IP address for the hostname queried.

The WINS resource record type is proprietary to Microsoft DNS implementations. There's an option not to replicate it, because servers running other DNS implementations, such as bind (Berkeley Internet Name Deamon), would reject WINS records when they're transferred.

WINS-R

The reverse *WINS resource record (WINS-R)* is another record type proprietary to Microsoft. Adding a WINS-R record to a reverse lookup zone allows the DNS server to try using WINS mechanisms to resolve IP addresses into names. The data supplied by a WINS-R record is just a domain suffix. When a DNS server receives a reverse lookup for an IP address for which it is authoritative but has no entry and a WINS-R record is configured for that zone, it will send a NetBIOS node adapter status request to the queried IP address. NetBIOS hosts will send a reply, including their NetBIOS name, and the WINS-R domain suffix will be appended to the WINS-R domain suffix to the NetBIOS hostname to answer the query.

Again, because WINS-R is proprietary to Microsoft DNS implementations, there's an option not to replicate it, because servers running other DNS implementations, such as bind, would reject WINS-R records when they are transferred.

DNS Servers

A *DNS server* is a computer that accepts incoming DNS requests, typically on port 53. With Windows NT and 2000 servers, you can install either Microsoft's or a third-party's DNS server service to make them function as DNS servers. Implementations of DNS are available for most other platforms, the most notable of which is bind. Bind is by far the most widely used DNS server on Unix platforms, and integration issues between Active Directory and bind are covered later in the chapter.

Each DNS server can host multiple zones, and these can be of any type, be it primary, secondary, or—in the case of Windows 2000 domain controllers only—Active Directory-integrated. A DNS server is said to be authoritative for zones for which it holds zone files and if an authoritative server fails to resolve a query for which it's authoritative, it won't refer to other DNS servers.

Query Types

When a client contacts a DNS server to perform a query, it usually performs a *recursive query*. Recursive queries must either be responded to positively or negatively. They're equivalent to asking your assistant to go and look up an obscure fact, such as the capital of Mongolia, and not come back until he has the answer or has tried every possible avenue.

The alternative to a recursive query is an *iterative query*. Iterative queries can be answered positively, negatively, or with a referral to another DNS server. This is analogous to your assistant asking your question to a friend at the canteen and being told to try the know-it-all in the corner.

Iterative queries are used by DNS servers contacting other DNS servers when attempting to resolve names that they aren't authoritative for. For example, if I launch the Web site **www.microsoft.com** from home, my service provider's DNS server is not authoritative for **microsoft.com**, so it's first task will be to send an iterative query to a root server to find a server authoritative for **.com**.

Once a server authoritative for **.com** is returned, my ISP's DNS server will then query it for the IP address of a DNS server authoritative for **microsoft.com**. Finally, another iterative query will be sent to the DNS server authoritative for

microsoft.com, and this should result in the desired IP address being returned. This is equivalent to your assistant being sent around the canteen until he finds the person who knows most about Mongolia and finally being told the capital is Ulaanbaatar.

Query Resolution

If a DNS server receives a query for a record in a zone that it's authoritative for, it will answer the query itself either by returning the result or returning an error message if no resource record matches the query. No communication will be entered into with other DNS servers, because the zone data is authoritative information.

If a DNS server receives a query for which it's not authoritative and holds no cached result, it will attempt to use other DNS servers to answer the query. The exact method it uses depends on configuration. It's possible to configure a list of alternate DNS servers, known as *forwarders*, to use as a first resort in the event that a query can't be answered locally. In such circumstances, these servers are contacted, in turn, until an authoritative answer is found or the list of forwarders is exhausted.

If an answer is found, it is cached and sent to the client that made the original query. If no answer is found, the behavior of the DNS server depends on configuration. If it's set up not to use recursion, it will return a DNS error to the requesting client. Such servers are known as *slaves*.

In the eventuality that all forwarders fail and recursion is allowed, or if no forwarders are configured, the DNS server will use *root hints* to try and resolve the query. Root hints are the IP addresses of DNS servers authoritative for the root of the namespace. The root hints file in Windows 2000 is %SystemRoot\system32\dns\cache.dns.

Reponses from forwarders or those obtained through recursion with root hints are cached for later use, until they expire. An addition to the DNS standard, documented in RFC 2308, is negative caching. Normally, DNS servers will store only successful name resolutions in their cache. If a large number of hosts all try to access the same Web site for which there isn't currently a host record, this would normally result in a large number of requests being sent out and all coming back negative. With negative caching, these authoritative, negative responses can be cached at the referring server, then function in the same way as traditional, positive cached entries.

In actual fact, there's no need for a DNS server to host any zone files at all. Such servers are known as caching-only servers, because they hold no authoritative information. Caching-only servers are still useful, though, because they provide a central cache of all DNS requests from a collection of hosts and thus can be used to save wide area network (WAN) traffic.

Caching

One of the purposes of DNS is to allow the underlying IP addresses of computers to change without affecting the information clients need to locate them. However, in practice, IP address changes aren't a regular occurrence.

This fact is exploited by DNS servers in order to reduce load and network bandwidth by caching the results of queries. Resource records that a DNS server isn't authoritative for are cached locally and considered authoritative for a short period of time. Although they're considered authoritative, they're used as the result of future queries.

For example, if the first thing that all of the engineers in your office do when they get into work at 11 A.M. is read **www.dilbert.com**, then only the first request will cause queries to go out onto the Internet, because accesses in subsequent minutes will be answered from cache.

When a record is cached, the time is noted along with the cached entry. Once its TTL has expired, the record is no longer considered authoritative, and it's deleted from the cache. The length of time to cache an entry is a balance between the fact that if you cache for too short a time, extra traffic and load will be created, but if you cache for too long, then when the IP address of servers is changed, there'll be a longer delay in loss of service.

If a Web server is moved between IP addresses, it's rarely a big deal, because a Web server can be configured on the old IP address to redirect to the new address. With LDAP, however, it's not this simple, so it's a good idea to clear server caches after changing the IP address of a domain controller.

Dynamic Updates

The traditional method of maintaining DNS information is by hand, with manually updated text files or a graphical interface. In large networks, this can be a time-consuming and laborious use of skilled labor and impossible in networks where dynamic host configuration is used. So instead of static IP addresses being assigned to each client, DHCP servers are used to allow computers, such as laptops, to move between subnets without reconfiguration.

A feature of DNS set out in RFC 2136 and first implemented by Microsoft in Windows 2000 is DNS dynamic update protocol. This is a mechanism that allows hosts on the network to dynamically register and deregister DNS entries. In Windows 2000, the netlogon service is responsible for dynamically registering and deregistering DNS entries. When a computer starts up, it will register its IP address, and when it shuts down it will deregister it. Periodically, while running, it will reregister it as a keep-alive to show that the entry hasn't been forgotten about.

TIP: *Stopping and restarting the netlogon service will force reregistration of DNS entries.*

For hosts that use DHCP to obtain their IP addresses, there's a choice. The default behavior for Windows 2000 DHCP clients is for the client to register the A record and the server to register the PTR record. This gives the client ownership of its name mapping and the server ownership of the IP address mapping. For downlevel clients, such as Windows NT 4 computers that don't support dynamic DNS, the DHCP server will have to register both the A and PTR resource records.

Replication

When more than one server contains authoritative information for a zone, there must be replication in place to transfer zone data between servers. With standard zones, the secondary servers receive replicas either from the primary server or from other secondary servers.

With Active Directory-integrated zones, the zone data is stored as objects in the directory itself and is replicated with the rest of the domain's information, using the mechanisms of Active Directory replication described in Chapter 8. These include notification, scheduling, and compression mechanisms. Replication to secondary DNS servers that aren't Active Directory-integrated happens in the same way as primary DNS servers that usually replicate to secondary servers.

The most basic, standard mechanism for replicating zone data between DNS servers is as follows:

1. A secondary server waits for the refresh period specified in the **SOA** record for the zone.

2. When this time has elapsed, it contacts an upstream server—either the primary or another secondary for the zone—and compares the serial number on the **SOA** record.

3. If it has a lower serial number, it requests that a full copy of the zone file be sent. This request is known as an *AXFR*.

In an environment that uses dynamic DNS, this scheme can cause several problems. First, updates aren't replicated in a timely manner, because the refresh period must elapse; and second, a large amount of network traffic is generated by sending a full copy of the zone file each time it's transferred.

These deficiencies are addressed by RFCs 1995 and 1996, which define incremental zone transfers and a notification mechanism (known as DNS notify), respectively. Incremental zone transfers, known as *IXFRs*, can be a more efficient method of replicating the full zone transfers.

Primary servers that support IXFR must also maintain a history of recent changes to the zone. When a secondary server contacts a master requesting an incremental transfer, it reports its serial number for the zone data. The master then uses this information to generate the list of changes, which need to be sent. If it doesn't have enough history stored to do this or if this list of changes would take more bandwidth than an entire transfer, it would reply with an AXFR instead.

With DNS notify in use, a master server maintains a list of secondary servers to inform when changes are received. After the master updates the zone file, it increases the serial number as usual, then sends this serial number in a notification message to each server on its notify list. Replication then proceeds as normal, with the secondary server comparing the new serial number with its current serial number, and requesting either a full or incremental zone transfer if it's out of date.

Windows 2000 DNS supports IXFR and DNS NOTIFY for standard primary and secondary zones, as well as transferring Active Directory-integrated zones to secondary servers. The replication scheme used by Active Directory is, however, more efficient than these mechanisms, because it optimizes the replication topology and can be tuned to your physical network with the use of sites.

Windows 2000 DNS

Not surprisingly, Microsoft's Windows 2000 DNS server implements all of the features that are both essential and recommended to support Active Directory. It also includes the new functionality of Active Directory-integrated zones, which are designed to make your DNS infrastructure more robust, secure, and efficient.

DNS Server Service

The Windows 2000 DNS server service is an optional component of the Windows 2000 Server family of operating systems. The executable file for the service is installed to %SystemRoot%\system32\dns.exe. In common with standard DNS servers, it operates by default on Transmission Control Protocol (TCP) and User Datagram Protocol (UDP) port 53.

Aging and Scavenging

When dynamic DNS is in use, it's possible for computers to become disconnected from the network without deregistering their DNS records. This will happen if a computer crashes or a laptop user undocks improperly, for example.

Aging and scavenging are features to stop the resulting "stale" records clogging up space on the DNS server, incorrectly answering queries and preventing other registrations from taking place. To enable scavenging, you must configure it for the server and enable it for each zone you wish to scavenge.

Windows 2000 clients that register DNS entries dynamically will periodically try to register their addresses, normally every 24 hours. Scavenging works by removing DNS records that haven't been updated recently. By default, only dynamically added resource records are scavenged, although you can individually enable scavenging of manually added entries (beware because this will cause them to eventually be deleted if they aren't updated).

Individual timestamps are held for each DNS record to be aged, and there are two configurable parameters:

- *No-refresh interval*—This specifies the length of time between updates being made to the timestamp on a record. It prevents excessive disk activity by timestamps being updated too frequently.
- *Refresh interval*—This specifies the length of time that must elapse after the no-refresh interval has expired before the record can be deleted by scavenging. Scavenging occurs at a predetermined interval or can be started manually.

Performance and Logging

A number of performance monitor counters are exposed for the DNS server through the DNS performance monitor object. These can be monitored in the Performance MMC Snap-in.

Once the DNS server service is installed, a DNS log is added to Event Viewer that records important information, such as zone version updates and the service starting. To view the DNS event log, use the Event Viewer Snap-in.

More verbose logging information is also available through the DNS Snap-in, and this provides the ability to log all DNS events, such as queries and actual responses sent. With a busy network, the data gathered from the debug logging mechanism grows large quickly: with all options enabled, a single recursive query takes several kilobytes of log file.

DNS Resolver

All computers running any version of Windows 2000 that have TCP/IP installed as a networking protocol have a DNS resolver service, listed as DNS Client in the Services MMC Snap-in. This intelligent resolver is responsible for performing all DNS queries requested by applications. It provides a caching service for DNS requests to reduce network load. For example, as you browse the Web and revisit a site, instead of sending out a lookup request for the same name again, the resolver will answer from its cache.

To prevent thoroughly out-of-date information being returned from the DNS resolver cache, each entry is added with a time-to-live (TTL) and once that TTL has expired, it's removed from the cache. It's also possible to manually purge the resolver cache.

Utilities

A number of utilities are available, either as part of all Windows 2000 systems or with the support tools, to enable DNS management and troubleshooting from the command line.

Ipconfig

The **ipconfig.exe** command-line utility is a standard IP diagnostic tool installed on all Windows 2000 systems running TCP/IP. It allows you to view detailed information about the IP configuration of the local host and all adapters, including all IP addresses, subnet masks, the default gateway, and DNS servers for each adapter.

Through command-line switches, **ipconfig.exe** also allows you to monitor and manage DHCP information by ending and renewing leases and configuring class IDs. Important for the purposes of this chapter, it also allows you to view and to clear the local DNS resolver cache. For example, **ipconfig.exe** is the tool to use if you know an out-of-date DNS lookup is cached locally and you wish to remove it.

NOTE: *There is no graphical equivalent to **ipconfig.exe** in Windows 2000, the Resource Kit, or Support tools. If you're used to **winipcfg.exe** from Windows 9x, then, unfortunately, you must learn to know and love **ipconfig.exe**.*

NsLookup

The **NsLookup** utility can either be run as a command-line utility by specifying arguments or in interactive mode as shown in Figure 3.2.

DNS and Active Directory

As we've seen, Active Directory requires a DNS server that's capable of supporting SRV resource records in order to function. It's also strongly recommended that dynamic updates and incremental transfers be supported to ease administration and network load.

Before you install Active Directory for the first time in your organization, you must choose the DNS domain name for the directory. With the release version of Windows 2000, it's impossible to rename a domain, so this choice must be made carefully.

Practical Limitations for Domain Names

The Active Directory installation wizard will allow UTF-8 DNS names for your Active Directory domains up to 64 bytes long. UTF-8 is a mechanism that, similar to Unicode, allows a wide variety of non-Roman alphabets to be stored

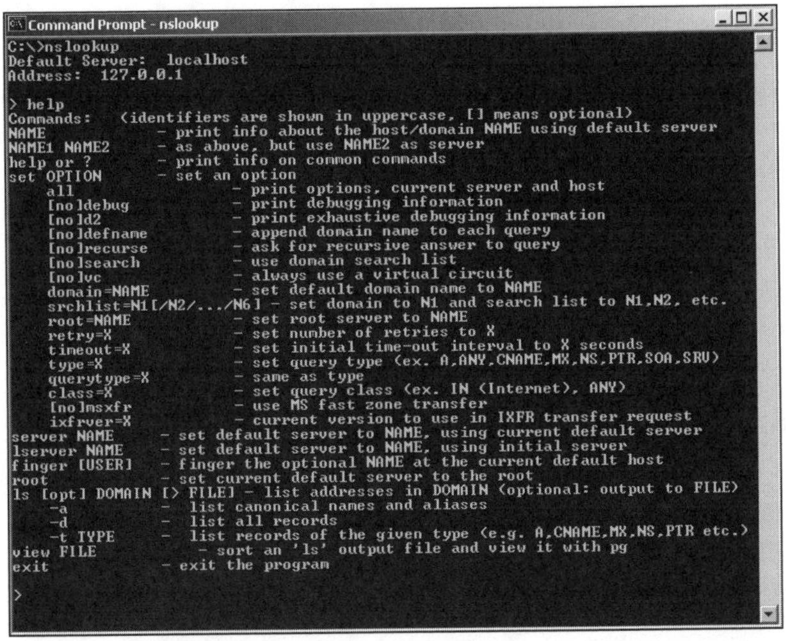

```
Command Prompt - nslookup                                          _ □ X
C:\>nslookup
Default Server:  localhost
Address:  127.0.0.1

> help
Commands:   (identifiers are shown in uppercase, [] means optional)
NAME            - print info about the host/domain NAME using default server
NAME1 NAME2     - as above, but use NAME2 as server
help or ?       - print info on common commands
set OPTION      - set an option
    all                 - print options, current server and host
    [no]debug           - print debugging information
    [no]d2              - print exhaustive debugging information
    [no]defname         - append domain name to each query
    [no]recurse         - ask for recursive answer to query
    [no]search          - use domain search list
    [no]vc              - always use a virtual circuit
    domain=NAME         - set default domain name to NAME
    srchlist=N1[/N2/.../N6] - set domain to N1 and search list to N1,N2, etc.
    root=NAME           - set root server to NAME
    retry=X             - set number of retries to X
    timeout=X           - set initial time-out interval to X seconds
    type=X              - set query type (ex. A,ANY,CNAME,MX,NS,PTR,SOA,SRV)
    querytype=X         - same as type
    class=X             - set query class (ex. IN (Internet), ANY)
    [no]msxfr           - use MS fast zone transfer
    ixfrver=X           - current version to use in IXFR transfer request
server NAME     - set default server to NAME, using current default server
lserver NAME    - set default server to NAME, using initial server
finger [USER]   - finger the optional NAME at the current default host
root            - set current default server to the root
ls [opt] DOMAIN [> FILE] - list addresses in DOMAIN (optional: output to FILE)
    -a          - list canonical names and aliases
    -d          - list all records
    -t TYPE     - list records of the given type (e.g. A,CNAME,MX,NS,PTR etc.)
view FILE       - sort an 'ls' output file and view it with pg
exit            - exit the program
>
```

Figure 3.2   **Nslookup** help information while running in Interactive mode.

on computers. Unlike Unicode, it does not represent each character by a fixed number of bytes but, instead, uses a variable length scheme so that standard 7-bit ASCII is a valid subset of UTF-8, and longer bytes are used to represent less common characters.

Although Windows 2000 DNS supports UTF-8 characters being used in DNS names, one of the limitations inherent in changing the rules for DNS servers is that, at some point, you may need to interoperate with a DNS server that still only supports the character set described in RFC 1035—that is, alphanumeric and hyphens only.

Obviously, you won't be using such a server to contain the zone used by Active Directory, but it may be that computers with your Active Directory need to be accessed by clients, which use such a server. It is, therefore, highly recommend to use only the RFC 1035 character set. For this reason, very few companies seem keen to implement Active Directory domains named using the myriad of non-Western characters allowed by UTF-8.

The restriction to 64 bytes is due to the fact that Active Directory domain names are used in Uniform Naming Convention (UNC) paths by the Windows 2000 login process to access items, such as login scripts. These paths also contain globally unique identifiers in text form—another 36 characters—and various other details, which increase length.

Because Windows 2000 contains a hard limit of 260 bytes in file paths known as *MAXPATH*, the arbitrary limit of 64 bytes for domain names was chosen to ensure that the 260-bytes limit isn't exceeded. Using standard ASCII characters, 64 bytes is actually quite a long domain name, so this shouldn't be a problem. For an idea of scale, the following domain name is exactly 64 bytes in length:

```
extra.long.domain.name.to.illustrate.that.64.bytes.is.plenty.com
```

As you can see, 64 characters is plenty long enough—especially for administrators to have to type over and over again—so the real decision is likely to be based on other factors and, mainly, this means existing DNS infrastructure.

Active Directory-Integrated Zones

When a zone is configured as Active Directory-integrated, the usual mechanism of storing resource records in a host file is replaced by storing them as Active Directory objects. DNS information is stored in the domain naming context beneath the following object:

```
cn=MicrosoftDNS,cn=System,dc=domain
```

As the information is stored within the domain naming context, it's replicated only to domain controllers within the same domain.

Secure Dynamic Updates

Although the DNS dynamic update mechanism saves administration, it also creates security problems. In short, allowing computers to register their own DNS names allows malicious computers to replace existing DNS names, thus allowing them to impersonate other computers. Attempts are made in other implementations of dynamic updates to mitigate this risk by only allowing updates from a specified set of IP addresses, but this approach is open to IP spoofing, whereby the malicious computer pretends to have, or "spoofs", one of the allowed IP addresses.

With Windows 2000 clients joined to Windows 2000 domains using Active Directory-integrated DNS zones, making use of the existing Windows 2000 authentication mechanism solves this problem. The client identity can be established by the computer account stored in Active Directory, and a discretionary access control list (DACL)—a list of permissions—is applied to each resource record, allowing only administrators and the creating computer to amend or replace them. The resource record objects themselves are owned by the creating computer account.

Secure dynamic updates are also available to downlevel clients if they obtain their IP addresses from a Windows 2000 DHCP server. The DHCP server won't, however, take ownership of these records, and, instead, leaves them open for the downlevel client to take ownership of if it's upgraded to Windows 2000. To achieve this, the DHCP server must be a member of the DnsUpdateProxy Global Group in the domain in which its performing the updates.

One crucial security point for secure dynamic updates is that if you use DHCP to provide secure dynamic registration for downlevel DHCP clients, then the DHCP server shouldn't be the DNS server. This is because the entire point of secure dynamic updates is to prevent "name hijacking" by applying security to DNS resource records, but if the DHCP server runs in the system context on the domain controller/DNS server, it will have enough privileges to overwrite any DNS record.

NOTE: *A new requirement in Windows 2000 is that Windows 2000 DHCP servers that are members of a domain must be authorized in the domain in order for them to function. This doesn't affect downlevel DHCP servers.*

Multiple Domains

A situation you must be aware of when using Active Directory-integrated zones arises when you use multiple domains. Because the directory-integrated DNS information is only replicated within its own domain, no DNS data will be replicated by default between domains. It is, therefore, a good idea to delegate subdomains of the DNS namespace to match the names of Active Directory domains before creating the child domain and also to install the DNS server to support the delegated zones before creating the child domain.

Choosing a Domain Name

When installing Active Directory for the first time, you require a DNS name for the root domain in your forest. This name should be chosen carefully, because, as of the first release of Active Directory, no mechanism exists for renaming the root domain of a forest. When faced with this decision, you can be in one of two situations: either there's already a DNS infrastructure in your organization, or there's no infrastructure.

No Existing DNS Infrastructure

If your network doesn't already have a DNS server, you'll need to add at least one DNS server. Windows 2000 DNS running Active Directory-integrated zones is the simplest and most efficient choice in this case.

The choice of domain name is slightly more difficult. Ideally, you should use an externally registered domain name so your domain can be located from the public Internet, either because it's already connected or in case you connect it in the future. If you already have an externally registered domain, such as **adamwood.com**, that's hosted at an ISP, which provides mail and Web services, then you shouldn't name your Active Directory domain after it. This is simply because doing so would prevent clients on your network from contacting your external Web server or from sending email to addresses in your domain, and they would resolve the IP addresses locally and not to the correct Internet addresses.

The solution is to use a subdomain of an existing address, for example, **ad.adamwood.com**. This would make your internal DNS server authoritative for **ad.adamwood.com** only, so requests for computers outside of this such as **www.adamwood.com** or email to **adam@adamwood.com** can be forwarded to external DNS servers.

If you have no intention of ever making your Active Directory servers accessible over the Internet and you don't wish to register a domain name, you should use a **.local** domain. The point here is that **.local** domains are a *de facto* standard for private domains and aren't registered on the public Internet and, thus, don't create any clashes.

The alternative is to pick a domain name that isn't registered to you at random, say **coriolis.com**. If you do this, then when you try to open **www.coriolis.com** from a client computer in your network, it will resolve to a local server (or fail), because your internal DNS is authoritative for this domain, instead of forwarding your request to an external DNS server that can resolve it to the IP address of the real **www.coriolis.com**.

Existing DNS Infrastructure

If your organization already has DNS deployed, things become trickier. Not just technically but also for political reasons. If it's often the case that DNS servers are operated by different parts of a large organization other than the Windows NT or 2000 servers, a conflict can ensue if the DNS team doesn't want to abdicate some or all DNS responsibility.

There are two main solutions to this:

- *Delegate a subdomain*—This delegated subdomain can be hosted on Windows 2000 DNS servers, benefiting from Active Directory-integration, and not impacting the existing DNS infrastructure. This is probably going to be the most popular method of deploying DNS in large organizations, and is actually what Microsoft uses, because its internal Active Directory forest is rooted at **corp.microsoft.com**.

- *Use existing DNS servers*—There is no requirement for Active Directory to use Microsoft DNS servers, and as long as SRV records are supported, it will work.

Exactly which solution best suits an organization will depend on a range of political factors and decisions based on the current infrastructure. At the very least, this includes whether the current DNS servers support SRV resource records and dynamic updates or whether they can be upgraded to do so in a timely manner.

Using Other DNS Servers

There's no necessity in using Windows 2000 DNS to support Active Directory. If an existing DNS is in place, it's most likely to be bind, so this section is dedicated to issues of integrating Active Directory and bind.

Bind

For domain controllers to be supported, DNS must support **SRV** resource records as defined in RFC 2052. The minimum version of bind to support **SRV** that Microsoft recommends is 4.9.6.

Beyond the minimum requirements, however, if you're using DHCP to assign IP addresses, then support for dynamic updates becomes a virtually essential feature. This requires at least version 8.1.1 of bind, although, due to serious security issues, 8.2.2 or later is a better choice.

Windows NT 4 DNS

Support for SRV resource records was added to Windows NT 4 DNS at Service Pack 4. It doesn't, however, support incremental zone transfers or dynamic update protocol, so it's a poor choice for large environments using Active Directory.

Unsurprisingly, Microsoft recommends upgrading existing Windows NT 4 DNS servers to run Windows 2000, although, delegating a subdomain is another option.

Immediate Solutions

Installing Windows 2000 DNS

The Windows 2000 DNS Server Service is an optional component of Windows 2000 Server. It isn't available as an option in Windows 2000 Professional. You can add it during installation of Windows 2000, after installation of Windows 2000, or allow it to be installed by the Active Directory installation wizard.

To install Windows 2000 DNS after Windows 2000 is installed:

1. Open the Control Panel by clicking Start|Settings|Control Panel.
2. Open the Add/Remove Programs applet.
3. Choose the Add/Remove Windows Components button.
4. DNS is situated under Networking Services. Select Networking Services in the Components list then click details.
5. To install DNS, check the corresponding box and click OK.
6. Click Next to install the necessary files.

The DNS server will then install, the service will be started, and a shortcut to the DNS MMC Snap-in will be added to the Administrative Tools menu. No zones will be loaded unless the server is also a domain controller in a domain with Active Directory-integrated zones.

Using the DNS MMC Snap-In

The graphical interface for DNS management is provided via the DNS Management Console Snap-in. A shortcut to it is created in the Administrative Tools menu once DNS is installed, and it is also added as an extension to the Services and Applications of Computer Management for DNS servers.

Related solution:	*Found on page:*
Creating a Customized Console	56

Managing Remote DNS Servers

In common with almost all MMC Snap-ins, the DNS console can be used to manage both local and remote DNS servers. To connect to an additional DNS server:

1. Select the DNS Snap-in in the left console pane.

2. Select Connect to Computer from the Action or context menu.

3. A dialog box prompts you to choose the local computer or provide the IP address or hostname of the DNS server to manage.

DNS Servers can be deleted from the computer's list by right-clicking their names, selecting Delete, and confirming.

Related solution:	*Found on page:*
Installing All Bundled MMC Snap-ins on Windows 2000	61

Viewing Cached Entries

By default, the DNS MMC Snap-in hides cached results from display. With Advanced view enabled for the DNS Snap-ins, Cached Lookups folders are added beneath each connected server, and cached lookups can be inspected, browsed, and individually deleted from within them.

To enable Advanced view from the DNS MMC Snap-in:

1. Select View from the standard menu actions menu bar.

2. Select Advanced.

The Cached Lookups folder should appear beneath the DNS server in the tree pane. Repeat the above steps to hide the Cached Lookups folder.

Refreshing the Display

The information held by a DNS server can, and does, change over time while the DNS Snap-in is in use as cached entries are added, zone transfers take place, and external tools are used to modify entries. The display in the Snap-in doesn't update automatically and must be manually refreshed.

To refresh the Snap-in display:

1. Right-click the container you wish to refresh in the left-hand tree. The refresh will only take place at this level and below.

2. Select Refresh from the context menu.

Installing the DNS WMI Provider

In order to remotely manage DNS via scripting, it's necessary to extend Windows Management Instrumentation on the DNS servers you wish to manage by installing Microsoft's DNS Windows Management Instrumentation (WMI) provider.

NOTE: *A WMI provider is a Component Object Model (COM) object that extends the capabilities of WMI. It's possible to write WMI providers for your own applications using the WMI SDK from* **http://msdn.microsoft.com/downloads/ sdks/platform/platform.asp.**

To obtain and install the DNS WMI provider:

1. Download it from **ftp.microsoft.com/reskit/win2000/dnsprov.zip**.

2. Unzip it, using a tool such as WinZip (**www.winzip.com**), to a temporary directory.

3. Copy the **dnsschema.mof** and **dnsprov.dll** from the temporary directory to %SystemRoot%\system32\wbem.

4. Start a Command Prompt and issue the following two commands from the %SystemRoot%\system32\wbem directory:

```
mofcomp dnsschema.mof
regsvr32 dnsprov.dll
```

With the WMI class information and the DLL registered, the provider is installed and can be used.

Managing Zones

The DNS namespace is broken into zones for management purposes. Even if you only use one zone on your network, you must still be familiar with basic zone management tasks for setting up and troubleshooting your network.

Adding Zones

The task of adding a new zone to a DNS server is required either when a brand-new zone is created or when you're configuring a server to hold a secondary copy of an existing zone.

To add a new zone with the DNS management console Snap-in:

1. Select the DNS server you wish to add the zone to.

2. Click Action then New Zone. The New Zone wizard appears.

3. Select the type of zone: Active Directory-integrated, standard primary, or standard secondary, as required.

4. Select whether you want to create a forward lookup zone to map names into addresses or a reverse lookup zone to map addresses into names.

TIP: *If you select Forward Lookup Zones in the console tree before launching the wizard, this screen will be skipped and a new forward lookup zone will be added. Similarly, if you select Reverse Lookup Zones first, the zone type will be assumed.*

---

5. Specify a zone name. This must be a fully qualified domain name, including the trailing period, for a forward lookup zone or with the network ID or explicit zone name in the form **something.in-addr.arpa** for a reverse lookup domain.

6. For standard zones only, you'll be prompted to specify a file to store the zone data in. Active Directory-integrated zones are stored in the directory itself.

To add a new zone with dnscmd.exe from the Windows 2000 Support Tools, the command to use is **/ZoneAdd**. The exact syntax and required options depend on the type of zone. To get help on the command type:

```
C:\>dnscmd /ZoneAdd /?
```

For example, to create a standard primary zone called **another.example.** to the server **dc1.example.com**, stored in **ae.dns** you would type (all on one line):

```
C:\>dnscmd dc1.example.com /ZoneAdd another.example. /Primary /file ae.dns
```

Many of the operations in this chapter can be carried out using the DNS WMI Provider, for example, the following script shows how to add a zone file:

Listing 3.1   ADBB-03-01-AddZone.vbs.
```
Option Explicit

' Declare Variables
Dim strMSDNS, strUserName, strPassword, strServer, objService, objDNSZone
Dim strZoneName, intZoneType, objLocator, objServer, objNull

' Specify Username and Password: NULL uses the current user
strUserName = NULL
strPassword = NULL
```

```
' Change these values to specify your DNS Server and Zone name
strServer   = "calvin.example.com"
strZoneName = "YourZoneHere."

' ZoneType: 0 = AD Integrated, 1 = Primary, 2 = Secondary
intZoneType = 0

' Constants
strMSDNS    = "root\microsoftdns"

' Connect to the DNS Server
Set objLocator = CreateObject("WbemScripting.SWbemLocator")
Set objService = objLocator.ConnectServer(strServer, strMSDNS, _
                                        strUserName, strPassword)
Set objServer  = objService.Get("MicrosoftDNS_Server.name=""."""")
Set objDNSZone = objService.Get("MicrosoftDNS_ZONE")

' Actually Create the Zone
Set objNull    = objDNSZone.CreateZone(strZoneName, intZoneType)
```

The above script shows how to connect to a DNS server by scripting and performing a simple operation. To customize the script, you should change the variable values in the highlighted lines to match your network and specify the full
zone name to add.

The script goes through the process of using WMI—also known as WBEM (Web
Based Enterprise Management)—to set the **objServer** variable as a connection
to the DNS provider on the specified server with current credentials, then create
objects representing the DNS Server and Zone. Only after the connection is made
is the zone created. Using the same initial framework and replacing only the final
line, the script in Listing 3.1 can be used as a basis to perform a variety of DNS
management tasks.

Delegating Subdomains

Delegation is the process where a separate zone is created for a DNS subdomain
and authority is set. This zone can then be managed completely separately from
its parent.

To delegate a subdomain using the DNS Management Console Snap-in:

1. Select the domain to delegate from by left-clicking in the tree windows.

2. Right-click and select New Delegation.

3. The New Delegation wizard appears. Click Next.

4. Type the delegated domain name. Periods are not valid. Click Next.

5. Specify the names and IP addresses of DNS servers that will host the zone file, so their requests can be referred to them.

6. Click Next then Finish to delegate the zone.

Delegating a subdomain is equivalent to adding NS records for the subdomain to an existing zone. To add an NS record type:

```
C:\>dnscmd servername /RecordAdd zone subdomain NS subdomainserver
```

For example, to delegate the subdomain **europe** beneath **example.com** from the local machine to **hobbes.example.com**, you would type:

```
C:\>dnscmd localhost /RecordAdd example.com. europe NS hobbes.example.com
```

Removing Delegations

If you wish to remove the delegation of a subdomain, you must both delete the delegation from the parent zone and delete the zone you're removing from all hosting servers. You should first delete all copies of the zone data, starting with secondary servers, then, finally, delete the zone delegation object, as if it were a resource record.

Deleting Zones

Deleting a zone will remove the zone from the current server only. If the current server holds the primary copy of the zone, then you should reconfigure any remaining secondary servers so one is a new primary and so they can all still receive updates.

To delete a zone using the DNS management console snap-in, simply select it, press the Delete key, and confirm.

To delete a zone using dnscmd.exe use the following syntax:

```
C:\>dnscmd server /ZoneDelete zonename
```

By default, this will prompt for confirmation. If you want to use this command unattended, confirmation can be skipped using the **/f** switch. For example, to delete a zone named **another.example** from a DNS server whose IP address is **10.0.87.1** without confirmation you would type:

```
C:\>dnscmd 10.0.87.1 /ZoneDelete another.example. /f
```

In the case of Active Directory-integrated zones, deletion will remove them from the directory service and, hence, all other domain controllers. When using the graphical user interface (GUI), an additional level of confirmation is required, and from the command line the **/dsdel** parameter must be specified after the zone name, otherwise the operation will fail with the error **DNS_ERROR_ INVALID_ZONE_TYPE**.

Manually Force Zone Replication

DNS replication is a pull mechanism, so for standard secondary zones only, you're able to initiate a transfer of the zone from a master server. Primary servers have no master, so they can't be updated in this way; Active Directory zones are updated by Active Directory replication, as described in Chapter 8.

To manually force zone replication from the DNS Management Console Snap-in:

1. Right-click on the zone to update.

2. Select "Transfer From master".

To manually force zone replication with **dnscmd.exe** from the Windows 2000 Support Tools, type the following at a command prompt:

```
dnscmd servername /ZoneRefresh ZoneName
```

Related solution:	Found on page:
Forcing Immediate Replication	208

Managing Resource Records

Within zones, data is stored in Resource Records. You can manage Resource Records by directly editing zone files, but it is more intuitive to use the graphical tools provided in the form of the DNS Snap-in.

Adding Resource Records

The basic procedure for adding a resource record from the DNS Management Console Snap-in is:

1. Select the zone to add the record to in the left-hand tree.

2. Right-click the zone and select "New Other Records".

3. Select the type of record from the list and click Create.

4. Fill in the necessary details on the property page of the record.

Common resource record types, such as hosts and aliases, have specific shortcuts on the context menu. To add records with the **dnscmd.exe** utility, use the

/RecordAdd switch. The syntax varies slightly with the type of record to be added, and help is available via the following command:

```
C:\>dnscmd /RecordAdd /?
```

Once added, records can also be modified through scripting or the MMC Snap-in. The **dnscmd.exe** tool doesn't support record modification.

TIP: *It's also possible to add resource records to standard zones by directly editing the zone file. You can create one using the DNS MMC Snap-in to determine the correct syntax. Actually, it's possible to add resource records to AD-integrated zones using **ADSIEdit**, although it's more trouble than it's worth.*

Deleting Resource Records

To delete a resource record or cached resource record using the DNS Management Console Snap-in:

1. Connect to a DNS server containing a writable copy of the record, which means either a primary or Active Directory-integrated server for authoritative records.

2. Single-click the record you wish to delete, right-click and select Delete (or press the delete key).

To delete resource records with the **dnscmd** utility, use the following basic syntax:

```
C:\>dnscmd server /RecordDelete Zone RecordName Type
```

To delete records, you must specify the server, zone, and record names, as well as the type of record to delete. Without specifying anything further, all records of the given type will be deleted. Additional data can be added to delete a specific record and the **/f** switch used to automatically conform the deletion. Instead of a fully qualified domain name, *zone* can specify the DNS server cache or root hints. For example, to delete a host record, which maps **calvin.example.com** to **10.0.87.2**, from the local DNS server, without prompting for confirmation, you would type:

```
C:\>dnscmd localhost /RecordDelete example.com. calvin A 10.0.87.2 /f
```

Preventing WINS and WINS-R Record Transfer

WINS and WINS-R resource records aren't defined in the standards and will, therefore, be rejected by non-Microsoft DNS servers. If you have non-Microsoft DNS servers hosting a zone, you can disable the replication of WINS and WINS-R resource records. If you do so, you must add them explicitly to each Windows NT/2000 DNS server.

To prevent WINS resource record transfer:

1. Start the DNS Management Console and connect to the server hosting the zone to configure.
2. Expand Forward Lookup Zones.
3. Right-click the zone you wish to configure WINS for and select Properties.
4. Switch to the WINS tab and check "Do Not Replicate This Record".

To prevent WINS-R resource record transfer:

1. Start the DNS Management Console and connect to the server hosting the zone to configure.
2. Expand Reverse Lookup Zones.
3. Right-click the zone you wish to configure WINS-R for and select Properties.
4. Switch to the WINS-R tab and check "Do Not Replicate This Record".

SRV Resource Records

Because Windows 2000 Domain Controllers use dynamic DNS by default, changing the properties of SRV resource records on a DNS server will have limited effect, because they'll be overwritten the next time the entries are refreshed.

Instead, to adjust the following **DWORD** values in the registry to alter the weight and priority of a domain controller's SRV resource records:

```
HKLM\SYSTEM\CurrentControlSet\Services\Netlogon\Parameters\LdapSrvPriority
HKLM\SYSTEM\CurrentControlSet\Services\Netlogon\Parameters\LdapSrvWeight
```

The **DWORD** value of these parameters specifies the values applied to the SRV resource records updated by dynamic registration.

WARNING! At this point in a book, it's traditional to have a "be very careful when editing the registry" warning. It should go without saying that making changes to the configuration of a computer that you aren't confident of being able to recover from is a very bad idea, and using a registry editor is just one such case.

Aging and Scavenging

I'll now discuss aging and scavenging.

Configuring Scavenging for a DNS Server

For any record to be scavenged, it must be enabled on a per-server basis. Aging and scavenging is only possible on primary and Active Directory-integrated zones and must also be enabled for each zone you wish to scavenge.

To enable scavenging for a DNS server:

1. Right-click the server to configure and select "Set Aging/Scavenging For All Zones".
2. Check the Scavenge stale resource records box to enable scavenging for this DNS server.
3. Configure the No-Refresh interval and Refresh interval. The Refresh interval should be longer than your DHCP lease, and the No-Refresh interval should be tuned according to server load, with lower values resulting in more disk activity.
4. Click OK when done.
5. On a domain controller, you'll be prompted to enable scavenging on Active Directory-integrated zones.

Configuring Scavenging for Zones

To enable aging/scavenging on individual zones, you must configure it for that zone and enable it on the server. To configure aging and scavenging for a zone:

1. Right-click the zone to configure and select Properties.
2. Click the Aging button.
3. Check the Scavenge stale resource records box to enable scavenging for this zone.
4. Configure the No-Refresh interval and Refresh interval. These values will default to the settings for the zone.
5. Click OK, then OK when done.

Scavenging Immediately

The scavenging process runs periodically, as defined by the Scavenging Period setting from the Advanced tab of a DNS server's Properties dialog box. It can also be started immediately as follows:

1. Right-click the server to scavenge.
2. Select Scavenge stale resource records.
3. Click OK to confirm scavenging stale resource records.

Configuring Forwarders

Forwarders are servers used as a first resort if the current DNS server can't authoritatively answer a query. The query is relayed to each forwarder in turn until an authoritative answer is found or the list is exhausted. They're configured on a per-DNS-server basis.

WARNING! If the option to enable forwarders is disabled, it's because your server is configured as a root server, that is to say, it's authoritative for the root zone '.'. Before you can enable forwarders, you must first delete the root zone. If you use dnscmd to add forwarders to a root server, the command will complete successfully but no forwarders will be added.

To configure forwarders using the DNS MMC Snap-in:

1. Open the Properties dialog of the DNS server to configure by right-clicking the server name and selecting Properties.

2. Change to the Forwarders tab.

3. Use the options on this tab to enable forwarders, add and remove them, rearrange the order in which they're contacted, and change the timeout delay.

4. If you wish to make this server a slave, check the "Do not use recursion" box.

To configure forwarders using the **dnscmd** utility from the Support Tools, you must replace the entire list of forwarders of each type. The following syntax is used:

```
dnscmd ServerNameOrIPaddress /ResetForwarders ipaddress1 ipaddress2 ..
```

Here **ipaddress1 ipaddress2 ..** is a list of forwarder IP addresses in the order in which they're to be contacted. Additional options can be specified with parameters after the IP address list:

- **/Slave**—This is equivalent to checking the "Do not use recursion" box in the MMC and configures the server as a slave DNS server. Omitting this, or explicitly specifying **/NoSlave**, allows recursive queries to be generated.

- **/TimeOut** n—This specifies that after n seconds have elapsed, the next forwarder in the list will be tried. The default value is 5 seconds.

For example, to configure the local machine as a slave that forwards to **131.111.8.42** and **131.111.12.20** as with 10-second timeouts, you would type:

```
dnscmd . /ResetForwarders 131.111.8.42 131.111.12.20 /Slave /TimeOut 10
```

Displaying IP Configuration Information

Seeing basic IP configuration information is useful for diagnosing and trouble-shooting connectivity problems. To view such information locally, use the **ipconfig.exe** utility from a command prompt as follows:

```
C:\>ipconfig
```

To display more detailed information, type:

```
C:\>ipconfig /all
```

Managing the Resolver Cache

I'll now discuss managing the Resolver Cache.

Viewing the Resolver Cache

The DNS client resolver cache is maintained separately on each computer on the network and is consulted first before DNS queries are sent. To view the contents of the cache, type the following at the command line:

```
C:\>ipconfig /displaydns
```

This gives gratuitous details about every cached entry DNS record and will more than likely scroll useful information straight off the top of the command prompt. To pipe it to a file named dnscache.txt for leisurely viewing, use the following syntax:

```
C:\>ipconfig /displaydns >dnscache.txt
```

Clearing the Resolver Cache

To enable clients to respond to changes on DNS servers in a more timely manner, you can delete all entries in the local resolver cache, so subsequent queries must be made to a DNS server. To clear the resolver cache, type:

```
C:\>ipconfig /flushdns
```

Controlling Dynamic DNS Registrations

I'll now cover controlling dynamic DNS registrations.

Preventing Domain Controllers Using Dynamic DNS

If you're not using dynamic DNS in your network, you should disable the registration of resource records to save resources and prevent error logs from filling up. To prevent domain controllers registering SRV resource records, set the following registry entry to 0:

```
HKLM\System\CurrentControlSet\Services\Netlogon\Parameters\UseDynamicDns
```

WARNING! Only change this registry entry if you are not using dynamic DNS registration and are adding all records manually for domain controllers. Disabling DDNS and not adding records manually will render your domain controller useless.

Preventing Clients from Registering Addresses

By default, Windows 2000 Professional computers and member servers will attempt to register DNS records dynamically for themselves. In environments where dynamic updates aren't in use or are not supported, this is wasteful of resources and can potentially fill server error logs.

To disable dynamic registration for a network connection:

1. Open the Network and Dial-up Connections folder from Control Panel.
2. Double-click the connection to modify (usually Local Area Connection).
3. Click Properties.
4. Select Internet Protocol (TCP/IP) from the components list and click Properties.
5. Click the Advanced button.

6. Select the DNS tab.

7. Clear the "Register This Connection's Address" in the DNS box.

8. Select OK three times to commit changes.

There's no need to reboot after changing TCP/IP configuration in Windows 2000.

NOTE: *Dynamic registration is also the default behavior for dial-up connections. Internet Service Providers are generally much happier if you go to the Networking tab of the dial-up connection properties dialog box, and repeat the above procedure to prevent dynamic registration being attempted.*

Reregister Host Records

If you wish to force the reregistration of dynamically added resource records, for example, if you delete them accidentally, you must stop and restart the net logon service.

To do this from a graphical interface:

1. Start the Computer Management console from the Administrative Tools menu.

2. If you need to reregister records for a remote computer, right-click Computer Management and select "Connect To Another Computer". Select or type the name or IP address of the computer you wish to connect to and click OK.

3. Expand the Services and Applications node.

4. Click Services.

5. In the details pane, right-click Net Logon and select Restart.

To restart the net logon service on a local computer from the command line, type:

```
C:\>net stop "net logon" | net start "net logon"
```

TIP: *The pipe character | is used to separate commands in the same line of input at the command prompt.*

To do the same on a remote computer, use the **sc.exe** tool from the Windows 2000 Server Resource Kit twice, as follows:

```
C:\>sc \\servername "net logon" stop | sc \\servername "net logon" start
```

Chapter 4

Installing Active Directory

In Depth

Installing Active Directory is, on the face of it, a straightforward task: run the wizard and it just happens. Reality is, of course, more complicated. As an administrator, you should understand what to do to prepare for Active Directory installation, the processes that take place during installation, and also how to remove Active Directory from a server.

Preparing for Active Directory

Before making a server into a domain controller, a certain number of steps must be taken to ensure that the process will run and do so as smoothly as possible.

Minimum Requirements

The essentials to be able to install Active Directory are the following:

- *NTFS Volume*—The domain controller's shared system volume (**Sysvol**) must be stored on an NT File System (NTFS) volume, so domain controllers should have at least one NTFS volume. The Active Directory database and log files need not be stored on NTFS volumes.

- *Static IP Address*—Domain controllers must be able to be located using Domain Name System (DNS), and the requirement for a static IP address makes this process less problematic.

- *250 MB Hard Disk Space Free*—This is the minimum required and should not be a problem on modern hardware. Because running out of hard disk space on a domain controller causes Active Directory to shut down, it's a good idea to have plenty of free space. More exact size requirements of Active Directory databases can be found in Chapter 8.

In addition, DNS must be configured appropriately. Probably the single largest cause of Active Directory installations failing is incorrectly configured DNS. If you're creating a brand-new forest, there are no existing domain controllers to contact, so the DNS issue is simple, because the DNS server service can be installed as part of promotion to a domain controller.

However, if you're adding a domain controller to an existing forest—either by creating a new domain or joining an existing domain—issues of authentication and replication require that other domain controllers be contacted. Therefore,

DNS has to be correctly configured so the service (SRV) resource records for existing domain controllers can be resolved.

Windows 2000 computers that aren't domain controllers maintain a local set of user and group accounts, which are used to assign permissions to resources on the local computer. Domain controllers don't have such local user and group accounts, so, instead, domain accounts are used to fulfill this role. The upshot of this is that when you convert a server to a domain controller, all local security accounts are lost, and permissions are reset.

In addition, because user accounts are deleted, all encryption keys are also deleted. Specifically, this means that any files encrypted using the Windows 2000 Encrypting File System will become unreadable unless you have exported the cryptographic keys used to protect them. For this reason, it's a very good idea to decrypt any files before promoting a server to be a domain controller. You can always re-encrypt them afterward.

Choosing Names

Renaming domains and domain controllers isn't supported in Windows 2000 Active Directory, although it may be in future revisions. It's thus essential that you choose names with care.

Domains

If you're creating a new domain, you'll require a unique DNS name for that domain, and you should either choose an internal name that's sufficiently unique or use a domain name registered externally, such as **example.com**. That is, don't choose **microsoft.com** as your domain name, even if your network isn't permanently connected to the Internet, because it will make it very hard for your computers to see a relatively important Web site. Instead, you should choose a **.local** address, such as **blackbook.local**, if you don't have an externally registered address.

It's far better to choose an externally registered address, because it may save restructuring at a later date. If your company already uses DNS internally, it could be your current domain name or a subdomain of it. If your company doesn't use DNS already, then you should register an address specially.

Domain Controllers

One limitation of Active Directory at present is that you can't rename a domain controller and must, instead, remove Active Directory, rename it, then reinstall it. Because this process is time-consuming and inefficient, it's best to name your domain controllers in a way that you're happy with before installing Active Directory.

Preparing DNS

Even though DNS can be added as part of the Active Directory installation process, when you create a new domain—particularly a child domain—it's beneficial to set up your DNS infrastructure before creating an Active Directory domain.

At the very least, this is good discipline, because it forces you to think about delegating zones to a child domain. Additionally, DNS must be configured on the second and subsequent domain controllers in your forest, because it must be able to contact other domain controllers to join a forest. It's less problematic to configure the DNS of the server to be promoted as you intend it finally, instead of having to move it between DNS servers at a later date.

Installing Active Directory

Active Directory can't be installed during the installation of Windows 2000 and must be added later. The installation process is started by executing **dcpromo.exe**, either directly or by using the Configure Your Server application, which starts automatically or can be found on the Administrative Tools menu. The Active Directory screen of the Configure Your Server application is shown in Figure 4.1.

Executing **dcpromo.exe** starts the Active Directory Installation Wizard, which guides you through the rest of the process.

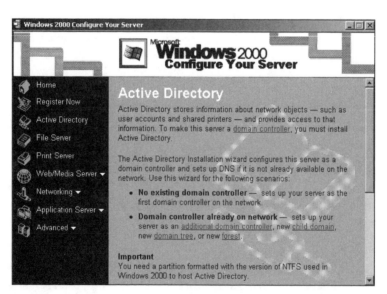

Figure 4.1   The Configure Your Server screen for adding Active Directory.

Installation Options

The same Wizard is used for all installations, from creating a new Active Directory forest to adding a new domain controller to an existing domain. For this reason, the Wizard starts with a series of questions that are summarized by Figure 4.2.

Domain Controller Type

The first decision is whether you're adding a domain controller to an existing domain or creating an entirely new domain. If you're adding a controller to an existing domain, there's no need to specify some of the more complex options for the installation, and, instead, only a set of credentials, the domain to join, and installation directories are required. If, instead, you're creating a new domain, there's an additional series of questions to determine whether you're creating a child domain or a new tree, which will either be part of an existing forest or an entirely new one.

Network Credentials

To prevent rogue domains or domain controllers from being added, authentication is required as part of the Active Directory installation process if you're adding to an existing Windows 2000 forest. The username, password, and domain name for authentication must be specified in downlevel (NetBIOS) form and not via user principal names (UPNs) or DNS domain names. By default, only members of the Enterprise Admins group can add domains to a forest, and only Enterprise or Domain Admins can add domain controllers to a domain.

New Domain Name

If a new domain is being created, a DNS name must be specified. A full DNS name is required for new trees, and an offset to the parent domain is needed for subdomains. A hard-coded limit of 64 bytes exists for the full DNS name of the new domain, because it must be used as part of file paths for Group Policy, and file paths are limited to 260 characters.

The domain name that you specify should be externally registered (even if your network isn't connected to the Internet at present) to guarantee global uniqueness and to allow your directory to be connected to the Internet at a later date. With Windows 2000 Active Directory, domains can't be renamed, so production domains should be named carefully.

Additionally, you must specify a downlevel domain name, used by NetBIOS functions, such as Windows NT 4 clients. This name must be unique within your enterprise and may be up to 15 characters (ideally alphanumeric for safety). Like DNS domain names, NetBIOS names aren't case sensitive.

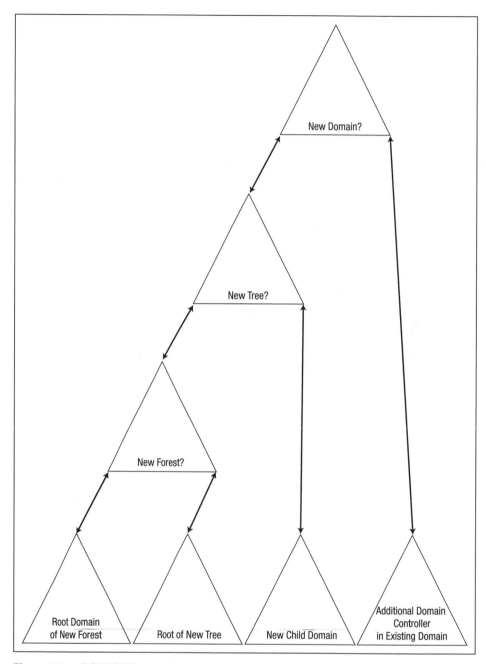

Figure 4.2   **DCPROMO** decision tree.

NOTE: *Out-of-the-box, Windows 2000 prevents you from using all numeric labels in DNS domain names, so it prohibits* **123.example.com** *being an Active Directory domain, for example. This is intended to prevent the use of IP addresses as domain names and also solves the problem that all numeric NetBIOS names are invalid. However, all numeric DNS labels are valid within the standard, so Microsoft has fixed this issue in Service Pack 1.*

File Locations

All new domain controllers must have three locations specified for file storage: for the database itself, for database transaction log files, and for the shared system volume (known as **Sysvol**). The Active Directory data is itself stored in a file called ntds.dit within the folder specified for database location. NTDS is a commonly found acronym within Active Directory internals and stands for NT Directory Service. DIT is a directory service acronym and stands for Directory Information Tree. A minimum of 200MB is allocated for the ntds.dit file.

When changes are made to the contents of Active Directory, they're first written to a log file and only then made to the directory database. The staging area is the transaction log files, and to increase performance, you're able to specify a separate location for these files from the directory database. A minimum of 50MB is required for log files, including 20MB for emergency log files in case the disk fills up.

The third location you must specify is for **Sysvol**. **Sysvol** is a shared folder used to make files, such as logon scripts, available to clients and to replicate domain controllers. The **Sysvol** structure must be stored on an NTFS volume. The database and log files are easily moved at a later time with the **ntdsutil** tool, but the **Sysvol** shared folder is an altogether more complicated object, because it uses advanced features of NTFS 5, known as junction points, that can't simply be moved.

Directory Services Restore Mode Password

The Active Directory Installation Wizard prompts for a password for all domain controllers. This is used to protect Directory Services Restore mode and also the recovery console on the domain controller (usually the local administrator password is used for the recovery console, but no local administrator is on a domain controller).

Directory Services Restore mode is an advanced startup option accessed by pressing F8 and selecting the appropriate menu item, when prompted during the Windows 2000 boot sequence. It doesn't load the directory into memory but is used for operations, such as restoring the directory, and for performing database maintenance, such as moving the database file to a different location.

The account information used to authenticate for Directory Services Restore mode is held in the Security Accounts Manager (SAM) in the same way that local accounts are on Windows 2000 Professional and member Server computers.

4. Installing Active Directory

Windows NT 4 domains also use the SAM to store account information. Because of this, the password can be compromised using **L0phtCrack** and **pwdump2**, which can be found at **www.l0pht.com/l0phtcrack** and **www.webspan.net/~tas/pwdump2**, respectively. Good security practice dictates that you should use different passwords for the Administrator account in the domain and Directory Services Restore mode, because if one is compromised, then the other won't be.

Even if you don't suspect that any malicious hackers lurk in your organization, it's still useful to use a different password for each so you can tell a junior administrator the password to get into Directory Services Restore mode without giving her administrative access to the domain.

Pre-Windows 2000 Compatible Access

As part of the Windows 2000 installation process, a group named Pre-Windows 2000 Compatible Access is created. This group is given read permissions to all user and group accounts in the directory.

If you select the Pre-Windows 2000 Compatible Access option, then the Everyone Group is nested inside the Pre-Windows 2000 Compatible Access Group. This means that everyone, whether authenticated or not, can read any property of any user and group account in the directory.

The setting is required if you're using Windows NT 4 Remote Access Service (RAS) or Routing and Remote Access Service (RRAS) servers to authenticate against Active Directory, but it's a security risk. Obviously the Microsoft answer to any security worries is to upgrade your RAS servers to Windows 2000 (which is, in all fairness, a good solution, because Windows 2000 RAS is much improved over Windows NT 4).

In fact, the Everyone Group can be added to the Pre-Windows 2000 Compatible Access Group even in a Mixed-mode domain by a special internal mechanism. It's possible to add and remove it as required, regardless of domain mode, to tighten or lessen security. This is described in the Immediate Solutions with this chapter.

What the Installation Process Actually Does

Once you've made all the necessary choices to install Active Directory and have finished the Wizard, the installation process itself starts. Exactly what this process does depends slightly on the options selected.

Object Creation

A domain controller object is created in the Active Directory to represent the domain controller. This is created in the Domain Controller's OU and contains objects for information, such as replication partners. The replication topology of the network is also automatically recalculated when a new domain controller is created, so it receives updates to the directory.

Domain Creation

If a new domain is being created in an existing forest, the domain-naming master must be contacted in order for the new domain name to be checked for uniqueness and registered in the configuration-naming context.

DNS Entries

In order for domain controllers to be located on the network, various resource records are added to DNS. The resource records are critical to your network, because they're used whenever any Windows 2000 computer wishes to find a domain controller of any description, including Global Catalog servers or the primary domain controller (PDC) Emulator.

For example, the logon process requires a domain controller for authentication, and searching across all domains in the forest requires a Global Catalog server. The DNS entries registered for a given domain controller are stored in %SYSTEMROOT%\System32\Config\netlogon.dns. If your DNS server supports dynamic updates, these records are registered each time the netlogon service starts or stops.

Migration of User Accounts

When you use **dcpromo** to promote to a domain controller, the existing Security Accounts Manager (SAM) containing local accounts is replaced by the SAM for Directory Services Restore mode, so what happens to accounts in the existing SAM?

On the first domain controller in each domain, they're migrated to the built-in Users container in Active Directory, so that they exist as domain accounts. This is the logical thing to do, because it allows you to migrate one server from a peer-to-peer, workgroup environment to an Active Directory domain. On subsequent domain controllers in a domain, local accounts are deleted, and they're lost.

One impact this does have is on service accounts. If you have an application, such as Internet Information Services (IIS), running on a member server that you promote to be an additional domain controller in an existing domain, all local accounts, and, hence, all service accounts will be deleted.

Some services, such as IIS, are able to deal with this by re-creating their service accounts if they're deleted. IIS does this through the IIS Admin service, which crucially logs on under the system context so it doesn't require a user account to log on. Other applications may not be this robust, so it's essential to document and be prepared to re-create service accounts after installing Active Directory.

4. Installing Active Directory

Groups Created

When you create a new domain, a number of predefined groups and accounts are created in the directory. These are to support a number of predefined roles within the domain and forest. The Global Groups are:

- Cert Publishers
- DnsUpdateProxy
- Domain Admins
- Domain computers
- Domain Controllers
- Domain Guests
- Domain Users
- Group Policy Creator Owners
- RAS and IAS Servers

The built-in Local Groups are:

- Account Operators
- Administrators
- Backup Operators
- Guests
- Pre-Windows 2000 Compatible Access
- Print Operators
- Replicator
- Server Operators
- Users

Additionally, for the root domain of a forest, only the following groups are added:

- *Enterprise Admins*—The Enterprise Admins Group holds administrative privileges for every domain in the forest, because they're added to each Domain Admins Group by default. Also, there are a number of functions that can, by default, only be performed by Enterprise Admins, such as adding new domains to the forest. Membership of Enterprise Admins should be very strictly limited.

- *Schema Admins*—As the name suggests, the Schema Admins Group is the one and only group that, by default, has permission to modify the schema of the forest. Changing the schema is a relatively infrequent task and membership of Schema Admins should be very tightly controlled because of the potential harm that can be caused by an incorrect or malicious schema modification.

Server Roles

The operation master roles that exist within a Windows 2000 network are required for the network to function normally and are, therefore, configured when domains and forests are created. When you create a new domain, the first domain controller holds the three domain operation master roles–PDC Emulator, Infrastructure Master, and relative identifier (RID) Master. Also, when you create a new forest, the two enterprise operation master roles—domain-naming master and schema master—are assigned to the first domain controller in the first domain in the forest. These roles are flexible and can be transferred to other domain controllers—within the domain for domain-specific roles and anywhere within the forest for the two enterprise roles. Because multiple-domain environments actually require a Global Catalog server for some authentication purposes, the first domain controller in a forest is designated as a Global Catalog server.

Removing Active Directory

There may come a time in the life of a domain controller when it no longer needs to be a domain controller. Unlike Windows NT 4, which required a complete reinstall (or a third-party utility), Windows 2000 provides an out-of-the-box mechanism to convert from a domain controller to a member server or standalone server. This process is known as *demotion* and uses the same program—**dcpromo.exe**— as promoting a server to be a domain controller. When a member of Domain Admins runs **dcpromo.exe** on a domain controller, he is given the option to remove Active Directory or cancel the Wizard.

Removal Options

The first option when removing Active Directory is whether or not this is the last domain controller in the domain. If it is, then the domain must be deleted from the forest. Credentials for a member of the Enterprise Admins Group must be specified to delete the objects that represent the domain from the configuration partition of the directory.

Finally, you must also specify the administrative password for the new local administrator account, because the computer will no longer contain domain accounts. If you're attempting to demote a Global Catalog server, the warning shown in Figure 4.3 will appear.

Figure 4.3   Global Catalog server demotion warning.

In multiple domain environments, Global Catalog servers must be contacted as part of the user authentication process in order to check Universal Group membership, because it's possible for a user account to belong to Universal Groups in other domains within the forest. Therefore, it's unwise to remove all Global Catalog servers from your network if you wish to be able to log on.

If you're demoting an operations master role holder, such as the PDC Emulator, for a domain, it will attempt to transfer any operations master roles to other eligible domain controllers before demotion. It doesn't hurt, however, to manually transfer any roles before demotion, because this will ensure they're moved to servers of your choice.

Troubleshooting Failed Removals

The Active Directory installation process is fairly robust and can cope with (and recover from) various failures throughout. It also has the option to cancel. The removal process is less robust and has no cancel option, simply because once you've started to remove Active Directory, stopping will leave you without a functioning domain controller.

However, the removal process can be stopped for you by various means, including power failure, and this may leave the computer in an inconsistent state. Of course, in an ideal world, you'd have a complete backup of all important data from the time just before **dcpromo** was run, so you could simply reformat the hard disk and reinstall Windows 2000 without losing any data.

Back in the real world, you'll be glad to know it's possible to recover under such circumstances by manually completing the removal of Active Directory. A common reason for removal to fail before it even begins is, again, DNS. Before a server is demoted, it first replicates all changes made to its directory, and if this replication fails, then demotion won't proceed. In addition, if you're removing a domain, the domain-naming master must be contacted in order for the objects representing the domain to be deleted from the configuration partition.

Immediate Solutions

Preinstallation Tasks

Here I'll cover the tasks that you need to know for preinstallation.

Converting a Drive to NTFS

The installation of Active Directory requires at least one volume formatted with the NT File System (NTFS) to host the shared system volume (**Sysvol**). If you didn't select an NTFS volume during installation, it's possible to convert an existing volume to NTFS without loss of data. To do so, start a command prompt and type something similar to

```
C:\>convert x: /fs:ntfs
```

where x should be replaced by the letter of the drive to convert to NTFS.

Decrypting Files

Any encrypted files on NTFS volumes will be rendered unreadable, because the cryptographic keys used to access them are associated with user accounts, which may be destroyed by promoting the computer to be a domain controller.

To decrypt a file or folder:

1. Start Explorer from the Accessories menu by pressing the Windows key and *E*.
2. Right-click on the file or folder to decrypt and select Properties.
3. Encryption is classified as an advanced attribute, so click the Advanced button.
4. Clear the Encrypt contents to secure the data checkbox and click OK.
5. Click OK to accept changes and close the Properties dialog box.

4. Installing Active Directory

Installing Active Directory

Now I'll cover the installation of Active Directory.

Installing the First Domain Controller in a New Forest

The series of questions asked by the Active Directory Installation Wizard varies, depending on which type of server you're installing. Follow these instructions to create the root domain of a new forest:

1. Click Start, Run, type **dcpromo.exe**, then click OK.

2. The Active Directory Installation Wizard begins. Click Next to continue.

3. You're creating a new forest and, hence, a new domain, so click Domain Controller for a New Domain, then Next.

4. A new forest requires a new tree, so select "Create A New Domain Tree", then click Next.

5. Finally, select "Create New Forest of Domain Trees" to specify that this is an entirely new forest.

6. In the next screen, type the fully qualified DNS domain name for your new domain in the form of a fully qualified domain, for example, **coriolis.com**. Click Next.

7. You must now specify a downlevel or NetBIOS domain name. This defaults to the first part of your fully qualified domain name, for example, CORIO-LIS. This name must be unique within your enterprise. Click Next to continue.

8. The Database Location and Logs Location boxes default to %SystemRoot%\ Ntds. You should specify the path to the local drives to hold the directory database and log files. For optimum performance, they should be located on separate, physical hard drives. Click Next.

9. In the Shared System Volume screen, the default location for **Sysvol** is %SystemRoot%\Sysvol. **Sysvol** must be hosted on an NTFS volume. Enter the desired path and click Next.

10. If no DNS server is available, a message stating "The wizard cannot contact the DNS server that handles the name Domain Name to determine if it supports dynamic update. Confirm your DNS configuration or install and configure a DNS server on this computer" appears. If this happens, you should click OK, then Next to accept the recommended option of installing Windows 2000 DNS.

11. In the Windows NT 4.0 RAS Server screen, choose whether or not you want to weaken permissions to allow Windows NT 4 Remote Access Services

(RAS) access to this server. This answer can easily be reversed at a later time. Click Next.

12. In the next screen, specify the password to use when you start the computer in Directory Services Restore mode. Click Next when done.

TIP: *This password can be changed by starting the domain controller in Directory Services Restore mode and changing your password in the usual way by pressing Alt+Ctrl+Del.*

---

13. The summary screen details the options selected. Click Next to confirm the choices and start the installation process.

14. Once Active Directory is installed, click Finish to close the Wizard, and then restart the computer.

Adding a Tree to an Existing Forest

The following steps should be followed if you're adding a new tree to an existing forest in order to create a new domain within the forest that has a separate DNS name.

1. Click Start, Run, type **dcpromo.exe**, then click OK.

2. The Active Directory Installation Wizard starts. Click Next to continue.

3. You are creating a new tree and, hence, a new domain, so click Domain Controller for a New Domain, and then click Next.

4. You're creating a new domain tree, so select "Create A New Domain Tree", and then click Next.

5. You aren't creating a new forest, so Click "Place This New Domain Tree In An Existing Forest", then click Next.

6. The next screen prompts for network credentials with sufficient privileges to perform this operation. Type the user name, password, and domain name for an account with Enterprise Admins membership.

7. In the next screen, type the fully qualified DNS domain name for your new domain in the form of a fully qualified domain, for example, **examcram.com**. Click Next.

8. You must now specify a downlevel or NetBIOS domain name. This defaults to the first part of your fully qualified domain name, for example, EXAMCRAM. This name must be unique within your enterprise. Click Next to continue.

9. The Database Location and Logs Location boxes default to %SystemRoot%\Ntds. You should specify the path to the local drives to hold the directory database and log files. For optimum performance, they should be located on separate, physical hard drives. Click Next.

10. In the Shared System Volume screen, the default location for **Sysvol** is %SystemRoot%\Sysvol. **Sysvol** must be hosted on an NTFS volume. Enter the desired path and click Next.

11. If no DNS server is available, a message stating "The wizard cannot contact the DNS server that handles the name Domain Name to determine if it supports dynamic update. Confirm your DNS configuration, or install and configure a DNS server on this computer" appears. If this happens, you should click OK, then Next to accept the recommended option of installing Windows 2000 DNS.

NOTE: *Your existing DNS configuration determines whether you need to install the DNS service on this server.*

---

12. In the Windows NT 4.0 RAS Server screen, choose whether or not you want to weaken permissions to allow Windows NT 4 Remote Access Services (RAS) access to this server. This answer can easily be reversed at a later time. Click Next.

13. In the next screen, specify the password to use when you start the computer in Directory Services Restore mode. Click Next when done.

TIP: *This password can be changed by starting the domain controller in Directory Services Restore mode and changing your password in the usual way by pressing Alt+Ctrl+Del.*

---

14. The summary screen details the options selected. Click Next to confirm the choices and start the installation process.

15. Once Active Directory is installed, click Finish to close the Wizard, and then restart the computer.

Installing the First Domain Controller in a New Child Domain

The following steps should be followed if you're adding a new child domain with a DNS name beneath an existing domain name in your forest:

1. Click Start, Run, type **dcpromo.exe**, then click OK.

2. The Active Directory Installation Wizard commences. Click Next to continue.

3. You're creating a new domain, so click Domain Controller for a New Domain, and then click Next.

4. You aren't creating a new domain tree, so select "Create A New Child In An Existing Domain Tree", and then click Next.

5. The next screen prompts for network credentials with sufficient privileges to perform this operation. Type the user name, password, and domain name for an account with Enterprise Admins membership.

6. In the next screen, type the full DNS name of the parent and the domain and specify a subdomain name for the child. For example, a parent called **coriolis.com** and a subdomain accounting would create a new Active Directory domain called **accounting.coriolis.com**.

7. You must now specify a downlevel or NetBIOS domain name. This defaults to the first part of your fully qualified domain name, for example, AC-COUNTING. This name must be unique within your enterprise. Click Next to continue.

8. The Database Location and Logs Location boxes default to %SystemRoot%\Ntds. You should specify the path to the local drives to hold the directory database and log files. For optimum performance, they should be located on separate, physical hard drives. Click Next.

9. In the Shared System Volume screen, the default location for **Sysvol** is %SystemRoot%\Sysvol. **Sysvol** must be hosted on an NTFS volume. Enter the desired path and click Next.

10. If no DNS server is available, a message stating "The wizard cannot contact the DNS server that handles the name Domain Name to determine if it supports dynamic update. Confirm your DNS configuration, or install and configure a DNS server on this computer" appears. If this happens, you should click OK, then Next to accept the recommended option of installing Windows 2000 DNS.

NOTE: *Your existing DNS configuration determines whether you need to install the DNS service on this server.*

11. In the Windows NT 4.0 RAS Server screen, choose whether or not you want to weaken permissions to allow Windows NT 4 Remote Access Services (RAS) access to this server. This answer can easily be reversed at a later time. Click Next.

12. In the next screen, specify the password to use when you start the computer in Directory Services Restore mode. Click Next when done.

TIP: *This password can be changed by starting the domain controller in Directory Services Restore mode and changing your password in the usual way by pressing Alt+Ctrl+Del.*

13. The summary screen details the options selected. Click Next to confirm the choices and start the installation process.

14. Once Active Directory is installed, click Finish to close the Wizard, and then restart the computer.

Installing an Additional Domain Controller for an Existing Domain

To install an additional Domain Controller for an existing domain perform the following:

1. Click Start, Run, type **dcpromo.exe**, then click OK.

2. The Active Directory Installation Wizard commences. Click Next to continue.

3. You aren't creating a new domain, so click Additional Domain Controller for an Existing Domain, then click Next.

4. The next screen prompts for network credentials with sufficient privileges to perform this operation. Type the user name, password, and domain name for an account with Enterprise Admins or Domain Admins membership.

5. In the next screen, type the full DNS name of the domain to add the current server to. Click Next when done.

6. The Database Location and Logs Location boxes default to %SystemRoot%\ Ntds. You should specify the path to the local drives to hold the directory database and log files. For optimum performance, they should be located on separate physical hard drives. Click Next.

7. In the Shared System Volume screen, the default location for **Sysvol** is %SystemRoot%\Sysvol. **Sysvol** must be hosted on an NTFS volume. Enter the desired path and click Next.

8. If no DNS server is available, a message stating, "The wizard cannot contact the DNS server that handles the name Domain Name to determine if it supports dynamic update. Confirm your DNS configuration, or install and configure a DNS server on this computer" appears. If this happens, you should click OK then click Next to accept the recommended option of installing Windows 2000 DNS.

NOTE: *Your existing DNS configuration determines whether you need to install the DNS service on this server.*

---

9. In the Windows NT 4.0 RAS Server screen, choose whether or not you want to weaken permissions to allow Windows NT 4 Remote Access Services (RAS) access to this server. This answer can easily be reversed at a later time. Click Next.

10. In the next screen, specify the password to use when you start the computer in Directory Services Restore mode. Click Next when done.

TIP: *This password can be changed by starting the domain controller in Directory Services Restore mode and changing your password in the usual way by pressing Alt+Ctrl+Del.*

---

11. The summary screen details the options selected. Click Next to confirm the choices and start the installation process.

12. Once Active Directory is installed, click Finish to close the Wizard, and then restart the computer.

Changing Pre-Windows 2000 Compatible Access

If you select to weaken permissions when creating a domain in order to support Windows NT 4 RAS servers, you thereby grant the Everyone Group read permissions to all objects in the domain. At a later time you can remove this setting by typing the following at the command line:

```
C:\>net localgroup "Pre-Windows 2000 Compatible Access" everyone /delete
```

Alternatively, you may have selected not to weaken permissions and find that a Windows NT application is unable to access user or group accounts or you wish to add an NT 4 RAS server to your domain. In such a situation, you should add the Everyone Group to Pre-Windows 2000 Compatible Access by typing:

```
C:\>net localgroup "Pre-Windows 2000 Compatible Access" everyone /add
```

Removing Active Directory

If you no longer require a server to be a domain controller, you can remove Active Directory from it by re-running **dcpromo**. This will leave you with a member server in the domain, or if you remove the last domain controller in a domain, you'll be left with a standalone server.

Before demoting a domain controller, you should ensure that it isn't the only Global Catalog server on the network, and as a best practice, you should manually transfer flexible single operations master roles to other servers.

WARNING! You can't cancel the demotion of a domain controller to a member server. If dcpromo.exe is stopped with Task Manager, kill.exe, or power failure, then you won't be able to remove or add Active Directory to the server until you manually complete the process.

1. Click Start, Run, type **dcpromo.exe**, then click OK.

2. The Active Directory Installation Wizard starts. Click Next.

4. Installing Active Directory

3. If the current computer is a Global Catalog server, you'll be warned to make sure that another exists within the forest.

4. Next, you're asked whether this is the last domain controller in the domain or not. If it is, check the box so the domain objects can be removed from the forest.

5. The next screen prompts for the local administrator account password on the server after Active Directory is removed. Type the password twice and click Next.

6. In the Summary screen click Next.

7. Once Active Directory has been fully removed, click Finish to quit the Wizard and restart the computer when prompted.

Related solution:	*Found on page:*
Configuring a Domain Controller as a Global Catalog Server	421
Seizing Operations Master Roles	422

Chapter 5

Domains and Domain Controllers

In Depth

Now that we've dealt with the preliminary concepts, tools, and installation of Active Directory, our attention turns to exploring the underlying processes and mechanisms of Active Directory. The first of these is Active Directory domains and the domain controllers that host them.

Domains

An Active Directory domain is a logical structure that contains objects that represent items on your network, such as users or computers. It's analogous to a Windows NT domain but can contain many more objects. Domains are physically hosted on one—or hopefully more than one—Windows 2000 Server computer running Active Directory, known as a domain controller.

Domain Modes

Active Directory domains exist in one of two modes: either Mixed or Native. The mode of operation reflects whether they're compatible with pre-Windows 2000 domain controllers or not. Mixed-mode domains are compatible with Windows NT 4 backup domain controllers (BDCs), because they don't implement features, such as group nesting, which Windows NT 4 has no method of storing in its Security Accounts Manager (SAM) database. All domains begin as Mixed mode, even if they're installed from scratch.

Once you've removed any Windows NT domain controllers, you must explicitly convert a domain to Native mode once it has been created, and this is a one-way process—it's impossible to convert back. Strictly speaking, you don't have to remove Windows NT domain controllers before converting to Native mode, although it's a very good idea to do so because they stop receiving updates and, hence, become worse-than-useless by holding out-of-date information.

It should be stressed that the mode of a domain only affects the type of objects that it stores and how certain internal functions work. Mode doesn't affect external trust relationships, and it's perfectly possible to mix both Native and Mixed-mode domains in a forest.

Domain Partitions

The contents of the directory are broken down into contiguous groups known as *partitions* for the purpose of replication. Each partition contains all of the

Lightweight Directory Access Protocol (LDAP) namespace beneath it, less any parts that are partitions themselves. Each partition is an autonomous unit for the purpose of replication.

Each domain controller carries replicas of at least three partitions—one for its domain, one for the forestwide schema, and one for the configuration partitions. In addition, Global Catalog servers hold partial replicas of every domain partition for the forest to enable fast searches of forestwide objects on frequently accessed properties. For example, the three partitions created for the root domain of a forest called **example.com** are:

- *dc=example,dc=com*—This is the domain partition that contains domain-specific information, such as all of the objects within the domain, as well as any integrated Domain Name System (DNS) information. It's only replicated in its entirety to domain controllers in the **example.com** domain.

- *cn=configuration,dc=example,dc=com*—The configuration partition contains forestwide information, such as service details and site information. It's replicated to every domain controller in the forest.

- *cn=schema,cn=configuration,dc=example,dc=com*—The schema partition contains details of the attributes and classes that can be stored within the forest. Again, the same schema partition is replicated to every domain controller in the forest, but unlike the configuration partition, it's singly mastered and can only be updated by the schema master.

Each additional domain in a forest will have its own domain partition, and its domain controllers will carry the forestwide schema and configuration partitions.

Active Directory enforces unique names regardless of prefix (dc, ou, or cn). This means that certain names can't be used for child domains. For example, the domain creation process for a subdomain called "configuration" beneath the forest root domain, **example.com**, would fail, because the **cn=configuratiom, dc=example,dc=com** already exists and conflicts with the **dc=configuration, dc=example,dc=com** object that would be created.

Composition of Domains

Unlike the flat structure within Windows NT domains, Active Directory allows objects to be contained beneath other objects. This logical structure allows objects, such as user accounts, to be arranged in a hierarchy of containers and have settings and management functions delegated, based on its position within containers.

Organizational Units

The most important type of container used to store objects within a domain is the Organizational Unit (OU). OUs can contain objects, such as users or other OUs, so it's possible to build a hierarchy of OUs within your organization that can be used to organize objects for administrative purposes. For example, desktop settings, such as wallpaper, startup scripts, software settings, software deployment, and, in fact, anything controlled by the registry, can be configured, based on the position of user and computer objects within the OU structure of a domain.

These settings are inherited to child OUs, so for example, companywide settings should be specified at the domain level, and additional levels of settings can also be configured. This mechanism is known as Group Policy, and as you would expect, some options can block or force inheritance. Group Policy is covered in detail in Chapter 12.

TIP: *It's also possible to assign Group Policy at the site level, and it's better to place geographically required settings there. This is because a user whose account is in the Europe OU doesn't want Europe-specific settings, such as help desk numbers on her wallpaper, if she's visiting the USA.*

A second major function for OUs is to delegate control. It's possible to give users or groups the right to manage objects at the OU level. For example, the following OU structure could be used to contain the printers within your organization (see Figure 5.1). The companywide printer administrator could be given permissions at the printer's OU level and local support teams given them at the office location level.

It's possible to use permissions to delegate very specific tasks, such as just giving the ability to add users to a group, but a Wizard is provided to allow quick assignment of common sets of permissions, such as resetting passwords, managing group membership, or modifying Group Policy. This functionality is provided through

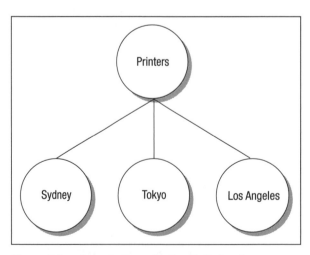

Figure 5.1   Sample Organization Unit structure.

the delegation of Control Wizard, which is accessed by right-clicking on an OU in Active Directory Users and Computers and selecting Delegate Control.

One thing you can't do with an OU is assign permissions on resources to the OU—the group mechanism must still be used for this. Other operating systems work differently, but there's good logic behind this design decision, because you may wish to move an object around the OUs within your domain (to allow a different administrator to manage the account, for example) without changing permissions. The alternative is to have accounts not being moved when they otherwise should be, purely to keep the correct permissions assigned to them.

TIP: *You can add all of the current members of an OU to a group by right-clicking the group in Active Directory Users and Computers and selecting "Add members to a group". You should remember, however, that the membership of the group won't update to reflect changes in the OU, and vice versa.*

A final important point to note about Organizational Units in Active Directory is that a user's location in the OU hierarchy is irrelevant to the user—there's no need (or possibility) to type your user account's distinguished name (DN) when logging in. This means that the OU structure can be used purely for Group Policy and administration, and internal company politics shouldn't interfere with OU design.

Other Containers

When you first create a domain, a number of default containers are created that are Container objects and not Organizational Units. These Containers, such as "Users" and "Built-in", exist for compatibility with downlevel clients, administration application programming interfaces (APIs), and domain controllers. They don't confer the advantages of OUs and can't contain OUs. Essentially, they exist to provide default locations for objects created by downlevel means, because it's not possible to specify where a user created by User Manager for Domains should be created; there must be a default location.

Finally, certain more common objects are, in fact, containers. For example, the domain controller objects that are created for each domain controller in the domain are containers, and beneath them are objects representing the directory replication topology. Similarly, printer objects are contained beneath printer objects. These types of container objects are dealt with later in Chapter 11.

Kerberos

Kerberos is a cross-platform network authentication protocol. Using strong cryptography, it allows clients and servers to verify each other's identity, and once this has been done reliably, other protocols can be used to encrypt network traffic. It was designed for use on the physically insecure campus network at the Massachusetts Institute of Technology (MIT) and assumes that all network communication can be intercepted, modified by attackers, or replayed at a later time. In general, networks are open in this way to disgruntled employees or compromised computers on Internet-based subnetworks between two communicating computers.

The name Kerberos comes from Greek mythology and is the three-headed dog that guards the entrance to Hades, the underworld. The Latin spelling of the name is Cerberus, and you'll often find that spelling in mythology texts; but for the purposes of the computer protocol, the Greek spelling, Kerberos, is used.

It's named after a three-headed dog, because three parties are involved in authentication:

- *Client*—The computer that requests authentication.
- *Server*—The computer the client authenticates with.
- *Trusted Third-Party*—The mediator between the client and the server.

An Example

Imagine that two people, Alice and Bob, wish to talk. They don't know anything about each other and can't recognize one another's voice. This is analogous to the computers communicating on an open wire, because it's possible to appear to be any other computer by using its name, IP address, or whatever. Because Alice and Bob know nothing about each other, they'll never be able to securely authenticate. Imagine, however, that they have a mutual friend, Charlie, and Charlie knows secrets about both Alice and Bob and is able to use these secrets to encrypt any messages he sends to them.

Now Alice, Bob, and Charlie could get together in the same room and authentication would happen, or if they're communicating by telephone, then they could have a conference call with Charlie each time they wish to talk. However, Charlie is probably the sort of person who knows everyone and is extremely busy, and, thus, doesn't have the time to listen in on all of the conversations of all of his friends. What Charlie needs is a way of allowing his friends to authenticate with each other, without having to keep track of who is talking to whom.

Protocol Basics

Kerberos is designed for this kind of a problem on a server that, like Charlie, doesn't have the resources to track every single connection that's made in the network. In addition, it doesn't require servers to track every single connection made to it and, instead, places all of the work on the client.

Here's how the Kerberos protocol works for the example with Alice, Bob, and Charlie:

1. Using their shared secret, the client, Alice, tells the trusted third party, Charlie, that she wishes to speak to the server, Bob.

2. Charlie makes up a new secret—the session key—and encrypts two copies of it, once with both Alice's secret and once with Bob's.

3. Both copies are sent to Alice.

4. Alice decodes the session key from the copy encrypted for her and uses it to encode some standard information about herself.

5. She then sends to Bob both this encoded information—the authenticator—and the session key encrypted for Bob.

6. Finally, Bob decrypts the session key, and then uses that to decrypt the authenticator. If it's in the standard form for an authenticator then he knows that he's speaking to Alice, so he and Alice now have a shared secret.

In practice, this is extended slightly to allow Alice to verify Bob's identity.

Tickets

In the language of Kerberos, authentication information is supplied in tickets. A ticket provides authentication for a limited time; when it expires, a new ticket must be obtained. Tickets are stored by clients and contain time and expiry information, the session key, and the session key encrypted with the server's long-term key. All of this is encrypted with the long-term key of the client. In Windows 2000, long-term keys are derived from user account passwords and from automatically managed computer account passwords.

Tickets are obtained from *Key Distribution Centers (KDCs)*. In the Windows 2000 implementation of Kerberos, KDCs are domain controllers (which play the role of Charlie in the story). How does the KDC know that a client requesting a ticket is who he or she says he or she is? The solution is simply to require a password, hence the account password for a user. However, tickets are required for all authentications, and it would become laborious to type your password in again each time you connected to a new server: so the solution, therefore, is a Ticket Granting Ticket (TGT).

Ticket Granting Tickets

When a client first accesses the network (a computer starting or a user logging in), he or she contacts a Key Distribution Center (KDC) and authenticates with his password to obtain a Ticket Granting Ticket. This ticket is just like a normal Keberos ticket, and it's used to authenticate with the Ticket Granting Service (TGS). The TGS is then responsible for actually issuing the ticket, assuming all authentication details in the TGT are genuine. The TGT is then reused for any subsequent requests for tickets.

Domain Controllers

An Active Directory domain itself is a logical collection of objects and their properties, but it can't exist without physical hosts. The Active Directory information is stored on a number of domain controllers in the domain. In every domain, it's a very good idea to have at least two domain controllers, because if you lose every working domain controller in a domain and have no useful backups, you'll have lost the unique security identifier of the domain and be unable to re-create it and its contents. This situation is best avoided, because the only solution would be to totally rebuild from scratch and re-create all objects and permissions.

LDAP

All Windows 2000 domain controllers are also Lightweight Directory Access Protocol (LDAP)-version-2 and version-3-compliant servers, which run the LDAP service on port 389. This isn't configurable, so this means that other LDAP services must be configured to use a different port. LDAP is an Internet Engineering Task Force (IETF) standard for access to directory services. It's described by a number of Request for Comments (RFCs), notably RFC 1487 and RFC 2251.

The LDAP protocol was developed as a simple, efficient alternative to Directory Access Protocol (DAP), which is used to query X.500 directories. Essentially, LDAP describes a method for clients to query directory services by providing a common definition for possible query types and responses. LDAP defines a number of operations that clients can perform on a server.

Operations

LDAP clients can perform a variety of operations against servers to query and update directory information. The most important of these are the following:

- *Bind*—The **bind** operation is used to connect to, and optionally authenticate with, a server. Anonymous access can be gained by sending a **NULL** username as part of the bind operation.

- *Search*—Probably the most widely used LDAP operation; a search allows you to find information from within the directory. You can specify a base object in the tree to search under, a scope (either the single object, a single level, or the entire subtree), a list of attributes to return, as well as a search filter, and some usual search options, such as a timeout interval and maximum number of results.

- *Modify*—As the name suggests, the modify operation is used to make changes to existing objects in the directory. A single modify operation can include changes to several different properties of an object.

- *Add*—The add operation allows LDAP clients to create objects in the directory if they have sufficient permissions.

- *Delete*—The delete operation is used to delete an object and all associated attributes.
- *Modify RDN*—The modify relative distinguished name (RDN) operation is used to rename the last portion of an object's name, optionally deleting attributes.

Additionally, the **compare** operation can be used to check data in a directory; the abandon operation will cancel a given operation, for example, it will stop a search; and the unbind operation will disconnect and implicitly abandon any outstanding operations.

The mechanics of LDAP are hidden from users by client programs that implement it. However, as an administrator, it's worth knowing the basics of LDAP to be able to troubleshoot it, especially because the extremely useful Active Directory Administration Tool (ldp.exe) is essentially a raw LDAP client, whose menu options and output bear striking resemblances to the LDAP protocol and application programming interface (API).

LDAP Search Filters

The most important part of the LDAP search operation to understand is the search filter. It's required when writing search scripts or using the Active Directory Administration Tool (ldp.exe). A simple example is:

```
(cn=Adam*)
```

This search filter returns all objects whose common name (cn) starts with "**Adam**", then has any other characters thereafter, as matched by the wildcard *. Sets of conditions can be grouped using Boolean logic with and (**&**), or (I), but not (!). These modifiers are used as prefixes to a list of conditions. For example, to find people whose account name starts with Adam in the accounting department, the filter would be:

```
(&(cn=Adam*)(department=accounting))
```

In addition to "**=**", you can use "**>=**" or "**<=**" to test greater than or less than, respectively. To test whether an attribute is present, "**=***" is permissible, so to match any entries without an existing telephone number, you use the following filter:

```
(!(telephoneNumber=*))
```

TIP: *If you wish to find the name of a property for use in a search filter, start Active Directory Service Interface (ADSI) Edit from the Support Tools and check the list of possible attributes on the Properties dialog box of an object that can have that property.*

Referrals

No LDAP server in the world contains information about the entire LDAP namespace. It is perfectly possible to send an LDAP search operation to an LDAP server that contains no information about a particular object or subtree. In such cases, an LDAP referral will be returned if the queried server knows a "better" server to answer the query.

Global Catalog Servers

An Active Directory forest has a single, comprehensive global catalog that contains a subset of properties of every object in every domain in the forest. This information is replicated to a number of domain controllers, which are designated Global Catalog servers. The first domain controller in the root domain of the forest is automatically created as a Global Catalog server.

The Global Catalog is defined as a subset of the attributes found in the forest-wide schema, and every instance of each attribute is replicated to each Global Catalog server in the forest. You can view and modify exactly which attributes are included in the Global Catalog through the schema Snap-in. This is discussed in Chapter 9.

Two main purposes of the Global Catalog are the following:

- *Logon processing*—In a multiple-domain environment, it's possible for a user account to belong to a Universal Group in a different domain. Such a group membership may confer permissions or restrictions that must be processed at logon. This means that the membership of all Universal Groups is required, so this information is published to the Global Catalog server.

- *Fast searching*—Having common details, such as names and telephone numbers, of all users in your organization stored on a single server means that only a single, quick search is needed to find information about users in your organization.

To allow for maintenance when no Global Catalog servers are available, members of the Domain Admins Group are able to log in to their domain in multiple-domain forests, even when no Global Catalog server is available.

Global Catalog servers run an additional LDAP service on port 3268, and all Windows 2000 Global Catalog operations use this port. It's also possible to configure other LDAP clients to query this port to enable them to search objects from the entire forest. If a Global Catalog server receives a request for an attribute that isn't part of the Global Catalog, such as someone's alternative home phone number, it will generate an LDAP referral to a domain controller in the relevant domain, which can return the information.

Operations Masters

Although Active Directory is mainly a multi-mastered directory, some functions are easiest to implement in a single-mastered way. By single-mastered, I mean that certain changes can only be made in one place, whereas the multi-mastering of most objects allows you to change properties of user accounts at any domain controller.

For each forest, two such flexible, single operations master roles exist:

- Schema Master
- Domain-naming Master

Also, three roles exist on a per-domain basis:

- PDC Emulator
- RID Master
- Infrastructure Master

Schema Master

The schema of the Active Directory defines exactly what information can be stored in it in terms of classes of objects, properties, and the associations between the two. This information is stored in the directory itself in the schema partition (**cn=schema,cn=configuration,dc=example,dc=com** for a forest whose root domain is **example.com**). The same schema partition is replicated to every domain controller in every domain of the forest.

The Schema Master operation role holder is the only domain controller in a forest that holds a writable copy of the schema. If there were no Schema Master and if the schema could be updated simultaneously on a different domain controller, a possibility would exist of conflicting updates being made. For example, if a property with the same name was added on two domain controllers but with a different data type on each, which of these should be used? Whatever decision is made, data will be lost.

Also, the Schema Master is used as a final arbiter in the event of schema problems. For example, an object that uses a change to the schema may be replicated to a domain controller before the change to the schema. In this instance, the Schema Master is contacted so an updated version of the schema can be obtained.

Domain-Naming Master

The other forestwide operations master role is the Domain-Naming Master. The Domain-Naming Master is the only domain controller in the forest capable of adding and removing domains from the forest. The reason for this is simply to prevent you from simultaneously adding two domains with the same name to a forest, because doing so would make distinguished names less than unique and, generally, result in an unpredictable mess. Instead, all domain-creating actions must contact the forest's domain-naming master first. Also, the domain-naming master is the only domain controller able to create cross-referenced objects to directories outside the forest.

NOTE: *The domain-naming master must also be a Global Catalog server to ensure that distinguished names (DNs) of objects don't clash with the DN of a new domain, to ensure that it truly is unique.*

PDC Emulator

The most obvious purpose of the Primary Domain Controller (PDC) Emulator's role is to masquerade as the PDC to computers, such as Windows NT 4 BDCs, that expect to be able to consistently locate a PDC for the domain. However, the role of each domain's PDC Emulator is broader than this and includes preferential replication of password changes, processing of account lockouts, and an elevated position in the time synchronization hierarchy of the forest.

Because password changes are multi-mastered, it's possible for a user's most up-to-date password to be rejected by domain controllers that aren't up-to-date. For example, a user may forget his password and have it reset by a member of the help desk, who is connected to a domain controller 1. If the user immediately tries to log in with his new password and if his logon process connects to any other domain controller, the logon will be refused with incorrect credentials, because the new password won't have had a chance to be replicated.

To solve this problem, password changes are pushed, on a best-effort basis, to the PDC Emulator. If authentication fails, the PDC Emulator is contacted to verify that the password really is bad before returning an error message. Account lockouts may be triggered when an incorrect password is used too frequently to prevent "brute force" attacks that cycle through every possible password combination. The PDC Emulator is used to centrally track account lockouts for a domain.

Synchronized time is critical to the Kerberos authentication protocol. To prevent loops, time synchronization is performed according to a hierarchy as follows:

- Clients and member servers synchronize time with their authenticating domain controller.

- Domain controllers synchronize time with the PDC Emulator for their domain.

- PDC Emulators synchronize with the PDC Emulator of the domain above them in their tree. The PDC Emulators at the roots of trees synchronize with the forest root domain's PDC Emulator.

The PDC Emulator of the root domain of a forest is authoritative in time for the entire forest and should be configured to connect to a Simple Network Time Protocol (SNTP) server on the Internet.

RID Master

Relative identifiers (RIDs) are components of the unique security identifiers (SIDs), which are allocated to every security principal in the directory. A *security principal* is an object, such as a user, computer, or group, that can have permissions granted to it. Each security principal in the forest must have a unique SID, which is comprised of its domain SID combined with a RID. Because every domain controller can create objects, they must all be issuing unique RIDs, and to do this, they're allocated unique groups of RIDs, known as *pools*. These pools of RIDs are allocated centrally from the domain's RID Master.

Infrastructure Master

The *Infrastructure Master* is responsible for updating "stale" references to objects from other domains in the forest. If an object is referenced, for example, as belonging to a group, it's stored by either its SID or its distinguished name (DN). SIDs change as objects are moved between domains and DNs change if objects are renamed or moved around in the directory. It's the responsibility of the Infrastructure Master to update links to objects in other domains when their SIDs or DNs changes.

References never become "stale" on Global Catalog servers, because they hold the SIDs and DNs of all objects in the forest. So if the Infrastructure Master Role is held on a Global Catalog server, it will never do anything (but will create Event Log entries to this effect). Domains whose domain controllers are all Global Catalog servers don't need the services of the infrastructure master, so it should be placed on any domain controller.

DNS Entries

For a domain controller to function and be found by clients, service (SRV) resource records must be present on DNS servers. An SRV resource record is a special form of DNS information that is used to locate a computer by service and not name. SRV resource records are generally structured in the form:

```
service.protocol.domain
```

It's often the case that the *service* and *protocol* portions are several components long to specify a detailed service, such as a Global Catalog server. The final component of the protocol is prefixed by an underscore to avoid conflicts with other DNS names. In the **example.com** domain, services that use TCP are identified by **_tcp** because **tcp.example.com** may already be in use for a host or subdomain.

The use of underscores may cause problems with some DNS implementations, and care should be taken to ensure that they aren't generating warning messages and unnecessarily filling up log files. You may have to disable strict name checking to prevent this, for example.

The following SRV resource records may be registered on behalf of domain controllers, depending on their function:

```
_ldap._tcp.DomainName
```

NOTE: *In the following examples, **DomainName** refers to the fully qualified DNS name of the Active Directory domain that the domain controller belongs to and **ForestName** refers to the fully qualified DNS name of the root domain of the forest. **DomainGUID** is used to represent the text form of the globally unique identifier of the domain (basically a unique and long string of hexadecimal digits) and **SiteName** is used to represent the name of the Active Directory site in which the domain controller is registered.*

This record is registered on behalf of all domain controllers, so clients can query for **_ldap._tcp.DomainName** and receive a list of all domain controllers in the domain.

```
_ldap._tcp.SiteName._sites.DomainName
```

One site record is registered for each domain controller, according to which site it belongs to. This record allows clients to query for all domain controllers in a given site and, hence, locate a nearby domain controller. It's also possible to register a domain controller in multiple sites to provide what is known as *site coverage*. Site coverage is discussed in detail in Chapter 7.

```
_ldap._tcp.pdc._msdcs.DomainName
```

The **_msdcs** protocol is used as a placeholder for special domain controller functions, and this record is used to locate the PDC Emulator role holder for a domain. The PDC Emulator is responsible for registering this record and removing any conflicting records from the DNS database. It is required because PDC Emulators serve a variety of special roles, such as priority replication of passwords, and don't just replace Windows NT 4 primary domain controllers.

```
_ldap._tcp.gc._msdcs.ForestName
```

A second **_msdcs** service type is **gc** for Global Catalog. Each Global Catalog server in the forest registers the above entry so that a Global Catalog server can be found. Note that this entry is under the domain name of the forest root;

because all Global Catalog servers are equal, a client will be agnostic to which domain a Global Catalog server is actually a domain of, as long as it is a Global Catalog server.

```
_ldap._tcp.SiteName._sites.gc._msdcs.ForestName
```

Similar to the site-specific record registered by all domain controllers, Global Catalog servers each register a record in the above form specific to their own site. Again, it's under the name of the forest, because all Global Catalog servers hold information about all objects in the forest.

```
_ldap._tcp.DomainGuid.domains._msdcs.ForestName
```

This record, located under the forest root's DNS domain name, allows domain controllers to be found based solely on the Globally Unique Identifiers (GUID) of their domains. It's registered for each domain controller in a domain. A GUID is a unique, 128-bit number generated for referencing directory objects.

In addition, an A (host) record is registered for each domain controller to enable it to be found by a normal means, and a CNAME (Canonical Name, also known as 'alias') record of the following form is registered to allow for the possibility of domain controllers to be renamed in Active Directory (this isn't yet a feature, but it may be in later versions):

```
ServerGUID._msdcs.DomainName
```

Here, **ServerGUID** is a text representation of the globally unique identifier of the domain controller.

Locating a Domain Controller

Numerous processes in Active Directory require that a domain controller be found. Sometimes a specific type of domain controller, such as the PDC Emulator or a Global Catalog server, is required, and other times the requirement is less strict, such as just a domain controller in a given domain.

Within Windows 2000, an application programming interface (API) call is used for this purpose, and it's also available for everyone's use (in case the programmer in you ever needs to find a domain controller in a hurry). The API call is **DsGetDcName** and takes the following input parameters:

- *ComputerName*—The name of the computer that the domain controller is being found for. Normally, it's left blank to specify the local machine.

- *DomainName*—The name of the domain to find a domain controller in. If this is unspecified, it uses the forest root domain if a Global Catalog server is being found, or the domain of the computer specified by **ComputerName**, otherwise. A **DomainName** may either be a flat, NetBIOS name or a DNS name.

- *DomainGUID*—An optional parameter that is used in the eventuality that the domain specified by **DomainName** has been renamed.

NOTE: Domain renaming isn't currently supported by Windows 2000 Active Directory, but it may be in a future version.

- *SiteName*—An optional parameter to specify a particular site to find a domain controller close to. If it's left blank, the site of the machine specified by **ComputerName** is used.
- *Flags*—Multiple options can be used to specify exactly what type of domain controller is required.

The following flags may be specified, in any comb.

- *DS_AVOID_SELF*—Quite simply, this flag requires a domain controller other than the computer specified by **ComputerName** that must be returned. It's useful for finding other domain controllers from a domain controller.
- *DS_DIRECTORY_SERVICE_PREFERRED*—If possible, a Windows 2000 (or later) domain controller will be returned.
- *DS_DIRECTORY_SERVICE_REQUIRED*—Will only return a Windows 2000 (or later) domain controller.
- *DS_FORCE_REDISCOVERY*—If a domain controller is found to be unavailable, this flag will return a different domain controller, if possible.
- *DS_GC_SERVER_REQUIRED*—Used to specify that a Global Catalog server must be returned. This can't be used with **DS_WRITABLE_REQUIRED** or **DS_PDC_REQUIRED**, because you can't guarantee that all conditions can be met in one domain controller.
- *DS_GOOD_TIMESERV_PREFERRED*—This is used by the Windows Time Service to locate servers that are configured as "reliable" timeservers, if possible. A timeserver is configured reliable by editing the registry appropriately.
- *DS_IP_REQUIRED*—As the name suggests, this flag forces the IP address of the domain controller to be returned.
- *DS_IS_DNS_NAME*—This flag is used to clarify that the specified name is a DNS name and not a flat (NetBIOS) name.
- *DS_IS_FLAT_NAME*—This is used to clarify that the **DomainName** parameter is a flat name. It may not be specified with the **DS_IS_DNS_NAME** flag.

- *DS_KDC_REQUIRED*—This requires that the returned domain controller be running the Kerberos Key Distribution Center (KDC) service.

- *DS_ONLY_LDAP_NEEDED*—The presence of this flag means that any suitable LDAP server will be returned, without regard to whether it's a domain controller or not. If this flag is specified, flags requiring a PDC Emulator, the KDC service, or any sort of timeserver are ignored.

- *DS_PDC_REQUIRED*—Requires that the returned DC be the primary domain controller (PDC) for the domain. This may not be set if either **DS_WRITABLE_REQUIRED** or **DS_GC_SERVER_REQUIRED** are set, because the full requirement may not be able to be satisfied.

- *DS_RETURN_DNS_NAME*—Means that the returned domain controller name and domain name should be DNS names. It may not be specified with the **DS_RETURN_FLAT_NAME** or **DS_IS_FLAT_NAME** flags. It also returns the IP address of the domain controller, so **DS_IP_REQUIRED** is implied.

- *DS_RETURN_FLAT_NAME*—Means that the returned domain controller name and domain name should be flat names. It may not be specified with the **DS_RETURN_DNS_NAME** or **DS_IS_DNS_NAME** flags.

- *DS_TIMESERV_REQUIRED*—Simply requires that the returned DC be currently running the Windows Time Service (W32Time).

- *DS_WRITABLE_REQUIRED*—Ensures that the domain controllers returned host a writable copy of the directory. If the specified domain name is a flat name, this flag is the same as **DS_PDC_REQUIRED**, because the PDC is the only guaranteed-writable domain controller when a NetBIOS name is used. If a DNS name is specified, writable domain controllers are found. Only the PDC Emulator is writable in a Mixed-mode Windows 2000 domain. This flag is included partly because future releases of Active Directory may allow for "read only" domain controllers. It may not be set with **DS_PDC_REQUIRED** or **DS_GC_SERVER_REQUIRED**.

Storage of Active Directory

All of the Active Directory information stored on a domain controller is kept within the single **ntds.dit** file, stored by default in %SystemRoot%\ntds\ntds.dit. The database engine used is Extensible Storage Engine (ESE), which is the same technology used previously in Microsoft Exchange, so Active Directory doesn't use a brand-new method of storing data.

Each object stored is represented as a single row in a database, regardless of whether it's in the domain controller's domain, the configuration partition, the schema partition, or from any other domain in the forest for a Global Catalog server. ESE uses a sparse storage engine, that is to say, that space is only used for attributes as they're created, instead of a large chunk being set aside for every possible attribute of an object when the object is created.

Ntds.dit

There are, in fact, two **ntds.dit** files on any given domain controller. The default locations are:

```
%SystemRoot%\ntds\ntds.dit
%SystemRoot%\system32\ntds.dit
```

The location and contents of the second of these is fixed—it's present on all Windows 2000 Server computers to allow you to promote them to become domain controllers, without needing the Windows 2000 Server CD-ROM. The first of these **ntds.dit** files is the one that's used to store data.

Extensible Storage Engine

The databases mechanism used by Active Directory is known as Extensible Storage Engine (ESE).

When a change is made to the database, the following sequence of events occurs:

1. The change is made to the copy of the data stored in memory on the domain controller.

2. Details of the change are written to a log file as what is known as a transaction. This ensures that the change will be applied even if the server is shut down at this point.

NOTE: *Software disk caching is disabled when Active Directory is installed. It adds the possibility that ESE thinks data has been written to disk when, in fact, it has only been written to cache, so if power fails, it will be lost and the directory will become inconsistent.*

Alongside this, the database engine reads the log files and applies the transactions to the **ntds.dit** file on disk. The method of logging is known as circular, because once a log entry has been used, it's marked as being safe to overwrite.

A checkpoint, stored in **edb.chk** in the log file directory, is used to record how far log files have been processed. When transactions are imported, this checkpoint is advanced.

Immediate Solutions

Converting a Domain to Native Mode

All domains are in Mixed mode when they're first created, regardless of whether they're brand-new or upgraded from Windows NT 4 domains. Conversion to Native mode is a one-way, irreversible process that enables additional features of Windows 2000, such as Security Group nesting and Universal Security Groups.

To convert a domain to Native mode, perform the following steps:

1. Open the Active Directory Domain and Trusts Snap-in, connected to a domain controller in the domain to convert.
2. Right-click on the domain to convert and select Properties.
3. Click Change Mode.
4. You're warned that this is a one-way process. Click Yes to proceed.

This is all that's required. You only have to make the change on one domain controller per domain, and there's no need to reboot it.

In fact, clicking the Change Mode button modifies the **nTMixedDomain** property of the domain from 1 to 0. This value is a property of the Active Directory object whose DN is the DN of the domain, such as **dc=example,dc=com** for the **example.com** domain.

For single value changes of directory objects, it's simpler to use ADSI Edit from the Windows 2000 Support Tools. To change a domain to Native mode with ADSI Edit:

1. Open the ADSI Edit Support Tool from the Windows 2000 Support Tools folder.
2. Right-click ADSI Edit in the root of the tree and select "Connect To" if you wish to change the domain.
3. Expand the Domain Naming Context (NC).
4. Right-click the first object beneath it that represents the domain itself. It's of class **domainDNS**.
5. Choose **nTMixedDomain** from the "Select A Property To View" list.
6. Type "0" in the Edit Attribute box and click Set.
7. Click OK.

WARNING! With the ADSI Edit technique to change domain mode, you could try to convert a domain back from native to Mixed mode. Fortunately, this is impossible, and you receive the confusing error message "A device attached to the system is not functioning."

Delegating Control with OUs

An important function of Organization Units (OUs) is to allow administrative control to be delegated. This is achieved by setting granting permissions on OUs and child objects. The usual recommendation of adding accounts to global groups, which are in turn added to domain local groups, that have permissions assigned (A-G-DL-P) applies.

Groups Scopes Revisited

In Active Directory, there are three possible *scopes* for group objects: Global Groups, Domain Local Groups, and Universal Groups.

- *Global Groups* can contain objects from any trusted domain and
- *Domain Local Groups* can contain objects from their own domain and can be granted permissions to objects to their own domain or any trusting domain, which includes all other domains in the forest.
- *Universal Groups* combine the facility to contain members from anywhere in the forest and the ability to be granted permissions in any domain in the forest. There is a performance cost of using Universal Groups and they are only available as security groups in Native Mode.

The simplest method of delegating management of an OU is with the Delegation of Control Wizard from the Active Directory Users and Computers Snap-in. To use the wizard:

1. Open Active Directory Users and Computers from the Administration Tools menu.

2. Navigate to the OU to delegate control of it in the tree pane.

3. Right-click the OU and select Delegate Control. The Delegation of Control Wizard appears. Click Next to begin.

4. Initially, you're prompted to select users and groups to assign control to. Use Add to select users and groups from a list. Click Next to continue.

5. Next, you're prompted to select task(s) to delegate. Either choose a combination of the common tasks or select "Create A Custom Task" to delegate. The possible Common Tasks are shown in Table 5.1.

Table 5.1   Common Tasks.

Task
Create, delete, and manage user accounts
Reset passwords on user accounts
Read all user information
Create, delete, and manage groups
Modify the membership of a group
Manage Group Policy links

6. If you create a custom task, you're prompted to select the type of objects to be managed and the exact permissions to grant.

7. Finally, click Finish to complete the Delegation of Control Wizard.

Managing Domain Controllers

Now we'll discuss the configuring of time synchronization.

Configure Time Synchronization

Time synchronization need only be configured on the PDC Emulator of the forest root domain. Other computers all synchronize automatically in a hierarchy, with the forest root's PDC Emulator at the top of the hierarchy.

To configure a list of timeservers, simply type the following at a command prompt:

```
C:\>net time /setsntp:serverlist
```

Where **serverlist** is a comma-separated list of the host names or IP addresses of SNTP servers, without any spaces. Ideally, you should use the SNTP server of your Internet Service Provider. If your ISP doesn't have an SNTP server, you can configure a public server instead. In fact, it's advisable to configure multiple SNTP servers for redundancy.

Internet timeservers are divided into levels, with high-level servers intended for only other timeservers to connect to them. Unless you have a large number of clients on your network, you should go with a second-level server. A list of public second-level servers is available at **www.eecis.udel.edu/~mills/ntp/clock2.htm**.

NOTE: *Many Internet documents refer to Network Time Protocol (NTP) servers and not SNTP servers. On the whole, NTP servers also support SNTP, so connecting to an NTP server should be fine.*

Viewing DNS Entries for Domain Controllers

To verify that clients can find a newly promoted domain controller, you can check for its SRV resource records in DNS.

NOTE: *For the following examples, it's assumed that the domain is **example.com**.*

Using **Nslookup**

The **nslookup.exe** utility provides an interactive method of querying DNS servers. To use it to verify the promotion of a domain controller, perform the following steps:

1. Open a Command Prompt from the Accessories menu.

2. Type **nslookup** to start it in Interactive mode.

3. Type **set type=all** and press enter.

4. Type **_ldap._tcp.dc._msdcs.example.com** and press enter to query for all domain controllers in the **example.com** domain.

5. A series of records (one per domain controller in the domain) is returned. One of these should correspond to the new domain controller.

Using DNS Snap-In

With the Management Console DNS Snap-in, you can browse the DNS entries in a zone in a tree-like fashion. To check that a domain controller has been added:

1. Start the Management Console DNS Snap-in and connect to a DNS server for the domain in question.

2. Browse to **_msdcs/dc/_tcp** in the zone in question.

3. There should be records for **_ldap** and **_kerberos** named after the new domain controller.

Load Balancing with SRV RRs

To influence the chances of clients connecting to a given domain controller, you can change the priority and weight fields of its SRV resource record entries. By default, domain controllers use dynamic DNS entries (DDNS), so any changes made on the server will be overwritten, so, instead, the following registry keys should be edited:

```
HKLM\SYSTEM\CurrentControlSet\Services\Netlogon\Parameters\LdapSrvWeight
HKLM\SYSTEM\CurrentControlSet\Services\Netlogon\Parameters\LdapSrvPriority
```

Both of these values are **REG_DWORD**s.

Recall that servers of lowest priority are contacted first. If multiple servers of the same priority exist, then the probability of connecting to a server is proportional to its weight. By default, all domain controllers have the same priority and weight. If DDNS isn't in use by domain controllers, then manually changing the SRV records on the DNS server is the way to make the change. In Windows 2000 DNS, this is achieved by editing the Properties of each DNS entry individually.

Active Directory Administration Tool

Included as part of the Support Tools, the Active Directory Administration Tool (**ldp.exe**) is, in effect, a raw LDAP client and can be used to connect to any LDAP-compliant server. The user interface is shown in Figure 5.2.

The main output of the Active Directory Administration tool is in the right-hand gray pane, where each command is output as an LDAP API call and where any results or error messages are output.

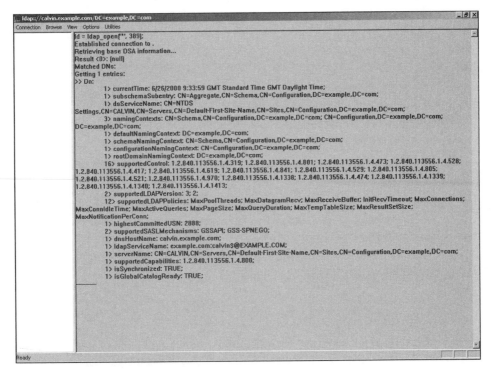

Figure 5.2   The Active Directory Administration Tool.

Connecting to a Server

To connect to an LDAP server:

1. Select Connect from the Connection menu.

2. Enter a DNS name for the server to connect to and the port number to connect on. The default LDAP port is 389. The Global Catalog port is 3268. The Connection dialog box is shown in Figure 5.3.

After a successful connection, information about the server is returned to the right-hand pane.

Binding

To authenticate with an LDAP server, you must supply credentials by binding to it. To do so:

1. Select Bind from the Connection menu.

2. You're prompted for a username and password. The username must be a User Principal Name (UPN) with the Domain checkbox cleared, or a downlevel account name if the Domain checkbox is ticked. The Domain textbox defaults to the current domain.

3. Click OK to bind.

NOTE: *Binding without an open connection will automatically connect to a domain controller.*

Searching

To perform an LDAP search:

1. Select Search from the Browse menu. The Search dialog box shown in Figure 5.4 appears.

2. Enter the Distinguished Name where you wish to start your search for Base Dn. For example, **dc=example,dc=com** if you wish to search the root of the **example.com** domain.

Figure 5.3   The Active Directory Administration Tool Connection dialog box.

Figure 5.4   The Search dialog box.

3. Select a Scope. Use Base to search the named object only, One-Level to search its direct child objects, or Subtree to search all objects beneath the Base DN.

4. In the Filter box, enter a text LDAP search-filter.

5. Advanced properties, including which attributes are returned, can be configured from the Options dialog.

6. Finally, click OK to execute the search.

Kerberos Tools

A number of utilities are available as part of the Windows 2000 Server Resource Kit that allow you to monitor and manage Kerberos tickets on clients.

Kerberos List

Kerberos List (**klist.exe**) is a command-line utility that displays current Kerberos tickets. To show details of the Ticket Granting Ticket (TGT) for the current session, type:

```
C:\>klist tgt
```

This will display details of the current ticket, including your username, authenticating domain, granting time, and expiry time. To show details of all service tickets, type:

```
C:\>klist tickets
```

Finally, it's also possible to delete tickets by typing:

```
C:\>klist tickets
```

and saying yes/no to each ticket in turn.

Kerberos Tray

Kerberos Tray (**kerbtray.exe**) provides graphical functionality similar to **klist.exe**. When run, it places a small, green icon in the system tray, which allows you to view and purge Kerberos tickets. To view tickets with Kerberos Tray:

1. Double-click on the green ticket icon. The dialog box shown in Figure 5.5 appears.

2. You can visually inspect tickets, including viewing a breakdown of the flag meanings.

3. Other tickets can be selected from the listbox at the top of the dialog.

To delete tickets with Kerberos Tray:

1. Right-click on the green ticket icon and select Purge Tickets.

WARNING! You aren't prompted for confirmation. Purging tickets may require you to log off and back on again to resume working with network resources.

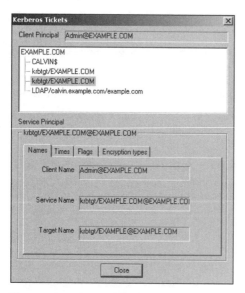

Figure 5.5   Kerbtray Ticket Inspector.

Chapter 6

Multiple Domains

In Depth

Not every organization is suited to a single Windows 2000 domain with all domain controllers containing every object in the directory. Having multiple domains will reduce the volume of data replicated around an organization and will allow greater flexibility in certain settings. The very sensible Microsoft recommendation, which is proven by experience, is to have just one domain if you can possibly manage it. The reason for this is simplicity: it's easier to help a single domain, and there's less that can go wrong.

This chapter covers issues surrounding multiple-Windows 2000 domains and trust relationships, including external trust relationships to downlevel domains. Additionally, the discussion of Kerberos from Chapter 5 is extended to cover authentication in multiple domains, as well as interoperability with non-Microsoft Kerberos systems. Some considerations that apply to multiple domains and trusts are also necessary for interoperating with partner companies, as when resources are shared during joint ventures, for example, so this information is also worth knowing even if you're sure that you'll never need to deal with a multiple-domain network.

Trees and Forests

An Active Directory *tree* is a collection of domains arranged hierarchically, with a common namespace and two-way, transitive trust relationships between parent and children. Each tree has a single root domain, after which the tree is named. A single domain is the most trivial example of a tree. An example tree with four domains is shown in Figure 6.1.

An Active Directory *forest* is a collection of Active Directory trees. In Windows 2000 Active Directory, a forest is identified by its root domain, which is the root of the first tree in the forest. The root domains of other trees are connected by transitive trusts to the forest root, so resources are accessible from all domains in a forest. Active Directory forests also define the boundaries of Exchange 2000 organizations. The simplest forest is a single tree, which itself is just a single domain. A more complex example is shown in Figure 6.2.

Using Multiple Domains

Within your organization, you may need to create several Windows 2000 domains. You may already have several Windows NT domains and may be upgrading to

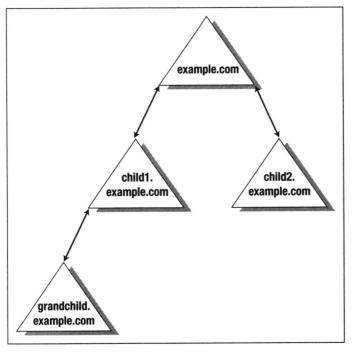

Figure 6.1 Sample Active Directory tree.

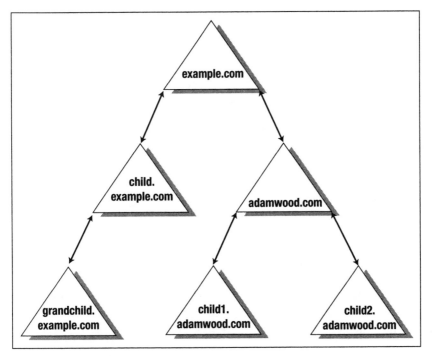

Figure 6.2 Sample Active Directory forest.

multiple-Windows 2000 domains (at least initially), or your company's circumstances may call for several domains. My general recommendation, however, is to use as few domains as possible and use only one domain if you can manage it. Doing so simplifies numerous operations and reduces IT costs, because you'll most likely require fewer domain controllers and Windows 2000 licenses.

If you wish to run Internet servers or use email addresses with additional DNS domain names, you don't require a tree. Creating one only affects the namespace of the directory and the DNS names of computers and domain controllers. Of course, if a company requires separate identities in terms of directory names, then it must create multiple trees and, hence, multiple domains.

Avoid if Possible

A multiple-domain model "just because you had one in NT 4" is a bad idea. The canonical recommendation is to work with a single domain model and add domains only if necessary. Active Directory has been shown to scale to 100 million objects in Native mode on sufficiently powerful hardware, so sheer scale isn't a good reason to use a second domain.

Don't be Confused by Mixed Mode and Native Mode

The terms Mixed mode and Native mode are often misunderstood. You should be clear that changing an Active Directory domain to Native mode in no way impairs the ability of non-Windows 2000 clients to authenticate with it. You can still use Win9x and other downlevel clients with no need to make changes on the client computers—they still see the domain controllers in the same way that they see Windows NT domain controllers or Windows 2000 domain controllers in Mixed mode.

The impact of changing to Native mode is to stop updates from being sent to Windows NT Backup Domain Controllers (although they really should be removed or upgraded before making the switch to Native mode). In hindsight, it would have been better for Microsoft to coin terms along the lines of "Windows NT BDC Compatibility Mode" and "No Windows NT BDC Compatibility Mode" to prevent confusion. This is how you should think of the modes, although the terminology is unlikely ever to catch on.

With Active Directory, scalability is only an issue for the very, very largest of companies. Using many domains may make sense for a company that's essentially a conglomeration of many unrelated companies, because it satisfies both the administrative and political requirements that arise from having several completely autonomous IT departments.

One advantage of using multiple domains is that it partitions your directory objects into smaller groups for replication purposes. This means that every branch office doesn't receive every update. However, to facilitate logon in a multiple-domain environment, a Global Catalog server must be contacted to examine Universal Group membership. Hence, the replication saving isn't as great as you would expect.

Usage Guidelines

Certain settings can only be performed at the domain level in Windows 2000 Active Directory. Obviously, if you wish to implement these settings in different ways throughout your organization, you'll have to have multiple domains.

The settings are as follows:

- *Password policy*—Settings pertaining to password restrictions, such as minimum password length, minimum and maximum password ages, and password complexity, can only be set at the domain level.

- *Account lockout policy*—This specifies how many unsuccessful account logon attempts can be made before an account is disabled. The default value of 0 means never lockout.

- *Kerberos policy*—Kerberos policy settings are used to specify settings, such as the maximum lifetimes of Kerberos tickets, as well as the tolerance to time differences for the domain.

If you wish to vary these settings within your organization, you'll have to use separate Windows 2000 Active Directory domains.

Possible Multiple Domain Models

The literature for Windows NT 4 is full of templates for "domain models" that specify simple arrangements of account domains and resource domains. These are no longer applicable in Windows 2000, because the concept of a resource domain containing no users is redundant, and many limitations are blown away by the scalability of Active Directory.

That said, many domains are possible in some instances, and the following are examples of how multiple-domain models could be used. The following examples don't name domains, so no distinction is made between trees and first-level child domains. Also, please note that the names given to these models are the author's own and aren't, by any means, official. The exact reasons for choosing one design over another are considered in detail in Chapter 19 after more of the inner workings of Active Directory have been examined, particularly in terms of physical operation.

Single Child

The basic idea of this model is to have a small forest root domain housing no more than a minimal number of Administrator accounts and a much larger child domain that houses all other resources. One possible reason for using this model in large organizations is to safeguard the Enterprise Admins Group membership and the default Administrator account in the forest root domain, because anyone who is a member of just the Domain Admins Group is able to reset the password on an Enterprise Admins account and, hence, gain unrestricted access to the network.

NOTE: *Even being a mere Domain Admin is still enough of a privilege to be able to irreparably damage the entire forest by taking ownership of items in the Schema and Configuration partitions of the directory and doing antisocial things, like deleting critical objects. This means that there's an issue with who in your forest has Domain Admins membership in any domain, so anyone in any Domain Admins Group must be suitably trusted. Organizational Units (OUs) should be used where possible to delegate administration.*

When using any design that calls for an empty forest root domain, be sure to have enough domain controllers and recent off-site backups in case of disaster, because the loss of a forest root domain is a *very bad thing indeed.*

Many Children

This model is similar to the last, usually with an empty root domain and a small number of roughly equal children. A common example would be to use the children to represent geographic parts of a company, such as three domains for the Americas, EMEA (Europe, Middle East, and Africa), and Asia-Pacific. A three-child example is shown in Figure 6.3.

A key point with a good multiple-children design is to keep it small. This model only makes sense with a small number of child domains—if you're considering a design with tens of child domains, then it's probably worth reconsidering. Even Compaq is

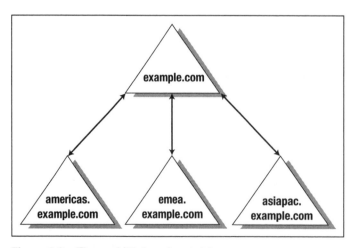

Figure 6.3   Three-child domain model.

using three children, and a major retailer with thousands of locations the world over is planning a single domain with domain controllers at every outlet.

In particular, a domain for every tiny branch office isn't necessary. Instead, a trade-off to consider is using a many-children model with a child domain for a group of branch offices. This will reduce replication to some extent but have increased costs in terms of manageability, hardware, and software.

Multiple Forests

In general, having multiple forests is an unnecessary complication within your network. With multiple forests, you have multiple Global Catalogs, so one of the points of having a single place to search for all information is lost. Additionally, information about transitive trusts is stored in the forestwide configuration partition and is, thus, not replicated out-of-forest. Out-of-forest trusts aren't transitive, so the management benefits of not having to maintain numerous manual trust relationships is lost.

When to Use Multiple Forests

The most important use of a second forest is for internal testing. To evaluate applications that make schema changes, you should use a second forest. Also, any schema modifications developed in-house should be thoroughly tested on a nonproduction forest. The reason for doing this is that changes made to the schema are made forestwide and are irreversible (they can be disabled but not deleted—see Chapter 9 for details). If you're simply evaluating an application, it's a bad idea for it to leave a permanent mark on your network. Beyond testing purposes, you should only use a second forest in extreme circumstances—make sure that what you're trying to achieve can't be done by having separate domains or using OUs within a domain.

Trusts

In Windows NT and Windows 2000, a *trust* is a relationship whereby a trusting domain accepts the authentication mechanism of a trusted domain. In this way, users can log into the trusted domain and access resources in the trusting domain (subject to having sufficient permissions to the resources in question, of course). Within an Active Directory tree, two-way transitive trust relationships are created automatically between parent and child domains so that every domain in the forest directly or indirectly trusts every other domain in the forest. These are known as *parent-child trusts*. The root domains of trees are connected to the forest root domain in a similar way, with what are unsurprisingly known as *tree-root trusts*.

Windows NT 4-style trusts are one-way and nontransitive. Trust in both directions is established by creating two one-way trusts. To create complete trust within a Windows NT 4 environment, you require two trusts for every pair of domains. This means that you need to have n times as many trusts for a complete-trust Windows NT 4 network than a Windows 2000 forest with n domains, which defaults to having complete trust. Additionally, the Windows 2000 trusts are configured automatically.

Why n Times More?

In a Windows 2000 forest, one trust relationship is created for each domain added after the first, so a forest with n domains will have, by default, $n-1$ trust relationships.

In the Windows NT 4 complete trust model, you add 0 trusts for the first domain created, 2 trusts for the second domain, 4 for the third, 6 for the fourth, and so on up to $2n-2$ for the nth. Adding all of these numbers, you find n terms that average to $n-1$, so the total is $n(n-1)$.

Trust Evaluation

When a client wishes to access resources in another domain, it must authenticate with that domain. To do so, it contacts a domain controller in its domain, and a trust *path* is constructed. Each domain holds information about each domain that it trusts directly and about every domain that trusts it. Using this information, a path between any domains in the same forest can be constructed by default by going via the forest root domain, but external trust relationships and shortcut trust relationships are also stored.

Shortcut Trusts

In Windows 2000 forests, a *shortcut trust* can be created between domains to speed and simplify cross-domain authentication. They're also called *cross-link trusts*. This is a useful efficiency boost if users of two domains in different "parts" of a forest frequently share resources. Shortcut trusts can only be created within Windows 2000 forests and are transitive and one-way (although, you can create a second shortcut in the opposite direction to give, in effect, a two-way shortcut trust). For an example of when shortcut trusts are necessary, consider the organization shown in Figure 6.4.

Now, it's likely that resources are shared within the New York office—say the color laser printer in New York is part of the sales domain. This means that whenever a user in the accounts domain connects to it, trust evaluation goes via the **multinational.example** root domain to verify credentials.

Because the **multinational.example** domain is located entirely in London, this will create transatlantic network traffic for authentication, which is likely to be

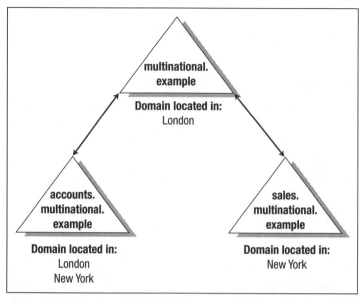

Figure 6.4   An Active Directory forest for multinational.example.

expensive. This network is a perfect candidate for a shortcut trust with the sales domain trusting accounting. With shortcut trusts in place, trust evaluation takes the shortest path between domains, so in this example, wide area network (WAN) traffic caused by printing is circumvented.

WARNING! Simply because sales and accounting are the example child domains above, it doesn't mean that sales and accounting departments need separate domains. They're just examples.

Downlevel Domain Controllers

In Mixed-mode Windows 2000 domains, there may still be Windows NT 4 (or earlier) domain controllers in operation and clients authenticated by these servers. Because Windows NT 4 domain controllers have no concept of transitive trusts and no copy of the directory configuration partition, they're unable to evaluate them and, instead, are only able to use direct relationships to domains adjacent in the tree.

If you have a Mixed-mode domain that isn't adjacent in the forest to a domain that it must access resources from, you should do one or more of the following:

- *Convert to Native mode*—This problem doesn't affect domains in Native mode, so upgrading all downlevel domain controllers and switching to Native mode is a simple answer.

- *Upgrade clients*—Windows 2000 clients preferentially authenticate with Windows 2000 domain controllers and are, thus, unaffected by the problem.

- *Add Explicit trust relationships*—If upgrades are impossible, explicit one-way, nontransitive NT 4-style trusts must be established, as would be required in a pure Windows NT 4 environment.

Trusting Pre-Windows 2000 Domains

Windows 2000 domains support trust relationships with Windows NT 4 (and earlier) domains. For these purposes, they appear like a Windows NT domain to the trusted/trusting downlevel domain. Because of the need for compatibility, all such trusts are one-way and nontransitive. As with all trusts, these are managed from Active Directory Domains and Trusts.

Kerberos Trusts

In addition to trusting other Windows NT or 2000 domains, a Windows 2000 domain can trust other Massachusetts Institute of Technology (MIT) Kerberos version 5 realms. Other Kerberos realms are typically found on Unix servers. These trusts can be one- or two-way and transitive or nontransitive. Note that transitivity is only supported within the Windows 2000 forest, so a transitive trust will cover all Windows 2000 domains but only one foreign realm.

Other limitations of foreign Kerberos trusts exist, including a limited range of cryptographic algorithms—only DES-CDC-MD5 and DES-CDC-CRC are available. Additionally, Windows 2000 client computers can be configured to use Kerberos authentication with non-Windows Kerberos realms.

Kerberos

Kerberos version 5 is the authentication protocol used to verify credentials in Windows 2000. The basics of how Kerberos is used within a single Windows 2000 domain were described in Chapter 5. However, Kerberos is also used to authenticate connections between Windows 2000 domains within a forest and can be used to interoperate with non-Microsoft systems.

Terminology

The following is an explanation of some of the basic terminology used in discussions of Kerberos and how they relate to the Windows 2000 implementation.

Secret Key

Like any cryptographic key, a secret key is just a number. When referring to cryptography, people often talk about "bit length", such as 128-bit encryption. The bit length is the number of 0s and 1s used to store the key within a computer, so an n-bit key can take any one of 2^n possible values. The least interesting way to break a cryptographic code is to guess the secret key. In that sense, having a higher bit length is good, although a high-bit length also increases processing power and is no use if your cryptographic system is so weak that there are other ways to break it.

A secret key is a shared secret between two parties, and its interception will compromise all communication. This contrasts with public key cryptography whereby the public key can be used to encrypt messages that require the private key (or a lucky guess) to decrypt. Public key cryptography is more processor-intensive than secret key cryptography due to the more complex mathematics behind it.

Session Key

A *session key* is a temporary secret key generated for the communication between a client and server for a limited period of time. Its lifetime is limited to the duration of a single logon session.

Long-Term Key

A *long-term key* is a secret that seldom changes over time. Long-term keys are used to authenticate logon. For user accounts in Active Directory, this is derived from the account password. For computer accounts, it is managed automatically by Active Directory.

Realm

A Kerberos realm is defined in the Kerberos standard as being an "organization". In effect, it's a group of Key Distribution Centers (KDCs) that can authorize the same accounts, as well as the clients and servers that they can authorize. In the Windows 2000 implementation, a Kerberos realm, therefore, maps to an Active Directory domain.

Key Distribution Center

Key Distribution Centers (KDCs) are the most important part of Kerberos realms. They're responsible for the issuing of Ticket Generating Tickets (TGT) to clients for their realm, and the issuing of Session Tickets to clients requesting resources in their realm. In Windows 2000, the domain controllers are the KDCs.

Authenticator

An *authenticator* is a piece of information used to prove knowledge of a secret key. It also contains a time stamp to prevent it from being intercepted on a network and used much later to impersonate the client. The entire authenticator is encrypted with the session key.

Ticket

A Kerberos ticket is central to authentication. Tickets are maintained by clients but are encrypted with the long-term keys of the servers for which they are used to obtain access. The information in a ticket includes the name and realm of both the server and client, the encrypted session key, any realms traversed to obtain the ticket, the initial authorization time, the start and end of authorization (to allow for post-dated tickets to be issued), a time until which a ticket can be renewed, and a number of flags. The flags that can be set are the following:

- *FORWARDABLE*—A forwardable TGT can be used by a client to request a TGT for a different client, that is, authentication from a forwardable ticket can be transferred from one host to another and used to obtain session or Ticket Granting Tickets by the new host.

- *FORWARDED*—A forwarded ticket is just that. This flag marks a ticket as having come from another host or as being granted based upon a forwarded TGT.

- *PROXIABLE*—Proxying is a lesser form of forwarding or a TGT that allows only session tickets to be issued based on the proxied ticket.

- *PROXIED*—This field indicates that a session ticket has been obtained based on a proxied TGT.

- *MAY-POSTDATE*—When applied to a Ticket Granting Ticket, this flag indicates that a session ticket with a start time in the future may be issued to allow future, but not immediate, access to a resource.

- *POSTDATED*—A ticket that was issued with a start time in the future.

- *INVALID*—A ticket that must be rejected by servers and which can only be validated by a KDC.

- *RENEWABLE*—A ticket whose lifetime may be extended before expiring up to a maximum specified in the ticket itself. A renewable ticket is presented to the granting server before expiring to obtain a replacement.

- *INITIAL*—The initial flag specifies that a ticket wasn't obtained with a TGT. This flag will be seen on the TGT obtained for a client's own realm.

- *HW_AUTHENT*—Specifies that the authentication of the client is based on hardware.

The flags applied to a ticket may be viewed using the **kerbtray.exe** utility from the Windows 2000 Server Resource Kit.

The krbtgt User Account

The astute users who have installed Active Directory will have noticed an account named krbtgt that's stored in the Users container of an Active Directory and is disabled.

This account exists to provide a password from which a long-term key is derived that's used to encrypt TGTs. Those presented to a domain controller are deciphered using this long-term key. There's a hard limitation; the krbtgt account can neither be deleted nor enabled, because it absolutely must exist but isn't needed for logon.

Basic Process

To recap, the essential points of a logon to a Kerberos realm are as follows:

- Initially, a user logs onto a workstation using her username and password. This password is used to compute the long-term key, which is cached locally by the Kerberos client service.

- The long-term key is used to encrypt a request for authentication, which the workstation sends to the KDC, along with the username that has logged on.

- The long-term key of the user from the Active Directory is used to decrypt the authenticator. If it checks out, the KDC replies with a session key that's encrypted with the user's long-term key and a TGT encrypted with the KDC's long-term key.

- The Kerberos client service then decrypts the session ticket with the user's long-term key (which it then discards) and stores the TGT.

- All subsequent requests from the client require a session key, an authenticator, and a ticket for the server. If no suitable ticket is cached, then it requests one from the KDC. This request is just like any other, and it uses the session key for the KDC obtained at logon, along with the TGT.

A request involves sending an authenticator and a ticket. The authenticator is in a common format, including a time stamp to prevent replay attacks, and is encrypted with the session key. The ticket is a copy of the session key encrypted with the server's long-term key. By decrypting the ticket, the server can then decrypt the authenticator and validate the client. To authenticate the server, the client can also request mutual authentication, whereby the server replies with the time stamp from the authenticator encrypted with the session key.

Inter-Domain Authentication

The process for Kerberos authentication operating between realms, such as between domains, has the same basic building blocks as authentication within domains. The place where it differs is that Ticket Granting Tickets must be issued from every realm in the trust path, starting with the client's realm and ending with the server's realm. Consider, for example, the Active Directory domain tree shown in Figure 6.5.

Here, the trust path of a client in **child1.example.com** connecting to a shared folder on a server in the **child2.example.com** domain is shown, and it passes through the root domain. This means that the communication process is as follows:

- Client logs on and requests a TGT from a KDC on **child1**.

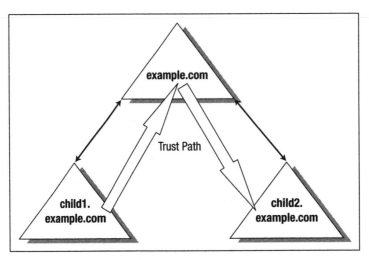

Figure 6.5   **Example.com** forest.

- Client contacts a domain controller from **example.com** and uses the TGT from **child1** to obtain a TGT for **example.com**. This TGT for **example.com** is known as a *referral ticket* and is encrypted with the interrealm, long-term key.

- Client contacts a domain controller from **child2.example.com** and uses the TGT from **example.com** to obtain a referral ticket for **child2**.

- Client uses the TGT from **child2** to obtain a session ticket for the desired server.

The important point to note here is that network traffic is generated to a domain controller in **example.com** for every authentication request between its children. This fact is important when you're planning the placement of domain controllers within your organization.

For example if all domain controllers from **child1** and **child2** were contained in a company's Glasgow office and if all domain controllers from **example.com** were in the London office, as shown in Figure 6.6, then WAN traffic would be generated.

Here, a shortcut trust with **child2** trusting **child1** would prevent the WAN traffic from being generated, because the trust path would be shortened to a direct trust between **child1** and **child2**. (If this situation occurs in your organization, you would want a second shortcut trust with **child1** trusting **child2** to prevent WAN traffic from being generated as resources are shared in the other direction.)

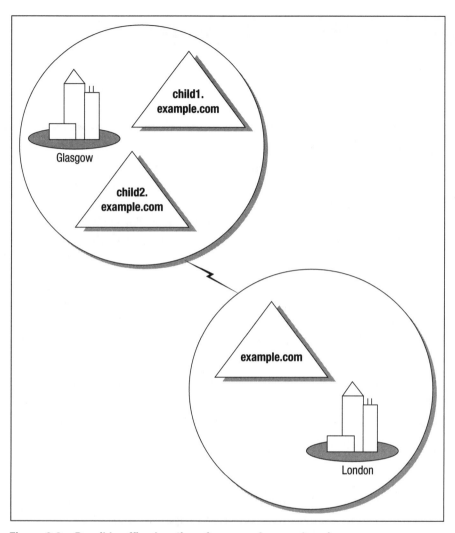

Figure 6.6   Possible office locations for **example.com** domains.

User Account Mapping

If trusts are established with non-Windows 2000 Kerberos realms, then in order to provide Windows 2000 services to users in these foreign realms, users in these foreign realms must be able to have Windows 2000 permissions applied to them.

In order to do this, a Windows 2000 user account must be associated with the user in the foreign realm. This process then allows the specified user of the foreign realm to exercise the privileges of the mapped Windows 2000 user. The mapping process can be performed through Active Directory Users and Computers.

6. Multiple Domains

Immediate Solutions

Managing Trust Relationships

Now we'll discuss managing trust relationships.

Viewing Trust Relationships

Trust relationships are stored on a per-domain basis. For each domain, separate lists of trusted and trusting domains are stored, along with the associated trust passwords. It's the trust passwords that enable the trust to function. The password must agree at each end of the trust.

Trust information is most easily managed through the Active Directory Domains and Trusts Snap-in. To view trust information:

1. Open Active Directory Domains and Trusts from the Administrative Tools menu.

2. Right-click on the domain you wish to view trust information for in the tree pane and select Properties.

3. Switch to the Trusts tab. You're presented with a list for incoming trusts and a list for outgoing trusts.

4. To view more details of a trust, select the trust from the list and click the corresponding Edit button.

5. Once you've finished examining trust information, click Cancel to discard any inadvertent changes from the trust Properties dialog box.

Because trust information is stored within the directory as objects of the **trustedDomain** class with a domain's naming context, it is possible to manipulate trust relationships as you would with any other directory object. For example, a trust to a domain named **adamwood.com** from **example.com** would be stored in the object:

```
cn=adamwood.com,cn=System,dc=example,dc=com
```

This means that it's simple to extract information about a domain's trusts programmatically. An example of how to create a list of trust relationships is shown in Listing 6.1.

Listing 6.1   ADBB-06-01-ViewTrust.vbs.

```
Option Explicit

Dim strPath, objConnection, objCommand, objRecordSet, strOut, strQuery

' Change this to match your domain

strPath = "LDAP://cn=System,dc=example,dc=com"

' Set up connection

Set objConnection            = CreateObject("ADODB.Connection")
Set objCommand               = CreateObject("ADODB.Command")
objConnection.Provider       = "ADSDSOObject"
objConnection.Open
Set objCommand.ActiveConnection  = objConnection
objCommand.Properties("Sort On") = "trustPartner"

' Write the LDAP Search Filter

strQuery = "<" & strPath & ">;(objectCategory=trustedDomain);trustpartner"
strQuery = strQuery & ",trusttype,trustdirection;onelevel"

' Obtain Results Set

objCommand.commandtext = strQuery
Set objRecordSet       = objCommand.execute

' Display Results

While Not objRecordSet.EOF

  select case objRecordSet.Fields(2)
    case 1 strOut = "Incoming "
    case 2 strOut = "Outgoing "
    case 3 strOut = "Bidirectional "
  end select

  select case objRecordSet.Fields(1)
    case 1 strOut = strOut & "downlevel "
    case 2 strOut = strOut & "Windows 2000 "
    case 3 strOut = strOut & "Kerberos "
  end select

  strOut = strOut & "trust with " & objRecordSet.Fields(0)
```

6. Multiple Domains

```
    Wscript.Echo strOut

    objRecordSet.MoveNext

Wend

' Clean Up

objRecordSet.Close
Set objRecordSet = Nothing
```

Adding a Trust Relationship

The process for adding a trust relationship shares common elements regardless of whether or not the inbound or outbound portion is being configured and regardless of exactly what type of trust is being created.

To create a trust relationship using Active Directory Domains and Trusts:

1. Open Active Directory Domains and Trusts from the Administrative Tools menu.

2. Right-click on the domain you wish to add a trust to in the tree pane and select Properties.

3. Switch to the Trusts tab. You're presented with a list for incoming trusts and a list for outgoing trusts.

4. Click either the Add button for incoming or the Add button for outgoing trusts, according to the task being performed.

5. You're prompted for the name of the domain to configure the trust with and a trust password, with confirmation. The same password must be entered at each end of the trust relationship, and it's this password that secures the trust. If a malicious person obtains the password for a trust, he can gain access to the trusting end of the relationship.

6. An attempt will be made to contact the domain to be trusted. Trusts to Windows domains will only be created if they can be contacted.

TIP: *If you wish to find the location of a file on a drive—for example, if you're wondering which set of add-on tools a utility came in—the command-line Resource Kit utility, **where.exe**, can be used to locate a file. You can simply type* **where netdom.exe** *to find which folder in which* **netdom.exe** *is located in if it exists.*

Setting the Domain's Managed by Property

Numerous objects in the Active Directory have a "managed by" attribute. This is stored as the distinguished name (DN) of a directory object. Being the manager of an object doesn't confer any special permissions, but it's useful to configure this property, nevertheless, to make your directory self-documenting. This property can be queried to discover which person is responsible for an object and, hence, find his contact details.

To set the "managed by" property of a domain:

1. Open Active Directory Domains and Trusts from the Administrative Tools menu.

2. Right-click on the domain you wish to change the manager of in the tree pane and select Properties.

3. Switch to the Managed By tab. You're presented with the details of the current manager if any.

4. Click Set to change the manager. You're presented with the standard Select User or Contact dialog box.

5. Select, or type the name of, the desired manager for the object. A typed name can either be a User Principal Name (UPN) or the relative distinguished name (RDN) of an object. Click OK. In the event of multiple objects of the same type having the same RDN, you're presented with a list to choose from.

6. The new manager's details should appear in the Properties dialog for the domain. Note again that no additional privileges are granted, based on this assignment.

7. Click OK to accept the changes to the domain's properties.

As with any other change to directory information, this change can be made using Active Directory Service Interface (ADSI) Edit. To do so:

1. Open ADSI Edit from the Tools folder beneath the Windows 2000 Support Tools menu item.

2. If necessary, use **Action -> Connect to** in order to access a domain controller in the domain you wish to configure.

3. Expand the Domain NC (Naming Context).

4. Right-click the object representing the domain in the tree pane and select Properties. If you're accessing **example.com**, this would be called **dc=example,dc=com**.

5. In the "Select A Property To View:" drop-down list, select **managedBy**.

TIP: *In Windows controls, such as list boxes and drop-down lists, typing the first letter of the item you wish to select will make it easier to find. In this case, with the default schema, typing m will take you straight to **managedBy**.*

---

6. In the Value field, type the full Lightweight Directory Access Protocol (LDAP) distinguished name (DN) of the object you wish to do the managing, such as **cn=Administrator,cn=Users,dc=example,dc=com**. Note that this is case-sensitive.

7. Now, click Set to commit the change. Failure to do so is a frustrating and common mistake, especially if you've just typed a long and complicated DN.

8. Click OK to accept the change and close the Properties dialog box.

Kerberos Interoperability

Now we'll discuss Kerberos interoperability.

Trust with a Kerberos Realm

The process of configuring functioning trust relationships with a general Kerberos realm is a multistep process. It consists of not just physically configuring the trust relationship, but also configuring client computers to access the foreign realm and creating account mappings for users in the foreign realm.

Setting up Hosts

When a trust is added to a foreign realm, computers wishing to access the realm must be made aware of its existence. This is performed by adding a specific registry entry under **HKLM\System\CurrentControlSet\Control\LSA\Kerberos\Domains**.

For each realm, a key must be added with the name of the realm and within which there is a multivalued string called **KdcNames** that contains the Domain Name System (DNS) names of the Key Distribution Centers (KDCs) for the realm. This entry can be added using the **ksetp.exe** utility from the Windows 2000 Support Tools. To add knowledge of the KDC **kdc.realm.example.com** from the realm **REALM.EXAMPLE.COM**, type the following:

```
C:\>ksetup /addkdc REALM.EXAMPLE.COM kdc.realm.example.com
```

As with any large-scale change of registry settings, it may be beneficial to use Group Policy to automate this process.

Related solution:	Found on page:
Group Policy Results	353

NOTE: *Out-of-the-box, there's an issue that may require the client to be rebooted for the change to be used by the Kerberos client service. This issue is resolved by Windows 2000 Service Pack 1.*

Configuring the Trust

Once mappings to a KDC of the foreign realm have been established on the domain controllers of a domain, you can configure the trust as normal from any domain controller in the domain. The user interface of Active Directory Domains and Trusts only allows nontransitive trusts to be created. Such a trust can be made transitive using the **netdom.exe** utility from the Support Tools. In addition, it can be created using **netdom.exe** as a transitive trust.

NOTE: *Only transitivity within the Windows 2000 forest is supported by such a trust, so while any domain in the forest will have an effective trust with the foreign realm, no domain will have access to other realms that trust the foreign realm, without additional direct trust relationships.*

Mapping Accounts

The process of mapping user accounts is performed with the Active Directory Users and Computers tool. The user interface elements involved are hidden, by default, and require Advanced Features to be enabled. To enable Advanced Features:

1. Start Active Directory Users and Computers from the Administrative Tools menu.

2. Open the View menu from the lower, Snap-in-specific menu bar.

3. If no tick is next to Advanced Features, click Advanced Features to enable them.

With Advanced Features enabled, Snap-ins show a greater choice of menu options. In the case of Active Directory Users and Computers, this includes the Name Mappings option used for X.509 and Kerberos name mappings.

To map a Kerberos principal name to a user account within Active Directory Users Computers:

1. Right-click the user object to map to and select Name Mappings (which, by default, will be the third option).

2. Switch to the Kerberos Names tab.

3. Click Add to create a new mapping.

4. Enter the name of the Kerberos principal to map in the form **user@REALM**, for example, **adam@REALM.ADAMWOOD.COM**. (Note that it's conventional for realms to have uppercase names.) Click OK.

5. Click OK again to close the Security Identity Mapping dialog box.

6. Multiple Domains

Chapter 7

Sites

In Depth

Active Directory sites are, technically, just groups of IP addresses. They're intended to represent physical locations within your organization and are used by a variety of processes to optimize your network. Site information is stored in the Configuration partition of the directory and is, thus, stored by all domain controllers in the forest.

Site information is published in the directory for use by applications and services. Perhaps the most important consumer of site information is the Active Directory itself. The process of Active Directory replication is optimized so that replication within a site is uncompressed and (almost) immediate, whereas replication between sites is heavily compressed, periodic, and can be scheduled.

This reflects the assumptions that: within a sites network, connectivity is plentiful; not compressing traffic saves processor cycles; and between sites, it's the network links that are the limiting factor. Applications using Active Directory sites should make the same assumption, and this must be borne in mind when designing the site topology for a network.

A second crucial use of Active Directory site information occurs in the Windows 2000 logon process. The **DsGetDcName** application programming interface (API) function discussed in Chapter 5 prefers, by default, to find domain controllers close to the calling computer. This means that logons are more responsive and more efficient, because the use of finite network bandwidth is minimized.

Sites

Active Directory site information is stored in terms of site objects in the directory. These objects are contained in the Configuration partition of a forest's directory and, hence, are replicated to all domain controllers in the forest. Site information can't usefully be shared between forests. Primarily, sites are administered through the Active Directory Sites and Services Snap-in shown in Figure 7.1. In addition to sites, the main service that this is used to manage is the Active Directory on a per-domain controller basis. Replication settings, for example, are managed through Active Directory Sites and Services.

By default, when you create a new Active Directory forest, a single site called Default-First-Site-Name is created. Generally, the rule of thumb is to create an

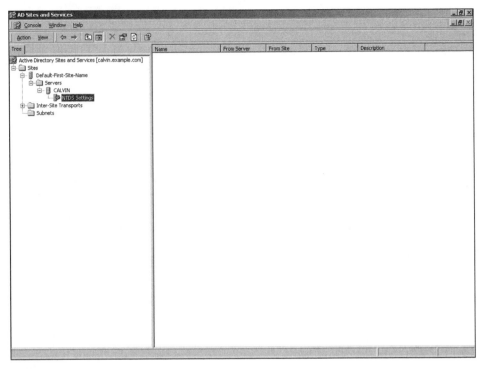

Figure 7.1   Active Directory Sites and Services.

Active Directory site for each physical location in your organization. This may be broken if you have well-connected locations with underutilized wide area network (WAN) lines whose speeds are comparable to a local area network (LAN). In this case, you may be inclined to define a single site for all such locations.

Site Membership

The current site for a client computer—either workstation or member server—is wholly dependent on its IP address. This allows laptop users to roam between sites and pick up new site information when they reach a different building. For multihomed computers that have more than one network card or even just multiple IP addresses in different site ranges, the site used depends only on the IP address used to contact the authenticating domain controller.

Computers, in fact, cache their site membership information to disk, so the next time they start up a domain controller, their old site is contacted first. This happens because it's likely that a computer hasn't moved between sites and between restarts. To cope with changes in site boundaries and mobile users moving between locations, referrals to other domain controllers will be generated if a client contacts a domain controller in her cached site and discovers that it's no longer in that site.

Domain controllers, on the other hand, must explicitly belong to a site. The initial site a domain controller is created in is based wholly on its IP address. Thereafter, a domain controller can be explicitly moved to a site where its IP address doesn't belong and, more importantly, must manually be moved if a new site is created, even if its IP address is part of that site.

Site Coverage

The concept of site coverage allows a domain controller to appear as if it's a member of multiple sites. It maintains membership of only one site, and its server object appears beneath only that site in Active Directory Sites and Services, but service (SRV) resource records are registered for its own and any covered sites.

This means that clients in covered sites will see covering domain controllers as if they're part of the site they're covering. They'll select between covering domain controllers and domain controllers in the site in the usual way with the aid of SRV resource records, weights, and priorities.

Bridgehead Servers

A *bridgehead server* is one responsible for managing a connection between sites. Logically, you can think of it as the gatekeeper sitting at the end of the connection between two sites, although this needn't be reflected in your physical network. Bridgehead servers are used for replication purposes, because interdomain replication only takes place between bridgeheads and is then disseminated within sites to avoid sending the same information down a WAN link several times.

The *Knowledge Consistency Checker (KCC)*, the automated process for generating a replication topology, will select bridgehead servers on its own. You can manually define servers as a preferred bridgehead on a per-transport protocol basis, and this will lead the KCC to choose only between preferred bridgehead servers.

Site Licensing Server

One server in the site—which need not be a domain controller—is designated the site licensing server. This server becomes responsible for logging license use within a site if you're using Windows 2000's license tracking features. The default site licensing server is the first domain controller in a site, although a site licensing server need not even be contained within the site (though it helps performance).

Subnets

In the context of Active Directory sites, a subnet is purely a range of IP addresses. It need not correspond to the subnet mask on client computers, but your network will doubtless be easier to maintain if it does. Although the Active Directory Sites and Services user interface protects you from having to specify subnet names manually—instead you're prompted for a network address and subnet mask—all it in fact does is convert your input into the corresponding network name.

Subnet Names

An example of a subnet name for an IP version 4 network is 10.0.87.0/28. It consists of two portions— the network address appears before the slash, and after the slash is a representation of the subnet mask. Instead of specifying the subnet mask like an IP address, the number of 1s is specified. All of these 1s form a contiguous block at the start of the subnet mask and are implicitly padded out to 32 characters with zeros. For example, a **/28** corresponds to:

```
Binary        :  11111111 11111111 11111111 11110000
Dotted Decimal:     255.     255.     255.     240
```

Here, the 32-bit IP version 4 address is split into groups of 8 bits (octets) and is also converted to the more familiar dotted decimal representation. Some common subnet masks and the corresponding slash notation are shown in Table 7.1.

This form of subnet naming prevents you from specifying a discontinuous subnet mask for a subnet object. A discontinuous subnet mask is one where not all of the 1s that comprise the binary representation of the subnet mask are in a group at the left. For example 255.0.255.255 (11111111 00000000 11111111 11111111) is a discontinuous subnet mask, and 10.0.87.1 with a netmask of 255.0.255.255 matches all IP addresses of the form 10.x.87.1.

These types of subnets can't be specified by slash notation, and this is with good reason—they may not be published to the public Internet and are, hence, only of use internally and must be aggregated before routes are published. It's always possible to design your network using contiguous subnet masks instead, and this makes for a more intuitive and easy-to-document network. Actually, the only argument I've ever seen in favor of discontinuous subnet masks is job security for administrators, because no one else will understand how your internetwork operates.

Table 7.1   Subnet Masks and Slash Notation.

Subnet Mask	Slash Notation
255.0.0.0	/8
255.255.0.0	/16
255.255.255.0	/24

7. Sites

Subnet Matching

Other than for domain controllers, the site that a computer is in depends on matching its IP address with a subnet object. In this, as with any other operation with IP addresses, it's best to think of what is happening at the binary level. The IP address matching doesn't even take into consideration the subnet mask that a host is configured with. Instead, the subnet objects are used in exactly the same way as in firewalls to match an IP address. This means that a general subnet **a.b.c.d/n** will match any IP address whose first **n** bits are the first **n** bits of **a.b.c.d**. In this way you can use a **/32** subnet to match exactly one host, if required.

Inter-Site Transports

Within Active Directory Sites and Services, there's a folder titled "Inter-Site Transports". This contains information about how the sites in the directory are connected. Connections can be either the more common IP, which is more correctly termed RPC over IP (Remote Procedure Calls over Internet Protocol), or the alternative, which is *Simple Mail Transfer Protocol (SMTP)*.

SMTP is the mechanism used to route Internet email. It can also be used as a transit mechanism for intersite, interdomain Active Directory replication data. To use SMTP replication, each participating domain controller must have the SMTP component of Internet Information Services (IIS) installed, and an Enterprise Certificate Authority must exist to enable security features to be used.

Site Links

A *site link* defines the connectivity between two or more Active Directory sites. The following key properties are available for each site link:

- *Transport protocol*—The transport protocol for a site link is decided at creation and can be either IP or SMTP. The use of SMTP site links for replication traffic is discussed in Chapter 8. For most requirements, IP site links are preferred. The transport protocol defines what form of communication can take place across a site link.

- *Cost*—The cost assigned to a site link is a number on an arbitrary scale that should reflect, in some sense, the expense of sending traffic along that link. Cost can be in the range 1 to 32,767, and lower costs are preferred.

- *Replicate every*—The "replicate every" setting specifies the interval for replication across a site link. This is the number of minutes that should elapse before replication is attempted.

- *Replication schedule*—With the replication schedule, you can define when a site link is available for replication and when it isn't. This can be to the resolution of one hour, and different settings can be applied for each week-day. The reason why the resolution is limited to one hour is so that it can be stored efficiently as 168-bit flags within one attribute in the directory. Figure 7.2 shows the Replication Schedule Configuration dialog box for a site link.

The magnitude of the cost of a site link only matters relative to other site link costs within your forest. Cost should be assigned to "guide" processes that use intersite communications. For example, the automatic mechanism known as the Knowledge Consistency Checker (KCC) that generates a replication topology tries to do so by using the lowest cost links possible.

The cost of a link should be inversely proportional to the effective bandwidth of a network connection between sites. For example, if you assign a cost of 32,000 to a 64kbps line, then you should assign 16,000 to a 128kbps line and 1,000 to a 2Mbps line. It makes sense to use a high number for the slowest link in your organization, because you wouldn't want to have to recost all links in the future. As technology improves and communication becomes cheaper, it's likely that future WAN lines will be faster than today's, so there's little sense in assigning a cost of two for your current 128kbps line and a cost of 1 for your 256kbps line, because quicker links can't be priced more cheaply. Also, it's important to consider only the bandwidth that you wish to be considered for replication when costing links, that is to say, the effective bandwidth. If you have a 2Mbps line connecting two offices that's constantly used by another process, then you should only consider it as a 1Mbps line for costing, for example.

Notification

A property of site links that can't be configured through the Microsoft Management Console (MMC) is that of *replication notification*. With this enabled, replication between sites in the site link happens as it does within sites, with notification

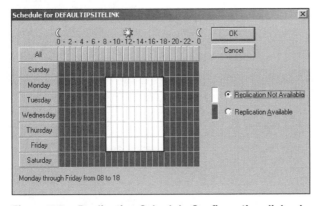

Figure 7.2   Replication Schedule Configuration dialog box.

messages being sent when changes are received, as opposed to the default intrasite behavior of periodic connections. This option is useful when you use multiple sites within a highly connected network to partition traffic but still want fast convergence when data is changed. For example, an office building may have network hubs on a per-floor basis, with each hub connected to a building backbone. To ensure that clients authenticate preferentially with domain controllers on their own floor, sites are created for each floor. However, the delays in intrasite replication may seem unnecessary, so change notification is an option. It's implemented by setting the first bit of the options property of the site link so it's enabled if the options property is set to an odd number. It should be noted that a regime of multiple sites within one building is relatively rare and should only be considered if your backbone is highly used.

Two-Way Sync

The *two-way sync option* is designed for use on dial-up connections to require replication in each direction during a single connection, such as when a telephone connection is on. It's controlled by the second bit of the options property for a site link. Using, for example, Active Directory Service Interface (ADSI) Edit, the values of the options attribute in Table 7.2 configure two-way sync and notification.

Site Link Bridges

A *site link bridge* is a collection of site links that are deemed transitive, so computers in any site are allowed to contact computers in any other site that they can trace a path to through a number of site links within the same site link bridge. By default, all site links for both the IP and SMTP transport protocols are bridged, so no site link bridges are necessary and, in effect, all site links form part of a single site link bridge. So when would you not want to use the default settings? The canonical example Microsoft uses is that of a network that isn't fully routed. Consider the example in Figure 7.3.

Table 7.2   Site Link Options values.

Value	Two-Way Sync	Notification
0	No	No
1	No	Yes
2	Yes	No
3	Yes	Yes

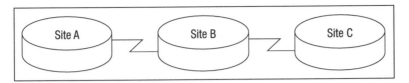

Figure 7.3 **A nonfully-routed network.**

Here, we assume that hosts in Site A can't communicate by the chosen transport mechanism with hosts in Site C. The reason is unimportant, although this will typically be due to router or firewall configuration. What matters is that a domain controller in Site A can't communicate with a domain controller in Site C. This means that if the KCC went away and created a replication object linking two such domain controllers, it would fail to replicate any data.

The solution would be to break site link transitivity for your chosen transport protocol, so no host in Site A attempts to contact a host in Site C, and vice versa. This still wouldn't require the use of a site link bridge, although if we add a Site D linked to Site C and able to communicate with Site B but not Site A, we could configure as shown in Figure 7.4.

A more likely reason to remove the default setting of all site links bridged and to implement site link bridges would arise in an office whose network topology shows a clear hierarchy of large data centers and branch offices.

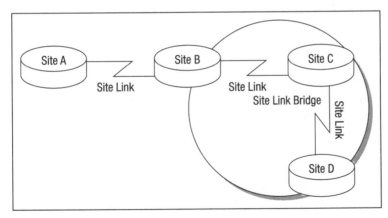

Figure 7.4 **Expanded, nonfully-routed network with site links and site link bridge shown.**

7. Sites

Site Design

Before deploying Active Directory, you should plan thoroughly. An essential part of this plan is to consider exactly which sites you should create and how they're linked in terms of site links and site link bridges. Site information is stored in the configuration partition under **cn=Sites,cn=Configuration,dc=ForestRoot**, and because of this, you can create sites and associated information at any point in your deployment of Active Directory. Ideally, you should do it as early as possible, because subsequent domain controllers will appear in the correct site to start with.

Microsoft correctly advises that site topology is technically unrelated to domain hierarchy—the two can be defined completely independently. However, common issues affect the design of both. The most important of these is replication. If you don't wish to have every property of objects replicated to domain controllers throughout your network, then you can create separate domains to partition objects within the directory. Because the reason for creating these domains was related to replication, it's likely that you'll have created domains based on physical locations and, hence, sites. Such situations are only relevant in very large organizations, because the actual volume of replication data between sites isn't that great, and with the ability to schedule it to run overnight, it need not impact WAN performance during business hours.

Delegating Administration of Sites

Two of the much-vaunted advantages of Windows 2000 are the ability to delegate the administration of actions and the diminished need for all-powerful administrator accounts within your organization. Because site information is stored as objects within the directory, delegating administration of site management is as easy as delegating administration of directory objects. From an operational perspective, site configuration is likely to be relatively static—ask yourself how often your company opens a new location (Starbucks employees need not answer). This means that sites, and their associated objects, can be administered centrally by a small group of people. This prevents junior administrators from unnecessarily tweaking the site configuration. Above all, you should aim for a relatively static and well-documented site structure, because constant change is probably unnecessary and of little benefit.

Sites

Sites themselves are stored as objects beneath the Sites object within the Configuration partition. Hence, to delegate administration to a group you should assign the following permissions:

- To the delegated Site Administration Group, assign Read and Create child objects on **cn=Sites,cn=Configuration,dc=ForestRoot** specified for *this object only* to allow new sites to be created.

- Give the special Creator-Owner Group full control of **cn=Sites, cn=Configuration,dc=ForestRoot** *for this object and all child objects* to allow sites to be managed.

- Deny Create Inter-Site Transports container objects for *this object only* to prevent site-only administrators from modifying any intersite transports.

NOTE: *More details about Windows 2000 Permissions are given in Chapter 10.*

Subnets

Along with delegating control of sites, it's likely that you would want junior administrators to be able to manage subnet objects (because, otherwise, they wouldn't be able to do much useful in the way of managing sites). The permissions required here are the following:

- To the delegated Subnet Administration Group, assign Read and Create child objects on **cn=Subnets,cn=Sites,cn=Configuration,dc=ForestRoot** specified for *this object only* to allow new subnets to be created.

- Give the special Creator-Owner Group full control of **cn=Subnets,cn=Sites, cn=Configuration,dc=ForestRoot** for *this object and all child objects* to allow subnets to be managed.

Site Links and Site Link Bridges

Site links and site link bridges influence the replication topology of your network, and a malicious administrator can seriously misconfigure your network if he has access to them. These permissions should only be granted to trusted employees. To delegate site link administration for the IP protocol:

- To the delegated Site Link Administration Group, assign Read and Create child objects on **cn=IP,cn=Inter-Site Transports,cn=Sites,cn=Configuration, dc=ForestRoot** specified for *this object only* to allow new site links and site link bridges to be created.

- Give the special Creator-Owner Group full control of **cn=IP,cn=Inter-Site Transports,cn=Sites,cn=Configuration,dc=ForestRoot** for *this object and all child objects* to allow site links and site link bridges to be managed.

The process for SMTP is identical, with the obvious change of IP to SMTP in the first component of the distinguished names (DNs).

7. Sites

Immediate Solutions

Managing Sites

Now we'll discuss managing sites.

Renaming a Site

One of the first tasks to perform when administering your site structure is to rename the default site. Even if an organization is housed in a single location, it makes sense to rename Default-First-Site-Name, because you never know when it will expand.

To rename a site perform the following steps:

1. Start Active Directory Sites and Services from the Administrative Tools menu.

2. Expand the Sites folder in the tree pane if necessary.

3. Sites are shown with icons of small, yellow office buildings. Right-click the site you wish to rename and select Rename.

4. Type the new name and press Enter.

When a domain controller becomes aware that its site has changed names, it will reregister its Domain Name System (DNS) records appropriately. Because of issues with cached DNS lookups and client caching of site names that will lead to temporary delays in connectivity directly after a rename, it's best to name and rename sites as early as possible in the deployment. Once you've renamed a site, it's advisable to manually force replication with other domain controllers in the same site.

Related solution:	*Found on page:*
Forcing Immediate Replication	208

Creating Sites

Site objects are created through the Active Directory Sites and Services Snap-in. To create a site:

1. Start Active Directory Sites and Services from the Administrative Tools menu.

2. Right-click the Sites folder in the left-hand tree pane and select New Site.

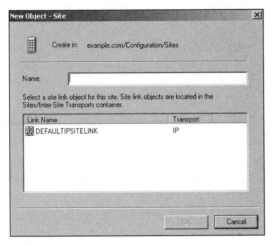

Figure 7.5   Site Creation dialog box.

3. A dialog box similar to Figure 7.5 appears.

4. Type a name, remembering that this will form part of a DNS resource record, so you should restrict yourself to alphanumeric characters and the dash ("-") only.

5. Select an initial site link for the site to be a member of. You can always reconfigure this and add it to multiple site links at a later time. Click OK when done.

6. You'll be reminded to add subnets and create appropriate site links. Click OK again.

Alternatively, you can create a site by script. A sample script to do this with VBScript and ADSI is given in Listing 7.1.

Listing 7.1   ADBB-07-01-SiteCreation.vbs.

```
Option Explicit
' Declare Variables
Dim strSite, oRootDSE, oSites, oNewSite, oNTDSObj, oLicense, oServers
strSite  = "New-Site-Name"
' Get Sites Object
Set oRootDSE = GetObject("LDAP://RootDSE")
Set oSites   = GetObject("LDAP://cn=Sites," & _
                     oRootDSE.Get("ConfigurationNamingContext"))
' Create the New Sites object and the three mandatory subobjects
Set oNewSite = oSites.Create("site", "cn=" & strSite)
oNewSite.SetInfo
Set oNTDSObj = oNewSite.Create("NTDSSiteSettings", "cn=NTDS Site Settings")
oNTDSObj.SetInfo
```

```
Set oLicense = oNewSite.Create("LicensingSiteSettings", _
oLicense.SetInfo
Set oServers = oNewSite.Create("ServersContainer", "cn=Servers")
oServers.SetInfo
```

Creating Subnets

Active Directory sites need one or more subnet objects to be associated with them in order to match client computers. A site can only be associated with one subnet. To create a new subnet:

1. Start Active Directory Sites and Services from the Administrative Tools menu.

2. Expand the Sites folder in the tree pane if necessary.

3. Right-click subnets and select **New Subnet**.

4. Enter the network address and subnet mask in dotted decimal notation.

5. Select a site to associate the subnet with from the list provided. You must select a subnet for the graphical user interface (GUI) to allow you to proceed.

Alternatively, you can use a script to create a site, as shown in Listing 7.2.

Listing 7.2   ADDB-07-02-SubnetCreation.vbs.

```
Option Explicit
' Declare Variables -- Replace the values of strSite and strSubnetName
'                      to suit your own network
Dim strSite, strSubnetName, oRootDSE, oSubnets, oNewSubnet
strSite       = "Site-For-Subnet"
strSubnetName = "192.168.0.0/16"
' Get Sites Object
Set oRootDSE = GetObject("LDAP://RootDSE")
Set oSubnets = GetObject("LDAP://cn=Subnets,cn=Sites," & _
                  oRootDSE.Get("ConfigurationNamingContext"))
' Create the new subnet object and associate it with a site
Set oNewSubnet        = oSubnets.Create("subnet", "cn=" & strSubnetName)
oNewSubnet.siteobject = "cn=" & strSite & ",cn=Sites," & _
                  oRootDSE.Get("ConfigurationNamingContext")
oNewSubnet.SetInfo
```

Managing Site Membership for Domain Controllers

Now we'll discuss managing site membership for domain controllers.

Moving a Domain Controller between Sites

The site of a domain controller doesn't change based upon its IP address. Instead, you must manually move it explicitly between sites. To do so:

1. Start Active Directory Sites and Services from the Administrative Tools menu.
2. Expand the Sites folder in the tree pane if necessary.
3. Expand the site the domain controller is currently a member of.
4. Expand the Server's folder.
5. Right-click on the domain controller to relocate and click Move.
6. Select the destination site from the list that appears and click OK.

Configuring Site Coverage

For a Windows 2000 domain controller to service clients from multiple sites, it must be configured to cover additional sites by registering the necessary SRV resource records for these sites. Because dynamic SRV resource record registration is managed by the netlogon service, you won't be surprised to learn that configuring site coverage is a matter of informing the registry which sites it should cover.

The registry entry in question is the **SiteCoverage** value beneath:

```
HKLM\System\CurrentControlSet\Services\Netlogon\Parameters
```

To enable site coverage, you should add a value **SiteCoverage** of type **REG_MULTI_SZ** beneath the key above and specify a list of site names to cover, separated by carriage returns, as the data for the value.

WARNING! Due to limitations of regedit.exe, you must use regedt32.exe when dealing with REG_MULTI_SZ values.

7. Sites

Managing Inter-Site Transports

IP and SMTP are two possible transport protocols for inter-site connections. The settings and tasks are performed on a per-protocol basis.

Disabling Default Bridging Behavior

By default, all SMTP site links and all IP site links are bridged, meaning sites are assumed to be allowed to communicate with any site that they can trace a path to through site links of the correct protocol. This behavior is stored separately as properties of the IP and SMTP objects. To modify it:

1. Start Active Directory Sites and Services from the Administrative Tools menu.
2. Expand the Sites folder in the tree pane if necessary.
3. Expand the Inter-Site Transports folder.
4. Right-click the object (SMTP or IP) to modify and select Properties. The dialog box shown in Figure 7.6 appears.
5. Uncheck the "Bridge all site links" box. Click OK to commit the change.

WARNING! This feature should be used with caution, and only then by those who know what they're doing. Idly turning it off in situations where there are several site links could prevent the forest from replicating fully, which is a very bad thing.

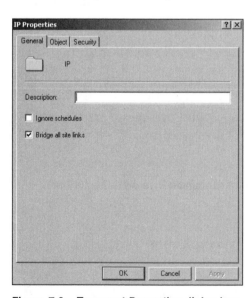

Figure 7.6 Transport Properties dialog box.

Bypassing Schedules

There may be exceptional circumstances when the schedule for inter-site replication must be bypassed temporarily, perhaps to propagate an important change during office hours. To achieve this, there's an option on a per-transport basis to ignore schedules. To ignore schedules:

1. Start Active Directory Sites and Services from the Administrative Tools menu.

2. Expand the Sites folder in the tree pane if necessary.

3. Expand the Inter-Site Transports folder.

4. Right-click the object (SMTP or IP) to modify and select Properties.

5. Toggle the "Ignore schedule" checkbox. Click OK to commit the change.

Once any critical objects have been replicated, don't forget to turn the option off by repeating the above.

Creating a Site Link

Site links are used to define connectivity between two or more sites. A site link can be used to specify a period for replication, as well as an arbitrary cost for the link. To create a site link:

1. Start Active Directory Sites and Services from the Administrative Tools menu.

2. Expand the Sites folder in the tree pane if necessary.

3. Expand the Inter-Site Transports folder.

4. Right-click the transport (SMTP or IP) that you wish the site link to use. Select New Site Link.

5. If there's only one site in your network, you'll be warned that a Site Link will be of little use, although it will still let you create one. You should, ideally, configure sites before site link bridges. The dialog box shown in Figure 7.7 appears.

6. Type a descriptive name for the site link.

7. Select the sites that the link connects and ensure only they are in the right-hand list. At least two sites must be selected for the link to have any effect. Click OK to finish.

Once you've created a site link, it appears under its transport protocol. It still remains to configure the cost and replication settings for a site link.

Configuring Site Links

The configuration of site links takes place through its Properties dialog box in Active Directory Sites and Services. To configure a site link:

7. Sites

Figure 7.7   Site link creation.

1. Start Active Directory Sites and Services from the Administrative Tools menu.

2. Expand the Sites folder in the tree pane if necessary.

3. Expand the Inter-Site Transports folder.

4. Left-click the transport (SMTP or IP) of the site link you wish to configure. A list of all site links appears in the right-hand details pane.

5. Double-click the site link to modify it, or right-click it and select Properties. The site link Properties dialog box appears.

Creating a Site Link Bridge

Site link bridges define groups of site links that replication connections can cross between. Site link bridges are unnecessary, by default, but if you've disabled the default "bridge everything" behavior, then you can create site link bridges to allow connections to occur between sites not explicitly linked.

To create a site link bridge:

1. Start Active Directory Sites and Services from the Administrative Tools menu.

2. Expand the Sites folder in the tree pane if necessary.

3. Expand the Inter-Site Transports folder.

4. Right-click the transport (SMTP or IP) that you wish to bridge the site links of. Select New Site Link Bridge.

NOTE: *You must have at least two site links of the current transport, or you'll be unable to create a site link bridge.*

5. Type a name for the site link bridge in the Name edit box.

6. Use the Add and Remove buttons to configure the list of site links you wish this object to bridge. Click OK when done.

The only other property of a Site Link Bridge to configure is the Description field, which should be completed (along with any other Description fields for objects) to make your directory self-documenting, so a new administrator can see, at a glance, the business and technical purpose of an object. It's configured from the object's Properties dialog box.

7. Sites

Chapter 8

Active Directory Replication

In Depth

An essential process for any domain with more than one domain controller (and all domains should have more than one domain controller) is *replication*. Replication is the process which ensures that all copies of the domain data are kept up-to-date, and it does this by sending information about changes from one domain controller to another.

Single Master Replication

Compared to Active Directory replication, the process for replicating singly mastered information is simple. Windows NT 4 domains and standard Domain Name System (DNS) zones are singly mastered, and both use a process similar to the following. The crucial point with single master replication is that only one server can make changes—the primary domain controller (PDC) in a Windows NT 4 domain or the primary name server for a DNS zone. This means that it's possible for secondary servers to connect to the primary server to obtain the latest changes. Alternatively, secondary servers could connect to other secondary servers. This is illustrated in Figure 8.1.

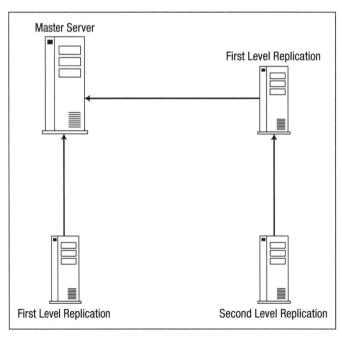

Figure 8.1   Single master replication.

In this scheme, it's necessary to know what changes need to be replicated to a given secondary server. The secondary server usually stores this information either as a "time of last replication," or if changes have associated numbers, as the number of the most recent change received.

Active Directory Replication

The Active Directory is, for the most part, multi-mastered. This means that information can be changed simultaneously on several different servers. Consider the example in Figure 8.2 that shows why simple information isn't enough to track what's going on.

Imagine a user, Susan, changes her password on Alpha at 10:00. Five minutes later the change—only Susan's new password data and not her entire user object—is replicated to Beta and a further minute later it's replicated to Gamma. The time is now 10:06.

Now when Beta next comes to replicate with Gamma, we find the time of the last update to Susan's password is later on Gamma than on Beta. However, it's the same password, and no change has been made, so relying on timestamps alone would endlessly replicate the same piece of information (because now Alpha's copy of the password is older than Beta's, and it would be replicated and continue similarly).

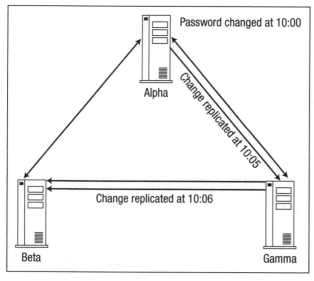

Figure 8.2 Replication example.

Instead, information about where the password was changed originally must be replicated around with the value of the password. If Beta stores this information, it will know the copy that Gamma has is the same that it already holds, so it will decline the update. This is known as *propagation dampening*.

Replication Meta-Data

To cope with the problems outlined above, Active Directory tracks information about each attribute of each object stored. This is known as *meta-data* (literally, second order data, that is, "data about data").

USNs

For each replication partner, the unique sequence number (USN) of the most recent change received is stored. USNs are counted separately on each domain controller, so as to provide a globally unique identifier of a change; they're combined with the Globally Unique Identifier (GUID) of the domain controller where the change was made. This means that Server A's USN 13 will, in general, be a different change to Server B's USN 13.

When replication happens, the domain controller that's to receive updates tells the replicating domain controller the USN of the most recent change that it has received, so only subsequent changes are sent. The USN of a domain controller is increased for each change operation to an object, regardless of whether it's replicated or performed locally. A change operation can contain an arbitrary number of changes to individual properties, so for example, both the telephone number and office address of a user can be modified in a single change operation.

NOTE: *USNs are 64-bit numbers, which means there are 2^{64} possible values. 2^{64} is less commonly written as 18,446,744,073,709,551,616, which is equivalent to over five hundred years' worth of a constant one billion changes per second. This means that you're unlikely to ever reach a USN of 2^{64} (if you have hardware that can cope with a billion updates per second, let me know). Even if you reach the maximum USN, it will wrap around and start again at 0, and Microsoft claims to have implemented an RFC-compliant method of dealing with wraparounds of USNs, but the author hasn't tested this one personally.*

It's a common mistake to assume that the latest USN should be about the same on all domain controllers. This isn't the case for many reasons. One reason for this concerns the optimizations Active Directory uses. If Susan changes her password twice in quick succession, then the USN on the domain controller where the changes happened will increase by two, but only the most recent change will be replicated, so other domain controllers will only increase their USN by 1.

Similarly, when an object is created through the management console, one change is used to create it, and if you immediately edit its properties, that will cause another change, producing a second increment to the USN of the domain controller that it's connected to. However, it's likely that both the creation of the object and property changes will replicate as a single change.

Most Recent Original Update

To test whether or not a server has already received a change, each property for each object in the directory has details of where the change actually happened. This is in the form of the GUID of the domain controller where the change was initially made and the USN of the change (on that domain controller). When a property is replicated, this information is replicated with it.

Each domain controller maintains a record of the USN of the most recent update it has had from every other domain controller (even those it doesn't replicate directly with). Using this information, each update replicated is tested to see whether or not it's more recent than that of the latest original update from the server where the change was initially made. If it isn't more recent, then it's discarded, because the change will already have been applied. If it's more recent, then it's applied, and the most recent USN for its originating server is changed to the USN of the new update on its originating server.

Attribute Version Number

Along with the originating server and USN for a property, additional meta-data is stored. The most important other meta-data is the version number of the attribute value. Quite simply, when an attribute is changed, its version number increases. This is used as the simplest way of determining whether an update that hasn't already been applied is needed—if an incoming update has a lower version number than the current value of an attribute, it's discarded.

Attribute Timestamp

Version numbers alone aren't always enough to resolve a collision. Consider, for example, the case where Susan changes her password on domain controller Alpha at 10:00, and before the change has replicated, an administrator changes it on Beta. Now both Alpha and Beta have the same version number for Susan's password, but the values are different. Which one should be kept?

This is a tricky question, because Windows 2000 has no way of knowing which one *should* be kept. It depends, for example, on whether Susan changed her password, instantly forgot the new value, and so asked an administrator to reset it (in which case the Administrator's change is the one we want to keep); or to leave on whether Susan's password became known to someone else, so it had to be changed. In this instance, through a lack of communication, both Susan and the administrator could have changed it, but because Susan will actually be using the account, it's her new change that should be kept. The way Windows 2000 deals with this problem is simple: in the case of duplicate version numbers, the value with the later timestamp is kept, so in the example above, it's the Administrator's change that will replace Susan's change and eventually be replicated to all domain controllers.

You may be wondering what happens if the version number and timestamp (down to the nearest second) for a property are the same. Well, to arbitrate in this instance, the GUID of the servers is used and, quite simply, the highest GUID wins. This situation is rare, but GUIDs are used as a deterministic, arbitrary method of deciding which change wins through.

Mechanics of Replication

What has been described so far are the elements in determining whether or not individual attributes are replicated. This section addresses the issues surrounding the actual transport mechanisms of directory replication.

Connection Objects

The replication of the Active Directory throughout domains and forests is achieved through a number of connection objects, each between two domain controllers. A *connection object* is stored beneath a domain controller's NT Directory Service (NTDS) Settings object in the Configuration partition of the directory and represents an inbound replication connection to the server specified by the name of the object. So for two-way replication to exist between servers, each requires a connection object for the other. Connection objects can be created manually, but it's usually easier to allow the automatic process known as the KCC (Knowledge Consistency Checker) to automatically build your replication topology.

Intra-Site Replication

The exact process of Active Directory replication depends on whether the communicating computers are in the same site or in different sites. Replication within a site, known as *intra-site* replication, is more immediate than inter-site replication, and is uncompressed.

Intra-site replication is notification-based: that is to say that a server that receives updates will inform replication partners when it has changes available. Because an overhead is involved in establishing a connection between domain controllers, there's a delay between a change being received and it being replicated. This delay defaults to five minutes and is configurable.

Updates often happen in batches, so this delay means that all changes are sent in one connection, instead of a new connection being negotiated for each individual update. This is particularly beneficial when a large script is running or when an administrator is updating several user accounts at once.

Inter-Site Replication

Replication between sites, known as *inter-site replication,* is more complicated and more configurable than intra-site replication. Instead of being notification-based, by default, it's schedule-based. This means that you specify the times of the week when inter-site replication can happen and the frequency with which it takes place. For example, you may wish to schedule replication not to happen when wide area network (WAN) links are otherwise congested, such as during office hours.

A further option for inter-site replication is the transport protocol used: it can either be remote procedure calls (RPCs) over IP or *Simple Mail Transport Protocol (SMTP),* the very same that's used to send email. Regardless of which transport is used, inter-site replication data is compressed usually between 10 and 15 percent of its original size (depending on exactly what sort of data is being sent—text compresses better, passwords don't compress as well, and so forth).

SMTP

SMTP connection objects are less common than RPC connections. This is because they're only available to replicate between domain controllers in different domains that are also located in different sites. Within domains, Active Directory replication consists of not just directory data but also the files that are replicated by the File Replication Service (FRS). SMTP replication doesn't support replicating files in Windows 2000 Active Directory, and file-based replication is required to synchronize, for example, logon scripts between domain controllers within the same domain.

To support SMTP replication, the domain controllers using it must be running the SMTP server service from Internet Information Services (IIS) 5, which is included on the Windows 2000 Server CD-ROM. SMTP is useful for connections that only support SMTP, are unreliable, and have low bandwidth or high latency. Replication data sent over SMTP is, of course, encrypted, and having Certificate Services installed in your enterprise is a prerequisite to using SMTP replication for this reason.

IP

The more common inter-site transport protocol is called *IP* in the user interface; it's, in fact, RPC over IP. The actual communication is, therefore, similar to intra-site replication. The IP transport will work over links that previous versions of Windows NT or Exchange are able to replicate over using RPC (and is actually more efficient than these two).

Using Inter-Site Notification

Enabling inter-site notification effectively turns several sites into a single site for replication purposes. That is, it means the replication process between these sites is exactly the same as it is within sites, with change notification and so forth.

The main (some say *only*) use of this feature is when you have deliberately created more sites than is strictly necessary. To use inter-site notification, the sites must be well connected enough to be able to be a single site, due to the additional replication traffic. However, it's sometimes useful to do this if a local area network (LAN) has bottlenecks. One example of this is a company located in an office block that has a single backbone linking floors. User logons, it turns out, take a great deal more network bandwidth than replication, so to save the over-used backbone from more load, sites were created for each floor to ensure users were authenticated by domain controllers on their own floor. Business requirements dictated that domain controllers should be as up-to-date as possible, so inter-site notification was turned on.

Points to Note

In addition to the basic process outlined above, a number of other key points and optimizations are in the Active Directory replication process that every administrator should know about.

Replicating Deletions—Tombstoning

When a user deletes an object in Active Directory, it isn't removed completely, because if it were, how would replication partners be informed that it's deleted? Instead, it's replaced by what is known as a tombstone. This tombstone retains key properties, such as the GUID of the original object, but the key properties are renamed and moved to a hidden Deleted Objects container (an object of Container class called "Deleted Objects" is located beneath the root of each partition of Active Directory. It's hidden even from Active Directory Service Interface ADSI Edit). The tombstone is replicated and indicates that the object it represents is deleted from the directory.

A garbage collection process runs on domain controllers (by default, every 12 hours) to remove tombstones that have exceeded the tombstone lifetime (a default of sixty days). After this time, the tombstone will no longer be replicated, so it's essential that all domain controllers receive the tombstone before it expires.

LostAndFound

Another special, but not-so-hidden, container is called *LostAndFound*. Each domain partition has a LostAndFound container beneath its root, and the configuration partition similarly has a *LostAndFoundConfig* container.

With multi-master replication, it isn't hard to dream up circumstances where an object can lose its Organizational Unit (OU). For example, imagine that administrators both add a new user account called Greg to the Publishing OU on Server A and delete the Publishing OU on Server B. What does Server B do when Greg's user account is replicated over? It can't go into Publishing—that's been deleted.

The answer is, of course, LostAndFound. Objects that are "lost" in this way are placed in the LostAndFound container. Administrators should occasionally check the LostAndFound container for straggling objects (probably by script).

Urgent Replication

The standard process of replication involves delays—either until the next scheduled replication between sites or the default 5-minute delay within sites. In some circumstances, replication should take place immediately. Urgent replication takes place to Windows 2000 domain controllers under three circumstances:

- *RID master operations master change*—If the holder of the domain-wide relative identifier (RID) master operations master role holder is changed, this generates an urgently replicated event.

- *LSA secret change*—The Local Security Authority is a protected subsystem of Windows 2000, and the LSA secret is securely stored data.

- *Account lockouts*—If an account is newly locked out, this fact is replicated urgently to prevent unauthorized access.

Urgent replication causes replication notifications to be sent immediately within sites for any changes currently queued and for the urgent change itself. Notifications aren't sent across site boundaries, by default, so urgent changes aren't replicated immediately to other sites (unless notification is enabled on the site link).

Password Replication

Passwords can be changed on any domain controller. This could cause confusion if, returning to the earlier example, Susan changes her password at Alpha but then immediately tries to authenticate with Beta using her new password. Because replication hasn't taken place, her credentials will fail at Beta. However, password changes at domain controllers are immediately pushed (on a best-effort basis) to the PDC Emulator role holder for the domain. Before a domain controller fails a password that doesn't correspond to its local copy, it will attempt to contact the PDC Emulator, and if the PDC Emulator accepts the credentials, it will authenticate anyway. This means that Alpha will push the password change to the domain's PDC Emulator (say it's Gamma) as soon as it's made, so after Susan's new password isn't recognized by Beta, Beta will pass the credentials on to Gamma, which authorizes her logon because the password supplied is correct. The pushing of passwords by domain controllers over WAN links can be disabled through the registry.

Not Everything Gets Replicated

Some attributes in the Active Directory schema aren't replicated. An example of this is a user's last logon time. In the early beta versions of Windows 2000 (NT 5 as it was then), a user's last logon time was replicated to give a clear answer to the question: "When did a user last log on?" Doing this creates a replication every time a user logs on or a computer starts up, which means a fair amount of extra replicated data, but for what end? In the author's experience, a last logon time isn't the sort of information that users or administrators eagerly look at as soon as they get into the office each day, so the decision was made to not replicate logon times, to remove the overhead, and to require you to query every domain controller if you want an authoritative answer to when a user last logged on.

Multi-Valued Attributes

Active Directory data is replicated at the attribute level. This means that small changes don't cause the entire object to be replicated but, instead, just the individual attribute is replicated. For multi-valued attributes, which are single properties of an object that can contain numerous pieces of information (such as telephone numbers), one change will cause the entire list to be resent.

The potential problem with this is that a multi-valued attribute may be changed independently on two different domain controllers. This will result in two distinct "values" (here the "value" is the list of multiple values) of the attribute with the same version number. The ordinary replication process will, therefore, keep the most recent of the two "values" when equilibrium is reached, and any changes made in the first modification are lost.

This isn't a major problem for a list of alternative telephone numbers, because they're unlikely to change all that often. It's a more serious issue for Windows 2000 group membership, because group membership is stored as a multi-valued attribute containing security identifiers (SIDs). If the membership of a group is changed in two or more places before replication takes place, then only one of the changes will have a lasting effect.

Inherited Permissions

Active Directory objects can have permissions applied to them to grant and deny users and groups access to the objects. These permissions can also be inherited, so you can apply a permission to an object and all of its children at once.

Inherited permissions are actually stored with the child objects; that is, if you give a group full control of an OU and all children, then this permission is stored separately with each child object. Doing this is an optimization that means permissions on all parent objects don't have to be checked whenever a user accesses an object in the directory, because all the necessary information is stored with the object itself. Of course, giving an inheritable permission to an object creates a change not just to that object but also to all objects beneath it. Fortunately, Active Directory replication is optimized so only the initial change to the top object is replicated, and all subsequent changes to child objects are applied individually by each domain controller and aren't replicated.

The Knowledge Consistency Checker

The *Knowledge Consistency Checker (KCC)* is a service that runs on each Windows 2000 domain controller, and it's responsible for generating (and checking) the Active Directory replication topology. Left to itself, the KCC will automatically build an efficient replication topology and be resilient to link failures. It will recalculate the topology by default every 15 minutes to cope with changes to the network, such as the addition or removal of domain controllers or the failure of WAN links.

If, however, you choose to manually modify the replication topology by creating or deleting connections, then the KCC will respect this. Essentially, what happens is that replication connection objects are flagged as either being owned by the KCC (in which case they can be modified by the KCC) or not owned by the KCC (and, hence, left alone). It's possible to alter the interval at which the KCC recalculates the topology or even to disable it altogether. Manually specifying a topology is particularly useful in networks with a very large number of sites—on the order of several hundred—simply because it may take the KCC longer to recalculate the inter-site topology than the interval before it starts again (not a pleasant experience).

Intra-Site Topology

On each domain controller in a site, the KCC runs independently and calculates what it thinks the replication topology should be for that site. The KCC on each domain controller then creates connection objects for its servers, which are inbound replication connections. These connection objects exist in the directory so are replicated normally to other domain controllers as part of the configuration partition. In a state of equilibrium where each domain controller knows the same (correct) information about the other domain controllers in its site, the KCC on each domain controller will reach the same result as to what the topology should be, so the correct topology will be generated.

Inter-Site Topology

The generation of *inter-site topology* is slightly different. Instead of every domain controller taking part, the KCC on only one domain controller per site is responsible for calculating what the topology should be and for creating inbound connections for the site. This domain controller is unsurprisingly known as the *Inter-Site Topology Generator (ISTG)*.

ISTG Keep-Alive

The domain controller that's the ISTG periodically writes to its own NTDS Settings object's *Inter-Site Topology Generator attribute* (by default, every 30 minutes). This change is then replicated to all other domain controllers in the site, so they know there's still a functioning ISTG in the site. If there's no ISTG keep-alive for a specified interval (by default, every 60 minutes), domain controllers will assume that there's no current ISTG and, thus, elect a new one.

Choosing the ISTG

A domain controller will assume it's the new ISTG if its GUID is the next highest to that of the current ISTG of all the domain controllers in the site. If no such domain controllers exist, the one with the lowest GUID assumes it's the ISTG. Domain controllers that don't assume they're the new ISTG will do nothing, and eventually the keep-alive written by the new ISTG will be replicated to them.

A potential problem exists with this, because with unconverged replication, two or more domain controllers will assume that they're the ISTG (for example, if the domain controller with the next highest GUID is new and if the domain controller with the second highest GUID doesn't know about the new domain controller, they'll both assume they're the ISTG). This will mean that, temporarily, several domain controllers will be creating inbound connection objects. This will be corrected and unnecessary objects deleted when replication next occurs, and of the several domain controllers that wrote their names as the new ISTG property in the directory, the one that did so last will prevail as the normal rules of replication apply.

Simple Directory Replication Example

The basic example of Active Directory replication that illustrates the use of the meta-data discussed earlier is that of three servers in the same site that all replicate with each other in a triangle, as illustrated in Figure 8.3.

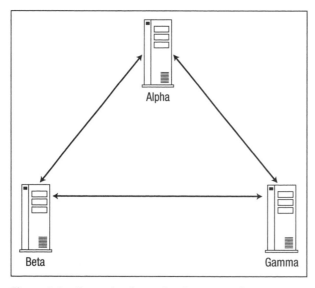

Figure 8.3   Example of a replication network.

For the purposes of this example, we'll consider changing the City Value property of a user account. Initially, the network has converged, so all three domain controllers contain the same information. Assume the values for replication meta-data in Table 8.1.

Here *Hf* is short for *highest from* and indicates the unique sequence number (USN) of the highest update received from the specified replication partner. *Horigf*, short for *highest original (update) from*, indicates the highest originating update received from, in this case, Alpha. Observe that this value is currently at 87, which means the last 12 updates performed at Alpha did not originate there. Now imagine the City Value property is changed to Cambridge at server Alpha. This change is given the USN 101 locally at Alpha, and the attribute version number is incremented accordingly, so the information is now as in Table 8.2.

After five minutes, change notification will be sent to both Beta and Gamma and the change replicated. Suppose, instead, that replication is initiated manually between Alpha and Beta. Alpha's current USN is above the highest replicated, so the latest change is replicated to Beta, and Beta accepts it as having local USN 201, updates the value and version accordingly, and increases its up-to-dateness and high water mark values for Alpha (see Table 8.3).

Now, suppose that the next replication that takes place is between Beta and Gamma. The changed password is replicated to Gamma, which, therefore, sees USN 201 from Beta, and updates the City Value and City Version. Also, the high watermark from Alpha is increased, because the password change originated at Alpha. The familiar data is now as shown in Table 8.4.

Table 8.1   Initial replication meta-data.

Server	Current USN	Hf Alpha	Hf Beta	HfGamma	HOrigf Alpha	City Version	City Value
Alpha	100		200	300		2	Crowborough
Beta	200	100		300	87	2	Crowborough
Gamma	300	100	200		87	2	Crowborough

Table 8.2   Replication metadata after the change at Alpha.

Server	Current USN	Hf Alpha	Hf Beta	HfGamma	HOrigf Alpha	City Version	City Value
Alpha	101		200	300		3	Cambridge
Beta	200	100		300	87	2	Crowborough
Gamma	300	100	200		87	2	Crowborough

Table 8.3   Replication meta-data after replication with Beta.

Server	Current USN	Hf Alpha	Hf Beta	HfGamma	HOrigf Alpha	City Version	City Value
Alpha	101		200	300		3	Cambridge
Beta	201	101		300	101	3	Cambridge
Gamma	300	100	200		87	2	Crowborough

Table 8.4   Replication meta-data after replication with Gamma.

Server	Current USN	Hf Alpha	Hf Beta	HfGamma	HOrigf Alpha	City Version	City Value
Alpha	101		200	300		3	Cambridge
Beta	201	101		300	101	3	Cambridge
Gamma	301	100	201		101	3	Cambridge

The change has now fully propagated to all domain controllers, but the directory isn't yet in equilibrium, because not all servers are fully up-to-date with each other. For example, Gamma still hasn't seen change 101 from Alpha. On seeing it, the change is discarded, because the high watermark means this update has already been applied, and the up-to-date USN is increased to 101 without any other change being made to the directory data.

Replication Traffic Sizing

A common query about Active Directory replication is: exactly how much traffic replication will it generate? The answer, unfortunately, is simply "it depends." It depends on what information you store in your directory, how many attributes you change in a time period, how frequent replication is, what transport protocol you use, and what sort of data is being replicated.

Database Sizing

The amount of disk space consumed by the Active Directory data (excluding log files) varies, depending on a variety of factors—not the least of which is how many objects you store and how much information you store in their attributes.

A certain overhead is generated in creating an object, even with a minimal set of properties that consists of storage space for things, such as security settings. A security principal (user accounts, computer accounts, groups) consumes roughly 4K and nonsecurity principals take roughly 2K.

Attribute values have an overhead, too, which is used to store replication meta-data and the like. This is roughly 90 bytes, so most values can be thought of as taking roughly 100 bytes in the directory. Binary files are stored slightly above actual size, and adding 25 percent to the file size is a rough guide.

Replication Traffic

The actual number of bytes sent down the wire for a single change is relatively large for a change of a few bytes. This is because of the overhead of establishing a replication connection between the servers. For actual attribute changes them-selves, the amount of data replicated is less than the disk space taken by the attribute.

Password changes consume nearly 1K as part of normal replication, and they don't compress well, because they're stored as a cryptographic hash and, by de-fault, cause additional traffic to the PDC Emulator role holder.

Microsoft provides detailed information for estimating replication traffic size, but ballpark figures are usually sufficient for most planning operations. When esti-mations aren't sufficient, the only way to get a true picture is to build a test lab that represents a company's unique conditions and requirements.

File Replication Service

The *File Replication Service (FRS)* is the least well-documented part of Win-dows 2000 and Active Directory replication. FRS isn't exclusive to Active Direc-tory, and other uses include synchronizing files between servers hosting copies of the same data. It replaces the LAN Manager Replication (LMREPL) service from Windows NT, which was used to replicate logon scripts and system policy settings between domain controllers. FRS uses a "last writer wins" mechanism for resolving multi-master conflicts. This means that, quite simply, the most re-cent copy of any file overwrites previous copies (and no concept of version num-bers exists as it does for Active Directory properties). Thus, it's ill suited to replicating files that are updated frequently by several people but quite suitable for items, such as logon scripts that are relatively static.

The FRS, through the NT File Replication Service (NTFRS), is responsible for replicating the shared system volume (sysvol) between domain controllers. It does this through remote procedure call (RPC) and doesn't compress data, regardless of whether it's operating between or within sites. FRS replicates at the file level, which means an entire file is replicated if it has changed, regardless of how small the change is.

Immediate Solutions

Configuring Replication

I'll now discuss how to configure replication.

Forcing Immediate Replication

Normally, data is replicated based upon change notification within sites. It you wish to force immediate replication, you can do so. To force the immediate replication of all data on a given connection in a single direction:

1. Start Active Directory Sites and Services from the Administrative Tools menu.

2. Expand Sites in the left-hand tree pane.

3. Expand the name of the site of the server you wish to replicate *to*.

4. Expand the name of the server you wish to replicate *to*.

5. Click that server's NTDS Settings object. The right-hand pane is populated with that server's inbound connection objects.

6. In the right pane, right-click the name of the server you wish to replicate *from* and select Replicate Now.

Replication can also be forced from the command line by using the **repadmin.exe** utility from the Support Tools with the following syntax:

```
C:\>repadmin /sync [Naming Context] [Dest Server Name] [Source Server GUID]
```

The GUID of a server can be found at the top of the output of the **repadmin / showreps** command.

Managing Replication

I'll now discuss managing replication.

Creating Connection Objects

If you wish to manually create a replication object, you can do so through Active Directory Sites and Services as follows:

1. Start Active Directory Sites and Services from the Administrative Tools menu.

2. Expand Sites in the left-hand tree pane.

3. Expand the name of the site of the server you wish to replicate to.

4. Expand the name of the server you wish to replicate out of.

5. Right-click that server's NTDS Settings object and select New Active Directory Connection. The Find Domain Controller's dialog box appears.

6. Once searching has finished, select the domain controller you wish to replicate from and click OK.

7. Type a name for the connection object (or accept the default of the incoming server name) and click OK.

Changing the Transport of a Connection Object

The transport type of a connection object can be managed through Active Directory Sites and Services and chosen from the list of IP, RPC, and SMTP. They can be used as described in Table 8.5.

It's possible to configure a connection object "illegally", such as an SMTP connection between domain controllers in the same site or an RPC connection between sites, but such connection objects won't function. By default, Active Directory Sites and Services creates intra-site connections as RPC and intra-site connections as IP.

To change the transport of a connection object:

1. Start Active Directory Sites and Services from the Administrative Tools menu.

2. Expand Sites in the left-hand tree pane.

3. Expand the name of the site of the server whose connection you wish to modify.

4. Expand the name of the server whose connection you wish to modify.

5. Click that server's NTDS Settings object. The right-hand pane is populated with that server's inbound connection objects.

6. In the right pane, right-click the name of the connection object you wish to modify and select Properties.

7. Use the drop-down list labeled Transport to choose the required Transport protocol.

Table 8.5   Connection Object Transport protocols.

Protocol	Use
RPC	All intra-site connections.
SMTP	Inter-site connections between domain controllers in different domains.
IP	All other inter-site connections.

8. Active Directory Replication

Setting Schedules

The schedule for replication on inter-site connection objects can be set to determine which hours of the week replication will take place. It can also be set for inter-site objects, but will have no effect. To change a replication schedule:

1. Start Active Directory Sites and Services from the Administrative Tools menu.

2. Expand Sites in the left-hand tree pane.

3. Expand the name of the site of the server whose connection you wish to modify.

4. Expand the name of the server whose connection you wish to modify.

5. Click that server's NTDS Settings object. The right-hand pane is populated with that server's inbound connection objects.

6. In the right pane, right-click the name of the connection object whose schedule you wish to modify and select Properties.

7. Click the Change Schedule button. The Schedule for dialog box appears as illustrated in Figure 8.4.

8. A schedule is defined by selecting how many times per hour replication can happen—either 0, 1, 2, or 4 corresponding to replication never, hourly, half-hourly, or quarter-hourly. To change the frequency for a group of hours, drag a rectangle around the hours and select the desired frequency from the list to the right.

Installing the SMTP Server Service

The *SMTP service* is required on a domain controller in order for SMTP-based replication to be possible. It's part of IIS 5 and is, in fact, included in the default install of Windows 2000.

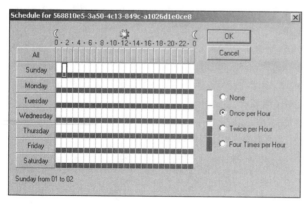

Figure 8.4   Schedule for dialog box.

To check if SMTP is already running on a server, type the following at a command prompt:

```
C:\>net start
```

The **net start** command will give an alphabetical list of services currently running. If **Simple Mail Transport Protocol (SMTP)** appears in the output, then it's already installed and running.

TIP: It's often useful to configure a high-screen buffer so that you can scroll back to previous output. This is achieved through the Command Prompt's properties dialog box (available from the system menu in the top left of the window).

If you need to install SMTP, do so as follows:

1. Click Start|Settings|Control Panel to launch the Control Panel window.
2. Launch the Add/Remove Programs applet.
3. Click Add/Remove Windows Components, the third large button down on the left-hand side.
4. After a short wait, the Windows Components Wizard appears, as shown in Figure 8.5.
5. Select Internet Information Services (IIS) and click Details. The list of items that comprise IIS appears.
6. Select SMTP Service and click OK.
7. Click Next in the Windows Components Wizard. The selected components will be installed. Insert the Windows 2000 Server CD-ROM if prompted.

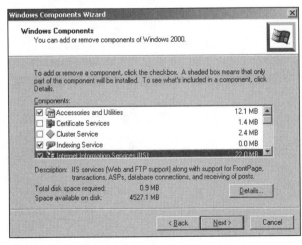

Figure 8.5   The Windows Components Wizard.

Replication Settings

Many aspects of directory replication can be controlled by registry entries on domain controllers or by modifying object properties in the directory.

Prevent Password Changes Being Pushed Over WAN Links

In domains spread across multiple sites, only one domain can have the PDC Emulator. This means that the default behavior of domain controllers in other sites to immediately send password changes to the PDC Emulator will cause WAN traffic, which may be undesirable with a dial-up connection. Setting the following registry entry to a **REG_DWORD** value of 1 will prevent this behavior from a domain controller:

```
HKLM\SYSTEM\CurrentControlSet\Services\Netlogon\Parameters\AvoidPdcOnWan
```

Enabling Site Link Notification

To enable notification on a site link, you must set the first bit of the *options* attribute of the site link object to one—this is equivalent to increasing the decimal value by 1, to make it an odd number. If it's already odd, then site link notification is already enabled. To change the options property of the site link object:

1. Launch ADSI Edit from the Windows 2000 Support Tools, Tools menu.

2. Drill down the configuration container through **cn=configuration, cn=yourdomain, cn=Sites, cn=Inter-Site Transports**.

3. Double-click the relevant transport (**cn=IP** or **cn=SMTP**) in the right-hand pane.

4. Right-click the site link you wish to modify and select properties.

5. In the "Select a property to view" list, select options.

6. To enable notification, enter a number one higher in the Edit Attribute box than is currently in the Value(s) box. A value of **<not set>** is equivalent to 0. To disable it, reduce the value by 1. This is equivalent to **XOR**ing the value with 1.

7. Click Set to commit the change, then click OK to close the dialog box.

Monitoring Replication

I'll now discuss monitoring replication.

Active Directory Replication Monitor

The *Active Directory Replication Monitor tool* (**replmon.exe**) included on the Windows 2000 Server CD-ROM as part of the Support Tools is a graphical interface that allows you to monitor and troubleshoot replication. Replication Monitor is, in fact, useful for more than just monitoring replication, because it's able to report other facts about domain controllers.

Adding a Server to Monitor

To add a server to the Monitored Servers list, the following steps are required:

1. Start Active Directory Replication Monitor from the Tools menu under the Windows 2000 Support Tools menu.

2. Right-click the Monitored Serves item at the root of the left-hand tree and select the only option—Add Monitored Server.

3. Either choose to Add the server explicitly by name (in which case you'll be prompted for a network name for the server) or search the directory. To search the directory, you must choose a domain so that the wizard can obtain a list of sites and servers. Click Next.

4. Either select a server from the site list, or type an appropriate name explicitly and click Finish.

Monitoring a server will log replication information about that server, as well as allowing monitoring and limited management of the server's replication. Adding a server will automatically add child entries for each directory partition held on the server.

Server Properties

The Server Properties dialog box is a great resource within Replication Monitor. To bring it up:

1. Right-click a server object in the left-hand tree and select Properties from the bottom of the long list.

The Properties dialog box then appears. It's a cool way to view important information about a domain controller. All of the data shown is available in other ways (mainly through the directory), but Replication Monitor brings it all together. Table 8.6 lists the available information.

Table 8.6   Information available through replmon's server properties.

Pane	Information
General	Shows basic information about the name of the domain controller, its computer account in Active Directory, and whether or not it's a preferred bridgehead.
Server Flags	Decodes the server flags information from the Active Directory to show whether Active Directory is write-enabled, whether the Win32Time service is running, whether the Key Distribution Centers (KDC) service is running, whether it's a Global Catalog server, and whether it's the PDC Emulator.
FSMO Roles	Shows which domain controllers the monitored server thinks holds the five operations master roles and allows you to test communications with them.
Credentials	Details the account used to authenticate with the domain controller to gain the other displayed information.
Inbound Replication Connections	Lists the connections under the server's NTDS Settings objects and gives a textual explanation of which partitions are replicated.
TCP/IP Configuration	Shows the IP addresses and other TCP/IP details (DNS, Windows Internet Name Service [WINS], and so forth) for the domain controller. It's similar to the output of **ipconfig.exe**.

Viewing the Replication Topology of a Network

The feature of Active Directory Replication Monitor that has the biggest "Wow!" factor is easily the ability to draw a replication topology. To be able to draw the replication topology based around a given server:

1. Right-click on the server to start from and select Show Replication Topologies.

2. The View Replication Topology Window appears.

Group Policy Object Status

Group Policy objects consist of two components: the directory objects that define them and the disk-based information, such as logon scripts, that they use. As you'll see in Chapter 12, for Group Policy to be applied, both the directory and disk-based portions must be synchronized.

To view the status of group policy object replication on a domain controller within Replication Monitor:

1. Right-click that server in the Monitored Servers pane and select Group Policy Object Status (seventh from top).

2. A window detailing the name, GUID, disk-based sysvol, and domain-based version numbers appears. For the items to be in sync, the version numbers must be the same.

Finding Bridgehead Servers

When examining your replication topology, it's useful to know which servers are acting as bridgeheads, channeling data between sites. You can easily obtain a list of *bridgehead servers* of a particular site or of all sites in the forest ("the enterprise") through Active Directory Replication Monitor as follows:

1. Add a domain controller from the site you wish to view the bridgehead servers of. If you want to see bridgeheads for all sites, then any domain controller will do.

2. Right-click that server in the Monitored Servers pane and move the mouse pointer over Show Bridgehead Servers.

3. Select either In This Server's Site or In The Enterprise.

Domain Trust Relationships

The trust relationships for a domain can be displayed through **replmon** as follows:

1. Add a domain controller from the domain you wish to view the trust relationships of.

2. Right-click that server in the Monitored Servers pane and select Show Trust Relationships (fifth from bottom).

3. A window displaying details of all trust relationships the domain is configured for is shown.

Object Meta-Data

Meta-data, such as attribute version numbers and USNs, can be shown on a per-object basis. This brings up a display of every attribute that has a value for the object and the meta-data for each attribute. To display meta-data:

1. Right-click on the server object on which the object to inspect resides and select Show Attribute Meta-Data for Active Directory Object (fourth from bottom).

2. You're prompted for credentials. This allows you to supply an alternative username and password to access the desired object under. Alternatively, you can use your current credentials.

3. Next, you're prompted to type the DN of the object you wish to inspect. Type carefully because it's common to get frustrated by mistyping a DN.

8. Active Directory Replication

TIP: *You can copy and paste the DN of an object by finding it in ADSI Edit, going to its property dialog box, and selecting then copying everything from the first CN onwards in the Path entry on the Attributes tab. Use either Ctrl+V or the Context menu to copy. You will probably have to move the cursor beyond the end of the Path to select the entire DN.*

---

4. A window appears showing meta-data, similar to Figure 8.6.

5. If you wish to compare attributes between domain controllers, you can use the Compare button to see the value of the attribute on every domain controller in the domain or forest.

Object meta-data can also be accessed through the command-line tool **repadmin.exe** as follows

```
C:\>repadmin /showmeta [DN]
```

where **[DN]** is the distinguished name of the object to inspect.

TIP: *This produces wide output, and before running the command, it's worth widening the command prompt to 110 or 120 characters so lines don't wrap.*

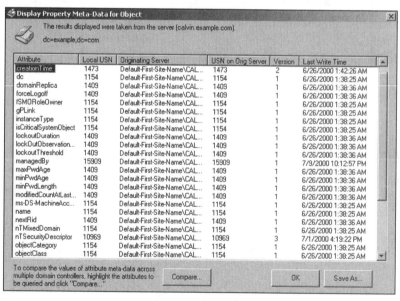

Figure 8.6   Example of object meta-data for dc=example,dc=com.

Replication Traffic Sizing

To calculate the amount of traffic that replication generates, it's necessary to make the traffic in some way unique then use a tool, such as a network monitor, to calculate the number of bytes on the wire.

RPC/IP

By default, a *remote procedure call (RPC)* uses dynamic port mapping for security—this means that the usual method of monitoring network traffic by port number won't work by default, because the port number isn't deterministic. However, it's possible to specify the port for RPC replication by setting a registry entry on a domain controller. The registry entry

```
HKLM\CurrentControlSet\Services\NTDS\Parameters\TCP/IP Port
```

can be added with the REG_DWORD value of the port number you wish to specify. You should use a relatively high port number to prevent conflict with other TCP/IP services. The task of measuring replication traffic between two domain controllers is then simply (!) a case of recording traffic between the domain controllers on the port you choose and totaling the bytes transmitted.

SMTP

The Simple Mail Transport Protocol (SMTP) is assigned port 25 in the standards documents, and directory SMTP replication uses this port also, so traffic monitoring should take place on port 25 to count bytes.

Chapter 9

Schema

In Depth

The *schema* of an Active Directory forest defines exactly what data can be stored in the directory. Information in the directory is stored in terms of *objects*. Everything from a user account to a site link is stored as an object. Each object is an instance of a *class*. In general, multiple instances of the same class of object are in the directory. For example, you'll have multiple user accounts, and each of these is an instance of the class User. Each user account will have data associated with it, such as the user's account name, password, full name, and telephone number. This data is stored as the values of *attributes*. Attributes are defined in the schema by name and permissible data type.

Each class has a number of attributes associated with it. These attributes are designated as either mandatory or optional for each class. All instances of the class must have a value for each mandatory attribute, whereas optional attributes need not be present. Up to 260 attributes may contain values for each object.

The two most important points to note about the schema are the following:

- *Only one schema exists for an entire forest.* This means that a schema change will have a network-wide impact, and a malicious schema change will be a network-wide catastrophe.

- *Schema changes cannot be deleted.* If you add a schema element, you can't delete it but, instead, can only deactivate it. This means careful planning is required for schema changes.

Classes

Schema classes define what attributes objects in the directory can and must contain. Class information is stored in terms of **classSchema** objects in the **cn=Schema, cn=Configuration,dc=ForestRootDomain** container of the directory (where **dc=ForestRootDomain** represents the DN of the root domain of the forest).

An important concept for schema classes is that of *inheritance*. Instead of each schema class being defined independently, they're arranged in a treelike fashion with child classes deriving all of the attributes of their parents. For example, the class hierarchy of the User class is as follows:

Top

Person

Organizational-person

User

Actually, three types of class objects are available:

- *Abstract classes*—These are building blocks of the class hierarchy. You can't create objects that belong to abstract classes. Their sole purpose is to allow you to build up a structure of classes and should be used for classes that you don't wish people to create instances of (*instantiate*).

- *Structural classes*—This is the only type of class that can be turned into actual directory objects and can be derived from either abstract or structural classes. Examples include the User class and **organizationalUnit**.

- *Auxiliary classes*—These can't be instantiated. Instead, they can be added to other classes in order to provide common groups of attributes across the class hierarchy. For example, Active Directory has a **securityPrincipal** auxiliary class, which contains all of the attribute information required to let an object have permissions assigned to it. Users, groups, and computer objects are all security principals, but their only common ancestor in the class hierarchy is top. Instead of deriving them all from the same place, they each have the **securityPrincipal** class added to them, so they can hold the necessary security values.

A child class, or subclass, inherits all of the mandatory and optional attributes of its parent class (which, in turn, inherits all attributes of its parent's class, and so forth). In addition, any number of auxiliary classes may be added to a class, and properties can explicitly be added to a class.

The following are the more interesting mandatory attributes of the **schemaClass** object:

- *cn*—This is the relative distinguished name of the object within the schema container. It has no other operational purpose.

- *governsID*—This is the unique object identifier of the class (see the "Object Identifiers [OIDs]" sidebar).

- *lDAPDisplayName*—This is the Lightweight Directory Access Protocol (LDAP) name of the schema class. It's the LDAP names that are used throughout this book to identify schema classes and attributes.

- *subClassOf*—This is the unique parent of the class (top is a subclass of itself for this purpose).

9. Schema

- *objectClassCategory*—This is an integer specifying whether this is a structural (value 1), abstract (value 2), or auxiliary (value 3) class.

Classes have attributes associated with them. These attributes are either mandatory or optional. Mandatory attributes can only be defined when a class is created as they must be present in all instances of an object, if you were able to add mandatory attributes later then you could end up with some instances of the class without mandatory attributes. Optional classes can be added at creation or later and need not be present in instances of the object. Objects can't hold values for attributes that don't belong to their class, and the class of an object can't be changed once it's created.

Object Identifiers (OIDs)

Object identifiers are a throwback to X.500 directories. They're globally unique identifiers, so in some sense similar to Globally Unique Identifiers (GUIDs), but they obey a strict hierarchy. In Active Directory, every schema element must have an OID, and these are comprised of several decimal numbers (components) separated by periods. The process of delegation can be thought of as being similar to Domain Name System (DNS), with the highest level being controlled by a central authority and lower levels of the tree being delegated to others, beneath which they're free to do as they choose.

Understanding OIDs

Consider for example the OID of the **defaultGroup** Active Directory attribute, which is 1.2.840.113556.1.4.480. From left to right, it's comprised of the following portions:

- 1—ISO
- 2—ANSI
- 840—USA
- 113556—Microsoft
- 1—Active Directory
- 4—Attributes
- 480—**defaultGroup** attribute

At the high levels, a portion of the namespace is allocated to another authority. So here the International Standards Organization (ISO) owns the entire space of OIDs and has delegated 1.2 to the American National Standards Institute (ANSI). ANSI has assigned 840 as the country code for the U.S.A. Microsoft has been assigned the number 113556 beneath this, so Microsoft owns the space of OIDs starting with 1.2.840.113556 and is free to do what it likes with them. Beneath this, a portion has been assigned for Active Directory and, within that, one for schema attributes.

It's essential that OIDs remain unique, because using the same OID twice will have unfortunate consequences (varying slightly by the situation, but that are bound to be unpleasant). To this end, you should only use an OID that you know is safe—*never* just "make up" an OID and hope for the best. To know an OID is safe, you should obtain an OID that you know is uniquely yours and use OIDs beneath it in the hierarchy by appending numbers.

When doing this, it's *essential* to record what OIDs you've used so you never repeat them. It's best to keep a file listing the OIDs that you've generated under version control using software, such as Visual SourceSafe or PVCS. Failure to do so will result in a situation familiar to the author where two people look at the list of assigned OIDs, use the next one in their program, deploy their program, and then come back to update the list later.

Obtaining OIDs

So how exactly do you get hold of an OID? The first possibility is to contact your regional authority and pay money. Microsoft rightly assumed this wouldn't be too popular a way of encouraging developers to embrace Active Directory in their applications, so alternatives are available. Both alternatives are based on the fact that Microsoft already has its own OID, so its free to assign OIDs beneath it.

The first is a utility in the Windows 2000 Server Resource Kit, **oidgen.exe**. Quite simply this allocates OIDs beneath the Active Directory base OIDs for classes and attributes based on the GUID of your computer and several very large random numbers. Because the GUID of your computer is very likely to be globally unique anyway, this OID is almost surely globally unique.

A second alternative, which is recommended for people looking to distribute their application, is to obtain ranges assigned by Microsoft. This can be achieved by emailing **oids@microsoft.com** (and asking nicely).

Attributes

Active Directory attributes define what data can be stored in the directory. The main components that define an attribute are the following:

- *cn*—The common name of the attribute, which is usually a descriptive name for the attribute.

- *LDAP Display Name*—The LDAP name of the attribute, which is the name most commonly used in scripts and programs to identify the attribute.

- *OID*—The unique X.500 OID of the attribute.

- *Syntax*—The data type of the attribute can be one of 23 different values, such as **Boolean**, **Large Integer**, **Unicode String**, or **Distinguished Name**.

- *Single-Valued*—Attributes can either be single-valued (in which case they can contain only one piece of data) or multi-valued (in which case they can contain a list of values, such as telephone numbers).

Attributes can be flagged as either mandatory or optional for an object. Mandatory objects must be present in all instances of a class.

Operational Attributes

An *operational attribute* isn't, in fact, an attribute at all. Instead, it's a trigger in the Directory, which triggers a task when it's set. For example, the following are all operational attributes of the **RootDSE**:

- **becomeDomainMaster**

- **becomeIntrastructureMaster**

- **becomePDC**

- **becomeRidMaster**

- **becomeSchemaMaster**

Setting each of these values to 1 will transfer the corresponding operations master role to the target server. Another example of an operation attribute of **RootDSE** is **schemaUpdateNow**, which is detailed later in this chapter.

RootDSE

The **RootDSE** is a server-specific object at the top level of an LDAP server's tree. For example, for the server **calvin.example.com**, the DN of the **RootDSE** is **cn=RootDSE,dc=calvin,dc=example, dc=com**.

RootDSEs are phantom objects, which describe their respective servers but have no object class. However, they have attributes, some of which are defined by the LDAP standards specifying exactly what the server supports, as well as optional vendor-specific attributes. More information can be found in Request for Comments (RFCs) 2251 and 2252.

Global Catalog

The *Global Catalog* is a partial replica of all information in the domains that comprise the forest. Technically, it comprises the values of a subset of attributes for the forest. This means that the Global Catalog is defined by flagging attributes for inclusion. It also means that you only have two choices for an attribute: in or out. In particular, you can't include an attribute for only a subset of classes in the directory, so you can't, for example, include the **telephoneNumber** of user objects but not contact objects: it's all or nothing.

The composition of the Global Catalog can be modified by altering which attributes comprise the Global Catalog. It's important to know that modifying the composition of the Global Catalog will cause it to be rebuilt from scratch on each Global Catalog server. This means that all of the current Global Catalog information is discarded, and all data from other domains will be replicated afresh to rebuild the Global Catalog. This additional replication load must be considered when planning changes to the Global Catalog composition.

Indexes

The underlying storage of Active Directory is in a database, and just like other database engines, Active Directory supports indexing. When an attribute is indexed, the disk space requirement increases, but the time to search on the attribute decreases. Besides needing more disk space, additional overhead is placed on the server when modifications to indexed attributes are received, because a background process also has to update the index. The best attributes to index are single-valued and highly unique, because the most benefit can be derived from indexing them. It's still possible to index any attribute, however.

Ambiguous Name Resolution (ANR)

Ambiguous Name Resolution is an extension to LDAP designed to allow a name to be matched across a number of attributes that may contain someone's name. It can be used in LDAP search filters with the token "**anr=**", so for example,

```
(anr=Adam Wood)
```

will perform an ANR search for **Adam Wood**. In fact, ANR searches for a match on any attribute that's enabled for Ambiguous Name Resolution and will return TRUE if any match is found. The default attributes enabled for ANR are **displayName**, **givenName**, **physicalDeliveryOfficeName**, **proxyAddresses**, and **sn** (surname). You can also enable other attributes for ANR.

Additionally, if the query string contains a space, then the two portions are checked against given names and surnames. This is known as First/Last and Last/First checking, because the pairs are tested in each direction.

```
(| (displayName=Adam Wood*)
   (givenName=Adam Wood*)
   (physicalDeliveryOfficeName=Adam Wood*)
   (proxyAddresses=Adam Wood*)
   (sn=Adam Wood*)
```

9. Schema

225

```
    (& (givenName=Adam*)(sn=Wood*))
    (& (givenName=Wood*)(sn=Adam*))
)
```

It's possible to control the First/Last and Last/First functionality to enable both, neither, or just one of the two possibilities.

Schema Operations

The Active Directory schema is comprised of attributes and classes stored in the configuration partition. The operations of the schema are slightly different to those of other directory objects, and the points made in the following sections must be borne in mind.

Schema Cache

A copy of the Active Directory schema is kept in memory on a domain controller. This is because every change made to the directory is verified against the schema to check legality. The schema is cached in memory to enhance performance. When modifications to the schema are detected, the cache and disk version of the schema fall out of synchronization. However, just as with directory replication, a delay between a schema change being received and the schema cache being rebuilt occurs. This delay is intended to ensure that all schema changes are replicated in before the new schema is loaded into memory (to prevent another new cache from being loaded immediately afterward, because moiré changes appear). It's possible to force an immediate update to the schema cache on a domain controller. This is achieved by writing a value of 1 to the **schemaUpdateNow** operational attribute on the **RootDSE** object.

Defunct Schema Entries

Elements of the Windows 2000 Active Directory schema can never be deleted—Microsoft avoided tricky questions about what to do with objects of deleted classes or values of deleted attributes and, instead, forbade the entire concept. Instead, you can disable a schema entry—either an attribute or a class. Doing so is as simple as setting the **isDefunct** attribute of the **schemaClass** or **schemaAttribute** object to TRUE. Making a class defunct prevents new instances from being created and existing instances from being modified. This is because the modification operations are compared against the schema cache found not to match the schema and, hence, discarded. Existing instances are still found by searches and deleted. Similarly, deactivated attributes can only be deleted completely and not have their values modified (which includes not being able to delete part of a multiple set of values).

When a **schemaClass** or **schemaAttribute** object is defunct, the only modification that can be made is to set **isDefunct** to FALSE. This will make all existing instances/values of the object modifiable again, as well as enabling new instances to be modified. It isn't possible to make defunct objects and classes that are part of the default schema of Active Directory. It's also not possible to make defunct classes that have subclasses or attributes that are mandatory for any classes.

WARNING! Because schema changes are irreversible you should never install a schema modification for test purposes on a production network. If you're developing a schema modification or evaluating a program that requires a schema change, it should be done on a separate test Active Directory forest. A separate domain or tree isn't sufficient, because the entire forest shares the schema.

Extending the Schema

One of the major benefits of Windows 2000 over previous versions of Windows NT is that the directory service has an extensible schema, which allows more than just the user's name and account to be stored in the directory. This allows other applications to use information in the directory; for example, the name and manager information that can be stored in Active Directory could be used to build an organization chart.

However, even the wide variety of built-in attributes isn't enough for applications Microsoft never considered during the development process, and certainly some of the most cunning uses of Active Directory require you to store objects of a different type, such as network routers or physical offices. To these ends, it's possible to extend the directory by adding attributes and classes and by extending existing classes with new attributes.

Schema Extension Notes

The following points about extending the Active Directory schema should be kept in mind. The limitations of Active Directory regarding schema entry names is an important issue for developers, and the replication note is of interest to anyone applying schema modification.

Naming Schema Extensions

The largest potential problem that arises from schema extensions in Windows 2000 Active Directory is as follows:

1. You install an application that updates the schema. Say it creates an attribute called **newAttribute** of syntax **Long Integer** for its own purposes.
2. A new application from a different software vendor comes out.

Of course, **newAttribute** is an unlikely name for a schema extension, but attributes such as **annualSalary** or **insideLegMeasurement** may be the first names chosen for software packages from several different vendors and would cause a clash.

The same problem also applies to classes, where you attempt to derive classes of the same name from several different places or even from the same place with a different set of attributes or auxiliary classes. For this reason, it's essential that any Active Directory schema extensions you make (either as an in-house developer or third-party software developer) have LDAP names that you're confident are going to be unique.

A simple way to achieve this is to prefix the names (both LDAP and common) of all new classes and attributes that you create with a string unique to your company. For example, if you work for Example Corporation, instead of adding **insideLegMeasurement** as a new attribute for your trouser management application, you would be better off to add **exampleCorpInsideLegMeasurement**. The extra long attribute names don't affect users in any way, and the mild inconvenience to programmers is more than overcome by the safety of additional uniqueness.

Replication
Changes can only be made on the Schema operations master, so the Active Directory schema is single-mastered. This ensures that the schema can't become inconsistent permanently, although delays in replication can cause temporary inconsistency. For example, consider the case where a schema extension is made and a new instance to that extension is quickly created. It's possible for the new object to be replicated to a domain controller before the schema extension is, hence, the replication will fail.

Active Directory is designed to cope with these failures. Once Server A rejects a replicated object from Server B due to a schema issue, Server B's schema is replicated to Server A, and an immediate schema cache update is triggered. Because Server B contains the object it's replicating, the object must match the new schema on Server A, so the object is re-replicated and all is well.

When to Extend the Schema
The Active Directory schema should be extended only if you wish to store additional information in the directory. Active Directory is best for storing relatively static data that is of wide interest. Rapidly updated, high volume data probably requires a dedicated database, and data only used by a small, geographically concentrated set of users may be better in a database, also.

Extending the Active Directory schema can mean one of several things: creating new attributes, adding attributes to existing classes, or creating additional classes. Obviously, creating attributes alone is of little use, because to actually use the attributes, they must be added to classes. New classes can be derived from existing classes so that they inherit all of the settings for the current class, but new attributes can be added. Alternatively, if you want to represent an entirely new object, you can start afresh. There's no such thing, however, as an entirely new class. Instead, classes that owe nothing to any other existing classes are created as a subclass of top.

New Class or Not?

Suppose you wish to track details about some members of your workforce. Perhaps you want to track the commission earned by your workforce and want to do this by storing data in a **yourCorpNameHereCommission** attribute. This can either be achieved by creating a new class of object (**userWithCommission**), derived from the User class, that has this attribute or by adding the **yourCorp NameHereCommission** attribute to the User class.

The advantage of the first approach is that the new class for sales people (who earn commissions) seems somewhat cleaner. However, doing this would mean you would have to create the **userWithCommission** objects for everyone in your sales force to replace their existing user accounts (as well as reassigning permissions and so forth). In this instance, it would be better to add the attribute to the User class, because not only would it save you from re-creating the objects of existing employees, but it would also save work if anyone ever transferred to a job where they could earn a commission.

When Not to Extend the Schema

The Active Directory isn't a suitable repository to store every sort of information. This is because anything stored in the directory will be replicated to every domain controller in the domain, and updates will be sent on every change. In some cases, the additional storage, processor, and replication overhead of keeping data everywhere may outweigh the benefits of directory-based storage.

It's important to know that you can use a combination of Active Directory and external storage for information. For example, if you have data that relates to objects in the directory, that changes frequently, and that's of interest only to a small number of people, you can eliminate duplicate storage by working on a view combining Active Directory and external data.

A very obvious example of data you wouldn't want to keep in the schema is stock prices. During trading hours, stock quotes change to some small degree by the minute, so replication events would be generated almost continuously. Most importantly, the cost of this replication traffic, in terms of server and network load, would probably exceed the benefits of having recent stock quotes on all domain controllers. (Actually, with replication latency, the quotes on far-flung domain controllers probably wouldn't be at all recent.) However, if you're a brokerage firm, you may choose to store some relatively static information about companies in your Active Directory, such as their ticker symbols, registered addresses, contact details, and perhaps summary stock information—the last closing price and 52-week highs and lows, for instance.

Applications that Extend the Schema

Installing an Active Directory schema extension only has to be done once per forest. An application that relies on schema extensions should be engineered so house a separate install process for installing the schema extensions. This means that a senior administrator (whose account is a member of the Schema Admins Group) only has to perform the initial installation of the schema extensions, then anyone can install the application itself without having to touch the schema again.

Obviously, this schema-install process must be installed before the application, and you should ensure (either manually or by waiting) that the new schema has replicated to the server before installing the new application on it. You shouldn't worry unduly if you never see the schema change. Microsoft Exchange 2000 has a Forest Preparation Only mode (that actually does more besides just update the schema), for example, but if you try to install Exchange 2000 without having run the setup program in Forestprep mode and if the currently logged in user has the correct privileges, schema modification will be enabled, the changes will be made, and it will be disabled again without user intervention.

Immediate Solutions

Registering the Active Directory Schema Snap-In

The Microsoft Management Console tool for managing the Schema, named Active Directory Schema, isn't available by default on domain controllers. Instead, it must be manually registered by typing the following at a command prompt:

```
C:\>regsvr32 %SystemRoot%\system32\schmmgmt.dll
```

NOTE: *Different instructions for performing this task appear in the release version of Windows 2000's Help system. Those instructions are incorrect, and the above should be used instead.*

The above method doesn't add a shortcut for Active Directory Schema to the Administrative Tools menu. Instead, you should start **mmc.exe** and add the Snap-in manually. If you're using a nondomain controller for administration, Active Directory Schema needs no special installation once **adminpak.msi** has been executed.

Related solution:	Found on page:
Adding Snap-Ins	56
Installing All Bundled MMC Snap-ins on Windows 2000	61

Enabling/Disabling Schema Modifications

The schema may only be modified at the Schema Operations Master role holder for the forest. Even then, it can't be modified by default, and a special registry setting must be present. To enable the Active Directory schema to be modified, the value, "Schema Update Allowed", beneath the following registry entry, must be set to a **DWORD** value of 1:

```
HKLM\System\Current Control Set\Services\NTDS\Parameters
```

9. Schema

It should be returned to a value of 0 to disable schema modifications. Alternatively, the Active Directory Schema Snap-in may be used as a graphical interface to modify this registry entry as follows:

1. Launch the Microsoft Management Console and add the Active Directory Schema Snap-in.

2. Right-click Active Directory Schema in the left pane and select Operations Master.

3. Check or clear the checkbox labeled "The Schema may be modified on the Domain Controller" as appropriate.

4. Click OK when done.

For security reasons, it's good practice to disable schema modifications once the current set of changes is complete on the schema master.

Using **oidgen.exe**

The Windows 2000 Resource Kit Utility, **oidgen.exe**, can be used to create an (almost surely) unique base pair of OIDs for classes and attributes that you can use for your own Active Directory extensions. To generate OIDs, simply run **oidgen** from any Windows 2000 Server with the resource kit as follows from a command prompt:

```
C:\>cd "Program Files"\"Resource Kit"
C:\Program Files\Resource Kit>oidgen
```

TIP: *The output of **oidgen.exe** is very wide, so make the command prompt wider before you execute it (95 or 100 characters should do).*

After you've run **oidgen** once, you should write down the OIDs returned, put that list in a safe place, and record all OIDs issued beneath them. If more than one person is responsible for issuing them, ensure that some form of change control software or procedure is used to prevent the same OID from being used twice.

Adding Attributes

Whenever you extend the schema, it's best to add attributes before meddling with classes. Quite simply, mandatory attributes for classes can't be altered once the class is created, so any attribute you wish to make mandatory had better exist before you design the class.

To add a new attribute through the user interface:

1. Launch the Microsoft Management Console and add the Active Directory Schema Snap-in.

2. Expand Active Directory Schema in the left-hand tree.

3. Right-click Attributes and select Create Attribute.

4. A warning informing you that the new attribute is for life appears. Click Continue to proceed.

5. The Create New Attribute dialog box shown in Figure 9.1 appears.

6. Fill in the fields in the dialog box. Specify a CN for the resulting **attributeSchema** object, give the unique LDAP Display Name (no spaces allowed) and the OID chosen as above, as well as the syntax of the attribute and other details.

7. Clicking OK can't be taken back. Only do so if you're sure the details given are correct.

NOTE: *The preferred method of modifying the schema is by script. The above is given mainly for informational purposes.*

Figure 9.1   Create New Attribute dialog box.

Including Attributes in the Global Catalog

Whether or not an Active Directory attribute is included in the Global Catalog, which is a partial replica of all domains in a forest replicated to domain controllers designated Global Catalog serves, can be controlled through the Active Directory Schema console and specifically through an Attribute's properties dialog box.

An Attribute's properties dialog (see Figure 9.2) is accessed as follows:

1. Launch the Microsoft Management Console and add the Active Directory Schema Snap-in.

2. Expand Active Directory Schema in the left-hand tree.

3. Click Attributes to populate the right pane with the attributes in the schema.

4. Right-click the attribute to enable and select Properties.

5. Check (or uncheck) the "Replicate this attribute to the Global Catalog" box, as appropriate.

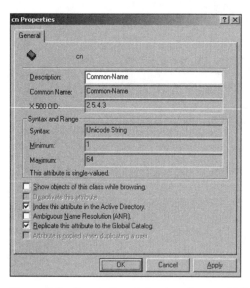

Figure 9.2   Properties dialog box for an **attributeSchema** object (cn).

Adding Classes

Before creating a new class, you should be sure that extending an existing class with new attributes isn't sufficient for your needs. If a new class really is required, then you should plan its position in the class hierarchy and, in particular, you should know the LDAP Display name of its parent class before starting. As a last resort, a class unrelated to any other should be a subclass of top.

New Active Directory classes are defined as follows:

1. Launch the Microsoft Management Console and add the Active Directory Schema Snap-in.

2. Expand Active Directory Schema in the left-hand tree.

3. Right-click Classes and select Create Class.

4. A warning informing you that the new class is for life appears. Click Continue to proceed.

5. The Create New Schema Class dialog box shown in Figure 9.3 appears.

6. Fill in the fields in the dialog box. Specify a CN for the resulting **attributeClass** object and give the unique LDAP Display Name (no spaces allowed) and the OID chosen as above. Also specify the LDAP Display Name of the parent class and the type (structural, abstract, or auxiliary).

7. Click Next to continue.

8. On the final page of the Wizard, add mandatory and optional attributes to the class. Mandatory attributes can't be modified after you click Finish, but optional ones can. Auxiliary classes can't have mandatory attributes.

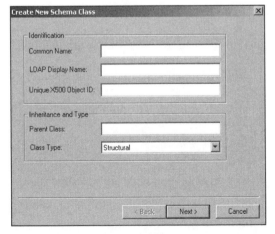

Figure 9.3   Create New Schema Class dialog box.

9. Schema

9. Before clicking Finish, use Back to review the first screen to ensure all details are correct. Only click Finish if you're sure all irreversible details are correct.

NOTE: *The preferred method of modifying the schema is by script. The above is given mainly for informational purposes.*

Managing Class Objects

I'll now cover managing optional attributes.

Managing Optional Attributes

The list of optional attributes—potential properties for instances of the class—isn't static and may be modified to either add or remove attributes to a class.

To add an optional attribute to a given class:

1. Launch the Microsoft Management Console and add the Active Directory Schema Snap-in.
2. Expand Active Directory Schema in the left-hand tree.
3. Click Classes to populate the right pane with the classes in the schema.
4. Right-click the given class and select Properties.
5. Change to the Attributes tab and click Add. A Select Schema Object dialog box listing attributes appears.
6. Select a single attribute to add (multiple selection isn't allowed) and click OK.
7. Click OK to accept the change.

To remove an optional attribute from a class, select the existing attribute from the list and click the Remove button.

Managing Auxiliary Classes

Sets of optional attributes may be added to a class in the form of an auxiliary class. Multiple auxiliary classes may be associated with a single class.

To add an auxiliary class to a given class:

1. Launch the Microsoft Management Console and add the Active Directory Schema Snap-in.
2. Expand Active Directory Schema in the left-hand tree.
3. Click Classes to populate the right pane with the classes in the schema.

4. Right-click the given class and select Properties.

5. Change to the Relationship tab and click the upper Add button. A Select Schema Object dialog box listing all auxiliary classes in the schema appears.

6. Select an auxiliary class to add (multiple selection isn't allowed) and click OK.

7. Click OK to accept the change.

To remove an auxiliary class, select it by name and click the appropriate Remove button.

Defining Possible Superiors

For an object to exist in the directory, it most likely has a parent object. The class of an object's parent must be one of the possible superiors for that child. For example, the use of superiors ensures that site objects can only appear in the appropriate container of Active Directory.

To modify the list classes of object that may act as parents to objects of a given class:

1. Launch the Microsoft Management Console and add the Active Directory Schema Snap-in.

2. Expand Active Directory Schema in the left-hand tree.

3. Click Classes to populate the right pane with the classes in the schema.

4. Right-click the given class and select Properties.

5. Change to the Relationship tab and click the lower Add button. A Select Schema Object dialog box listing all classes in the schema appears.

6. Select a possible superior class to add (multiple selection isn't allowed) and click OK.

7. Click OK to accept the change.

To remove a possible superior, select it by name and click the appropriate Remove button.

Scripting Schema Modifications

Due to the irreversibility of schema modifications, it isn't something that's worth modifying through the user interface. A typo in the object name is an inconvenience, but creating an attribute of the wrong syntax is an awful error that can't be undone.

9. Schema

Instead, the preferred method of modifying the schema is to use a script and develop/verify that script (and any application that relies on the schema change) on a test forest before making the change live on a production network.

One method of scripting schema extensions is to use LDAP Directory Interchange Format (LDIF). LDIF is a syntax for text files for adding data to LDAP directories, and it has a wide variety of purposes, which are explored fully in Chapter 16. LDIFDE is the command-line tool used to import and export LDIF to and from Active Directory. Here we consider only a sample piece of LDIF, which could be used to create a schema attribute (but don't use it!).

```
dn: CN=test,CN=Schema,CN=Configuration,DC=example,DC=com
changetype: add
adminDisplayName: test
attributeID: 1.2.3.4.5.6.7.8.9
attributeSyntax: 2.5.5.12
cn: test
instanceType: 4
isSingleValued: TRUE
lDAPDisplayName: testAttribute
distinguishedName: CN=test,CN=Schema,CN=Configuration,DC=example,DC=com
objectCategory:
 CN=Attribute-Schema,CN=Schema,CN=Configuration,DC=example,DC=com
objectClass: attributeSchema
objectGUID:: GSv7UmlMlOyrRVI5Tf1FtQ==
oMSyntax: 64
name: test
schemaIDGUID:: dsKawfjhVEiL4jxJgAsfgA==
showInAdvancedViewOnly: TRUE
```

Related solution:	Found on page:
Working with LDIF Files	428

Ambiguous Name Resolution

I'll now discuss ambiguous name resolution.

Enabling an Attribute for ANR

Attributes that contain string data can be enabled for ANR. This means that any attribute of syntax Case Insensitive String, IA5-String, Print Case String or Unicode String may be enabled for ANR.

Enabling an attribute called **attrib** for ANR means that any query for

```
(anr=value)
```

will return objects matched by the LDAP query filter

```
(attrib=value*)
```

To enable an attribute for ANR:

1. Launch the Microsoft Management Console and add the Active Directory Schema Snap-in.
2. Expand Active Directory Schema in the left-hand tree.
3. Click Attributes to populate the right pane with the attributes in the schema.
4. Right-click the attribute to enable and select Properties.
5. If it isn't already enabled, check the box labeled "Index this attribute" in the Active Directory.
6. Check the box labeled Ambiguous Name Resolution (ANR).
7. Click OK.

The ANR setting on an attribute is stored as the third bit of **searchFlags** property of an **attributeSchema** object. Setting the bit to 1 enables ANR. Setting bit 1 enables indexing, so the **searchFlags** should have a value of 5 to enable ANR alone (adding other flags will result in other values).

Performing an ANR Search

An Ambiguous Name Resolution search may be performed in the usual way from an LDAP search filter with the token "**anr=**". For example, to match "value", you would filter as follows:

```
(anr=value)
```

It's possible to use Active Directory Users and Computers to perform an ANR search as follows:

1. Launch Active Directory Users and Computers from the Administrative Tools menu.
2. If necessary, right-click Active Directory Users and Computers in the root of the left-hand tree and connect the domain or domain controller you wish to search.
3. Right-click on the container you wish to search under and select Find. This container could be the entire domain or an Organizational Unit (OU) within the domain. The Find dialog box appears as in Figure 9.4.

9. Schema

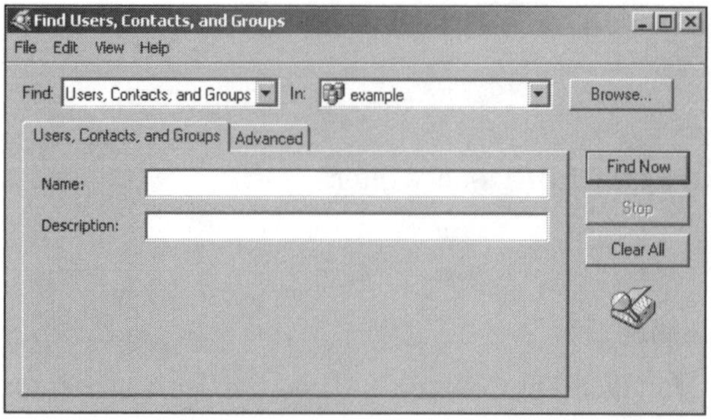

Figure 9.4   Find dialog box.

4. Expand the Find drop-down list and select Custom Search from the bottom of the list.

5. Switch to the Advanced tab.

6. Enter the filter you wish to search on in the Enter LDAP query box. For example, **(anr=value)**.

7. Click Find. A list of search results appears. Double-click on an object to view its properties or right-click for the usual context menu.

Controlling First/Last and Last/First Behavior

First/Last and Last/First searching are configured on a per-forest basis through an object in the configuration partition. The value of the **dSHeuristics** attribute on the **cn=Directory Service,cn=Windows NT,cn=Services,cn=Configuration, dc=ForestRootDomain** object controls the behavior. **dSHeuristics** is a string attribute, and the values of the first two characters are significant for this purpose. The accepted values and their effects are listed in Table 9.1.

Table 9.1   Possible values of **dSHeuristics** for First/Last and Last/First control.

Value	First/Last	Last/First
00	Enabled	Enabled
01	Enabled	Disabled
10	Disabled	Enabled
11	Disabled	Disabled

Schema Documentation

All aspects of your network should be well documented, but perhaps none more so than the Active Directory schema. It's possible to write scripts to detail the schema using techniques from this chapter and others in this book, but Microsoft is nice enough to provide a special tool for the purpose: the Active Directory Schema Documentation Program (**schemadoc.exe**).

To obtain the tool, download it from **www.microsoft.com/windows2000/library/operations/activedirectory/schema.asp**.

To use it:

1. Register the associated DLL file (XMLSchema.dll), if you haven't done so already, by typing the following (in the directory where XMLSchema.dll is):

```
C:\>regsvr32 XMLSchema.dll
```

2. Start the client application, **schemadoc.exe**.

3. Fill in the fields appropriately. The DN of your schema partition should already be populated. You can specify a prefix to return only the subset of schema elements whose LDAP names start with a common element. Also, you must specify the output file for the XML output.

4. Either specify user credentials for binding to the directory or leave the Credentials fields blank to perform an anonymous bind.

5. Click Next to proceed to the Vendor Information page.

6. The Vendor Information page allows you to add extra details to the output. Click Next when done.

7. The Product Information page allows product and version details to be added to the XML output.

8. Click Execute to generate and launch the XML report.

9. Schema

Chapter 10

Permissions, Users, and Groups

In Depth

Having dealt with the underlying technology in Active Directory in previous chapters, attention now turns to more practical aspects.

Permissions

The entire directory doesn't have to be accessible and freely modifiable to every user. On the contrary, allowing everyone in your organization equal privileges to directory data may be a daringly egalitarian notion, but it's one that quickly becomes unstuck when the unhappy employee you just fired destroys all of the user accounts.

To counter such happenings, everything in Active Directory can have permissions applied at the object or attribute level. This allows you to hide entire objects or simply make data read-only. For example, it's usual to configure user objects so that a user can modify her personal information, but everyone else (except administrators) can only read the data.

It's also quite possible to hide attributes on objects. For example, if you've extended the schema to include salary information, then this is probably best restricted so the entire company can't see it.

Security Architecture

The *security architecture* of Active Directory is strikingly similar to that of the NT file system (NTFS). This is obviously useful for people who are familiar with NTFS permissions, although it isn't difficult to pick up from scratch once you penetrate the jargon.

ACE

An *access control entry (ACE)* specifies a user/group and a degree of access. An ACE can apply to a single user or to a group of users and can either allow or deny one or more permissions or audit an event. They can apply to a single object only, or they can sit on a subtree of the directory.

A permission could be anything from Full Control (do whatever you like to an object) to the specific ability to read the contents of a telephone number field. The ACEs don't store the user/group to which they apply by name but, instead, use the unique Security Identifier (SID) for the object.

This means you can rename an object without affecting its security settings, because the SID won't change. It also means that deleting an object then re-creating one with the same name will give the new object the security settings of the old one, because it will have a different SID.

Well-Known SIDs

Windows 2000 contains the concept of a well-known SID. These are predefined and can't be changed, and they apply to certain built-in and calculated groups, such as Everyone. In addition, some users and groups that are part of a domain have a well-known Relative Identifier (RID). For example the Administrator account for a domain always has the same RID, so its SID always ends in the same value.

DACL

The *Discretionary Access Control List (DACL)* is the list of ACEs that define the permissions on an object and its properties. Each object in the directory has its own DACL, and the ACEs that apply to an object are stored within that DACL. Access control lists are ordered and can contain zero or more ACEs. Permissions are only granted if they're explicitly specified in a DACL (which may include settings inherited from parent objects). If no setting is specified, then permission isn't granted.

SACL

The *System-audit Access Control List (SACL)* is also a list of access control entries that trigger audit events but only if auditing is enabled. The SACL for an object can be accessed through the Advanced button on its Security page. Adding an entry to the SACL isn't enough in itself to enable auditing. In addition, auditing must specifically be enabled through Group Policy, and only then are SACLs evaluated to audit object access. For more information on auditing, see Chapter 17.

Ownership

Just like file system objects, directory objects have owners. The owner of an object is initially its creator, although this can be transferred. Ownership of an object can confer additional permissions to an object. In Windows 2000, ownership can never be given to another user. Instead, you can give someone the ability to take ownership, but he must actually click to take the ownership of an object. This preserves the authenticity of ownership information and prevents files being planted in the ownership of others (a feature that would have disappointed the administrators when I was at school, because they delighted in assigning ownership of illicit files to others).

An object doesn't have to belong to a specific individual. For administrative accounts (direct or indirect members of the Administrators Group), objects are, by default, owned by the Administrative Group and not by users themselves, although this is configurable on a per-object basis. The reasoning behind this is that administrative accounts shouldn't be used on a day-to-day basis. Objects created with them were created by someone wearing her "administrator's hat", so they belong to the administrators, in general.

Investigating Permissions

Access control lists and ownership information can usually be found on the Security tab of an object's Properties dialog box. Perhaps the most obvious place to look at this is the main source for low-level directory information: Active Directory Service Interface (ADSI) Edit from the support tools.

For the objects visible in Active Directory Users and Computers, security can be managed through that application when Advanced view is enabled, although all of the examples at the end of this chapter use ADSI Edit for object neutrality.

The Security Tab

The initial port of call for managing security is the Security tab of an object's properties. An example is shown in Figure 10.1. This provides a simple user interface to the most common permissions set for an object. It lists all users and groups who have any permissions set, along with what those permissions are (and perhaps a note that they can only be fully displayed on the Advanced tab).

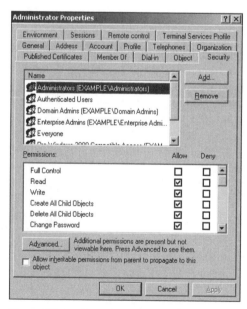

Figure 10.1   Security tab for a user object.

Permission boxes can be cleared, checked, or grayed. A clear box means that a setting isn't applied; a checked box indicates that it is. A grayed check indicates that a permission is inherited from an ACE on a parent object so can't be modified here.

Evaluating Permissions

A user may have several different sets of permissions to an object. This can come about easily when a user is a member of several groups, each of which has been assigned permissions.

The mechanism for calculating the effective permission is as follows:

- *Allow permissions*—Allow permissions are combined on a most-permissive basis: If a user has permission from any one of its groups, then it does indeed have that permission allowed.

- *Deny permissions*—Deny permissions are combined in the same way: if one group denies a permission, then that permission really is denied.

- *Deny beats allow*—If a permission is both denied and allowed, then it isn't granted.

- *Neither denied nor allowed*—If a permission is neither denied nor allowed, then it isn't granted, and that action can't be performed.

Advanced

As with so much in Windows, the real options lie behind the Advanced button. Clicking it brings up the dialog box shown in Figure 10.2.

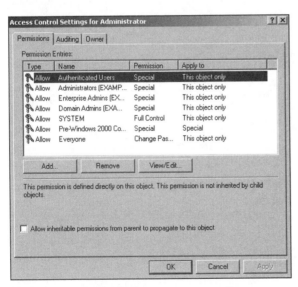

Figure 10.2   Advanced Security dialog box.

The three tabs of this dialog box correspond to DACL (Permissions), SACL (Auditing), and Ownership of an object. The first two of these tabs are similar, and both list ACEs, as well as allow orphaning (that is, blocking inheritance by disassociating from parents). ACEs can either allow or deny a set of permissions to a user or a group. Editing an ACE involves the dialog box shown in Figure 10.3.

The two tabs of the Permission Entry dialog box list objectwide and attribute-specific permissions. The exact settings available depend on the class of the object being inspected (its possible attributes, essentially).

NOTE: *An ACE can only consist of Allow permissions or Deny permissions and not a combination of the two. If you use the user interface to create an ACE with some permissions allowed and others denied, then two separate ACEs will actually be created.*

Finally, the Owner tab (see Figure 10.4) displays the current owner of an object and, if applicable, allows you to take ownership of an object.

Users

A user object in Active Directory represents a login to the Windows 2000 domain trusting resources. User accounts are stored in the domain partition on a domain controller, so their data is replicated only to other domain controllers in the same domain.

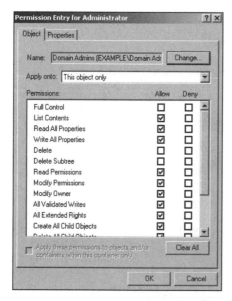

Figure 10.3   Edit Permission Entry dialog box.

Figure 10.4   Owner tab.

Mapping People to User Objects

Although by no means a necessity, life is so much simpler if only one person uses each user object. Having groups of people all using the same network logon introduces issues of accountability if the account is misused. Experience shows that once a password is shared among a small group of people, it gets shared among a large group of unauthorized people, too.

The converse of this isn't true, however. Many situations exist where one person should have multiple-user accounts. The first of these is anyone with elevated privileges, because it's very bad practice to log on and do day-to-day work with any kind of "super user account". Unnecessary privileges can (and probably will) be exploited by any trojan, virus, or passing malevolent person when a user's back is turned.

For these situations, simply have two user accounts for a person—a day-to-day account and an administrative account. The new **RunAs** service in Windows 2000 (similar to **su** in Unix) allows individual applications (such as administrative tools) to be launched with elevated privileges, which apply to that instance of the application only.

A final possibility, aside from many-to-one (for administrators) and one-to-one (for users), is, of course, one-to-zero: that is, a user account that doesn't represent any particular person. Such users are generally service accounts that are used by a server application to log on. For example, the **IUSR_computername** account is used by Internet Information Services but represents no particular person.

The general rule with service accounts is that they need no management. You could consider creating a separate Organizational Unit (OU) to file them all neatly in the directory, but by and large, you can leave them alone (except perhaps to apply permissions as necessary).

The krbtgt User

The Key Distribution Center Service (KDCS) that runs Windows 2000 domain controllers has a user object called **krbtgt**. The unique thing about this service account is that the KDCS doesn't use it to log on, and the account is actually disabled and should stay that way.

This account exists to act as the service principal name for the KDC itself in Keberos and to provide a long-term password for encrypting the realm's Ticket Granting Tickets (TGTs). You can't delete it or rename it, so just leave it alone.

Managing User Objects

The main graphical interface for managing user accounts is Active Directory Users and Computers (see Figure 10.5). Its operation is typical of a Management Console Snap-in.

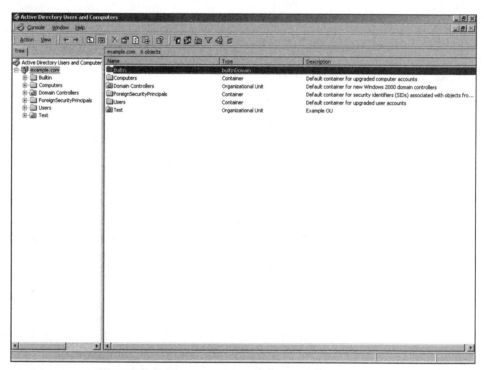

Figure 10.5   Active Directory Users and Computers.

The left-hand portion is a tree view, which displays the OU and structure of the domain, and the right-hand details pane shows the contents of each container. By organizing accounts into OUs, administrators are able to drill down and easily find the desired user account without pages upon pages of scrolling.

Once an OU is selected, its contents, including user accounts, are listed in the main right-hand pane. From here it's easiest to right-click on an object to manage it. Right-clicking brings up the Context menu (see Figure 10.6), which lists some actions you can perform on the object.

The most important option on the Context menu is the Properties option. The Properties dialog box for a user object allows most settings to be configured. Like the Context menu, the Properties dialog box can be customized, so applications that extend the schema or expose new options can piggyback on it for their own configuration. For example, Windows 2000 Terminal Services adds property pages, as does Exchange 2000.

It may seem fairly pointless to type personal information about the users in your network into their user object, but it will be beneficial in the long term. One of the key ideas behind Active Directory is that it becomes a central repository for this sort of information, so it only has to exist in one place in your network and can be updated centrally. As you start to use Active Directory-enabled applications, they'll make use of this data, and custom applications can be written that also make use of it.

Groups

In Windows 2000, although permissions can be assigned directly to user objects, it's always recommend that a group be used instead. Permissions applied to a group also apply to all members of the group, so you simply have to add users to a group to grant them the permissions assigned to the group.

Figure 10.6   User Object Context menu.

By creating role-based groups, instead of assigning permissions directly to user accounts, it becomes easier to manage permissions as users' job descriptions change. This means that if you want someone else to take over a task that involves multiple sets of permissions, instead of manually modifying every access control list twice, you just have to remove one user from the group for this task and add the replacement.

Group Types

Windows 2000 introduces the concept of group type: either security or distribution. Regardless of a group's type, the directory object for it is of *Group* class.

Security Groups

The majority of Windows 2000 groups tend to be *Security Groups*, and if you've experienced Windows NT 4, then Security Groups correspond directly to Windows NT 4 groups. As the name suggests, the primary purpose of a Security Group is to allow permissions to be assigned to members. All groups are security principals and have unique Security Identifiers (SIDs) assigned at creation time. The SIDs of Security Groups can be added to access control lists, so permissions can be granted and denied to their members.

Distribution Groups

Distribution Groups can perform a subset of the function of Security Groups—in fact, all they can't do is have security settings applied to them. As the name suggests, their primary purpose is to allow you to contact multiple people at the same time, for example, by sending email (if you have an application that supports doing so).

A unique fact to note about Distribution Groups is that they have a security descriptor assigned to them on creation, even though they can't be used in ACLs. The reason for this is simply that you can (potentially) convert a Distribution Group to a Security Group at a later date.

Why Use Distribution Groups at All?

This is a reasonable question to ask, because Security Groups can do everything a Distribution Group can, and more.

However, Distribution Groups have two advantages:

- *Mixed-mode domain*—In a Mixed-mode domain, the only way to create a Universal Group is to create a Universal Distribution Group.

- *Logon performance*—Distribution Groups don't affect logon performance. When a user logs on, every Security Group she belongs to must be processed to create an access token. This isn't required for Distribution Groups, so if you only want to send email, use a Distribution Group. You can always convert it later.

Group Scope

Orthogonal to the concept of group type is a group's scope: either domain local, global, or universal for groups in Active Directory. In addition, nondomain controllers can also have local groups, which exist only on that computer.

Domain Local

Domain Local Groups can contain users, computers, contacts, and Global/Universal Groups from any trusted domain and may be added to ACLs on objects in their own domain—either on domain controllers or member computers.

Because Domain Local Groups can be added to access control lists on any resource in their domain, but not other domains, it's usual to use them to grant permissions on resources. It isn't usual, however, to add users directly to them. Instead, use Global Groups as an intermediary. This may not seem important in a single domain environment, but it does create the abstraction between groups of permissions and groups of people. Domain Local Groups should be used to create logically similar groups of permissions, such as a "Database Access" Group, or an "Able To Add Domain Controllers Group".

WARNING! You should not use Domain Local groups to assign permission to directory-based objects. Only use them for assigning permissions on the filesystem.

Global

Global Groups can contain users, computers, contacts, and Global Groups, from their own domains, and they may be added to ACLs and groups in any trusted domain.

The role taken by Global Groups is to contain similar people by function. For example, it's usual to create Global Groups by department and for any set of people who need similar access control, such as help desk staff, managers, directors, project teams, or whatever. These groups are then added to Domain Local Groups to specify permissions. For example, you may add both the Server Support Team Group and Help Desk Supervisor Group to the "Able To Add Domain Controllers Group".

Universal

Universal Groups are new to Windows 2000 Native mode and combine the ability of Domain Local Groups to have members from anywhere and the ability of Global Groups to be added to Local and Domain Local groups that reside anywhere (anywhere in the forest, that is).

Because Universal Groups cover the entire forest and because accounts from any domain can be a member of a given Universal Group, Global Catalog servers are used extensively. Whenever a user logs in to a multiple-domain forest, a Global Catalog server must be contacted to determine Universal Group membership, because an ordinary domain controller doesn't know about Universal Groups from other domains.

For a small organization with a single site (no wide area network [WAN] links), the additional overhead of using Universal Groups for every task isn't a problem, but if you want a large group, then replicating its entire membership to every Global Catalog server in your enterprise can potentially be a problem.

Of course, there's no necessity to use Universal Groups (Global and Domain Local are sufficient between them), but situations exist where they simplify things—essentially, when you want to assign access to resources in multiple domains to the same set of people. They're made more useful by another new feature available in Native mode—group nesting.

Nesting Groups

A new feature in Windows 2000 is the ability to add a Global Group to another Global Group, and more. In Windows NT 4 and in Mixed mode, it's possible to add Global Security Groups to Domain Local Groups—this is the whole point of Global Groups—but in Native mode, the restrictions of the Windows NT Security Accounts Manager (SAM) are lifted, and almost anything is possible. Here *almost anything* is defined in Table 10.1.

Accounts can be user accounts, computer accounts, or even humble contact objects. Group A being nested into Group B simply means that all settings that apply to Group B's members also apply to Group A's members. Oh, and before you try it, logic is in Windows 2000 intended to spot recursive group nesting and ignore it (that is, adding Group A to Group B and also adding Group B to Group A).

Group nesting is a useful feature, especially considering that group membership is stored as a single, multi-valued attribute. This means that the entire membership of a group gets replicated whenever it gets changed. As a group gets large, this traffic becomes more and more significant. The number Microsoft floats around as a recommended practical size for a large group is 5,000 users. Group nesting is a useful way to simplify management and reduce replication traffic.

For example, instead of creating a huge "Whole Organization" Group, why not simply create Departmental Groups and add those groups to one single "Whole

Table 10.1   Group Memberships in Native Mode.

Group Scope	May Contain
Domain Local	Accounts, Domain Local Groups from the same domain, Global Groups, Universal Groups
Global	Accounts, Global Groups from the same domain
Universal	Accounts, Global Groups, Universal Groups

Company" Group? You could take it even further and have Subdepartment Groups that nest into Department Groups, which, in turn, nest into the "Whole Organization" Group, if your company is large enough.

Nesting also overcomes the replication problem associated with having large Universal Groups—you can nest one Global Group per domain into a Universal Group. This way the Universal Group's membership is almost totally static (it only changes when you add or remove domains).

Implicit Groups

In Windows 2000, not all groups are represented by objects in Active Directory and have their membership defined by a static list. Instead, some groups have their membership dynamically calculated. The groups listed in Table 10.2 are implicit.

Table 10.2   Implicit Groups.

Group Name	Contains
ANONYMOUS LOGON	Users who have logged on anonymously.
Authenticated User	All users that have logged on.
BATCH	Users who have logged on as part of batch queue facility, such as a scheduled task.
CREATOR GROUP	The primary group of the object's current owner.
CREATOR OWNER	The object's current owner.
DIALUP	Users logged on via dial-up connections.
ENTERPRISE DOMAIN CONTROLLERS	All domain controllers in the forest.
Everyone	Absolutely everything, whether authenticated or not.
INTERACTIVE	Users logged on locally.
NETWORK	Users connected over the network.
SELF	The object itself.
SERVICE	All users logged on as a service.
SYSTEM	The local system.
TERMINAL SERVICE USER	Users connected via Terminal Services.

Immediate Solutions

Managing Users

I'll now discuss the management of users.

Creating Users

The standard user interface for account management is the MMC Snap-in Active Directory Users and Computers. To create a user account with Active Directory Users and Computers, perform the following steps:

1. Open Active Directory Users and Computers from the Administrative Tools menu.

2. Use the left-hand tree to drill down to the OU or container where you wish to create the new user object.

3. Right-click on the OU/container and hover the mouse over New.

4. Click User in the resulting menu. The New Object—User Wizard appears (see Figure 10.7).

5. Type the First name, Initials, and Last name of your user. This will automatically populate the Full name edit box.

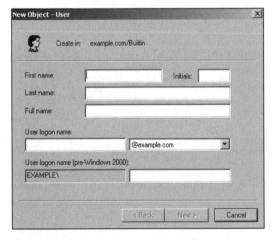

Figure 10.7   New Object—User Wizard.

WARNING! Pay close attention to full stops in the Full name for users with two or more middle initials. A full stop is added automatically to the Full name after the last initials, but not between them, so if someone's middle names are Michael William then you should type M. W. into the Initials box to get M. W. in the Full name box.

6. Next, type the first portion of the user logon name and select the User Principal Name (UPN) suffix from the list. The Windows 2000 logon name will also be the default for the NetBIOS (down-level, pre-Windows 2000) account name.

7. Click Next to continue.

8. Enter the initial password for the user account and set password options. You also have the opportunity to create the account initially disabled.

9. Click Next to continue.

10. Click Finish to complete the Wizard.

The new user account now appears within its OU/container. You can now use its Properties dialog box to configure more options.

---

*TIP: The tool **addusers.exe** from the Windows 2000 Server Resource Kit can be used to perform a bulk creation of user accounts from a comma-separated file. See the Windows 2000 Server Resource Kit Tools Help for details.*

Specifying Additional UPN Suffix Options

The New Object—User Wizard and User Object Properties dialog box only allow you to choose User Principal Name suffixes from a prepopulated list.

By default, this list contains the Domain Name System (DNS) names of the current domain and forest root domains. However, the value can be arbitrary, and custom entries can be added as follows:

1. Open Active Directory Domains and Trusts from the Administrative Tools menu.

2. Right-click Active Directory Domains and Trusts at the root of the left-hand tree pane and select Properties.

3. On the UPN Suffixes tab, type the suffix you wish to specify and click Add.

4. Click OK to accept the change.

Cloning a User Account

Numerous occasions come up when you may wish to clone a user account. For one thing, it's a simple way of adding a user object for a new hire whose role is similar to an existing member of the staff.

To clone a user account:

1. Open Active Directory Users and Computers from the Administrative Tools menu.

2. Navigate through your OU structure to the account to copy.

3. Right-click the user to clone and select Copy.

4. The New Object—User Wizard appears. Fill in the details as you would when creating a new user.

The new user account is situated in the same OU/container as the original and will retain some data from the original. Exactly which property values are maintained is determined by the **Copy This Attribute When User Is Duplicated** flag on the **schemaAttribute** objects.

The potential to copy accounts is another good reason to use groups to assign permissions, because the cloned account will maintain group memberships but not permissions assigned directly to the original.

Resetting a User's Password

A user forgetting his password is a common occurrence. To allow the user to log on again, someone with sufficient permissions on the forgotten user account must reset the password to a new value. For security reasons, it isn't possible to go in and view the existing password.

To reset a user account's password (observe this doesn't involve the Property dialog box):

1. Open Active Directory Users and Computers from the Administrative Tools menu.

2. Navigate through your OU structure to the account whose password needs resetting.

3. Right-click the user object in question and select Reset password.

4. Type the new password (twice for confirmation) into the Reset Password dialog box (see Figure 10.8).

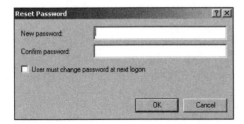

Figure 10.8   Reset Password dialog box.

5. If you're giving out a password that may be overheard, you may wish to force the user to change his password at next logon with the checkbox provided.

6. Click OK to complete the operation.

Alternatively, you can use the command-line tool **cusrmgr.exe** (Console User Manager) with the following syntax (**Username** is the account name and **NewPasswordHere** is the password to assign):

```
C:\>cusrmgr -u Username -P NewPasswordHere
```

You can even force the new password to be changed as follows:

```
C:\>cusrmgr -u Username -P NewPasswordHere +s MustChangePassword
```

Disabling a User Account

For a variety of reasons, you may wish to prevent an account from being used but not delete it entirely. For example, the security conscious may disable the accounts of users when they're on extended leave to ensure there's no misuse, and many companies disable (but don't delete) user accounts of ex-employees in case they or their permissions are ever needed.

Enabled accounts can be disabled in one of two ways through Active Directory Users and Computers. The simplest method is from the Context menu:

1. Open Active Directory Users and Computers from the Administrative Tools menu.

2. Navigate through your OU structure to the account to disable.

3. Right-click the user object in question and select Disable Account.

4. Confirmation appears. Click OK.

NOTE: *When an account has been disabled, a cross appears on its user icon in Active Directory Users and Computers.*

Alternatively, it can be done through the Properties dialog box:

1. Open Active Directory Users and Computers from the Administrative Tools menu.

2. Navigate through your OU structure to the account to disable.

3. Right-click the user object in question and select Properties.

4. Switch to the Account tab.

5. Scroll down in the list until you see "Account Is Disabled".

6. Click the checkbox next to "Account is disabled".

7. Click OK to accept the change.

A user account can be enabled, essentially, by repeating either of the above. The interface term in the Context menu reads "Enable Account" for those that are currently disabled.

You can also disable an account from the command line with **cusrmgr.exe**. For example, to disable an account called **Username**:

```
C:\>cusrmgr -u Username +s AccountDisabled
```

Unsurprisingly, to enable an account from the command line you reverse the **AccountDisabled** switch like so:

```
C:\>cusrmgr -u Username -s AccountDisabled
```

Moving a User Account within the Domain

There may be times when you wish to move a user object around within the OU structure of the current domain. This may be necessary when a person changes roles or the OU structure is reorganized (or a slip of a finger meant the account got created in the wrong place).

Active Directory Users and Computers doesn't provide a drag-and-drop interface, so moving a user account is just like moving any other directory object:

1. Open Active Directory Users and Computers from the Administrative Tools menu.

2. Navigate through your OU structure to the account to disable.

3. Right-click the user object in question and select Move.

4. The Move dialog box appears (Figure 10.9). Select the destination OU/ container and click OK.

Moving users (and other objects) between domains and forests is slightly more complex, and is covered in Chapter 20.

Modifying User Properties

The general properties that can be stored with a user account are many and varied. At first glance, it may not seem useful to fill in all of the details for every user—particularly if your organization doesn't yet employ any software that makes use of it. However, it's a good idea to fill such details in early and give users the permissions to update their own personal information. User properties can be modified as follows:

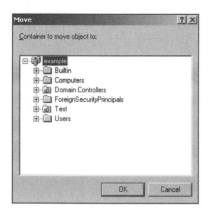

Figure 10.9   Move dialog box.

1. Open Active Directory Users and Computers from the Administrative Tools menu.

2. Navigate through your OU structure to the account to modify.

3. Right-click the user object in question and select Properties.

4. Make the desired alterations and click OK when done.

Managing Users by Script

A frequent task is to make the same change to several users at once. The Active Directory Users and Computers interface doesn't let you perform too many tasks with multiple users selected (Move, Enable, Disable, Send Mail, and Add to Group is about it).

A solution, therefore, is to use VBScript and ADSI to make the changes. The process used when scripting access to the directory in this way is to use a Lightweight Directory Access Protocol (LDAP) search filter to return one or more objects, rather like querying a database, then to perform actions on each of these objects.

Obtaining a List of Users

The first step is to connect to the directory, specify a search, and obtain a results set. It goes something like this:

```
option explicit

Dim objConnection, objCommand, objRecordSet, strSearch

' Define the LDAP Search String
```

```
strSearch = "<LDAP://dc=example,dc=com>:(objectClass=user);adspath;subtree"

' Initialize Connection
Set objConnection            = WScript.CreateObject("ADODB.Connection")
objConnection.Provider       = "ADsDSOObject"
objConnection.Open             "Active Directory Provider"

' Initialize and Execute Command
Set objCommand               = WScript.CreateObject("ADODB.Command")
Set objCommand.ActiveConnection = objConnection
objCommand.CommandText       = strSearch
Set objRecordSet             = objCommand.Execute
```

The above code snippet contains the generic code required to perform an ADO (ActiveX Data Objects) search of a directory. The nature of the search depends on the selected line, that is to say, the value of the **strSearch** variable. This is used as the value for the ADODB Command object's **CommandText** and consists of four parts:

- *ADsPath*—For example, **<LDAP://dc=example,dc=com>**

- *LDAP Search Filter*—For example, **(objectClass=user)**

- *Return Properties*—For example, **ADsPath**

- *Search depth*—Either **base**, **onelevel**, or **subtree**

Together, these specify what should be searched, the search criteria, and what data should be returned. The above example searches all of **example.com** (more precisely, the subtree rooted at **dc=exmple,dc=com**) for objects of the **user** class and returns the **ADsPath** of the objects found.

That means that this example will match every user in your domain. Instead, you may wish to match on a narrower or wider field. For example, to search a specific OU, use the distinguished name (DN) of the OU in the **ADsPath**:

```
<LDAP://ou=sample,dc=example,dc=com>
```

For example, to search the Global Catalog, use the **GC://** syntax and the name of your forest root domain in the **ADsPath**:

```
<GC://dc=example,dc=com>
```

You can also use the LDAP search filter to further restrict the results obtained, for example, by searching for users from a list of names (with judicious use of the OR operator), or perhaps users in a particular group, or with a particular address.

The next step is to process the objects returned. The generic way of doing this is to use a **While ... Wend** block and advance through the record set until the end is reached as follows:

```
' Loop through the records
While Not objRecordset.EOF
    ' Put some code here to do something useful
    ' For example echo the ADsPath of the object as follows
    ' Wscript.Echo objRecordset.Fields.Item("ADsPath").Value

    objRecordSet.MoveNext
Wend
```

Opening a User Object

Once you have the **ADsPath** of a user you wish to process, the actual task of opening an object is simply a case of using the following line of code:

```
Set objUser = Getobject(strADsPath)
```

This assumes that you wish to use **objUser** to manipulate the user object later in your script and **strADsPath** is a string containing the **ADsPath** of the object to open. In the above solution for obtaining a list of **ADsPaths**, **objRecordSet. Fields("Adspath").Value** will return the **ADsPath** of the current record. What the above code actually does is read the object's attributes into the client's memory, from where they can easily be accessed and manipulated.

Reading and Setting Properties

For many attributes of an object, there's a simple way to read and set their values. All ADSI objects have properties, such as **.Name** and **.ADsPath**, but many other properties can be accessed simply as follows:

```
Set objUser = Getobject("LDAP://cn=Adam Wood,cn=Users,dc=example,dc=com")

' Set the Decsription Field
objUser.Description = "The Author"

' Print the email address
Wscript.Echo objUser.mail

objUser.SetInfo
```

Alternatively, all properties can be manipulated using **.Get** and **.Put** as follows:

```
Set objUser = Getobject("LDAP://cn=Adam Wood,cn=Users,dc=example,dc=com")
```

```
' Set the Decsription Field
objUser.Put "Description", "The Author"

' Print the email address
Wscript.Echo objUser.Get("mail")

objUser.SetInfo
```

Any manipulation you perform only happens to the locally cached copy of an object, initially. To write changes to the directory itself, you must call **SetInfo** on the object as follows:

```
objUser.SetInfo
```

As ever, when you've finished with an object, it's a good idea to specify that by setting it to **nothing**.

```
Set objUser = nothing
```

Obtaining All Properties

The above example is fine if you know what properties you wish to retrieve for an object, but what about if you just want to know the value of every property there is? Fortunately, properties can also be retrieved through an array, and the size of that array is given by **.PropertyCount**. The Listing 10.1 will output all properties specified for the object and works just as well for any other class as it does for users.

Listing 10.1   ADBB-10-01-DumpAllProperties.vbs.

```
option explicit

Dim strObject, objObject, objProperty, intI

' Specify the ADsPath of the Object
strObject = "LDAP://cn=Administrator,cn=Users,DC=example,DC=com"

' Open the object
Set objObject = GetObject(strObject)

objObject.GetInfo

' Enumerate the Properties
For intI = 0 to objObject.PropertyCount - 1
  Set objProperty = objObject.Item(intI)
  Wscript.Echo objProperty.Name
Next
```

```
' Tidy Up
Set objProperty = nothing
set objObject   = nothing
```

RunAs

Windows 2000 lets you start processes with a different set of credentials to those you're currently logged in as. This is achieved through the **RunAs** service.

To launch a shortcut with alternate credentials:

1. Hold down and right-click the shortcut or menu item and select Run As.

TIP: Not all shortcuts require Shift+right-click to get the Run As option (although holding down Shift doesn't usually hurt). Shortcuts to .MSC files (Management Consoles), for example, don't need the Shift.

---

2. The Run As Other User dialog box (see Figure 10.10) appears. Enter an alternate username, password, domain name or UPN, and password.

3. Click OK.

It's also possible to use Run As functionality from the command line with **runas.exe**. It's found in %SystemRoot%\system32 on the Path by default, so all you have to type is something like:

```
C:\>runas /user:EXAMPLE\Administrator sol.exe
C:\>runas /user:administrator@example.com sol.exe
```

You're then prompted for a password. Additional options are available: type **runas /?** at a command prompt for a full list.

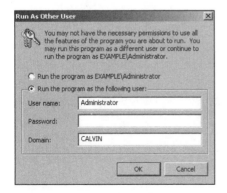

Figure 10.10   Run As Other User.

Managing Groups

I'll now discuss the management of groups.

Creating a Group

To be able to assign permissions through Security Groups or make contact through Distribution Groups, it's first necessary to create the group. A group is created as follows through the Active Directory Users and Computers Snap-in:

1. Open Active Directory Users and Computers from the Administrative Tools menu.

2. Use the left-hand tree to drill down to the OU or container where you wish to create the new group object.

3. Right-click on the OU/container and hover the mouse over New.

4. Click Group in the resulting menu. The New Object—Group Wizard appears (see Figure 10.11).

5. Fill in the name fields. The Group name becomes the relative distinguished name (RDN) of the object and the name by which it's usually known. The pre-Windows 2000 Group name is the NetBIOS name of the group.

6. Select the desired mode and scope of the group. In Mixed-mode domains, Universal Security Groups are unavailable.

7. Click OK to create the group.

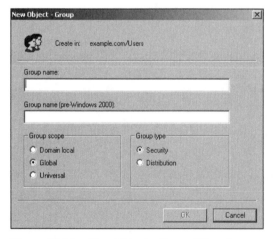

Figure 10.11   New Object—Group Wizard.

Related solution:	*Found on page:*
Converting a Domain to Native Mode	143

Adding Users to a Group

Numerous ways exist to add users to a group from Active Directory Users and Computers. You can do it either by looking at a group and selecting which users to add or by looking at a user and selecting group membership for that user. It's also possible to create a group with a snapshot of the members of an OU. To add users to a group, you must be able to write to its members' property (and ideally read it).

From the Group Object

To add one or more users to a particular group:

1. Open Active Directory Users and Computers from the Administrative Tools menu.

2. Navigate through your OU structure to the group whose membership you wish to manage.

3. Right-click the group and select Properties.

4. Switch to the Members tab. A list of joined members is displayed as in Figure 10.12.

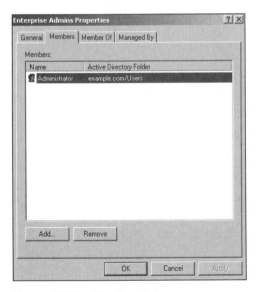

Figure 10.12   Members tab.

5. Click Add. The Select Users, Computers, Contacts, or Groups dialog box appears.

6. Select any members you wish to add and click OK.

Members can also be removed in a similar way.

From a User Object

To add a particular user to one or more groups:

1. Open Active Directory Users and Computers from the Administrative Tools menu.

2. Navigate through your OU structure to the account to add to one or more groups.

3. Right-click the user whose group membership you wish to modify and select Properties.

4. Switch to the Member of tab. A list of joined groups is displayed.

5. Click Add. The Select Group dialog box appears with multiple selections enabled (see Figure 10.13). Either select one or more groups from the list (use Ctrl or Shift in the normal way), or type a semicolon-separated list of group names in the space below.

6. Click OK.

Group memberships can also be removed in this way.

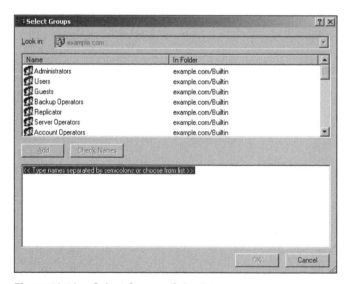

Figure 10.13   Select Groups dialog box.

Adding an Entire OU

The current contents of an OU can be added to an existing group as follows:

1. Open Active Directory Users and Computers from the Administrative Tools menu.

2. Use the left-hand tree to drill down to the OU whose contents you wish to add to the group.

3. Right-click the OU and select "Add Members To A Group".

4. The Select Group dialog box appears. Type or choose the group to add to and click OK.

5. You're now prompted to confirm the addition. You'll be prompted further for each container within the OU as to whether to add its contents to the group, also. Click Yes to proceed or Yes to All to add the entire subtree.

Changing Group Scope and Type

With certain limitations, which depend on the mode of the domain, it's possible to change the scope and type of a group once it has been created. Distribution Groups can always be converted to the equivalent Security Group. Security Groups can also be converted to Distribution Groups, although it will negate any access control settings currently in place on the group.

In Native mode only, Domain Local Groups can be converted to Universal Groups, and Global Groups can also be converted to Universal Groups. Universal Groups can be converted to any other group scope.

To change the scope or type of a group:

1. Open Active Directory Users and Computers from the Administrative Tools menu.

2. Navigate through your OU structure to the group whose scope/type you wish to modify.

3. Right-click the group and select Properties.

4. Modify the Scope and Type as appropriate from the General tab. Invalid options will be disabled (grayed out).

5. Click OK when done. If you're converting a Distribution Group to a Security Group, you'll be warned about the loss of permissions this may result in. Click OK to continue or cancel to abort.

Chapter 11

Other Directory Objects

In Depth

The previous chapter dealt with two of the most common types of objects you'll encounter in the Active Directory: users and groups. In this chapter, attention turns to some of the other more common types of objects in the directory.

Chief among these are computer objects and domain controller objects. In addition, the myriad of objects that make up the configuration partition will be examined. A discussion of shared folder objects and printer objects is delayed until Chapter 15, when these two important areas are given a full treatment. This chapter starts, however, with contact objects.

Contacts

An Active Directory contact object represents a person but isn't a security principal as a user account would be. Instead, contact objects used to represent people without user accounts in your organization—literally, external contacts. With the use of contact objects in Active Directory, an organization can centralize its address book to a single distributed database available to everyone and can have security permissions applied just like other directory objects.

Contact Object Class

Contact class is descended from Organizational-Person, just as the User class is. This common ancestry means that contacts and users share many of the same properties.

Top

    Person

        Organizational-person

            User

In fact, all that user objects have, in addition to the abstract Organizational-Person class, are attributes that relate to the mechanics of authentication and account-specific information, such as home folder location. All that contact objects have, in addition to the Organizational-Person class, is a Notes field.

Keep Information Original

It may not be possible when Active Directory is first deployed, but a long-term goal of any organization should be to avoid duplicating information. This comes back to the point that should be driving IT: cost savings.

Personally, it would be great if there were a single "directory in the sky" that one could go to whenever contact details changed. This was a particularly acute problem at the university, with frequent changes along the lines of nine weeks at college, a few weeks at home, a few weeks away working, and so on. Mail kept being redirected around the country on a catch-up basis, and it got to the point where it wasn't worth staying on top of the most up-to-date forwarding address.

Now, a global, central information store for contact details that's accessible to everyone is a little unrealistic. However, within a single company, it isn't an unrealistic target. Even the smallest company running Active Directory will have a full-service Lightweight Directory Access Protocol (LDAP) directory at its disposal, and it should be made available. An obvious use of the directory is as a central information store for personal information—contact details, customer details, and so forth. Over time, applications can be rewritten to use the directory to store static information, such as names and addresses, and to link that information to other databases.

Searching the Active Directory

With a directory chock-full of information about employees and business contacts, it's of course essential to be able to utilize that information. Because Active Directory is an LDAP-compliant directory service, you can use any tool that allows an LDAP server to be searched. For example, LDAP servers can be added to Microsoft Outlook (and Outlook Express for that matter), and even used to check email addresses of recipients.

There are also various means of searching the directory built in to Windows 2000 itself, catering both to users and administrators. Finally, as ever, directory searches are perfect examples of something that's scriptable. The possibilities for custom scripts are numerous and range from quick and dirty command-line administrative "hacks" to a beautifully designed Web interface on the corporate intranet.

Within Windows 2000

The Windows 2000 user interface provides a generic method for searching the Active Directory accessible from the Start menu. With the Start| Search| For People option, you're able to search an LDAP directory—either from the preconfigured list or from specifying your own through the registry. The Find People dialog box is shown in Figure 11.1. Using the People tab, you can search by email address; and the Advanced tab also allows a slightly more detailed set of search options.

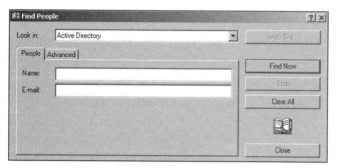

Figure 11.1   Find People dialog box.

The area to search is labeled Active Directory (and should more precisely be Active Directory Global Catalog). The server name is specified as NULL in the Account properties so that Windows 2000 contacts a default Global Catalog server for the current domain. Hence, the impact of the search on the wide area network (WAN) will be minimized, because a nearby Global Catalog server will be chosen.

This approach of using a NULL server name and specifying a search of the Global Catalog by using port 3268 (and not the LDAP default of 389) will insure that a nearby server is contacted and the entire forest is searched. Specifying a server by name is a bad idea, because it will place an extra load on a single server and have bad implications if you specify it for computers on remote sites. (Even if you're clever and specify a different one on each site, experience shows that it won't be long before a desktop PC or laptop gets moved between sites and look-ups start going over the WAN.) Also, by leaving it up to the usual Domain Name System (DNS)-based methods to find an LDAP server, you don't leave yourself open to problems if a single server is decommissioned or down for maintenance (either scheduled or, more likely, unscheduled).

Active Directory Users and Computers

The Active Directory Users and Computers interface allows for more advanced searches than those available with the Find People dialog box. These searches are made against the currently connected domain controller. Active Directory Users and Computers allows you to right-click on a container and select Find to bring up a search dialog box (see Figure 11.2), from which you can employ the user interface to build a query or simply to type an LDAP search filter.

Because Active Directory Users and Computers is primarily an administrative tool, it isn't a good idea to make it available to users. For one thing, it's best to make the Organizational Unit (OU) structure transparent to users in your organization. Instead, if you wish to let users perform more advanced searches than are

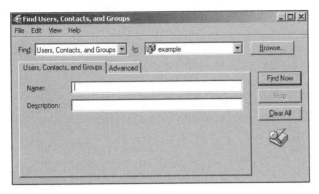

Figure 11.2   Active Directory Users and Computers search dialog box.

allowed by the Find People dialog box, it's probably best to use some kind of custom application, perhaps by using ADSI scripting from a Web page.

Active Directory Management Tool

The Active Directory Management Tool from the Windows 2000 Support Tools (often just called **ldp.exe** because it's quicker to say) is a general LDAP client. Looking deeper than the rudimentary interface, you'll find a powerful way of searching Active Directory. Using the **Search** command (on the Browse menu, where else?) you can specify just about any parameter of an LDAP search and type a custom LDAP search filter. Instead of the nice, clickable graphical list of results you get from Active Directory Users and Computers, all you get back in response is raw output. However, **ldp.exe** is more powerful, because you can use it to search the Global Catalog or other partitions, except for the domain partition.

Script

With *script* or a custom application, it's possible to do just about anything. Examples in previous chapters have demonstrated the use of ActiveX Data Objects (ADO) to script searches of the Active Directory with VBScript, but it's possible to use just about any programming language to search the directory. One particularly popular application, especially when aiming at end users, is to create an intranet page to search the directory using scripting.

Search.vbs, part of the Windows 2000 Support Tools, is an example that provides a command-line mechanism for performing directory searches. Common parameters, such as a search filter, base, and scope, are specified as parameters, and the script can also be edited to change other values (not to mention customized for your own purposes).

Computers

Windows 2000 Active Directory domains require computer accounts for Windows NT and Windows 2000 computers that you wish users to be able to log on from. Computer accounts aren't, however, required for Windows 95, 98, or Millennium Edition (ME) machines. The reason they exist at all is principally to allow a secure channel to be established for authentication, but they also allow computers to be uniquely identified within a domain.

When a workstation or server has been connected to a computer account (that is, it's *joined* to the domain), you can add users and groups from the domain to access control lists on the computer. This means that a user only has to log on once to be able to use resources (which she has appropriate permissions for), regardless of whether these resources are on a domain controller or on another computer in a domain.

Group Policy

By having accounts in the directory, computers can have Group Policy applied to them if they're running Windows 2000 and later (specifically, not previous versions of NT). To recap briefly, *Group Policy* is the replacement for System Policy from Windows NT 4, and it allows customized settings to be applied to users and computers. For example, registry settings to alter the desktop, hide menu items, or alter application behavior can be set through Group Policy.

But the great thing is that Group Policy can be applied to specific computers as well as to users, so for example, the software installation settings can be configured on a per-computer basis. This way, software is installed whenever a computer is rebooted—this is perfect for fixes to the operating system and software that's to be deployed on a company-wide basis (as well as useful if you want specific software on specific computers, such as the ones with scanners attached, regardless of who logs in on them).

Because the determination for exactly what Group Policy is applied to on a computer is based upon its position in the OU hierarchy of your domain—its Security Group membership and site membership—you should use an OU structure and Security Groups to specify group policy for computers exactly as you would for users.

For example, if a number of workstations are designated as kiosk machines for public use, perhaps in the lobby of a building, then you could use a separate OU for these computers. Similarly, OUs can be used to define computers that require broadly similar software installation settings.

NOTE: *The site an ordinary computer belongs to is based solely on its IP address, specifically, the IP address it uses initially to contact a domain controller during the logon process.*

Operating System Details

One of the really useful features of Active Directory Users and Computers is that it displays the current operating system version and service pack details for a computer object. In addition, hotfix details are stored in the directory.

NOTE: *Hotfixes are patches released between service packs designed to address specific problems. In general, the advice is not to apply a hotfix unless you're experiencing or may experience a specific problem.*

This information is stored in the directory and is, thus, accessible in the usual way for creating reports, for scripting, or for displaying in Web pages.

Computer Location

Anyone who has ever opened a browse list in an organization that uses numbers as computer names (PC0001, PC0002, and so forth) has probably wondered once in a while exactly where (physically) a computer is located.

Windows 2000 introduces the concept of location. By using a hierarchical naming convention, the idea is that you can specify exact locations of objects. Subnet objects can be given a base location to represent the office they're in, and beneath these bases, the locations of computers and printers can be specified, perhaps down to the room number. As well as administrators, this information is useful to users who may, for example, also be looking for a nearby color printer.

Choosing a Good Location Name

The basic syntax you should use for a location name is a series of identifiers separated by forward slashes (*/*). Although the identifiers can technically be 32 characters long and the entire location string for an object can be anything up to 260 characters, it's best to keep them short and snappy, so users are able to type them quickly.

For example, **Europe/Great Britain/Cambridge/St. Catherine's** would work, but users have to type these locations, so you could leave out anything unnecessary (for example, it's doubtful that there's any real need for a continent) and shorten names where possible. Also, it's worth leaving out spaces and special characters to make typing easier.

When using abbreviations, stick to common ones well known to users. For example, in a really large organization **GBR/Cam/Catz** would be ideal for the above, but in a smaller business with operations in only one country, just **Cam/Catz** would do.

Beneath the name of an office, further levels of detail should be specified for individual objects. The most important thing here is consistency. It's usual to use something along the lines of floors and room numbers (but the exact convention used should follow any existing any one). Again, make sure locations are exact, unambiguous, and easily understood by new recruits.

Of course, the main problem you're likely to encounter with the Computer Location field is that it wasn't updated when someone moved the computer six months ago. This is a procedural issue within the company, but at the very least, if the Managed By information is filled in for a computer, you get somebody to blame.

Domain Controllers

Windows 2000 Servers configured as domain controllers are represented in the directory by both computer objects and server objects.

Domain Controllers OU

The computer objects for domain controllers are, by default, added beneath the Domain Controllers OU in the domain partition for their Active Directory domain. Just after it's created, an Active Directory domain only contains one Organizational Unit, that for domain controllers. The reason behind this is Group Policy; its objects can't be applied to Containers (such as the built-in Users and Computers' Containers), so to apply a unique Group Policy Object (GPO) to the domain controllers in a domain, they're organized into their own OUs.

Of course, you don't need to leave the computer objects for domain controllers in this single OU, but it's usually the easiest way. If you need to segregate domain controllers for management or Group Policy purposes, you could create a hierarchy of OUs beneath Domain Controllers or have several domain controller OUs within a wider structure (as long as you link the Default Domain Controllers Group Policy Object to any new domain controller OUs so that certain settings apply to all domain controllers.)

Server Objects

Server objects are used to represent Windows 2000 Domain Controllers in the configuration partition for a forest. They're organized beneath site objects to reflect the site membership of the domain controller they represent.

These server objects are managed through Active Directory Sites and Services, as described in Chapter 8. Beneath them are NT Directory Service (NTDS) Settings objects, which store the configuration of Active Directory on the domain controller (NTDS is another, older name for Active Directory).

Adding Downlevel Domain Controllers

One curious point to note is that to add a Windows NT computer as a backup domain controller (BDC) to an Active Directory domain, you must create the computer account for that domain controller first.

Do this by adding a computer object with the downlevel (NetBIOS) name to be specified when Windows NT is installed as a domain controller. Group Policy won't apply to that object, but for neatness, it's probably best to place it in the same OU as other domain controllers.

Of course, you can only (sensibly) add Windows NT BDCs to Active Directory domains that are still in Mixed mode, and you should remove or upgrade them before converting to Native mode (otherwise, they'll stop receiving Security Accounts Manager (SAM) updates and become worse than useless).

Other Objects

As well as the visible objects discussed in this and previous chapters that represent commonly accessed contents of the directory, such as users and computers, a whole host of other objects exist beneath the surface.

These objects, usually concealed from view, contain information either to support additional services or to support services essential to Active Directory functioning. For example, Active Directory-integrated DNS information must clearly be contained in the directory somewhere. It has already been stated in previous chapters that Active Directory-integrated DNS is stored at the domain level, so it must be stored somewhere within a domain partition.

The best tool to go poking around the innards of Active Directory with is Active Directory Service Interface (ADSI) Edit. Opening a typical Domain Naming Context will give the first-level containers shown in Figure 11.3.

Discounting the OUs and containers we already know about, the most striking candidate for storing hidden meta-data about the domain is **cn=System**. Sure enough, beneath **cn=System** there will be a **cn=MicrosoftDNS** object whose children are **dnsZone** objects, and their children are **dnsNode** objects (which take the role of individual lines in a zone file). The first-level containers within the configuration partition are considered next.

Display Specifiers

The objects in the *Display Specifiers* container relate to the user interface elements presented by certain Active Directory applications. So, you can modify what gets displayed and also extend the user interface to support new classes. For example, when you right-click in Active Directory Users and Computers and go to the New item on the Context menu, you get a list of items to add. The names listed here are read from display specifiers, and it's perfectly possible to change it so that OU is displayed instead of Organizational Unit (if you're so inclined).

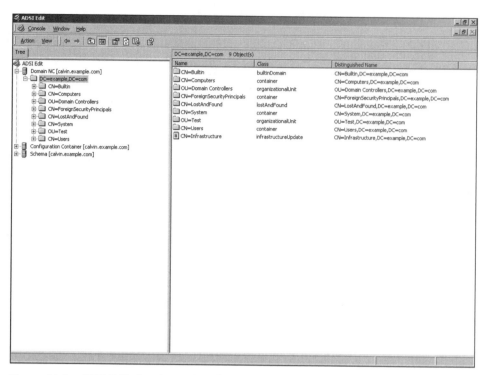

Figure 11.3   ADSI Edit showing a domain naming context.

Beneath the Display Specifiers container is a bunch of numbers. Looking more closely, you can see that the presence of the letters *A–E* gives away that these are hexadecimal numbers. They represent different locales. For example 1033 (409 Hex) is the U.S. English locale and 2057 (809 Hex) is the U.K. English locale. If color objects were ever added to the directory (you never know...), display specifiers could then be used to customize the Context menus so that "color" is spelled correctly for British administrators.

Extended Rights

Extended rights are just that—extensions of the permissions that can be granted to security principals. Most permissions either relate to specific attributes of objects or to the ability to act on entire objects (create, delete, or whatever). However, other types of rights relate to operations. For example, Group Policy (met in detail in Chapter 12) can be filtered so that it doesn't apply to every object. This is done by granting or denying the Apply Group Policy permission, which is an extended right. It's possible for developers to add their own extended rights to a forest to support their own applications.

Partitions

As the name betrays, the *Partitions container* lists each Active Directory partition in the forest. A single partition will exist for the forestwide schema, a single partition for the forestwide configuration, then one domain partition per Active Directory domain in the forest. Downlevel Windows NT domains can't join a forest and, hence, can't have entries here.

The purpose of these objects is to specify a complete list of partitions (for example, for building the Global Catalog), as well as to provide authoritative information on the DNS and NetBIOS names of the domains in the forest and to aid forestwide search resolution.

Physical Locations

The *Physical Locations* container is reserved for future use (that is, it doesn't do anything in Windows 2000 except look intriguing and make people waste time looking up what it's for).

Services

The objects in the *Services* container represent services (in the Windows 2000 sense, that is, server services running on domain controllers and member services). These objects store information of interest to the entire domain, such as public key infrastructure and remote access.

Well-Known Security Principals

The configuration partition houses a container called **cn=WellKnown Security Principals** whose function is purely to map the names of the predefined security principals, such as **Everyone** and **Self**, to their SIDs (Security Identifiers). This allows the SIDs stored on Access Control Lists (ACLs) to be mapped back to nice, friendly names for the user interface.

These SIDs are allocated by Microsoft, and there's no reason whatsoever to alter the objects initially in the Well-Known Security Principals container, or for that matter, to add to it. The objects listed in this container correspond to the Well-Known Security Principals detailed in Chapter 10.

Immediate Solutions

Creating Contacts

Contact objects are created in much the same way as user objects are. Before creating a contact, it's useful to have an idea where in your Organizational Unit structure it's to go.

To create a contact object:

1. Open Active Directory Users and Computers from the Administrative Tools menu.

2. Use the left-hand tree to drill down to the Organizational Unit or Container where you wish to create the new contact.

3. Right-click on the OU/Container and hover the mouse over New.

4. Click Contact in the resulting menu. The New Object—Contact dialog box appears (see Figure 11.4).

5. Type the appropriate information for the new contact and click OK when done.

The new contact object is created devoid of any contact details. To add these, right-click on the resulting object and select Properties. Information, such as email addresses and telephone numbers, can then be added.

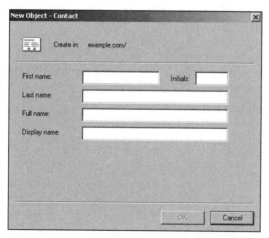

Figure 11.4   New Object—Contact dialog box.

Searching Active Directory

Numerous interfaces to searching Active Directory (more than discussed in this chapter, in fact) are available. The following solutions illustrate how to search Active Directory in a variety of ways.

Find People Dialog Box

Anyone, including end users, with a Windows 2000 computer is able to use the Find People dialog box to perform searches of LDAP directories.

To Launch the Find People Dialog Box

The Find People dialog box can easily be accessed from the Start menu as follows:

1. Click Start.

2. Move the mouse pointer over Search then select For People. The Find People dialog box will appear.

Using the Find People Dialog Box to Search Active Directory

The Find People dialog box is used to search both the local address book and LDAP servers. To use it to perform a simple search on Active Directory (or, indeed, any LDAP server):

1. Select the name of the LDAP Server in the Look in dialog box. Select Active Directory to search the Global Catalog of the current domain.

2. If you simply wish to search by name or email address, enter the text to search for (which could be just an initial fragment) as required.

3. Click Find Now.

Alternatively, you can perform a detailed search from the Advanced tab. This allows you to build up a query using combinations of conditions. Specifically, all conditions specified are **AND**ed together. The fields available are Name, E-mail Address, First Name, Surname, and Organization; the operators are **contains**, **is**, **starts with**, **ends with**, and **sounds like**.

To build an Advanced query:

1. Select the name of the LDAP Server in the Look in dialog box. Select Active Directory to search the Global Catalog of the current domain.

2. Switch to the Advanced tab.

3. Now build one or more conditions. Any records returned must meet all conditions. Each condition is built by selecting a field and an operator and by typing a string to match, then clicking Add.

NOTE: *If you enter two or more conditions then remove the first, a spurious **And** is left on display. This is only a user interface glitch and can safely be ignored.*

---

4. Finally, click Find Now to execute the search. The dialog box expands to display the search results. The resulting objects can be managed by right-clicking.

Editing Find People LDAP Servers

The list of LDAP servers that appears in the Look in list of the Find People dialog box is stored under the following registry key:

```
HKCU\Software\Microsoft\Internet Account Manager\Accounts
```

Although the entries can be configured by hand, perhaps the easiest way to create an account with the desired settings is to use Outlook Express, because it's the same list of LDAP servers used by Outlook Express that appears in the Find People dialog box. To edit the list using Outlook Express:

1. Launch Outlook Express, either from the Programs menu or the Taskbar short-cut. If you need to launch it directly, the path will likely be %ProgramFiles%\ Outlook Express\msimn.exe.

2. If you're prompted to make Outlook Express your default mail client, click No, because it's only being used to configure the LDAP server list.

3. Click the Tools menu then Accounts. The Internet Accounts dialog box appears.

4. Switch to the Directory Service tab to display only directory service accounts.

From here, you can edit the properties of existing accounts by selecting an account and clicking Properties.

Additional accounts added can be exported to an iaf file and distributed (perhaps via logon script), or registry changes could be made throughout your organization by means of Group Policy.

Search with Active Directory Users and Computers

Administrators can use the Active Directory Users and Computers Microsoft Management Console (MMC) Snap-in to search for objects in a domain. To do so:

1. Open Active Directory Users and Computers from the Administrative Tools menu.

2. Use the left-hand tree to drill down to the Organizational Unit or Container to use as the root of the search. The domain itself may be used as the root of the search.

3. Right-click the root of the search and select Find. The Find dialog box appears.

4. Use the Find list to select the object type(s) to search for. This will affect the search options available.

TIP: *To enter an LDAP search filter, select Custom Search, then the Advanced tab.*

---

5. Use the In drop-down list or the Browse button to alter the scope of the search if necessary.

6. Either enter a basic search criterion on the first tab or switch to the Advanced tab and construct a more advanced query to match all criteria specified. Each criterion consists of an attribute, an operator (**Starts With**, **Ends With**, **Is (exactly)**, **Is Not**, **Is Present**, **Is Not Present**), and a string to search for if applicable.

7. Click Find Now to execute the search. The dialog box expands to display the search results. The resulting objects can be managed by right-clicking.

Search with Active Directory Management Tool (ldp.exe)

The Active Directory Management Tool is a raw LDAP client and can be used to search any LDAP-compliant directory service. To search an LDAP directory with **ldp.exe**:

1. Start the Active Directory Management Tool from the Windows 2000 Support Tools, Tools menu.

2. Select Connect from the Connection menu and specify a server and port to connect to. The default LDAP port is 389, and the Global Catalog port is 3268. Either specify explicitly the name of a server or domain to connect to or leave the Server field blank to connect to the current domain.

3. Select Bind from the Connect menu and provide alternate credentials with the server if necessary.

4. Select Search from the Browse menu. The Search dialog box (Figure 11.5) appears.

5. Specify the Distinguished Name to start the search from (for example, **cn=Users,dc=example,dc=com**, the LDAP search filter, and the depth of the search.

Figure 11.5 **ldp.exe** Search dialog box.

Figure 11.6 Search options.

6. Click Options to verify and configure additional settings. The dialog box shown in Figure 11.6 appears. In particular, you can define the list of attributes that the search should return.

7. When all options are set, click OK.

8. Click Run to execute the query. Results are returned as text output on the right of **ldp.exe**.

Search by Script

The **search.vbs** script included in the Windows 2000 Support Tools can be used to search an LDAP directory. By now you should recognize the search parameters detailed in Table 11.1.

Table 11.1 Search.vbs parameters.

Parameter	Description	Default Value	Example
ADsPath	The **ADsPath** of the root of the search. This parameter is mandatory.	**LDAP://dc=example, dc=com**	
/C:criteria	An LDAP search filter	**/C:objectClass=***	**objectClass=user**

(continued)

Table 11.1   Search.vbs parameters *(continued)*.

Parameter	Description	Default Value	Example
/P:properties	A comma-separated list of the LDAP names of attributes to return	**/P:adspath**	**/P:cn,adspath**
/S:scope	The scope of the search: Base, OneLevel, or **SubTree**	**/S:OneLevel**	**/S:SubTree**
/O:outputfile	Optional output file if omitted results are displayed in the Command Prompt		**/O:search.txt**
/U:username	Optional username, so alternative credentials can be specified.	By default, the current logged-on user's credentials are used.	**/U:administrator @example.com**
/W:password	Required password if **/U** is used		**/W:HardTo GuessPassword**
/Q	Suppresses all output		

For example, the following command will perform a search for users in or beneath the Test Organizational Unit of **example.com**, and output their UPNs:

```
C:\>cscript search.vbs LDAP://ou=Test,dc=example,dc=com /C:objectClass=user
  /P:userPrincipalName /S:SubTree
```

Implementing an LDAP search in your own script is a common occurrence and one that is used many times throughout this book. For a detailed example, see the "Managing Users by Script" solution.

Related solution:	*Found on page:*
Managing Users	256

Adding a Windows 2000 Computer to a Domain

One easy way to add a Windows 2000 computer to a domain is to do so during installation of the operating system, when prompted. However, it's of course possible to add a computer to a domain at a later date.

To add a Windows 2000 computer to a domain:

1. From the computer to add, click Start|Settings|Control Panel and launch the System Applet.

2. Switch to the Network Identification tab.

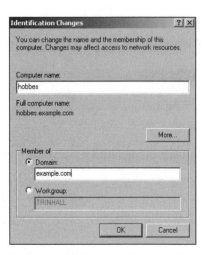

Figure 11.7   Network Identification dialog box.

3. Click the Properties button. The Identification dialog box appears (see Figure 11.7).

NOTE: *The properties button is disabled on a domain controller, because you can't rename or change the current domain without first removing Active Directory.*

4. In the Member of radio group, select Domain and enter the DNS name of the domain to join.

5. Click OK. You're now prompted for domain credentials.

6. Enter the username and password with authority for adding the computer to the domain and click OK.

7. The computer is joined to the domain, and, if necessary, a new computer account with the correct name is created in the built-in Computers container.

WARNING! It's vital to configure DNS correctly on a client computer before joining it to the domain. Failure to do so will result in errors locating domain controllers.

Creating Computer Accounts

As well as being able to create computer accounts when you add a machine to the domain, you can also precreate them to allow specific users to add computers to the domain or to prestage Remote Installation Services (RISs) clients.

To create a computer account:

1. Open Active Directory Users and Computers from the Administrative Tools menu.

2. Use the left-hand tree to drill down to the Organizational Unit or Container where you wish to create the computer account.

3. Right-click on the OU/Container in question and select New|Computer. The New Object—Computer dialog box appears (see Figure 11.8).

4. Type a Computer name. This will, by default, be used as the leading portion of the DNS name for the computer. The downlevel computer name will be populated automatically, but this may be amended as necessary.

5. Select a user or group to be able to add computers to that account. Selecting a user/group here will grant permission to join a computer to this account.

6. If you wish to allow Windows NT computers to connect to the account, tick the Allow pre-Windows 2000 computers to use this account box.

7. Click OK.

Figure 11.8   New Object—Computer dialog box.

Managing Computer Accounts

Computer accounts are Active Directory objects just like user accounts, and in many ways, managing them is exactly the same as managing user objects. Active Directory Users and Computers is the main user interface, and general properties, group memberships, and object movements are handled exactly as for user objects.

TIP: *If you right-click on a computer account in Active Directory Users and Computers and then select Manage, the Computer Management MMC console is launched and focused on that machine.*

Related solution:	Found on page:
Managing Users	256

Resetting Computer Accounts

Resetting a computer's account breaks the link between the computer object and the Windows NT or Windows 2000 computer joined to that account. It effectively removes the computer from the domain without deleting the account. For example, if a hard drive fails, and after replacing it you want the new installation of Windows 2000 to have the same identity, you would reset the computer account.

To reset a computer account:

1. Open Active Directory Users and Computers from the Administrative Tools menu.

2. Use the left-hand tree to drill down to the organizational unit or container where the computer account you wish to reset is located. Left-click on the OU/container in question to list its contents.

3. Right-click on the computer account and select Reset Account.

Disabling Computer Accounts

Disabling a computer account will prevent it from being used as part of the domain until it's reenabled. You can't disable domain controllers.

To disable a computer account:

1. Open Active Directory Users and Computers from the Administrative Tools menu.

2. Use the left-hand tree to drill down to the organizational unit or container where the computer account you wish to disable is located. Left-click on the OU/container in question to list its contents.

3. Right-click on the computer account and select Disable Account.

Delegating Permission to Create and Join Computer Accounts

It's inefficient for someone with an administrative password to physically walk to the machine each time you reinstall Windows 2000 or buy a new computer. It's also plain negligent to give out an administrative password to a user so he can do it himself.

Instead, two options are available: to delegate the permission to create a brand new computer account (perhaps to the engineer responsible for configuring the new computer at the user's desk) or to delegate the permission to join a computer to an existing account.

The latter option means the computer account must already exist in the directory and simply gives a user the permission to associate the Windows 2000 machine he's sitting at with that account. This option becomes particularly important if Remote Installation Services (RISs) is used. See Chapter 14 for more details on RIS.

Create Computer Accounts

To create computer accounts in an Organizational Unit or container, the Create Computer Objects permission should be granted. This can be found on the Advanced permissions for the OU/container object. A simpler way to grant this permission is to use the Delegation of Control Wizard as follows.

Join Computers to Existing Accounts

To join a computer to an existing account, the following four permissions are required over the account object:

- Reset Password
- Validated write to DNS hostname
- Validated write to service principal name
- Write account restrictions

Adding the **RootDSE** to ADSI Edit

By default, the **RootDSE** object for a domain controller isn't visible through ADSI Edit, and it must, instead, be added manually. Because **RootDSE**s are local to their respective domain controllers, you should also specify which domain controller's **RootDSE** you wish to load.

To load a **RootDSE** into ADSI Edit:

1. Launch ADSI Edit from the Windows 2000 Support Tools menu.

2. Right-click ADSI Edit at the top of the left-hand tree and select Connect to. The Connection dialog box shown in Figure 11.9 appears.

3. In the Connection Point Group, select the Naming Context radio button and choose **RootDSE** from the accompanying list.

4. In the Computer Group, select the first option and type the DNS name of the server whose **RootDSE** you wish to inspect/modify.

5. If necessary, use the Advanced tab to specify alternative credentials and port number.

6. Click OK. The **RootDSE** is added within ADSI Edit, and the single object can be modified and inspected as normal.

A similar technique can be applied to add partitions of other domains and forests to ADSI Edit (with appropriate permissions, of course).

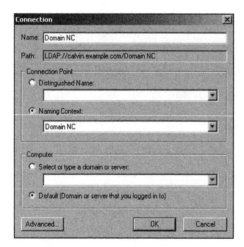

Figure 11.9   Connection dialog box.

Chapter 12

Understanding Group Policy

In Depth

Group Policy allows administrators to specify settings for users and computers and to have those settings enforced by the operating system. Group Policy can be specified at numerous levels: sites, domains, and Organizational Units (OUs). When a computer starts up, the computer applies the Computer Policy portion of Group Policy objects linked to the current site, current domain, and the hierarchy of OUs that contain the computer account. When a user logs in, the computer applies the User Policy portion of the GPOs linked to the site, domain, and OU hierarchy, based on the location of the user object.

Group Policy is the Windows 2000 replacement for Windows NT System Policy. It allows greater flexibility and finer control, and it actually removes itself when a user logs off or the computer shut down (as appropriate). Group Policy requires Windows 2000 (or later) clients, as well as an Active Directory domain. Windows 2000 still supports System Policy for down-level clients. For Windows 2000 clients that do not form part of a domain, Local Policy provides similar functionality to Group Policy.

What Can Have Group Policy?

Group Policy Objects can apply to users or computers. User policy is applied at logon and computer policy at startup. Group Policy is refreshed periodically, and new settings will take effect immediately thereafter. Exceptions to this exist for policies that only make sense to apply at logon or when a computer starts up, such as software installation (upgrading an application that is currently in use isn't ideal). When a user logs in or when a computer starts up, the appropriate Group Policy is applied.

What Can Group Policy Do?

Group Policy is far more capable than Windows NT System Policy and isn't just limited to desktop lockdown. It can be used to install software, run multiple logon and logoff scripts (and startup and shutdown scripts for computers), redirect folders, configure Internet Explorer, and perform various other tasks, including applying custom registry changes through Administrative Templates. This chapter is concerned more with the mechanisms behind Group Policy. Specific capabilities are dealt with in Chapter 13. And, best of all, it actually gets removed when a user logs off (instead of hanging around in the Registry until another policy replaces it).

The individual settings that comprise Group Policy Objects are referred to by their hierarchical names, for example:

```
Computer Configuration/Windows Settings/Security Settings/Account Policies
```

To find the settings referenced here, simply drill down the tree of a Group Policy Object as you would when navigating to a particular folder in Windows Explorer or to a particular key in a Registry Editor.

Where Can Group Policy be Applied?

Group Policy can be applied at several different levels within Active Directory. It can be applied to an entire site, to an entire domain, or to part of a domain (in the form of the subtree beneath an OU). As we'll see later, it's possible to alter the processing of Group Policy by restricting policy objects to only certain Security Groups, as well as by changing the default inheritance.

Sites

Specific Group Policy settings can be applied to users or computers based upon their current Active Directory site. Although they're only stored in a single domain, site-based policies are applied to computers and users in a site regardless of their domain. This means if there's a Group Policy for the site London in Domain A, then users in Domain B who are situated in London will also have to contact a domain controller in Domain B before they log on. This will slow down the logon process slightly, according to network conditions and server load.

Domains

Group Policy can be set at the domain level, so it applies to all users and computers within the domain. Domain-level settings will override site settings under the normal inheritance rules.

Certain options set via Group Policy can only be applied at the domain level in Windows 2000 Active Directory. The items that fit into this category are the following:

- *Everything beneath Computer Configuration/Windows Settings/Security Settings/Account Policies*. Namely:
  - *Password Policy*—This policy contains six settings relating to minimum password length, complexity, age, and so forth.
  - *Account Lockout Policy*—This policy contains three settings, which dictate how accounts get locked out after failed logon attempts.
  - *Kerberos Policy*—This policy contains five settings, including ticket life times and computer clock difference tolerance.

- *The following items beneath Computer Configuration/Windows Settings/ Security Settings/Local Policies/Security Options*:

  - Automatically log off users when logon time expires.

  - Rename administrator account.

  - Rename guest account.

The technical reason that settings can only be set from domain-level policy is that they are processed only by domain controllers, and domain controllers are hard coded in Windows 2000 to ignore these settings from other Group Policy Objects. If several domain-level GPOs specify these settings, they're processed in the normal way.

Collectively, these particular settings are often referred to as per-domain or domain-level-only settings. If you wish to vary any of these settings for different portions of your organization, you must create separate domains to do so.

Organizational Units

Group Policy can also be associated with Organizational Units. In fact, an object processes Group Policy from every Organizational Unit above it in the directory. As an example, for the user Andrej in Figure 12.1, the only OUs from which Group Policy is applied are the Research and Engineering OUs.

Group Policy Objects

Group Policy settings are stored in terms of Group Policy Objects (GPOs). A GPO is stored in a specific domain, and consists of a directory-based portion and a file-based portion. These are both backed up with the rest of the Active Directory information from within Windows NT backup (see Chapter 16).

Why Is it Called "Group Policy"?

Group Policy consists of groups of policies, so a Group Policy Object is an object that groups policies together. It has nothing to do with Active Directory Security Groups, and it isn't a method of applying policy to Security Groups, because Group Policy can't apply directly to Security Groups—only to users and computers.

Group Policy Container

The directory-based portion of a GPO is stored in what is known as a Group Policy Container. The actual information is stored in the domain partitions of Active Directory beneath the **cn=Policies,cn=System,dc=DomainName** object. The information stored includes the version of the GPO, status information, and settings for software installation.

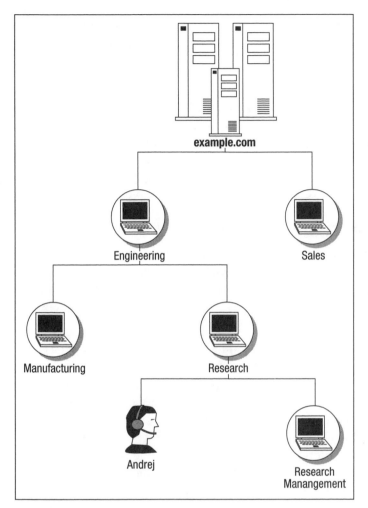

Figure 12.1   Example of Organizational Unit hierarchy.

Group Policy Template

The *Group Policy Template (GPT)* contains the disk-based portion of Group Policy. It's here that logon script files, custom administrative templates, and other data are stored. Group Policy Templates are stored by the Globally Unique Identifier (GUID) within a domain's **SYSVOL** share. The path of a typical GPT is:

```
%SystemRoot%\SYSVOL\sysvol\example.com\Policies\
                         {0B29CA90-8E86-426D-AB9A-C81DEFA42051}
```

Beneath this version information, settings and administrative templates are stored, and this data is replicated via the File Replication Service (FRS) to all domain controllers in the domain.

NOTE: *Because Group Policy Objects exist in two parts that are replicated by different mechanisms, it's possible for these two parts to become out of sync. If they're out of sync, then the entire GPO isn't processed.*

External Data

Group Policy Objects can use data stored externally to the container or template. To be useful, this data must be referenced in either the Group Policy Container or Group Policy Template. For example, setting software installation options doesn't copy the software to be installed into Active Directory—instead, just a share where the installation files can be found is stored, and these files are used to actually install software when the software installation Group Policy is processed.

Linking Group Policy Objects

Conceptually, a single long list of Group Policy objects for each domain is in the forest. The list references them by GUID, not name, so they can be freely renamed without impact to operations. The usual caveats about deleting then re-creating an object with the same name and not bringing back security settings apply.

These Group Policy Objects are then linked to sites, domains, and OUs (collectively, *containers* in this context). A single Group Policy Object can be linked to none, one, or more containers, and these containers can be from the GPO's own domain or from other domains in the forest. Linking allows the same GPO to apply to several different parts of the directory yet maintain a single instance, so when you change that GPO, its effects change for everyone together. The alternative to this would be to create two identical GPOs, one for each container that needs the same policy, and even with the best will in the world, they would likely fall out of sync sooner or later.

GPOs linked between domains obviously have a performance overhead, because clients and users will have to contact a second domain controller to log on. The exact overhead this causes will vary depending upon the environment. Experience shows that it isn't a major problem with multiple domains in the same site with well-specified servers and good network connectivity. However, in environments where there isn't a domain controller from each domain in every branch office, the potential for wide area network (WAN) traffic during logon makes any additional administrative burden from maintaining the same GPO in two different domains the lesser evil.

Of course, if a network structure is simple enough for linked GPOs not to be a problem, but a multiple domain Active Directory environment exists, then it's more than likely that there's either an administrative or political reason for not having a single domain model. In these instances, GPOs tend not to be linked between domains.

Group Policy Evaluation

As discussed earlier, Group Policy can be relatively complicated, with multiple GPOs linked to the same container and multiple containers all conveying Group Policy to be processed.

Windows 2000 uses a deterministic order to process Group Policy. Computer Policy is first processed when a machine first starts and user policy is first processed at logon. During each of these times there is a particular order that GPOs are processed in.

Processing Order

Group Policy Objects can be assigned at various levels: site, domain, and within many layers of OU. Note that Group Policy isn't inherited from other domains in a forest; a child domain, for example, doesn't apply the domain Group Policy of its parent domain.

Site, Domain, Organization Unit (SDOU)

The order in which the levels of Group Policy are processed is site, domain, and OU. GPOs for all OUs above the object in question are processed with the highest first. The acronym SDOU comes from this processing order. As shown in Figure 12.2, this order corresponds to processing the most distant GPO first.

It's very important to realize that the order in which GPOs are processed is the reverse order of precedence of their settings. Quite simply, the settings in the last processed GPO will overwrite conflicting settings from previous GPOs in memory. The default inheritance behavior can be modified, however. This means that the GPO closest to the user or computer takes precedence at a conflict. For example, if a site-level GPO disables Control Panel and if a domain-level GPO enables Control Panel, then the result is that Control Panel will be enabled.

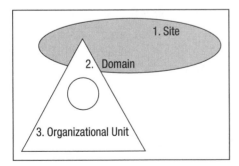

Figure 12.2   Group Policy Application order.

Local Policy

In addition to directory-based policy, Windows 2000 computers (whether they're part of a domain or not) can have Local Policy settings. *Local Policy* is, in effect, an additional Group Policy Template on the local computer. It's processed before any directory-based policies and, hence, has the lowest precedence of any policy.

Multiple GPOs at One Level

It is quite normal to assign several Group Policy Objects at the OU, domain, or site. It's, then, natural to ask in what order they're processed (and applied). If you examine a Group Policy tab (reference Figure 12.3), you can see an ordered list of GPOs within the container.

This list is processed in reverse order, so when the container is evaluated, the GPO at the bottom is applied first, then each in turn up to the GPO at the top. This means that settings in a higher GPO take precedence over a lower GPO, because they're applied later and, hence, not overwritten.

Filtering GPOs

Group Policy Objects can only be applied to users and computers, but, specifically, not to Security Groups. However, occasions exist where it's desirable to apply a GPO only to members of a particular Security Group or to grant an exception to members of a Security Group. Because GPOs are objects in the directory, they have permissions associated with them, and one of these permissions is Apply

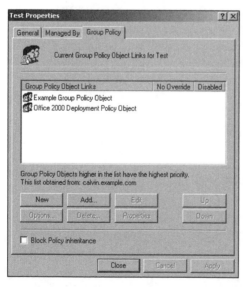

Figure 12.3   Group Policy tab for an Organizational Unit.

Group Policy. If, for whatever reason, a particular user doesn't have the Apply Group Policy and Read permissions for a particular GPO, then it isn't processed. This means you could create a Security Group with Apply Group Policy denied for a particular GPO, so it isn't processed by members of the Security Group. It's preferable, however, to avoid deny permissions wherever possible, because they have a habit of being forgotten about and causing unexpected results in the future. Instead, positive filtering is preferred. This means removing Authenticated Users from the Access Control List of a GPO and specifically adding the Security Groups you want to apply it to.

No Override

Individual Group Policy Objects can be flagged as No Override for a particular container. This means that in the event of conflicting policies, the No Override setting is applied. For example, if there's a domain-level policy to disable the **Run** command from everyone's desktop that's set to No Override, then an OU-level policy to enable the **Run** command will have no effect.

As soon as a setting from a GPO flagged as No Override is processed, that setting can't be replaced. In particular, it isn't overridden by subsequent GPOs with No Override set. This means that in the case of a conflict, the highest GPO in the SDOU hierarchy takes precedence.

Block Inheritance

A domain or OU can be flagged to block Group Policy Inheritance. This means that any settings from higher-level GPOs, such as sites and perhaps also domain and parent OUs, are ignored. The one exception to this is No Override settings, which aren't blocked. The reasoning here is that if control of GPOs for a portion of the domain are delegated, then that delegated administrator shouldn't have the ability to block centrally-mandated GPOs.

In general, it's best to minimize the use of No Override and Block Inheritance settings. One reason for this is that there's usually another way to achieve the desired result that's more elegant and less likely to cause future problems. Block Inheritance, for example, is all-or-nothing. It isn't possible to selectively block GPOs. If you find yourself wanting to selectively block GPOs, then it's usually indicative of needing to redesign your OU structure.

Synchronous or Asynchronous Processing

If a user or computer processes Group Policy synchronously, then all Group Policy Objects will finish processing before a user gets the opportunity to log on or before applications can be launched. Asynchronous processing is faster, but user logon/the Start menu bar appearing doesn't wait for GPOs to be applied.

For example, with asynchronous processing, a user may have the opportunity to use the **Run** command before the GPO setting to remove it is applied. By default, all Group Policy processes synchronously, although this is configurable. The only possible reason to switch to asynchronous processing is performance, and even then, only if the performance gain is compelling.

Group Policy Refresh

Unlike Windows NT System Policy, Group Policy isn't applied at logon/startup and forgotten. In addition to the initial settings being read, Group Policy is updated periodically, and new settings automatically replace old ones. This period, which is controlled through Group Policy, is, by default, 5 minutes for domain controllers and 90 minutes for other computers. With these periods goes a random offset that defaults at up to 30 minutes for other computers.

The random offset is there to spread the network and server load from Group Policy refreshes. If it didn't happen in companies where employees all come in and turn on their computers at exactly the same time, then there would be traffic spikes at 9 A.M., 10:30 A.M., 12:00 P.M., and so forth. Instead, the default random offset will cause the first wave of updates to take place between 10 A.M. and 11 A.M., preventing concentrated spikes of activity.

Not all Group Policy settings refresh. For example, folder redirection doesn't refresh (to avoid situations where a file is locked open and its folder name suddenly changes) nor does software deployment (to avoid trying to upgrade applications while you're still currently using them). When Group Policy refreshes, the Windows shell also refreshes. This causes a brief flicker of the screen and all Context menus to close, which, in short, may interrupt the user. For this reason and for reasons relating to network bandwidth, it's usual not to refresh too often, and the default settings are fine for most environments.

Delegating Control of Group Policy Objects

Just like many other functions of Active Directory, it's possible to delegate control of Group Policy. You can assign permission to manage specific GPOs or to manage all Group Policy settings for a specific container or to manage any combination of these. Two separate privileges can be assigned: the ability to edit particular Group Policy Objects, and the ability to link (and unlink) GPOs. The intention here is that when you've created OUs based on your administrative structure, the permission to apply Group Policy at these levels is delegated to the administrator who also controls the user accounts. In this way, Group Policy can be configured at local levels according to local needs.

The delegation of control of Group Policy is, like everything else that can be delegated, a case of setting the correct permissions on the appropriate objects in the directory. It's possible to use the Delegation of Control Wizard to automate this task.

Design Considerations

Along with the administrative model, Group Policy is one of the two main technical driving forces behind the design of an Active Directory forest and the OUs within a domain.

Chapter 19 is dedicated to design considerations, but before considering how to implement Group Policy, here are five aims of Group Policy design and implementation.

- Keep it simple.
- Group policies on a functional basis.
- Disable when possible.
- Avoid Block Inheritance.
- Use No Override sparingly.

Keep It Simple

It's very true to say that as far as Group Policy is concerned, *there's more than one way to do it*. For example, most GPOs can be created at domain level and filtered entirely by Security Group, or the objects that it's to be applied to can be placed in an exclusive subtree of the domain and the GPO can be applied at the root of the subtree.

Here, any general rule would be to prefer the subtree approach, because the Security Group filter increases processing time for members of that Security Group, adds administrative work, and will probably result in the Security Group being hijacked for other unrelated purposes by another administrator.

Group Policies When Meaningful

A single Group Policy Object can contain a great many settings or only a very small number. A trade-off is to be made here: If you use a small number of GPOs that have numerous settings each—perhaps one per container—then processing becomes relatively fast, because only a small number of objects exist to enumerate. But you lose flexibility and may end up having to duplicate settings.

The alternative extreme is to use a separate GPO for each individual setting. Although this gives the greatest degree of flexibility, it will increase processing time and also perhaps make administration more complex, with an awful lot of GPOs to manage and browse through. Instead, you should create GPOs somewhere between these two extremes. Having a small number is an advantage for logon processing, so policy settings should be placed in the same GPO where they'll always be applied together. For example, if a business need is to fully lock down a desktop, then a fully locked down desktop GPO should be created.

Disable When Possible

Group Policy evaluation takes a little time. Every Group Policy Object that applies to a user or computer must be read through in its entirety to check for applicable settings. GPOs are split into two portions—one for users and one for computers. To speed processing, it's possible to disable one portion of a GPO.

For example, imagine a domain-level GPO that has been introduced to apply certain settings to all computers, so there's no filtering in place. Even though this GPO has no user settings configured, it will still be processed by each user logging on to check this. It's possible to prevent unnecessary processing by disabling the user portion of a GPO or the computer portion of a GPO through the Management console (see Figure 12.4).

Disabling even half of a GPO will prevent that half from being processed at all, whether or not it includes any settings.

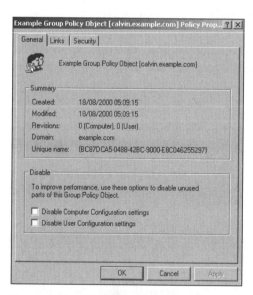

Figure 12.4   Disabling the user portion of a Group Policy Object.

Avoid Block Inheritance

It's easy to overuse the Block Inheritance option, which isolates an OU from higher Group Policy Objects. A simple test is that whenever you consider blocking inheritance, you should wonder why you couldn't just move the container out of its current position in the OU tree to avoid any inherited policies. After all, an OU structure should (in theory) be designed with only Group Policy and administration in mind, so if Block Inheritance is considered, then often a simple change to the delegation of administration will suffice.

Use No Override Sparingly

Similarly to trying to avoid inheritance blocks, No Override creates a situation where confusion may arise at a later date when policies aren't applied, as you expect they might. It goes against the self-documenting nature of the directory, and the fact that there can only be one No Override setting means that exceptions can never be created.

The usual reasons given for using Block Inheritance are to force organization-wide settings everywhere, regardless of what local administrators want. If such a rule really does cover everyone with no exceptions, and it's thought likely that local administrators may try to change the setting for whatever reason, then Block Inheritance is necessary.

Immediate Solutions

Creating and Opening Group Policy Objects

Group Policy is administered through its own Management Console Snap-in, called Group Policy. However, no shortcut is available for the Group Policy Snap-in created by default on the Administrative Tools menu. Instead, you must load it explicitly or as an extension Snap-in.

Creating and Opening Arbitrary Group Policy Objects

Each instance of the Group Policy Snap-in displays a single Group Policy Object. You can select exactly which GPO to load by starting the Group Policy Snap-in explicitly as follows:

1. Start a blank instance of the Microsoft Management console by clicking Start|Run, typing **mmc,** and clicking OK.

2. Click Console|Add/Remove Snap-in (or just press Ctrl+M).

3. On the Standalone tab, click Add.

4. Select Group Policy and click Add from the resulting dialog box. The dialog box is shown in Figure 12.5.

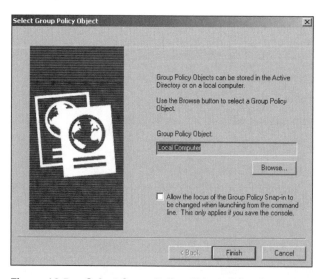

Figure 12.5   Select Group Policy Object dialog box.

5. By default, the Local Computer Policy (for the current machine) is selected. Click the Browse button to select any Group Policy Object from the forest or the Local Computer Policy for any computer. The Browse for a Group Policy Object Wizard appears (see Figure 12.6).

6. An existing GPO can be selected either by its position in domain/OU or by site. Local Computer Policy can be loaded by computer name or by browsing, and in addition, Group Policy Objects for a domain can be viewed by name from the All tab.

    Alternatively, a new Group Policy Object can be created in the current container with the middle of the three unlabelled buttons (marked in Figure 12.6).

7. Highlight the GPO to edit and click OK, then click Finish to load the Snap-in.

Creating and Opening Group Policy from Other Snap-Ins

Instead of having to create consoles for every Group Policy Object, it's possible to access the GPOs associated with a given site, domain, or OU as properties of these objects within other Active Directory administration tools.

Site Group Policy

Group Policy Objects that apply to sites are dealt with through Active Directory Sites and Services MMC Snap-in and, in particular, through the Properties dialog boxes for individual site objects.

To view the list of Group Policy Objects for a site:

1. Start Active Directory Sites and Services from the Administrative Tools menu.

2. Right-click on the site in question and select Properties.

3. Switch to the Group Policy tab (see Figure 12.7).

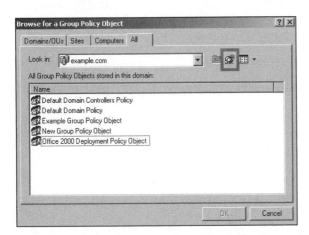

Figure 12.6   Browse for a Group Policy Object Wizard.

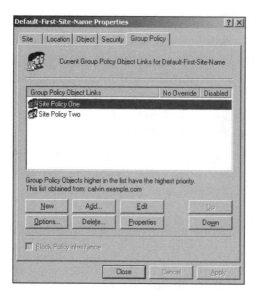

Figure 12.7   Group Policy Properties tab.

The list of Group Policy Objects linked to a site is shown in the main list. To open a Group Policy Snap-in focused on a particular GPO:

1. Left-click the GPO to view in the Group Policy Object Links list.

2. Click Edit.

To create a new GPO for the site, use the New button from the dialog box.

Domain and Organizational Unit Group Policy

Group Policy Objects that apply to domains and OUs are, in effect, the same thing (if you consider the domain root as an OU above all other OUs). Group Policy is configured for both in the same way through the Active Directory Users and Computers MMC Snap-in. The Group Policy tab of the Properties dialog box is (almost) the same for domains/OUs as it is for sites.

To view the list of Group Policy Objects for a domain or OU:

1. Start Active Directory Users and Computers from the Administrative Tools menu.

2. Right-click on the domain/OU in question and select Properties.

3. Switch to the Group Policy tab.

The list of Group Policy Objects linked to a site is shown in the main list. To open a Group Policy Snap-in focused on a particular GPO:

1. Left-click the GPO to view the Group Policy Object Links list.

2. Click Edit.

To create a new GPO for the site, use the New button from the dialog box.

Linking Group Policy Objects to Containers

As well as being able to create entirely new Group Policy Objects, you can also add GPOs that already exist in the directory to another container. This process is known as *linking*.

To link a GPO to a container:

1. Start Active Directory Sites and Services or Active Directory Users and Computers from the Administrative Tools menu.

2. Right-click on the container to link a GPO to it and select Properties.

3. Switch to the Group Policy tab.

4. Click the Add button. The Add a Group Policy Link dialog box appears.

5. Select a GPO to link, either by its existing links to domains, OUs, and sites or from a list of all GPOs for a particular domain.

6. Click OK when done.

Changing Group Policy Processing Order within a Container

It's possible to add several Group Policy Objects to the same site, domain, or OU. In such circumstances, the order of application becomes important, because it affects the order of precedence that the settings take in the case of conflict.

The various Group Policy Objects linked to a particular container are listed in its Properties tab (see Figure 12.8). The GPO at the bottom of the list is processed first. This means that the settings of the top GPO take precedence over all others (unless No Override is used for lower settings).

To adjust the processing order, it's possible to float links up and down on a per-container basis. To do this, select a Group Policy Object Link and use the Up and Down buttons.

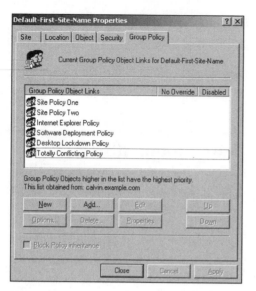

Figure 12.8   A site with numerous linked Group Policy Objects.

Setting No Override

No Override is set on a per-GPO link basis. Settings from the GPO that are linked to a container and flagged for No Override won't be replaced by any policies that are processed later, regardless of whether Block Inheritance is used or whether subsequent GPOs are also No Override.

To set a link to be No Override:

1. Use Active Directory Sites and Services or Active Directory Users and Computers to locate the site/domain/OU to have the No Override GPO applied to, as appropriate.

2. Right-click on the site/domain/OU in question and select Properties.

3. Switch to the Group Policy tab.

4. Select the GPO to set No Override for.

5. Click Options. The Options dialog box (see Figure 12.9) appears.

6. Check the No Override box. A Confirmation dialog box appears.

7. Click OK to close the Options dialog box.

8. Click OK again.

Figure 12.9   Group Policy Object Options dialog box.

Setting Block Inheritance

Blocking Group Policy Inheritance prevents all but No Override Group Policy settings from higher levels over the site/domain/OU hierarchy. Block Inheritance can be set at either the domain or OU level. The option is disabled for sites (because nothing is available to block).

To Block Inheritance for a domain or OU:

1. Use Active Directory Sites and Services to locate the site in question or Active Directory Users and Computers to locate the domain/OU in question.

2. Right-click on the object to Block Inheritance on and select Properties.

3. Switch to the Group Policy tab.

4. Check the Block Policy Inheritance box.

5. Click OK.

Disabling a Group Policy Object for a Container

This solution refers to disabling an entire Group Policy Object from a single container (that is, the link from the GPO to that container). It doesn't disable a portion of the GPO or affect it in another container.

One of the main uses for this feature is troubleshooting Group Policy problems. To disable a GPO from a container:

1. Use Active Directory Sites and Services or Active Directory Users and Computers to locate the site/domain/OU in question, as appropriate.

2. Right-click on the object to disable a GPO from and select Properties.

3. Switch to the Group Policy tab.

4. Select the GPO to disable.

5. Click Options. The Options dialog box appears.

6. Check the Disabled box. A Confirmation dialog box appears. Click Yes to accept.

7. Click OK to close the Options dialog box.

8. Click OK again.

Disabling Portions of Group Policy Objects

To speed Group Policy processing, and, hence, reduce boot and logon times, it's possible to disable any unused portions of GPOs. Each GPO has two portions: computer and user. Disabling a portion will prevent that half of the GPO from being processed. Because reading a GPO with only default values takes time, disabling an unused portion saves time. Disabling portions will also prevent any settings in them from being processed. It's possible to disable both halves of a GPO in this way, although the preferred method is simply to disable the GPO altogether.

An unused portion can be disabled as follows:

1. Open the Group Policy Object to partially disable in the Group Policy MMC Snap-in.

2. Right-click the GPO's name in the left-hand tree and select Properties.

3. At the bottom of the General tab, check the appropriate box to disable a portion of the GPO.

4. A Confirmation dialog box appears. Click Yes to accept. You won't be prompted for confirmation again until you close and reopen the Properties dialog box.

5. Click OK.

Deleting a Group Policy Object

When deleting a GPO, you can either simply delete a single link of the GPO to a particular container (thus leaving the GPO alive and well in the directory), or you can delete it in its entirety.

To do either for a GPO that is currently linked to a container:

1. Use Active Directory Sites and Services or Active Directory Users and Computers to locate the site/domain/OU linked to the GPO in question, as appropriate.

2. Right-click on the object to delete the GPO from and select Properties.

3. Switch to the Group Policy tab.

4. Select the GPO to delete.

5. Click Delete. The Delete dialog box (see Figure 12.10) appears.

6. Use the radio button to choose whether you wish to remove the GPO from this container but leave it in the directory ("Remove the link from the list", the default) or do both that and delete it from Active Directory ("Remove the link and delete the Group Policy Object permanently").

7. Click OK.

8. Click OK again.

TIP: *If you wish to delete a GPO that's no longer linked to anything, use the Group Policy Snap-in to find it in the domain list, right-click it, and select Delete.*

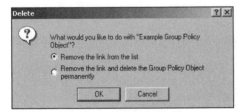

Figure 12.10   Group Policy Object Delete question.

Immediately Refreshing Group Policy

There may be times when you wish changes in Group Policy to happen right away, instead of having to wait until the next refresh interval or logging out the current user/restating the computer. In order to force an immediate refresh of either user or computer Group Policy, use the **secedit.exe** command line tool that is included with Windows 2000. To refresh computer policy type:

```
C:\>secedit /refreshpolicy machine_policy /enforce
```

And to refresh user policy type:

```
C:\>secedit /refreshpolicy user_policy /enforce
```

12. Understanding Group Policy

Chapter 13

Implementing and Troubleshooting Group Policy

In Depth

The mechanics of Group Policy and the basics of managing Group Policy Objects were introduced in Chapter 12. This chapter is devoted to exploring exactly what you can achieve with Group Policy and how you can achieve it.

Group Policy is an extremely complex area, and there are a great many settings available to administrators with a multitude of different effects and subtleties. One chapter is not enough to explain every setting in nauseating detail and it is not my intention to do so.

Instead, this chapter lists all settings with cursory explanation, but will explain the most important ones in detail. With the Windows 2000 Server Resource Kit, there is a help file (gp.chm) that explains most Group Policy settings in great detail.

Computers

The first portion in the Group Policy Snap-in is for settings that apply when the GPO is used on a computer object. Like all of Group Policy, this is divided into a tree-like structure of folders, which contain policy leaves and other folders. The Group Policy MMC Snap-in is shown focused on computer settings in Figure 13.1.

NOTE: *Cases exist where the same option is found in both the Computer and User sections of Group Policy. If the same setting is applied to a computer and a user logging on to that computer, the computer settings will take precedence (because at bootup, computer policy is applied first). For example, many offline file's policy settings are handled in this way.*

Software Settings

Group Policy allows software packages that employ the Microsoft Installer technology (msi files) to be deployed to users or computers. In the case of computers, deployed software is automatically installed as the computer boots up. Unlike most other settings, software installation policy isn't refreshed periodically, and computers must be restarted for new software to be installed if it's assigned to computers.

TIP: *Windows 2000 computers can be restarted remotely using the **shutdown.exe** tool with the **/R** switch from the Windows 2000 Resource Kit.*

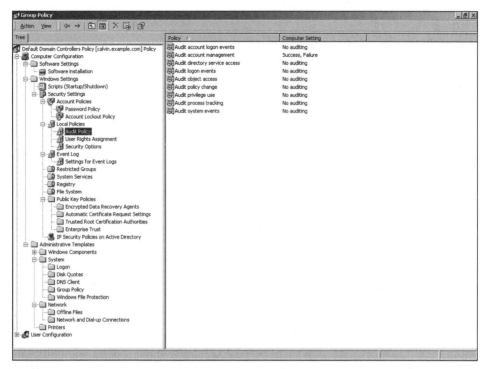

Figure 13.1   MMC Console showing Computer Group Policy settings.

Software deployment is a complex subject that you need to fully understand. For this reason, it deserves a chapter to itself, so it's covered in Chapter 14. A quick point to note that often concerns people who hear about software installation for the first time is that you can prevent software installation over slow links—installing several hundred megabytes of Office 2000 over a modem connection must be anything but pretty.

Scripts (Startup/Shutdown)

The Windows Settings structure can contain a variety of policies that apply to the operating system and its components. In the case of computers, for example, it allows you to run startup and shutdown scripts, as well as to define a whole host of security-related settings.

Two lists of scripts can be defined: one each for startup and shutdown scripts. Startup scripts are executed before users log in, and shutdown scripts run after a user logs off and the system is being shut down. Scripts are added to a GPO with the dialog box shown in Figure 13.2 or with the Shutdown equivalent.

Scripts can be added and removed with the buttons to the right, and the processing order can also be modified. In effect, any file that Windows can execute can

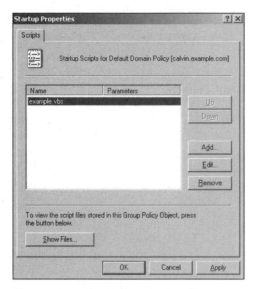

Figure 13.2   Startup Properties dialog box.

be added as a startup script: batch files (bat) can be used, Windows Scripting Host (vbs files, and so forth) can, of course, be used and are becoming the norm, but executable files can also be used, for example. Script parameters can also be specified. Startup and shutdown scripts run in the system context on the local computer.

Security Settings

Security settings cover a variety of policies that relate to account lockout, password complexity, auditing, logon rights, the event log, as well as a whole host of others such as IPSec and public key cryptography.

Account Policies

Account Policies comprise three distinct sets of polices, which are applied only at domain controllers: They're divided into three areas:

Password Policy comprises settings that are used to set restrictions on user passwords. Simple passwords are easy to guess and crack, and a single cracked password may be able to be used by an intruder to obtain a foothold before compromising a network more fully. For this reason many organizations, particularly those with Internet connections, enforce complex passwords on their users. Usually this would take the form of a minimum length, some form of complexity, and a history to prevent passwords being recycled. The available options for Password Policy are the following:

- *Enforce password history*—If enabled, this sets the number of passwords to remember (up to 24). When a password is changed, it's compared against the list and discarded if it's a repeat. The idea here is to prevent users from reusing the same password again and again.

NOTE: *Without a "minimum password age" also in place, this setting could be useless, because all a user has to do is change her password 24 times in quick succession, then change it back to its old value if she doesn't want to keep remembering a new password.*

- *Maximum password age*—This is used to specify the maximum number of days until a user has to change his password, except that a setting of 0 is identified with never having to change a password.

- *Minimum password age*—The minimum number of days between password changes.

- *Minimum password length*—The minimum number of characters in a password. The value of 0 (default) means that no password is required.

- *Passwords must meet complexity requirements*—If enabled, this setting ensures that all password changes and creations meet the requirements set down in passfilt.dll. By default, these requirements are: a length of at least six characters, a stipulation that no part of the account name can be in the password, and a stipulation that characters from three of the following four classes must be present—lowercase letters, uppercase letters, numbers, and nonalphanumeric characters.

- *Store password using reversible encryption for all users in the domain*— Usually, passwords are stored as hash functions without the information to derive the password text from the hash (this is reversible, because no encryption is truly unbreakable—it's just very hard to reverse), but an additional reversible version of the password is needed in some circumstances. Macintosh logins require reversible passwords for the associated user account, for example. Reversible encryption can be configured on a per-user basis through Active Directory Users and Computers. This setting is not normally required and, as it presents some form of security loosening, should only be enabled if necessary, for example to support downlevel RAS servers or Macintosh connectivity.

Account Lockout Policy determines the behavior of locking out accounts for failed passwords. Crackers may try to repeatedly log on to an account with a range of common passwords using an automated tool and perhaps a dictionary and list of names. To thwart this, you should lock out an account that has repeated failed logon attempts.

The need to do this, however, must be balanced against extra calls to the helpdesk that would be generated by a user who can't type. Typically something like 3 or 5 logon attempts is usual before an account gets locked out.

The available policy settings are:

- *Account lockout duration*—When an account is locked out through bad logon attempts, this policy specifies the number of minutes until it is automatically re-enabled. A value of 0 means that the account must explicitly have the lockout removed.

- *Account lockout threshold*—The number of failed logon attempts that must occur before an account is locked out.

- *Reset account lockout counter after*—The number of minutes before the account lockout count is reset to zero. This value should really be lower than account lockout duration, or an account won't be reenabled as expected.

Kerberos Policy is used to configure the Kerberos authentication protocol for a domain. These settings are generally suitable for most organizations.

- *Enforce user logon restrictions*—If enabled, this causes an extra step to be taken when a session ticket is requested to verify that the user has the right to Log On Locally or to Access This Computer From The Network (as appropriate).

- *Maximum lifetime for service ticket*—The maximum duration that a service ticket is valid for (in minutes, and anything from 10 minutes to the Maximum Lifetime For User Ticket, and 600 minutes by default).

- *Maximum lifetime for user ticket*—The number of hours that a Ticket Granting Ticket can be used before renewal (10 by default).

- *Maximum lifetime for user ticket renewal*—When a ticket lifetime has expired, you can allow it to be renewed by setting this value (a number of days, seven by default).

- *Maximum tolerance for computer clock synchronization*—The maximum number of minutes that can differ between the timestamp on ticket requests and the current timestamp on computers. A large value here is less secure, because it opens up the possibility of replay attacks that reuse intercepted authenticators. The default of 5 minutes should be fine for most purposes.

Week/Day/Hour/Minute/Second Conversions

Many Group Policy settings require times to be specified in seconds or minutes. The following bullets list common conversion values:

- One minute is 60 seconds.
- Five minutes is 300 seconds.

- Ten minutes is 600 seconds.
- Thirty minutes is 1,800 seconds.
- One hour is 60 minutes or 3,600 seconds.
- Five hours is 300 minutes or 18,000 seconds.
- Ten hours is 600 minutes or 36,000 seconds.
- One day is 24 hours or 1,440 minutes or 86,400 seconds.
- One week is seven days, or 168 hours, or 10,080 minutes, or 604,800 seconds.

Local Policies

Local Policies comprise three areas: audit policies that determine whether or not certain events are audited, user rights assignment that allows specific rights to be granted to or denied from people using the current computer, and various security options that relate to system-wide security configuration, such as renaming certain accounts or disabling Ctrl+Alt+Del at logon.

Audit Policy can be used to set whether or not nine types of events are enabled or disabled for auditing. Each setting can be Not Audited, or Audited for Success, Failure, or both.

- Audit account logon events
- Audit account management
- Audit directory service access
- Audit logon events
- Audit object access
- Audit policy change
- Audit privilege use
- Audit process tracking
- Audit system events

Auditing consumes resources and disk space, and is of course only useful if you actually bother to read the audit logs. In general, it may be worth auditing some failed events, but auditing successes except in specific instances is unwise due to the overheads created.

The User Rights Assignment folder of policies consists of the following settings, and each policy item can have users or groups added to it:

- Access this computer from the network
- Act as part of the operating system
- Add workstations to domain

- Back up files and directories
- Bypass traverse checking
- Change the system time
- Create a pagefile
- Create a token object
- Create permanent shared objects
- Debug programs
- Deny access to this computer from the network
- Deny logon as a batch job
- Deny logon as a service
- Deny logon locally
- Enable computer and user accounts to be trusted for delegation
- Force shutdown from a remote system
- Generate security audits
- Increase quotas
- Increase scheduling priority
- Load and unload device drivers
- Lock pages in memory
- Log on as a batch job
- Log on as a service
- Log on locally
- Manage auditing and security log
- Modify firmware environment values
- Profile single process
- Profile system performance
- Remove computer from docking station
- Replace a process level token
- Restore files and directories
- Shut down the system

NOTE: *The option, Synchronize Directory Service Data, is present but not functional in the initial release of Windows 2000.*

- Take ownership of files or other objects

In the Default Domain Controllers GPO, it is necessary to give users the right to log on locally if you wish them to use the domain controller console. Other settings here are important, and not setting them may be the cause of "access denied"-type error messages.

The final type of Local Policies is Security Options, and the following settings are available:

- *Additional restrictions for anonymous connections*—Restrictions can be placed either on the enumeration of users and shares (remember that a prerequisite to gaining unauthorized access to a resource is knowledge that it exists) or all anonymous access not explicitly allowed.

- *Allow server operators to schedule tasks (domain controllers only)*—This permits members of the Server Operators Group to use the **AT** command to submit jobs. It doesn't apply to the Task Scheduler.

- *Allow system to be shut down without having to log on*—This enables the Shut Down option on the Windows 2000 Logon box. This is enabled by default in Windows 2000. Of course, leaving it disabled doesn't prevent people from using the power switch.

- *Allowed to eject removable NTFS media*—This specifies who may eject NT File System (NTFS). By default, it's Administrators only, but just Power Users or Interactive (anyone logged on locally) may be added.

- *Amount of idle time required before disconnecting session*—The time in minutes that must elapse before a server drops a Server Message Block (SMB) session. The default is 15 minutes.

- *Audit the access of global system objects*—This setting is equivalent to setting a System-audit Access Control List (SACL) on system objects, so that if Audit object access is also configured, then access to objects, such as mutexes, events, semaphores, and DOS devices, will be audited.

- *Audit use of Backup and Restore privileges*—Any exercise of Backup or Restore privileges will be audited if this setting is enabled and Audit privilege use is also.

- *Automatically log off users when logon time expires*—Enabling this will force any user in the domain to be logged off out of logon hours. Otherwise, they'll still have access to resources after they log off.

- *Automatically log off users when logon time expires (local)*—Enabling this will force any user on the local computer to be logged off.

- *Clear virtual memory pagefile when system shuts down*—Windows 2000 uses a pagefile on disk as an extension to RAM, and systems that hibernate dump the contents of their RAM to disk before hibernating. Memory, and

13. Implementing and Troubleshooting Group Policy

hence these files, may contain data meant to be kept secure. Enabling this policy option will erase the contents of these files when a user logs off and a system returns from hibernation.

- *Digitally sign client communication (always)*—This prevents man-in-the-middle attacks on SMB communication by always using a digital signature on client communication. Connections to servers that don't support signing will fail. The digital signature is computed from the packet contents at the client, then recalculated and verified at the server. A man-in-the-middle attack would change the data in transit and, hence, invalidate the signature.

- *Digitally sign client communication (when possible)*—This attempts to negotiate digitally signed SMB communication but will use unsigned ones if signing isn't supported by the server.

- *Digitally sign server communication (always)*—This will only support signed SMB packets.

- *Digitally sign server communication (when possible)*—This will attempt to negotiate SMB packet signing.

- *Disable Ctrl+Alt+Del requirement for logon*—Windows 2000 usually requires Ctrl+Alt+Del to be pressed before a user logs on (a key combination that can't be sent across a network). This often confuses users, and if utmost security isn't a priority, it can be disabled with this policy setting.

- *Do not display last user name in logon screen*—Windows 2000 usually populates the username of the login screen with the last user to log on. The thinking here is that the same person often uses the same workstation day in, day out. This can be disabled, because it isn't appropriate in highly secure environments where usernames are kept secret or in public environments, such as cyber cafés or universities, where the same person rarely logs in twice in a row.

- *LAN Manager Authentication Level*—LAN Manager (a pre-Windows NT Microsoft product) has three methods of authentication: LM, NTLM, and NTLM v2. This policy allows various combinations of them to be supported and others explicitly ignored.

- *Message text for users attempting to log on*—A dialog box can be displayed to users as they log on, perhaps giving some important information about how to use the system or providing a legal disclaimer. This policy specifies the text in the box.

- *Message title for users attempting to log on*—This policy specifies the title bar value for the message defined with the previous policy.

- *Number of previous logons to cache (in case domain controller is not available)*—If a domain controller is unavailable, it's still often desirable for users to be able to log on to get on with any work they can. To support this, local computers must cache a number of sets of credentials. This policy can vary from 0 (disabled cache) through 50. Values above 50 are taken to mean 50, and 10 is the default.

- *Prevent system maintenance of computer account password*—For security reasons, computer account passwords are changed automatically every seven days. This policy will prevent these automatic changes from taking place.

- *Prevent users from installing printer drivers*—Enabling this policy will stop members of Users (but not Power Users) from adding printers that don't already have a driver installed on the system.

- *Prompt user to change password before expiration*—Specifies the number of days before a password is due to expire that warnings start appearing for users.

- *Recovery Console: Allow automatic administrative logon*—If this is enabled, restarting with the Windows 2000 Recovery Console (a simple command-line interface) will give automatic administrative access.

- *Recovery Console: Allow floppy copy and access to all drives and all folders*— Enabling this allows certain flags to be specified within the Recovery Console to extend functionality.

- *Rename administrator account*—This policy allows you to specify a new name for the built-in Administrator account. Organizations often rename their Administrator account to thwart attackers (if they don't know the logon name they can't get in), although this technique is only effective if they also can't enumerate the accounts on the computer.

- *Rename guest account*—Allows you to specify a new name for the built-in guest account.

- *Restrict CD-ROM access to locally logged-on user only*—This prevents CD-ROM drives from being accessed via the network.

- *Restrict floppy access to locally logged-on user only*—This policy prevents floppy disk drives from being accessed via the network.

- *Secure channel: Digitally encrypt or sign secure channel data (always)*— Secure channels are established between domain members and domain controllers through computer account passwords to ensure sensitive requests are authenticated. Not all such requests are encrypted by default. Enabling this policy forces all such requests to be encrypted (a processor overhead does this), and secure channels can't be established if the other party doesn't support them.

- *Secure channel: Digitally encrypt secure channel data (when possible)*— This policy will encrypt secure channel data if both ends are configured to support it but will rely on authentication only if necessary.

- *Secure channel: Digitally sign secure channel data (when possible)*—If this is enabled, all secure traffic will be signed to prevent man-in-the-middle attacks.

- *Secure channel: Require strong (Windows 2000 or later) session key*—If enabled, the requested encryption key strength will be such that only Windows 2000 or later domain controllers support the secure channel.

- *Secure system partition (for RISC platforms only)*—This policy is designed to secure the file allocation table (FAT) system partition on reduced instruction set computing (RISC) machines. What it's still doing in Windows 2000 after Alpha processor support was dropped many months before release is anyone's guess.

- *Send unencrypted password to connect to third-party SMB servers*—This option allows authentication with non-Microsoft SMB servers to be negotiated with clear text (unencrypted) passwords sent over the network. Unencrypted authentication is, in general, a Very Bad Thing as it's trivial to scan for passwords on a network. Only use this option if you really have to.

- *Shut down system immediately if unable to log security audits*—On highly secure systems you don't want to miss any security events from the log. If for any reason a logging fails, then this policy will shut the system down.

- *Smart card removal behavior*—If smart-card logon is used, this policy gives the option of locking the workstation, logging the user off, or continuing normally if the smart card is removed.

- *Strengthen default permissions of global system objects (for example, Symbolic Links)*—Prevents nonadministrators from modifying system objects.

- *Unsigned driver installation behavior*—In an effort to provide users with a method to identify high-quality drivers, Microsoft has introduced the concept of digitally signed drivers that can have their authenticity verified by the Windows Hardware Quality Lab. The options are to prevent the use of unsigned drivers, prompt (default), or silently install (that is, ignore the fact that they aren't signed).

- *Unsigned non-driver installation behavior*—Software applications can also be signed by their creators. This policy also offers the choice of ignoring the lack of digital signature, warning about it, or refusing to install unsigned software.

Event Log

The *Event Log policy folder* contains only one child: Settings for Event Logs. Beneath that, the following policy options can be configured to manage the access to and the size of event logs.

In Windows 2000, several Event Logs exist and are used by a variety of components, services, and applications to record information (particularly errors and warnings). They can be accessed on servers and workstations with the Event Viewer MMC Snap-in.

The options that can be configured are the following:

- Maximum application log size
- Maximum security log size
- Maximum system log size
- Restrict guest access to application log
- Restrict guest access to security log
- Restrict guest access to system log
- Retain application log
- Retain security log
- Retain system log
- Retention method for application log
- Retention method for security log
- Retention method for system log
- Shut down the computer when the security audit log is full

Restricting guest access to log files prevents guest users from viewing particular logs. In all cases, users require the "Manage Auditing And Security Log" right in order to access the security log.

Maximum log sizes are specified in kilobytes and default to half a megabyte each. Computers can be configured to shut down if the security log is full to prevent people from performing actions that can't be audited or from those that cause old audit events to be lost. This is particularly applicable in high-security environments where certain types of actions must be audited for business or security reasons.

Log retention can either be for a fixed period (that can be specified in days) by the last n kilobytes (so old items are overwritten as needed), or logs can be retained until they're manually deleted.

Restricted Groups

The idea behind *Restricted Groups* is that there are certain Security Groups that it's desirable to have tight membership control over, so through Group Policy, it's possible to specify the membership of these groups and also the groups that they're members of. When Group Policy is applied, the membership of these groups will be reverted back to that specified by Restricted Groups. It's normal only to use Restricted Groups for nondomain controllers, and not for domain administration.

System Services

The *System Services folder* gives a list of the services that run on Windows 2000 and allows their startup to be configured and permissions to be applied to them. A typical service Policy Setting dialog box is shown in Figure 13.3. With this policy, it's possible to centrally manage which services start on sets of computers, and who can manage them.

Registry

The *Registry folder* allows you to set security on registry keys and, hence, lockdown items from prying users. In common with all of Group Policy, it's applied securely (that is, users cannot override these settings) and will be removed when the Group Policy Object no longer applies.

File System

Similar to the Registry folder, the *File System folder* allows you to set security on various files and folders on the computer, just as you would through Windows Explorer.

Public Key Policies

Public Key Policies are used to configure aspects of public key cryptography on computers. You can add users to the list of recovery agents able to read all data encrypted with Encrypting File System (EFS) and have computers automatically request and install a client certificate so they can participate in activities that require them. Also, additional Certificate Authorities can be trusted, so common trust exists for all applicants of the Group Policy Object (GPO).

More information on public keys, and public key cryptography (often called PKI—Public Key Infrastructure) can be found on the Web at **www.microsoft.com/windows2000/library/planning/security/pki.asp**.

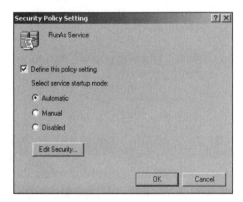

Figure 13.3   Typical service Policy Setting dialog box.

IP Security Policies on Active Directory

IP Security (IP Sec) is an encrypted form of IP communications. IP Sec policies dictate how computers make and respond to IP Sec requests. This area of Group Policy allows you to specify common IP Sec policies for computers. It's possible to assign one of the three default policies that require or request IP Sec for servers or clients. IP Security is beyond the scope of this book. Information can be found on the Web at **www.microsoft.com/windows2000/library/technologies/security**.

Administrative Templates

Administrative Templates are essentially text files of a certain specification, which are contained in the Group Policy Template for a particular GPO. They're used to configure arbitrary registry settings on client computers. Microsoft provides a number of Administrative Templates for Windows 2000, and it's possible to edit these and to add your own.

Windows Components

The first Administrative Template in the list deals with software components in Windows. The only setting under the Netmeeting folder is Disable Remote Desktop Sharing. *Netmeeting* is an online collaboration application that usually comes with Internet Explorer. One of its features allows a user running Netmeeting to permit a person she's in a meeting with to take over her desktop remotely, in a similar but more restrictive way than using products such as PC Anywhere. This policy setting allows you to prevent a computer's desktop from being shared.

The following Internet Explorer options can be configured:

- Security Zones: Use only machine settings.

- Security Zones: Do not allow users to change policies.

- Security Zones: Do not allow users to add/delete sites.

- Make proxy settings per-machine (rather than per-user).

- Disable Automatic Install of Internet Explorer components.

- Disable Periodic Check for Internet Explorer software updates.

- Disable software update shell notifications on program launch.

- Disable showing the splash screen.

The Windows 2000 Task Scheduler (a vast improvement on the **AT** command) also has a number of settings that can be configured:

- Hide Property Pages

- Prevent Task Run or End

- Disable Drag-and-Drop
- Disable New Task Creation
- Disable Task Deletion
- Disable Advanced Menu
- Prohibit Browse

Finally, in this template, a number of settings for the Windows Installer service can be configured for the computer:

- Disable Windows Installer
- Always install with elevated privileges
- Disable rollback
- Disable browse dialog box for new source
- Disable patching
- Disable IE security prompt for Windows Installer scripts
- Enable user control over installs
- Enable user to browse for source while elevated
- Enable user to use media source while elevated
- Enable user to patch elevated products
- Allow admin to install from Terminal Services session
- Cache transforms in secure location on workstation
- Logging

System

The following settings, broadly titled System, cover various aspects of operating system configuration:

- Remove Security option from Start menu (Terminal Services only)
- Remove Disconnect item from Start menu (Terminal Services only)
- Disable Boo/ Shutdown/Logon/Logoff status messages
- Verbose versus normal status messages
- Disable Autoplay
- Don't display welcome screen at logon
- Run these programs at user logon
- Disable the run once list
- Disable legacy run list

- Do not automatically encrypt files moved to encrypted folders
- Download missing COM components

Also beneath system settings are the following, which pertain to user logon:

- Run logon scripts synchronously
- Run startup scripts asynchronously
- Run startup scripts visible
- Run shutdown scripts visible
- Maximum wait time for Group Policy scripts
- Delete cached copies of roaming profiles
- Do not detect slow network connections
- Slow network connection timeout for user profiles
- Wait for remote user profile
- Prompt user when slow link is detected
- Timeout for dialog boxes
- Log users off when roaming profile fails
- Maximum retries to unload and update user profile

Disk Quotas are a new feature in Windows 2000 that can track and limit disk space by users on a per-volume basis. They're managed through the Quota tab on the volume in question, accessed through Windows Explorer, for example. The available Group Policy settings are the following:

- Enable disk quotas
- Enforce disk quota limit
- Default quota limit and warning level
- Log event when quota limit exceeded
- Log event when warning level exceeded
- Apply policy to removable media

Beneath the DNS Client option, the Primary Domain Name System (DNS) Suffix for the computer can be configured. Windows 2000 also supports connection-specific DNS naming as well as just the primary suffix, which is used to create the primary DNS name.

A variety of Group Policy settings are configured through Group Policy. They're as follows:

- *Disable background refresh of Group Policy*—Enabling this policy will prevent Group Policy from being updated periodically when computers are on or users are logged in.

- *Apply Group Policy for computers asynchronously during startup*—By default, Group Policy is applied synchronously, which takes longer but is more predictable than asynchronous processing, because each task waits for the previous one to finish before starting. This policy causes computer policy to be processed asynchronously, that is quickly and not necessarily sequentially.

- *Apply Group Policy for users asynchronously during logon*—This policy causes user policy to be processed asynchronously.

- *Group Policy refresh interval for computer*—Used to specify the refresh interval and random offset in minutes for Group Policy refresh on nondomain controllers. The default is 90 minutes with a 30 minutes offset. A value of zero is identified with seven seconds.

- *Group Policy refresh interval for domain controllers*—Used to specify the refresh interval and random offset in minutes for Group Policy refresh on domain controllers. The default is five minutes with zero minute offset. A value of zero is, again, identified with seven seconds.

- *User Group Policy loopback processing mode*—Normally the computer portions of GPOs that apply to the computer and the user portions of GPOs that apply to the user are processed. With loopback processing enabled, the user portion of GPOs that apply to the computer can also be processed either instead of (replace) or after (merge) normal user GPOs. Lookback processing happens last, so its policies will win through in the event of conflicts. Loopback processing can be enabled on a per-computer basis, so for example, it can be used with Terminal Services to provide a different (perhaps more restricted) user experience.

- *Group Policy slow link detection*—This policy sets the threshold (in Kbps) for what's considered a slow link for Group Policy purposes. The default is 5,000Kbps.

Each of the nine policy processing options allows you to specify whether or not a particular subset of policies are applied and whether they're applied over slow links when policy is refreshed, regardless of whether they've changed.

- Registry policy processing

- Internet Explorer Maintenance policy processing

- Software Installation policy processing

- Folder Redirection policy processing

- Scripts policy processing

- Security policy processing

- IP Security policy processing

- EFS recovery policy processing

- Disk Quota policy processing

The final four system options come under the heading Windows File Protection (WFP). Windows File Protection is a mechanism designed to stop you from ruining the operating system. Quite simply, on a default installation of Windows 2000, you can delete a file protected by WFP and it will be re-created.

- *Hide the file scan progress window*—Enabling this will stop the scan progress window being displayed to prevent it from confusing anyone.

- *Limit Windows File Protection cache size*—WFP requires disk space to be able to keep copies of critical files to make replacements with. This policy lets you set a maximum number of megabytes for the file cache.

- *Set Windows File Protection scanning*—This option allows you to configure WFP to scan files at every startup or just the next startup. This doesn't affect the normal operation of Windows File Protection, which replaces critical system files if they're ever deleted.

- *Specify Windows File Protection cache location*—This option allows you to move the cache from its default, hidden (%SystemRoot%\system32\dllcache) location.

Network

A new feature in Windows 2000 is Offline Files. In effect, it is to network shares what Internet Explorer's Temporary Internet Files is to the Internet: an offline cache. More than that, it allows you to open files when disconnected from the network, edit them, and then synchronize them back into the main file server when you return to the network.

- *Enabled*—This policy setting enables Offline Files on the computer.

- *Disable user configuration of Offline Files*—Setting this policy will prevent end users from reconfiguring Offline File support.

- *Synchronize all offline files before logging off*—Two levels of synchronization are available: quick and full. Enabling this policy performs a full synchronization that ensures that files are complete and up-to-date. A quick synchronization only ensures that all files are synchronized and doesn't check their timestamps.

- *Default cache size*—Sets the size of the Offline File cache as a percentage of disk space.

- *Action on server disconnect*—When a network connection is lost, this policy can specify whether or not files can be used.

- *Non-default server disconnect actions*—This policy allows override to the previous one for specific servers.

- *Disable "Make Available Offline"*—Normally, users are able to choose certain files to use offline. This policy disables that option but still allows files designated on their server for offline use to be cached.

- *Prevent use of Offline Files folder*—This disables a button to show the contents of the offline folder from Offline Files configuration. It doesn't stop users from viewing the folder in other ways, though.

- *Files not cached*—This is a semicolon-separated list of file extensions that should not be cached.

- *Administratively assigned offline files*—A list of Uniform Naming Convention (UNC) paths to folders that are made offline.

- *Disable reminder balloons*—Normally, periodic reminders appear near the system tray to warn a user that he or she is offline. This policy allows those reminders to be disabled.

- *Reminder balloon frequency*—This is the number of minutes between reminder balloons.

- *Initial reminder balloon lifetime*—The duration in seconds that the first reminder is shown for.

- *Reminder balloon lifetime*—The duration in seconds that subsequent reminders are shown for.

- *At logoff, delete local copy of user's offline files*—This clears the offline file cache at logoff, even if changes have been made to the offline files.

- *Event logging level*—Allows you to specify one of four levels of logging that range from logging data corruption only to logging when servers are available.

- *Subfolders always available offline*—Usually, the option to include subfolders is presented when a folder is marked for offline use. With this policy enabled, all existing and new subfolders of offline folders are made available offline without user intervention.

The only option beneath Network and Dial-up Connections is Prohibit Configuration Of Connection Sharing. Connection sharing is a feature built in to Windows 2000, which is great for allowing a small network to share a single Internet connection but inappropriate for a large office from a security perspective.

Printers

The following options are available to configure printing for computers:

- Allow printers to be published

- Automatically publish new printers in Active Directory

- Allow pruning of published printers
- Printer browsing
- Prune printers that are not automatically republished
- Directory pruning interval
- Directory pruning retry
- Directory pruning priority
- Check published state
- Web-based printing
- Custom support URL in the Printers' folder's left pane
- Computer location
- Pre-populate printer search location text

Users

The second portion of each GPO is applied at login time based on the user's location in the Active Directory. Any policies that are previously configured by computer Group Policy Objects can't be overwritten by values in user Group Policy Objects.

Software Settings

Similar to computers, software can be deployed to users with Group Policy. It can either be published, so users have the option to install it, or assigned so it's always available (and installed at logon if it isn't currently available). Chapter 14 covers software installation in detail.

Windows Settings

The next folder in the user portion of Group Policy is called Windows Settings and contains everything else except Administrative Templates.

Internet Explorer Maintenance

The following folders are available to configure Internet Explorer for users.

The Browser User Interface folder can be customized with the following:

- *Browser Title*—This allows you to add custom text to the title of Internet Explorer and change the background image behind the toolbar buttons.
- *Animated Bitmaps*—This allows you to replace the animated Internet Explorer logo with a custom animated bitmap.
- *Custom Logo*—This allows you to replace the static Internet Explorer logo with a custom bitmap.

- *Browser Toolbar Buttons*—This allows you to customize the toolbar by adding or removing buttons.

The Connection folder allows the following to be configured:

- *Connection Setting*—Essentially, this lets you specify the values in the Connection tab of the Internet Properties dialog box.

- *Automatic Browser Configuration*—This allows a URL for an auto-configuration script to be specified.

- *Proxy Settings*—This permits proxy settings to be specified, such as the IP address and port of a Web proxy server.

- *User Agent String*—This lets you add a custom string to the HTTP User Agent String. User Agent Strings are sent with all HTTP requests, are logged by Web servers, and can be used programmatically by Web designers to influence page behavior and page display.

The URL folder allows customization of favorites, links, homepage, search page, and online support URL. Also, you can customize the channels available. The headings to configure these items under are the following:

- Favorites and Links

- Important URLs

- Channels

From the Security folder, you can establish Security Zones, Content Ratings, and Authenticode Settings for recipients of the Group Policy Object, so for example, you can centrally define security zones for computers and enforce ratings in schools. The Programs folder allows you to customize the Programs page of the Internet Options dialog box and, hence, set features, such as the default mail and news clients, for a computer.

Scripts (Logon/Logoff)

Scripts can be designed to run for users to execute at logon and logoff in exactly the same way as described previously for computer startup and shutdown scripts.

Security Settings

The only security setting that can be configured on a per-user basis is Certificate Trust Lists.

Remote Installation Services

Remote Installation Services (RIS, pronounced as "rizz") is a Windows 2000 technology that can be used to deploy Windows 2000 Professional (and Server, although this is unsupported). Client computers boot using either their network card or a special boot disk, and users are then able to install Windows 2000 and perhaps one of several different customized versions with appropriate applications

- Disable application Sharing
- Prevent Application Sharing in true color
- Prevent Control
- Prevent Desktop Sharing
- Prevent Sharing
- Prevent Sharing Command Prompts
- Prevent Sharing Explorer windows

The Audio and Video policies are as follows:

- Disable Audio
- Disable full duplex Audio
- Limit the bandwidth of Audio and Video
- Prevent changing DirectSound Audio setting
- Prevent receiving Video
- Prevent sending Video

The Options Page policies are as follows:

- Disable the Advanced Calling button
- Hide the Audio page
- Hide the General page
- Hide the Security page
- Hide the Video page

If you thought there were too many policy settings for NetMeeting, you'll want to skip the next few pages that chronicle every possible way to disable obscure Internet Explorer menu items. The main Internet Explorer settings are as follows:

- Disable AutoComplete for forms
- Disable Internet Connection Wizard
- Disable caching of Auto-Proxy scripts
- Disable changing Advanced page settings
- Disable changing Automatic Configuration settings
- Disable changing Calendar and Contact settings
- Disable changing Messaging settings
- Disable changing Profile Assistant settings

- Disable changing Temporary Internet files settings
- Disable changing accessibility settings
- Disable changing certificate settings
- Disable changing color settings
- Disable changing connection settings
- Disable changing default browser check
- Disable changing font settings
- Disable changing history settings
- Disable changing home page settings
- Disable changing language settings
- Disable changing link color settings
- Disable changing proxy settings
- Disable changing ratings settings
- Disable external branding of Internet Explorer
- Disable importing and exporting of favorites
- Disable the Reset Web Settings feature
- Display error message on proxy script download failure
- Do not allow AutoComplete to save passwords
- Identity Manager: Prevent users from using Identities
- Search: Disable Find Files via F3 within the browser
- Search: Disable Search Customization
- Use Automatic Detection for Dial-up Connections

Individual pages of the Internet Control Panel can also be disabled with these policies:

- Disable the Advanced page
- Disable the Connections page
- Disable the Content page
- Disable the General page
- Disable the Programs page
- Disable the Security page

Offline Pages and channels can be managed, also. The subscription limits can specify times, size limits, and link depth. The policies are as follows:

- Disable adding channels
- Disable adding schedules for offline pages
- Disable all scheduled offline pages
- Disable channel user interface completely
- Disable downloading of site subscription content
- Disable editing and creating of schedule groups
- Disable editing schedules for offline pages
- Disable offline page hit logging
- Disable removing channels
- Disable removing schedules for offline pages
- Subscription Limits

The following menu items can be disabled:

- Disable Context menu
- Disable Open in New Window menu option
- Disable Save this program to disk option
- File menu: Disable New menu option
- File menu: Disable Open menu option
- File menu: Disable Save As Web Page Complete
- File menu: Disable Save As...menu option
- File menu: Disable closing the browser and Explorer windows.
- Help menu: Remove "For Netscape Users" menu option
- Help menu: Remove "Send Feedback" menu option
- Help menu: Remove "Tip Of The Day" menu option
- Help menu: Remove "Tour" menu option
- Hide Favorites menu
- Tools menu: Disable Internet Options...menu option
- View menu: Disable Full Screen menu option
- View menu: Disable Source menu option

Toolbars can be locked down with these three settings:

- Configure Toolbar Buttons
- Disable customizing Browser Toolbar buttons
- Disable customizing Browser Toolbars

13. Implementing and Troubleshooting Group Policy

Per-domain and per-file limits can be imposed for sites using DHTML Persistence behavior in each Internet Explorer zone to preserve disk space. The following policies can set limits in kilobytes:

- File size limits for Internet zone
- File size limits for Intranet zone
- File size limits for Local Machine zone
- File size limits for Restricted Sites zone
- File size limits for Trusted Sites zone

Finally, for Internet Explorer, Administrators can prevent the use of various add-ins and controls:

- Carpoint
- DHTML Edit Control
- Investor
- MSNBC
- Media Player
- Menu Controls
- Microsoft Agent
- Microsoft Chat
- Microsoft Scriptlet Component
- Microsoft Survey Control
- NetShow File Transfer Control
- Shockwave Flash

Someone's use of Windows Explorer can be controlled with the following settings:

- Disable DFS tab
- Disable UI to change keyboard navigation indicator setting
- Disable UI to change menu animation setting
- Disable Windows Explorer's default context menu
- Do not request alternate credentials
- Do not track Shell shortcuts during roaming
- Enable Classic Shell
- Hide Hardware tab
- Hide these specified drives in My Computer
- Hide the Manage item on the Windows Explorer context menu

- Maximum number of recent documents
- No "Computers Near Me" in My Network Places
- No "Entire Network" in My Network Places
- Only allow approved Shell extensions
- Prevent access to drives from My Computer
- Remove "Map Network Drive" and "Disconnect Network Drive"
- Remove File menu from Windows Explorer
- Remove Search button from Windows Explorer
- Remove the Folder Options menu item from the Tools menu
- Request credentials for network installations

Through a subfolder, these settings can also be configured to configure the Common File Open dialog box, as used by most applications:

- Hide the common dialog back button
- Hide the common dialog places bar
- Hide the drop-down list of recent files

Someone's ability to use the Microsoft Management Console can be restricted with the following two options:

- Restrict the user from entering author mode
- Restrict users to the explicitly permitted list of Snap-ins

If the latter of these is enabled, then users can only access explicitly permitted Snap-ins. It's possible to explicitly deny or permit the use of Snap-ins by name through the Restricted/Permitted Snap-Ins folder. Beneath this lie options for Extension Snap-ins and options to control access to individual parts of Group Policy.

A user's ability to use the Task Scheduler can be controlled with the following options:

- Disable Advanced menu
- Disable Drag-and-Drop
- Disable New Task Creation
- Disable Task Deletion
- Hide Property Pages
- Prevent Task Run or End
- Prohibit Browse

13. Implementing and Troubleshooting Group Policy

The following options can be configured for the Windows Installer service:

- Always install with elevated privileges
- Disable media source for any install
- Disable rollback
- Search order

Start Menu and Taskbar

The following options can each either be enabled or disabled to establish Start Menu possibilities for users:

- Remove user's folders from the Start menu
- Disable and remove links to Windows Update
- Remove common program groups from Start menu
- Remove Documents menu from Start menu
- Disable programs on Settings menu
- Remove Network and Dial-up Connections from Start menu
- Remove Favorites menu from Start menu
- Remove Search menu from Start menu
- Remove Help menu from Start menu
- Remove Run menu from Start menu
- Add Logoff to the Start menu
- Disable Logoff on the Start menu
- Disable and remove the Shut Down command
- Disable drag-and-drop context menus on the Start menu
- Disable changes to Taskbar and Start menu settings
- Disable Context menus for the taskbar
- Do not keep history of recently opened documents
- Clear history of recently opened documents on exit
- Disable Personalized menus
- Disable user tracking
- Add "Run in Separate Memory Space" check box to Run dialog box
- Do not use the search-based method when resolving shell shortcuts
- Do not use the tracking-based method when resolving shell shortcuts
- Gray unavailable Windows Installer programs Start menu shortcuts

Desktop

Desktop configuration covers several different areas of the Windows 2000 user interface. First, for the desktop itself, you can set the following self-explanatory options:

- Hide all icons on Desktop
- Remove My Documents icon from desktop
- Remove My Documents icon from Start menu
- Hide My Network Places icon on desktop
- Hide Internet Explorer icon on desktop
- Do not add shares of recently opened documents to My Network Places
- Prohibit user from changing My Documents path
- Disable adding, dragging, dropping, and closing the Taskbar's toolbars
- Disable adjusting desktop toolbars
- Don't save settings at exit

Active Desktop (a series of enhancements introduced with Internet Explorer 4 and not to be confused with Active Directory) is built in to Windows 2000, and the following options can be set:

- Enable Active Desktop
- Disable Active Desktop
- Disable all items
- Prohibit changes
- Prohibit adding items
- Prohibit deleting items
- Prohibit editing items
- Prohibit closing items
- Add/Delete items
- Active Desktop wallpaper
- Allow only bitmapped wallpaper

Finally, in the Desktop administrative template, a number of Active Directory settings can be configured:

- *Maximum size of Active Directory searches*—This policy is a limit on the number of search results for general directory operations, such as browsing for objects (for example, when adding users to a group). The default is 10,000.

- *Enable filter in Find dialog box*—The filter bar is an extension to the Windows 2000 Find dialog box that allows search results to be refined further. Enabling this policy makes the filter bar available to users (see Figure 13.5).

- *Hide Active Directory folder*—By default, users are able to browse the Active Directory through My Network Places. Enabling this policy prevents that.

Control Panel

The Windows 2000 Control Panel, although slightly reorganized from the Windows NT Control Panel, is still used to configure numerous system tasks. Its settings can be controlled by Group Policy, and it can be locked down, so users can't access it.

- *Disable Control Panel*—Enabling this will hide Control Panel shortcuts from users and prevent them from running any control panel applets by preventing **control.exe** from running.

- *Hide specified control panel applets*—This allows a list of cpl files to be hidden from the current user to be specified.

- *Show only specified control panel applets*—This removes all but the specified cpl files from the current user.

NOTE: If both Hide Specified Control Panel applets and Show Only Specified Control Panel applets are configured, then Show Only Specified Control Panel applets is ignored.

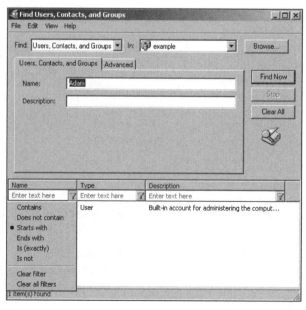

Figure 13.5   Find dialog box with filter bar.

Sidebar: **13. Implementing and Troubleshooting Group Policy**

One of the Control Panel applets that can be locked down is Add/Remove programs:

- *Disable Add/Remove Programs*—This applet prevents users from launching the Add/Remove Programs applet.

- *Disable Support Information*—This one removes the "click here for support information" hyperlink that appears next to some installed applications, when they're selected.

- *Go directly to Components Wizard*—The applet hides the "Set up services" part of Add/Remove Programs that appears if system services, such as Remote Installation Services (RIS), have been installed but not configured.

- *Hide Add New Programs page*—This option doesn't display the Add New Programs button, which prevents users from adding software published with Group Policy, from using Add/Remove Programs to connect to Windows Update, or from using the Run Installation Program Wizard.

- *Hide Add/Remove Windows Components page*—This applet doesn't display the Add/Remove Windows Components button and, hence, prevents the installed Windows components from being reconfigured.

- *Hide Change or Remove Programs page*—By selecting this option, you hide the main page that lists installed applications and allows their removal or reinstallation.

- *Hide the "Add a program from CD-ROM or floppy disk" option*—This applet removes the chance to launch the Run Installation Program Wizard from the Add New Programs page.

- *Hide the "Add programs from Microsoft" option*—This one removes the Windows Update button from the Add New Programs page.

- *Hide the "Add programs from your network" option*—This removes this option from the Add New Programs page.

- *Specify default category for Add New Programs*—Categories are used when publishing software to break down potentially huge lists of available applications within a company. This policy sets the default category to display on the Add New Programs page.

The Display applet (often accessed by right-clicking on the Windows desktop) allows you to configure the appearance of Windows. Some of the settings from the applet can be configured from the Administrative Template:

13. Implementing and Troubleshooting Group Policy

NOTE: *Certain display properties, such as screen resolution; color depth; and refresh rate, can't be set by Group Policy, because they're hardware-dependent.*

- *Activate screen saver*—Disabling this policy prevents screen savers from being run.

- *Disable Display in Control Panel*—This disables the entire Display applet.

- *Disable changing wallpaper*—This stops a user from changing the desktop wallpaper and other settings on the Background tab.

- *Hide Appearance tab*—This policy prevents the Appearance tab from being shown. The Appearance tab is used to configure colors and fonts.

- *Hide Background tab*—This policy keeps the Background tab from being shown. The Background tab is used to configure a background image/HTML document and pattern.

- *Hide Screen Saver tab*—This prevents the Screen Saver tab from being shown and, hence, any screen saver or energy saving monitor configuration from taking place.

- *Hide Settings tab*—Selecting this option prevents the Settings tab from being shown, so desktop size and color depth can't be configured.

- *Password protect the screen saver*—Enabling this policy password protects the screen saver, so users must employ their password.

- *Screen Saver timeout*—This policy specifies the time in minutes of inactivity required to initialize the screen saver.

- *Screen saver executable name*—Specifies the exe file of the screen saver to use.

The Printers' section allows control over what a user can do with the Printers' applet in Control Panel:

- *Browse a common web site to find printers*—Windows 2000 is able to add new printers through Web links. This policy allows you to specify a custom URL that users browsing for printers will be directed to.

- *Browse the network to find printers*—This policy exists so that it can be disabled and force users to look in Active Directory to find printers.

- *Default Active Directory path when searching for printers*—Location tracking is another method users can employ in a search for printers. Specifying a value for this policy provides a default location string. For example, it could represent the office that objects in a particular OU are present in.

- *Disable addition of printers*—Enabling this policy prevents users from adding extra printers.

- *Disable deletion of printers*—With this policy enabled, users can't delete printers that are already configured.

The sole option beneath Regional Options allows you to Restrict Selection Of Windows 2000 Menus And Dialogs Language. With Windows 2000, it's possible to have multiple languages available on the same computer, and with this policy setting, you can restrict a user to a particular language.

Network

The Offline Files options are identical to those in the computer portion. In the event of a conflict, the computer settings take precedence because they're applied first and are secured, as all Group Policy options are.

- Action on server disconnect
- Administratively assigned offline files
- Disable "Make Available Offline"
- Disable reminder balloons
- Disable user configuration of Offline Files
- Event logging level
- Initial reminder balloon lifetime
- Non-default server disconnect actions
- Prevent use of Offline Files folder
- Reminder balloon frequency
- Reminder balloon lifetime
- Synchronize all offline files before logging off

The following Network and Dial-up Connections options are all self-explanatory and are designed to prevent users from tinkering with their network options.

- Prohibit TCP/IP advanced configuration
- Prohibit access to current user's RAS connection properties
- Prohibit access to properties of RAS connections available to all users
- Prohibit access to properties of a LAN connection
- Prohibit access to properties of components of a LAN connection
- Prohibit access to properties of components of a RAS connection
- Prohibit access to the Advanced Settings item on the Advanced Menu
- Prohibit access to the Dial-up Preferences item on the Advanced Menu
- Prohibit access to the Network Connection Wizard
- Prohibit adding and removing components for a LAN or RAS connection
- Prohibit configuration of connection sharing
- Prohibit connecting and disconnecting a RAS connection
- Prohibit deletion of RAS connections

- Prohibit deletion of RAS connections available to all users

- Prohibit enabling/disabling a LAN connection

- Prohibit enabling/disabling components of a LAN connection

- Prohibit renaming LAN connections or RAS connections available to all users

- Prohibit renaming of RAS connections belonging to the current user

- Prohibit viewing of status statistics for an active connection

System

The following options control the behavior of aspects of the operating system:

- *Century interpretation for Year 2000*—To back millennium issues, Windows has a feature to support the interpretation of two-digit years. This policy specifies the highest two-digit year assumed to be in the twenty-first century. The default is 29, so 1/1/29 is interpreted as January 1, 2029, whereas 1/1/30 is interpreted as January 1,1930.

- *Code signing for device drivers*—If you're trying to install unsigned device drivers, this specifies the appropriate response: block, warn, or ignore.

- *Custom user interface*—This option allows you to specify an executable file to use as an alternative to the Explorer user interface.

- *Disable Autoplay*—Disables the default behavior of running the application specified by autorun.inf on CD-ROMs and DVD-ROMs. The default options are to set this for all drives or just for CD-ROM drives (which, in fact, disables it on drives of unknown type, removable drives, CD-ROM drives, and network drives).

- *Disable registry editing tools*—This option, when selected, prevents a user from employing **regedit.exe** and **regedt32.exe**. It doesn't prevent third-party registry editors or scripts from being used to edit the Registry, so it's ineffective against determined troublemakers without setting permissions on the Registry.

- *Disable the command prompt*—This keeps the command prompt (**cmd.exe**) from being used.

- *Don't display welcome screen at logon*—The option suppresses the Getting Started with Windows 2000 screen.

- *Don't run specified Windows applications*—Selecting this option keeps a list of executables from being run.

- *Download missing COM components*—If the operating system can't find a required COM component to provide certain functionality, it will search Active Directory in an attempt to find it if this policy is enabled. The default behavior is equivalent to disabling this policy.

- *Run only allowed Windows applications*—When you select this option, you can prevent a user from executing any application, except those specified.

Settings beneath Logon/Logoff control behavior relating to users logging on or off and associated events, such as changing their password or locking a workstation.

- *Connect home directory to root of the share*—Windows 2000 has redefined the %HOMESHARE% and %HOMEPATH% environment variables and maps %HOMEDRIVE% to slightly different places than Windows NT 4 (although combinations of them will still work as intended). Enabling this policy restores the Windows NT 4 behavior, which may be required if you use the environment variables in nonstandard ways.

- *Disable Change Password*—This option stops a user from changing his password unless prompted to by the system, for example, when his password is about to expire.

- *Disable Lock Computer*—Stops a user from locking a computer.

- *Disable Logoff*—This prevents a user from logging off by any method.

- *Disable Task Manager*—This option keeps a user from launching Task Manager, which is used to display system information, process information, and launch tasks.

- *Disable legacy run list*—Disables the list defined by Run These Applications At Startup.

- *Disable the run once list*—Opting for this policy prevents the applications listed in HKLM\Software\Microsoft\Windows\CurrentVersion\RunOnce from being executed at startup.

- *Exclude directories in roaming profile*—This policy provides a semicolon-separated list of folders to exclude from a user's roaming profile. History, Local Settings, Temp, and Temporary Internet Files are excluded, by default, through other means.

- *Limit profile size*—This specifies a maximum size for a user's profile in KB, along with options for warning her about it.

- *Run legacy logon scripts hidden*—If you want to hide the output of batch files that run at logon, select this policy option.

- *Run logoff scripts visible*—This policy outputs the instructions of logoff scripts as they execute.

- *Run logon scripts synchronously*—If you want to keep Windows Explorer from starting before all logon scripts have completed running, use this option.

- *Run logon scripts visible*—This policy outputs the instructions of logon scripts as they execute.

- *Run these programs at user logon*—This specifies a list of programs to run when a user first logs in to a computer.

The following Group Policy options can be configured for users:

- *Create new Group Policy Object links disabled by default*—If enabled, the selection of this policy means that creating a new Group Policy Object in a container or adding a new link to an existing GPO will leave the link disabled by default to prevent it from being processed until the creator is ready.

- *Disable automatic update of ADM files*—Normally when the Group Policy Snap-in is opened, the ADM files are updated automatically. Enabling this policy prevents that, which means they must be refreshed manually.

- *Enforce Show Policies Only*—Administrative Templates can contain both "true" policies (anything specified in the Registry under Software\Policies or Software\Microsoft\Windows\CurrentVersion\Policies) and preferences (everything else). Enabling this setting hides the options for everything else from the Group Policy Snap-in.

- *Group Policy domain controller selection*—This policy determines how a domain controller is located when the Group Policy Snap-in is used. The primary domain controller (PDC) Operations Master role holder, a domain controller found in the normal way, or the same domain controller that Active Directory Users and Computers (or Sites and Services) is connected to can be used.

- *Group Policy refresh interval for users*—This policy specifies how often Group Policy is refreshed for users, and it specifies the random offset. The default is 90 minutes, with 30 minutes offset.

- *Group Policy slow link detection*—This option specifies the threshold in Kbps for what constitutes a slow link for user policy.

Immediate Solutions

Group Policy Results

Often, the first concern when troubleshooting Group Policy is to know exactly what policies have been applied. A client-side utility to test Group Policy application is **gpresult.exe** from the Windows 2000 Server Resource Kit.

The command-line tool, **presult.exe**, will output a report detailing the Group Policy that has been applied. By default, it will display information for the current computer and the current user policies. To restrict it to just computer policy, use the **/c** switch and use the **/u** switch to display just user policies.

Three levels of detail are available: default (no switch), verbose (**/v**) and super verbose (**/s**). Default output includes the following:

- *System information*—This option provides the time of the report, operating system version, and whether Active Directory or terminal services are installed.

- *Object information*—This gives you the current user/computer, domain and site name, as well as profile information for users.

- *Security Group membership*—Because they can be used to filter GPOs, the security groups that the user/computer belongs to are listed.

TIP: *If you need a quick list of security group memberships* **gpresult.exe** *is useful to get that.*

- *Last GPO application information*—This policy provides the time that Group Policy was last applied and the domain controller it was applied from.

- *GPOs Applied*—This is a list of setting areas and the Group Policy Objects that applied them.

In Verbose mode, additional information is present:

- *Security privileges*—For user information, privileges, such as whether a user can change the system time, are displayed.

- *GPOs Applied*—Instead of just listing setting areas, the exact GPO revision, Globally Unique Identifier (GUID), and container that it's linked to are displayed, as well as the settings themselves (script file names, Registry changes, and so forth). Binary registry values are suppressed.

In binary registry, values are displayed as hex dumps. The command prompt width should be increased to at least 85 so these display correctly. In general, Verbose mode is sufficient and Superverbose mode need only be checked if you wish to view the binary Registry data.

Even Default mode produces a lot of information, and you must increase the buffer length for the Command Prompt (from Properties on its System Menu) or redirect the output to a file using **>filename** at the end of the command line. For example, to pipe verbose output for the current computer to a file called GPOInfo.txt, type:

```
C:\>gpresult /v /c >GPOInfo.txt
```

Group Policy Verification

A second command-line tool from the Windows 2000 Server Resource Kit for Group Policy management and troubleshooting is **gpotool.exe**. One of the main uses of GPO tool is to perform a health check on Group Policy Objects around the domain.

In Verbose mode, it also reports the version numbers of each GPO verified on each domain controller specified. By default, all GPOs are tested on every domain controller in the current domain.

The following options are available:

- */gpo:GPOName,GPOName…*—The **/gpo** switch specifies the name or names of Group Policy Objects to verify. If omitted, all GPOs are verified. The Group Policy Objects names given may be partial matches.

- */domain:DomainName*—The **/domain** switch is used to specify an Active Directory domain, other than the current domain, to test Group Policy for.

- */dc:DomainController,DomainController…a*—The **/dc** switch allows you to specify a list of domain controllers to verify on. Not specifying a list will check all DCs in the domain.

- */checkacl*—This is an additional test to verify that the Access Control List on sysvol can be specified.

- */verbose*—In addition to checking GPOs, Verbose mode outputs status information, such as version numbers and extension GUIDs.

Chapter 14

Change and Configuration Management

In Depth

Change and Configuration Management is a buzz phrase that refers to a number of Windows 2000 features responsible for managing user preferences, user data, software, and remote installation of Windows 2000.

NOTE: *Another buzzword, Intellimirror, specifically refers to the first three of these technologies.*

Data and software management functionality is tied up in roaming profiles, Group Policy, and other filing system capabilities covered in Chapters 12, 13, and 15. This chapter focuses on the Software Deployment options available in Group Policy and remote operating system installation through what is known as Remote Installation Services (RIS).

Software Deployment

With the aid of Group Policy, software can be deployed to computers running Windows 2000 operating systems. Software can be associated with users or computers, so for example, a user can always have a certain application available, and fixes can be deployed to computers. In technical terms, Software Deployment options let you run Windows Installer (msi) files on the target systems. This means that you can deploy anything that an msi file can contain—be it a driver update, set of company files, or even an application.

Windows Installer Technology

The msi files are intended as a replacement for **setup.exe** files used to install applications on Windows 2000. They add additional features to improve software management, and in particular, make uninstallation easier. They do this by using a common cache of installed files, so when an application is removed, the correct files are removed with it.

Another benefit of Windows Installer Technology is that this file cache is used to make applications self-healing. For example if **winword.exe** is deleted and Microsoft Word) is subsequently executed, the fact that winword.exe is missing is noticed and attempts will be made to replace it. In the case of software installed from the network, it will then be replaced automatically, and for other installs, the user will be prompted for the original installation media.

Other features include just-in-time installation where additional attributes are made available through menu items but are not actually present on disk and only installed on first use. For example, numerous converters are available for obscure word processing formats, so instead of installing them all by default, they can be installed only as needed.

In addition to msi files, transformations in the form of mst files and patches in msp files are used to customize application installations and patch applications, respectively. Transforms are used to set installation options, and patch files are similar to msi files except they can only upgrade existing msi files and are limited in exactly what they can do (essentially, they can only add/replace features, not remove them). Software Deployment can take place through Group Policy in three ways.

Assigning Software to Computers

Applications can be assigned to computers as part of machine Group Policy. Software Deployment settings are only processed when a computer restarts, and all msi files housed within the settings (and any other method by Group Policy) install under Elevated Privileges. Software assigned to a computer is available, by default, to all users of a computer.

TIP: *The **shutdown.exe** tool from the Windows 2000 Resource Kit can be used to remotely restart computers if you need Software Deployment policy to be processed immediately.*

Assigning Software to Users

Software can also be assigned to users, so it follows them around as they move from computer to computer. For example, an administrator could assign herself the Windows 2000 Server Resource Kit and Support Tools for Organizational Units that contain Windows 2000 Server Computers, so they are always available to her on these machines. Assigned software will be installed during a user's logon process if it's not already present on the machine.

TIP: *A threshold can be set for Software Deployment Group Policy processing so software doesn't get installed over painfully slow links. If you don't want to experience an installation of Office 2000 over a dial-up link, make sure that slow links are defined appropriately in Group Policy and Software Installation isn't allowed over a slow network connection.*

Publishing Software to Users

In addition to software being assigned to users, it can also be published to them. Unlike assigned software, packages that are published aren't added by default and, instead, must be invoked. Invocation can either be through the Add/Remove

Programs applet, clicking on a shortcut for the application, or by document invocation. Extensions associated with software assigned by Group Policy are stored in Active Directory, and if no local application is associated with the extension of a document that is clicked on, a request will go to the directory. If this request is matched by a suitable application that can be installed, then it will be.

Software Maintenance

Group Policy Software Deployment options don't just cover the basics of installing software on computers. They also provide the ability to manage software once it has been deployed. Software packages can be patched, redeployed, upgraded, and removed.

Patching Packages

In addition to msi files, Windows Installer also uses patch files known as msp files. Application writers can create an msp file to patch an existing application. When installing software interactively, users can use msp files to update applications. With Group Policy Software Deployment, msp files aren't deployed directly and, instead, should be applied to msi files on distribution servers. These msi files can then be redeployed to clients.

Redeploying Packages

The option exists within Group Policy to redeploy an existing application. Redeployment will simply reinstall the package on systems that it's already deployed to. The main purpose of redeploying an application is to make updates available to users. For example, if you replace the msi file of an application on disk, then redeploying the package will cause the new msi file to be installed on client systems. Similarly, if a software vendor supplies a patch (msp) file, then this can be run on the source msi file to update it, and the package can then be redeployed.

Redeploying applications doesn't change the friendly name of the application nor does it update association with file extensions. For example, if you're supplied with a new msi file that should have a different description to the package it replaces (Office 2000 Service Release 1, for example), then redeployment isn't the best option. Instead, you should deploy the new msi file as an upgrade to the previous package.

Upgrading Packages

A feature of Windows Installer Technology is the ability to upgrade other software. An upgrade package is deployed in place of an old package and can either be a mandatory upgrade or an optional upgrade. Msi packages can be configured to upgrade existing packages. For example, A package for a newer version of Microsoft Office can be configured to upgrade the already-deployed package for Office 2000. Various options exist to control the upgrade behavior; for example, you can either install the new msi file on top of the old package, or remove the old one before installing afresh. In another instance, if a new version of Microsoft Office becomes available, you could deploy it as an optional upgrade to Office 2000. In this way, any workers relying on specific features or custom templates for Office 2000 can continue using them, but other users will be able to have the latest version available.

Removing Packages

Packages deployed by Group Policy can also be removed by Group Policy. To do this, select the package targeted for removal. Removing a package gives you one of two choices:

- Immediately uninstalling the software from users and computers.

- Allowing users to continue using the software but preventing new installations.

The former of these options will completely remove the software the next time that software policy is processed. You should select this choice if the application is no longer to be used—for example, if your license to use it expires, if it's no longer needed, or if company policy dictates that it should be removed. It will also remove the package from the GPO, so it can no longer be installed.

The second choice will only remove the package from the GPO and not affect any currently installed instances of the packages. These instances will have to be deleted manually using Add/Remove Programs on individual desktops.

Repackaging Applications

Not every application comes with an msi file. In fact, the technology was only introduced with Microsoft Office 2000, so a great many applications developed before that date exist without them, as well as many applications published since then that don't use msi files.

One technique to get msi files for these applications is to nicely ask the company that publishes the software. Although this approach may work if you're a big customer of a friendly software house, the request will usually fall on deaf ears. An alternative is to create your own. With the aid of the WinInstall LE software bundled with Windows 2000, it's possible to take a "before" image of a system, make arbitrary changes, and take an "after" snapshot that's differenced against the "before" snapshot; the results are saved as an msi file. This msi file can then be edited using a supplied console to add files, Registry entries, shortcuts, and so forth.

When repackaging applications by imaging, it's essential to understand that all changes made between the two snapshots—and only changes made in that period—are saved as part of the msi file. For example, if you install an application that requires a shared DLL that's already on the system, then this DLL doesn't become part of the msi file. Hence, if the package is deployed to a computer without the DLL, then the application won't function. Conversely, if you make an unrelated change to the computer, such as getting a new Minesweeper high score (which changes a Registry setting), then this also becomes part of the package file.

It's essential, therefore, to repackage only applications deployed on a completely vanilla installation of Windows 2000, and to ensure that inadvertent changes are not made to the Registry or other files. Instructions on repackaging applications are included in the "Immediate Solutions" with this chapter.

ZAP Files

Zero Administration Windows application package (ZAP) files are text files with the .zap extension. They can be created for applications that don't have msi installation files and that you haven't repackaged and used to publish the applications to users via Group Policy.

Software published with zap files can't be assigned and is, instead, only published in Add/Remove Programs or made available through document invocations. Because zap files aren't installed by the Windows Installation Service, they don't install with elevated privileges and, in effect, the old setup.exe is simply executed, so user intervention may be required. This means that zap files can only be associated with users, not with computers.

Software Deployment and Systems Management Server

One of the first questions from anyone familiar with SMS who hears about Windows 2000 Software Deployment technology is quite simple: How do the two relate? For one thing, Systems Management Server has many more features than Windows 2000—it contains inventory and network management tools, for example. Also, its Software Deployment supports multiple-operating systems and not just Windows 2000.

Remote Installation Services

Remote Installation Services (RIS) is a Windows 2000 technology that allows Windows 2000 Professional to be deployed to client computers over a network with minimal intervention at the user end. In fact, RIS is designed as a method for end users to install (or reinstall) the operating system and preconfigured applications over the network.

To use RIS, you need an Active Directory domain and a Dynamic Host Configuration Protocol (DHCP) server on your network, as well as a RIS server. At the client side, you need either network adaptors supporting at least Pre-boot eXecution Environment (PXE) version .99c or a network card supported by the RIS boot disk.

WARNING! *Clients installed with the default RIS image will have a NULL administrator password. This isn't a problem if you know about it and deal with it, so this warning is here to make you aware of the fact.*

Overview

At the client side, all it takes to install a copy of Windows 2000 via Remote Installation Services is a supported network card and sufficient logon credentials. The ability to add new computers to a domain can be delegated to ordinary users. Security can be employed to specify that only particular machines can be added and also to restrict a user's choice of which RIS image to use.

The RIS installation process actually installs Windows 2000 with no user intervention required, and then adds settings and files as required. This means that it's hardware-independent and the Hardware Abstraction Layer (HAL) of the computer Windows 2000 is being deployed to doesn't matter (except for RIPrep images).

RIS Architecture

Remote Installation Services consists of three server-side processes that are installed by the installation option of adding RIS from the Windows 2000 Components Wizard. These services are as follows:

- *Boot Information Negotiation Layer (BINL)*—BINL is a main RIS responsible for responding to client requests.

- *Trivial File Transfer Protocol Daemon (TFTPD)*—Trivial FTP is a low overhead method of transferring files over a network, and it's employed to send files to RIS clients from the RIS server.

- *Single Instance Store (SIS)*—The single instance store is responsible for saving space on the drive containing images. It manages multiple copies of the same file by deleting all but one and storing references in place of the others.

RIS Client Process

Clients use PXE to obtain an IP address and the details of a RIS server. When RIS is initialized at the client end, a DHCP discover packet is sent out. This discover packet asks for both an IP address and a boot server. Hopefully, one or more DHCP offer packets are sent. DHCP servers use offer packets to alert clients to their presence and ability to assign IP addresses; a RIS server will also respond with an offer.

The client will then request an IP address from a DHCP server (which is acknowledged with the IP address), and request a boot server from the RIS server (which is acknowledged with the RIS server's IP address and the address of the first file to download).

NOTE: *If the RIS server is also a DHCP server, then only one request packet will be sent to it, and one acknowledgment will cover all details.*

RIS servers can be configured to respond only to known clients. This option increases security because it means that only machines that already have computer accounts in the directory can have an operating system installed via RIS. A RIS server configured to respond only to known clients will ignore requests from unknown computers, and no offer packet will be sent to them.

RIS Images

When a client connects to a RIS server to install an operating system, it receives a list of possible configurations to install, known as images. An image can be anything from a simple, no-intervention installation of Windows 2000 to a fully configured system with numerous applications configured. By default, only a basic Windows 2000 Professional image is installed.

SIF Files

Setup answer files, also known just as *answer files*, are text files that specify how Windows 2000 should be configured. They can be created by hand according to specifications in the unattend.doc document contained in the \support\tools\deploy.cab cabinet file on the Windows 2000 Server CD-ROM or via the Setup Manager Wizard (**setupmgr.exe**) from the same location. They're, in effect, Windows INI files with a different name, and they can be used to specify custom settings, such as post-installation tasks, and specific Windows components to install (or not). For example, you can use a sif file to ensure that Windows 2000 games aren't installed.

RIPrep Images

Remote Installation Preparation (RIPrep) images are complete images of the source computer. They're more restrictive than other images, because the computers that they are deployed to must have a matching HAL. RIPrep images are created by configuring a Windows 2000 computer as required, and then running a wizard over the network to copy the current configuration to a RIS server.

Using Multiple RIS Servers

In general, large organizations may require multiple RIS servers. Each must be installed, configured, and authorized properly. So the servers can all offer the same installation images to clients, the images must be copied between them. An option to do so exists within the management interface for RIS servers, or it's possible to copy images to disk (if that is more convenient, as it often is between locations where the disk can be couriered to reduce wide area network [WAN] traffic).

Because DHCP discover packets are used by clients to locate RIS servers, the usual DHCP rules apply, and the first RIS server to respond will service a client. RIS clients pay no attention to the available bandwidth when requesting installation, so you must be careful if a client is able to contact a RIS server over a WAN link.

NOTE: *Installing by RIS over a WAN link is only possible if a DHCP relay agent is in use on the local subnet or if the router has Boot Protocol (BOOTP) forwarding enabled—the two ways of allowing DHCP clients to obtain addresses from DHCP servers on remote subnets.*

When multiple RIS servers exist, it's possible to steer particular clients to particular servers by a process known as prestaging—effectively adding a computer account for the client to the network in advance and associating it with a particular RIS server.

Prestaging Clients

A RIS client is *prestaged* if a computer account is created for it in Active Directory and associated with the Globally Unique Identifier (GUID) of the client. The Globally Unique Identifier used by RIS is based on its network card's media access control (MAC) address. Existing computers that already have Windows 2000 installed can be prestaged, so if RIS is ever used to reinstall the operating system, the appropriate RIS server is used. Also, new computers can be prestaged, which requires you to enter its GUID. The facility exists to import a text file containing multiple GUIDs, and the hope from Microsoft is that vendors will supply a list of the GUIDs of new computers in a suitable format, if you ask nicely.

Configuring Remote Installation Services

Remote Installation Services can be installed through the Windows 2000 Components Wizard, either at setup time or later through Add/Remove Programs. Once it has been installed and the server rebooted, it must be configured. RIS is configured through the Set up services view of the Add/Remove Programs dialog box (see Figure 14.1), which will appear by default if you open Add/Remove Programs when there are services to configure.

To configure RIS, you need at least two volumes on the RIS server. The single instance store (SIS), which manages RIS images, can't run against a Windows 2000 system partition (the one with the %SystemRoot% directory, usually c:\winnt). This is because the SIS is responsible for managing duplicate files in the installation images and ensuring that data, such as the Windows 2000 install files, is only on the disk once, and running the SIS on the system partition would lead to difficulties with the copy of Windows 2000 that is actually running.

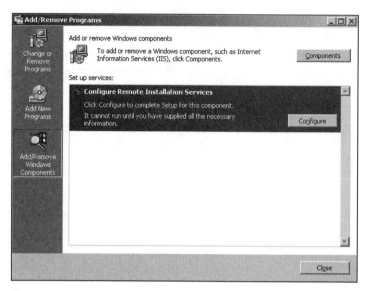

Figure 14.1   Set up services.

The volume that the RIS images are stored on must also be formatted NTFS, because new features of NTFS version 5 are required for the SIS to function. In addition, RIS servers should have static or reserved IP addresses, because they must be authorized in DHCP. To complete the configuration of a RIS server, you need a Windows 2000 Professional CD-ROM to supply the first default image that will enable a basic installation of Windows 2000 to take place over the network.

Computer Naming

The format of computer names generated for RIS-installed workstations can be specified on a per-RIS server basis. A naming format can be specified on the Advanced Settings dialog box under the Remote Install tab of a RIS server's computer object in Active Directory Users and Computers.

The special tokens available are the following:

- *%First*—Installing user's first name
- *%Last*—Installing user's last name
- *%Username*—Installing user's account name
- *%MAC*—Computer's media access control address
- *%#*—Incremental number to ensure uniqueness

These fields can be modified with a decimal number between the % and field name to specify a maximum number of letters, so for example, **%1First** gives just the first initial of a user. A variety of preconfigured naming schemes can be selected or a completely custom one entered.

NOTE: *Unfortunately, there's no way to pad out the incremental number to a given length.*

Immediate Solutions

Deploying a Package Using Group Policy

To deploy an msi file or a zap file by Group Policy, it must be associated with a Group Policy Object. To add a package to a GPO:

1. Open the GPO to add the package to the Group Policy Snap-in.

2. Expand either User Configuration or Computer Configuration (depending on whether you want the package associated with users or computers).

3. Expand Software Settings.

4. Click Software Installation in the left-hand pane. A list of existing packages appears.

5. Right-click Software Installation and select New, then Package. An Open file dialog box appears. Select the package to deploy or enter a filename. This should be in the form of a Uniform Naming Convention (UNC) path to a network location to ensure all clients can install the package. For large organizations it may be beneficial to use a DFS path here. DFS is covered in Chapter 15.

NOTE: *The Open dialog box for the User portion of a GPO allows you to select msi files or zap files. The Computer portion only allows msi files to be selected.*

---

6. If you didn't specify a network location in Step 5, you'll receive a warning.

7. The Deploy Software dialog box (see Figure 14.2) prompts you to select whether the package is Published, Assigned, or Advanced. Selecting Advanced allows transformations to be applied. Not all options may be available, depending on whether the package is associated with users or computers.

8. Click OK.

If Advanced was selected, then the package's Properties dialog box is launched. Do *not* click OK on the Properties dialog box until all transforms (mst files) are added to the Modifications tab, because they can't be modified later.

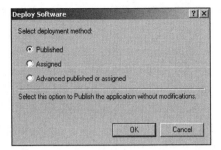

Figure 14.2   Deploy Software dialog box.

Patching an msi File

Vendors may supply updates to msi files in the form of msp files. To apply an msp patch file to an existing msi file use the **msiexec.exe** tool as follows:

```
C:\>msiexec /a example.msi /p patch.msi
```

Obviously, replace **example.msi** and **patch.msi** with the paths to the package and patch files, respectively. Once patched, the package should be redeployed.

Once a patched msi file is installed, the patch is inseparable from the application, and the only way to remove the patch alone is to remove the entire application and reinstall the unpatched .msi file.

Redeploying a Package

A package that has had its underlying msi file or msp file replaced should be redeployed so that it's reinstalled by all clients and users that the policy affects. Either replace or patch the msi file prior to performing these steps.

To redeploy a package:

1. Open the GPO containing the package with the Group Policy Snap-in.
2. Navigate to the package in question beneath Computer/User Configuration, then Software Settings, and finally, Software Installation.
3. Right-click the package, hover over All tasks, then select Redeploy application.
4. You're prompted to confirm. Click Yes. The package is redeployed.

14. Change and Configuration Management

Upgrading a Package

To upgrade a software package that has already been deployed, a new package must be created containing the upgrading msi file. This new package should then be configured to upgrade the old one as follows:

1. Open the GPO containing the new package with the Group Policy Snap-in.

2. Navigate to the package in question beneath Computer/User Configuration, then Software Settings, and finally, Software Installation.

3. Right-click the new package and click Properties.

4. Switch to the Upgrades tab (see Figure 14.3).

5. Click Add to specify another package to upgrade.

6. Select the GPO containing the package to upgrade, browsing if necessary.

7. Select the exact package to upgrade from the list.

8. Choose the upgrade method—either uninstall first, or install on top—and click OK.

9. Tick the Required upgrade for existing packages box if you wish to make this a mandatory upgrade.

10. Click OK to accept the changes to the Properties dialog box.

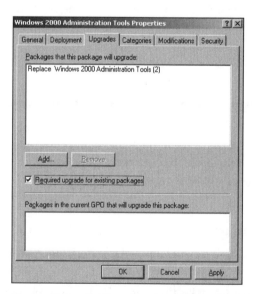

Figure 14.3   Software package Upgrades tab.

Transforming a Package

Transforms are used to customize the installation of Windows Installer (msi) files. To actually create transforms, you'll either need an authoring tool or an application that provides a method of creating transforms. The procedure for creating a transform is application-specific. For example, Microsoft Office 2000 ships with the Office Custom Installation Wizard that can be used to create mst files for Office.

To add a transform to a deployed package:

1. Create a package and select Advanced Published Or Deployed as the deployment type.

2. When the Properties dialog box appears, change to the Modifications tab (see Figure 14.4).

3. Click Add. An Open dialog box appears.

4. Use the Open dialog box to select a transform to apply.

NOTE: *Repeat Steps 3 and 4 until all transforms are applied.*

---

5. Click OK.

WARNING! Transforms can only be added at creation time. You cannot go back and transform a package that is already created.

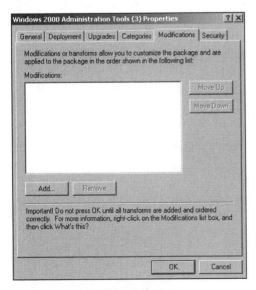

Figure 14.4   Modifications tab.

Repackaging an Application

The process of creating an msi file from an arbitrary application or set of files is as follows:

1. Perform a basic install on Windows 2000 onto a completely fresh computer. Don't customize any settings or add any other application. This is the computer to be imaged.

2. On a second computer, install Wininstall LE by executing \valueadd\ 3rdparty\mgmt\winstle\swiadle.msi from the Windows 2000 Server CD-ROM. No user interaction is required in the install process.

3. Use Windows Explorer to share the %ProgramFiles%\VERITAS Software\Winstall directory on the second computer. (Right-click, select Sharing, click Share this folder, then click OK.)

4. On the computer to image, start a Command Prompt and use the **net use** to connect to the Winstall share on the second computer. Run **discoz.exe** from the share and follow the instructions to take a "before" snapshot.

5. On the computer to be imaged, install and configure the application to repackage.

6. Don't restart the computer, even if prompted after the application installation.

NOTE: *This instruction is here because restarting may cause unrelated changes to the system that will show up in the package. If the application asked you to restart and the package created when using this step failed, try starting this solution again and ignoring Step 6.*

---

7. Delete any uninstallation shortcuts. Applications that have been repackaged can only successfully be removed by removing their package, not by running the original uninstall program. Also delete any Startup folder shortcuts.

8. Wait a short period to ensure that any temporary files have been deleted.

9. Again, run **discoz.exe** from the Winstall share to take an "after" snapshot.

10. Copy the resulting msi file to a network share.

It's essential that a completely fresh computer be used as a reference computer to image, to ensure that all shared DLLs used by the application to repackage are actually installed. It's also best to repackage only one application at a time.

Creating a ZAP File

To publish an application without an msi file via Group Policy without repackaging the application, it's necessary to create a simple text file in a specific format and, in effect, publish that file. The file is known as a ZAP file because it should be saved with the extension .zap, and it takes the Windows INI file format. Such files can be created with any text editor, such as Notepad.

The outline for a simple ZAP file is given in Listing 14.1. (Lines staring with a semicolon (;) are comments.)

Listing 14.1   Example of a ZAP file for you to customize.

```
[Application]
; FriendlyName is required and is the display name of the application.
FriendlyName = "Application Name Goes Here"

; SetupCommand is required, the command line to install the application.
; Long file names must be quoted and parameters may be specified.
SetupCommand = "\\server\share\directory name\setup.exe" /parameter

; Optional Information for Add/Remove Programs
DisplayVersion = 3.1415
Publisher = Coriolis
URL = http://www.coriolis.com


[ext]
; An optional list of the file extensions the application will
; auto-install for. Leading dots are optional. The = signs are required.
HTM=
TXT=
.ETC=
```

Testing Application Deployment

It isn't generally a good idea to configure an application to be deployed and leave it, with no testing, until the first user processes the new software installation policy and phones the help desk to complain when it all goes horribly wrong (which, let's face it, is inevitable if you don't test the package). Instead, by using permissions and security groups, you can filter the newly modified GPO so that it only applies to designated test users. To do this, remove the GPO's Apply Group Policy permission from everyone except the test group.

Installing RIS on a Windows 2000 Server

To use Remote Installation Services, you must install RIS on one or more Windows 2000 Server computers.

To install RIS:

1. Click Start|Settings|ControlPanel.

2. Open the Add/Remove Programs applet.

3. Click Add/Remove Windows Components. The Add/Remove Windows Components Wizard appears.

4. Check the box next to Remote Installation Services in the Components list.

5. Click Next, and insert the Windows 2000 Server CD-ROM if prompted.

6. Reboot your computer when prompted.

7. After logging on, launch Add/Remove Programs again and switch to Add/Remove Windows Components.

8. In the Set up services list, click Configure next to Configure Remote Installation Services. The Remote Installation Services Setup Wizard appears (see Figure 14.5).

9. Click Next on the first screen.

10. Enter the path to the folder on an NTFS partition you wish the Remote Installation images to be stored on. This partition should have plenty of free space for images, and can't be the system partition. Click Next.

Figure 14.5   Remote Installation Services Setup Wizard.

11. By default, RIS servers are disabled. If you wish to enable the server immediately, check the Respond to client computers requesting service box. If you wish to limit support to prestaged computers, also check the Do not respond to unknown client computers box. These options can also be reconfigured later. Click Next to continue.

12. Now, you are prompted to give the path to Windows Installation files. Either specify the root directory of the Windows 2000 Professional CD-ROM or a copy of the i386 directory. Click Next.

13. Enter a folder name for the image. The default of win2000.pro is usually acceptable. Click Next.

14. Enter a description and help text for the default image. Again, the defaults are usually fine for the first image added. Click Next to continue.

15. Click Finish to begin the copying process.

16. Click Done when the copying process is complete.

Sharing the RIS Administration Tools

It's often useful to have the RemoteInstall directory shared. This allows you to access administration tools such as **rbfg.exe** over the network. To share the RemoteInstall directory:

1. Start Windows Explorer from the Accessories menu (or press Windows Key+E).

2. Navigate to the RemoteInstall folder (that is, the folder specified when RIS was installed on the server).

3. Right-click on the folder and select Sharing.

4. Select Shared As.

5. Click OK.

Authorizing a RIS Server

For a RIS server to be able to operate, it must be authorized to do so. This authorization is set with the DHCP Management Console Snap-in and the process is exactly the same as that for authorizing a DHCP server:

1. Open the DHCP console from the Administrative Tools menu.

2. Right-click the DHCP object in the root of the tree and select Manage authorized servers. The Manage Authorized Servers dialog box appears (see Figure 14.6).

3. Click Authorize to add a server.

4. Type the name or IP address of the RIS server to authorize and click OK.

TIP: *For a multihomed RIS server, repeat Steps 3 and 4 for each IP address.*

---

5. Click Close to return to the DHCP console.

NOTE: *The BINL (Boot Information Negotiation Layer) service won't start on a server that isn't authorized in the directory.*

The authorization information is held in the Active Directory configuration partition as objects named after the IP addresses of DHCP servers beneath the **cn=NetServices,cn=Services,cn=Configuration,dc=ForestRootDomain** container.

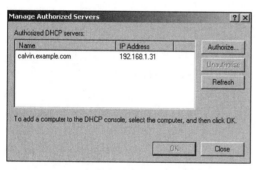

Figure 14.6   Manage Authorized Servers dialog box.

Creating Additional Images

Now I'll discuss the creation of additional RIS images. The default is to have a single image containing a basic copy of Windows 2000 Professional. It is possible to add extra images to install Windows 2000 Server, non-default installs of Windows 2000 Professional, or even a fully configured setup including applications.

Adding Windows 2000 Server as an Installation Option

Microsoft only supports the installation of Windows 2000 Professional by RIS. That said, it's actually possible to deploy any of the Windows 2000 Server versions by RIS if you wish to. In essence, this method involves modifying the

Windows 2000 Server installation files so that it looks like Windows 2000 Professional, installing the image to the RIS server, then modifying the installation files on the RIS server back to their original state.

The setting in question is the **ProductType** value in the **[SetupData]** section of **Txtsetup.sif**. A value of 1 represents a server product, and a value of 0 represents Professional.

Thus, the steps to take are as follows:

1. Copy the contents of the i386 directory from the Windows 2000 Server CD-ROM to disk.
2. Use an editor such as Notepad to change the value of **ProductType** in the **[SetupData]** section of **Txtsetup.sif** to 0.
3. Start Active Directory Users and Computers at the RIS server console.
4. Navigate to the RIS server's computer object, double-click it, and select Properties.
5. Switch to the Remote Install tab and click Advanced Settings.
6. Change to the Images tab and click Add.
7. Select Add a new installation image and click Next.
8. The Remote Installation Services Setup Wizard launches. Click Next.
9. Specify the path of the modified Windows 2000 Server i386 directory from Steps 1 and 2. Click Next.
10. Change the default pathname to say **win2000.srv**. Click Next.
11. Specify the Friendly Description and Help Text. The friendly description should be accurate but the help text won't be. Click Next when done.
12. Select Use the old client installation screens, to preserve any customizations made. Click Next.
13. Review the settings. Click Finish.

A similar process can be used to add other versions of the Windows 2000 (or later) i386 directory (the directory from the CD-ROM that contains the actual operating system install files) to a RIS server. For example, by a process known as *slipstreaming*, it's possible to apply a Service Pack to the i386 directory, then the resulting Windows 2000 and Service Pack i386 directory can be added, so RIS clients can install the operating system with the Service Pack already applied.

Using the Setup Manager Wizard

The Setup Manager Wizard (**setupmgr.exe** from the Windows 2000 Server Resource Kit) is used to create answer files. Answer files have many uses, including automating cloned systems that are duplicated with **sysprep**, specifying answers to questions in the Windows 2000 installation process for disk- or CD-based installations, and also for customizing RIS images.

To create an answer file with the Setup Manager Wizard:

1. Click Start|Run and type **setpmgr**.

2. Click Next on the welcome screen of the Windows 2000 Setup Manager Wizard.

3. Click Next again to create a new answer file.

4. Select Remote Installation Services and click Next.

5. Select the user interaction level from the options provided that range from Fully automated (no user intervention) to Provide defaults (the options specified become the default values and may be overridden by users). It's normal for RIS answer files to be fully automated.

6. If you selected Fully automated, check the accept box on the license agreement page, because during a fully automated installation, the user isn't prompted with the license agreement.

7. Configure Windows 2000 installation options as prompted.

8. Finally, choose a location and save the answer file. It can then be associated with an image to create a RIS installation option

Related Solution	Found on page
Installing the Windows 2000 Server Resource Kit Utilities	63

Editing SIF Files by Hand

Setup Information Files (sif Files) are, in effect, text files that follow the same format as Windows INI files that are characterized by:

```
[Section]
Key = Value
```

You can edit sif files using Notepad, and the full list of options that can be specified is contained in the Unattend.doc file published by Microsoft. The unattend.doc file is located in the deploy.cab file found in the \Support\Tools directory of the Windows 2000 CD-ROM.

Using RIPrep

RIPrep is a method of imaging an existing computer and replicating that image exactly to other machines using RIS. Unlike general RIS images, RIPrep isn't Hardware Abstraction Layer (HAL)-independent.

On the client machine to image, perform the following:

1. Install a basic configuration of Windows 2000 via RIS on the computer (you'll see it later in this chapter).

2. Install and configure additional applications, as required.

3. Click Start|Run.

4. Enter the Universal Naming Convention (UNC) path of the **riprep.exe** utility and click OK. For example **\\Server\Share\RemoteInstall\ Admin\i386\riprep.exe**.

5. Click Next on the Welcome screen.

6. Specify the RIS server to copy the image to, then click Next.

7. Specify the folder name to copy the image to, then click Next.

8. Give a Friendly Description and Help text. These are shown to users selecting which image to install, so they should be descriptive and aimed at end users. Click Next to continue.

9. A list of programs and services currently running appears. Close any applications that are running and click Next.

10. Click Next twice, after reviewing the information provided. The image is replicated to the RIS server specified.

Setting Permissions to Use RIS

Not every RIS image on a server has to be made available to each user accessing the server. Instead, images can be restricted. The process of restricting an image is simply setting permissions on its sif file: If a user has Read permission on a sif file, then he can attempt to install the image (obviously he needs to be able to read all of the files that comprise it to actually be able to install the image).

Creating a RIS Boot Disk

A RIS boot disk can be used on clients with supported network cards that can't use Pre-boot eXecution Environment (PXE) to connect to a RIS server. To create a RIS boot disk do the following:

1. Run **d:\RemoteInstall\Admin\i386\rbfg.exe** (where **d:\RemoteInstall** should be replaced by the folder you specified in Step 10 of Installing RIS on a Windows 2000 Server).

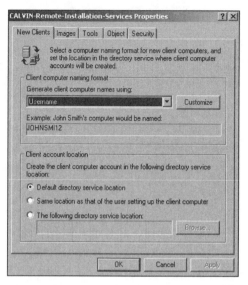

Figure 14.7   Installing RIS on a Windows 2000 Server.

2. The Installing RIS on a Windows 2000 Server appears (see Figure 14.7).

3. Insert a formatted floppy disk in the A: or B: drive, select the appropriate destination drive, and click Create Disk.

4. Once the disk is created, you'll be prompted to create another.

A list of supported network cards can be obtained by clicking the Adapter List button. Note that the **rbfg.exe** utility only works under Windows 2000.

Prestaging RIS Clients

For security and load balancing, it's possible to create computer accounts in Active Directory for computers that are to have the operating system installed by RIS. This task is known as *prestaging* the computers, and it's an additional option in the New Computer Wizard that becomes available after RIS is installed.

To prestage a computer:

1. Create a computer account and fill in the computer name details as per normal.

2. On the Managed tab, check This Is A Managed Computer.

3. Type the computer's Globally/Universal Unique Identifier (GUID/UUID) from its BIOS, or accompanying documentation. The Next button will be

enabled when an exactly 32-character hexadecimal string has been typed. Don't enter any other characters.

4. Click Next.

5. If you wish to load balance, assign the host to a specific RIS server from the Host Server tab. Click Next.

7. Click Finish when done.

These settings are stored in the **netbootGUID** and **netbootMachineFilePath** properties on the computer object, and may be modified through its Properties dialog box.

Related Solution	Found on Page
Creating Computer Accounts	288

Chapter 15

File and Print Services

In Depth

So far, only the mechanics of actually creating a Windows 2000 Active Directory domain and configuring users and groups have been discussed, and although a corporate directory is useful in itself, one of the main purposes of actually having a corporate network is to share resources.

Two such resources are files and printers. Hosting file shares on servers has numerous benefits including shared access and centralized backup—many organizations forbid users from keeping data on their desktop PCs to avoid having to back them up

File Services

Windows 2000 has a number of new features that make files easier to manage in a large network, as well as new features that add functionality for end users. Not all of these require Active Directory, but some are enhanced by it, and knowledge of many of them is useful when planning and administering a Windows 2000 Active Directory domain.

User Profiles

Just like Windows NT, users in Windows 2000 have profiles. A profile is a collection of user-specific settings, such as registry entries, application data, shortcuts and desktop configuration. In Windows 2000, profiles are now stored by default in **c:\Documents and Settings**, instead of the Windows NT 4 default of **c:\ winnt\profiles**.

Default User Profile

When a user logs on to a computer for the first time and there's no other profile stored for her, the computer's default user profile is copied for her to a directory beneath Documents and Settings. For example, if a user is called Jstockton, then the contents of Documents and Settings\Default User will be copied to the newly created Documents and Settings\JStockton. Now, whenever changes are made to application or desktop layout, they're saved beneath a user's profile directory, so when she next logs on, they'll still be available.

All Users Profiles

In addition to user-specific settings, machine-specific settings are often required. Well-written applications will prompt the installer as to whether they should be available to all users or just the current user—this doesn't affect NT File System (NTFS) permissions but, instead, whether the current profile or the All Users profile has settings added to it.

Anything in the All Users profile for a computer is made available to everyone who logs on to the computer. For example, having a desktop shortcut in the All Users profile will place that shortcut on the desktop of everyone who logs on to the workstation. The All Users profile is contained in the Documents and Settings\All Users directory.

Customizations aren't saved to the All Users profile, however. For example, after an application has been installed with its registry defaults in the All Users profile, if a user chooses to customize it by, for example, configuring her name, then this modification is saved to the user's own profile at logon. Any conflicts between a user's personal profile and the All Users profile are resolved in favor of personal profiles, which means that next time our user logs on, her name will be correctly configured in the application.

Roaming Profiles

Having a separate profile on every single computer is extremely wasteful and annoying. If JStockton logs on to 25 different computers, then she'll have 25 different user profiles with different settings taking up disk space on each computer. In particular, changes she makes on one machine won't be made on any others.

Although this is the default behavior in Windows 2000, it's often replaced by what's known as a *roaming profile*. With roaming profiles, the user profile is stored on a network share and copied to the client computer at logon and copied back to the network at logoff. This way, settings persist between logons to different computers. It's also possible to create a Default User profile on the network for new users.

However, with default profiles in use, the problem of the build-up of old profiles on client computers persists. For example, if 100 different people all log on to the same computer over the course of several months, then by default, a profile directory will exist for each of them. A way around this is to automatically have user profiles deleted at logoff by setting a DWORD value of 1 to the Registry entry HKLM\Software\Microsoft\WindowsNT\CurrentVersion\WinLogon\DeleteRoamingCache. A value of 0 or deleting the entry disables the deletion.

Mandatory Profiles

Some circumstances exist where you don't want to give users the freedom to customize their own profiles. Prime examples of this are schools and cyber cafés, where most users aren't given the freedom to change settings, and you don't want to store profiles for everyone.

Mandatory profiles allow users to change settings during the current session but don't save changes on logout. Instead, the same profile is downloaded again at the next logon. You can flafòa profile as mandatory by renaming a .dat profile to a man file. However, this only prevents settings from being saved to the profile on logout and doesn't prevent a user from actually replacing the man file with a profile of his choice. Hence, to actually secure a mandatory profile, you have to lock it down with appropriate access control settings (read-only for users).

Encrypting File System

The *Encrypting File System (EFS)* feature of Windows 2000 isn't unique to systems running Active Directory. However, it bears mentioning. It's many times more useful to organizations that use Active Directory, because user profiles serve as a repository for encryption keys.

EFS uses a Microsoft technology called *Pstore (Protected Storage)* to store unique, per-user cryptographic keys as part of the user profile. These keys are used to transparently encrypt and decrypt files with no additional intervention—quite simply, if a user has the ability to decrypt an encrypted file. In fact, no administrative effort is required to enable EFS (although it can be disabled with Recovery policy.)

It's best to implement EFS at the folder level rather than the file level. The simple reason for this is that many applications, such as Microsoft Word, create temporary files in the same directory as the source file. Because every file in an encrypted directory is encrypted by default, this will mean that the temporary file is also encrypted, so it's not vulnerable itself.

How EFS Works

The Encrypting File System uses both public key cryptography and symmetric key cryptography, in common with many modern cryptographic systems. Users have a public/private key pair associated with them. These keys are either stored in Certificate Services or generated the first time a file is encrypted by that user. Each time a file is encrypted, a "session key" is created for the encryption operation and is stored with the file.

The reason for this is simple: public key cryptography allows for one key to be published but makes for slow encrypting and decrypting because of the complex formulae required to make a public key algorithm secure. Symmetric key systems, on the other hand, are comparatively fast but require a method of secure key exchange. The public key cryptography provides this key exchange.

In the case of EFS, the symmetric algorithm used is DESX: a stronger variant on DES (the US Government's Data Encryption Standard), which has a second encryption key. This second key is logically **XOR**ed against the beginning of the plain text before DES is applied. In essence, this means any brute force attack has to work out what the second "whitening" key is, as well as calculating the DES key.

DES works by splitting the message to encrypt (the *plaintext*) into small chunks known as blocks. The first of these blocks is encrypted using the symmetric DES algorithm. The encrypted version of this first block is the **XOR**ed.

Moving/Copying Encrypted Files

Because EFS is a function of the NTFS version 5 file system, encrypted files can only exist on Windows 2000 computers with NTFS hard drives. When an encrypted file is copied over the netwok, it's copied in plaintext and encrypted again at the other end if possible.

In fact, encryption will always take priority when moving/copying files. For example, if you move an encrypted file to an NTFS volume, then it will stay encrypted, and if you move an unencrypted file to an encrypted folder, then it will be encrypted. Similarly for copying, files that are encrypted when copied stay encrypted, and when files are copied to encrypted directories, they become encrypted. Files that are renamed obviously just retain their previous encryption state.

When moving/copying an encrypted file to a file allocation table (FAT) volume, it can't be encrypted at the other end and, thus, remains plaintext. When an encrypted file is sent to a remote computer, it will remain encrypted if you use Windows 2000 Backup to move it. In this case, your encryption certificate must be available on the remote computer for the file to be accessible.

Recovering Encrypted Data

In Windows 2000 domains, only members of the Domain Admins Group are designated recovery agents, who are able to decrypt any files. In standalone Windows 2000 systems, the Administrator account fulfills this role. Recovery agents have special recovery cryptographic keys, which allow them to decrypt any files. Obviously, being a recovery agent is a sensitive role and when planning an Active Directory domain that intends to implement EFS, you should consider this when deciding whom to make a Domain Admin.

EFS Caveats

Several points need to be noted when using EFS. The first of these is to remember that EFS keys are tied to users. This means that if a user account is lost, then a recovery agent must be used. This is really only a problem when an entire system is lost. For example, if you take a server that's part of a workgroup and install Active Directory, then all existing user accounts are deleted and, hence, their encryption keys are also deleted.

This renders encrypted files useless. The way around this problem is to decrypt all encrypted files before installing Active Directory. The same point also applies to people reinstalling Windows 2000 Professional on home systems. Because of the way that EFS is implemented within NTFS, it is not possible to compress encrypted files. In general, encrypted data is less compressible than unencrypted data, but due to NTFS internals, it isn't sensible to be able to do both to the same file.

The fact that Windows 2000 uses single-sign-on to provide transparent encryption must also be borne in mind, because if an attacker gains access to an unlocked workstation with a user currently logged in, then that person can read encrypted files exactly as the current user can. Solving this problem requires user education—in terms of locking unattended computers and especially of insuring that laptops are locked when they're suspended or hibernated. However, no encryption is "unbreakable". Granted, it may take considerable effort and know-how beyond the man in the street to crack EFS but rest assured that it's possible (just very, very expensive with current technology).

Finally, you should remember that a clever intruder will always attack the weakest link in your security system, and that is rarely the computers. For example, if you implement EFS on corporate laptops to protect sensitive data in the event of theft, just make sure senior managers don't use their age, date of birth, or wife's name as a password, or worse still, write it on a note stuck to the laptop keyboard (yes, it really happens).

Offline Files

Another feature new to Windows 2000 but not unique to networks employing Active Directory is Offline Files. Offline Files and folders are to network shares what Temporary Internet Files are to web and FTP sites—essentially a local cache that can be used offline. Offline Files and folders allow people disconnected from the corporate network, such as laptop users, to access their shared files as if they were still connected to the network.

Offline File Cache

Windows 2000 stores local copies of offline files in its offline file cache located beneath %SystemRoot%\csc (CSC stands for Client-Side Cache). A certain proportion of your system drive can be allocated to the offline file cache through the Offline Files property tab (from the Tools|Folder Options in Windows Explorer).

Caching Files

Exactly which files are cached depends both on administrators and users. At the administrator's side, each file share can have caching enabled or disabled. If caching is enabled, then one of the following three settings must be specified on the Caching Settings dialog box for the share:

- *Automatic Caching for Documents*—With this setting, files are cached automatically and the server-side version is used in preference to the client-side version when working online. This insures a file is locked when it should be and minimizes conflicts.

- *Automatic Caching for Programs*—With this setting, files are cached automatically, but the client-side version is used in preference. This is best for read-only documents (and not just program files).

- *Manual Caching for Documents*—This is the default. Like automatic document caching, the server version is opened in preference when working online, but with this option, files must explicitly be specified for files or folders.

If manual caching is selected, then end users must choose to cache a folder or individual files from within.

Synchronization

Offline files are of little use if they aren't up to date, and changes aren't synchronized back onto the network. With Windows 2000's offline files feature, synchronization can be configured when users log off (or forced manually) and also when users first log in to the network.

File Shares in Active Directory

Another type of object that can be published to Active Directory is a shared folder. *Shared folder objects* represent *file shares* on computers within a domain. These shared folders can then be browsed through My Network Places, and keywords can be associated with them to enable users to search for them. For example, folders that are of interest to everyone, such as company policy documents or software installation points, can be shared in the directory. This means that users can either navigate to their contents (if they know where in a domain's OU structure the folders are) or can search by keyword.

To navigate to a folder's contents, you can use My Network Places, then drill down beneath Entire Network, Domain, then your domain name and OU structure to find the shared folders. Of course, you could place all shared folder objects in the same OU and create a shortcut to that OU for users to browse from.

Distributed File System

Following on the theme from other features in this chapter: distributed file system (Dfs) isn't new in Windows 2000, but it's enhanced by Active Directory. *Dfs* is a method of providing a single, logical hierarchy for network shares, regardless

15. File and Print Services

of where they physically live. With Dfs, a user only needs to know one share name (the Dfs root) and other shares can be placed beneath the Dfs root by an administrator to create a seamless folder structure.

For example, in an organization with numerous user accounts, home folders and profiles may be spread over several different servers. However, you don't want administrators to have to worry about which server an individual home folder is hosted on, so you create a Dfs structure to deal with this.

Beneath a single Dfs root, say **\\example.com\home**, you add links for each home folder, regardless of which server it's hosted on. This way you can move home folders around between servers without users noticing any effect (besides a half-hour period until their old cached location for the Dfs link expires).

To be able to use Dfs, end users require a Dfs client on their operating system. Windows 2000, Windows NT 4, Windows 98, and Windows ME ship with a Dfs client included. A Dfs client must be obtained separately for Windows 95. Dfs has two main advantages: the first is that users only have one share name to remember (and only one share to browse through Windows Explorer), and the second is that share names are abstracted a level. This presents the same level of abstraction as DNS does to IP addresses, because it allows you to move a share to a different server without affecting end user configuration—all you have to do is update the Dfs link.

Stand-Alone Dfs

In true Microsoft style, what people are used to calling Dfs has been renamed *Stand-Alone Dfs*. Stand-alone Dfs uses a single server called the Dfs root server to provide the mapping service that resolves requests for virtualized directories via Dfs to actual physical shares on servers.

Shares added to the Dfs tree are known as *links*, and these links can be organized arbitrarily within the Dfs structure. For example, you could add all links coming off the Dfs root, or you could add some beneath other links to form a deeper structure. Whichever method you choose, making a share available through Dfs doesn't affect permissions—which are still derived from the actual share permissions and NTFS permissions on the shared folder in the normal way.

The Dfs root server is the weakest link in stand-alone Dfs because if it's unavailable, then clients are unable to resolve requests to actual shares and, hence, can't access the data referred to by links. To overcome this and to add the possibility of multiple replicas of the same link, Windows 2000 introduces domain Dfs.

Domain Dfs

Domain Dfs (formerly known as Fault Tolerant Dfs) requires a Windows 2000 domain, as the name suggests. It also allows for fault tolerance with replica child nodes. Domain Dfs roots must be housed on member servers, and the Domain Dfs topology is stored in Active Directory and, hence, replicated to all domain controllers. This means that it's possible to instantly create a new Dfs root if the old one fails.

Fault tolerance comes from the ability to assign replicas to links. This means that you can load balance between two identical shared folders: for example, software installation points. Better than that, domain Dfs is site-aware, so clients will resolve the closest link. In the example of using domain Dfs to house software installation points, this means that the same share path will always resolve to the closest installation point.

For example, if Office 2000 is installed over the network, with some features configured for install on demand, then when features not yet installed are first activated, the original install point will be contacted to add the requested feature. If a laptop user is in a remote site when this happens, there will be wide area network (WAN) traffic. If Office 2000 was installed from a domain Dfs share and a local replica is in place, requests to the original install point will be resolved locally, and no WAN traffic will result. Domain Dfs is also useful when deploying software by Group Policy, because it means the same software installation policy can be used, regardless of physical site.

Print Services

Printing is a service that often causes the biggest headaches to administrators. Somehow the combination of end users, third-party drivers, network shares, and paper jams conspires to wreck havoc. Windows 2000 has introduced driver signing in an effort to insure quality, and just like Windows NT, printer drivers can be installed at the server for use by Windows 2000 clients, without them ever needing to be installed locally. New features in Windows 2000 make it much easier for end users to find and connect to printers, as well as making it easier to delegate administrative control of printers.

Printer Shares in Active Directory

Windows 2000 computers that host shared printers and belong to a domain will publish the printers in Active Directory, by default. Shared printers whose queues are hosted on pre-Windows 2000 computers must be added explicitly to the domain.

Windows 2000 Printers

Printers hosted on Windows 2000 computers are stored as directory objects beneath their host computers. These **printQueue** objects aren't displayed in Active Directory Users and Computers, however, because all management functions are controlled through the usual properties dialog box from the Printers applet on Control Panel.

Windows 2000-hosted printer shares are published to the directory by default, although this behavior can be controlled on an individual printer's properties. For example, if a printer is only intended for use by certain members of staff (such as upper management), there may be little point publishing it in the directory, especially if ordinary users don't have sufficient permissions on the printer. However, **printQueue** objects, just like any other objects, can have permissions set for them, so it's, of course, possible to hide printers from those who have no need to see them.

Pre-Windows 2000 Printers

Any printers shared from pre-Windows 2000 computers aren't published in the directory, by default. Instead, they must be added manually in Active Directory Users and Computers. Manually adding a **printQueue** object with Active Directory Users and Computers requires the share to be available. Once added, normal printing configuration, such as drivers and permission to print, should be configured as normal, and directory-specific settings, such as functionality (for searches) and location strings, should be configured in the directory.

Location Tracking

The Windows 2000 interface allows users to search for printers through Search|For Printers from the Start menu. The resulting dialog box allows you to search by printer name, model, or any number of advanced features relating to paper handling and other capabilities (see Figure 15.1).

However, as a rule, users don't care about the make or model of a printer. It doesn't really matter to them, because all they really want is a hard copy of their particular

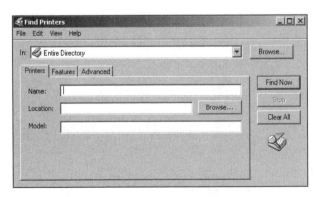

Figure 15.1   The Find Printers dialog box.

document and who cares whether it's a LaserJet 4000 or a 4050 that it comes out of? So if a user has no knowledge or interest in the current printers available to him, how can he find the best printer? The solution is by location, and this also lends itself to the problems of users moving between offices, as well as providing the possibility of using printers to send hard copy documents around a company.

Locations Strings

Location tracking works by using *location strings*, which take the form of a series of slash-separated components, such as London/BakerSt. These can be of arbitrary depth, so for example, a printer location can be specified right down to the office building, floor, and room (for example, London/BakerSt/221b/2ndFloor/Study).

Searches based on location strings aim to match the initial components, so for example, searching for London/BakerSt/221b would return any printers whose location strings start like that, so it finds all printers in that particular house. Fortunately, a Browse button is available, so users don't even have to remember the location string specified. However, it's a good idea to keep location names short, snappy, and descriptive. Location strings are associated with Active Directory sites, and to aid users searching by location, it's possible to have the current site's location appear by default in the Printer Search dialog box (by using Group Policy's). This is done by enabling the **Computer Configuration\Administrative Templates\Printers\Pre-Populate Printer Search Location Text Policy** setting. The location of a printer hosted in Windows 2000 is set using its Properties dialog box on the print server. Details, such as double-sided printing and color capabilities, are specified automatically by the installed drivers (although they can be overridden using Active Directory Service Interface [ADSI] Edit).

For pre-Windows 2000 print servers, a directory object representing the printer must be added manually, and the properties of this object allow the location string and other information to be configured.

15. File and Print Services

Immediate Solutions

Profiles

Now we'll discuss how to configure and manage profiles in Windows 2000, including copying profiles so that settings can be moved or shared between users. In addition to the techniques described here it is also possible to share elements of a profile by, for example, copying the individual shortcut files from one profile to another.

Configuring Roaming Profiles

The following solutions cover the basic steps involved in creating and assigning user profiles. They can easily be adapted to, for example, replacing the current All Users profile or Default User profile with an existing profile.

Creating a Profiles Share

Roaming profiles must be stored on the network and be accessible to users. The first step in making this possible is creating a suitable share. It's, of course, possible to use multiple shares across many servers (perhaps using Dfs) to host user profiles, but the basics are still the same:

1. Start Windows Explorer from the Accessories menu.
2. Create a folder called (for example) Profiles.
3. Right-click the new folder and click Sharing.
4. Share it as Profiles. Grant Full Control permissions to Authenticated Users.

Assigning Profiles

To actually make roaming profile take effect, the user must have the network path to her roaming profile specified as a property of her user account.

To set a user's profile location:

1. Start Active Directory Users and Computers from the Administrative Tools menu.
2. Navigate to the user whose profile you wish to change.
3. Right-click the user and select Properties.
4. Switch to the Profile tab (see Figure 15.2).

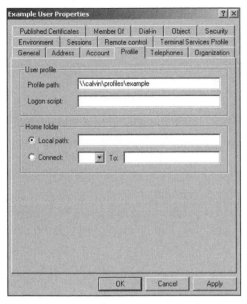

Figure 15.2   A User Properties Profile tab.

5. In the Profile path box, type the UNC name of a directory for the user's
    profile. This directory need not exist. For example,\\serve r\profiles\Jbloggs.

6. Click OK.

If the directory specified doesn't exist, the profile will be created next time a user
logs in. The %UserName% environment variable will *not* work in the Profile path
box. If you have a template profile you wish a user to use, copy that profile into
the folder specified using the next solution.

NOTE: *By default, Administrators don't have access to a user's profile. Instead, they must Take Ownership before they
can assign themselves any control or access. This is done through the Owner tab of the Advanced Control Settings,
accessible through the Security tab of the Profile folder's Properties dialog box.*

Copying Profiles

User profiles are copied most easily using a dedicated function.

To copy a user profile:

1. On the desktop, right-click My Computer and select Properties (alterna-
    tively launch the System applet from Control Panel).

2. Switch to the User Profiles tab.

3. Select the profile to copy from the list and click Copy To.

4. Browse to or type the location to copy to. Specifying a new folder will create it when you click OK.

5. Use the Change button to select a user or group to give permissions over the copied profile to.

6. Click OK.

The User Profiles tab of the System applet can also be used to manage profiles in other ways, such as deleting them or changing their status between Local and Roaming.

Creating a Mandatory Profile

Mandatory user profiles are preconfigured profiles for users whose settings you don't wish to change. The process of creating a mandatory user profile can be broken down into three stages:

- Creating the profile
- Publishing the profile
- Assigning the profile

To create a mandatory user profile, simply create a new user account, log in with that user, and customize away until you're happy with the current configuration. Then log out and log back in as an administrator.

The next step is to copy the resulting profile to a network share using the method of the previous solution. Now, the most important step is to rename the NTUser.dat file to NTUser.man on the network share.

Finally, assign the resulting profile to the desired users by specifying its profile in the same way that you would change the profile path to create roaming profile.

TIP: *The environment variable, %LogonServer%, can be used in profile paths to specify the authenticating server. For example, you can copy the same mandatory profile to every domain controller, share it beneath the Profiles share, and use the profile path \\%LogonServer%\Profiles\NTUser.man to insure that users pick up their profile from the authenticating domain controller.*

Encrypting the File System

Now we'll discuss encrypting the file system, the mechanism introduced in Windows 2000 that allows transparent encryption of files on disk so that their contents can only be read by those with the appropriate decryption key. This is more powerful that just applying NTFS access control, because access control can be bypassed with third-party software to read NTFS drives such as that available from **www.sysinternals.com**.

Encrypting Files and Folders

Encrypting a file or folder is a simple enough task in Windows 2000. Assuming an NTFS file system and no policy to prevent it, a user may encrypt a file/folder from Explorer as follows:

1. Start Windows Explorer from the Accessories menu.

2. Navigate to the item to encrypt and right-click it.

3. Select Properties.

4. From the General tab, click the Advanced button in the Attributes section. The Advanced Attributes dialog box appears (see Figure 15.3).

5. Check the Encrypt contents to secure data box.

NOTE: *The Compress contents to save disk space box will clear, if it's checked.*

---

6. Click OK.

7. If prompted, confirm whether the attribute change should apply to the current folder only, or include all subfolders and files.

8. Click OK.

The process can be repeated, by clearing the checkbox, to decrypt files.

Alternatively, files can be encrypted or decrypted from the command line using the **cipher.exe** tool. The following command-line options listed in Table 15.1 are available.

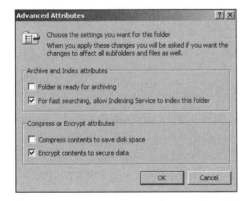

Figure 15.3   Advanced Attributes dialog box.

Table 15.1   cipher.exe command-line options.

Switch	Description
/E	Encrypt the specified files/folders. May not be used with **/D**.
/D	Decrypt the specified files/folders. May not be used with **/E**.
/S:*dir*	Perform the current operation on the specified directory and on all subdirectories.
/A	Operate on files and directories.
/I	Ignore errors and continue processing. By default, the operation will be halted when an error is encountered.
/F	Force encryption. This will encrypt already encrypted objects (which would otherwise be skipped).
/Q	Quiet mode. A lower level of detail will be output.
/H	Encrypts hidden and system files (which would otherwise be skipped).
/K	Creates a new encryption key for the current user. If specified, all other switches will be ignored.

For example, to decrypt every file that you can beneath the current directory:

```
C:\>cipher /d /s:. /a
```

Or, if an entire directory structure isn't being operated on, a pathname should be specified. For example, to encrypt all Word (doc) files in the current directory:

```
C:\>cipler /e *.doc
```

Create a New Encryption Key for a User

By default, a user without any other encryption key will have one created the first time she uses EFS. However, should you wish to regenerate an encryption key, you can do so for the current user as follows:

```
C:\>cipher /k
```

Examining Encrypted Files

The **efsinfo.exe** command-line utility from the Windows 2000 Server Resource Kit allows you to display information about encrypted files and folders. For example, running **efsinfo** on a sample directory containing one encrypted file gives the following output:

```
C:\temp\

sample.xml: Encrypted
  Users who can decrypt:
    EXAMPLE\administrator (CN=administrator,L=EFS,OU=EFS File Encryption
Certificate)

SchemaDoc.doc: Not Encrypted

SchemaDoc.exe: Not Encrypted

XML.CFG: Not Encrypted

XMLSchema.dll: Not Encrypted
```

Other options are available for **efsinfo.exe** in the form of the command-line switches shown in Table 15.2.

A path can also be specified at the end of the command line to operate on a specific directory or file. By default, the current directory is used. As an example, for the display recovery agent information for all files and subdirectories beneath C:\winnt, you would type:

```
C:\>efsinfo /r /s c:\winnt
```

Disabling EFS with Group Policy

If you do not wish EFS to be used on a particular set of computers, you can disable it. This is done through the auspices of Group Policy, so any such set of

Table 15.2   efsinfo.exe command-line switches.

Switch	Description
/U	Displays the users able to decrypt specific files. This is the default and, hence, leads to output, such as the example given earlier.
/R	Displays the recovery agent for specific files. The output is similar to the **/U** output (just with different accounts listed).
/C	In addition to information shown by **/U**, this adds the 'thumbprint' of the user's certificates.
/I	Ignores errors.
/Y	Displays the current certificate thumbnail.
/S	Recurses subdirectories.

computers must either be in the same OU hierarchy or in a security group. You can disable EFS for a domain by performing this solution on the Default Domain Policy GPO.

To disable EFS perform the following steps:

1. Open the appropriate GPO to disable EFS in the Group Policy Snap-in.

2. Navigate to the **Computer Configuration\Windows Settings\Security Settings\Public Key Policies\Encrypted Data Recovery Agents** policy setting and left-click it.

3. Delete any certificates in the right-hand side by right-clicking on them and selecting Delete.

4. Right-click Encrypted Data Recovery Agents in the tree-pane and select **Delete Policy**.

5. Right-click Encrypted Data Recovery Agents in the tree-pane again, and select **Initialize Empty Policy**.

Configuring Offline Folders

Offline folders allow network file shares to be cached on mobile or remote computers and used when the network is disconnected. The default settings in Windows 2000 allow Windows 2000 Professional users to cache file shares from Windows 2000 Servers, but beyond this default there are a number of options that can be configured. Here we will discuss them.

Configuring Client Offline Folder Properties

At the client side, a number of settings exist to control Offline Folders. These settings are controlled through the Offline Files properties tab. To access these settings, perform the following:

1. Launch Windows Explorer from the Accessories menu (or press Windows Key+E).

2. Select Folder Options from the Tools menu.

3. Switch to the Offline Files tab (see Figure 15.4).

From here, the settings that control Offline Files can be changed, including the amount of disk space made available.

NOTE: *These settings can be configured through Group Policy. See Chapters 12 and 13 for details.*

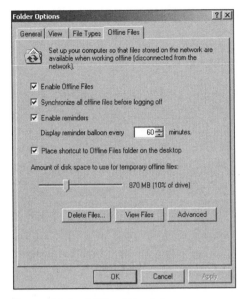

Figure 15.4   Offline Files tab.

Marking a Folder for Offline Use

There are two ways of marking a folder for offline use: at the server or at the client. Here we will discuss how to implement them.

At the Server

At the server side, shared folders can be configured for offline use from the Share Properties tab. To configure a shared folder for offline use:

1. Open Windows Explorer from the Accessories menu.

2. Navigate to the shared folder to configure for offline use.

3. Right-click the folder and select Sharing (or Properties, then switch to the Sharing tab).

4. Click the Caching button. The Caching Settings dialog box appears.

5. Insure that the Allow caching of files in this shared folder box is checked to allows files to be cached. Clearing this checkbox will prevent document caching (but won't prevent users from taking a copy of a file and replacing it manually).

6. Choose either Manual Caching for Documents, Automatic Caching for Documents, or Automatic Caching for Applications, as appropriate.

7. Click OK, twice.

At the Client

On client computers, to locally cache shared folders that are enabled for manual caching, perform the following steps:

1. Open Windows Explorer from the Accessories menu.

2. Navigate to the file or folder to configure for offline use.

3. Right-click the item in question, and click Make Available Offline.

If the Make Available Offline option is disabled (grayed out), this means that it's made available offline by a setting on a Parent folder. Files marked for offline use show two blue arrows on their icons.

Synchronizing Offline Folders

Synchronization can take place automatically at logon or logoff. To force it manually, perform the following steps:

1. Launch Synchronization Manager (%SystemRoot%\system32\syncapp.exe).

2. Open the Tools menu.

3. Click Synchronize.

Individual offline files and folders can be synchronized by right-clicking them in Windows Explorer and selecting synchronize. The Setup button can be used to configure other synchronization options.

Shared Folders

We'll now discuss shared folders, which are used extensively to make data available to users over the network. Here we discuss shared folder objects in Active Directory.

Publishing Shared Folders in Active Directory

Shared folders are published by creating objects for them in the Active Directory. These objects are created and managed through Active Directory Users and Computers.

To create a shared folder object:

1. Start Active Directory Users and Computers from the Administrative Tools menu.

2. Navigate to the OU beneath which you wish to create the shared folder object.

15. File and Print Services

3. Right-click the OU in question and select New then Shared Folder.

4. Type the descriptive name of the shared folder. This will be the common name (cn) of the resulting object.

5. Type the Network path to the shared folder.

6. Click OK.

NOTE: *The object won't be created unless the network path can be verified.*

Once the object is created, right-click it, select Properties and configure Keywords from the General tab to allow meaningful searches to be performed.

Searching Shared Folders in Active Directory

Administrators can use the Find dialog box from Active Directory Users and Computers to search shared folders in the directory. For users, who generally may be restricted from using this application, alternative arrangements are necessary. To launch the same Find dialog box, all they need to do is execute the following command line:

```
C:\>rundll32 dsquery,OpenQueryWindow
```

To search for folders, they must next choose Shared Folders in the Find drop-down list. A shortcut could be created for this command on users' desktops.

Distributed File System

Now we'll discuss distributed file systems. Dfs is a technology that allows a single logical view to be used to access disparate file shares. Its use makes it easy to move file shares between servers, as user configuration need not change. Also it allows multiple replicas of static data to exist within an enterprise, providing fault-tolerant access to the nearest copy of the data.

Creating a Dfs Root

Distributed file systems are managed through the Distributed File System MMC Snap-in. Initially, with no Dfs root configured, the Snap-in appears as shown in Figure 15.5.

To add a new Dfs root:

1. Launch the distributed file system console from the Administrative Tools menu.

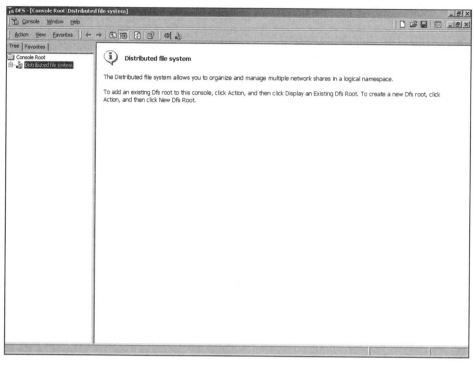

Figure 15.5   Distributed file system Snap-in.

2. Right-click Distributed file system in the left-hand tree and select New Dfs Root. The New Dfs Root Wizard appears.

3. Click Next to proceed.

4. Select whether you wish to create a domain Dfs root or a standalone Dfs root. Click Next.

5. If you selected a domain Dfs root, choose the domain to host it. Click Next.

6. Select or type the name of the server to host the Dfs root. Click Next.

7. Choose the share to be the Dfs root. This can either be an existing share or a new share that can be created. Click Next.

8. Type a name for the Dfs root and a descriptive comment. Click Next.

NOTE: *The name can't be changed in the case of a standalone Dfs root, instead, the Dfs root name will match the share name.*

---

9. Review your selections and click Finish when done.

You're now able to create Dfs links beneath the new Dfs root.

Adding Dfs Links

Once you've added a Dfs root, the next task is to make shares available beneath it by adding Dfs links. To do this, perform the following steps:

1. Launch the distributed file system console from the Administrative Tools menu.

2. Expand the name of the Dfs root to add a link to.

3. Right-click the Dfs root and select New Dfs link. The Create a New Dfs Link dialog box appears (see Figure 15.6).

4. Enter a link name (the path to house the folder beneath the Dfs root), the physical location of the shared folder, a comment, and a timeout value in seconds for the referral.

5. Click OK to create the link.

NOTE: *When you add Dfs links, folders bearing the names of the links appear beneath the Dfs root. These folders are inaccessible to users and are there as markers to prevent you from duplicating the link name with another folder.*

Adding Link Replicas

For fault tolerance, Domain Dfs allows you to replicate links. To do this perform the following steps:

1. Launch the distributed file system console from the Administrative Tools menu.

2. Expand the name of the Dfs root to add a replica to, and navigate to the link to create the replica of.

3. Right-click the link and select New Replica.

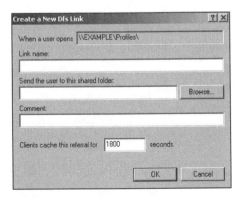

Figure 15.6   Create a New Dfs Link.

4. Enter the name of the replica shared folder or Browse to find it.

5. Select whether you wish to be manually responsible for synchronizing data between replicates, or whether you wish synchronization to be carried out by the File Replication Service (FRS).

6. Click OK when done.

Publishing Printers in Active Directory

We'll now discuss publishing printers in Active Directory. Printer queues are represented by directory objects, which can be used by clients and administrators to find and manage printers in the enterprise.

Windows 2000

Shared print queues hosted on Windows 2000 computers are published to Active Directory by default. They're represented by printQueue objects contained within their host's computer accounts in the directory. These objects are hidden within Active Directory Users and Computers.

To manage these printers, for example to set location strings and control publication, you must use the Printers applet from Control Panel on their host computers. A location string and comment may be configured from the General tab, and the directory listing is controlled from the Sharing tab (see Figure 15.7).

Pre-Windows 2000

The first stage in publishing a shared printer based on a pre-Windows 2000 computer in Active Directory is to create the share on the printer server.

Once this is done, perform the following steps from Windows 2000:

1. Open Active Directory Users and Computers from the Administrative Tools menu.

2. Navigate to the OU that is to contain the printer object.

3. Right-click the OU and select New then Printer.

4. Type the UNC network path to the printer in the form \\Server\Share.

5. Click OK.

NOTE: *This wizard requires the printer to be available to add it. If you wish to add an unavailable printer, you can do so manually using ADSI Edit. The mandatory attributes such as **printerName** and **serverName** are self-explanatory. As ever, if you need to know the default value of a particular attribute, have a look at an existing instance of the object.*

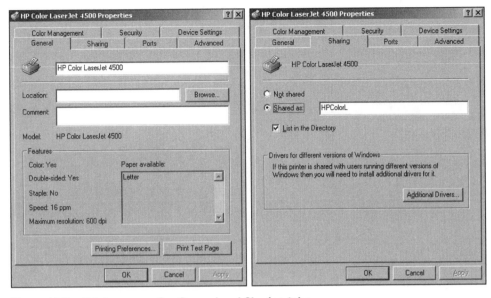

Figure 15.7   Printer properties General and Sharing tabs.

6. To configure the new printer, right-click its object in Active Directory Users and Computers and click Properties.

7. On the General tab, specify the location string for the printer and describe the model and its capabilities, so users can search effectively on these items.

8. On the Managed By tab, click Change, then select the user designated to be in charge of the printer.

9. Click OK when done.

Chapter 16

Managing Domain Controllers

In Depth

This chapter deals with the process of maintaining the computers that physically make up your Active Directory domains and forest: the domain controllers. Having created a healthy network of domain controllers, it's important that they're kept that way.

Operations Master Roles

In Windows 2000 Active Directory, there are five operations master roles (previously known as flexible single master operations roles (FSMOs)—flexible or floating single masters of operations). These roles can all be held by the same server or split across numerous servers. In fact, by default, the first domain controller of a forest—the first in the forest root domain—will hold five operations master roles.

Two of the operations master roles exist on a per-forest basis and can be held by any domain controller in the forest. These are as follows:

- *Schema master*—The only domain controller where the schema may be modified. The current role holder is stored as the **fSMORoleOwner** property of **cn=Schema,cn=Configuration,dc=ForestRootDomain**.

- *Domain Naming master*—The only domain controller where partitions (and, hence, domains) may be added or removed from the forest. The current role holder is stored as the **fSMORoleOwner** property of **cn=Partitions,cn= Configuration,dc=ForestRootDomain**.

Three operations master roles exist for each and every domain. These are as follows:

- *PDC Emulator*—The primary domain controller (PDC) Emulator acts as a Windows NT PDC for downlevel clients, and performs a special role in processing password changes and checking account lockouts. In addition, when running in Mixed Mode, the PDC emulator also replicates domain information to Windows NT BDCs. The current role holder is stored as the **fSMORoleOwner** property of **dc=Domain**.

- *RID master*—The Remote Installation Services (RIS) master is responsible for allocating pools of Relative Identifiers (RIDs) to other domain controllers in a domain. The current role holder is stored as the **fSMORoleOwner** property of **cn=RID Manager$,cn=System,dc=Domain**.

- *Infrastructure master*—The infrastructure master is responsible for cleaning up stale links. The current role holder is stored as the **fSMORoleOwner** property of **cn=Infrastructre,dc=Domain**.

Transferring Operations Master Roles

One of the key aspects of operation master roles in Windows 2000 is that they aren't tied to an individual computer and can, instead, be transferred freely between domain controllers. As a matter of course, operations master roles should be transferred off of a server before it's demoted.

For example, a possible scenario is to upgrade a Windows NT 4 primary domain controller (PDC) to Windows 2000 with Active Directory, add other domain controllers, then decommission the first domain controller, because it may be running older hardware or because you would prefer a clean installation of Windows 2000. In such circumstances, you should transfer all of the operations master roles from this server before removing it (as well as making sure another Global Catalog server is on the network).

Seizing Operations Master Roles

Transferring operation master roles is all very well if both the server you wish to take the role and the current role holder are online and functioning properly. However, if the current role holder isn't available, then the network may suffer problems. For example, if the RID master is offline for an appreciable amount of time, then other domain controllers may exhaust their pools of relative identifiers and, hence, be unable to create additional security principles, or if the PDC Emulator is offline, then certain functionality relating to account lockout counts will be lost temporarily.

The answer to such problems is, in extreme circumstances, to seize the operations master role for another computer by using the **ntdsutil** utility available on any domain controller. **ntdsutil** is a command-line tool that allows you to perform a variety of operations on Active Directory.

It's important to stress that seizing operations master roles is something not to be taken lightly and, in general, isn't necessary if a computer will be back online soon. It's necessary, however, if a hardware failure renders a domain controller inoperable and you don't have the backups or the hardware to restore it.

You should only seize an operations master role if you don't intend to return the current role holder to the network. This is because having two computers that think they hold the role on the network can be, at best, unpredictable. Normally, such situations will have a period of instability while Active Directory replication takes care of informing all domain controllers, which is the real holder of a particular role (in fact, it will be the domain controller that seized the role which will win).

Optimizing Operations Master Role Placement

The most important rule for operations master role placement is that you should avoid placing a domain's infrastructure master on a Global Catalog server. This is simply because Global Catalog servers will never suffer from stale links, because they hold partial copies of every attribute in the directory.

Global Catalog

In an Active Directory forest, the Global Catalog contains a subset of attributes for every object in the forest. Global Catalog servers are computers, which are also domain controllers, hosting a copy of the Global Catalog. Global Catalog servers, therefore, receive replication updates not just from their own partition and the configuration and schema partitions but also from all other domain partitions in the forest. Because these partial replicas of domain partitions are read-only and common to all Global Catalog servers, they can either be replicated from another Global Catalog server or a domain controller in the corresponding domain (but partial replicas don't replicate to domain controllers of that particular domain).

Domain controllers can be configured as Global Catalog servers through their NT Directory Service (NTDS) Settings object in Active Directory Sites and Services. You should always have at least one Global Catalog server in a forest, and in multiple-domain environments, you should aim to have one in every site to allow Universal Group membership to be fully evaluated (or else disable this behavior). The first domain controller in a forest is a Global Catalog server, by default.

Actually, in single domain environments, nothing is lost by configuring every domain controller as a Global Catalog server, because very little additional traffic is created, and all domain controllers will then function on port 3268 (the Global Catalog port), as well as on port 389. Certain functions, such as the Search For People option from the Start menu, use Global Catalog servers by default, instead of any domain controller, so specifying this setting will share such a load between all domain controllers.

The composition of the Global Catalog can be affected by specifying whether or not a particular attribute is included. Be warned, though, that altering the Global Catalog's composition will cause all Global Catalog servers to rebuild all of their Global Catalog data from scratch and will, hence, have replication implications.

Specifying Domain Controllers

An often-asked question truly difficult to answer is quite simply: What specification computer should a particular company use as a domain controller? The answer, unfortunately, is "it depends". Microsoft's Active Directory Size tool (available for download from **www.microsoft.com/downloads/deployment/sizer**) will ask a series of questions and suggest server specifications.

One important point to note is that the clustering of domain controllers isn't supported in Windows 2000. For one thing, it isn't really necessary, because load balancing is performed by Domain Name System (DNS), and data is shared efficiently between domain controllers, making shared storage less important than it would be for, say, an Exchange cluster.

In terms of physical storage, domain controller requirements are low by modern standards, unless, of course, they're used for other services, such as hosting user profiles or home directories. Under normal operation, a domain controller may be simultaneously accessing its system files, virtual memory, directory database, and log files. Hence, to optimize performance, these four components should be placed on separate physical disks. Given limited resources, the most important two components to separate are the ntds.dit file and the log files.

Directory Services Restore Mode

A Windows 2000 startup option available on domain controllers is Directory Services Restore. In this mode, Active Directory doesn't start and administrators are, thus, able to perform maintenance operations on the directory database files, such as restoring them from backup or compacting the files. Directory Services Restore mode can be entered either through the F8 menu on startup or from an entry on the Boot menu. Using the new **/SAFEBOOT:DSREPAIR** switch in the boot.ini file, it can be added as an option on the Start menu.

In fact, this can even be used to make it the default, which opens up the possibility of using Directory Services Repair mode over terminal services, by replacing the normal boot.ini with one that defaults to DS Repair mode. In this way, the server can be rebooted, the terminal services can be connected to, the maintenance taken care of (if needed), the boot.ini file replaced, and the server rebooted again.

Directory Database Maintenance

The most important data stored on a domain controller is the Active Directory data. The data is contained in the three locations specified at installation: the ntds.dit file, the log files, and the shared system volume (sysvol).

Backup and Restore

An important task in the maintenance of any server is taking regular backups and testing them to ensure they can be restored properly. Even though Active Directory is a distributed database with fast convergence within a site, backups are still vital. For one thing, offsite backups should still be taken as a defense against Acts of God and the like. Another, more common scenario that will require backups is the replacement of objects that are deleted accidentally.

Backup

Windows 2000 includes its own backup utility, which is much improved from the built-in Windows NT Backup from NT 4. Found on the System Tools menu, beneath Accessories in the Start | Programs menu structure, Windows 2000 Backup can be driven either by wizards or by commands located on the tabs of its main display (see Figure 16.1).

Emergency Repair Disks

Emergency Repair Disks (ERDs) are a last resort if a system won't start with the aid of Safe mode or with using the Recovery Console. They're used in conjunction with the Windows 2000 CD-ROM or setup floppies to replace system files and the boot sector in order to get Windows 2000 starting. As single floppy disks, they obviously don't contain full system backups.

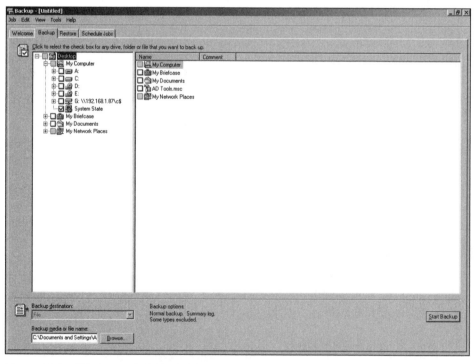

Figure 16.1   Windows 2000 Backup Backup tab.

To back up the Active Directory, the System State data must be selected. Backing up System State data is an all-or-nothing operation, although System State includes components labeled Active Directory, Boot Files, the COM+ Class Registration Database, the Registry, and Sysvol.

When Active Directory is backed up, the domain controller is obviously still running and servicing clients. This means that there can be changes to the database file while backup is in progress. This potential problem is very real, because the database can be of the order of a hundred megabytes for a reasonably large enterprise.

The solution implemented is quite simple: Essentially, all transactions that occur on the database during the backup will be replayed after it's restored. This is made possible by the checkpoint file (edb.chk), which records the most recently applied transaction and is used, in general, to ensure that the correct transactions are applied each time the database is opened.

Restore

Restoring Active Directory is slightly more complicated than backing it up. For one thing, you can't restore Active Directory while the directory service is running and must, instead, reboot into a special Directory Services Restore mode to be able to replace the directory database.

A second issue with restoring Active Directory concerns deleted objects. Consider, for example, the scenario where you delete your boss's user account by mistake, realize five or so minutes later, and hope to restore it from backup tape. After taking a domain controller into Directory Services Restore mode, restoring the backup, and rebooting normally, what happens? Replication. As part of this replication, the tombstone for your boss's user object will be replicated back in, and hence, your freshly restored copy of her user account will be deleted.

The way to avoid this is by performing an authoritative restore. This means that before you reboot the computer after restoring the backup, you mark one or more subtrees as authoritatively restored (of course, these subtrees could be single objects). This will mean that they aren't deleted by the existing tombstone and will, instead, replace it and replicate normally. Objects are marked as authoritatively restored with **ntdsutil**.

The final point to note about restoring Active Directory is that you shouldn't restore backups older than the tombstone lifetime (60 days, by default), because some objects that have been deleted since the backup will be restored after their tombstones have expired. For example, say your most recent backup is three months old, and you restore that backup, and the tombstone lifetime is the default of about two months. Any object deleted between two and three months ago that was present exactly three months ago will be on the backup tape. However, the tombstone marking this object as deleted will now have expired when the tape is restored, so these objects will be returned to the network when such an old backup tape is restored.

Defragmentation

Just as hard disks become fragmented, the ntds.dit file becomes fragmented also. This is because the database engine used is optimized for writing data quickly to fill database pages and as a result, the distribution of data within the file isn't usually optimal from a reading point of view.

Online

Online defragmentation takes place as the last step of the periodic garbage collection process, and, thus, occurs while Active Directory is running. Its only effect is to rearrange the data within the file.

Offline

The Active Directory database file (ntds.dit) is held permanently open while the directory service is running. This has several consequences, two of which are that the file never shrinks (even when numerous objects are deleted) and also that the correct file size may not be reported.

To reclaim unused space from ntds.dit and to determine the exact file size, it's necessary to perform offline defragmentation. This can only take place in Directory Services Restore mode, and actually copies the ntds.dit file to a new location and defragments that file. It's then possible to back up the old ntds.dit file and copy the defragmented file into its place.

Moving Active Directory Components

During the installation of Active Directory, the **dcpromo.exe** Wizard gives you the opportunity to specify the locations for the directory database file (ntds.dit), log files, and sysvol. By reason of poor planning or unexpected growth, there may be occasions upon which you wish to move the location of these objects.

The database file and log files may be moved easily using **ntdsutil.exe** when a domain controller is booted into Directory Services Repair Mode. Sysvol is altogether more complicated, and it isn't advisable to attempt to move it.

Database Import/Export

The import and export of data from Active Directory is an important area. It often comes up in relation to test environments, where you rapidly wish to populate the directory with data (and may frequently rebuild the test lab from scratch) and is also an issue in live environments where the initial import of directory data is an issue.

In addition to techniques, such as scripting via Active Directory Service Interface (ADSI), and importing with a dedicated tool, such as the Active Directory Connector (ADC) for Exchange 5.5, Microsoft provides two utilities with Windows 2000 that can import and export Active Directory data.

LDIF

The *LDAP Data Interchange Format (LDIF)* is an Internet Engineering Task Force (IETF) standard for import/export of directory data. LDIF is supported by numerous directory service implementations and can, thus, be used to transfer data between different directory services, as well as be used for import/export of Active Directory data.

The standards document for LDIF is RFC 2849, although Windows 2000 was released before the RFC was published, so the version implemented was based on a draft specification. LDIF files are, in effect text files, which contain a series of commands separated by blank lines. These commands correspond to the LDAP operations **add**, **delete**, **modrdn** (move), and **modify**. They must be valid (UTF)-8 (Universal Text Format-8) files, and fortunately, the Windows 2000 version of Notepad has the option to save a file as UTF-8. 7-bit ASCII is valid UTF-8, so unless you're using localized characters or those with ASCII values over 127, you don't have to worry about explicitly using UTF-8 encoding.

Although Microsoft's examples often omit it, the first line of an LDIF file should specify the version number in use. For Windows 2000 Active Directory, this means version 1, as follows:

```
version: 1
```

In fact, all values in LDIF files are specified on separate lines in a similar fashion with a command (or attribute name), a separator (usually a colon), and a value. The # sign is used to comment lines out.

Add

We'll now discuss the **add** operation, and start with an example in Listing 16.1.

Listing 16.1   ADBB-16-01-AddExample.ldf.

```
version: 1
dn: CN=Ed,CN=Users,DC=example,DC=com
changetype: add
cn: Ed
```

```
objectCategory: CN=Person,CN=Schema,CN=Configuration,DC=example,DC=com
objectClass: user
name: Ed
sAMAccountName: Ed
userPrincipalName: Ed@example.com
```

Listing 16.1 is a small example of a simple LDIF file. Here, there's only one action, which is to add a new user account called Ed. The first line of the entry starts **dn:** and specifies the distinguished name of the object that this entry corresponds to. The next line, **changetype**, tells us that this is an **add** operation and the following lines specify the attributes to populate and their values.

Modify

The next example (see Listing 16.2) shows a **modify** operation. Here, changes to a number of different attributes can be specified in a single entry if they're delimited by a line containing only a single dash (-). Here, each change can either be an **add**, a **delete**, or a **replace**.

Listing 16.2   ADBB-16-02-ModifyExample.ldf.

```
version: 1
dn: CN=Ed,CN=Users,DC=example,DC=com
changetype: modify
add: telephoneNumber
telephoneNumber: 555 1234
-
delete: streetAddress
-
replace: otherTelephone
otherTelephone: 555 2345
otherTelephone: 555 3456
-
```

Here **add** simply appends the value specified to the existing values (so adds another value to a multivalue attribute), whereas **replace** will delete any existing values for the specified attribute with those given in the LDIF file.

Delete

Deleting an object with LDIF is altogether easier than adding or modifying. Listing 16.3 gives an example of how to do it:

Listing 16.3   ADBB-16-03-DeleteExample.ldf.

```
version: 1
dn: CN=Ed,CN=Users,DC=example,DC=com
changetype: delete
```

Modrdn

Renaming or moving an object requires the **modrdn** operation. This is a two-stage process: first, to change the relative distinguished name (RDN) and second, to change the parent object's distinguished name (DN). An example is given in Listing 16.4.

Listing 16.4   ADBB-16-04-ModrdnExample.ldf.

```
version: 1
dn: CN=Ed,CN=Users,DC=example,DC=com
changetype: modrdn
newrdn: CN=Edward
deleteoldrdn: 1
newsuperior: OU=Test,DC=example,DC=com
```

CSV (Comma-Separated Variable)

If LDIF seems too complicated (although it isn't, honestly), then comma-separated variable files provide a simpler method of importing and exporting directory objects—although, no modifications or deletions are possible. The utility included in Windows 2000 to work with Active Directory CSV imports and exports is **csvde.exe**.

The required format for a CSV file is the first line lists the attributes for the new objects, with subsequent lines each containing a single object. For example, the CSV equivalent of the simple LDIF **add** operation (Listing 16.1) is given in Listing 16.5:

Listing 16.5   ADBB-16-05-CSVUser.csv.

```
dn,cn,objectCategory,objectClass,name,sAMAccountName,userPrincipalName
"CN=Ed,CN=Users,DC=example,DC=com",Ed,"CN=Person,CN=Schema,
 CN=Configuration,DC=example,DC=com",user,Ed,Ed,Ed@example.com
```

NOTE: *The second line of the above listing is artificially wrapped to fit it onto the page. CSV files shouldn't wrap and, consequently, they have very long lines. Use a CSV-aware application, such as Microsoft Excel, or a good text editor, such as TextPad (**www.textpad.com**), because Notepad can only display 1024 characters in a single line.*

Event Logs

In Windows 2000, several event logs are available, which applications and system components can write to in order to record diagnostic details or inform administrators. These logs can be read through the Management Console Snap-in Event Viewer (for which there is a shortcut on the Administrative Tools menu).

The main logs of specific interest on domain controllers are the following:

- System Log

- Directory Service Log

- File Replication Service Log

It's a good idea to periodically scan these logs on servers to ensure that they're functioning properly. If you encounter an error, there should a description of it. If this doesn't include a solution to a problem, then the first course of action should be to search for the event ID and source application in the knowledgebase, either through a local copy of TechNet or at **http://support.microsoft.com**.

Miscellaneous Utilities

In addition to the major areas discussed in this chapter, a number of utilities are available that can help in the management of Active Directory domain controllers. The uses of the utilities are discussed below, and the mechanics of their use are illustrated in the "Immediate Solutions" section of this chapter.

Dcdiag

The command-line domain controller diagnostics tool (**dcdiag.exe**), which ships as part of the Windows 2000 Support Tools, can be used to test numerous aspects of one or more domain controllers.

The following tests can be performed with **dcdiag.exe**, whether on a specific domain controller, on all domain controllers in a site, or on all domain controllers in a forest:

- *Connectivity*—Performs connectivity tests, including testing DNS registrations, **ping**, LDAP connectivity, and RPC connectivity.

- *Replications*—Tests domain controller replication.

- *Topology*—Checks that there are no disconnected domain controllers through the current topology.

- *CutoffServers*—Checks that there are no disconnected domain controllers through partner failure.

- *NCSecDesc*—Checks that appropriate permissions exist on the directory for replication.

- *NetLogons*—Checks that appropriate logon permissions exist for replication.

- *Advertising*—Checks that domain controllers are advertising themselves.

- *KnowsOfRoleHolders*—Checks whether operations master role holders are known.

- *Intersite*—Checks for intersite replication failures.
- *FsmoCheck*—Checks whether operations master role holders can be contacted.
- *RidManager*—Checks that the RID operations master role holder is operational and responding.
- *MachineAccount*—Checks that the domain controller has a proper computer account in Active Directory.
- *Services*—Checks that all necessary services for a fully functioning domain controller are running. These services are the following:
  - Dnscache
  - NtFrs
  - IsmServ
  - kdc
  - SamSs
  - LanmanServer
  - LanmanWorkstation
  - RpcSs
  - RPCLOCATOR
  - w32time
  - TrkWks
  - TrkSvr
  - NETLOGON
  - Dnscache
  - NtFrs
- *OutboundSecureChannels*—Checks secure channels to all domain controllers in the current domain.
- *ObjectsReplicated*—Checks that machine account and Directory System Agent (DSA) objects have replicated by default, and can also be used to check additional objects.
- *frssysvol*—Checks that sysvol is ready for file replication.
- *kccevent*—Checks that the Knowledge Consistency Checker is free of errors.
- *systemlog*—Checks that the system log is running without errors.

NOTE: dcdiag.exe *has numerous options that allow these tests to be run individually or all together. Type* **dcdiag.exe /?** *at a command prompt window to see a full list of options. Be sure to have a large screen buffer, because the options go on for numerous lines.*

Dsastat

To produce summary statistics on a particular directory server, **dsastat.exe** can be used. For example, it can return the number of objects matching certain criteria and perform a comparison over several servers. This tool is part of the Windows 2000 Server Support Tools found on the Windows 2000 Server CD-ROM. An example of its usage is found in the "Immediate Solutions" for this chapter.

Esentutl

The *Extensible Storage Engine (ESE)* is the database storage engine used for the ntds.dit file. The management utility, **esentutl.exe**, is for ESE database files in general that are found in the %SystemRoot%\system32 directory. For Active Directory, **ntdsutil.exe** provides its own interface to **esentutl.exe**, although it's still possible to use it directly on the database file. However, to use this utility on the Active Directory database, you must restart in Directory Services Restore mode, because the directory database must not be locked for exclusive use.

Immediate Solutions

Configuring a Domain Controller as a Global Catalog Server

To configure a domain controller as a Global Catalog server:

1. Start Active Directory Sites and Services from the Administrative Tools menu.

2. Navigate to the server to configure as a domain controller beneath Sites, the name of the server's site, then Servers.

3. Expand the server's object.

4. Right-click its NTDS Settings object and click Properties. The Properties dialog box appears (see Figure 16.2).

5. Check or clear the Global Catalog box, as appropriate.

6. Click OK.

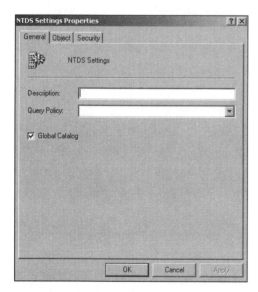

Figure 16.2   NTDS Properties General tab.

Disabling Global Catalog Requirement at Logon

To disable the requirement for a Global Catalog server to be contacted when a user logs in, the following registry key can be specified at the domain controller:

```
HKLM\System\CurrentControlSet\Control\Lsa\IgnoreGCFailures
```

Setting it with a DWORD value of 1 will ignore Global Catalog failures. The Global Catalog requirement exists to determine accurate Global Group membership but doesn't apply for Domain Admins by default.

Operations Master Roles

I'll now discuss operations master roles.

Seizing Operations Master Roles

Operations master roles can be seized with the **ntdsutil.exe** utility, installed by default on Windows 2000 domain controllers. To seize an operations master role with **ntdsutil**:

1. Launch a command prompt from the Administrative Tools menu.

2. Type **ntdsutil**. **Ntdsutil** launches.

   ```
   c:\>ntdsutil
   ```

3. At the **ntdsutil** prompt, type **Roles**.

   ```
   ntdsutil: Roles
   ```

4. Next, we need to connect to the server that you wish to seize the role of. Type **Connections**.

   ```
   fsmo maintenance: Connections
   ```

5. If you wish to specify alternate credentials to the current user, enter **Set creds** and the domain name of the user (NetBIOS or DNS), username (no User Principal Names [UPNs]), and password to authenticate with.

   ```
   server connections: Set creds domain user password
   ```

6. Now type **Connect to server,** and enter the DNS or NetBIOS name of the server to connect to. Status messages appear.

```
server connections: Connect to server server.to.transfer.to
Binding to server.to.transfer.to as user(user) in domain(domain) ...
Connected to server.to.transfer.to as user(user) in domain domain) ...
```

7. Return to the previous menu system by typing **quit**.

```
server connections: quit
```

8. Enter one of the following, appropriate to the role for seizure.

```
fsmo maintenance: Seize domain naming master
fsmo maintenance: Seize infrastructure master
fsmo maintenance: Seize PDC
fsmo maintenance: Seize RID master
fsmo maintenance: Seize schema master
```

9. You're then prompted to confirm the seizure. Click Yes if you're sure.

10. Finally, exit **ntdsutil** by typing **quit** twice.

```
fsmo maintenance: quit
ntdsutil: quit
Disconnecting user(user) in domain(domain) from server.to.transfer.to ...
```

Before seizure takes place, a transfer of the role will be attempted. At any point in **ntdsutil**, you can type **help** for a list of all available commands and **quit** to go back up a menu level (or exit at the root level).

Starting in Directory Services Restore Mode

Directory Services Restore mode is an option from the F8 startup menu. To restart in Directory Services Restore mode:

1. Restart the computer by clicking Start, Shutdown and then selecting Restart in the list and clicking OK.

2. If prompted, select the appropriate Windows 2000 installation from the boot menu.

3. When prompted, press F8 for Advanced Startup Options.

4. Select the seventh option to start in Directory Services Restore mode.

5. When prompted, log on with the Directory Services Restore mode password specified when Active Directory was installed on this domain controller.

Creating an Emergency Repair Disk

Emergency repair disks (ERDs) can be used with Windows 2000 installation media to replace critical boot and system files. To create an emergency repair disk in Windows 2000:

1. Launch Backup from the System Tools menu, beneath Accessories.

2. Click the icon labeled Emergency Repair Disk from the Welcome tab. The Emergency Repair Diskette dialog box (see Figure 16.3) appears.

3. Insert a blank, formatted floppy into drive A:

4. If you wish, click to back up the Registry. This will copy the current state of the registry to %SystemRoot%\repair so you can recover to the current state of the Registry with your ERD.

5. Click OK to create the ERD.

Figure 16.3   Emergency Repair Diskette dialog box.

Active Directory Backup and Restore

Now, I'll discuss the backup and restoration of Active Directory.

Backing Up Active Directory

Although third-party products are available, Windows 2000 includes a backup utility that is perfectly capable of backing up and restoring Windows 2000 computers running Active Directory—and now it even has the ability to schedule backup jobs and use media other than tape drives.

To back up Active Directory, you must back up the System State Data on a domain controller. To do this, perform the following:

1. Launch Backup from the System Tools menu, beneath Accessories.

2. Click the icon labeled Backup Wizard from the Welcome tab. The Backup Wizard appears.

3. Click Next at the welcome screen.

4. On the What to Back Up page, select Only back up the System State Data. Click Next.

5. On the next screen, choose the destination for the backup. Windows 2000 backup files have the .bkf extension. Click Next.

6. On the final page of the Backup Wizard you can click Finish to back up now, or use the Advanced button to set more options, including backup type and various media options that apply mainly to tape backups.

Restoring Active Directory

By default, once a server is rebooted, the directory service will start again and replicate in any changes made since the backup was taken. In particular, this means that if you restore a deleted object, it will be deleted again by its tombstone replicating in from another domain controller on the network.

To restore a backup of System State Data made with Windows 2000 Backup:

NOTE: *You can only restore System State Data on a local machine.*

---

1. Restart the domain controller to restore to in Directory Services Repair mode.

2. Launch Backup from the System Tools menu, beneath Accessories.

3. Click the icon labeled Backup Wizard from the Welcome tab. The Restore Wizard appears.

4. Click Next.

5. Drill down through the listed backups (or import a file) to find the System State to restore. Check the box next to the appropriate System State and click Next to continue.

6. Click Finish to restore the backup. Advanced options only give you the choice of restoration location, which doesn't really apply for System State Data.

To make restored objects shrug off the fact that they're tombstoned, the restoration must be marked as authoritative. This is done before rebooting the computer.

16. Managing Domain Controllers

Performing an Authoritative Restore

Once you've restored System State Data on a domain controller, you can mark subtrees of the restored directory as authoritative. To do so perform the following:

1. Boot into DS Restore mode, restore the applicable System State backup, but don't reboot the computer when prompted.

2. Launch a Command Prompt from the Accessories menu.

3. Type **ntdsutil** and press enter. **Ntdsutil** starts.

4. At the **ntdsutil** prompt, type **Authoritative restore**.

   ```
   ntdsutil: Authoritative restore
   ```

5. At the **authoritative restore** prompt, type **Restore subtree** *DN*. For example:

   ```
   authoritative restore: restore subtree ou=test,dc=example,dc=com
   ```

   Alternatively, type **Restore database** to mark the entire restoration authoritative.

   ```
   authoritative restore: restore database
   ```

Performing Offline Defragmentation

Offline defragmentation of the directory database file takes place in Directory Services Restore mode.

NOTE: *Offline defragmentation shouldn't be required as a matter of course. Use it only to reclaim large amounts of lost space or to accurately assess the database size.*

---

1. Restart the computer in Directory Services Restore mode.

2. Launch a command prompt and type **ntdsutil** and press Enter,

   ```
   C:\>ntdsutil
   ```

3. Type **files** and press Enter.

   ```
   ntdsutil: files
   ```

4. Type **compact to** followed by the directory to hold the new ntds.dit and press Enter. For example:

```
file maintenance: compact to "c:\temp folder"
```

5. Exit **ntdsutil**.

```
file maintenance: quit
ntdsutil: quit
```

The new ntds.dit can now be copied over the old one. Obviously, you should take backups before starting this process, as well as making backups of the old ntds.dit file.

Changing Active Directory File Locations

I'll now discuss changing Active Directory file locations, in particular, how to move the database and log file locations for Active Directory.

Moving the Database Directory

The database file—ntds.dit—can be moved using **ntdsutil.exe** from within Directory Services Restore mode. To do so:

1. Restart the computer in Directory Services Restore mode.

2. Launch a command prompt and type **ntdsutil** and press Enter.

```
C:\>ntdsutil
```

3. Type **files** and press Enter.

```
ntdsutil: files
```

4. Type **move DB to** followed by the directory to hold the new ntds.dit and press Enter. For example:

```
file maintenance: move DB to "d:\Active Directory"
```

5. Exit **ntdsutil**.

```
file maintenance: quit
ntdsutil: quit
```

Moving Log Files

Similarly to moving ntds.dit, you can also move the log files directory post-installation. To do this:

1. Restart the computer in Directory Services Restore mode.

2. Launch a command prompt and type **ntdsutil** and press Enter.

   ```
   C:\>ntdsutil
   ```

3. Type **files** and press Enter.

   ```
   ntdsutil: files
   ```

4. Type **move logs to** followed by the directory to hold the new ntds.dit and press Enter. For example:

   ```
   file maintenance: move logs to "e:\new log directory"
   ```

5. Exit **ntdsutil**.

   ```
   file maintenance: quit
   ntdsutil: quit
   ```

Working with LDIF Files

The LDAP Data Interchange Format (LDIF) provides a convenient way of dumping data, transferring data between directories and applying changes with text files. The LDIF standard (RFC 2849) dictates that LDIF files comply with UTF-8 (see **www.unicode.org**.) UTF-8 includes simple 7-bit ASCII as a subset, and the Windows 2000 version of notepad can generate UTF-8 files.

LDIF files need not have any particular extension, but .ldf and .ldif are favorites.

Directory Exports

Export is the default operation for LDIFDE. A simple export can be obtained by typing:

```
C:\>ldifde -f example.ldif
```

This will, however, export the entire current domain. The objects exported can be restricted with additional parameters including **-r** followed by a search filter, **-d** followed by a DN to base the query at, and **-p** to specify a scope (base object only, one level, or a subtree). By default all objects in the subtree rooted at the current domain naming context will be exported.

You can also filter exported data by including (**-l**) or excluding (**-o**) a comma-separated list of attributes. The **-n** switch is also useful, as it suppresses binary values being exported.

Directory Imports

Files can be imported using LDIFDE's **–i** switch. Additional useful switches include **-k** (which suppresses certain error messages) and **-y** (which uses lazy commit and hence speeds up the execution of LDIFDE). To import a file called example.ldif you would simply type:

```
C:\>ldifde -I -f example.ldif
```

A final switch that can be used for both export and import is **-c**, followed by two DNs. This replaces occurrences of the first DN with the second. For example, consider the following:

```
C:\>ldifde -i -f example.ldif -c "dc=example,dc=com" "dc=coriolis,dc=com"
```

This imports the contents of **example.ldif** and replaces all **dc=example, dc=om DNs with dc=coriolis,dc=com**. This command is useful if you have exported objects from the **example.com** domain and wish to import them to the **coriolis.com** domain.

Configuring Passwords

Configuring user passwords with LDIF is a non-trivial matter. For one thing you don't want to be able to change a password by transmitting the new password in clear text over the network.

Therefore, there are a number of criteria that must be adhered to when setting passwords with LDIF. These are as follows:

- *128-bit SSL*—There must be a 128-bit SSL session between the client and domain controller.
- *BER-encoded Unicode passwords enclosed in quotes*—The passwords must be enclosed in quotes, converted to Unicode and then encoded as an octet string data with the ASN.1 BER encoding scheme (Abstract Syntax Notation 1 Basic Encoding Rules).

16. Managing Domain Controllers

- *Base64 encoding*—BER data is an octet string, and in LDIF octet strings must be Base64-encoded.

We now examine how to meet the above requirements.

Installing 128-bit Encryption

Windows 2000 has a 128-bit encryption add on that is available in most countries around the world. It is often distributed on a single floppy disk (the high encryption disk) or can be downloaded from **www.microsoft.com/windows2000/ downloads/recommended/encryption**.

NOTE: *There may be certain restrictions on the export or import of 128-bit encryption. If in doubt, please check with your local laws.*

To install the High-Encryption pack, execute **encpack.exe** or install direct over the Internet from the address above.

Installing and Configuring Certificate Services

To provide a public key infrastructure for SSL, you must establish an Enterprise Root certificate authority in the forest. To do so you must install Certificate Services as follows:

1. Click Start, Settings, and then Control Panel.
2. Double-click Add/Remove Programs.
3. Click Add/Remove Windows Components and then Next.
4. Check the Certificate Services check box, accept the warning, and click Next.
5. Select an Enterprise Root CA, and then click Next.
6. Complete the identifying information for your organization, and click Next.
7. Specify the data storage locations, and click Next.
8. If it is running, you will be prompted to stop IIS so the installation can proceed. Click OK if prompted.
9. Insert the Windows 2000 CD-ROM (if prompted).
10. Click Finish to compete the installation.

Encoding Passwords

A password cannot be added as-is to an LDIF file. Instead it must be converted to Unicode, enclosed in double quotes, BER-encoded, and then Base64 encoded. The resulting alphanumeric value should then be set as the **unicodePwd** attribute, with a double colon (::) separator, as the value is Base64 encoded.

To actually perform the encoding, the easiest language to use is Perl, as libraries are available for performing BER and Base64 encoding. A sample Perl script to perform the encoding process on a supplied password is given in Listing 16.6.

Listing 16.6 ADBB-16-06-EncodePassword.pl.

```
use Convert::BER;
use MIME::Base64;

$ber    = new Convert::BER;
$pwd    = $ARGV[0];
$string = chr(0)."\"";
$l      = length $pwd;

for ($i = 0; $i < $l; $i++)
{
  $string .= chr(0);
  $string .= substr $pwd, $i, 1;
}

$string .= chr(0)."\"".chr(0);
$ber->encode(STRING => $string);
$encoded = encode_base64($ber->buffer);

print substr $encoded, 4, length($encoded) - 5;
```

This script takes a single parameter which is the password to encode (7-bit ASCII only), and prints out the encoded value. This should then be copied and pasted into an LDIF file. The syntax to do this with Perl is:

```
C:\>perl ADBB-16-06-EncodePassword.pl password
```

An example add operation that creates an account with a password of **password** is given below:

```
dn: cn=Test123,cn=Users,dc=example,dc=com
changetype: add
unicodePwd::IgBwAGEAcwBzAHcAbwByAGQAIgA=
cn: Test123
sAMAccountName: Test123
userPrincipalName: test123@example.com
```

The Perl language is included in the Windows 2000 Server Resource Kit, and the latest version can be found at **www.activestate.com**. More information about the language can be found in the accompanying documentation or from **www.perl.com**.

Importing LDIF over SSL

Once you have created your LDIF file and configured SSL, the final step is to import it. The syntax to do so is:

```
C:\>ldifde -i -f file.ldif -t 636 -b administrator domain password
```

Here **file.ldif** should be replaced with your file name and **administrator domain password** should be replaced by the user, domain, and password to authenticate with. The **-t 636** specifies that port 636 is used, which is the default SSL port for LDAP.

NOTE: An "Unwilling to perform" error will return if SSL/128-bit encryption is not configured correctly and a "Constraint Violation" will be reported if the password attribute is not correctly encoded and in the right format.

Working with CSV Files

CSV files are imported and exported with **csvde.exe**. Type **csvde /?** At a command prompt to see the full range of options available, but the examples of the main options are given below:

Import a file called **file.csv** to a specific domain controller:

```
C:\>csvde -i -f file.csv -s server.example.com
```

Import a file to the currently connected domain controller, and change all DNs from **example.com** with **coriolis.com**.

```
C:\>csvde -i -f file.csv -c "dc=example,dc=com" "dc=coriolis,dc=com"
```

Export all objects beneath **ou=test,cn=example,cn=com** (export is implicit):

```
C:\>csvde -f file.csv -d "ou=test,cn=example,cn=com"
```

Export only user objects in the Test OU:

```
C:\>csvde -f file.csv -d "ou=test,cn=example,cn=com" -p OneLevel -r
        "(objectClass=user)"
```

Export only the User Principal Name (UPN) and email address of a specific object:

```
C:\>csvde -f file.csv -d "ou=test,cn=example,cn=com" -p Base -l
        "userPrincipalName,mail"
```

Chapter 17

Troubleshooting Active Directory

In Depth

This chapter's attention turns to the part science, part black art that is trouble-shooting. In particular, we look at troubleshooting Active Directory (after all, it's what the book is about). Troubles with Active Directory can be categorized either as connectivity problems or "real" Active Directory problems. Connectivity issues are, by far, the most common problems, although they're, of course, indistinguishable from "real" directory problems until they're investigated.

DNS and IP Troubleshooting

Probably the single largest cause of "Active Directory-related" problems is Domain Name System (DNS) configuration (and the lack thereof). However, the most basic area to check before DNS can be investigated is the network connectivity itself.

Can You Ping It?

Before examining DNS configuration, the very first step is to insure that you actually have network connectivity to an end system. This usually means checking first to determine whether you can **ping** a domain controller by IP address and, second, that you can **ping** your DNS server by IP address.

Ping is a utility that that sends **ECHO_REQUEST** packets and expects **ECHO_REPLY**s to come back, and it's named after the sound made by a sonar system. It's widely used as the simplest test of IP network connectivity and is available in Windows 2000 through the ping.exe program. Quite simply, from a command prompt you can type something like:

```
C:\>ping 192.168.0.1
```

If an **ECHO_REPLY** is returned from the destination, then a reply, such as the following, will be displayed:

```
Reply from 192.168.0.1: bytes=32 time<10ms TTL=128
```

If **ping** replies are received, then network connectivity exists. Unfortunately, a lack of reply doesn't necessarily mean that a connection doesn't exist or that the server isn't up and responding.

The reason for this is that on many networks, routers are configured to block **ECHO_REQUEST**s and **ECHO_REPLY**s to thwart potential intruders and denial-of-service attacks. If you know or suspect this to be the case between the client and domain controller, then an alternative way to check basic connectivity is required.

What about Telnet to Port 389?

If Internet Control Message Protocol (ICMP) **ECHO_REQUEST**s are blocked at the router level, then an alternative way to check that network packets will reach an Active Directory domain controller is to telnet to port 389. This method will, of course, only work on computers running a service on port 389.

Because port 389 is the default Lightweight Directory Access Protocol (LDAP) port that domain controllers will all use, they should, of course, respond to requests on it. Telnetting to it is just a matter of typing something like the following command:

```
C:\>telnet 192.168.0.1 389
```

In this case, the desired response is a blank telnet window (indicating that an LDAP request is expected), because this shows a connection has been made. If a connection can't be established, you'll see a message similar to:

```
Connecting To 192.168.0.1...Could not open a connection to host on port 389
 : Connect failed
```

A failure like this from a domain controller means that it's either not functioning properly (no LDAP server is running) or, more likely, network problems exist that need to be resolved.

Client Configuration

The most likely cause of Active Directory connectivity problems is misconfigured DNS settings, but IP address configuration can also cause more fundamental errors. DNS is used as the primary locator service by Windows 2000 clients to locate directory services, so if a DNS server that's aware of Active Directory is unavailable, you won't be able to add a computer to a domain or log on, for example.

The IP configuration of the current computer can be examined with the command-line tool **ipconfig.exe**. Unfortunately, there's no graphical equivalent similar to **winipcfg.exe** in Windows 2000. Most importantly, it's essential that clients are using a DNS server that holds the zone that domain controllers are registering their service (SRV) resource records in. If you're using Active Directory-integrated DNS, this means that clients should use a domain controller as a DNS server.

The reason for this is that clients (and domain controllers) must be able to resolve the SRV resource records that are registered by domain controllers into IP addresses.

TIP: *DNS uses a local cache, which may contain outdated information. To clear the cache, type **ipconfig /flushdns** at the command line.*

DNS Registration

If clients have their DNS settings configured correctly, the next stage is to check that the DNS server is operational with the correct resource records registered. The best way to do this is using **netdiag /test:dns /debug**, but **nslookup.exe** can also be used to query the DNS server.

NsLookup (name server lookup) is a command-line utility, which simply queries a specific domain controller for a specified resource record. When configured to query for SRV resource records, it will return all the configurable options for the records, such as priority and weight. For example, domain controllers should register the following resource records:

```
_ldap._tcp.DomainName.
_ldap._tcp.gc._msdcs.DomainName.
_ldap._tcp.<DomainGUID>.domains._msdcs.ForestRootDomainName.
<ServerGUID>._msdcs.DomainName.
_kerberos._tcp.dc._msdcs.DomainName.
_ldap._tcp.dc._msdcs.DomainName.
_kerberos._tcp.DomainName.
_kerberos._udp.DomainName.
_kpasswd._tcp.DomainName.
_kpasswd._udp.DomainName.
_ldap._tcp.<SiteName>._sites.DomainName.
_ldap._tcp.<SiteName>._sites.gc._msdcs.DomainName.
_kerberos._tcp.<SiteName>._sites.dc._msdcs.DomainName.
_ldap._tcp.<SiteName>._sites.dc._msdcs.DomainName.
_kerberos._tcp.<SiteName>._sites.DomainName.
```

In addition, the primary domain controller (PDC) Emulator Master should be identified by the following DNS resource record:

```
_ldap._tcp.pdc._msdcs.DomainName.
```

Finally, Global Catalog servers should be identified by these two resource records:

```
_gc._tcp.ForestRootDomainName.
_gc._tcp.<SiteName>._sites.ForestRootDomainName.
```

To reregister resource records in Windows 2000, you can stop and then start the netlogon service using the Services Snap-in, found, for example, within Computer Management.

Event Log

A key area to inspect in case of trouble is the Windows 2000 Event Log. Using the Event Viewer Snap-in, you can connect to the Event Logs of remote computers (or perhaps create a custom Microsoft Management Console [MMC] containing the logs of every important server on your network).

Services and system components write status and error messages to the Event Log. In fact, the Event Log is divided into a number of separate logs, such as System, Security, Application, and Directory Service. Entries in the Event Logs have a number of common features shown in the sample Event Properties dialog box (see Figure 17.1).

Perhaps chief among these for troubleshooting purposes are the source of the event, the event ID, and the description. For example, the event shown above will occur periodically on the PDC Emulator of a forest root domain that doesn't have external time synchronization configured. This is because that machine is the authoritative source of time for the entire forest, and, hence, should be getting its information (indirectly) from some Internet-based atomic clock.

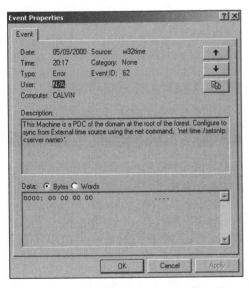

Figure 17.1 Sample Event Properties dialog box.

17. Troubleshooting Active Directory

With the Event ID and source, it's usually possible to pin down the exact cause and resolution of an event from the manufacturer of a program. In the case of Microsoft, this usually means searching the online knowledge base for reports of the error.

Replication Troubleshooting

Replication is key to the success (or otherwise) of an Active Directory installation. Without efficient and functioning replication, directory data isn't shared in a timely manner, and the directory may as well not be there. Again, replication issues often boil down to connectivity—can the domain controller actually resolve the SRV resource records for its replication partners? Is there sufficient connectivity for remote procedure call (RPC) communication? Are options, such as schedules, preventing replication from happening?

A number of tools exist to help with these problems. RPC connectivity can be tested by the RPC **ping** applications (**rpings.exe** and **pringc.exe** from the Windows 2000 Resource Kits.) The **replmon.exe** and **repadmin.exe** utilities, both in the Windows 2000 Support Tools, can be used to show object metadata and, in particular, details of the last time a new value was received (including the originating server).

Administration

So far, we've looked mainly at troubleshooting Active Directory connectivity problems. Another side to troubleshooting is dealing with issues that relate to adding objects to the directory. When adding an object to the directory, the key constraint is that it has a unique distinguished name (DN), which, in turn, means having a unique relative distinguished name (RDN) within its parent container. This can lead to the seemingly peculiar situation where a user object whose RDN is **cn=Joanna Smith** can validly exist in the Marketing OU, but when you try to move her to the Sales OU where a **cn=Joanna Smith** already exists, the operation will fail.

In this case, the solution would be to rename the user object. Active Directory users have several different names and, crucially, the common name (cn) of a user's object isn't the be-all and end-all in terms of display name. Instead, when you try to rename an object using the Active Directory Users and Computers Microsoft Management Console (MMC) Snap-in, you're presented with the dialog box shown in Figure 17.2.

Here, the Full Name edit box corresponds to the **cn** of the object, the first and last names to the **givenName** and **sn** attributes, and the Display name is the **displayName** of the object. Other possible errors when creating and renaming objects come from the lack of a contactable Global Catalog server. For example, if you create a user

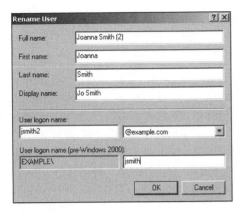

Figure 17.2 Rename User dialog box.

account without a GC server available, the UPN can't be verified as enterprise-unique. In this case, the account will actually be created with that caveat (and you'll be warned of this). This is because the User Principal Name (UPN) of an object must be unique within an enterprise. Additionally, the NetBIOS name of an object must be unique within its domain (and, hence, the domain\username form will be unique within the enterprise).

Windows 2000 Recovery Console

The *Windows 2000 Recovery Console* is a stripped-down, command-line interface made accessible through a boot option or by starting from the Windows 2000 CD-ROM. It's available in both Windows 2000 Server and Professional. With the Recovery Console, you can configure services to start up (or not), replace system files (for example from CD), and perform other basic tasks, such as fixing the master boot record, formatting disks, and even running an equivalent of **fdisk** (to repartition hard drives).

Things That You Can't Do

Unfortunately, not all problems in Active Directory have solutions. Sometimes they're symptomatic of product limitations.

Rename Domains

It just can't be done in Windows 2000. The only way would be to delete the domain by demoting all domain controllers, then re-creating it (which is more like re-creating the domain than renaming it). If you wish to preserve objects, you can use a holding domain. Essentially, the process would be to create a brand new domain, export objects to this domain, delete the domain you wish to rename, create a new domain with the correct name, and reimport the objects. Depending on hardware requirements, you could simply create a new domain with the correct name and import the objects into that, then delete the old domain.

Of course, this process becomes more complex in forests that contain several domains, because the process of destroying and re-creating a domain will also destroy trust links (the replacement domain will have a different Security Identifier [SID], and trusts are stored in terms of SIDs). In particular, this means that "renaming" a forest root domain for anything but a one-domain forest is out of the question.

Rename Domain Controllers

Windows 2000 doesn't support renaming domain controllers. The only solution is to remove Active Directory (so that the server is no longer a domain controller), rename the computer, then reinstall Active Directory.

Move Domain Controllers between Domains

A domain controller is tied to the domain that it's a member of. Moving it between domains would mean deleting the current domain's naming context and adding the naming context of the new domain. Again, the only way to perform this task is to remove the domain controller from its current domain and promote it, again, as a domain controller in the new domain.

NOTE: *Upgrading to Windows 2000 Active Directory is covered in Chapter 20. Troubleshooting upgrades is also dealt with in the same chapter.*

Immediate Solutions

Pinging a Remote Host

Pinging a remote host is a simple task, which can be performed from the command line as follows (here **hostname** can be a hostname or IP address):

```
C:\>ping hostname
```

For a good connection, results akin to the following will be displayed:

```
Pinging 192.168.0.1 with 32 bytes of data:

Reply from 192.168.0.1: bytes=32 time<10ms TTL=128
Reply from 192.168.0.1: bytes=32 time<10ms TTL=128
Reply from 192.168.0.1: bytes=32 time<10ms TTL=128
Reply from 192.168.0.1: bytes=32 time<10ms TTL=128

Ping statistics for 192.168.0.1:
    Packets: Sent = 4, Received = 4, Lost = 0 (0% loss),
Approximate round trip times in milli-seconds:
    Minimum = 0ms, Maximum =  0ms, Average =  0ms
```

By default, the **ping** command will send four **ICMP ECHO_REQUEST**s and wait for the replies. The **-n** switch followed by a number can be used to alter the number of echos sent by a **ping** command.

If the remote host isn't responding or if echoes are being blocked en route, you'll see the following response:

```
Pinging 192.168.1.1 with 32 bytes of data:

Request timed out.
Request timed out.
Request timed out.
Request timed out.

Ping statistics for 192.168.1.1:
    Packets: Sent = 4, Received = 0, Lost = 4 (100% loss),
Approximate round trip times in milli-seconds:
    Minimum = 0ms, Maximum =  0ms, Average =  0ms
```

If you try pinging a host when no known route to them exists, **Destination host unreachable** will be reported. Also, if you try to ping a hostname that can't be resolved to an IP address, **Unknown host** will be reported.

---

*TIP: A number of other options on the **ping** command are available, including the ability to ping indefinitely and to **ping** alter the default timeout value. Type **ping /?** at a command prompt for details.*

Telnetting to a Server

Telnet is another command prompt-based application that can be used for trouble-shooting. It can also be used for remote administration. To telnet into a specific port on a particular server, type the following at a command prompt:

```
C:\>telnet server port
```

Where **server** can either be an IP address or hostname and **port** should be replaced by the decimal port number you wish to connect to. Alternatively, you can start the telnet application and connect interactively by typing "telnet" at the Command Prompt/Run dialog box, then typing "open server port" with the same meanings for server and port as before. For example to telnet to the LDAP server on 192.168.0.1:

```
C:\>telnet

Microsoft (R) Windows 2000 (TM) Version 5.00 (Build 2195)
Welcome to Microsoft Telnet Client
Telnet Client Build 5.00.99201.1

Escape Character is 'CTRL+]'

Microsoft Telnet> open 192.168.0.1 389
```

Windows 2000 Telnet Service

Included with Windows 2000 (Server and Professional) is a new telnet service. This is installed (but not started) on all Windows 2000 systems by default. In effect, it gives a remote command prompt to users connecting via telnet. It's licensed for up to two simultaneous connections.

The Windows 2000 Telnet Service defaults to accepting only connections from clients using a telnet client capable of NT Lan Manager (NTLM) authentication (basically Windows 2000), although this and other options can be changed to accept normal plaintext authentication via the **tlntadmn.exe** administration utility (option 3, then option 7).

IP and DNS Configuration

Troubleshooting network problems often involves verifying and correcting IP and DNS configuration.

Checking IP and DNS Configuration

To examine the IP configuration of a local computer, you can type the following at a command prompt:

```
C:\>ipconfig /all
```

This will display a number of settings for the computer, under the heading of Windows 2000 IP Configuration, as well as settings for each network adapter in the computer.

An example of output is shown below:

```
Windows 2000 IP Configuration

        Host Name . . . . . . . . . . . . : calvin
        Primary DNS Suffix  . . . . . . . : example.com
        Node Type . . . . . . . . . . . . : Broadcast
        IP Routing Enabled. . . . . . . . : No
        WINS Proxy Enabled. . . . . . . . : No
        DNS Suffix Search List. . . . . . : example.com

Ethernet adapter Local Area Connection:

        Connection-specific DNS Suffix  . :
        Description . . . . . . . . . . . : NE2000 Compatible
        Physical Address. . . . . . . . . : 00-00-00-00-00-00
        DHCP Enabled. . . . . . . . . . . : No
        IP Address. . . . . . . . . . . . : 192.168.1.31
        Subnet Mask . . . . . . . . . . . : 255.255.255.0
        Default Gateway . . . . . . . . . : 192.168.0.63
        DNS Servers . . . . . . . . . . . : 127.0.0.1
```

The most important setting here for Active Directory is the last—the IP address of the DNS server.

Setting IP and DNS Configuration

If you've diagnosed a problem with IP address configuration, to resolve the issue you should change the configuration. If you use Dynamic Host Configuration Protocol

(DHCP) for client configuration, then the following don't apply. Instead, the correct options must be configured at the DHCP server console.

Manually

Manual configuration is carried out on a per-connection basis in Windows 2000 through the Network and Dial-up Connections folder.

1. Open Network and Dial-up Connections from the Settings portion of the Start menu. The Network and Dial-up Connections folder appears.

2. Double-click Local Area Connection (the default name for the LAN).

3. On the Status dialog box, click Properties.

4. Select Internet Protocol (TCP/IP) in the components list and click Properties. A Properties dialog box similar to Figure 17.3 appears.

5. Configure the IP address, default gateway, and subnet mask as appropriate to your network.

6. Configure the IP addresses of one or two DNS servers that carry the appropriate zone for the computer's domain.

TIP: *Use the Advanced button to specify additional IP addresses, gateways, DNS servers, Windows Internet Name Service (WINS) servers, and options for IP Sec and filtering.*

---

7. Click OK, OK again, then Close.

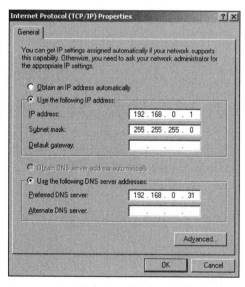

Figure 17.3   Internet Protocol (TCP/IP) Properties dialog box.

By Script

Static IP addresses can be configured using the **netsh.exe** utility. The following two lines set the IP address/subnetmask/default gateway (in that order) and DNS server respectively.

```
netsh interface ip set address "Local Area Connection" static 192.168.0.1
  255.255.255.0 192.168.0.1 1
netsh interface ip set dns "Local Area Connection" static 192.168.10.31
```

NOTE: *This is only two separate lines, and the first has wrapped.*

Resolving SRV Resource Records

To test that the necessary SRV resource records have been registered by a domain controller, you can simply query the server for them from any client. Additionally, to verify that a client has DNS connectivity, you can perform these tests from the client.

To verify that a particular SRV resource record exists with **nslookup.exe**:

1. Launch a Command Prompt from the Accessories menu.

2. Type **nslookup** and press return to enter interactive mode.

```
C:\>nslookup
```

3. By default, **nslookup** will query the currently configured DNS server. To query a specific server, use the server command with an argument of the IP address or hostname of the server to use:

```
> server 192.168.1.31
```

4. To query specifically for SRV records, type the following:

```
> set type=srv
```

5. Enter the fully qualified domain name of a record to query for (including the trailing dot). All matching SRV resource records will be displayed. For example, to display all domain controllers in the **example.com** domain:

```
> _ldap._tcp.example.com
Server:  calvin.example.com
```

```
Address:   192.168.1.31

_ldap._tcp.example.com   SRV service location:
        priority      = 0
        weight        = 100
        port          = 389
        svr hostname  = calvin.example.com
_ldap._tcp.example.com   SRV service location:
        priority      = 0
        weight        = 0
        port          = 389
        svr hostname  = mach.example.com
calvin.example.com       internet address = 192.168.1.31
mach.example.com internet address = 192.168.1.32
```

6. To leave nslookup, type **exit** (I've lost count of how many times I've queried nslookup for a host called "quit").

```
> exit
```

Checking SRV Resource Record Registration

Before clients can resolve SRV resource records (RRs) to IP addresses, the relevant RRs must exist within DNS. In the case of networks whose DNS servers support dynamic DNS registration, these records should be registered automatically.

To check this, you can use **nslookup.exe** to manually query for the appropriate records or use **netdiag.exe** to run a test. To use the utility, launch a command prompt and type:

```
C:\>netdiag /test:DNS
```

Windows 2000 Recovery Console

I'll now discuss the Windows 2000 Recovery Console, a new feature in Windows 2000 that provides a limited command-line interface to Windows 2000.

Installing the Recovery Console

The recovery console can't be installed as part of the normal installation process and, instead, should be added later.

To do this:

1. Insert the Windows 2000 Server CD-ROM.

2. Start a Command Prompt from the Accessories menu.

3. Change to the CD-ROM drive, for example.

```
c:\>d:
```

4. Change to the i386 directory and execute **winnt32 /cmdcons**.

```
d:\>cd i386
d:\i386>winnt32 /cmdcons
```

5. A Confirmation dialog box (see Figure 17.4) appears. Click Yes to proceed.

Starting the Recovery Console

The first step in using the Recovery Console is launching it.

From Disk

If the Recovery Console has been installed locally, it's added as an option on the Boot menu. To use it:

1. Restart the computer.

2. Select Microsoft Windows 2000 Recovery Console when prompted to select the operating system to start.

From CD-ROM

If a system doesn't have the Recovery Console installed locally, it's still possible to use the Recovery Console (it's just a little more time-consuming to get started.) To use the Recovery Console on an arbitrary Windows 2000 system:

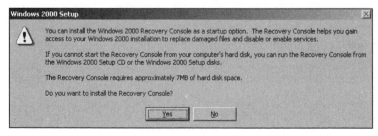

Figure 17.4   Confirmation for Recovery Console installation.

1. Be sure the computer is configured to boot from its CD-ROM drive before the hard drive/SCSI. Refer to manufacturer or motherboard instructions for precise details (although this usually involves going into the BIOS).

2. Insert the Windows 2000 Server CD-ROM and boot the computer.

3. Press a key to boot from CD, when prompted.

4. When prompted, press R to recover.

5. Next press C to start the Recovery Console.

NOTE: *Booting from the CD-ROM-based Recovery Console means you're always limited to the version that shipped with Windows 2000. Disk-based versions of the recovery console can and will be updated by Service Packs.*

Using the Recovery Console

Once you've started the Recovery Console by whatever means, the next step is to actually use it. Once the Recovery Console has started:

1. Type the number of the installation of Windows 2000 to run the console against from the list shown, and press Enter.

2. Enter the local administrative password for the computer. For domain controllers, this is the password specified during Active Directory installation.

3. The Recovery Console command prompt appears, focused on the system root directory of the installation chosen.

You can then use a small number of commands to manage the system. These commands are listed below:

- **attrib**
- **batch**
- **cd**
- **chdir**
- **chkdsk**
- **cls**
- **copy**
- **del**
- **delete**
- **dir**
- **disable**
- **diskpart**

- **enable**
- **exit**
- **expand**
- **fixboot**
- **fixmbr**
- **format**
- **help**
- **listsvc**
- **logon**
- **map**
- **md**
- **mkdir**
- **more**
- **rd**
- **ren**
- **rename**
- **rmdir**
- **set**
- **systemroot**
- **type**

TIP: *Alt+Ctrl+Delete doesn't work under the recovery console. Instead type **exit** to reboot the computer.*

If you wish to use removable media, such as floppy disks from the recovery console, you must type the following command:

```
C:\>set AllowRemovableMedia=true
```

Chapter 18

Advanced Scripting

In Depth

Scripting is a large and important topic, too large for a single book. Throughout this book, you've been exposed to examples of how to perform various tasks by script. This chapter is intended to bring together and expand upon the scripting repertoire presented thus far.

The VBScript Language

All of the scripting content in this book has focused on VBScript. However, other scripting languages are available for use with the Windows Script Host, most notably Jscript and Perl. This chapter, however, is dedicated to scripting either with native methods or VBScript (although many of the techniques for VBScript apply to other languages to some extent).

Accepting User Input

The scripts presented in this book all have hard-coded values. This is okay for one-time scripts and good for readability, but in practice, many scripts will be used time and time again with different values. An alternative, therefore, is to accept user input whenever a script is run, either as a parameter or interactively.

Command-Line Parameters

One way of passing data to scripts is through command-line parameters, so instead of just typing:

```
C:\>cscript scriptname.vbs
```

You instead type:

```
C:\>cscript scriptname.vbs param1 param2 …
```

Within your script, command-line parameters are available as an array. For example, to print out the contents of this array:

```
Set objArgs = WScript.Arguments

For intI = 0 to objArgs.Count - 1
    WScript.Echo objArgs(intI)
Next
```

So, after setting a variable (**objArgs**) to **Wscript.Arguments**, individual arguments are addressed as elements of this array, starting with the index 0 for the first argument, 1 for the second, and so forth.

Prompting for User Input

A second alternative is to prompt for user input midway through a program. One way to do this is with a message box as follows:

```
strValue = InputBox("Prompt text:","Dialog box title","Default Value")
```

Here, the user will be prompted with the dialog box shown in Figure 18.1, and whatever is present in the edit field will be set as the value of **strValue** once OK is pressed. Pressing cancel will set **strValue** to nothing and proceed with script execution.

Subroutines

The normal linear flow of control through a script file is okay for small scripts, such as the examples presented in this book, but it becomes less useful and harder to maintain in longer programs. In common with other programming languages is the concept in VBScript of a subroutine. A subroutine is a block of code that isn't processed "normally" and can, instead, be called from another place in a script multiple times if necessary.

The syntax for writing a subroutine is as follows:

```
Sub name
'   statements go here

End Sub
```

This is known as *declaring* a subroutine, and a declared subroutine isn't executed until its name is explicitly used elsewhere to invoke it. The name of a subroutine is the word that follows the **Sub** statement and is *name* in the example above. To invoke a subroutine, you simply type the name on a line of script. For example:

```
name
```

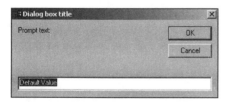

Figure 18.1   Dialog box title example.

Arguments

Subroutines can also have arguments passed to them. To do this, a list of variables is included in parentheses on the declaration line. For instance:

```
Sub name(strVar1, intVar2)
  '   statements go here

End Sub
```

Now, to call the subroutine, you should list the values for parameters after the subroutine name as follows:

```
name "string value",1234
```

You shouldn't use brackets to enclose the parameters.

Exit Sub

A useful trick to use within a subroutine is the **Exit Sub** statement to end execution of a subroutine and return to the calling statement. For example, you can use it with an **If** statement to affect execution.

```
Sub name
  If condition = FALSE Then
    Exit Sub
  End If
  ' more statements go here

End Sub
```

Functions

Functions are similar to subroutines but have one key difference: functions return a value. Functions have a name, take arguments, and are declared analogously to subroutines. For example:

```
Function name
  '   statements go here
  name = 1
End Function
```

Apart from using **Function name**…**End Function**, the key difference is that the name of the function is used as a variable, and its value at the termination of the function is the return value.

For instance, the following function will return the current season:

```
Function season
  If (Month(Date) < 2) or (Month(Date) = 11) Then
    season = "Winter"
  Elseif Month(Date) < 5 Then
    season = "Spring"
  Elseif Month(Date) < 8 Then
    season = "Summer"
  Else
    season = "Autumn"
  End If
End Function
```

Automating Active Directory Installation

Installing Active Directory on Domain Controllers was covered in Chapter 4. However, actually standing next to the server, filling out the wizard, and manually rebooting the server at the end of the process is time consuming. Instead, it's possible to script the wizard with the aid of an Answer file. The syntax and examples are given in the "Immediate Solutions" of this chapter.

Answer files can also be used in other circumstances—particularly to fully automate the installation of Windows 2000. This is thoroughly documented in the unattend.doc file contained in the deploy.cab file in the \support\tools directory of the Windows 2000 CD-ROM. The creation of the Answer files is made easier by the Setup Manager Wizard (**setupmgr.exe**).

Scripting Users and Groups

The management of all Active Directory objects can be scripted, and any property of an object can be set by its **lDAPDisplayName**. The "Immediate Solutions" of this chapter give basic examples of how to create users and groups. To set more detailed properties of an object, you can simply use the **Put** method with the **lDAPDisplayName** of the attribute and specify a value as the second parameter, as follows:

```
ObjUser.Put "attribute", "value"
```

To read an attribute, use the **.Get** method. For example to read **objUser**'s email address into the variable **strMail**:

```
strMail = objUser.Get("mail")
```

File Management

The use of Active Directory Service Interface (ADSI) scripts isn't limited to just manipulating directory objects. ADSI and VBScript can also be used to, for example, manipulate Windows file shares and to create folders.

VBScript has a built-in object for manipulating the file system, called the **FileSystem** object. To use the **FileSystem** object, you need to create it and set a variable to use. As an example:

```
Set objFileSystem = CreateObject("Scripting.FileSystemObject")
```

Having done this, you can use a variety of methods to perform operations on files and folders. The following are some of the more interesting methods available.

- *CopyFile*—This is used to copy a file around. Quite simply:

```
objFileSystem.CopyFile "c:\source\file.txt", "c:\destination folder", False
```

  The optional final Boolean parameter determines whether the file will be overwritten if it already exists in the destination. It defaults to **True**.

- *CopyFolder*—Similar to the above, this will copy an entire folder from one location to another.

- *CreateFolder*—This will make a new folder with the path specified. It's useful, for example, in a user-creation script that not only creates the user but also makes a home directory and so forth.

- *DeleteFile*—Quite simply, this deletes the file specified as a parameter. A second parameter can be set to **True** in order to delete read-only files. For instance, to delete all files in a folder, even if they're read only:

```
objFileSystem.DeleteFile "c:\temp\*.*", True
```

- *DeleteFolder*—This is the same as **DeleteFile**, except that it's used on folders instead of files.

- *FileExists*—This one can be used to test whether a specified file exists. It's usually used as part of an **If** block, perhaps before creating a file. For example:

```
If objFileSystem.FileExists("c:\temp\file.txt") Then
   ' Because the file already exists, perhaps open it
Else
   ' Because the file doesn't exist, perhaps create it
End If
```

- *FolderExists*—This is similar to **FileExists**, except that it tests folders. Again, this could be used before creating a folder, such as a user's home folder.

- *MoveFile*—This can be used to move a file to a new location. It takes two parameters (source, destination) similarly to **MoveFolder**.

- *MoveFolder*—Use this to move a folder. For example:

```
objFileSystem.MoveFile "c:\source folder\*.txt", "c:\destination folder"
```

Logon Scripts

Another use for scripting in general (and VBScript in particular) is writing Windows 2000 logon scripts. With the opportunities presented by VBScript, these can be richer than simple batch files used in Windows NT. Of course, in Windows 2000, you can use Group Policy to set scripts not just for Logon but also for Logoff, as well as Startup and Shutdown of computers. The general technique for writing all of these script types is the same, however.

Testing Group Membership

A common task in logon scripts is to test Group Membership. Although, to some extent, it could be avoided with Group Policy and security group filtering, logon script actions often depend on whether or not a user is a member of a particular group. Because this is a common test to make, it's best implemented as a function that returns either **True** or **False,** so it can be used many times in the same script. A sample function for achieving this is given below:

```
Function isMemberOf(strGroup)

    ' Declare variables
    Dim strADsPath, objUser, objGroup, objNetwork

    ' Assume the worst
    isMemberOf = False

    ' Open the current user
    Set objNetwork = CreateObject("Wscript.Network")
    Set objUser    = GetObject("WinNT://" & objNetwork.UserDomain & "/" _
                               & objNetwork.UserName & ",user")

    ' Test each group
    For Each objGroup in objUser.Groups
```

```
      If strGroup = objGroup.Name Then
        ' Exit if there is a match

        isMemberOf = True
        Exit Function
      End If

   Next

End Function
```

Running Programs

Running programs and, more generally, executing arbitrary commands is achievable through the **Run** method of the **Wscript.Shell** object. An application is launched as follows:

```
Dim objShell
Set objShell = CreateObject("Wscript.Shell")
ObjShell.Run("application.exe")
```

Registry Access

The **Wscript.Shell** object also allows Registry access through the **RegRead**, **RegWrite,** and **RegDelete** methods.

Examples of reading and writing to the Registry are given below:

```
Dim objShell
Set objShell = CreateObject("Wscript.Shell")

' Write a string value
objShell.RegWrite "HKCU\Software\ADBB\Example", "Test String", "REG_SZ"

' Echo that string value to screen
Wscript.Echo objShell.RegRead("HKCU\Software\ADBB\Example")

' Delete the value
objShell.RegDelete "HKCU\Software\ADBB\Example"

Set objShell = nothing
```

Here, the first parameter of each method is the registry key in question, and in the case of **RegWrite**, the second is the value and the third the datatype. The supported types are **REG_SZ**, **REG_EXPAND_SZ**, **REG_DWORD**, and **REG_BINARY**.

To specify a hive of the registry, either the short or long names can be used, as listed in Table 18.1. Note that shortened forms can't be used for **HKEY_USERS** and **HKEY_CURRENT_CONFIG**.

Mapping Network Drives

The **Wscript.Network** object provides a convenient interface to mapping network drives. Quite simply, for example, to map drive D: to **\\Server\Share**:

```
Dim objNetwork
Set objNetwork = CreateObject("Wscript.Network")
objNetwork.MapNetworkDrive "D:", \\Server\Share
```

Additional, optional parameters may be specified to enable persistence (a **True**/**False** value that defaults to **False**) and two optional string values allow for alternate username and password. For example, to connect to the same share as **Example\Administrator** (whose password, as ever, is **"password"**) and to make the connection persistent, the selected line would be changed to:

```
objNetwork.MapNetworkDrive "D:", "\\Server\Share", True, _
                      "Example\Adminstrator", "password"
```

Table 18.1   Registry Hive name for Wscript.Shell registry functions.

Short Name	Long Name
HKCU	**HKEY_CURRENT_USER**
HKLM	**HKEY_LOCAL_MACHINE**
HKCR	**HKEY_CLASSES_ROOT**
	HKEY_USERS
	HKEY_CURRENT_CONFIG

18. Advanced Scripting

Immediate Solutions

Automating dcpromo.exe

When setting up domain controllers, it's possible to automate the task of answering the questions posed by the Active Directory Installation Wizard. To do this, you need to create a text file in a specific format to specify the necessary options. This file is known as an Answer file and can be specified as a parameter of **dcpromo.exe** as follows:

```
C:\>dcpromo /answer:file.txt
```

Where file.txt is the Answer file, the format of the Answer file is the same as Windows INI files, with a single **[DCInstall]** section and a number of possible keys and values as outlined separately for automating installation and removal of Active Directory.

Installing Active Directory

The first option needed when promoting a new server to a domain controller is whether to create a new domain (and if so, what type of domain).

The first parameter to set is **ReplicaOrNewDomain**. It has two possible values:

- *Replica*—This is the default and will add a domain controller to the existing domain specified by the **ReplicaDomainDNSName** parameter.

- *Domain*—This creates a new domain. The **TreeOrChild** parameter is then required in addition to specify the type of domain (and perhaps in turn the **CreateOrJoin** parameter to determine whether a new forest is required).

The **TreeOrChild** parameter can have two possible values:

- *Tree*—Using this value creates a new tree and requires **NewDomainDNSName** to be specified for the name of the tree. Create or Join should also be specified to determine whether or not this is a new forest.

- *Child*—This value adds a child domain to an existing domain. Values are, hence, required for the **ParentDomainDNSName** and **ChildName** settings.

CreateOrJoin can have two possible values and can be specified if a new tree is being formed:

- *Create*—This value creates a brand-new forest of domains.

- *Join*—This one adds the new tree to an existing forest.

Whenever a domain controller is being upgraded, a number of domain names must be specified either to indicate which domain is being joined or to name a new domain. The following names can be specified:

- *ReplicaDomainDNSName*—The DNS name or the domain to add a domain controller to.

- *NewDomainDNSName*—The DNS name of a new tree.

- *ParentDomainDNSName*—The DNS name of a domain to add a new child to.

- *ChildName*—The relative name of a new child to its parent (that is, just the new portion of the child DNS name, such as **child** if you were adding **child.example.com** as a new child domain of **example.com**)

- *DomainNetBiosName*—The required downlevel or NetBIOS name for a new domain.

All domain controllers store information in three places—sysvol, the database itself, and the log directory. These locations are configured with the following three settings:

- SysVolPath

- DatabasePath

- LogPath

Any **dcpromo** operations, with the exception of creating a brand-new forest, will require credentials in the existing forest. These are specified with the following parameters:

- UserName

- UserDomain

- Password

For security, the **Password** setting is deleted from the Answer file on a successful promotion.

An additional setting available for new forests is **SiteName**, which allows something other than the usual Default-Site-Name to be the initial site name in the enterprise.

DNS is, of course, important to Active Directory, and three settings exist for its configuration:

- *DNSOnNetwork*—A **Yes/No** value that defaults to **Yes** but can be set to **No** to skip autoconfiguration of DNS.

18. Advanced Scripting

- *AutoConfigDNS*—Another **Yes/No** value that, if set to **Yes** (the default), will allow a DNS server to be configured on the first domain controller in a new forest if no server that supports dynamic updates can be found.

Finally **RebootOnSuccess** (a **Yes** or **No** question) allows the domain controller to be rebooted when the operation is complete. It defaults to **No**, although a reboot is, of course, required to start the directory. Bringing all of this together, a sample Answer file to install a new forest is given in Listing 18.1

Listing 18.1   ADBB-18-02-NewChildAnswer.txt.

```
[DCInstall]
; Create a new Forest
ReplicaOrNewDomain=Domain
TreeOrChild=Tree
CreateOrJoin=Create

; Call it example.com
NewDomainDNSName=example.com
DomainNetBiosName=EXAMPLE

; No database locations are set, so the defaults are accepted.

; Setup DNS Automatically (Yes is the default, but we'll be explicit).
AutoConfigDNS=Yes
```

As a contrast, a sample to create a new child domain called test beneath **example.com** is given in Listing 18.2

Listing 18.2   ADBB-18-01-NewForestAnswer.txt.

```
 [DCInstall]
; Create a new Child
ReplicaOrNewDomain=Domain
TreeOrChild=Child

; Call it test.example.com
ParentDomainDNSName=example.com
ChildName=test
DomainNetBiosName=TEST

; Database locations
SysVolPath=%SystemRoot%\SYSVOl
DatabasePath=e:\NTDS
LogPath=d:\Logs

;Credentials
UserName=administrator
```

```
UserDomain=example.com
Password=password
```

Removing Active Directory

The removal of Active Directory can also be automated. Here, there are fewer options available.

- *IsLastDCInDomain*—The default is **No**, but a value of **Yes** indicates that this is the last domain controller in a given domain and, hence, any metadata for the domain will be removed from the forest's configuration partition at demotion.

- *RebootOnSuccess*—Exactly as for installation, a **Yes** value will reboot once **dcpromo.exe** has finished successfully.

- *AdministratorPassword*—Specifies the new local administrator password for the demoted computer. This is deleted from the Answer file after demotion for security.

Adding Organizational Units

Adding an Organizational Unit (OU) is a relatively simple affair with ADSI and is illustrated in Listing 18.3.

Listing 18.3   ADBB-18-03-NewOU.vbs.

```
option explicit

' Declare Variables
Dim objParent, objOU, strOU, strParent

' Populate string variables
strOU     = "ou=Test"
strParent = "dc=example,dc=com"

' Open the parent object for the OU (which could be another OU).
Set objParent = GetObject("LDAP://" & strParent)
Set objOU     = objParent.Create("organizationalUnit", strOU)

' Commit changes
objOU.SetInfo

' Tidy up.
Set objParent = nothing
Set objOU     = nothing
```

18. Advanced Scripting

Adding Users

The first step in adding a user to Active Directory is creating a user object. Part of creating any object is populating a minimal set of properties, and in the case of a user, this means the User Principal Name (UPN) and downlevel logon name (the Security Accounts Manager [SAM] logon name). The script in Listing 18.4 is about as simple as you can get to create a user object.

Listing 18.4   ADBB-18-04-NewUser.vbs.

```
option explicit

' Declare Variables
Dim objParent, objUser, strParent, strCN, strPassword, strUPN, strSAMName

' Populate string variables
strParent    = "ou=Test,dc=example,dc=com"
strCN        = "cn=Adam Wood"
strSAMName   = "adamwood"
strUPN       = "adam@example.com"
strPassword  = "password"

' Open the object for the parent of the user to create and actually.
' create the new user object.
Set objParent = GetObject("LDAP://" & strParent)
Set objUser   = objParent.Create("user", strCN)

' Populate a minimal set of properties
objUser.Put "sAMAccountName",    strSAMName
objUser.Put "userPrincipalName", strUPN
objUser.SetInfo

' Retreive any changes made by the directory. This isn't necessary in this
' simple script but may be if you're doing something more advanced.
objUser.GetInfo

' Set the user's password.  The SetPassword method only works on
' existing objects.
objUser.SetPassword strPassword
objUser.AccountDisabled = False
objUser.SetInfo

' Finally, tidy up.
Set objParent = nothing
Set objUser   = nothing
```

Here, the initial blocks of code are used to declare and populate variables. First, as with creating any new object, you must use **GetObject** to retrieve its parent, then use the **Create** method to make a child. The **Create** method takes two arguments—the first is the class of the new object, and the second is the relative distinguished name of the new object.

After this, values are given to the two attributes that must be set explicitly for all user accounts—the downlevel account name (also known as the SAM account name or NetBIOS name) and the UPN. These must both be unique within the domain and forest, respectively.

Before setting a user's password, the changes must be committed and this process will also cause operations within the directory service to, for example, assign a Security Identifier (SID) to the new user. At or before this point, other attributes of the user account can be populated in the same way as **sAMAccountName** and **userPrincipalName**. For example, a user's name, email address, and telephone number can be added here.

The password is set to the value in the **strPassword** variable (as ever, be aware that plain text copies of passwords should be safeguarded), and the account is enabled, because it would be disabled by default. Finally, **SetInfo** is called to commit the changes from the local property cache back to the directory, and it's a good habit to **Set** previously assigned variables to **nothing**.

Moving Objects

Another task, which is simple to script, is moving objects around within a directory. It's implemented as a method of the new parent object, which is the container that you're moving the object to. For example, if you're moving a user from the Sales OU to the Marketing OU, to perform this operation you must call a method on the Marketing OU to move the user to its new parent. You also have the option to rename the moved object. Listing 18.5 demonstrates how to move a user from the Users container to the Test OU.

Listing 18.5   ADBB-18-05-MoveObject.vbs.

```
option explicit

' Declare Variables
Dim objOU, objUser, strNewParent, strObjToMove, strNewRDN

' Populate string variables
' A NULL value for strNewRDN indicates that the existing RDN is used.
```

```
strNewParent = "LDAP://ou=Test,dc=example,dc=com"
strObjToMove = "LDAP://cn=Adam Wood,cn=Users,dc=example,dc=com"
strNewRDN    = "cn=Adam Wood"

' Open the new parent object
Set objOU    = GetObject(strNewParent)

' Use the MoveHere method to move an existing object beneath the parent
Set objUser  = objOU.MoveHere(strObjToMove, strNewRDN)

' Tidy up
Set objOU    = nothing
Set objUser  = nothing
```

TIP: *By moving an object to its current parent but changing the RDN, you can rename it.*

Creating Groups

The creation of a group object is much like any other, including the user and OU examples in this chapter. An example of creating a Global Security Group is given in Listing 18.6.

Listing 18.6   ADBB-18-06-CreateGroup.vbs.

```
option explicit

' Declare Variables
Dim objParent, strGroupName, strGroupNetBiosName, intGroupType, strParent,
objGroup

' Populate variables
strGroupName        = "cn=Group"
strGroupNetBiosName = "group"
strParent           = "ou=Test,dc=example,dc=com"
intGroupType        = &H80000002

' Open the parent object for the Group (which could be an OU or domain).
Set objParent = GetObject("LDAP://" & strParent)

' Create the new Group Object
Set objGroup  = objParent.Create("group", strGroupName)

' Set the necessary attributes
objGroup.Put "sAMAccountName", strGroupNetBiosName
```

```
objGroup.Put "groupType",          intGroupType
objGroup.SetInfo

' Tidy up
Set objParent = nothing
Set objGroup  = nothing
```

The important difference when creating other types of groups is in the **groupType** attribute, set here by the **intGroupType** variable. This value should be set by using one of the combinations of constants given in Table 18.2.

NOTE: *The &H before a number means that the value should be treated as hexadecimal. &B is used similarly for binary data.*

In practice, it's more usual to declare constants at the start of your script representing these numbers, and use these constants in your program for added readability. The constant names used correspond with those available by default in certain other programming languages (see Listing 18.7).

Listing 18.7   ADBB-18-07-GroupConstants.vbs.

```
' Constant declarations
Const ADS_GROUP_TYPE_GLOBAL_GROUP       = &H00000002
Const ADS_GROUP_TYPE_DOMAIN_LOCAL_GROUP = &H00000004
Const ADS_GROUP_TYPE_UNIVERSAL_GROUP    = &H00000008
Const ADS_GROUP_TYPE_SECURITY_ENABLED   = &H80000000
```

With these in place, the highlighted line of Listing 18.6 could be replaced as follows:

```
intGroupType        = ADS_GROUP_TYPE_GLOBAL_GROUP Or _
                      ADS_GROUP_TYPE_SECURITY_ENABLED
```

Here, the logical **Or** operator is used to combine the two hexadecimal values and signify that this is both a Global Group and a Security Group.

Table 18.2   ADSI Constants for Group Creation.

Scope	Type	Hex Value
Global	Distribution	&H00000002
Global	Security	&H80000002
Domain Local	Distribution	&H00000004
Domain Local	Security	&H80000004
Universal	Distribution	&H00000008
Universal	Security	&H80000008

18. Advanced Scripting

Add Members to a Group

The process of adding a user to a group with ADSI is quite simple: open the object representing the group and use its **Add** method with the **ADsPath** of the object (user/computer/group/whatever) to add.

Adding a Single Member

The simplest illustration of this process is to add a single member by script. Listing 18.8 shows how.

Listing 18.8   ADBB-18-08-AddToGroup.vbs.

```
option explicit

' Declare variables
Dim strGroupName, strUserName, objGroup

' The Group Name and the User to add
strGroupName = "cn=The New Group,dc=example,dc=com"
strUserName  = "cn=Adam Wood,ou=test,dc=example,dc=com"

' Open the Group
Set objGroup = GetObject("LDAP://" & strGroupName)

' Add the User
objGroup.Add("LDAP://" & strUserName)
objGroup.SetInfo

' Tidy up
Set objGroup  = nothing
```

Adding an OU to a Group

Scripting a single addition to a group will probably take longer than using the equivalent management tool, so a more complex example is called for. Here, Listing 18.9 demonstrates opening an Organizational Unit, iterating each object contained within, and adding users to a group.

Listing 18.9   ADBB-18-09-AddOUToGroup.vbs.

```
option explicit

' Declare variables
Dim strGroupName, strOU, objGroup, objOU, objChild, objClass

' The Group Name and the User to add
strGroupName = "cn=Group,ou=test,dc=example,dc=com"
strOU        = "ou=test,dc=example,dc=com"
```

```
' Open the Group and OU
Set objGroup = GetObject("LDAP://" & strGroupName)
Set objOU   = GetObject("LDAP://" & strOU)

' Iterate through the objects in the group
For Each objChild in objOU

  ' Test for user objects.  objChild.ObjectClass is an array of all
  ' objectclasses of the object.
  '
  ' To match a user object, we look for an object with three classes,
  ' one of which is "user".

  If Ubound(objChild.ObjectClass) = 3 then
    For Each objClass in objChild.ObjectClass
      If objClass = "user" then
        ' Add the object
        objGroup.Add(objChild.ADsPath)
      End If
    Next
  End If

Next

' Commit changes
objGroup.SetInfo

' Tidy up
Set objGroup  = nothing
Set objOU     = nothing
```

By using this method of enumerating every object in an OU when testing for users, it's necessary to match both the number of **ObjectClasses** and the fact that one of them is "user". This is because computer objects would be matched without specifying the number of **ObjectClasses** allowed. An alternative approach to the above would be to use a search and add each object returned by the search to a specific group.

Directory Object Access Control: Remove SELF from All Users

The script given in Listing 18.10 is an example of manipulating access control settings. The result of the script is to iterate through all user objects beneath the OU specified as part of the value of the **strSearch** variable and remove SELF from their access control lists. This prevents users from having access to their own object by virtue of being that object (see Listing 18.10).

Listing 18.10   ADBB-18-10-DSPermissions.vbs.

```
option explicit


' Declare variables
Dim objConnection, objCommand, objRecordSet, strSearch, strAdmin
Dim objX, objDACL, objACE, objNamespace, objSD, strPass


' Define the Strings:
' Search String, including the OU to remove SELF from
strSearch = _
 "<LDAP://ou=Test,dc=example,dc=com>;(objectClass=user);adspath;subtree"


' Administrator DN and Password
strAdmin  = "cn=administrator,dc=example,dc=com"
strPass   = "password"


' Initialize Connection
Set objConnection      = WScript.CreateObject("ADODB.Connection")
objConnection.Provider = "ADsDSOObject"
objConnection.Open      "Active Directory Provider"


' Initialize and Execute Command
Set objCommand                   = WScript.CreateObject("ADODB.Command")
Set objCommand.ActiveConnection = objConnection
objCommand.CommandText           = strSearch
Set objRecordSet                 = objCommand.Execute


' Loop through the records
While Not objRecordset.EOF

  Wscript.Echo objRecordset.Fields.Item("ADsPath").Value

  ' Open the DACL of the object
  Set objNamespace = GetObject("LDAP:")
```

```
Set objX         = objNamespace.OpenDSObject( _
                     objRecordset.Fields.Item("ADsPath").Value, _
                     strAdmin, strPass, 1)
Set objSD        = objX.Get("ntSecurityDescriptor")
Set objDacl      = objSD.DiscretionaryAcl

' Enumerate the ACEs, and remove any for "NT AUTHORITY\SELF"
For Each objACE In objDACL
   If objACE.Trustee = "NT AUTHORITY\SELF" Then
     objDACL.RemoveAce objACE
   End If
Next

' Put the new DACL back on the object
objSD.DiscretionaryAcl = objDACL
objX.Put                 "ntSecurityDescriptor", Array(objSD)
objX.SetInfo

' Advance to the next object
objRecordSet.MoveNext

Wend
```

The value of this example is not merely something to do. It illustrates how to manipulate access control lists and access control entries.

Manipulating Files and Folders

Another use for VBScript is to deal with the file system. Here we explore the use of the **Filesystem** object and creating file shares.

The **FileSystem** Object

The built-in Windows Scripting Host (WSH) **FileSystem** object allows files and folders to be manipulated. For example, the following folder tests whether or not a folder exists:

```
Dim objFileSystem, strFolder

strFolder = "c:\temp"

Set objFileSystem = CreateObject("Scripting.FileSystemObject")
```

```
If objFileSystem.FolderExists(strFolder) Then
  ' Do something
Else
  ' Perhaps create the folder
  objFileSystem.CreateFolder(strFolder)
End If
```

Here the **CreateFolder** method is used to create a folder if it doesn't exist.

Creating Shares

Another example is manipulating shared folders. Here an existing folder is shared.

```
option explicit

' Declare variables
Dim objComp, objShare, strShareName, strSharePath, strComp

' Populate string variables
strShareName = "temp"
strSharePath = "c:\temp"
strComp      = "calvin.example.com"

' Open the LanManServer object of the computer to host the share
Set objComp = GetObject("WinNT://" & strComp & "/LanManServer")

' Create the share and set its path
Set objShare = objComp.Create("FileShare", strShareName)
objShare.Path = strSharePath
objShare.SetInfo
```

Chapter 19

Active Directory Design

In Depth

Before implementing Active Directory in an organization, it's absolutely vital to plan every step of the process. With a step-by-step written plan of the tasks that need to be undertaken, you'll be able to optimize the implementation of Active Directory by spotting inefficiencies, eliminating redundant steps, and, hopefully, spotting problems before they arise. The first step in creating any plan, however, is to know where you're going—that is, to design the finished solution.

Business Needs

The first aspect to consider when planning Active Directory for an organization is the business's needs. There's no point implementing expensive (but cool) technology for its own sake; instead, it must be able to justify itself within an organization.

Hand in hand with this, Active Directory presents a number of new features and opportunities that organizations can use. For example, the entire IntelliMirror™ raft of technologies, which revolve around software deployment and making files and folders more available, are new to the operating system. The decision on whether (and how) to implement them should, again, be based on business reasons.

Of course, the prime business reason for doing anything is making money (or, for nonprofit organizations, serving more efficiently), so the overriding reasons to implement Windows 2000 should be cost and efficiency. For example, creating a single address book through contact and user objects will make people more productive, because they have a central storage area for all contact details. Using a smaller number of Windows 2000 domains than Windows NT domains will save money if fewer domain controllers are required and if support becomes less complex.

One definite business need for any Active Directory implementation is for the whole project not to fail so spectacularly that it leaves the network in a horrible mess. A failure like this takes days to resolve and prevents much useful work from being done.

It's impossible to utterly eliminate every potential failure during a large project, but part of the intention of a design and the project plan should be to minimize any risk. A back-out contingency plan should be available, at least in the early stages, which would allow the implementation of Active Directory and Windows 2000 to be reversed.

One way of reducing the time (and, hence, cost, measured in network downtime) of an Active Directory implementation is to script simple but arduous tasks, such as the definition of sites and subnets. To mitigate risk here, all such scripts should be thoroughly tested in a lab environment.

Collecting Information

To nail down exactly what Active Directory can do for an organization and how it should be implemented, it's necessary to know precisely where you are today.

IP and DNS Implementation

When planning Active Directory, it's vital to know the current extent to which IP and Domain Name System (DNS) are used within an organization. From the point of view of planning Active Directory sites, you should know the current IP subnets in use in various parts of the organization. To ensure that DHCP servers work post-upgrade to Windows 2000 and Active Directory, you should be sure to know the IP addresses of your Windows 2000 Dynamic Host Configuration Protocol (DHCP) servers, so they can be authorized in Active Directory. The Windows 2000 DHCP service will first check the Active Directory when it starts, and it will not start if its server is part of a domain and not authorized in Active Directory. Authorization does not affect other DHCP servers.

DNS is perhaps a more important service to collect current information about, because it provides a crucial role in locating domain controllers and, thus, in allowing Active Directory clients (and servers) to talk to each other. What existing DNS servers are there in your organization? Do they support service (SRV) resource records? Do they support dynamic updates? Organizations without existing DNS servers have it relatively easy, because they'll be able to use Windows 2000 DNS, which obviously supports all of the necessary and desirable features. However, such companies will obviously have the issue of registering a DNS name.

If existing DNS servers are in place, whether or not they support SRV resource records is key, because SRV resource records are essential for Active Directory to function. The use of dynamic DNS registration is technically optional but is far simpler to administer and, hence, is a cost saving.

Current WAN and LAN Topology

Knowing the physical structure of a network is essential for planning Active Directory sites. To design a site structure and to plan the placement of domain controllers and their replication topology, you must know about the current network. Not only should you determine the capacities of links, but you should also determine the current usage levels (probably over time). With this data, the period and schedule for replication can be planned. One point to bear in mind is that intersite Active Directory replication is less demanding on network resources than Windows NT domain replication.

Current Domain Structure

One aspect, which will have a large bearing on the Windows 2000 domain structure you end up with, is any existing Windows NT domain structure. The entire process of migrating from Windows NT 4 is covered in more detail in Chapter 21.

Essentially two main approaches are available for migrating from Windows NT to Windows 2000. The first and simplest is to upgrade all existing domains to Windows 2000 in place (that is, simply upgrading the existing domain controllers). The second is to create a new Windows 2000 domain structure and move the contents of existing domains into the new domain or domains.

Which of these paths is best in a given circumstance depends both on the intended domain structure and the current domain structure. An organization with a single Windows NT domain that wishes to move to a single Windows 2000 domain is probably better off upgrading in place, because this is the simplest (that is, quickest and least risky) solution.

On the other hand, a company with a tangled web of 20 Windows NT 4 domains that trust each other to varying degrees would do well to consider restructuring to a smaller number of domains. As well as the topology of Windows NT domains, other information about them, such as the number of domain controllers, member computers, and users accounts, is important. If you're considering upgrading in place, it's, of course, useful to know whether the current domain controllers have sufficient resources to run Windows 2000 acceptably.

Current Administrative Model

It's very important to realize that Windows 2000 allows for much more flexible delegation of administration than Windows NT currently does. However, regardless of the current operating environment, you should know who actually does what at present. You should use this information as a basis for planning the administrative model you intend to employ with Active Directory, because it will contribute to Organizational Unit planning.

For example, if you have a multiple-domain environment, there may be several different people who are domain administrators in one or more of the domains of the network. The new structure should take into account these current domains and the role of the administrators when it's designed.

Other Network Services

Anything else that currently uses a network should at least be considered when planning an Active Directory deployment. If an organization has existing Lightweight Directory Access Protocol (LDAP) servers, it may be possible to utilize these directories to import data into Active Directory.

For example, Microsoft provides a tool for use with Exchange Server 5.5 known as the Active Directory Connector (ADC), which allows synchronization of data between the two. Another example is if your organization already has an LDAP server, LDAP Directory Interchange Format (LDIF) could be used to initially populate your directory.

Designing a Domain and OU Structure

All aspects of directory design rely on others to some extent—domain design can be influenced by site design and wide area network (WAN) links, Organizational Unit design obviously depends on domain structure and the design of the DNS namespace, and placement of zones depends on what domains are decided upon. Therefore, design is an iterative process, feeding decisions made about one area back into other decisions, until a suitable result is reached. Perhaps the most important thing to keep in mind, however, is that simple structures are best from the point of view of manageability and later extension.

Choosing Domain Names

Windows 2000 Active Directory domains can't be renamed, so it's important to get the names right the first time. The choice of a domain name for a company with an existing Internet presence is relatively easy: use your existing name.

For small companies that have a dial-up connection to the Internet and a registered domain name (**example.com**) with hosted Web and email at their ISP, one solution would be to have a subzone, such as **ad.example.com** or **corp.example.com**, delegated to their DNS servers, with that zone used as the domain name. This way, host names of computers on the local network can't conflict with computers on the Internet.

Larger companies may have the opposite problem—too many domain names. It's important to realize that the names of Active Directory domains don't affect an organization's ability to use other domain names for Web servers, email addresses, or indeed, any other service. This means there's no need to create an additional domain purely because you have a particular Web site. Instead, the domain name only really affects the Distinguished Names of objects in LDAP servers and, of course, a DNS name of computers.

Simple Structures

The basic building blocks of the logical directory structure should be based on consistent types of division. For example, there's little sense in having first-level organizational units called "Boston", "Managers", and "Researchers". Instead, the structure could be divided on purely departmental, geographic, functional, or administrative grounds.

Departmental

Departmental organization would have domains or OUs based on department names. Although this approach allows delegation on clear departmental boundaries, a major problem exists: reorganizations. Many companies, Microsoft included, seem to delight in reorganizing every year or so. If an Active Directory is structured along these lines and if it's to keep up with the latest changes in structure and names or departments, considerable resource is required to rename/move objects and verify that settings and permissions are maintained during the reorganization. For example, a company may have an engineering division and two smaller groups, research and manufacturing, which are also part of this division (see Figure 19.1).

NOTE: *Even though examples of multiple-domain structures based on departments, job function, and simple administrative boundaries are available, this book is in no way suggesting that these structures are ever appropriate—they're just examples. Designs should try to minimize the number of Active Directory domains in use and certainly shouldn't create them frivolously.*

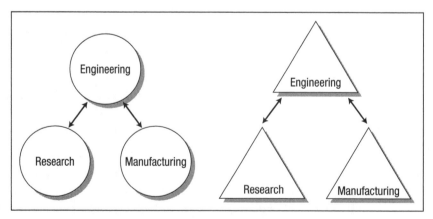

Figure 19.1   Department OU or domain examples.

Geographic

A geographic domain structure has a certain appeal over a departmental division. For one thing, place names rarely change. If an organization has administrators at all locations, a geographic division may also correspond to a rough administrative division, which is also a good thing. However, some single locations may be very large, so a geographic approach alone may not be suitable if different departments or divisions with differing security needs exist in one place. For example, domains or OUs could be created by continent, by country, and by office location, depending on company size. An example is pictured in Figure 19.2.

Functional

By functional, I mean division by job title, so there could be an OU for all programmers, another for all managers, another for all recruitment staff, and so forth. This has a certain appeal for small companies but obviously less so when a company has a vast number of employees with the same function or when those employees are spread throughout the world.

For example, imagine certain settings that apply to the entire help desk, a small additional number of settings that apply only to help desk managers, and perhaps some restrictions that are to be placed on ordinary help desk staff. In this case, a structure of OUs similar to Figure 19.3 may make sense.

Administrative

Because the OU structure of your organization isn't exposed to ordinary users and because a variety of permissions and settings can be assigned at the OU level, it's strongly recommended that you use an OU structure that (at some level) reflects the administrative structure of the organization.

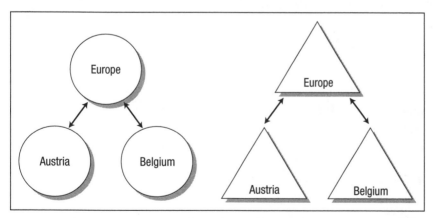

Figure 19.2   Geographic OU or domain examples.

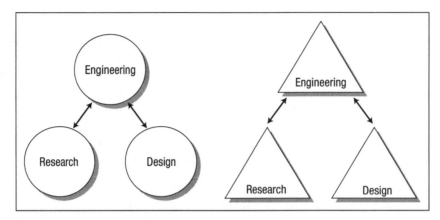

Figure 19.3   Functional OU or domain examples.

An administrative structure allows for permissions to be assigned against similar users and for Group Policy to flow naturally in a hierarchy. Of course, the administrative model of your company may closely follow the geographic or departmental boundaries, but it need not. For instance, it's common for large IT departments to be divided into teams based upon the system supported. Figure 19.4 gives an example of administrative breakdown (albeit one that applies perhaps more to OUs than domains.)

Composite Structures

It's unlikely that any of the preceding simple structures will entirely suit an organization of any size. If a geographic division is chosen and if there are multiple departments or administrators within a single office location, further subdivision by administrative model may be necessary.

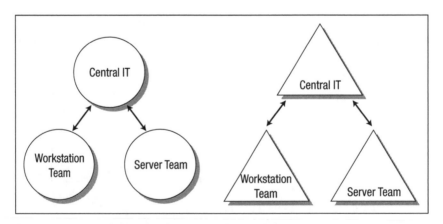

Figure 19.4   Administrative OU or domain examples.

As soon as you decide to structure by multiple levels, you have a decision to make: what order do you organize the groupings in? Should you decide to use departmental and geographic structures, do you organize by department then by geography, or do you organize by geography and then department? (See Figure 19.5).

Here, we have a fictitious company with just two departments and with operations in two countries deciding whether to structure OUs based first on country or first on department. The answer to this question will vary from company to company on a number of factors, but primarily, it will come down to which structure makes most sense for Group Policy and delegation of control.

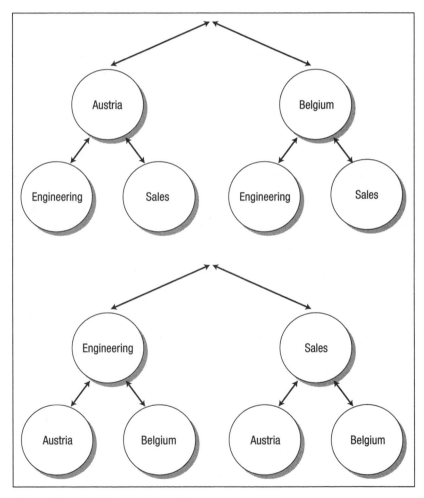

Figure 19.5   Which way around?

Remember that site-level Group Policy Objects can be used to apply geographic settings, so from a Group Policy perspective Possibility 1, with geography above department, is perhaps not necessary. Having said this, it may be the case that the administration is done squarely by geography, with local IT teams in each country, and in that case, Possibility 1 would be favored, because it allows control to be delegated in a simple way.

Domain-Only Issues

Certain settings in Windows 2000 Active Directory can only be configured at the domain level. Other items, such as domain replication, can't be configured as such but must take place at the domain level.

Replication

One reason to require a separate domain is if you need to use Simple Mail Transfer Protocol (SMTP)-based replication. This is because the File Replication Service (FRS) doesn't support SMTP as a transport protocol, and FRS is required to replicate the contents of each domain's shared system volume (sysvol). However, creating a separate domain means that sysvol needn't be replicated, so SMTP can be used.

Even if you aren't using SMTP, replication may still be a consideration. For example, imagine an Internet company that uses Active Directory to store the registrations at its Web site. Just like every other optimistic start-up, the company predicts several million registered users very quickly. It has servers at two locations: its offices and its ISP (where the Web servers are located), and a leased line connects the two locations.

In this scenario, there may be good reasons for having two separate domains: one for the company's employees and one for the registered Web users. This means that the bulk of the data and updates for the Web users will only be replicated around the ISP's data center. Although some will, of course, still replicate through to the main office in the Global Catalog, here, the volume of data will be much lower than replicating everything, particularly if the schema has been extended to support additional fields to power the Web site.

Other Settings

The other domain-only settings are found as part of Group Policy and are as follows: Everything beneath Computer Configuration/Windows Settings/Security Settings/Account Policies, namely:

- *Password Policy*—This policy contains six settings relating to minimum password length, complexity, age, and so forth.

- *Account Lockout Policy*—This policy contains three settings, which dictate how accounts get locked out after failed logon attempts.

- *Kerberos Policy*—This policy contains five settings, including ticket lifetimes and computer clock difference tolerance.

The following items beneath Computer Configuration/Windows Settings/Security Settings/Local Policies/Security Options are also domain-only:

- Automatically log off users when logon time expires.

- Rename administrator account.

- Rename guest account.

Multiple Forests

Although generally recommended against, a few scenarios exist when it actually makes sense to implement multiple forests in production. Remember that separate Active Directory forests are no worse than separate Windows NT 4 domains from the point of view of administration.

Of course, you lose the two-way transitive trust relationships, single Enterprise Admins Group, and comprehensive Global Catalog when you implement multiple forests, but you gain some things, (which may be good or bad):

- Lack of comprehensive Global Catalog

- Lack of common schema

- Greater separation of administrative powers

In a very large company that's structurally a number of loosely affiliated autonomous companies, it may make at least political sense to have separate forests for these organizations. Any decision to do this must balance the additional administration required against any benefits of additional security or feelings of autonomy that it brings.

Of course, you should always use a separate forest to pilot a sizable Windows 2000 Active Directory deployment, and also to evaluate applications that change the directory schema, as well as to test any in-house applications that modify the schema.

Designing Sites

Windows 2000 sites are, technically, collections of IP addresses (defined by subnets) with high connectivity. They're used by services and applications, such as the Active Directory itself, to build a physical picture of the network in order to optimize processes. As an example, Active Directory uses sites to alter how replication works, and distributed file system (Dfs) uses sites to locate the closest replica of a domain Dfs child node.

Site membership is determined by IP address for clients and explicitly for servers, based on the location of its server object in the configuration partition of the directory (although it defaults to the site corresponding to its IP address at install time). This means that care must be taken when changing site configuration to make sure the servers end up in the correct site.

One Site per Location

The starting point for planning sites is to plan one Active Directory site per physical location. A site need not have a domain controller (although it obviously helps speed logons if a site does have one), because even sites without a DC may have one added later. It will be easier to organize sites correctly the first time than have to redesign them later.

Remember /32 Subnet Masks

If you have a particularly complicated TCP/IP setup, you should remember that it's possible to use a "subnet mask" of 255.255.255.255 with a subnet object, so individual IP addresses can be matched to particular sites.

Designing Domain Controller Placement

Hand in hand with working out what sites to define in your organization should go planning how many domain controllers should be placed in each site and what domains they belong to. To repeat, it's *essential* to have two domain controllers in a domain—and, hopefully, more. How many domain controllers you need comes down to the number of users that need to be supported and the cost of that support.

Global Catalog Server Placement

In a single domain environment or even in a domain model where one small container domain and a single domain containing the vast majority of objects exist, every domain controller should be a Global Catalog server. In more complex domain structures, Global Catalog placement becomes an issue in its own right. To service logons, there should be at least one Global Catalog server in every site.

Design Replication

A replication topology need not be designed explicitly, because the Knowledge Consistency Checker (KCC) is capable of managing it transparently. However, you may wish to plan which servers to designate as bridgeheads between sites.

Another part of replication design is calculating convergence times. Particular convergences may be specified as business needs, and the costs, based on these goals, may have to be presented back to decision makers (that is, the financial controller) until a compromise between cost and functionality can be reached. For example, an unrealistic business requirement may be the replication of all changes globally within an hour. This is, of course, possible with Windows 2000 but may be extremely expensive. A more realistic synchronization period may be 24 or 36 hours, because overnight replication can be taken advantage of.

Designing DNS

Critical to the functionality of Active Directory is its name resolution and location service: DNS. Probably the vast majority of Active Directory errors can be traced back to DNS, so a well-planned DNS infrastructure will, doubtless, save time and money in later troubleshooting.

DNS Server Placement

Exactly where DNS servers are located within an organization will have an impact on service levels and response times. If the business requires that users be able to access local domain controllers even if all WAN links are down, each site should have its own local DNS server.

Multiple Domains

The hardest time to design Active Directory DNS is when several Windows 2000 domains are in an enterprise and when Active Directory-integrated DNS is being used. Because Active Directory-integrated DNS zones are stored in the domain partition of the directory, they can't be shared between domains with Active Directory-integration. Of course, DNS servers can be configured to hold standard secondary copies of zones for other domains, but this loses the replication benefits of Active Directory-integration.

This isn't such a problem for the forward lookup zones that hold SRV resource records, host records, CNAME records, and so forth, because zones can be delegated corresponding to Active Directory domain names and the appropriate zone hosted on each domain. The problem comes with the reverse lookup zones. However, unless you're in the fortunate position of having the IP addresses used by computers running in different domains dividing exactly at the octets of the addresses, there'll be an issue with reserve lookup zones.

This will possibly mean that you only have one reverse lookup zone for the entire organization, and this means it can only be housed in a single domain as Active Directory-integrated. The choice, therefore, is one of the following:

• Use standard zones for reverse lookup.

• Use a single Active Directory-integrated zone for reverse lookup.

Choosing the former somewhat negates the point of using Active Directory-integrated zones for dynamic registration in the first place, because it introduces a single point of failure.

The latter—using a single AD-integrated zone—seems, therefore, to be the better option. When doing so, it's logical to place the zone in the forest root domain and have clients use that for registration. Of course, Active Directory-integrated zones can have standard secondaries, and good arguments exist for carrying secondary copies of the reverse lookup zone on domain controllers from other domains that are also acting as DNS servers.

One possibility is to have a domain controller from the forest root domain in each site. This would also be running DNS, with an Active Directory-integrated reverse lookup zone. Registrations are, thus, dealt with in-site, and other domain controllers in the site can then hold secondary copies of this zone to service client requests. An additional advantage of this is quicker trust evaluation, because the domain controller from the forest root domain will also be able to provide Kerberos tickets for trust paths from one child domain to another.

Interoperability with BIND

There's no technical reason why Active Directory systems need to use Windows 2000-based DNS. There are certainly advantages, such as secure, dynamic updates; integration with Active Directory replication; and multiple, "primary" zone holders, to be had through Active Directory-integrated DNS zones.

Indeed, Berkeley Internet Name Daemon (BIND) or other DNS servers that support SRV resource records will work with Windows 2000. Recent versions of BIND also support dynamic registration of DNS records (the quoted minimum version for this is 8.2.1, but obviously, more recent releases are likely to correct security and other issues). However, BIND only uses what Microsoft calls standard zones, so all dynamic registration will have to be routed via the single primary server for a particular zone.

If the primary zone server is over a WAN link, this will create WAN traffic when computers and domain controllers boot up and shut down. There will also be a delay before the registration replicates back to any local DNS servers, which in turn causes a temporary lack of resolution for the newly registered records.

Interoperability with BIND doesn't necessarily mean using BIND to host all DNS services. If a particularly entrenched culture of DNS is being run by the Unix team within a company, it may not be politically possible to replace the DNS servers with Windows 2000 computers, even though the business decision has been taken to maximize security and redundancy by using Active Directory-integrated zones.

In such situations, a zone could be delegated for Active Directory, such as **ad.example.com**, if the Unix servers currently hold **example.com**. In this way, the BIND servers don't need reconfiguring or upgrading, and the Active Directory-integrated zone can be used. Quite simply, the root domain in the forest would now be **ad.example.com**, and all computers and child domains would have DNS names beneath this. Using a system like this doesn't affect what people's email addresses have to be or doesn't affect their User Principal Names (UPNs). So in this example, you could still use **example.com** as the UPN suffix for all accounts, so users need not know that their domain is called **ad.example.com**.

Another alternative would be to delegate only the subdomains used for SRV resource records as zones (that is, the underscore zones: _msdcs, _sites, _tcp, and _udp), and host these on the domain controllers. This has the benefit of allowing domain controllers to register these resource records but doesn't allow the full benefit of host records being securely and dynamically registered.

Designing for Redundancy

Complicated systems should not, as a general rule, have a single point of failure. After installing dual redundant power supplies, expensive Redundant Array of Independent Disks (RAID), and a meshed WAN topology, the last thing you want is for the network to grind to a halt because the only DNS server that a domain controller is able to update at is unavailable.

For this reason, if dynamic DNS is being used, it's well worth considering Active Directory-integrated DNS (at least for SRV resource records). This is because domain controllers running the Microsoft DNS servers act as primary servers and are, hence, able to update the directory. So, as long as clients have a suitably long list of DNS servers configured, they should either always be able to register their DNS records (in the absence of another, more serious, network problem).

Review your Designs

Anyone's first attempt at anything is rarely her best, so an important step in designing an Active Directory is to reconsider the finished design. In particular, review carefully any design decisions that deviate from the simplest possibility.

Because some elements of a design can't be changed once implemented, they should be thoroughly tested in a lab environment before being used. It's also advisable to have them reviewed as widely as possible within an organization by representatives of not just the IT department and management but by end users as well.

Immediate Solutions

Visio 2000 Enterprise

With Microsoft's purchase of Visio, it was able to integrate Active Directory design functionality into the Enterprise Edition of the product. Not only does it have a number of predefined shapes to represent Active Directory objects, so designs can be drawn, but it also has an online mode that allows you to work against a live Active Directory.

Installing Visio 2000

Before using Visio 2000 Enterprise Edition, you must install it. To install Visio:

1. Insert the Visio 2000 Enterprise CD-ROM into the computer.

2. If the splash screen doesn't appear, execute **setup.exe** from the root directory of the CD-ROM.

3. From the splash screen, click Install Visio 2000.

4. You're offered the chance to install Microsoft Data Engine. It's required by Visio's network autodiscovery functionality but isn't needed to work with Active Directory. Clear the checkbox if you don't need it, and click Update to proceed.

5. Click Accept to agree to the license agreement.

6. After some processing, you're prompted to restart the computer. Click OK.

7. Once Windows 2000 has restarted, log back in.

8. The Visio Installation Manager starts automatically. Click Next to begin.

9. On the License Agreement page, select I accept, then click Next.

10. Enter your name, the company name, and the Product ID on the Registration page and click Next to continue.

11. On the Setup Type page, select Custom Install and specify an installation directory. Click Next.

12. On the Custom Setup page, ensure that the Visio/Solution/Directory Services feature is set to Install locally, and select other options as appropriate. Click Next to proceed with installation.

13. Review the list of selected components and click Next again. The file copying process begins.

14. At the end of installation, you're prompted to register online if desired. Deal with this as is appropriate.

15. Finally, click Finish. By default, Visio will now launch.

Creating a New Active Directory Diagram

Once you've installed Visio, the next step is using it to design a directory. The first step in this process is to create a drawing to design with:

1. Launch Visio 2000 from the Start menu.

2. At the Welcome to Visio 2000 dialog box, select Create new drawing type, select Choose drawing type, then click OK.

3. Select Network Diagram in the category list, then Active Directory from the Drawing type, and click OK.

4. The Connect to Directory dialog box (Figure 19.6) appears. Two options are available: to work offline and create a directory structure "on paper" or to import the current structure from an existing domain.

To import from a live directory:

1. Select Import from a live directory.

2. Click Browse. If prompted, enter credentials (with the username in Domain\Username format). A directory browser appears.

3. Select the root object to import from and click OK.

4. Select the objects to import: either all objects, just containers, or a specified subset.

5. Either select to import the entire subtree or just a specified number of levels.

6. Click OK to begin the import.

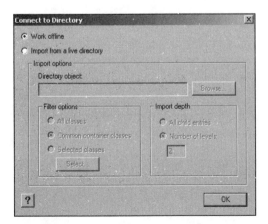

Figure 19.6   Connect to Directory dialog box.

Working offline is simpler: simply select Work offline and click OK. A blank drawing page is then created.

Working with Objects

The Active Directory structure "behind" the current drawing is shown in the Directory Navigator window (see Figure 19.7).

Objects in the directory browser can be dragged and dropped into the drawing to display them. When a container object is dropped, you're prompted whether or not to add its children. New objects can be added by dragging and dropping from the object palette to the left of the Visio window. These objects are then added, by default, at the root level of the directory browser and can be dragged/dropped within that to give them a position in the directory. Links will automatically be created on the drawing when this is done. All objects can be modified by right-clicking and by editing their properties (see Figure 19.8). These changes will then be reflected in any changes exported.

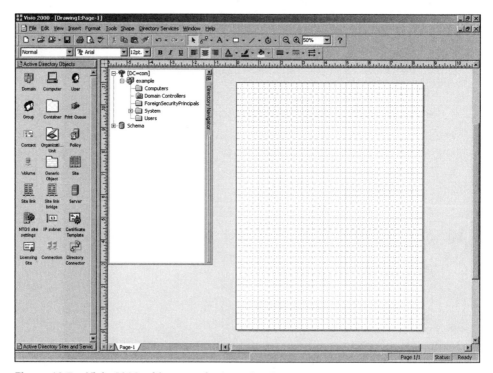

Figure 19.7   Visio 2000 with **example.com** structure open.

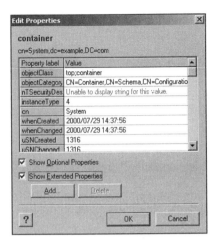

Figure 19.8   Editing object properties in Visio.

Exporting Changes

Any modification made in Visio can be applied to Active Directory through LDIF. To export a drawing to LDIF:

1. Open the Directory Service menu.

2. Select Export to LDIF.

3. Choose either Export changes (to create an LDIF file of changes made to the structure) or Export entries to export all objects in the loaded domains.

Delegating Administrative Control

To use a small number of domains effectively, there should be only very limited access to true domain and Enterprise administrator accounts. Instead, day-to-day administration tasks should be delegated to a number of domain local groups, and membership of these groups given to Global Groups. The following solutions document the necessary permissions to give to such groups.

Creating Child Domains

The default behavior requires an Enterprise administrator to add a new domain to a forest. In order to delegate the creation of child domains, an Enterprise administrator must precreate the domain using the **ntdsutil** utility. To do so:

1. Open a command prompt from the Accessories menu.

2. Type **ntdsutil** and press enter.

```
C:\>ntdsutil
```

3. Type **domain management** and press enter.

```
ntdsutil: domain management
```

4. Type **connections** and press enter.

```
domain management: connections
```

5. Connect to an existing domain controller. For example, to connect to a server named **calvin.example.com**:

```
server connections: connect to server calvin.example.com
```

TIP: *Alternative credentials can be set at this point. Type help at the server connections prompt for syntax.*

---

6. Type **quit** and press enter.

```
server connections: quit
```

7. Use the **precreate** command with the first parameter, the distinguished name of the new domain, and the second as the DNS name of the first domain controller for that domain. For example:

```
domain management: precreate dc=test,dc=example,dc=com srv.test.example.com
```

For the domain to be added, whoever is adding it must be able to bring up the first domain controller in that domain. Doing so involves replicating in copies of the Configuration and Schema partitions of Active Directory. Hence, the following permissions must be granted to the Child Domain Creation Group:

• Manage Replication Topology

• Read

• Replicating Directory Changes

• Replication Synchronization

Adding a domain controller also means adding it to a site, so the Child Domain Creation Group should also have:

• Read

• Create child objects

For this object and all child objects for the site use (**cn=sitename,cn=Sites, cn=Configuration,dc=ForestRootDomain**). Also, you should give **CREATOR OWNER** full control at the same level, so the Child Domain Creation Group members can manage the objects they create.

Creating Domain Controllers in Existing Domains

The permissions required to add a new domain controller to an existing domain include those required to add a new domain—namely, the ability to replicate in the Configuration and Schema Domain partitions and to create the server object. Also, a Domain Controller Addition Group will require rights to replicate in the relevant domain partition, namely:

- Add/Remove Replica in Domain
- Manage Replication Topology
- Read
- Replicating Directory Changes
- Replication Synchronization

Because the computer that becomes the new domain controller must be an existing member of the domain and because it will end up with its computer object in the Domain Controllers OU, it's simplest, as a domain administrator, to move it manually. Finally, the Domain Controller Addition Group must be able to log on locally to the computer in order to start Active Directory.

Delegating Management of Sites

Site information is stored in the configuration partition of Active Directory beneath **cn=Sites,cn=Configuration,dc=ForestRootDomain** (see Figure 19.9).

To delegate complete management of sites, a group should be granted Read, Delete, and Create child objects permissions on **cn=Sites,cn=Configuration, dc=ForestRootDomain**, and **CREATOR OWNER** should be given *full control* to the DN and all child objects.

To delegate management of subnets, similar permissions can be set on the Subnets container within the Sites container. And similarly, again, Site Link/Site Link Bridge management can be delegated by giving Read, Delete, and Create child objects permissions to the management group and *full control for this object and all child objects* to the **CREATOR OWNER** Group.

TIP: *Deny access control entries can be used on particular object types or subcontainers of **cn=Sites,cn=Configuration, dc=ForestRootDomain** to give groups only specific powers over site manipulation.*

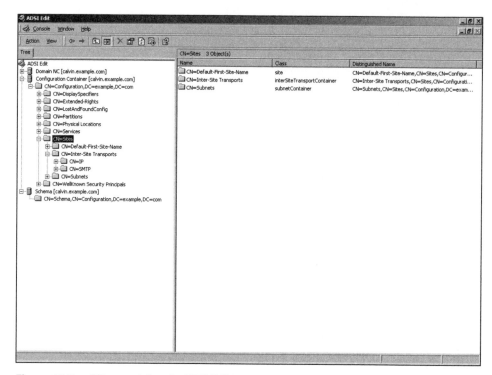

Figure 19.9   Sites container in ADSI Edit.

Chapter 20

Migrating to Windows 2000

In Depth

Chapter 20 addresses the process of moving from Windows NT to Windows 2000. Microsoft has specific definitions for words in the area of moving from Windows NT to Windows 2000, and this chapter adheres to these definitions for clarity.

Migration is a general term for going from a Windows NT domain infrastructure to Windows 2000. Within this, two main possibilities are available. An *upgrade* to Windows 2000 specifically refers to installing Windows 2000 on the existing Windows NT 4 domain controllers and is sometimes referred to as an *upgrade in place*.

The alternative is to *restructure* domains by developing a Windows 2000 infrastructure parallel to an existing Windows NT 4 infrastructure, then using one of a variety of techniques to move objects from the Windows NT 4 structure to Windows 2000.

In general terms, *restructuring* is the path of choice for organizations with highly complex Windows NT domain configurations that are looking to move to a smaller number of larger Windows 2000 domains. On the other hand, upgrading in place is a simpler procedure and more suited to basic Windows NT installations.

Upgrade or Restructure?

The first choice to be made when migrating from Windows NT to Windows 2000 is whether you should restructure your existing NT domains or upgrade in place. Of course, the migration process is flexible, and the tools used to restructure Windows NT domains into Windows 2000 domains can also be used to restructure post-migration. For example, this means you can perform an upgrade in place to Windows 2000, then restructure at a later date, perhaps as resources allow.

Advantages of Upgrading

Upgrading a current domain model in place is the simplest solution because, if planned correctly, it can be done with no impact on the production environment—a short interval will occur where the primary domain controller (PDC) of a domain is unavailable while Windows 2000 then Active Directory are installed, but nothing else.

As a corollary to being the simplest solution, it's also the fastest and, hence, cheapest solution to migrating to Windows 2000, because it doesn't require lengthy planning and testing of migration. It also carries low risk, because rollback during migration is relatively straightforward. Perhaps the best way to prepare for this is to take a backup domain controller from each Windows NT domain offline during the upgrade (known as putting "backup domain controllers [BDC] in a cupboard"). Full backups of all domain controllers should also be taken.

These offline BDCs can then quickly be plugged back in; any other domain controllers turned off; and after promoting a BDC from each domain to be the PDC, you'll have a functioning domain again. An upgrade in place, of course, maintains the original domain structure so it doesn't alter the existing administrative structure vis-à-vis the administrative boundaries already in place. This is an advantage for simple domain structures with perhaps a few domains in complete trust but is a disadvantage if you have a sprawling mass of Windows NT domains resulting from takeovers, mergers, and overenthusiastic architects who've misread one Windows NT 4 Server in the Enterprise study guide too many times (and created too many domains simply because they can).

In a single domain environment, upgrading to Windows 2000 in place is the obvious solution. Many people (including the author) prefer to avoid operating system upgrades opting, instead, for a clean install if at all possible, but this argument doesn't prevent an upgrade in place. This is because once the Windows NT PDC is upgraded to Windows 2000, additional Windows 2000 domain controllers can be brought online from clean installations, and (after configuring a Global Catalog server and transferring operations master roles) the original domain controller—the old PDC—can be removed.

Advantages of Restructuring

Restructuring outright generally involves creating a new, parallel Windows 2000 structure and moving objects in at a later date. It will chiefly reduce the complexity of your environment by resulting in fewer domains, which means fewer domain controllers and, hopefully, lower management costs.

The new Windows 2000 environment can be created in parallel to the existing Windows 2000 structure and objects moved at the last minute. Restructuring provides an IT department with a welcome opportunity to, in some sense, start with a blank piece of paper for its administrative and domain designs.

Advantages of Upgrading Then Restructuring

Upgrading in place then restructuring later means that the move to Windows 2000 can be achieved as quickly as possible. If you're nervous about the upgrade and want to be able to recover more easily to the old environment, you perform a straight restructure. When upgrading and restructuring, you should upgrade all domains into a single Windows 2000 forest, then use tools, such as the Active Directory Migration Tool, to restructure domains into their parents.

Domain Upgrades

The process of upgrading a Windows NT domain to Windows 2000 starts with installing Windows 2000 on the PDC. Once this installation is complete and the computer restarts in Windows 2000, the Active Directory Installation Wizard (**dcpromo.exe**) starts and you have the option to create a new domain. This new domain can be the root of a new forest, or it can join an existing Windows 2000 forest as a new tree or new child domain.

NOTE: *As ever, one of the biggest problems encountered in domain upgrades is Domain Name System (DNS). Make sure the PDC is configured to use a suitable DNS server before installing Windows 2000 (or use Windows 2000 DNS on the newly upgraded PDC).*

This means that the first step in upgrading a Windows NT domain infrastructure is to create the forest root domain. You do this either by upgrading a Windows NT domain or by creating an entirely new, empty Windows 2000 domain as the forest root and upgrading Windows NT domains as its children. The order of upgrades and structure formed will depend upon your current Windows NT domain structure.

Windows NT Domain Models

To illustrate domain upgrades here, we need to consider some of the fundamental Windows NT domain models and look at possibilities for upgrading them to Windows 2000 forests. Of course, reality is rarely as simple as the textbook-style configurations, but these examples should provide ideas for dealing with more esoteric situations.

Complete Trust

A complete trust Windows NT domain model, such as that illustrated in Figure 20.1, has a number of domains that all trust each other. Such an arrangement is obviously suited to a single Windows 2000 forest in order to preserve complete trust between the domains.

Exactly what configuration of domains is chosen depends on the relative merits of these domains. For example, consider a company with three domains in a complete trust model called AMERICA, EUROPE, and ASIA. These three are peers in terms of their scope, so creating a Windows 2000 domain structure, such as that shown in Figure 20.2, would be inappropriate.

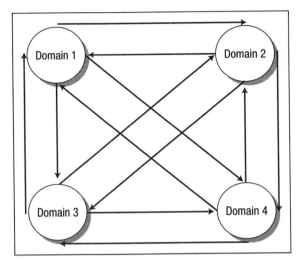

Figure 20.1   A Windows NT complete trust model (four domains).

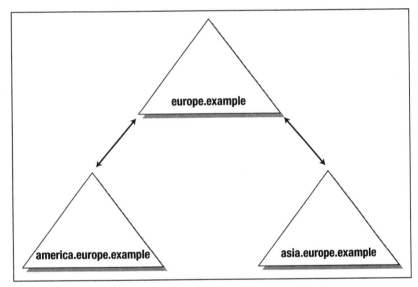

Figure 20.2   A possible Windows 2000 domain configuration.

Instead, this would be a perfect example of where an empty Windows 2000 forest root domain could be created from scratch and the existing domains promoted to be children of this domain. (Of course, this approach doesn't just apply to geographical divisions but to domains divided by department as well.)

Another possibility for a complete trust model is where some domains are logically children of others. For example, there may be the main corporate domain

(**EXAMPLE**), then separate domains for two particular departments (**PAYROLL** and **RESEARCH**, say), with all other departments having their resources in the main **EXAMPLE** domain. In this case, an upgrade in place may use **EXAMPLE** as the forest root with the other domains as children (see Figure 20.3).

Faced with this sort of scenario, either of the two possibilities are equally acceptable from the point of view of getting to a pure Windows 2000 forest as quickly as possible. If anything, it is non-technical factors that determine whether a new domain is created for the forest root or whether an existing domain is appropriate.

Incomplete Trust

An alternative to a complete trust model in an organization of several peered domains is one where every domain doesn't trust every other domain. For example, a company may be comprised of several divisions, each of which doesn't necessarily trust the other divisions. An example is pictured in Figure 20.4.

Here, the decision of what to do in an upgrade is harder. Moving to a single Windows 2000 forest will necessarily create trusts between all domains. Although this will make tasks operationally easier for users and perhaps simplify administration, it may not be politically desirable within an organization.

For example, no division may wish an administrator of any other division to have the use of a member of the Enterprise Admin Group. Actually, this problem can be overcome by using an empty forest root domain with only a handful of highly trusted central IT staff (say, from the head office) having access to it and delegating as many tasks as possible to the divisions that make up the company. However, using multiple forests in Windows 2000 will also be necessary if differing views exist within an organization about schema modifications, because each forest can only have one schema.

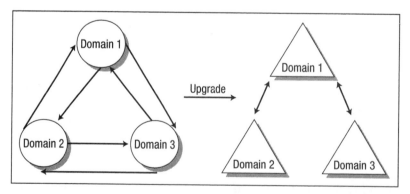

Figure 20.3   Upgrading a complete trust domain to a corresponding single tree.

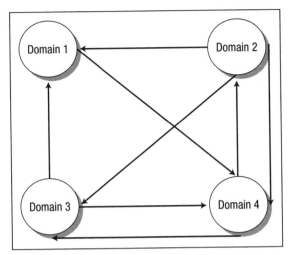

Figure 20.4   Example of a Windows NT domain structure without complete trusts.

Although using several forests is, in many ways, no worse than using separate Windows NT domains, it negates many of the benefits of Windows 2000 to an enterprise and must be considered very carefully—not least because, currently, no ways are available to graft forests together in Active Directory. Restructuring would have to be undertaken to make it possible.

Single Master Domain

A master domain model in Windows NT is a situation where one or more account domains exist housing user objects and where a number of (usually smaller) resource domains contain servers, workstations, printers, and so forth (see Figure 20.5).

The reasons resource domains tend to be employed are either related to delegating administration or the scalability of Windows NT, and these reasons go away when Active Directory is introduced. This means that the eventual aim of an organization with master domains and resource domains should be to restructure the resource domains into their masters. However, this process can take place before or after upgrading to Windows 2000.

Multiple-Master Domains

The multiple-master domain environments, which for scalability reasons have several master domains and perhaps an overlapping mesh of resource domains, can be thought of as a combination of the master domain scenario and the complete or incomplete trust scenarios. An example of the multiple-master domain model is pictured in Figure 20.6.

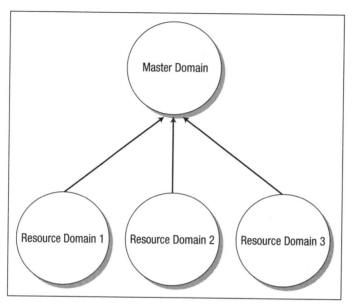

Figure 20.5   A single master domain model.

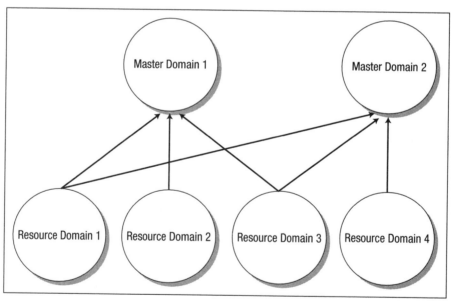

Figure 20.6   An example of a multiple-master domain model.

By that, I mean that master domains should be organized into trees, a forest, or forests, depending upon the relationship between the master domains. Resource domains should be upgraded beneath their masters as for the single-master domain model, then, hopefully, restructured into their master domains.

One potential problem, illustrated in Figure 20.6 with the **RESOURCE1** domain, is the issue of a resource domain being shared between masters. In such an instance, it isn't clear which it should be upgraded to, be a child of, and later migrated into.

Where the master domains are rolled up into a single forest isn't an issue at the logical design level, because the complete trust model, stemming from two-way, transitive parent-child trusts in Active Directory forests, makes a trust path available by default.

However, if the master domains are promoted into separate forests, this isn't possible. One solution here would be to upgrade the resource domain as a child of one of the masters, then use an explicit, interforest Windows NT-style trust to the out-of-forest master. In such situations, the resource domain should be promoted to be a child of a trusted master domain, so it can later be restructured into that master and still make its resources available to the other domain.

Planning an Upgrade

Once upgrading has been chosen as a migration path and once the intended Windows 2000 forest, site, and administrative structures have been designed and planned, the next steps are to actually, physically upgrade to Windows 2000.

Upgrading Windows NT to Windows 2000

Until this point in the chapter, the broad term, Windows NT, has been used to cover all possible versions of Windows NT. In fact, differences exist in upgrading the various versions. The main difference is that only Windows NT 3.51 and above can be upgraded to Windows 2000. Windows NT 3.1 and Windows NT 3.5 must first be upgraded via Windows NT 3.51 or NT 4 before computers can be upgraded to Windows 2000.

NOTE: *Before upgrading a computer, Microsoft recommends that you should apply the latest service pack available for its operating system and ensure it meets the hardware requirements for the version you are upgrading to.*

Planning for Recovery

The last thing you want to have happen is for the upgrade to fail—perhaps through a power cut or hardware failure—and be left without a working Windows 2000 domain and have no way of reverting to Windows NT. Thus, as for any major IT operation, you should carefully plan and test a recovery strategy. At a minimum, you should do the following:

- Ensure that at least two domain controllers exist in every domain.
- Synchronize all backup domain controllers (BDCs) to ensure convergence.

- Take full backups of all domain controllers.

- Test these backups.

- Take a BDC off the network.

This offline BDC can be used to quickly restore the Windows NT domain. It should periodically be added to the network again, synchronized, then removed again to keep its database up-to-date. Obviously you can only do this while a domain is still in Mixed mode.

Upgrade Order

The aims of upgrading should be to perform the following steps:

- *Upgrade/Create the new forest root*—The first domain in any forest must be the forest root domain.

- *Upgrade master or complete trust domains*—Where several domains exist, you should use the following considerations when planning which to upgrade first:

  - *Minimize risk*—The first upgrade is probably going to be the riskiest, so choose a relatively simple master domain without far-flung domain controllers or low bandwidth connections.

  - *Most important first*—If domains need to be in Windows 2000 in order for you to proceed with later stages of your migration plan, upgrade these first. For example, if you intend to restructure, upgrade the domains to receive restructured objects early.

  - *Upgrade resource domains*—Once master domains have been upgraded, resource domains can be upgraded and made children of the master domains. Again, if several exist, use the following considerations to plan an order:

  - *Use Windows 2000 Only Applications/Features*—If domains will host Windows 2000-only applications, such as Exchange 2000, these should be upgraded first. Also, domains that host workstations could be upgraded early to take advantage of software deployment and other Group Policy features.

  - *Restructuring targets*—If part of your later restructuring plan is to roll up resource domains into other resource domains, obviously the resource domains that will contain objects from restructured domains should be upgraded early, so restructuring can take place as soon as possible.

Within domains, the PDC must be upgraded first and BDCs should then follow—at least one other Windows 2000 domain controller should be added quickly in order to provide fault tolerance, but after that, it's perhaps more important to upgrade other domains that add tens of Windows 2000 domain controllers to one domain (although these tasks could go on in parallel).

Before upgrading domain controllers, it's vital to check their DNS configuration by making sure they can access the zone for their new domain and that the zone supports service (SRV) resource records and (ideally) dynamic registration of DNS records. It's also vital to ensure that domain controllers to be upgraded have an NT File System (NTFS) partition to host sysvol.

Switching to Native Mode

The final task of upgrading a domain is to make the switch to Native mode. This is a once-only, irreversible action that should be undertaken only when all BDCs have been upgraded to Windows 2000.

Native mode Windows 2000 domains support Universal Security Groups and other features not available in Mixed mode, when the accounts in Active Directory must remain compatible with the Windows NT Security Accounts Manager (SAM) structure.

Once a domain has been switched to Native mode, downlevel domain controllers will no longer receive updates to the SAM database, and downlevel domain controllers can no longer be added to the domain.

TIP: *The switch is made from a domain's Properties dialog box in Active Directory Domains and Trusts.*

Performing a Successful Upgrade

Several considerations must be taken into account when upgrading a Windows NT network to Windows 2000. This is because there are several areas where the two products operate in different ways. DNS, for example, is essential in Windows 2000 but need not be present in a Windows NT network. Other services may have to be reconfigured, and some items such as System Policy no longer apply.

DNS

DNS is absolutely vital to Active Directory (if you haven't gotten the message by now, let me know, and I'll stress it a little more in future editions). Before the Active Directory installation is performed, it's absolutely essential that a DNS server supporting SRV records is available. For Microsoft DNS servers, this means either Windows 2000 or Windows NT 4 with Service Pack 4 installed.

To avoid having to manually add SRV resource records, it is suggested that a server that supports dynamic updates be used, so probably Windows 2000 DNS server. This can be achieved by installing a Windows 2000 member server to the domain, by installing DNS, and by adding a secondary copy of the relevant zone and making that the primary zone.

Configure the PDC to use this new DNS server; this means that dynamic DNS registrations will be possible in the domain. The next step for DNS management could be to add DNS to the first domain controller and make the domain's zone Active Directory-integrated.

DHCP

Two issues exist with DHCP during domain upgrades: authorizing servers and providing DHCP services while Windows 2000 is installed on DHCP servers. Ideally, before a DHCP server is upgraded to Windows 2000, its IP address should be added to the authorized list for the forest in Active Directory. When the Windows 2000 DHCP service starts up, it checks Active Directory for authorization and will fail to start if it isn't authorized. To minimize the impact of DHCP servers being offline during the upgrade, alternative servers could be brought up (temporarily), or the upgrade could be performed during off-hours when DHCP requests are infrequent.

Windows NT LAN Manager Replication

Windows NT uses LAN Manager Replication to distribute scripts between Windows NT domain controllers. To continue to support this, the LAN Manager replication export server should be the last domain controller in the domain to be upgraded. This may mean transferring the export server responsibility from the PDC to another BDC. However, Windows NT doesn't receive updates from Windows 2000 to the replicated information and doesn't export updates to Windows 2000. Instead, a manual or scheduled process must be initiated to provide this service.

The Windows 2000 Server Resource Kit includes the lbridge.cmd file to automate the process of copying scripts from Windows 2000 to an NT export server, from where it normally will be replicated to other Windows NT domain controllers. This operation can be scripted, so updates become automatic. As domain controllers are upgraded, the LAN Manager replication service should be gradually reconfigured *not* to update newly upgraded domain controllers.

Logon Scripts

When domain controllers are upgraded to Windows 2000, logon scripts aren't affected. They're still available from NETLOGON shares and are still processed by clients—both Windows NT and Windows 2000. They're replicated between Windows 2000 domain controllers via File Replication Service (FRS) and between Windows NT domain controllers via local area network (LAN) manager replication. Replication from Windows 2000 to the Windows NT export server must be done manually, as described previously.

Domain Restructuring

An alternative to upgrading in place, or perhaps a task to perform later, is domain restructuring. This can either take the form of creating a parallel Windows 2000 infrastructure, creating trust relationships and restructuring users in, or it can take the form of wholly/partially upgrading a Windows NT domain structure then migrating resource domains or small domains into large domains.

Interforest Restructuring

The process of interforest restructuring involves copying user accounts and groups to a Windows 2000 domain from outside its forest. This means copying either from a Windows NT 4 domain or another Windows 2000 forest.

Interforest restructuring can copy user-defined users and security groups between Windows 2000 forests. It can't copy built-in users and groups, because these have the same Security Identifiers (SIDs) in every domain, and SIDs must be unique within a domain. This process requires using one domain controller in each forest. The domain controller in the source domain must be the PDC (emulator). The restructure process itself uses tools, such as the Active Directory Migration Tool, **netdom.exe**, or **ClonePrincipal**, and is run on the target domain controller, which can be any domain controller in the target Windows 2000 domain.

To restructure successfully between forests, the following conditions must be met:

- The target domain must be a Windows 2000 domain in Native mode.
- The user account used to restructure requires administrative privileges in both the source and target domains.
- The source domain controller must have a registry **DWORD** value of 1 for the following key:

```
HKLM\SYSTEM\CurrentControlSet\Control\Lsa\TcpipClientSupport
```

NOTE: *After making this change, you must reboot the domain controller for it to take effect.*

- An empty local group named after the source domain with three dollar signs—such as **example$$$**—must be created in the source domain.
- Account auditing must be enabled on both the source and target domains as follows:
  - Success and Failure for Account and Group Management must be enabled on a Windows NT 4 source domain controller.

- The Audit account management Group Policy option must be enabled in a Windows 2000 domain's Default Domain Controllers GPO.

Cloning

Intra-forest restructuring relies on copying users and groups from one domain to another, a process known as *cloning*. Cloning an account copies its properties from the source domain to a Native mode, Windows 2000 domain where a new account with a new SID is created.

The SID of the migrated account is added to this account's **sIDHistory** attribute, which means that the account still has the permissions assigned to its predecessor. Group membership is also maintained when users and groups are cloned by restoring it once both users and groups have been cloned. It's even possible to clone multiple groups into one. Such a merge operation is useful if you're combining domains and if parallel group structures exist in each. Local Groups on Windows NT domain controllers can be cloned to Domain Local Groups in Active Directory.

The tools used in cloning are the Active Directory Migration Tool (ADMT) and **ClonePrincipal**. More details on the use of these tools can be found in the "Immediate Solutions" of this chapter.

SID History

The SID History (sIDHistory) attribute for an object contains the object's old SIDs. Because object SIDs are based a domain's SID, when an object moves between domains it is assigned a new SID. However, in order to keep permissions on resources the object (such as a user) has already been assigned, as well as group memberships, the object's old SID is copied to a multi-valued attribute called sIDHistory.

When a user logs on, an access token is created at the authenticating domain controller. This access token will contain not just the user's current SID, but also any previous SIDs associated with the account. This means that when you migrate a user between domains, permissions are not lost.

The reason that native mode is required for migrating accounts with sIDHistory is that Windows NT domain controllers are not able to generate an access token that includes an account's old SIDs.

Computer Accounts

Computer accounts can't be migrated as such. Instead, the computers must be joined to the new domain, either remotely using ADMT or using the command-line **netdom.exe** utility (or scripting if ADSI is installed, or even manually…).

Joining a computer to a different domain doesn't affect its SID. Hence, local groups hosted on the domain are unaffected—although, as with cloned groups, you must ensure that the target domain of the restructuring trusts the domains whose members are in the group. Similarly, domain controllers can't be migrated and must, instead, be upgraded to Windows 2000 (if applicable), joined to the target domain, and optionally have Active Directory installed.

Intraforest Restructuring

The alternative to interforest restructuring is intra-forest restructuring. This is the process of moving objects between domains within a forest. Note that it isn't possible to clone objects within a forest, because, for example, this could lead to two user objects with the same user principal name in a forest and one SID would be associated with two user accounts.

The requirements for intraforest restructuring are broadly similar to interforest restructuring, namely:

- The target domain must be in Native mode.

- The user account used to restructure requires administrative privileges in both the source and target domains.

- The source domain controller must have a registry **DWORD** value of 1 for the following key:

```
HKLM\SYSTEM\CurrentControlSet\Control\Lsa\TcpipClientSupport
```

NOTE: *After making this change, you must reboot the domain controller for it to take effect.*

- Account auditing must be enabled on both the source and target domains: that is, the Audit account management Group Policy option must be enabled in a Windows 2000 domain's Default Domain Controllers GPO.

The only difference is the lack of a requirement for a Domain$$$ Group in the source domain.

Moving Security Principals

Interforest restructuring allows security principals—users, security groups, and computer accounts—to be moved between domains. This causes a new SID to be generated based on the new domain and the old SID to be retained as part of the **sIDHistory** attribute, exactly as for interforest restructuring.

Moving users is a one-way process, and it crucially deletes the account from the source domain. This means that unlike cloning users, no easy fallback is available in the event of error.

Closed Sets

One important restriction in moving users and Global Groups is that only *closed sets* can be moved. This means that:

- If you move a user, you must move all of the Global Groups the user belongs to.

- If you move a Global Group, you must move all of its members.

The second of these points may be recursive, because Global Groups may be nested, so the membership of all those groups must also be moved.

Closed sets also apply to Domain Local Groups and domain controllers—if Domain Local Groups have any access control entries (ACEs) on discretionary access control lists (DACLs) on resources on a domain controller, moving the Doman Local Groups will also cause the domain controller to have to be moved. Similarly, moving a domain controller will require all Domain Local Groups that it references to be moved. In this way, you can see that each of these objects in a domain will fall into exactly one closed set, and the moving process is essentially a case of migrating domains closed set by closed set.

Breaking Closed Sets

It may not always be convenient to restructure on a closed-set-by-closed-set basis. Instead, you may wish to migrate only some of the members of a particular group. To beat this restriction, you have several options. One of these options is to use Universal Groups. Because Universal Groups can have membership from any domain in a forest, you can convert Global Groups to Universal Groups to prevent their membership counting toward closed sets. A drawback with this approach is that the membership of Universal Groups is stored in the Global Catalog and, hence, has replication implications for the network. This could be overcome by creating additional groups and nesting them within the Universal Group, although access control settings would have to be duplicated to the new groups.

Another possibility is to create a parallel group structure in the new domain, then migrate accounts to the new domain. Again, access control entries would have to be set on the new groups.

Immediate Solutions

Using **lbridge.cmd** for LAN Manager Replication

The **lbridge.cmd** file is included in the Windows 2000 Resource Kit for synchronizing script files from Windows 2000 Domain Controllers to the Windows NT domain controllers.

Running **lbridge.cmd**

The **cmd** (command) file for copying files for LAN Manager replication from Windows 2000 domain controllers to the Windows NT export server is called **lbridge.cmd** and is contained in the Windows 2000 Server Resource Kit. The syntax is as follows:

```
C:\>lbridge.cmd destination
```

For example:

```
C:\>lbridge.cmd \\bdc\netlogon\scripts
```

Editing **lbridge.cmd**

An alternative to using a command-line parameter every time you wish to execute **lbridge.cmd** is to actually edit the file itself. The line to change is line number 29 of the file. It's the last line of the block quoted below:

```
:Variables
@Rem ------------------------------------------
@Rem ! Variables
@Rem !     You may edit or pass-in L-Destination
@Rem ------------------------------------------
Set L-Destination=%1
```

The **%1** sets the variable to be the first command-line parameter. Instead, you could hardcode it to be the LAN Manager export server. For example if your export server is called **bdc** you could change the line to:

```
Set L-Destination=\\bdc\netlogon\scripts
```

It's then recommended that you save the file in a new location and execute that file instead of the original.

Scheduling **lbridge.cmd**

You can schedule the execution of **lbridge.cmd**—or indeed an application or script file—with the Windows 2000 Task Scheduler. To do so perform the following steps:

1. Click Start and mouse over Programs|Accessories|System Tools, then click Scheduled Tasks. The Scheduled Tasks folder opens in an Explorer window.

2. Double-click Add Scheduled Task. The Scheduled Task Wizard (see Figure 20.7) appears.

3. Click Next.

4. Click Browse.

5. Navigate to lbridge.cmd in the Common File Open dialog box ("Select Program to Schedule"). For example, with a default install, it will be in c:\Program Files\Resource Kit\lbridge.cmd. Click OK.

6. Select to perform the task daily and click Next.

7. Alter the time of day (if desired) and click Next. The schedule will be modified again in a moment.

8. Enter logon credentials to run the task under and click Next.

WARNING! An account with minimal privileges is strongly preferred, so ideally, you should create an account specifically for this. Remember that once it's scheduled, anyone with access to lbridge.cmd can edit the file to run an arbitrary command in the context of the account specified in this step.

9. On the final screen, check the box to launch the Advanced Properties dialog box and click Finish. The Advanced Properties dialog box appears.

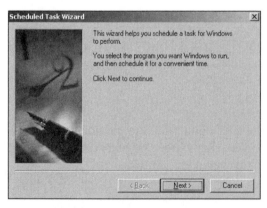

Figure 20.7   Scheduled Task Wizard.

10. On the Task tab, add any necessary command-line parameter at the end of the Run field.

11. On the Schedule tab, click Advanced.

12. Check the Repeat task box, and configure it to execute every two hours. Increase the duration to 24 hours.

13. Click OK twice.

Using the Active Directory Migration Tool for Restructuring

Now, I'll discuss using the Active Directory Migration Tool for restructuring. The ADMT is a downloadable utility for Windows 2000 that allows security principals to be migrated between domains, for example in restructuring operations.

Obtaining, Installing, and Launching the ADMT

The ADMT can be downloaded from the Microsoft Web site. At the time of writing, the correct URL is **www.microsoft.com/windows2000/downloads/deployment/ admt**. Once downloaded, the ADMT can be installed by running the admt.exe executable file. It should be installed. Following the wizards will add the migratory.msc Microsoft Management Console (MMC) Snap-in (see Figure 20.8) and a variety of supporting files.

The Active Directory Migration Tool adds an entry to the Administrative Tools menu, and its Snap-in can be launched from there or added to any other custom management console.

Migrating Security Principals

The ADMT can be used to migrate a variety of security principals. The process is wizard-based. The following solution illustrates migrating user accounts:

1. Launch the Active Directory Migration Tool Snap-in from the Administrative Tools menu.

2. Right-click Active Directory Migration Tool at the root of the console, and select User Migration Wizard. The User Migration Wizard launches.

3. Click Next.

4. Decide whether you wish to test a migration or actually migrate. It's recommended to test first in order to minimize risk. Click Next.

5. Type or select the NetBIOS names for the source domain (to migrate from) and the destination domain (to migrate to). Click Next.

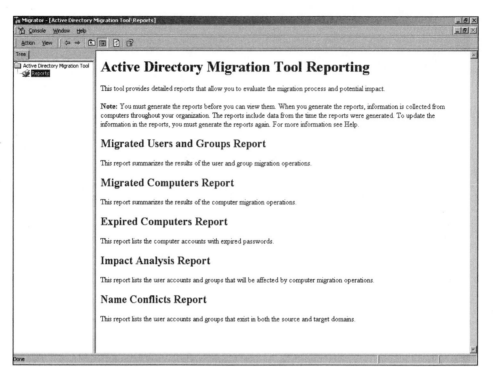

Figure 20.8   Active Directory Migration Tool.

6. On the User Selection page, use the Add button and the resulting User Selection dialog box to pick account(s) to migrate. Click Next when done.

7. Now type (or browse to get) the distinguished name (DN) of the Organizational Unit to migrate to.

8. Next, you have a choice about passwords—either a file can be created or the new accounts get passwords named after them. Click Next.

9. Decide whether you wish to disable the source on both or neither user accounts.

10. Optionally, specify an expiry date for the source account and decide whether or not to migrate the source account's SID to the **sIDHistory** attribute of the destination account. Click Next.

11. If you selected to migrate the SID, specify administrative credentials for the source domain and click Next.

12. On the User Options page (see Figure 20.9), specify which (if any) additional details to migrate or post migration tasks to perform, and click Next.

13. Choose a behavior for resolving naming conflicts and click Next.

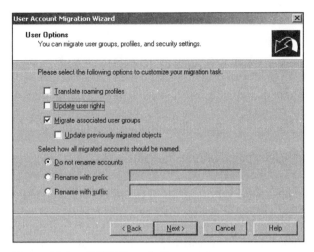

Figure 20.9   ADMT User Options page.

14. Click Finish. A progress window appears. Details of errors are reported. Use the View Log button at completion to see details of the steps performed.

15. Click Close to exit.

ClonePrincipal

ClonePrincipal is a Component Object Model (COM) object (**clonepr.dll**) supplied with five sample VBScript files in the Windows 2000 Support Tools that can be used to copy users and groups from source Windows NT or Windows 2000 domains to a Windows 2000 domain. The five sample script files are as follows:

- *clonegg.vbs*—Clones Global Groups.
- *cloneggu.vbs*—Clones Global Groups and Users.
- *clonelg.vbs*—Clones shared/Domain Local Groups.
- *clonepr.vbs*—Clones a single user or group.
- *sidhist.vbs*—Copies the SID from a source principal to the **sIDHistory** of a destination security principal.

The capabilities and functionality of the **ClonePrincipal** COM object are documented in the clonepr.doc file that forms part of the Windows 2000 Support Tools. Here we discuss only the sidhist.vbs sample file.

sidhist.vbs

This example script file demonstrates copying the SID from a security principal to the SID history of a security principal in a Windows 2000 domain. This will give the destination security principal the permissions of the source security principal. The parameters required specify the NetBIOS names of the source and destination domain controllers, the NetBIOS name of the source domain, the DNS name of the destination domain, and the NetBIOS names of the source and destination accounts.

For example, to copy the SID from **NT4DOMAIN\ADAM** to the **awood** account in **example.com**, with **NT4PDC** and **CALVIN** being the respective domain controllers to perform the operation on, you would type (all on one line):

```
C:\>cscript sidhist.vbs /srcdc:NT4PDC /srcdom:NT4DOMAIN /srcsam:ADAM
 /dstdc:CALVIN /dstdom:example.com /dstsam:awood
```

NOTE: *Administrative privileges are required in the source and destination domains.*

MoveTree

Another utility from the Windows 2000 Support Tools is **movetree.exe**. This is used to move a subtree of one Active Directory domain to another domain within the forest. A sample **movetree** syntax is:

```
C:\>movetree /start /s SrcServ /d DestServ /sdn SrcDN /ddn DestDN
```

Here, **SrcServ** is the DNS name of the domain controller in the source domain, **DestServ** is the DNS name of the domain controller in the destination domain to move to. **SrcDN** is the distinguished name of the source subtree (for example, **ou=Test,dc=child,dc=example,dc=com**), which, along with all of its children, will be moved to **DestDN**. **DestDN** is, of course, the distinguished name of the destination subtree, so if we wanted to move the **ou=Test** from **child.example.com** to **example.com** we would specify the **SrcDN** given earlier and a **DestDN** of **ou=Test,dc=example,dc=com**.

The **/start** command not only performs the operation but, first, runs a test to ensure uniqueness of things, like **sAMAccountName** in the destination domain. Other options, instead of **/start**, include **/startnocheck** (which performs the operation but not the check) and the **/continue** option, which resumes an operation that has previously gone wrong.

Netdom

Netdom is a versatile command-line tool from the Windows 2000 Support Tools that has been featured in other "Immediate Solutions" throughout this book. Its full list of uses can be found by typing the following at a command line:

```
C:\>netdom /help
```

The common thread connecting all of the uses of netdom.exe is managing computers and domains. In domain consolidation scenarios, its use is to move computer accounts from one domain to another. The syntax is as follows:

```
C:\>netdom move computername /d:domainname /ud:username /up:password
```

The source domain can be either Windows NT or Windows 2000, and the destination must be Windows 2000. You can even add a **/reboot:n** to reboot the machine in **n** seconds.

Chapter 21

Downlevel Computers

In Depth

Up until this point, the general assumption of this book has been a pure Windows 2000 network. Of course, during a migration this is an unrealistic assumption for domain controllers, because there must, at some point, be a mixture of Windows 2000 and non-Windows 2000 computers. Also, there's no compulsion whatsoever to use Windows 2000 clients with a Windows 2000 network (though Windows 2000 is better than previous versions of Windows in just about every way), so client issues with other operating systems are also addressed.

Windows 9x Clients

Computers running Windows 95, Windows 98, or Windows ME (which is morally matched by the term *Windows 9x*—think of it as Windows 9A if it makes things easier) can all connect to Active Directory domains, just as they can connect to Windows NT domains.

NOTE: *Domain mode doesn't affect clients, so downlevel clients, such as Windows 95 or Windows NT Workstation, can log in to Windows 2000 domains regardless of whether the domain is in Mixed or Native mode. Domain mode only affects downlevel domain controllers.*

Just like previous versions of Windows NT, Windows 9x clients don't need—and can't connect to—computer accounts in the domain. This means there's no server-end configuration to use a Windows 9x computer as part of a domain—just plug it in, configure it to authenticate against a domain, reboot, and log in.

Directory Services Client

The Windows 9x Directory Services Client is an optional install for Windows 9x computers that connect to Windows 2000 domains. It isn't absolutely necessary, and without it, client computers will function exactly as they would when connecting to Windows NT 4 domains. However, with the Directory Services Client installed, computers become site-aware. This is achieved by sending—as normal—a datagram to every domain controller in the domain at logon. Windows NT backup domain controllers (BDCs) will respond normally, offering logon services, but Windows 2000 domain controllers respond with additional information, such as their site, the client's site, and their Domain Name System (DNS) name.

Computers with the Directory Services Client installed prefer Windows 2000 domain controllers, and among these, they prefer Windows 2000 domain controllers in their own site. If no Windows 2000 domain controller in their own site responds, they'll explicitly query the first Windows 2000 domain controller from another site to respond to find a domain controller in their own site. If no Windows 2000 domain controller is available in their own site, they'll use a random Windows 2000 domain controller from any other site. If no Windows 2000 domain controllers respond, the fallback is to use a Windows NT BDC.

The same procedure is used by Windows 9x directory service-enabled clients to locate distributed file system (DFS) replicas. A final result of installing the Directory Services Client is to change password update behavior: instead of making changes at the primary domain controller (PDC) emulator, as would usually be the case, the domain controller location process described above would be used.

Policy Settings

Windows 9x clients don't support Group Policy, which is a Windows 2000 (or later) phenomenon. Instead, good old System Policy must still be used, exactly as it is under Windows NT domains. This means that the config.pol file from the netlogon share is used.

System policy settings are applied at logon and overwrite defaults in the Windows 9x Registry. They can be used, for example, to enforce system configuration and deploy Registry settings for users and can then be applied either individually or to groups.

Windows NT Clients

At the time of this writing, Microsoft has yet to release a Directory Services Client for Windows NT 4, although it has announced its plans to as part of Service Pack 7. The absence of a Directory Services Client means that the normal Windows NT-style logon procedure is required.

This means NetBIOS resolution is used to locate domain controllers, either by broadcast or through LMHOSTS or WINS resolution. Once a domain controller is located, logon proceeds as normal, and in the case of Windows 2000 domain controllers, it does so in a fully Windows NT-compatible fashion.

WINS Enhancements in Windows 2000

Unfortunately, WINS can't fully go away in Windows 2000, because it's usually required to support downlevel clients. However, Microsoft has introduced a number of enhancements to WINS services in Windows 2000.

At the server side, Windows 2000 WINS servers support persistent connections, which eliminate the overhead relating to continuously opening and closing replications connections and also speeds up replication. In addition, manual tombstoning of records is supported, a number of new and improved features are in the Dynamic Host Configuration Protocol (DHCP) Microsoft Management Console (MMC) Snap-in, including export to file; multiple selection of records, so they can all be operated upon at once; and the ability to filter the current view or search for records.

At the client side, Windows 2000 computers that use WINS can have up to 12 servers configured for fault tolerance and are also able to dynamically reregister their NetBIOS-IP mappings without rebooting.

Using the Active Directory as an Address Book

Even though no explicit client is available for Active Directory, applications that use Lightweight Directory Access Protocol (LDAP) servers, such as the Windows Address Book, can still be used to query Active Directory. To do this, LDAP queries should be directed at a specific domain on the Global Catalog port (3268). Depending on your network, you could either specify a particular Global Catalog server for each client to query or use a domain name, so they receive Global Catalog servers from the domain in rotation. Sadly, it isn't possible to make such searches site-aware until a Windows NT Directory Service Client is available and the **DsGetDcName** API function is implemented.

Policy

Like Windows 9x clients, Windows NT computers don't support Windows 2000's Group Policy, so Group Policy settings aren't applied for either users or computers under NT. Instead, System Policy is used. Again, exactly as for Windows 9x, **poledit.exe** can be used to create policy files, and it should be run on the target operating system (in this case NT), because of the different Registry structures that Windows 9x and Windows NT have.

Windows NT policy is stored separately to Windows 9x policy—in the file ntconfig.pol—but it's, again, stored in the netlogon share and downloaded automatically by clients at logon. Once you've seen the power and flexibility of Windows 2000 Group Policy, however, you probably won't want to go back to System Policy. The deployment of client operating systems is orthogonal to domain upgrades—you can upgrade clients to Windows 2000 either before, during, or after a domain upgrade—but the full power and flexibility of Windows 2000 is only available once Group Policy is. I've even known people to disable System Policy from clients during a domain upgrade then roll out Windows 2000 as quickly as possible, before implementing Group Policy.

Downlevel Domain Controllers

Downlevel—that is, Windows NT—backup domain controllers can be part of Windows 2000 Active Directory domains that are configured in Mixed mode. This can either be the result of upgrading a Windows NT 4 domain to Windows 2000 or adding explicitly to an Active Directory domain after it's created.

It isn't possible to have a Windows NT 4 primary domain controller in an Active Directory domain. This is because a PDC is designed to be the only write-enabled server for domain information, and this fact is incompatible with the multimastered Active Directory directory database. In fact, if you upgrade a Windows NT domain to Windows 2000 and Active Directory, the first step is to upgrade the PDC and install Active Directory on it.

Replication

Downlevel domain controllers don't receive the entire Active Directory through replication. Instead, they only receive updates to the records that are compatible with Windows NT domain controllers. Of course, because backup domain controllers can't make changes to the directory, they don't replicate any information back to Active Directory (and, instead, changes made by their clients go to the PDC Emulator role holder). Hence, no replication topology or Active Directory replication metadata concerning downlevel domain controllers is available, because they only receive changes and nothing else.

Native Mode

When a domain is switched to Native mode, updates are no longer sent to downlevel domain controllers, because new features that they don't support, such as Universal Security Groups and group nesting, become available. In addition, backup domain controllers can no longer be added to a Native mode domain.

No requirement, as such, to actually remove all Windows NT BDCs before switching to Native mode exists, because no checking is done as the switch is made. Instead, updates just stop being retrieved. The fact that no updates are getting through generates a number of Event Log entries on the affected domain controllers. Specifically Event 5716 will be raised by the netlogon service (every five minutes, by default), and this should inform savvy administrators that something is wrong.

The best practice is, of course, to remove or upgrade all downlevel domain controllers before changing to Native mode. Just make sure that they each have at least one DNS configured correctly, no rogue entries in the LMHOSTS file, and at least one NT File System (NTFS) volume to host sysvol if you want them to be Windows 2000 domain controllers. However, no compunction exists for an upgraded

Windows NT BDC to become a domain controller, and you can, instead, select "Leave as member server" when **dcpromo** runs after the upgraded exdomain controller is first rebooted into Windows 2000.

Removal

In reality, there's usually no good reason to continue using Windows NT BDCs in a Windows 2000 Active Directory domain, because it prevents the realization of some of the key benefits by switching a domain to Native mode. To change to Native mode, you should upgrade your Windows NT BDCs to Windows 2000 as soon as possible. One point to note is that there's no compulsion to make an upgraded BDC be a domain controller—you can install it as a member server if desired. Of course, just like any other installation of Windows 2000, it can later be promoted and demoted to and from being a domain controller at will.

A possible exception to this is if BDCs are hosting applications incompatible with Windows 2000. If reinstallation is out of the question, one option is to use a product, such as U-Tools U-Promote (**www.u-tools.com/Utools**), to demote the BDC down to a member server.

Immediate Solutions

Installing the Windows 9x Directory Services Client

Although not necessary, the functionality of Windows 9x clients can be improved with the Directory Services Client from the Windows 2000 Server CD. This allows them to use DFS as well as to make them site-aware. To install it:

1. Start the Windows 9x computer and log in normally.

2. Launch the \Clients\Win9x\Dsclient.exe file from the Windows 2000 Server CD-ROM.

3. The Directory Service Client Setup Wizard appears (see Figure 21.1). Click Next to proceed.

4. Click Next again to install.

5. Click Finish when it has installed.

6. When prompted, click Yes to restart the computer.

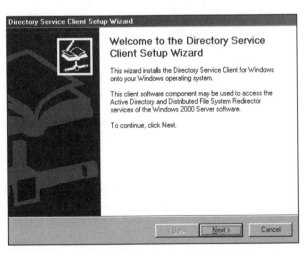

Figure 21.1 Directory Service Client Setup Wizard.

21. Downlevel Computers

The Directory Services Client can be removed through Add/Remove Programs from Control Panel, in the normal way. However, removing it doesn't remove the Active Directory address book entry, which will no longer work after removal, because it uses a **NULL** server name (so that the best domain controller is found in any given circumstance), and a **NULL** server name can't be interpreted correctly without the directory service client software.

Using the Windows 9x Directory Services Client

The Directory Services Client is, for the most part, invisible to the user. The use of site information at logon and password changes, for example, and the distributed file system (DFS) 5.0 client functionality are all-transparent. One area it does change is the Find menu accessed from the Start button. It adds a Printers entry with a similar dialog box found in Windows 2000 for searching printers. This is used exactly as in Windows 2000 and is pictured in Figure 21.2.

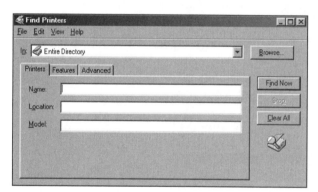

Figure 21.2   Windows 9x Find Printers dialog box.

Using Active Directory as an Address Book from Windows NT

If you wish to enable Windows NT users to search the Active Directory for user information from their desktop, you should add an entry for an Active Directory LDAP server to the Find People dialog box. To do so:

1. The first step in doing this is to install Internet Explorer 5, so the Address Book is added.

2. Open the Address Book from the Accessories menu.

3. Open the Accounts dialog box by clicking Tools|Accounts.

4. Click Add. The Internet Connection Wizard starts.

5. Type the name of a domain controller to use or a domain name to load balance the query via DNS.

6. Check the My LDAP Server Requires Me To Log On box and click Next.

7. Enter an account name (in Domain\Username form) and password to use to authenticate with the directory service. Click Next.

8. Select Yes or No, depending on whether you wish the directory to be used to check emails by default, and click Next.

9. Click Finish to create the account. The Wizard closes and the new account appears in the Accounts dialog box list.

10. Select the newly created account, then click the Properties button.

11. Switch to the Advanced tab.

12. If you wish to search just the directory of the specified server, enter the LDAP DN for the domain in the Search base box (for example, **dc=example,dc=com**). If you wish to search the Global Catalog (recommended), change the Directory Service port number to 3268.

13. Click OK.

System Policy

The following Immediate Solutions deal with System Policy under Windows 98, although the editing procedures are the same under Windows NT and other Windows 9x operating systems, and the installation process can be achieved by copying files.

Installing System Policy Editor

System Policy Editor can be installed from the Windows 98 CD-ROM or copied onto a system from Windows 2000. To use System Policy Editor on Windows 98, you need poledit.exe, common.adm, and windows.adm. To install it:

1. Insert the Windows 98 CD-ROM.

2. Launch the Add/Remove Programs applet from Control Panel.

3. Switch to the Windows Setup tab and click Have Disk.

4. In the Install From Disk dialog box, click Browse and locate the \tools\reskit\netadin\poledit folder, then click OK.

5. In the resulting dialog box, check the System Policy Editor dialog box then click OK.

The System Policy Editor is installed to the \Windows directory, so it can be launched by simply typing poledit in the Run dialog box.

Configuring Windows 98 to Use System Policy

A prerequisite to using System Policy is to configure Windows 9x to use User-level access control. To do so:

1. Right-click on the Network Neighborhood icon on the Windows 9x desktop.
2. Switch to the Access Control tab.
3. Select the User-level access control option.
4. In the Obtains lists of users and groups from field, type the NetBIOS name of the Windows 2000 domain that the computer is used in.
5. Click OK.
6. Reboot the computer when prompted.

Editing System Policy

System Policy Editor (see Figure 21.3) provides an intuitive user interface for creating system policy. The main part of the display shows the users and groups that policies are defined for. Users and groups can be added from the Edit menu.

Individual polices can be edited by double-clicking the icons/entries representing them, which will cause the corresponding Properties dialog box to appear (see Figure 20.4). In this dialog box you'll find a tree corresponding to the available options that can either be enabled (checked), disabled (cleared), or ignored (grayed).

Where users belong to multiple groups with policies defined, the Group Priority command (from the Options menu) can be used to order the groups with policy that are applied to them—the highest group's policy will thus take precedence.

Making System Policy Available

Once a policy file—either config.pol for Windows 9x or ntconfig.pol for Windows NT—has been created, the next step is to make it available. This is done by attempting to open the appropriate file from the netlogon share of the appropriate domain controller. This means placing it in the %SystemRoot%\ SYSVOL\sysvol\<domainname>\scripts folder (which is shared as \\server\netlogon) on a Windows 2000 domain controller, and using manual synchronization to place it on any Windows NT LAN Manager replication export server.

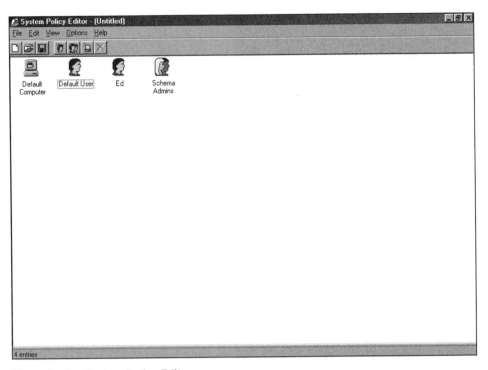

Figure 21.3   System Policy Editor.

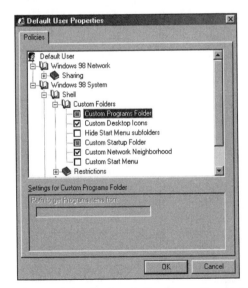

Figure 20.4   System Policy Properties dialog box.

Adding Downlevel Domain Controllers

The process for adding a Windows NT BDC to a Windows 2000 Active Directory domain running in Mixed mode is as follows:

1. Launch the Windows 2000 version of Server Manager for Domains, clicking Start|Run and typing srvmgr. It's included, by default, on Windows 2000 Server and is part of the Windows 2000 Professional Resource Kit.

2. Use the Computer|Select Domain command to connect to the correct domain, if necessary (the current domain will be opened by default).

3. Click Computer|Add To Domain. The Add Computer To Domain dialog box appears (see Figure 21.5).

4. Select Windows NT Backup Domain Controller from the Computer Type radio button group.

5. Type the NetBIOS name for the new domain controller in the Computer Name field.

6. Click Add. The computer account is created in the Domain Controller's OU of the domain. The common name of its object matches the NetBIOS name specified.

NOTE: *The computer account was only created in the Domain Controller's OU, because Windows NT Backup Domain Controller was selected. Ordinarily, computer accounts created this way appear in the Computers container. When creating accounts with Server Manager, the NetBIOS name for the new computer must be unique in the domain and also unique as a common name (cn) in the appropriate container, or a warning, such as in Figure 21.6, appears.*

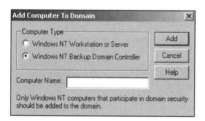

Figure 21.5   Server Manager's Add Computer to Domain dialog box.

Figure 21.6   Duplicate computer name warning.

7. Click Close to dismiss the Add Computer to Domain dialog box.

8. Close Server Manager.

Alternatively, the same results can be achieved the long way as follows:

1. Use Active Directory Users and Computers to create a computer account for the Windows NT BDC, marked for use by downlevel computers.

2. Start Active Directory Service Interface (ADSI) Edit from the Windows 2000 Support Tools, Tools menu.

3. Navigate to the new computer account object, right-click it and select Properties. The object's Properties dialog box appears (see Figure 21.7).

4. Select userAccountControl in the Select a property to view list.

5. In the Edit Attribute box, type the value 8192 and click Set.

6. Click OK.

This second approach is more amenable to scripting, of course.

Once a suitable account has been created in the domain, all that remains is to install the Backup Domain Controller as per the usual method for the operating system. When prompted, you should specify the downlevel name of the precreated account, downlevel domain name, and sufficient credentials to add a computer to the precreated account.

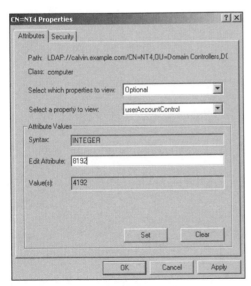

Figure 21.7 Modifying the userAccountControl attribute with ADSI Edit.

Related Solution	Found on page
Creating Computer Accounts	288

Administering Downlevel Domains

Windows 2000 includes a couple of tools to administer Windows NT domains. Specifically, these are Windows 2000 versions of Server Manager and User Manager for Domains. They are both included as part of Windows 2000 Server and as part of the Resource Kit (including the Professional Resource Kit). They're the executable files **srvmgr.exe** and **usrmgr.exe** respectively. These utilities are used in the same way as their Windows NT counterparts.

NOTE: *Windows 2000's* **usrmgr.exe** *can't be used to administer Active Directory on Windows 2000 servers.*

Chapter 22

Directory Interoperability

In Depth

This, the final chapter of the book, looks beyond the confines of how Active Directory functions in itself to the issues surrounding its interaction with other directory services. Specifically, three areas will be examined: metadirectory services, interaction with Novell networks running Novell Directory Services (NDS) and Microsoft Exchange—both Exchange 5.5 and Exchange 2000.

Metadirectories

A *metadirectory service* is, literally, a directory of directories. The idea behind metadirectories is that they provide a single, central repository of information and the ability to synchronize management of data. In particular, metadirectories provide a unified view of data. For example, imagine an organization has both Microsoft and Novell directory services, perhaps a Lotus Notes email organization, and an enterprise resource management system of some kind. Add to this a heady mix of employee databases of one form or another, and you have an awful lot of systems to keep in check (see Figure 22.1).

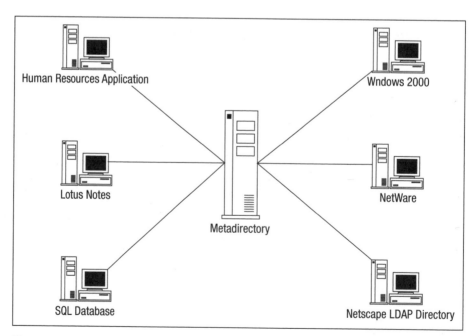

Figure 22.1   An example of an organization with multiple directories.

This whole area is known as *identity management* and is a particular problem, because an enterprise with disparate applications doesn't have a common interface to manage applications from. This is where metadirectories come in.

Metadirectories often provide a single administration interface of their own, as well as providing the ability to synchronize a definable subset of data from between sources in one or both directions. This data is joined together in the metadirectory, and rules can be used to define exactly what data flows in which direction between the constituent directories.

Areas where metadirectories help are:

• In the creation and deletion of user accounts ("hire/fire scenarios")

• In the provision of a global address book

• In the synchronization of data with partner companies

• Single-sign on

Using a metadirectory will also mean that existing administration tools can be used. Changes will be synchronized to the metadirectory and other applications, so it's cheaper and less risky than a huge consolidation project (and, hopefully, will also lack the company politics that go with a consolidation of systems controlled by different departments, teams, and warring factions within a company).

Metadirectory Architecture

Metadirectories work by detecting changes. When a piece of data changes on a system monitored by the metadirectory, this change is synchronized on the metadirectory then distributed to other systems. For example, if a user's telephone number is updated in Windows 2000, this change will be synchronized (how isn't important yet) with the metadirectory. Then, next time the metadirectory server pushes information to subscribing systems, such as open database connectivity (ODBC) databases, the change will be applied. Metadirectories support the aggregation of information, ensure the consistency of information, and distribute changes to other supported sources.

Microsoft Metadirectory Services

Microsoft's metadirectory product is imaginatively named Microsoft Metadirectory Services (MMS). It's a server product that runs on Windows 2000 Advanced Server (or above), and because it's a Lightweight Directory Access Protocol (LDAP) server in its own right, it isn't recommended that MMS be run on a domain controller.

MMS uses a number of Management Agents specific to the directories that are connected to MMS. These Management Agents connect through the Connector

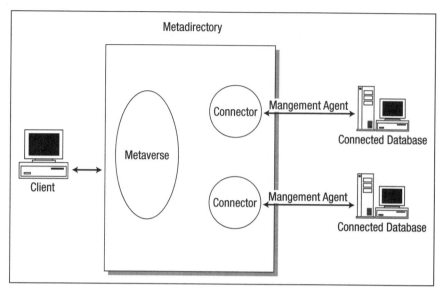

Figure 22.2   MMS architecture.

Namespace to the metadirectory's universe ("Metaverse"), which clients can connect to and manage. This is illustrated in Figure 22.2.

Management Agents

Management Agents are directory-specific. MMS ships by default with MAs for common directories, such as Windows NT, NDS, Active Directory, Microsoft Exchange, Lotus Notes, and cc:Mail. These software components vary in detail but are generally responsible for moving data between MMS and the connected directory and for reconciling it, based on either a periodic comparison or on a log of recent changes (depending on the target system).

Configuration is performed by script or other settings files, and these can determine exactly what data is synchronized, which side of the connection owns particular attributes, and so forth. Other details of connections, such as the frequency of synchronization, can also be set by script.

Compass

Compass is an LDAP client supplied with Microsoft Metadirectory Services. Although MMS is an LDAP server and, as such, Microsoft Metadirectory Services can be administered by any LDAP-enabled application, the application provided by Microsoft could be used to get the most out of managing MMS. Compass provides a familiar tree view of the entire directory and can be used to perform a variety of administration tasks, such as editing object properties and setting access control options. In addition to an installable client application, Microsoft provides ActiveX and Hypertext Transfer Protocol (HTTP)-based methods of administration.

NDS

NDS is the Novell Directory Service for its Netware network operating system. Organizations that are running either this or the NetWare 3.x bindery services may wish to synchronize with Active Directory, perhaps as a first step in migration.

Microsoft Directory Synchronization Services (MSDSS) is a tool available from Microsoft that provides two-way synchronization services between Active Directory and NDS bindery. It supports synchronization of various object types and attributes, including passwords, which means it can help reduce management by allowing users to change their password in one place for both Windows 2000 and NetWare.

With MSDSS, a company can use its existing NetWare objects to populate Active Directory and run the two systems in parallel, while only having to manage one of the two directory services. Either one- or two-way synchronization is supported, and the two directories need not have the same structure, because individual objects can be synchronized, regardless of their location in the directory tree. With this, object-specific synchronization and object moves are ignored by MSDSS, but changes to attributes are synchronized between directories.

The alternative is location-specific synchronization (the default), which the same object properties and the same object structures (for example, Organizational Units) between directories. This is easier to administer (no confused administrators wondering where an object is in the other directory service), but organizing both NDS and Active Directory in the same way will impact on flexibility. You have to delegate administration and apply Group Policy.

MSDSS is part of Microsoft's Directory Synchronization Services for NetWare's 5 suite, which includes a variety of other utilities for tasks, such as migrating files (with access control settings intact) from NetWare to Microsoft Windows file servers.

Microsoft Exchange

Exchange is Microsoft's email and messaging server product. Perhaps one of the most compelling reasons to use Active Directory is because it's required by Microsoft Exchange 2000, which, consequently, only runs under Windows 2000.

Exchange 5.5

The version of Microsoft Exchange available prior to Exchange 2000 is Exchange 5.5. It has its own directory service—including an LDAP server—and doesn't use Active Directory. Exchange 5.5 (with Service Pack 3 or better) is the earliest version that will run under Windows 2000.

In fact, if you install Exchange 5.5 under Windows 2000, you may be greeted with an error message warning that it's incompatible with Windows 2000. If this happens, you can ignore it by clicking Run Program and installing it normally. Once Exchange 5.5 is installed, you must apply at least Service Pack 3.

Because Exchange 5.5 servers also run their own LDAP server, issues running Exchange 5.5 on a Windows 2000 domain controller exist. In fact, what happens is that the Exchange LDAP server must be configured to use nondefault LDAP ports, because Active Directory can't be modified from port 389.

Active Directory Connector

To leverage existing data from an Exchange 5.5 installation in Active Directory, you'll use a Microsoft tool called the Active Directory Connector (ADC). This tool allows one- or two-way synchronization between Exchange 5.5 and Windows 2000 Active Directory. For example, you could use one-off, one-way synchronization from Exchange to Active Directory to add data to a test Windows 2000 forest prior to migration. After migration, you can use the ADC to automatically synchronize changes between the two systems. This, for example, allows administration to be performed in Exchange, and the modifications will be transferred automatically to Active Directory and vice versa.

Key Features

The key features of the ADC are the following:

- *Attribute-level synchronization*—Objects are compared, and only changed attributes are communicated.

- *Configurable bidirectional synchronization*—You can synchronize either one or both ways between Active Directory and Exchange.

- *Configurable attributes*—You can configure Exchange and Active Directory attributes to synchronize between systems.

The Active Dirtctory Connector requires Exchange 5.5 with Service Pack 1, or above.

ADC Architecture

The Active Directory Connector is a Windows 2000 service that need not reside on either an Exchange server or on a domain controller. Instead, you establish a relationship known as a *connection agreement* from the ADC hosting server, which connects to a particular Exchange 5.5 site and a particular Active Directory domain server (see Figure 22.3).

Multiple-connection agreements can be hosted on a single server running the ADC, linking different combinations of domains and Exchange 5.5 sites, although only one instance of the ADC can run on a given computer.

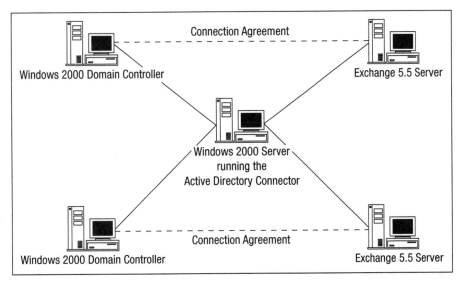

Figure 22.3 ADC architecture.

Connection Agreements

The settings for synchronizing data between Exchange 5.5 and Active Directory are stored in terms of the connection agreement. A single connection agreement links a Windows 2000 domain to an Exchange 5.5 organization and can be used to synchronize objects in one or both directions. Each connection agreement can be highly configured to synchronize only certain attributes in certain directions.

For example, the ADC and a simple import-only connection agreement can be used to create users in Active Directory from existing Exchange mailboxes. This could be used, for example, for populating a test Windows 2000 domain in a lab environment. Two-way synchronization would be more appropriate in environments where you wish to run Exchange 5.5 and Windows 2000 in parallel and continue to administer each separately.

Connection agreements have a number of important properties associated with them, not the least of which is the requirement for credentials to the Active Directory and Exchange 5.5 servers. It's important that these accounts have sufficient permissions to create and delete users and mailboxes in all containers and domains that the connection agreement will require.

Handling Deletions

One potentially tricky area for ADC connections is deleting objects. Connection agreements allow you to specify whether deletions should be automatically applied or whether they should be logged.

Automatically applying deletions may have unintended consequences (for example, if you wish to remove someone's mailbox but not delete his user account), and not doing so may cause a security problem (deleting someone's Windows 2000 user account when he leaves the company won't automatically delete his mailbox).

The alternative to synchronizing deletions will create two files in a connection agreement-specific directory called Ex55.csv and Win2000.ldf. These comma-separated and LDAP Directory Interchange Format (LDIF) files are respectively ready for import into Exchange and Windows 2000 to apply the deletions. One advantage of this method is that you can edit them before application, for example, to remove accounts that you don't wish to be deleted.

NOTE: *Two versions of the ADC are available: one supplied with Exchange 2000 and one supplied with Windows 2000. This chapter covers the Windows 2000 version. The Exchange 2000 version is more recent and has more features—be especially careful using its interorganization connection agreements, however.*

Exchange 2000

Exchange 2000 is the first version of Exchange to drop its own directory service and switch to using the Active Directory. This means, for one thing, that there are several changes to terminology. For example, the Exchange 5.5 concept of a mailbox is replaced by a mailbox-enabled user, custom recipients become mail-enabled contacts, and distribution lists become mail-enabled groups (either Distribution or Security).

This is made possible because Exchange 2000 extends the Active Directory schema for its own ends, such as mailbox-enabling users. It also extends administration tools, such as Active Directory Users and Computers, so that additional property pages appear for users, and these allow Exchange settings to be configured. Schema extensions are also used by Exchange to store routing information to facilitate message delivery. The **cn=Microsoft Exchange,cn=Services,dc=ForestRoot** hierarchy is used to store settings.

Instant Messaging

A new feature of Exchange 2000 is instant messaging (IM). Popularized by Internet-based services, such as ICQ, AOL IM, and MSN Messenger, instant messaging has now been added to the grown-up corporate communications server, Exchange.

In essence, users install software that registers with an IM server when they're logged in, and this conveys status information, such as Available, Away, Do Not Disturb, and so on. Each user has a contact list, which displays the current status information of all of their contacts by way of icons. From this list, you can double-click on someone to initiate a text-based chat.

Asynchronous text-based chat is a useful communications method if you want more urgency than an email without the disturbance of a phone call. When an incoming chat request is made, a window will open on the user's desktop. From here, messages can be typed, additional participants invited, and so on. Of course, the usefulness of IM isn't just limited to chatting, because the status information can also be used to determine whether someone is at her desk (and, thus, whether or not to phone her).

Conferencing

A new server-side feature of Exchange 2000 is conferencing. This allows standards-compliant voice and data conferences to be scheduled and hosted by the Conferencing edition of Exchange Server 2000. Conferencing supports H.323 and T.120 protocols, and individual conferences are joined by special URLs. Conferences are represented in the directory by mail-enabled user objects, and conferences allow people to connect over a local network or over the Internet and communicate in realtime with video, audio, and chat.

Active Directory Design

The reason for Exchange 2000's inclusion in this book, however, is that as a major Active Directory-enabled application, a decision to install it could influence Active Directory design. For one thing, the schema changes made by Exchange 2000 will influence capacity planning on domain controllers and should be made early in a deployment, because changing the Global Catalog (which Exchange does, considerably) causes it to be rebuilt. It's better that this is done at the very beginning than when 100 Global Catalog servers are already deployed over five continents. To do this, the **/forestprep** installation option should be used with Exchange to prepare the forest for its installation (one part of which is the schema modifications).

In Exchange 5.5, developers using the concept of Exchange Organizations were able to span multiple NT domains. In Windows 2000, the explicit idea of an Exchange organization is gone. Instead, the Active Directory forest is the Exchange organization boundary. In terms of directory design, this makes having separate Windows 2000 forests within one company less desirable.

Beyond this, little impact occurs to domain design from Exchange 2000. To some extent, a desire to homogenize UPNs with email addresses (or not, for security reasons) may affect user account creation. The possibilities for enabling mail and creating distribution groups may cause changes to group design, but apart from that, there's no reason to create more or fewer domains because of Exchange 2000.

Immediate Solutions

Installing the Active Directory Connector

The ADC is shipped on the Windows 2000 Server CD-ROM. It can be installed in
two separate portions: the server service and the management components.

To install it:

1. Insert the Windows 2000 Server CD-ROM and run the \valueadd\msft\mgmt\
   adc\setup.exe from the CD-ROM.

2. The Microsoft Active Directory Connector Setup Wizard appears. Click Next.

3. Select whether to install the Service component, Management component,
   or both (see Figure 22.4) and click Next.

4. Specify an installation location by browsing to the desired folder, or accept
   the default of %ProgramFiles%\MSADC. Click Next.

5. If you've chosen to install the ADC Service, specify credentials for the
   service to run under. Click Next.

6. Copying begins.

7. Click Finish.

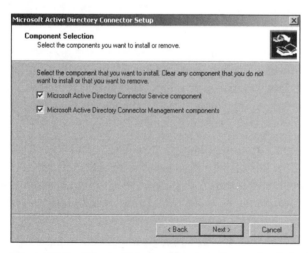

Figure 22.4   Microsoft Active Directory Connector Setup Wizard Component Selection.

Creating Connection Agreements

To link a Windows 2000 Active Directory to an Exchange 5.5, a Connection Agreement must be created. To do so, perform the following steps:

1. Launch Active Directory Connector Management from the Administrative Tools menu (see Figure 22.5).

2. Right-click Active Directory Connector, mouse-over to New, and click Connection Agreement. The Properties dialog box of the new connection agreement appears (see Figure 22.6).

3. On the General tab, specify the name of the Connection Agreement.

4. Select whether the replication will be two-way or in a specific direction.

NOTE: *As you change the replication direction option, you're prompted to ensure the accounts to be used have sufficient permissions to write to the target directory or directories. Click OK to accept the warnings.*

5. Select an ADC server to host the Connection Agreement.

6. Switch to the Connections tab and enter the details of the Windows 2000 domain controller and Exchange server to connect to (including the LDAP

22. Directory Interoperability

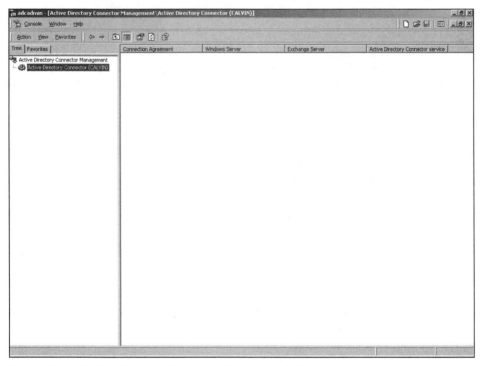

Figure 22.5   Active Directory Connector Management Snap-in.

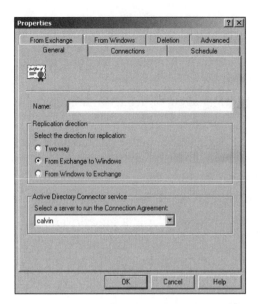

Figure 22.6   New Connection Agreement.

port number of the Exchange server, if it's nondefault). Also specify credentials using the Modify buttons for each end. These credentials are stored securely in Active Directory.

7. On the Schedule tab, specify when you want synchronization to take place. Ideally, this should be set to Always (that is, every five minutes, or as determined by the **HKEY_LOCAL_MACHINE\SYSTEM\CurrentControlSet\ Services\MSADC\Parameters\Sync Sleep Delay (secs) REG_DWORD** value).

Alternatively, you can define a period in which to replicate or disable replication altogether by selecting Never. The Replicate the entire directory checkbox should be selected initially to synchronize the directories and can be used later in operations to ensure consistency.

8. Use the From Exchange to determine what data is replicated from Exchange 5.5 to Windows 2000. The checkboxes can be used to filter by object type, individual Exchange Recipient containers used to replicate should be specified by the Add button, and the default destination should also be specified.

9. The From Windows tab is identical to the From Exchange tab, except that it specifies which (if any) Active Directory objects are to be synchronized and whether or not access control should be used to determine which objects are synchronized.

10. The Deletion tabs allow you to specify on a per-direction basis, whether deletions are synchronized or logged for possible later manual application.

11. On the Advanced tab, the paged results values can be left at default if you've left the LDAP paged results parameters on the Exchange and Active Directory servers at default. Otherwise, they should be adjusted, so they're no larger than the server values.

12. Specify whether or not you wish this connection to be primary in one or both directions. Primary connections will create new objects in the destination directory. Nonprimary connections won't.

13. Click OK to create the Connection Agreement.

Appendix A

Active Directory Classes

This appendix lists the built-in Active Directory classes along with some of their commonly referred to attributes.

Table A.1   ACS-Policy.

Class Property	Value
adminDisplayName	ACS-Policy
adminDescription	ACS-Policy
governsID	1.2.840.113556.1.5.137
lDAPDisplayName	aCSPolicy
objectClassCategory	1 (structural)
subClassOf	top
systemMayContain	aCSTotalNoOfFlows
	aCSTimeOfDay
	aCSServiceType
	aCSPriority
	aCSPermissionBits
	aCSMinimumDelayVariation
	aCSMinimumLatency
	aCSMaximumSDUSize
	aCSMinimumPolicedSize
	aCSMaxTokenRatePerFlow
	aCSMaxTokenBucketPerFlow
	aCSMaxPeakBandwidthPerFlow

(continued)

Table A.1   ACS-Policy *(continued).*

Class Property	Value
	aCSMaxDurationPerFlow
	aCSMaxAggregatePeakRatePerUser
	aCSIdentityName
	aCSDirection
	aCSAggregateTokenRatePerUser
systemMustContain	

Table A.2   ACS-Resource-Limits.

Class Property	Value
adminDisplayName	ACS-Resource-Limits
adminDescription	ACS-Resource-Limits
governsID	1.2.840.113556.1.5.191
IDAPDisplayName	aCSResourceLimits
objectClassCategory	1 (structural)
subClassOf	top
systemMayContain	aCSMaxTokenRatePerFlow
	aCSServiceType
	aCSMaxPeakBandwidthPerFlow
	aCSMaxPeakBandwidth
	aCSAllocableRSVPBandwidth
systemMustContain	

Table A.3   ACS-Subnet.

Class Property	Value
adminDisplayName	ACS-Subnet
adminDescription	ACS-Subnet
governsID	1.2.840.113556.1.5.138
IDAPDisplayName	aCSSubnet
objectClassCategory	1 (structural)
subClassOf	top
systemMayContain	aCSServerList
	aCSRSVPLogFilesLocation

(continued)

Table A.3   ACS-Subnet *(continued)*.

Class Property	Value
	aCSRSVPAccountFilesLocation
	aCSNonReservedTxSize
	aCSNonReservedTxLimit
	aCSNonReservedTokenSize
	aCSNonReservedPeakRate
	aCSNonReservedMinPolicedSize
	aCSNonReservedMaxSDUSize
	aCSMaxTokenRatePerFlow
	aCSMaxSizeOfRSVPLogFile
	aCSMaxSizeOfRSVPAccountFile
	aCSMaxPeakBandwidthPerFlow
	aCSMaxPeakBandwidth
	aCSMaxNoOfLogFiles
	aCSMaxNoOfAccountFiles
	aCSMaxDurationPerFlow
	aCSEventLogLevel
	aCSEnableRSVPMessageLogging
	aCSEnableRSVPAccounting
	aCSEnableACSService
	aCSDSBMRefresh
	aCSDSBMPriority
	aCSDSBMDeadTime
	aCSCacheTimeout
	aCSAllocableRSVPBandwidth
systemMustContain	

Table A.4   Address-Book-Container.

Class Property	Value
adminDisplayName	Address-Book-Container
adminDescription	Address-Book-Container
governsID	1.2.840.113556.1.5.125
lDAPDisplayName	addressBookContainer
objectClassCategory	1 (structural)

(continued)

Table A.4   Address-Book-Container *(continued).*

Class Property	Value
subClassOf	top
systemMayContain	purportedSearch
systemMustContain	displayName

Table A.5   Address-Template.

Class Property	Value
adminDisplayName	Address-Template
adminDescription	Address-Template
governsID	1.2.840.113556.1.3.58
lDAPDisplayName	addressTemplate
objectClassCategory	1 (structural)
subClassOf	displayTemplate
systemMayContain	proxyGenerationEnabled
	perRecipDialogDisplayTable
	perMsgDialogDisplayTable
	addressType
	addressSyntax
systemMustContain	displayName

Table A.6   Application-Entity.

Class Property	Value
adminDisplayName	Application-Entity
adminDescription	Application-Entity
governsID	2.5.6.12
lDAPDisplayName	applicationEntity
objectClassCategory	1 (structural)
subClassOf	top
systemMayContain	supportedApplicationContext
	seeAlso
	ou
	o
	l
systemMustContain	presentationAddress
	cn

Table A.7   Application-Process.

Class Property	Value
adminDisplayName	Application-Process
adminDescription	Application-Process
governsID	2.5.6.11
lDAPDisplayName	applicationProcess
objectClassCategory	1 (structural)
subClassOf	top
systemMayContain	seeAlso
	ou
	l
systemMustContain	cn

Table A.8   Application-Settings.

Class Property	Value
adminDisplayName	Application-Settings
adminDescription	Application-Settings
governsID	1.2.840.113556.1.5.7000.49
lDAPDisplayName	applicationSettings
objectClassCategory	2 (abstract)
subClassOf	top
systemMayContain	notificationList
	applicationName
systemMustContain	

Table A.9   Application-Site-Settings.

Class Property	Value
adminDisplayName	Application-Site-Settings
adminDescription	Application-Site-Settings
governsID	1.2.840.113556.1.5.68
lDAPDisplayName	applicationSiteSettings
objectClassCategory	2 (abstract)
subClassOf	top
systemMayContain	notificationList
	applicationName
systemMustContain	

Table A.10   Attribute-Schema.

Class Property	Value
adminDisplayName	Attribute-Schema
adminDescription	Attribute-Schema
governsID	1.2.840.113556.1.3.14
lDAPDisplayName	attributeSchema
objectClassCategory	1 (structural)
subClassOf	top
systemMayContain	systemOnly
	searchFlags
	schemaFlagsEx
	rangeUpper
	rangeLower
	oMObjectClass
	mAPIID
	linkID
	isMemberOfPartialAttributeSet
	isEphemeral
	isDefunct
	extendedCharsAllowed
	classDisplayName
	attributeSecurityGUID
systemMustContain	schemaIDGUID
	oMSyntax
	lDAPDisplayName
	isSingleValued
	cn
	attributeSyntax
	attributeID

Table A.11   Builtin-Domain.

Class Property	Value
adminDisplayName	Builtin-Domain
adminDescription	Builtin-Domain
governsID	1.2.840.113556.1.5.4

(continued)

Table A.11 Builtin-Domain *(continued).*

Class Property	Value
IDAPDisplayName	builtinDomain
objectClassCategory	1 (structural)
subClassOf	top
systemMayContain	
systemMustContain	

Table A.12 Category-Registration.

Class Property	Value
adminDisplayName	Category-Registration
adminDescription	Category-Registration
governsID	1.2.840.113556.1.5.74
IDAPDisplayName	categoryRegistration
objectClassCategory	1 (structural)
subClassOf	leaf
systemMayContain	managedBy
	localizedDescription
	localeID
	categoryId
systemMustContain	

Table A.13 Certification-Authority.

Class Property	Value
adminDisplayName	Certification-Authority
adminDescription	Certification-Authority
governsID	2.5.6.16
IDAPDisplayName	certificationAuthority
objectClassCategory	1 (structural)
subClassOf	top
systemMayContain	teletexTerminalIdentifier
	supportedApplicationContext
	signatureAlgorithms
	searchGuide
	previousParentCA
	previousCACertificates

(continued)

Table A.13   Certification-Authority *(continued).*

Class Property	Value
	pendingParentCA
	pendingCACertificates
	parentCACertificateChain
	parentCA
	enrollmentProviders
	domainPolicyObject
	domainID
	dNSHostName
	deltaRevocationList
	currentParentCA
	crossCertificatePair
	cRLObject
	certificateTemplates
	cAWEBURL
	cAUsages
	cAConnect
	cACertificateDN
systemMustContain	cn
	certificateRevocationList
	cACertificate
	authorityRevocationList

Table A.14   Class-Registration.

Class Property	Value
adminDisplayName	Class-Registration
adminDescription	Class-Registration
governsID	1.2.840.113556.1.5.10
lDAPDisplayName	classRegistration
objectClassCategory	1 (structural)
subClassOf	leaf
systemMayContain	requiredCategories
	managedBy
	implementedCategories

(continued)

Table A.14 Class-Registration *(continued)*.

Class Property	Value
	cOMTreatAsClassId
	cOMProgID
	cOMOtherProgId
	cOMInterfaceID
	cOMCLSID
systemMustContain	

Table A.15 Class-Schema.

Class Property	Value
adminDisplayName	Class-Schema
adminDescription	Class-Schema
governsID	1.2.840.113556.1.3.13
lDAPDisplayName	classSchema
objectClassCategory	1 (structural)
subClassOf	top
systemMayContain	systemPossSuperiors
	systemOnly
	systemMustContain
	systemMayContain
	systemAuxiliaryClass
	schemaFlagsEx
	rDNAttID
	possSuperiors
	mustContain
	mayContain
	lDAPDisplayName
	isDefunct
	defaultSecurityDescriptor
	defaultHidingValue
	classDisplayName
	auxiliaryClass
systemMustContain	subClassOf
	schemaIDGUID

(continued)

Table A.15   Class-Schema *(continued)*.

Class Property	Value
	objectClassCategory
	governsID
	defaultObjectCategory
	cn

Table A.16   Class-Store.

Class Property	Value
adminDisplayName	Class-Store
adminDescription	Class-Store
governsID	1.2.840.113556.1.5.44
IDAPDisplayName	classStore
objectClassCategory	1 (structural)
subClassOf	top
systemMayContain	versionNumber
	nextLevelStore
	lastUpdateSequence
	appSchemaVersion
systemMustContain	

Table A.17   Com-Connection-Point.

Class Property	Value
adminDisplayName	Com-Connection-Point
adminDescription	Com-Connection-Point
governsID	1.2.840.113556.1.5.11
IDAPDisplayName	comConnectionPoint
objectClassCategory	1 (structural)
subClassOf	connectionPoint
systemMayContain	monikerDisplayName
	moniker
	marshalledInterface
systemMustContain	cn

Table A.18   Computer.

Class Property	Value
adminDisplayName	Computer
adminDescription	Computer
governsID	1.2.840.113556.1.3.30
lDAPDisplayName	computer
objectClassCategory	1 (structural)
subClassOf	user
systemMayContain	volumeCount
	siteGUID
	rIDSetReferences
	policyReplicationFlags
	physicalLocationObject
	operatingSystemVersion
	operatingSystemServicePack
	operatingSystemHotfix
	operatingSystem
	networkAddress
	netbootSIFFile
	netbootMirrorDataFile
	netbootMachineFilePath
	netbootInitialization
	netbootGUID
	managedBy
	machineRole
	location
	localPolicyFlags
	dNSHostName
	defaultLocalPolicyObject
	cn
	catalogs
systemMustContain	

Table A.19   Configuration.

Class Property	Value
adminDisplayName	Configuration
adminDescription	Configuration
governsID	1.2.840.113556.1.5.12
IDAPDisplayName	configuration
objectClassCategory	1 (structural)
subClassOf	top
systemMayContain	
systemMustContain	cn

Table A.20   Connection-Point.

Class Property	Value
adminDisplayName	Connection-Point
adminDescription	Connection-Point
governsID	1.2.840.113556.1.5.14
IDAPDisplayName	connectionPoint
objectClassCategory	2 (abstract)
subClassOf	leaf
systemMayContain	managedBy
	keywords
systemMustContain	cn

Table A.21   Contact.

Class Property	Value
adminDisplayName	Contact
adminDescription	Contact
governsID	1.2.840.113556.1.5.15
IDAPDisplayName	contact
objectClassCategory	1 (structural)
subClassOf	organizationalPerson
systemMayContain	notes
systemMustContain	cn

Table A.22   Container.

Class Property	Value
adminDisplayName	Container
adminDescription	Container
governsID	1.2.840.113556.1.3.23
IDAPDisplayName	container
objectClassCategory	1 (structural)
subClassOf	top
systemMayContain	schemaVersion
	defaultClassStore
systemMustContain	cn

Table A.23   Control-Access-Right.

Class Property	Value
adminDisplayName	Control-Access-Right
adminDescription	Control-Access-Right
governsID	1.2.840.113556.1.5.77
IDAPDisplayName	controlAccessRight
objectClassCategory	1 (structural)
subClassOf	top
systemMayContain	validAccesses
	rightsGuid
	localizationDisplayId
	appliesTo
systemMustContain	

Table A.24   Country.

Class Property	Value
adminDisplayName	Country
adminDescription	Country
governsID	2.5.6.2
IDAPDisplayName	country
objectClassCategory	2 (abstract)

(continued)

Table A.24   Country *(continued).*

Class Property	Value
subClassOf	top
systemMayContain	co
	searchGuide
systemMustContain	c

Table A.25   CRL-Distribution-Point.

Class Property	Value
adminDisplayName	CRL-Distribution-Point
adminDescription	CRL-Distribution-Point
governsID	2.5.6.19
IDAPDisplayName	cRLDistributionPoint
objectClassCategory	1 (structural)
subClassOf	top
systemMayContain	deltaRevocationList
	cRLPartitionedRevocationList
	certificateRevocationList
	certificateAuthorityObject
	authorityRevocationList
systemMustContain	cn

Table A.26   Cross-Ref.

Class Property	Value
adminDisplayName	Cross-Ref
adminDescription	Cross-Ref
governsID	1.2.840.113556.1.3.11
IDAPDisplayName	crossRef
objectClassCategory	1 (structural)
subClassOf	top
systemMayContain	trustParent
	superiorDNSRoot
	rootTrust
	nETBIOSName

(continued)

Table A.26   Cross-Ref *(continued).*

Class Property	Value
	Enabled
systemMustContain	nCName
	dnsRoot
	cn

Table A.27   Cross-Ref-Container.

Class Property	Value
adminDisplayName	Cross-Ref-Container
adminDescription	Cross-Ref-Container
governsID	1.2.840.113556.1.5.7000.53
IDAPDisplayName	crossRefContainer
objectClassCategory	1 (structural)
subClassOf	top
systemMayContain	uPNSuffixes
systemMustContain	

Table A.28   Device.

Class Property	Value
adminDisplayName	Device
adminDescription	Device
governsID	2.5.6.14
IDAPDisplayName	device
objectClassCategory	2 (abstract)
subClassOf	top
systemMayContain	serialNumber
	seeAlso
	owner
	ou
	o
	l
systemMustContain	cn

Table A.29   Dfs-Configuration.

Class Property	Value
adminDisplayName	Dfs-Configuration
adminDescription	Dfs-Configuration
governsID	1.2.840.113556.1.5.42
IDAPDisplayName	dfsConfiguration
objectClassCategory	1 (structural)
subClassOf	top
systemMayContain	
systemMustContain	

Table A.30   DHCP-Class.

Class Property	Value
adminDisplayName	DHCP-Class
adminDescription	DHCP-Class
governsID	1.2.840.113556.1.5.132
IDAPDisplayName	dHCPClass
objectClassCategory	1 (structural)
subClassOf	top
systemMayContain	superScopes
	superScopeDescription
	optionsLocation
	optionDescription
	networkAddress
	mscopeId
	dhcpUpdateTime
	dhcpSubnets
	dhcpState
	dhcpSites
	dhcpServers
	dhcpReservations
	dhcpRanges
	dhcpProperties
	dhcpOptions

(continued)

Table A.30   DHCP-Class *(continued)*.

Class Property	Value
	dhcpObjName
	dhcpObjDescription
	dhcpMaxKey
	dhcpMask
	dhcpClasses
systemMustContain	dhcpUniqueKey
	dhcpType
	dhcpIdentification
	dhcpFlags

Table A.31   Display-Specifier.

Class Property	Value
adminDisplayName	Display-Specifier
adminDescription	Display-Specifier
governsID	1.2.840.113556.1.5.84
IDAPDisplayName	displaySpecifier
objectClassCategory	1 (structural)
subClassOf	top
systemMayContain	treatAsLeaf
	shellPropertyPages
	shellContextMenu
	scopeFlags
	queryFilter
	iconPath
	creationWizard
	createWizardExt
	createDialog
	contextMenu
	classDisplayName
	attributeDisplayNames
	adminPropertyPages
	adminContextMenu
systemMustContain	

Table A.32 Display-Template.

Class Property	Value
adminDisplayName	Display-Template
adminDescription	Display-Template
governsID	1.2.840.113556.1.3.59
lDAPDisplayName	displayTemplate
objectClassCategory	1 (structural)
subClassOf	top
systemMayContain	originalDisplayTableMSDOS
	originalDisplayTable
	helpFileName
	helpData32
	helpData16
	addressEntryDisplayTableMSDOS
	addressEntryDisplayTable
systemMustContain	cn

Table A.33 DMD.

Class Property	Value
adminDisplayName	DMD
adminDescription	DMD
governsID	1.2.840.113556.1.3.9
lDAPDisplayName	dMD
objectClassCategory	1 (structural)
subClassOf	top
systemMayContain	schemaUpdate
	schemaInfo
	prefixMap
	dmdName
systemMustContain	cn

Table A.34 Dns-Node.

Class Property	Value
adminDisplayName	Dns-Node
adminDescription	Dns-Node

(continued)

Table A.34   Dns-Node *(continued).*

Class Property	Value
governsID	1.2.840.113556.1.5.86
lDAPDisplayName	dnsNode
objectClassCategory	1 (structural)
subClassOf	top
systemMayContain	dNSTombstoned
	dnsRecord
	dNSProperty
systemMustContain	dc

Table A.35   Dns-Zone.

Class Property	Value
adminDisplayName	Dns-Zone
adminDescription	Dns-Zone
governsID	1.2.840.113556.1.5.85
lDAPDisplayName	dnsZone
objectClassCategory	1 (structural)
subClassOf	top
systemMayContain	managedBy
	dnsSecureSecondaries
	dNSProperty
	dnsNotifySecondaries
	dnsAllowXFR
	dnsAllowDynamic
systemMustContain	dc

Table A.36   Domain.

Class Property	Value
adminDisplayName	Domain
adminDescription	Domain
governsID	1.2.840.113556.1.5.66
lDAPDisplayName	domain
objectClassCategory	2 (abstract)
subClassOf	top

(continued)

Table A.36   Domain *(continued)*.

Class Property	Value
systemMayContain	
systemMustContain	dc

Table A.37   Domain-DNS.

Class Property	Value
adminDisplayName	Domain-DNS
adminDescription	Domain-DNS
governsID	1.2.840.113556.1.5.67
lDAPDisplayName	domainDNS
objectClassCategory	1 (structural)
subClassOf	domain
systemMayContain	managedBy
systemMustContain	

Table A.38   Domain-Policy.

Class Property	Value
adminDisplayName	Domain-Policy
adminDescription	Domain-Policy
governsID	1.2.840.113556.1.5.18
lDAPDisplayName	domainPolicy
objectClassCategory	1 (structural)
subClassOf	leaf
systemMayContain	qualityOfService
	pwdProperties
	pwdHistoryLength
	publicKeyPolicy
	proxyLifetime
	minTicketAge
	minPwdLength
	minPwdAge
	maxTicketAge
	maxRenewAge
	maxPwdAge

(continued)

Table A.38   Domain-Policy *(continued)*.

Class Property	Value
	managedBy
	lockoutThreshold
	lockoutDuration
	lockOutObservationWindow
	ipsecPolicyReference
	forceLogoff
	eFSPolicy
	domainWidePolicy
	domainPolicyReference
	domainCAs
	defaultLocalPolicyObject
	authenticationOptions
systemMustContain	

Table A.39   DSA.

Class Property	Value
adminDisplayName	DSA
adminDescription	DSA
governsID	2.5.6.13
IDAPDisplayName	dSA
objectClassCategory	1 (structural)
subClassOf	applicationEntity
systemMayContain	knowledgeInformation
systemMustContain	

Table A.40   DS-UI-Settings.

Class Property	Value
adminDisplayName	DS-UI-Settings
adminDescription	DS-UI-Settings
governsID	1.2.840.113556.1.5.183
IDAPDisplayName	dSUISettings
objectClassCategory	1 (structural)
subClassOf	top

(continued)

Table A.40   DS-UI-Settings (continued).

Class Property	Value
systemMayContain	dSUIShellMaximum
	dSUIAdminNotification
	dSUIAdminMaximum
systemMustContain	

Table A.41   File-Link-Tracking.

Class Property	Value
adminDisplayName	File-Link-Tracking
adminDescription	File-Link-Tracking
governsID	1.2.840.113556.1.5.52
lDAPDisplayName	fileLinkTracking
objectClassCategory	1 (structural)
subClassOf	top
systemMayContain	
systemMustContain	

Table A.42   File-Link-Tracking-Entry.

Class Property	Value
adminDisplayName	File-Link-Tracking-Entry
adminDescription	File-Link-Tracking-Entry
governsID	1.2.840.113556.1.5.59
lDAPDisplayName	fileLinkTrackingEntry
objectClassCategory	1 (structural)
subClassOf	top
systemMayContain	
systemMustContain	

Table A.43   Foreign-Security-Principal.

Class Property	Value
adminDisplayName	Foreign-Security-Principal
adminDescription	Foreign-Security-Principal
governsID	1.2.840.113556.1.5.76
lDAPDisplayName	foreignSecurityPrincipal

(continued)

Table A.43 Foreign-Security-Principal *(continued)*.

Class Property	Value
objectClassCategory	1 (structural)
subClassOf	top
systemMayContain	foreignIdentifier
systemMustContain	objectSid

Table A.44 FT-Dfs.

Class Property	Value
adminDisplayName	FT-Dfs
adminDescription	FT-Dfs
governsID	1.2.840.113556.1.5.43
lDAPDisplayName	fTDfs
objectClassCategory	1 (structural)
subClassOf	top
systemMayContain	
systemMustContain	remoteServerName
	pKTGuid
	pKT

Table A.45 Group.

Class Property	Value
adminDisplayName	Group
adminDescription	Group
governsID	1.2.840.113556.1.5.8
lDAPDisplayName	group
objectClassCategory	1 (structural)
subClassOf	top
systemMayContain	primaryGroupToken
	operatorCount
	nTGroupMembers
	nonSecurityMember
	member
	managedBy
	groupMembershipSAM

(continued)

Table A.45   Group *(continued)*.

Class Property	Value
	groupAttributes
	mail
	desktopProfile
	controlAccessRights
	adminCount
systemMustContain	groupType

Table A.46   Group-Of-Names.

Class Property	Value
adminDisplayName	Group-Of-Names
adminDescription	Group-Of-Names
governsID	2.5.6.9
lDAPDisplayName	groupOfNames
objectClassCategory	2 (abstract)
subClassOf	top
systemMayContain	seeAlso
	owner
	ou
	o
	businessCategory
systemMustContain	member
	cn

Table A.47   Group-Policy-Container.

Class Property	Value
adminDisplayName	Group-Policy-Container
adminDescription	Group-Policy-Container
governsID	1.2.840.113556.1.5.157
lDAPDisplayName	groupPolicyContainer
objectClassCategory	1 (structural)
subClassOf	container

(continued)

Table A.47   Group-Policy-Container *(continued).*

Class Property	Value
systemMayContain	versionNumber
	gPCUserExtensionNames
	gPCMachineExtensionNames
	gPCFunctionalityVersion
	gPCFileSysPath
	flags
systemMustContain	

Table A.48   Index-Server-Catalog.

Class Property	Value
adminDisplayName	Index-Server-Catalog
adminDescription	Index-Server-Catalog
governsID	1.2.840.113556.1.5.130
lDAPDisplayName	indexServerCatalog
objectClassCategory	1 (structural)
subClassOf	connectionPoint
systemMayContain	uNCName
	queryPoint
	indexedScopes
	friendlyNames
systemMustContain	creator

Table A.49   Infrastructure-Update.

Class Property	Value
adminDisplayName	Infrastructure-Update
adminDescription	Infrastructure-Update
governsID	1.2.840.113556.1.5.175
lDAPDisplayName	infrastructureUpdate
objectClassCategory	1 (structural)
subClassOf	top
systemMayContain	dNReferenceUpdate
systemMustContain	

Table A.50   Intellimirror-Group.

Class Property	Value
adminDisplayName	Intellimirror-Group
adminDescription	Intellimirror-Group
governsID	1.2.840.113556.1.5.152
IDAPDisplayName	intellimirrorGroup
objectClassCategory	1 (structural)
subClassOf	top
systemMayContain	
systemMustContain	

Table A.51   Intellimirror-SCP.

Class Property	Value
adminDisplayName	Intellimirror-SCP
adminDescription	Intellimirror-SCP
governsID	1.2.840.113556.1.5.151
IDAPDisplayName	intellimirrorSCP
objectClassCategory	1 (structural)
subClassOf	serviceAdministrationPoint
systemMayContain	netbootTools
	netbootServer
	netbootNewMachineOU
	netbootNewMachineNamingPolicy
	netbootMaxClients
	netbootMachineFilePath
	netbootLocallyInstalledOSes
	netbootLimitClients
	netbootIntelliMirrorOSes
	netbootCurrentClientCount
	netbootAnswerRequests
	netbootAnswerOnlyValidClients
	netbootAllowNewClients
systemMustContain	

Table A.52   Inter-Site-Transport.

Class Property	Value
adminDisplayName	Inter-Site-Transport
adminDescription	Inter-Site-Transport
governsID	1.2.840.113556.1.5.141
lDAPDisplayName	interSiteTransport
objectClassCategory	1 (structural)
subClassOf	top
systemMayContain	replInterval
	options
systemMustContain	transportDLLName
	transportAddressAttribute

Table A.53   Inter-Site-Transport-Container.

Class Property	Value
adminDisplayName	Inter-Site-Transport-Container
adminDescription	Inter-Site-Transport-Container
governsID	1.2.840.113556.1.5.140
lDAPDisplayName	interSiteTransportContainer
objectClassCategory	1 (structural)
subClassOf	top
systemMayContain	
systemMustContain	

Table A.54   Ipsec-Base.

Class Property	Value
adminDisplayName	Ipsec-Base
adminDescription	Ipsec-Base
governsID	1.2.840.113556.1.5.7000.56
lDAPDisplayName	ipsecBase
objectClassCategory	2 (abstract)
subClassOf	top
systemMayContain	ipsecOwnersReference

(continued)

Table A.54   Ipsec-Base *(continued).*

Class Property	Value
	ipsecName
	ipsecID
	ipsecDataType
	ipsecData
systemMustContain	

Table A.55   Ipsec-Filter.

Class Property	Value
adminDisplayName	Ipsec-Filter
adminDescription	Ipsec-Filter
governsID	1.2.840.113556.1.5.118
lDAPDisplayName	ipsecFilter
objectClassCategory	1 (structural)
subClassOf	ipsecBase
systemMayContain	
systemMustContain	

Table A.56   Ipsec-ISAKMP-Policy.

Class Property	Value
adminDisplayName	Ipsec-ISAKMP-Policy
adminDescription	Ipsec-ISAKMP-Policy
governsID	1.2.840.113556.1.5.120
lDAPDisplayName	ipsecISAKMPPolicy
objectClassCategory	1 (structural)
subClassOf	ipsecBase
systemMayContain	
systemMustContain	

Table A.57   Ipsec-Negotiation-Policy.

Class Property	Value
adminDisplayName	Ipsec-Negotiation-Policy
adminDescription	Ipsec-Negotiation-Policy
governsID	1.2.840.113556.1.5.119

(continued)

Table A.57   Ipsec-Negotiation-Policy *(continued).*

Class Property	Value
lDAPDisplayName	ipsecNegotiationPolicy
objectClassCategory	1 (structural)
subClassOf	ipsecBase
systemMayContain	iPSECNegotiationPolicyType
	iPSECNegotiationPolicyAction
systemMustContain	

Table A.58   Ipsec-NFA.

Class Property	Value
adminDisplayName	Ipsec-NFA
adminDescription	Ipsec-NFA
governsID	1.2.840.113556.1.5.121
lDAPDisplayName	ipsecNFA
objectClassCategory	1 (structural)
subClassOf	ipsecBase
systemMayContain	ipsecNegotiationPolicyReference
	ipsecFilterReference
systemMustContain	

Table A.59   Ipsec-Policy.

Class Property	Value
adminDisplayName	Ipsec-Policy
adminDescription	Ipsec-Policy
governsID	1.2.840.113556.1.5.98
lDAPDisplayName	ipsecPolicy
objectClassCategory	1 (structural)
subClassOf	ipsecBase
systemMayContain	ipsecNFAReference
	ipsecISAKMPReference
systemMustContain	

Table A.60   Leaf.

Class Property	Value
adminDisplayName	Leaf
adminDescription	Leaf

(continued)

Table A.60   Leaf *(continued)*.

Class Property	Value
governsID	1.2.840.113556.1.5.20
lDAPDisplayName	leaf
objectClassCategory	2 (abstract)
subClassOf	top
systemMayContain	
systemMustContain	

Table A.61   Licensing-Site-Settings.

Class Property	Value
adminDisplayName	Licensing-Site-Settings
adminDescription	Licensing-Site-Settings
governsID	1.2.840.113556.1.5.78
lDAPDisplayName	licensingSiteSettings
objectClassCategory	1 (structural)
subClassOf	applicationSiteSettings
systemMayContain	siteServer
systemMustContain	

Table A.62   Link-Track-Object-Move-Table.

Class Property	Value
adminDisplayName	Link-Track-Object-Move-Table
adminDescription	Link-Track-Object-Move-Table
governsID	1.2.840.113556.1.5.91
lDAPDisplayName	linkTrackObjectMoveTable
objectClassCategory	1 (structural)
subClassOf	fileLinkTracking
systemMayContain	
systemMustContain	

Table A.63   Link-Track-OMT-Entry.

Class Property	Value
adminDisplayName	Link-Track-OMT-Entry
adminDescription	Link-Track-OMT-Entry

(continued)

Table A.63   Link-Track-OMT-Entry *(continued)*.

Class Property	Value
governsID	1.2.840.113556.1.5.93
IDAPDisplayName	linkTrackOMTEntry
objectClassCategory	1 (structural)
subClassOf	leaf
systemMayContain	timeRefresh
	oMTIndxGuid
	oMTGuid
	currentLocation
	birthLocation
systemMustContain	

Table A.64   Link-Track-Vol-Entry.

Class Property	Value
adminDisplayName	Link-Track-Vol-Entry
adminDescription	Link-Track-Vol-Entry
governsID	1.2.840.113556.1.5.92
IDAPDisplayName	linkTrackVolEntry
objectClassCategory	1 (structural)
subClassOf	leaf
systemMayContain	volTableIdxGUID
	volTableGUID
	timeVolChange
	timeRefresh
	seqNotification
	objectCount
	linkTrackSecret
	currMachineId
systemMustContain	

Table A.65   Link-Track-Volume-Table.

Class Property	Value
adminDisplayName	Link-Track-Volume-Table
adminDescription	Link-Track-Volume-Table

(continued)

Table A.65   Link-Track-Volume-Table *(continued).*

Class Property	Value
governsID	1.2.840.113556.1.5.90
lDAPDisplayName	linkTrackVolumeTable
objectClassCategory	1 (structural)
subClassOf	fileLinkTracking
systemMayContain	
systemMustContain	

Table A.66   Locality.

Class Property	Value
adminDisplayName	Locality
adminDescription	Locality
governsID	2.5.6.3
lDAPDisplayName	locality
objectClassCategory	1 (structural)
subClassOf	top
systemMayContain	street
	st
	seeAlso
	searchGuide
systemMustContainl	

Table A.67   Lost-And-Found.

Class Property	Value
adminDisplayName	Lost-And-Found
adminDescription	Lost-And-Found
governsID	1.2.840.113556.1.5.139
lDAPDisplayName	lostAndFound
objectClassCategory	1 (structural)
subClassOf	top
systemMayContain	moveTreeState
systemMustContain	

Table A.68   Mail-Recipient.

Class Property	Value
adminDisplayName	Mail-Recipient
adminDescription	Mail-Recipient
governsID	1.2.840.113556.1.3.46
lDAPDisplayName	mailRecipient
objectClassCategory	3 (auxiliary)
subClassOf	top
systemMayContain	userCertificate
	userSMIMECertificate
	userCert
	textEncodedORAddress
	telephoneNumber
	showInAddressBook
	legacyExchangeDN
	garbageCollPeriod
	info
systemMustContain	cn

Table A.69   Meeting.

Class Property	Value
adminDisplayName	Meeting
adminDescription	Meeting
governsID	1.2.840.113556.1.5.104
lDAPDisplayName	meeting
objectClassCategory	1 (structural)
subClassOf	top
systemMayContain	meetingURL
	meetingType
	meetingStartTime
	meetingScope
	meetingRecurrence
	meetingRating

(continued)

Table A.69   Meeting *(continued)*.

Class Property	Value
	meetingProtocol
	meetingOwner
	meetingOriginator
	meetingMaxParticipants
	meetingLocation
	meetingLanguage
	meetingKeyword
	meetingIsEncrypted
	meetingIP
	meetingID
	meetingEndTime
	meetingDescription
	meetingContactInfo
	meetingBlob
	meetingBandwidth
	meetingApplication
	meetingAdvertiseScope
systemMustContain	meetingName

Table A.70   ms-Exch-Active-Directory-Connector.

Class Property	Value
adminDisplayName	ms-Exch-Active-Directory-Connector
adminDescription	ms-Exch-Active-Directory-Connector
governsID	1.2.840.113556.1.5.7000.62.4
lDAPDisplayName	msExchActiveDirectoryConnector
objectClassCategory	1 (structural)
subClassOf	top
systemMayContain	
systemMustContain	

Table A.71   ms-Exch-Base-Class.

Class Property	Value
adminDisplayName	ms-Exch-Base-Class
adminDescription	ms-Exch-Base-Class
governsID	1.2.840.113556.1.5.7000.62.14
lDAPDisplayName	msExchBaseClass
objectClassCategory	3 (auxiliary)
subClassOf	top
systemMayContain	
systemMustContain	

Table A.72   ms-Exch-Configuration-Container.

Class Property	Value
adminDisplayName	ms-Exch-Configuration-Container
adminDescription	ms-Exch-Configuration-Container
governsID	1.2.840.113556.1.5.176
lDAPDisplayName	msExchConfigurationContainer
objectClassCategory	1 (structural)
subClassOf	container
systemMayContain	templateRoots
	addressBookRoots
	globalAddressList
systemMustContain	

Table A.73   ms-Exch-Connection-Agreement.

Class Property	Value
adminDisplayName	ms-Exch-Connection-Agreement
adminDescription	ms-Exch-Connection-Agreement
governsID	1.2.840.113556.1.5.7000.62.3
lDAPDisplayName	msExchConnectionAgreement
objectClassCategory	1 (structural)
subClassOf	top
systemMayContain	
systemMustContain	

Table A.74   ms-Exch-Custom-Attributes.

Class Property	Value
adminDisplayName	ms-Exch-Custom-Attributes
adminDescription	ms-Exch-Custom-Attributes
governsID	1.2.840.113556.1.5.7000.62.6
lDAPDisplayName	msExchCustomAttributes
objectClassCategory	3 (auxiliary)
subClassOf	top
systemMayContain	
systemMustContain	

Table A.75   ms-Exch-Mail-Storage.

Class Property	Value
adminDisplayName	ms-Exch-Mail-Storage
adminDescription	ms-Exch-Mail-Storage
governsID	1.2.840.113556.1.5.7000.62.5
lDAPDisplayName	msExchMailStorage
objectClassCategory	3 (auxiliary)
subClassOf	top
systemMayContain	
systemMustContain	

Table A.76   ms-Exch-Multi-Media-User.

Class Property	Value
adminDisplayName	ms-Exch-Multi-Media-User
adminDescription	ms-Exch-Multi-Media-User
governsID	1.2.840.113556.1.5.7000.62.17002
lDAPDisplayName	msExchMultiMediaUser
objectClassCategory	3 (auxiliary)
subClassOf	top
systemMayContain	
systemMustContain	

Table A.77   ms-Exch-Schema-Map-Policy.

Class Property	Value
adminDisplayName	ms-Exch-Schema-Map-Policy
adminDescription	ms-Exch-Schema-Map-Policy
governsID	1.2.840.113556.1.5.7000.62.1
lDAPDisplayName	msExchSchemaMapPolicy
objectClassCategory	1 (structural)
subClassOf	top
systemMayContain	
systemMustContain	

Table A.78   MSMQ-Configuration.

Class Property	Value
adminDisplayName	MSMQ-Configuration
adminDescription	MSMQ-Configuration
governsID	1.2.840.113556.1.5.162
lDAPDisplayName	mSMQConfiguration
objectClassCategory	1 (structural)
subClassOf	top
systemMayContain	mSMQSites
	mSMQSignKey
	mSMQServiceType
	mSMQRoutingServices
	mSMQQuota
	mSMQOwnerID
	mSMQOutRoutingServers
	mSMQOSType
	mSMQJournalQuota
	mSMQInRoutingServers
	mSMQForeign
	mSMQEncryptKey
	mSMQDsServices

(continued)

Table A.78   MSMQ-Configuration *(continued)*.

Class Property	Value
	mSMQDependentClientServices
	mSMQComputerTypeEx
	mSMQComputerType
systemMustContain	

Table A.79   MSMQ-Enterprise-Settings.

Class Property	Value
adminDisplayName	MSMQ-Enterprise-Settings
adminDescription	MSMQ-Enterprise-Settings
governsID	1.2.840.113556.1.5.163
lDAPDisplayName	mSMQEnterpriseSettings
objectClassCategory	1 (structural)
subClassOf	top
systemMayContain	mSMQVersion
	mSMQNameStyle
	mSMQLongLived
	mSMQInterval2
	mSMQInterval1
	mSMQCSPName
systemMustContain	

Table A.80   MSMQ-Migrated-User.

Class Property	Value
adminDisplayName	MSMQ-Migrated-User
adminDescription	MSMQ-Migrated-User
governsID	1.2.840.113556.1.5.179
lDAPDisplayName	mSMQMigratedUser
objectClassCategory	1 (structural)
subClassOf	top
systemMayContain	mSMQUserSid
	mSMQSignCertificatesMig
	mSMQSignCertificates
	mSMQDigestsMig

(continued)

Table A.80 MSMQ-Migrated-User *(continued)*.

Class Property	Value
	mSMQDigests
	objectSid
systemMustContain	

Table A.81 MSMQ-Queue.

Class Property	Value
adminDisplayName	MSMQ-Queue
adminDescription	MSMQ-Queue
governsID	1.2.840.113556.1.5.161
lDAPDisplayName	mSMQQueue
objectClassCategory	1 (structural)
subClassOf	top
systemMayContain	mSMQTransactional
	mSMQQueueType
	mSMQQueueQuota
	mSMQQueueNameExt
	mSMQQueueJournalQuota
	mSMQPrivacyLevel
	mSMQOwnerID
	mSMQLabelEx
	mSMQLabel
	mSMQJournal
	mSMQBasePriority
	mSMQAuthenticate
systemMustContain	

Table A.82 MSMQ-Settings.

Class Property	Value
adminDisplayName	MSMQ-Settings
adminDescription	MSMQ-Settings
governsID	1.2.840.113556.1.5.165
lDAPDisplayName	mSMQSettings
objectClassCategory	1 (structural)

(continued)

Appendix A Active
Directory Classes

Table A.82   MSMQ-Settings *(continued)*.

Class Property	Value
subClassOf	top
systemMayContain	mSMQSiteNameEx
	mSMQSiteName
	mSMQServices
	mSMQRoutingService
	mSMQQMID
	mSMQOwnerID
	mSMQNt4Flags
	mSMQMigrated
	mSMQDsService
	mSMQDependentClientService
systemMustContain	

Table A.83   MSMQ-Site-Link.

Class Property	Value
adminDisplayName	MSMQ-Site-Link
adminDescription	MSMQ-Site-Link
governsID	1.2.840.113556.1.5.164
lDAPDisplayName	mSMQSiteLink
objectClassCategory	1 (structural)
subClassOf	top
systemMayContain	mSMQSiteGatesMig
	mSMQSiteGates
systemMustContain	mSMQSite2
	mSMQSite1
	mSMQCost

Table A.84   MS-SQL-OLAPCube.

Class Property	Value
adminDisplayName	MS-SQL-OLAPCube
adminDescription	MS-SQL-OLAPCube
governsID	1.2.840.113556.1.5.190
lDAPDisplayName	mS-SQL-OLAPCube

(continued)

Table A.84 MS-SQL-OLAPCube *(continued)*.

Class Property	Value
objectClassCategory	1 (structural)
subClassOf	top
systemMayContain	mS-SQL-Keywords
	mS-SQL-PublicationURL
	mS-SQL-InformationURL
	mS-SQL-Status
	mS-SQL-LastUpdatedDate
	mS-SQL-Size
	mS-SQL-Description
	mS-SQL-Contact
	mS-SQL-Name
systemMustContain	

Table A.85 MS-SQL-OLAPDatabase.

Class Property	Value
adminDisplayName	MS-SQL-OLAPDatabase
adminDescription	MS-SQL-OLAPDatabase
governsID	1.2.840.113556.1.5.189
lDAPDisplayName	mS-SQL-OLAPDatabase
objectClassCategory	1 (structural)
subClassOf	top
systemMayContain	mS-SQL-Keywords
	mS-SQL-PublicationURL
	mS-SQL-ConnectionURL
	mS-SQL-InformationURL
	mS-SQL-Status
	mS-SQL-Applications
	mS-SQL-LastBackupDate
	mS-SQL-LastUpdatedDate
	mS-SQL-Size
	mS-SQL-Type
	mS-SQL-Description
	mS-SQL-Contact

(continued)

Table A.85   MS-SQL-OLAPDatabase *(continued)*.

Class Property	Value
	mS-SQL-Name
systemMustContain	

Table A.86   MS-SQL-OLAPServer.

Class Property	Value
adminDisplayName	MS-SQL-OLAPServer
adminDescription	MS-SQL-OLAPServer
governsID	1.2.840.113556.1.5.185
lDAPDisplayName	mS-SQL-OLAPServer
objectClassCategory	1 (structural)
subClassOf	serviceConnectionPoint
systemMayContain	mS-SQL-Keywords
	mS-SQL-PublicationURL
	mS-SQL-InformationURL
	mS-SQL-Status
	mS-SQL-Language
	mS-SQL-ServiceAccount
	mS-SQL-Contact
	mS-SQL-RegisteredOwner
	mS-SQL-Build
	mS-SQL-Version
	mS-SQL-Name
systemMustContain	

Table A.87   MS-SQL-SQLDatabase.

Class Property	Value
adminDisplayName	MS-SQL-SQLDatabase
adminDescription	MS-SQL-SQLDatabase
governsID	1.2.840.113556.1.5.188
lDAPDisplayName	mS-SQL-SQLDatabase
objectClassCategory	1 (structural)
subClassOf	top
systemMayContain	mS-SQL-Keywords

(continued)

Table A.87   MS-SQL-SQLDatabase *(continued).*

Class Property	Value
	mS-SQL-InformationURL
	mS-SQL-Status
	mS-SQL-Applications
	mS-SQL-LastDiagnosticDate
	mS-SQL-LastBackupDate
	mS-SQL-CreationDate
	mS-SQL-Size
	mS-SQL-Contact
	mS-SQL-Alias
	mS-SQL-Description
	mS-SQL-Name
systemMustContain	

Table A.88   MS-SQL-SQLPublication.

Class Property	Value
adminDisplayName	MS-SQL-SQLPublication
adminDescription	MS-SQL-SQLPublication
governsID	1.2.840.113556.1.5.187
lDAPDisplayName	mS-SQL-SQLPublication
objectClassCategory	1 (structural)
subClassOf	top
systemMayContain	mS-SQL-ThirdParty
	mS-SQL-AllowSnapshotFilesFTPDownloading
	mS-SQL-AllowQueuedUpdatingSubscription
	mS-SQL-AllowImmediateUpdatingSubscription
	mS-SQL-AllowKnownPullSubscription
	mS-SQL-Publisher
	mS-SQL-AllowAnonymousSubscription
	mS-SQL-Database
	mS-SQL-Type
	mS-SQL-Status
	mS-SQL-Description
	mS-SQL-Name
systemMustContain	

Table A.89   MS-SQL-SQLRepository.

Class Property	Value
adminDisplayName	MS-SQL-SQLRepository
adminDescription	MS-SQL-SQLRepository
governsID	1.2.840.113556.1.5.186
IDAPDisplayName	mS-SQL-SQLRepository
objectClassCategory	1 (structural)
subClassOf	top
systemMayContain	mS-SQL-InformationDirectory
	mS-SQL-Version
	mS-SQL-Description
	mS-SQL-Status
	mS-SQL-Build
	mS-SQL-Contact
	mS-SQL-Name
systemMustContain	

Table A.90   MS-SQL-SQLServer.

Class Property	Value
adminDisplayName	MS-SQL-SQLServer
adminDescription	MS-SQL-SQLServer
governsID	1.2.840.113556.1.5.184
IDAPDisplayName	mS-SQL-SQLServer
objectClassCategory	1 (structural)
subClassOf	serviceConnectionPoint
systemMayContain	mS-SQL-Keywords
	mS-SQL-GPSHeight
	mS-SQL-GPSLongitude
	mS-SQL-GPSLatitude
	mS-SQL-InformationURL
	mS-SQL-LastUpdatedDate
	mS-SQL-Status
	mS-SQL-Vines
	mS-SQL-AppleTalk
	mS-SQL-TCPIP

(continued)

Table A.90   MS-SQL-SQLServer *(continued).*

Class Property	Value
	mS-SQL-SPX
	mS-SQL-MultiProtocol
	mS-SQL-NamedPipe
	mS-SQL-Clustered
	mS-SQL-UnicodeSortOrder
	mS-SQL-SortOrder
	mS-SQL-CharacterSet
	mS-SQL-ServiceAccount
	mS-SQL-Build
	mS-SQL-Memory
	mS-SQL-Location
	mS-SQL-Contact
	mS-SQL-RegisteredOwner
	mS-SQL-Name
systemMustContain	

Table A.91   NTDS-Connection.

Class Property	Value
adminDisplayName	NTDS-Connection
adminDescription	NTDS-Connection
governsID	1.2.840.113556.1.5.71
lDAPDisplayName	nTDSConnection
objectClassCategory	1 (structural)
subClassOf	leaf
systemMayContain	transportType
	schedule
	mS-DS-ReplicatesNCReason
	generatedConnection
systemMustContain	options
	fromServer
	enabledConnection

Table A.92   NTDS-DSA.

Class Property	Value
adminDisplayName	NTDS-DSA
adminDescription	NTDS-DSA
governsID	1.2.840.113556.1.5.7000.47
lDAPDisplayName	nTDSDSA
objectClassCategory	1 (structural)
subClassOf	applicationSettings
systemMayContain	serverReference
	retiredReplDSASignatures
	queryPolicyObject
	options
	networkAddress
	managedBy
	lastBackupRestorationTime
	invocationId
	hasPartialReplicaNCs
	hasMasterNCs
	fRSRootPath
	dMDLocation
systemMustContain	

Table A.93   NTDS-Service.

Class Property	Value
adminDisplayName	NTDS-Service
adminDescription	NTDS-Service
governsID	1.2.840.113556.1.5.72
lDAPDisplayName	nTDSService
objectClassCategory	1 (structural)
subClassOf	top
systemMayContain	tombstoneLifetime
	sPNMappings
	replTopologyStayOfExecution
	garbageCollPeriod
	dSHeuristics
systemMustContain	

Table A.94   NTDS-Site-Settings.

Class Property	Value
adminDisplayName	NTDS-Site-Settings
adminDescription	NTDS-Site-Settings
governsID	1.2.840.113556.1.5.69
lDAPDisplayName	nTDSSiteSettings
objectClassCategory	1 (structural)
subClassOf	applicationSiteSettings
systemMayContain	schedule
	queryPolicyObject
	options
	managedBy
	interSiteTopologyRenew
	interSiteTopologyGenerator
	interSiteTopologyFailover
systemMustContain	

Table A.95   NTFRS-Member.

Class Property	Value
adminDisplayName	NTFRS-Member
adminDescription	NTFRS-Member
governsID	1.2.840.113556.1.5.153
lDAPDisplayName	nTFRSMember
objectClassCategory	1 (structural)
subClassOf	top
systemMayContain	serverReference
	fRSUpdateTimeout
	fRSServiceCommand
	fRSRootSecurity
	fRSPartnerAuthLevel
	fRSFlags
	fRSExtensions
	fRSControlOutboundBacklog
	fRSControlInboundBacklog
	fRSControlDataCreation
	frsComputerReference
systemMustContain	

Table A.96   NTFRS-Replica-Set.

Class Property	Value
adminDisplayName	NTFRS-Replica-Set
adminDescription	NTFRS-Replica-Set
governsID	1.2.840.113556.1.5.102
IDAPDisplayName	nTFRSReplicaSet
objectClassCategory	1 (structural)
subClassOf	top
systemMayContain	schedule
	managedBy
	fRSVersionGUID
	fRSServiceCommand
	fRSRootSecurity
	fRSReplicaSetType
	fRSReplicaSetGUID
	fRSPrimaryMember
	fRSPartnerAuthLevel
	fRSLevelLimit
	fRSFlags
	fRSFileFilter
	fRSExtensions
	fRSDSPoll
	fRSDirectoryFilter
systemMustContain	

Table A.97   NTFRS-Settings.

Class Property	Value
adminDisplayName	NTFRS-Settings
adminDescription	NTFRS-Settings
governsID	1.2.840.113556.1.5.89
IDAPDisplayName	nTFRSSettings
objectClassCategory	1 (structural)
subClassOf	applicationSettings
systemMayContain	managedBy
	fRSExtensions
systemMustContain	

Table A.98   NTFRS-Subscriber.

Class Property	Value
adminDisplayName	NTFRS-Subscriber
adminDescription	NTFRS-Subscriber
governsID	1.2.840.113556.1.5.155
lDAPDisplayName	nTFRSSubscriber
objectClassCategory	1 (structural)
subClassOf	top
systemMayContain	schedule
	fRSUpdateTimeout
	fRSTimeLastConfigChange
	fRSTimeLastCommand
	fRSServiceCommandStatus
	fRSServiceCommand
	fRSMemberReference
	fRSFlags
	fRSFaultCondition
	fRSExtensions
systemMustContain	fRSStagingPath
	fRSRootPath

Table A.99   NTFRS-Subscriptions.

Class Property	Value
adminDisplayName	NTFRS-Subscriptions
adminDescription	NTFRS-Subscriptions
governsID	1.2.840.113556.1.5.154
lDAPDisplayName	nTFRSSubscriptions
objectClassCategory	1 (structural)
subClassOf	top
systemMayContain	fRSWorkingPath
	fRSVersion
	fRSExtensions
systemMustContain	

Table A.100   Organization.

Class Property	Value
adminDisplayName	Organization
adminDescription	Organization
governsID	2.5.6.4
lDAPDisplayName	organization
objectClassCategory	1 (structural)
subClassOf	top
systemMayContain	x121Address
	userPassword
	telexNumber
	teletexTerminalIdentifier
	telephoneNumber
	street
	st
	seeAlso
	searchGuide
	registeredAddress
	preferredDeliveryMethod
	postalCode
	postalAddress
	postOfficeBox
	physicalDeliveryOfficeName
	l
	internationalISDNNumber
	facsimileTelephoneNumber
	destinationIndicator
	businessCategory
systemMustContain	0

Table A.101   Organizational-Person.

Class Property	Value
adminDisplayName	Organizational-Person
adminDescription	Organizational-Person
governsID	2.5.6.7

(continued)

Table A.101   Organizational-Person *(continued)*.

Class Property	Value
lDAPDisplayName	organizationalPerson
objectClassCategory	2 (abstract)
subClassOf	person
systemMayContain	x121Address
	comment
	title
	co
	primaryTelexNumber
	telexNumber
	teletexTerminalIdentifier
	street
	st
	registeredAddress
	preferredDeliveryMethod
	postalCode
	postalAddress
	postOfficeBox
	thumbnailPhoto
	physicalDeliveryOfficeName
	pager
	otherPager
	otherTelephone
	mobile
	otherMobile
	primaryInternationalISDNNumber
	ipPhone
	otherIpPhone
	otherHomePhone
	homePhone
	otherFacsimileTelephoneNumber
	personalTitle
	middleName
	otherMailbox

(continued)

Table A.101   Organizational-Person (continued).

Class Property	Value
	ou
	o
	mhsORAddress
	manager
	thumbnailLogo
	l
	internationalISDNNumber
	initials
	givenName
	generationQualifier
	facsimileTelephoneNumber
	employeeID
	mail
	division
	destinationIndicator
	department
	c
	countryCode
	company
	assistant
	homePostalAddress
	streetAddress
systemMustContain	

Table A.102   Organizational-Role.

Class Property	Value
adminDisplayName	Organizational-Role
adminDescription	Organizational-Role
governsID	2.5.6.8
lDAPDisplayName	organizationalRole
objectClassCategory	1 (structural)
subClassOf	top
systemMayContain	x121Address

(continued)

Table A.102 Organizational-Role *(continued).*

Class Property	Value
	telexNumber
	teletexTerminalIdentifier
	telephoneNumber
	street
	st
	seeAlso
	roleOccupant
	registeredAddress
	preferredDeliveryMethod
	postalCode
	postalAddress
	postOfficeBox
	physicalDeliveryOfficeName
	ou
	l
	internationalISDNNumber
	facsimileTelephoneNumber
	destinationIndicator
systemMustContain	cn

Table A.103 Organizational-Unit.

Class Property	Value
adminDisplayName	Organizational-Unit
adminDescription	Organizational-Unit
governsID	2.5.6.5
lDAPDisplayName	organizationalUnit
objectClassCategory	1 (structural)
subClassOf	top
systemMayContain	x121Address
	userPassword
	uPNSuffixes
	co
	telexNumber

(continued)

Table A.103   Organizational-Unit *(continued)*.

Class Property	Value
	teletexTerminalIdentifier
	telephoneNumber
	street
	st
	seeAlso
	searchGuide
	registeredAddress
	preferredDeliveryMethod
	postalCode
	postalAddress
	postOfficeBox
	physicalDeliveryOfficeName
	managedBy
	thumbnailLogo
	l
	internationalISDNNumber
	gPOptions
	gPLink
	facsimileTelephoneNumber
	destinationIndicator
	desktopProfile
	defaultGroup
	countryCode
	c
	businessCategory
systemMustContain	ou

Table A.104   Package-Registration.

Class Property	Value
adminDisplayName	Package-Registration
adminDescription	Package-Registration
governsID	1.2.840.113556.1.5.49

(continued)

Table A.104   Package-Registration *(continued)*.

Class Property	Value
lDAPDisplayName	packageRegistration
objectClassCategory	1 (structural)
subClassOf	top
systemMayContain	versionNumberLo
	versionNumberHi
	vendor
	upgradeProductCode
	setupCommand
	productCode
	packageType
	packageName
	packageFlags
	msiScriptSize
	msiScriptPath
	msiScriptName
	msiScript
	msiFileList
	managedBy
	machineArchitecture
	localeID
	lastUpdateSequence
	installUiLevel
	iconPath
	fileExtPriority
	cOMTypelibId
	cOMProgID
	cOMInterfaceID
	cOMClassID
	categories
	canUpgradeScript
systemMustContain	

Table A.105   Person.

Class Property	Value
adminDisplayName	Person
adminDescription	Person
governsID	2.5.6.6
lDAPDisplayName	person
objectClassCategory	2 (abstract)
subClassOf	top
systemMayContain	userPassword
	telephoneNumber
	sn
	seeAlso
systemMustContain	cn

Table A.106   Physical-Location.

Class Property	Value
adminDisplayName	Physical-Location
adminDescription	Physical-Location
governsID	1.2.840.113556.1.5.97
lDAPDisplayName	physicalLocation
objectClassCategory	1 (structural)
subClassOf	locality
systemMayContain	managedBy
systemMustContain	

Table A.107   PKI-Certificate-Template.

Class Property	Value
adminDisplayName	PKI-Certificate-Template
adminDescription	PKI-Certificate-Template
governsID	1.2.840.113556.1.5.177
lDAPDisplayName	pKICertificateTemplate
objectClassCategory	1 (structural)
subClassOf	top
systemMayContain	pKIOverlapPeriod
	pKIMaxIssuingDepth

(continued)

Table A.107   PKI-Certificate-Template *(continued)*.

Class Property	Value
	pKIKeyUsage
	pKIExtendedKeyUsage
	pKIExpirationPeriod
	pKIEnrollmentAccess
	pKIDefaultCSPs
	pKIDefaultKeySpec
	pKICriticalExtensions
	flags
	displayName
systemMustContain	

Table A.108   PKI-Enrollment-Service.

Class Property	Value
adminDisplayName	PKI-Enrollment-Service
adminDescription	PKI-Enrollment-Service
governsID	1.2.840.113556.1.5.178
lDAPDisplayName	pKIEnrollmentService
objectClassCategory	1 (structural)
subClassOf	top
systemMayContain	signatureAlgorithms
	enrollmentProviders
	dNSHostName
	certificateTemplates
	cACertificateDN
	cACertificate
systemMustContain	

Table A.109   Print-Queue.

Class Property	Value
adminDisplayName	Print-Queue
adminDescription	Print-Queue
governsID	1.2.840.113556.1.5.23
lDAPDisplayName	printQueue

(continued)

Table A.109   Print-Queue *(continued)*.

Class Property	Value
objectClassCategory	1 (structural)
subClassOf	connectionPoint
systemMayContain	priority
	printStatus
	printStartTime
	printStaplingSupported
	printSpooling
	printShareName
	printSeparatorFile
	printRateUnit
	printRate
	printPagesPerMinute
	printOwner
	printOrientationsSupported
	printNumberUp
	printNotify
	printNetworkAddress
	printMinYExtent
	printMinXExtent
	printMemory
	printMediaSupported
	printMediaReady
	printMaxYExtent
	printMaxXExtent
	printMaxResolutionSupported
	printMaxCopies
	printMACAddress
	printLanguage
	printKeepPrintedJobs
	printFormName
	printEndTime
	printDuplexSupported
	printColor

(continued)

Table A.109   Print-Queue *(continued)*.

Class Property	Value
	printCollate
	printBinNames
	printAttributes
	portName
	physicalLocationObject
	operatingSystemVersion
	operatingSystemServicePack
	operatingSystemHotfix
	operatingSystem
	location
	driverVersion
	driverName
	defaultPriority
	bytesPerMinute
	assetNumber
systemMustContain	versionNumber
	uNCName
	shortServerName
	serverName
	printerName

Table A.110   Query-Policy.

Class Property	Value
adminDisplayName	Query-Policy
adminDescription	Query-Policy
governsID	1.2.840.113556.1.5.106
lDAPDisplayName	queryPolicy
objectClassCategory	1 (structural)
subClassOf	top
systemMayContain	lDAPIPDenyList
	lDAPAdminLimits
systemMustContain	

Table A.111   Remote-Mail-Recipient.

Class Property	Value
adminDisplayName	Remote-Mail-Recipient
adminDescription	Remote-Mail-Recipient
governsID	1.2.840.113556.1.5.24
lDAPDisplayName	remoteMailRecipient
objectClassCategory	1 (structural)
subClassOf	top
systemMayContain	remoteSourceType
	remoteSource
	managedBy
systemMustContain	

Table A.112   Remote-Storage-Service-Point.

Class Property	Value
adminDisplayName	Remote-Storage-Service-Point
adminDescription	Remote-Storage-Service-Point
governsID	1.2.840.113556.1.5.146
lDAPDisplayName	remoteStorageServicePoint
objectClassCategory	1 (structural)
subClassOf	serviceAdministrationPoint
systemMayContain	remoteStorageGUID
systemMustContain	

Table A.113   Residential-Person.

Class Property	Value
adminDisplayName	Residential-Person
adminDescription	Residential-Person
governsID	2.5.6.10
lDAPDisplayName	residentialPerson
objectClassCategory	1 (structural)
subClassOf	person
systemMayContain	x121Address
	title
	telexNumber

(continued)

Table A.113　Residential-Person *(continued)*.

Class Property	Value
	teletexTerminalIdentifier
	street
	st
	registeredAddress
	preferredDeliveryMethod
	postalCode
	postalAddress
	postOfficeBox
	physicalDeliveryOfficeName
	ou
	l
	internationalISDNNumber
	facsimileTelephoneNumber
	destinationIndicator
	businessCategory
systemMustContain	

Table A.114　RID-Manager.

Class Property	Value
adminDisplayName	RID-Manager
adminDescription	RID-Manager
governsID	1.2.840.113556.1.5.83
lDAPDisplayName	rIDManager
objectClassCategory	1 (structural)
subClassOf	top
systemMayContain	
systemMustContain	rIDAvailablePool

Table A.115　RID-Set.

Class Property	Value
adminDisplayName	RID-Set
adminDescription	RID-Set
governsID	1.2.840.113556.1.5.129

(continued)

Table A.115   RID-Set *(continued).*

Class Property	Value
IDAPDisplayName	rIDSet
objectClassCategory	1 (structural)
subClassOf	top
systemMayContain	
systemMustContain	rIDUsedPool
	rIDPreviousAllocationPool
	rIDNextRID
	rIDAllocationPool

Table A.116   Rpc-Container.

Class Property	Value
adminDisplayName	Rpc-Container
adminDescription	Rpc-Container
governsID	1.2.840.113556.1.5.136
IDAPDisplayName	rpcContainer
objectClassCategory	1 (structural)
subClassOf	container
systemMayContain	nameServiceFlags
systemMustContain	

Table A.117   rpc-Entry.

Class Property	Value
adminDisplayName	rpc-Entry
adminDescription	rpc-Entry
governsID	1.2.840.113556.1.5.27
IDAPDisplayName	rpcEntry
objectClassCategory	2 (abstract)
subClassOf	connectionPoint
systemMayContain	
systemMustContain	

Table A.118   rpc-Group.

Class Property	Value
adminDisplayName	rpc-Group
adminDescription	rpc-Group
governsID	1.2.840.113556.1.5.80
lDAPDisplayName	rpcGroup
objectClassCategory	1 (structural)
subClassOf	rpcEntry
systemMayContain	rpcNsObjectID
	rpcNsGroup
systemMustContain	

Table A.119   rpc-Profile.

Class Property	Value
adminDisplayName	rpc-Profile
adminDescription	rpc-Profile
governsID	1.2.840.113556.1.5.82
lDAPDisplayName	rpcProfile
objectClassCategory	1 (structural)
subClassOf	rpcEntry
systemMayContain	
systemMustContain	

Table A.120   rpc-Profile-Element.

Class Property	Value
adminDisplayName	rpc-Profile-Element
adminDescription	rpc-Profile-Element
governsID	1.2.840.113556.1.5.26
lDAPDisplayName	rpcProfileElement
objectClassCategory	1 (structural)
subClassOf	rpcEntry
systemMayContain	rpcNsProfileEntry
	rpcNsAnnotation
systemMustContain	rpcNsPriority
	rpcNsInterfaceID

Table A.121   rpc-Server.

Class Property	Value
adminDisplayName	rpc-Server
adminDescription	rpc-Server
governsID	1.2.840.113556.1.5.81
lDAPDisplayName	rpcServer
objectClassCategory	1 (structural)
subClassOf	rpcEntry
systemMayContain	rpcNsObjectID
	rpcNsEntryFlags
	rpcNsCodeset
systemMustContain	

Table A.122   rpc-Server-Element.

Class Property	Value
adminDisplayName	rpc-Server-Element
adminDescription	rpc-Server-Element
governsID	1.2.840.113556.1.5.73
lDAPDisplayName	rpcServerElement
objectClassCategory	1 (structural)
subClassOf	rpcEntry
systemMayContain	
systemMustContain	rpcNsTransferSyntax
	rpcNsInterfaceID
	rpcNsBindings

Table A.123   RRAS-Administration-Connection-Point.

Class Property	Value
adminDisplayName	RRAS-Administration-Connection-Point
adminDescription	RRAS-Administration-Connection-Point
governsID	1.2.840.113556.1.5.150
lDAPDisplayName	rRASAdministrationConnectionPoint
objectClassCategory	1 (structural)
subClassOf	serviceAdministrationPoint
systemMayContain	msRRASAttribute
systemMustContain	

Table A.124 RRAS-Administration-Dictionary.

Class Property	Value
adminDisplayName	RRAS-Administration-Dictionary
adminDescription	RRAS-Administration-Dictionary
governsID	1.2.840.113556.1.5.156
lDAPDisplayName	rRASAdministrationDictionary
objectClassCategory	1 (structural)
subClassOf	top
systemMayContain	msRRASVendorAttributeEntry
systemMustContain	

Table A.125 Sam-Domain.

Class Property	Value
adminDisplayName	Sam-Domain
adminDescription	Sam-Domain
governsID	1.2.840.113556.1.5.3
lDAPDisplayName	samDomain
objectClassCategory	3 (auxiliary)
subClassOf	top
systemMayContain	treeName
	rIDManagerReference
	replicaSource
	pwdProperties
	pwdHistoryLength
	privateKey
	pekList
	pekKeyChangeInterval
	nTMixedDomain
	nextRid
	nETBIOSName
	ms-DS-MachineAccountQuota
	modifiedCountAtLastProm
	minPwdLength
	minPwdAge
	maxPwdAge

(continued)

Table A.125 Sam-Domain *(continued)*.

Class Property	Value
lSAModifiedCount	
	lSACreationTime
	lockoutThreshold
	lockoutDuration
	lockOutObservationWindow
	gPOptions
	gPLink
	eFSPolicy
	domainPolicyObject
	desktopProfile
	description
	defaultLocalPolicyObject
	creationTime
	controlAccessRights
	cACertificate
	builtinModifiedCount
	builtinCreationTime
	auditingPolicy
systemMustContain	

Table A.126 Sam-Domain-Base.

Class Property	Value
adminDisplayName	Sam-Domain-Base
adminDescription	Sam-Domain-Base
governsID	1.2.840.113556.1.5.2
lDAPDisplayName	samDomainBase
objectClassCategory	3 (auxiliary)
subClassOf	top
systemMayContain	uASCompat
	serverState
	serverRole
	revision
	pwdProperties

(continued)

Table A.126   Sam-Domain-Base *(continued)*.

Class Property	Value
	pwdHistoryLength
	oEMInformation
	objectSid
	nTSecurityDescriptor
	nextRid
	modifiedCountAtLastProm
	modifiedCount
	minPwdLength
	minPwdAge
	maxPwdAge
	lockoutThreshold
	lockoutDuration
	lockOutObservationWindow
	forceLogoff
	domainReplica
	creationTime
systemMustContain	

Table A.127   Sam-Server.

Class Property	Value
adminDisplayName	Sam-Server
adminDescription	Sam-Server
governsID	1.2.840.113556.1.5.5
IDAPDisplayName	samServer
objectClassCategory	1 (structural)
subClassOf	securityObject
systemMayContain	
systemMustContain	

Table A.128   Secret.

Class Property	Value
adminDisplayName	Secret
adminDescription	Secret

(continued)

Table A.128   Secret *(continued).*

Class Property	Value
governsID	1.2.840.113556.1.5.28
IDAPDisplayName	secret
objectClassCategory	1 (structural)
subClassOf	leaf
systemMayContain	priorValue
	priorSetTime
	lastSetTime
	currentValue
systemMustContain	

Table A.129   Security-Object.

Class Property	Value
adminDisplayName	Security-Object
adminDescription	Security-Object
governsID	1.2.840.113556.1.5.1
IDAPDisplayName	securityObject
objectClassCategory	2 (abstract)
subClassOf	top
systemMayContain	
systemMustContain	cn

Table A.130   Security-Principal.

Class Property	Value
adminDisplayName	Security-Principal
adminDescription	Security-Principal
governsID	1.2.840.113556.1.5.6
IDAPDisplayName	securityPrincipal
objectClassCategory	3 (auxiliary)
subClassOf	top
systemMayContain	supplementalCredentials
	sIDHistory
	securityIdentifier
	sAMAccountType

(continued)

Table A.130 Security-Principal *(continued)*.

Class Property	Value
	rid
	tokenGroupsNoGCAcceptable
	tokenGroupsGlobalAndUniversal
	tokenGroups
	nTSecurityDescriptor
	altSecurityIdentities
	accountNameHistory
systemMustContain	sAMAccountName
	objectSid

Table A.131 Server.

Class Property	Value
adminDisplayName	Server
adminDescription	Server
governsID	1.2.840.113556.1.5.17
IDAPDisplayName	server
objectClassCategory	1 (structural)
subClassOf	top
systemMayContain	mailAddress
	serverReference
	serialNumber
	managedBy
	dNSHostName
	bridgeheadTransportList
systemMustContain	

Table A.132 Servers-Container.

Class Property	Value
adminDisplayName	Servers-Container
adminDescription	Servers-Container
governsID	1.2.840.113556.1.5.7000.48
IDAPDisplayName	serversContainer
objectClassCategory	1 (structural)

(continued)

Table A.132 Servers-Container *(continued)*.

Class Property	Value
subClassOf	top
systemMayContain	
systemMustContain	

Table A.133 Service-Administration-Point.

Class Property	Value
adminDisplayName	Service-Administration-Point
adminDescription	Service-Administration-Point
governsID	1.2.840.113556.1.5.94
lDAPDisplayName	serviceAdministrationPoint
objectClassCategory	1 (structural)
subClassOf	serviceConnectionPoint
systemMayContain	
systemMustContain	

Table A.134 Service-Class.

Class Property	Value
adminDisplayName	Service-Class
adminDescription	Service-Class
governsID	1.2.840.113556.1.5.29
lDAPDisplayName	serviceClass
objectClassCategory	1 (structural)
subClassOf	leaf
systemMayContain	serviceClassInfo
systemMustContain	serviceClassID
	displayName

Table A.135 Service-Connection-Point.

Class Property	Value
adminDisplayName	Service-Connection-Point
adminDescription	Service-Connection-Point
governsID	1.2.840.113556.1.5.126
lDAPDisplayName	serviceConnectionPoint

(continued)

Table A.135   Service-Connection-Point *(continued)*.

Class Property	Value
objectClassCategory	1 (structural)
subClassOf	connectionPoint
systemMayContain	serviceDNSNameType
	serviceDNSName
	serviceClassName
	serviceBindingInformation
systemMustContain	

Table A.136   Service-Instance.

Class Property	Value
adminDisplayName	Service-Instance
adminDescription	Service-Instance
governsID	1.2.840.113556.1.5.30
IDAPDisplayName	serviceInstance
objectClassCategory	1 (structural)
subClassOf	connectionPoint
systemMayContain	winsockAddresses
	serviceInstanceVersion
systemMustContain	serviceClassID
	displayName

Table A.137   Site.

Class Property	Value
adminDisplayName	Site
adminDescription	Site
governsID	1.2.840.113556.1.5.31
IDAPDisplayName	site
objectClassCategory	1 (structural)
subClassOf	top
systemMayContain	notificationList
	mSMQSiteID
	mSMQSiteForeign
	mSMQNt4Stub

(continued)

Table A.137   Site *(continued)*.

Class Property	Value
	mSMQInterval2
	mSMQInterval1
	managedBy
	location
	gPOptions
	gPLink
systemMustContain	

Table A.138   Site-Link.

Class Property	Value
adminDisplayName	Site-Link
adminDescription	Site-Link
governsID	1.2.840.113556.1.5.147
lDAPDisplayName	siteLink
objectClassCategory	1 (structural)
subClassOf	top
systemMayContain	schedule
	replInterval
	options
	cost
systemMustContain	siteList

Table A.139   Site-Link-Bridge.

Class Property	Value
adminDisplayName	Site-Link-Bridge
adminDescription	Site-Link-Bridge
governsID	1.2.840.113556.1.5.148
lDAPDisplayName	siteLinkBridge
objectClassCategory	1 (structural)
subClassOf	top
systemMayContain	
systemMustContain	siteLinkList

Table A.140 Sites-Container.

Class Property	Value
adminDisplayName	Sites-Container
adminDescription	Sites-Container
governsID	1.2.840.113556.1.5.107
IDAPDisplayName	sitesContainer
objectClassCategory	1 (structural)
subClassOf	top
systemMayContain	
systemMustContain	

Table A.141 Storage.

Class Property	Value
adminDisplayName	Storage
adminDescription	Storage
governsID	1.2.840.113556.1.5.33
IDAPDisplayName	storage
objectClassCategory	1 (structural)
subClassOf	connectionPoint
systemMayContain	monikerDisplayName
	moniker
	iconPath
systemMustContain	

Table A.142 Subnet.

Class Property	Value
adminDisplayName	Subnet
adminDescription	Subnet
governsID	1.2.840.113556.1.5.96
IDAPDisplayName	subnet
objectClassCategory	1 (structural)
subClassOf	top
systemMayContain	siteObject
	physicalLocationObject
	location
systemMustContain	

Table A.143   Subnet-Container.

Class Property	Value
adminDisplayName	Subnet-Container
adminDescription	Subnet-Container
governsID	1.2.840.113556.1.5.95
IDAPDisplayName	subnetContainer
objectClassCategory	1 (structural)
subClassOf	top
systemMayContain	
systemMustContain	

Table A.144   SubSchema.

Class Property	Value
adminDisplayName	SubSchema
adminDescription	SubSchema
governsID	2.5.20.1
IDAPDisplayName	subSchema
objectClassCategory	1 (structural)
subClassOf	top
systemMayContain	objectClasses
	modifyTimeStamp
	extendedClassInfo
	extendedAttributeInfo
	dITContentRules
	attributeTypes
systemMustContain	

Table A.145   Test-Class.

Class Property	Value
adminDisplayName	Test-Class
adminDescription	
governsID	1.2.3.4.5.6.7.8.11
IDAPDisplayName	testClass
objectClassCategory	1 (structural)
subClassOf	top

(continued)

Table A.145   Test-Class *(continued).*

Class Property	Value
systemMayContain	
systemMustContain	

Table A.146   Top.

Class Property	Value
adminDisplayName	Top
adminDescription	Top
governsID	2.5.6.0
IDAPDisplayName	top
objectClassCategory	2 (abstract)
subClassOf	top
systemMayContain	url
	wWWHomePage
	whenCreated
	whenChanged
	wellKnownObjects
	wbemPath
	uSNSource
	uSNLastObjRem
	USNIntersite
	uSNDSALastObjRemoved
	uSNCreated
	uSNChanged
	systemFlags
	subSchemaSubEntry
	subRefs
	siteObjectBL
	serverReferenceBL
	sDRightsEffective
	revision
	repsTo
	repsFrom
	directReports

(continued)

Table A.146   Top (continued).

Class Property	Value
	replUpToDateVector
	replPropertyMetaData
	name
	queryPolicyBL
	proxyAddresses
	proxiedObjectName
	possibleInferiors
	partialAttributeSet
	partialAttributeDeletionList
	otherWellKnownObjects
	objectVersion
	objectGUID
	distinguishedName
	nonSecurityMemberBL
	netbootSCPBL
	mS-DS-ConsistencyGuid
	mS-DS-ConsistencyChildCount
	modifyTimeStamp
	masteredBy
	managedObjects
	lastKnownParent
	isPrivilegeHolder
	memberOf
	isDeleted
	isCriticalSystemObject
	showInAdvancedViewOnly
	fSMORoleOwner
	fRSMemberReferenceBL
	frsComputerReferenceBL
	fromEntry
	flags
	extensionName
	dSASignature

(continued)

Table A.146 Top *(continued)*.

Class Property	Value
	dSCorePropagationData
	displayNamePrintable
	displayName
	description
	createTimeStamp
	cn
	canonicalName
	bridgeheadServerListBL
	allowedChildClassesEffective
	allowedChildClasses
	allowedAttributesEffective
	allowedAttributes
	adminDisplayName
	adminDescription
systemMustContain	objectClass
	objectCategory
	nTSecurityDescriptor
	instanceType

Table A.147 Trusted-Domain.

Class Property	Value
adminDisplayName	Trusted-Domain
adminDescription	Trusted-Domain
governsID	1.2.840.113556.1.5.34
lDAPDisplayName	trustedDomain
objectClassCategory	1 (structural)
subClassOf	leaf
systemMayContain	trustType
	trustPosixOffset
	trustPartner
	trustDirection
	trustAuthOutgoing
	trustAuthIncoming

(continued)

Table A.147   Trusted-Domain *(continued)*.

Class Property	Value
	trustAttributes
	securityIdentifier
	initialAuthOutgoing
	initialAuthIncoming
	flatName
	domainIdentifier
	domainCrossRef
	additionalTrustedServiceNames
systemMustContain	

Table A.148   Type-Library.

Class Property	Value
adminDisplayName	Type-Library
adminDescription	Type-Library
governsID	1.2.840.113556.1.5.53
lDAPDisplayName	typeLibrary
objectClassCategory	1 (structural)
subClassOf	top
systemMayContain	cOMUniqueLIBID
	cOMInterfaceID
	cOMClassID
systemMustContain	

Table A.149   User.

Class Property	Value
adminDisplayName	User
adminDescription	User
governsID	1.2.840.113556.1.5.9
lDAPDisplayName	User
objectClassCategory	1 (structural)
subClassOf	organizationalPerson
systemMayContain	userCertificate
	userWorkstations

(continued)

Table A.149　User *(continued).*

Class Property	Value
	userSharedFolderOther
	userSharedFolder
	userPrincipalName
	userParameters
	userAccountControl
	unicodePwd
	terminalServer
	servicePrincipalName
	scriptPath
	pwdLastSet
	profilePath
	primaryGroupID
	preferredOU
	otherLoginWorkstations
	operatorCount
	ntPwdHistory
	networkAddress
	msRASSavedFramedRoute
	msRASSavedFramedIPAddress
	msRASSavedCallbackNumber
	msRADIUSServiceType
	msRADIUSFramedRoute
	msRADIUSFramedIPAddress
	msRADIUSCallbackNumber
	msNPSavedCallingStationID
	msNPCallingStationID
	msNPAllowDialin
	mSMQSignCertificatesMig
	mSMQSignCertificates
	mSMQDigestsMig
	mSMQDigests
	mS-DS-CreatorSID
	maxStorage

(continued)

Appendix A Active
Directory Classes

Table A.149   User *(continued).*

Class Property	Value
	logonWorkstation
	logonHours
	logonCount
	lockoutTime
	localeID
	lmPwdHistory
	lastLogon
	lastLogoff
	homeDrive
	homeDirectory
	groupsToIgnore
	groupPriority
	groupMembershipSAM
	dynamicLDAPServer
	desktopProfile
	defaultClassStore
	dBCSPwd
	controlAccessRights
	codePage
	badPwdCount
	badPasswordTime
	adminCount
	aCSPolicyName
	accountExpires
systemMustContain	

Table A.150   Volume.

Class Property	Value
adminDisplayName	Volume
adminDescription	Volume
governsID	1.2.840.113556.1.5.36
lDAPDisplayName	volume

(continued)

Table A.150   Volume *(continued).*

Class Property	Value
objectClassCategory	1 (structural)
subClassOf	connectionPoint
systemMayContain	lastContentIndexed
	contentIndexingAllowed
systemMustContain	uNCName

Appendix B

Further Reading

Windows 2000 is a large topic, and a single book can't begin to cover it all. The Coriolis Group offers a broad range of available titles in its Black Book and Little Black Book series, and in other publications not part of a series. Below are some of the other useful books I've discovered, along with some pointers to Internet resources.

Books

Perhaps the single most important book to recommend is the *Microsoft Windows 2000 Server Resource Kit* (Microsoft Press, January 2000, ISBN: 1572318058). In fact, this is a package of seven books with more than 7,000 pages and, most importantly, the resource kit utilities are on CD. An alternative way to access the same information and tools is through the subscription versions of MSDN (Microsoft Developer Network) and TechNet.

You should also look out for periodic supplements that appear with updates and new utilities. The frequency of these supplements varies somewhat, although historically you can expect them to appear annually, or slightly more frequently. The first supplement is unsurprisingly *Microsoft Windows 2000 Server Resource Kit Supplement One* (Microsoft Press, November 2000, ISBN: 073561279X.)

Microsoft Windows 2000 Professional Resource Kit (Microsoft Press, March 2000, ISBN: 1572318082) is also available and covers desktop issues. It, too, contains numerous utilities.

For more information on Domain Name System (DNS), you should consider reading Cricket Liu's, Paul Albitz's, and Mike Loukides's, *DNS and BIND* (3rd edition, O'Reilly & Associates, September 1998, ISBN: 1565925122), which provides a solid background on the protocol, although it doesn't cover the specifics of Windows 2000 DNS.

If you want to know more about scripting, a good book to read is Tim Hill's *Windows 2000 Windows Script Host* (Macmillan Technical Publishing, 1999, ISBN: 1578701392).

Finally, for anyone who wants to delve a little deeper into Windows 2000—whether they're developers or not—they should read David A. Solomon's and Mark Russinovich's *Inside Microsoft Windows 2000* (3rd edition, Microsoft Press, September 2000, ISBN: 0735610215). It's highly recommended.

Subscriptions

Microsoft provides two CD/DVD subscription options for IT professionals or enthusiasts to get up to date information, software, and patches delivered to their door. These take the form of TechNet and MSDN, each of which comes in a variety of flavors.

TechNet

TechNet is a CD or DVD based subscription that contains technical information aimed at system administrators such as deployment guides, resource kits, white papers and the on-line knowledgebase of technical articles and fixes.

Also included on the disks are the latest service packs and patches for almost all Microsoft business products, as well as a variety of extras such as trial versions of software and on-line training material.

A more expensive level of subscription—TechNet Plus—also includes some beta software. TechNet subscription information can be found on-line at **www.microsoft.com/technet/subscription**.

Microsoft Developers Network (MSDN)

As the name suggests, MSDN subscriptions are aimed at developers and they come in three levels that range from just-information, to more software than one person can ever use properly.

The most basic, *Library*-level subscription includes a quarterly-updated information set that contains development tools documentation, software development kit (SDK) documentation, sample code, and technical articles. A slightly reduced version of the information is available online at **msdn.microsoft.com/library**.

One step up is the *Professional* subscription that includes everything in a Library subscription, as well as the actual software development kits and development copies of all Microsoft operating systems.

The highest level—*Universal*—also includes development copies of the Microsoft Servers family of products such as Exchange Server and SQL Server, as well as a licensed versions of Visual Studio, Office Developer, and other desktop software.

MSDN Universal and Professional subscribers also have access to some beta versions of the products included in those subscriptions. Subscription information including the latest, localized pricing can be found at **msdn.microsoft.com/ subscriptions**.

Newsgroups

Many people (especially people in the media) often equate the World Wide Web with the Internet. This is unfortunate, because it overlooks the other valuable resources that the Internet has to offer. One of these is newsgroups, and Microsoft provides a news server available to the public that hosts more than 1,000 different forums for discussing aspects of its products.

Although some of these newsgroups may be available from your local ISP, it's best to read directly from Microsoft's own public server, which is **news.microsoft.com**. The groups of particular interest to readers of this book are the following:

- microsoft.public.active.directory.interfaces

- microsoft.public.scripting.vbscript

- microsoft.public.win2000.active_directory

- microsoft.public.win2000.dns

These groups aren't officially monitored by Microsoft, but Microsoft employees sometimes answer questions (usually from their home email addresses). A number of regular respondents also are available, some of whom have been selected as Microsoft's Most Valuable Professionals (MVPs) as a reward for the their past performances answering questions.

Unfortunately, no guarantee is available that any given question will be answered, but there's a good chance a well-worded question will be, and there's every chance that any answers will be peer reviewed by pedants eager to point out mistakes. Even if you don't want to ask questions, it's often informative to "lurk" in the various newsgroups and read the questions and replies.

The Web

The most important Windows 2000 Web site is Microsoft's own, which is located at **www.microsoft.com/windows2000**. Here you'll find important information, such as downloadable updates, for Windows 2000 and some highly recommended white papers that deal with specific technology areas.

A second Microsoft site that's important for every system administrator to review regularly (not to mention, subscribe to and read the email alerts from) is the Microsoft

Security Web site at **www.microsoft.com/security**. If you ever have technical problems, the first place to search is Microsoft's online knowledge base at **support.microsoft.com**. Useful information can also be found at the online TechNet site—**www.microsoft.com/technet**.

If you're looking for more information on scripting technologies, the Microsoft Developers Network sites at **msdn.microsoft.com** and, in particular, **msdn.microsoft.com/scripting** are useful, as is the script library at **cwashington. netreach.net.** It's probably the best around.

There are many other Web sites that cover Windows 2000 and related technologies. Two particularly worth mentioning are the general Windows 2000-oriented **www.labmice.net**, and the security site **ICSA.net** (which includes the invaluable NTBugTraq security mailing list).

Finally, to repeat the URLs from the introduction, more information from the publisher can be found at **www.coriolis.com**, and the author's Web site, which is **www.adamwood.com**.

Glossary

access control—The mechanism of allowing or denying access to objects (such as files on disk or directory-based objects, such as users and Organizational Units) and to security principals (users, computers, and Security Groups).

access control entry (ACE)—An entry in an access control list that specifies a security identifier (SID) and a bitmask of permissions/auditable events.

access control list (ACL)—A group of access control entries. Objects and properties have access control lists, whose contents define security permissions on the object. There are two types of ACLs: discretionary access control lists (DACLs), which set permissions, and system access control lists (SACLs), which control auditing.

ACE—An entry in an access control list that specifies a security identifier (SID) and a bitmask of permissions/auditable events.

ACL—A group of access control entries. Objects and properties have access control lists, whose contents define security permissions on the object. There are two types of ACLs: discretionary access control lists (DACLs), which set permissions and system access control lists (SACLs), which control auditing.

Active Directory—Microsoft's directory service first included with Windows 2000. Active Directory stores and makes available information about objects on a network.

Active Directory Connector (ADC)—A Microsoft-supplied directory synchronization agent for linking Active Directory and the Exchange 5.5 directory.

Active Directory-integrated zone—A DNS zone that's stored within the domain partition of Active Directory and replicated to all domain controllers in a particular domain. Usually DNS zones are stored in zone files.

Active Directory replication—The process whereby changes made at one domain controller are synchronized with another domain controller. Each partition of Active Directory has its own replication topology, and the mechanics of replication depend on whether it crosses site boundaries.

Active Directory Service Interfaces (ADSI)—A set of programming interfaces used to access a variety of applications, including Active Directory. ADSI provides the ability for programs and scripts to easily manipulate and read directory data.

Active Directory Users and Computers—A Windows 2000 administration tool used to manage users, groups, and computers in Active Directory. It's installed by default on domain controllers and can be added to clients by installing adminpak.msi. It's found by default on the Administrative Tools menu or can be added to a Custom Management Console Snap-in. See also MMC.

ADC—Active Directory Connector. A Microsoft application for synchronizing Active Directory and Exchange 5.5.

.adm—Administrative Templates. These contain Registry settings that can be added to Group Policy.

ADSI—Active Directory Service Interfaces. A set of programming interfaces used to access a variety of applications, including Active Directory. ADSI provides the ability for programs and scripts to easily manipulate and read directory data.

attribute—Active Directory objects store information as attributes. The attributes associated with a class determine what type of information it can store.

auditing—The process of logging user actions.

authoritative restore—Active Directory data that is restored from backup must be marked as restored authoritatively for this data to survive when directory services are restarted. This is because the default action is to replicate in changes after the database is restored, so any recently deleted data will be deleted again by these changes. This can be overcome by marking portions of the restored data as authoritative, and this means that replicated changes will be discarded, and the restored data replicated out as the correct, up-to-date version.

AXFR—A full DNS zone transfer.

backup domain controller (BDC)—A Windows NT domain controller that can query but not make updates to the Security Accounts Manager (SAM) account database. For Windows 2000 servers, there's no concept of backup domain controllers (although you can add Windows NT BDCs to a Windows 2000 domain in mixed mode.)

BIND—Berkeley Internet Name Daemon. A commonly used Domain Name System (DNS) server product available for Unix, Windows, and other platforms. See **www.isc.org/products/BIND**.

boot—To start a computer.

bridgehead server—A server that collates and forwards traffic, such as Active Directory replication traffic, from one site to another.

caching-only server—A DNS server that does not authoritatively host any zones, but instead, forwards only queries and returns, and stores results.

Certificate Services—A Windows 2000 service that's responsible for issuing and managing digital certificates used in cryptographic processes.

checkpoint—In Jet databases, such as the Active Directory database, a checkpoint file is used to record the latest transaction processed.

child domain—A Windows 2000 domain located directly beneath another. For example, **domain.example.com** could be a child of the **example.com** domain.

child object—A child of a given object is any other object whose distinguished name is one component longer, and ends with the given object's DN. For example, **cn=Administrator,cn=Users,dc=example,dc=com** is an immediate child object of **cn=Users,dc=example,dc=com**.

ciphertext—Encrypted data. When a message is encrypted, it's said to be in ciphertext.

cleartext—In cryptography, a decoded message is said to be in cleartext or plaintext.

client—A computer that connects to another. In Windows 2000 domains, clients are any members of the domain that aren't domain controllers.

ClonePrincipal—A DLL and set of scripts found in the Windows 2000 Resource Kit that facilitate copying security principals between Windows NT domains to Active Directory or between Active Directory forests.

Comma Separated Value Directory Exchange (CSVDE)—A Windows 2000 utility used to import and export Active Directory data in comma separated format.

computer account objects—Active Directory objects that represent Windows NT / Windows 2000 computers in a domain.

connection object—A directory object stored beneath a domain controller's NT Directory Service (NTDS) Settings object that represents an inbound replication connection.

console—The command line or command prompt, **cmd.exe**, which is often incorrectly referred to as a DOS box. In the sense of "working at the console", it can also mean physically sitting at a PC (as opposed to accessing it over the network.)

container object—Either a specific class of Active Directory object or a more general family of objects that can have others added beneath them.

convergence—The process whereby, if no changes are made, data replicated or synchronized among disparate systems will become the same on every system. An Active Directory that's configured properly will converge over time.

cross-reference object—An object in a Lightweight Directory Access Protocol (LDAP) directory that contains knowledge of a foreign directory partition. These are used to generate LDAP referrals.

Data Encryption Standard (DES)—A 56-bit, U.S. government-approved encryption standard. It's weak in modern terms and is commonly used in a modified form, such as DESX.

decryption—The opposite of encryption, that is, the process of converting ciphertext to cleartext.

Dfs—Distributed file system. A Windows 2000 service that provides a single, logical view of network file shares. Dfs uses links as connections to shared folders, and these are hosted beneath a Dfs root. Dfs roots can be either stand-alone or domain-based. Domain Dfs (formerly known as fault-tolerant Dfs) provides for redundancy through multiple replicas of the same shared folder and a fault-tolerant Dfs root.

DHCP—Dynamic Host Configuration Protocol. A method of centrally assigning TCP/IP address and configuration information to clients at boot time.

directory partition—A logical division of the directory namespace for replication purposes.

disabled user account—A user account can be marked so it can't be used without actually deleting it. This process is known as *disabling* the account and can be achieved through Active Directory Users and Computers.

discontiguous namespace—Namespace based on several different root domains, such as **example.com** and **another.example**.

discretionary access control list (DACL)—A list of access control entries that specify permissions on an object.

DNS—Domain Name System. A hierarchical name system used in its simplest form to map IP addresses to host names and vice versa. In addition to mapping host names to IP addresses, other types of resource records perform other functions. For example, SRV resource records map services to hostnames.

DNS server—A computer running a DNS server service.

domain—In Windows 2000, a domain is a logical division of the network that shares a common Active Directory database.

domain consolidation—The process of migrating to a small number of domains by combining objects from existing domains.

domain controller—A computer that provides authentication and security services to a domain. In Windows 2000, domain controllers have Active Directory installed.

domain hierarchy—A structure of Windows 2000 domains in parent-child relationships.

Domain Name System (DNS)—A hierarchical name system used to map IP addresses to host names and vice versa.

domain naming master—The forest-wide Windows 2000 operations master role responsible for ensuring that newly created Windows 2000 domains don't conflict with other domains in the tree.

domain tree—A logical arrangement of Windows 2000 domains that form a contiguous DNS namespace, so that all domain names end in the name of the tree-root domain.

dotted decimal notation—A commonly used method of representing IP addresses that converts each octet of a 32-bit IP address into a decimal number in the range 0–255.

dynamic update—A DNS mechanism whereby clients or DHCP servers are responsible for maintaining records in the DNS database (instead of it having to be managed manually).

EFS—Encrypting File System. A feature of the new version of NTFS in Windows 2000 that allows files and folders to be transparently encrypted. EFS also supports recovery and key management.

emergency repair disk (ERD)—A floppy disk containing vital system recovery information. In Windows 2000. ERDs can be generated with the Backup utility.

Encrypting File System (EFS)—A feature of the new version of NTFS in Windows 2000 that allows files and folders to be transparently encrypted. EFS also supports recovery and key management.

Glossary

File Replication Service—A Windows 2000 service responsible for replicating files between computers. It can be used to synchronize replica of fault-tolerant Dfs links and is used by domain controllers to replicate the sysvol folder structure between domain controllers.

flexible single master operations (FSMO)—An old name for the operations master roles (schema, domain naming, primary domain controller [PDC] Emulator, Relative Identifiers [RIDs], and infrastructure).

folder redirection—A mechanism that allows My Documents, My Pictures, Desktop, Start menu, and Application Data.

forest—A collection of Active Directory trees that share a common root, common schema, single Global Catalog, and two-way transitive trusts between tree-root domains.

forward lookup—A DNS query that converts a hostname into an IP address.

forwarder—A DNS server that isn't a root server and is configured to pass on queries that it can't authoritatively resolve to external DNS servers.

fragmentation—The process in database files or hard disks whereby parts of rows of data or files are scattered throughout the file or disk. This improves write times but impacts performance.

FSMO—Flexible single master operations. An old name for the operations master roles (schema, domain naming, PDC Emulator, RID, and infrastructure).

full replica—A complete copy of a directory partition that's held by a domain controller. This contrasts with the partial replica of some partitions held by Global Catalog servers.

full zone transfer (AXFR)—A DNS replication operation where an entire zone file is copied, instead of individual updates.

garbage collection interval—The time period between Active Directory's garbage collection process. The default interval is 12 hours, and after this time, processes, such as the removal of expired tombstones and online defragmentation, take place.

Global Catalog—A forest-wide subset of Active Directory attributes used to accelerate query operations and make information from other domains more highly available.

Global Catalog server—A Windows 2000 domain controller that also hosts a copy of the Global Catalog.

Global Group—A Windows 2000 group scope.

Group Policy—The Windows 2000 replacement for Windows NT system policy. Group Policy is used to provide specific settings for users and computers, such as desktop lockdown, application assignments, and startup scripts.

Hardware Compatibility List (HCL)—A Microsoft-produced document detailing hardware compatibility with a given operating system. For Windows 2000, it can be found in the \support\hcl folder of the installation CD.

incremental zone transfer (IXFR)—The DNS replication process whereby only changes to a zone are replicated, as opposed to the entire zone files.

infrastructure master—A Windows 2000 operations master role responsible for cleaning up stale links to other objects in the forest. This role shouldn't be placed on a Global Catalog server (unless all domain controllers in a domain are Global Catalog servers).

inheritance—The process whereby a child object obtains settings or permissions because they were assigned to its parent object. In Windows 2000, for example, hard disk permissions are inherited.

IXFR—Incremental zone transfer. The DNS replication process whereby only changes to a zone are replicated, as opposed to the entire zone files.

Kerberos—A three-headed authentication protocol in Windows 2000 that uses a key distribution center to grant tickets to clients, which use these tickets to access services.

Key Distribution Center (KDC)—In Kerberos, the KDC is the center for trust and security in a network, because it issues tickets to clients. In Windows 2000, domain controllers are KDCs.

Knowledge Consistency Checker (KCC)—A Windows 2000 process that runs periodically to calculate the optimum Active Directory replication topology.

LDAP—Lightweight Directory Access Protocol. A standard method of directory service access. Windows 2000 Active Directory supports LDAP versions 2 and 3.

LDAP Data Interchange Format (LDIF)—A standardized text-based representation of entries and changes to LDAP directories. LDIF can be used to export directories and to make changes through the **ldifde.exe** utility.

load balancing—A process whereby client traffic is distributed between several potential servers. Active Directory operations are load balanced by DNS, and other services can be load balanced with the aid of Windows 2000 Advanced Server.

Glossary

Local Group—A group hosted on a member server or workstation, local in scope to that machine.

local policy—Policy settings similar to Group Policy that are applied to an individual computer.

log file—Usually a text file written to sequentially, with status information from a process. For example, Web servers use log files to record client requests, adding a new line for each "hit".

log off—Stop using a network connection or local computer.

log on—The process of authenticating with a computer or network resource.

mandatory attributes—Attributes of a directory object that must be specified.

master domain—A Windows NT domain that holds user accounts and is usually trusted by one or more resource domains. It's also known as an account domain.

master server—A DNS server that's the source of a zone transfer for a secondary server for the zone. A master server could either be a primary zone server, or another secondary server that (directly or indirectly) replicated from the primary server.

member server—A computer running Windows NT or 2000 Server that's joined to a domain but not configured as a domain controller. In many respects, such as local user and group management, member servers behave in the same way as client computers joined to the domain.

metadata—Data stored about data, such as replication information stored with objects in Active Directory.

metric—An arbitrary number used to specify the cost in an IP routing table or the replication cost between Active Directory sites.

Microsoft Management Console (MMC)—The common framework for Windows 2000 administration tools. Individual tools take the form of Snap-ins.

migrate—To move from one system to another. In the context of Windows 2000, migration is a general term that refers to both upgrading to Windows 2000 or moving to a parallel Windows 2000 environment by means of restructuring and copying objects.

Mixed mode—One of the two possible Windows 2000 domain modes. Mixed-mode domains support Windows NT backup domain controllers (BDCs) at the expense of certain new features, such as Universal Groups that are unavailable. Mixed-mode domains can be converted to Native mode with Active Directory Users and Computers.

MMC—Microsoft Management Console. The common framework for Windows 2000 administration tools. Individual tools take the form of Snap-ins.

.msi—Microsoft Installer files. These msi files have replaced the traditional setup.exe file as the installation files for applications. They may deployed to users and computers via Group Policy.

.msp—Patch files. Vendor-provided patches can be applied to msi files to update them to the latest version. A patched software application should be redeployed by Group Policy so that it's reinstalled by client system.

.mst—Transform files. They may be attached to msi files deployed via Group Policy to provide custom settings. They may only be added at deployment time.

multi-master—An environment where multiple copies of the same data exist but where each hosting server can make authoritative changes to the underlying data.

mutual authentication—A process whereby a client and server each verify the other's identity.

name resolution—The process whereby a name (NetBIOS, DNS, or whatever) is converted into an address (such as an IP address). This function can be performed in a number of ways, such as by DNS, Windows Internet Name Service (WINS), a hosts file, or an lmhosts file.

name server—A DNS server.

name server (NS) resource record—A DNS resource record that specifies an authoritative name server for a zone.

naming context—Another term for directory partition. An Active Directory forest has one schema naming context, one configuration naming context, and one naming context per domain.

Native mode—One of two possible Windows 2000 domain modes. Native mode domains don't support downlevel Windows NT domain controllers, which are incompatible with the new features, such as group nesting and Universal Group scopes that it enables. The switch to Native mode from Mixed mode is one-way and doesn't affect any clients—only downlevel domain controllers.

NDS—Novell Directory Services. The directory service included with Novell's NetWare network operating system. It's also available for other platforms, such as Unix and Windows NT.

nested groups—In Windows 2000 Native mode domains, Global Groups can be placed inside Global and Universal Groups, and Universal Groups within other Universal Groups, in order to assign permissions to group members. This process is known as group nesting.

NetBIOS—Network Basic Input/Output System. The network application programming interfaces (API) used by Windows NT domain operations.

NetBIOS name—A computer, user, group, or domain name that's compatible with NetBIOS operations.

Netdiag—A Windows 2000 command-line utility used to diagnose and fix network and connectivity problems. It is found in the Windows 2000 Support Tools.

Netdom—A Windows 2000 command-line utility used to manage Windows 2000 domains and trusts.

Netsh—A Windows 2000 command-line utility used to manage and script network configuration.

network basic input/output system (NetBIOS)—The network API used by Windows NT domain operations.

nontransitive trust relationship—Trust relationships that don't flow through. Interforest and Windows NT trust relationships are intransitive.

Novell Directory Services (NDS)—The directory service included with Novell's NetWare network operating system. It's also available for other platforms, such as Unix and Windows NT.

Nslookup—A command-line utility used to query name servers. For Windows 2000 Active Directory, it's useful for diagnosing DNS problems.

octet—A group of eight. Particularly, it refers to one quarter of an IP v4 address (8 of 32 bits).

one-level search—A search of an Active Directory that tests only immediate children of the target. For example, a one-level search of the Sales OU would match user accounts directory in that OU, but not user accounts in child OUs.

operations master—A domain controller that holds one of the operations master roles, such as a PDC Emulator or schema master.

Organizational Unit (OU)—An Active Directory child object used to divide domains. OUs can be used for administrative delegation or Group Policy linkage.

originating update—In Active Directory, an originating update is only made by the domain controller where a change was made to the directory, as opposed to an update that was made elsewhere and replicated in.

owner—In Windows 2000 security, each object has an owner. The owner of an object can grant permissions on an object to other people.

parent-child trust relationship—The two-way transitive trust relationship created automatically between Windows 2000 domains in a tree.

parent domain—In an Active Directory tree, the parent directory of a nonroot domain is its immediate superior. For example, the parent of **foobar.example.com** would be **example.com**.

parent object—The object immediately superior to an object. For example, **cn=Users,dc=example,dc=com** is the parent object of **cn=Jo Smith,cn= Users,dc=example,dc=com**.

partial replica—A subset of attributes for all objects in a given replica. In the context of Active Directory, Global Catalog servers hold partial replicas of each domain partition in the forest.

plaintext—An unencrypted message.

pointer (PTR) resource record—A DNS resource record used to map an IP address to the corresponding hostname.

primary domain controller (PDC)—A Windows NT domain controller that is fully authoritative for a domain. It is the only domain controller that is fully authoritative for a domain. It is the only domain controller that can update domain data. There is no PDC in a Windows 2000 domain, although some PDC functions are performed by the PDC Emulator role holder.

primary domain controller emulator—A per-domain Active Directory operations master role that designates a Windows 2000 domain controller as the pseudo-PDC for the purposes of downlevel clients and domain controllers. It also has a special role to play in other operations, such as account lockout.

primary zone—A copy of a DNS zone that isn't just authoritative but can be updated either manually or (depending on the server) dynamically.

public-key encryption—A class of encryption algorithms that rely on "hard" mathematical problems to use distinct encryption and decryption keys. The "hard" mathematics linking these keys makes it secure enough to publish the encryption (public) key. The other (private) key is then retained to decrypt messages.

Registry—A database on Windows computers that stores computer-, user-, and application-specific settings.

registry key—The Registry is organized hierarchically and the containers that it's organized along—analogous to folders on a hard disk—are known as registry keys.

relative distinguished name (RDN)—The leading component of a distinguished name, that is, the additional component that makes an object's DN different from its parents. For example, the RDN of **cn=Jo Smith,cn=Users, dc=example,dc=com is cn=Jo Smith**.

Remote Installation Service (RIS)—A Windows 2000 service that can be used to deploy Windows 2000 to client computers over the network.

replication—The process of distributing changes between homogenous systems. For Active Directory, it's the process of replication.

resource domain—A term given to a Windows NT domain used to host computers and servers, but only few user accounts.

resource record (RR)—An entry in a DNS zone file. DNS host records provide a mapping from computer names to IP addresses.

RID master—A per-domain Active Directory operations master role whose holder is responsible for allocating pools of relative identifiers to domain controllers, so unique security identifiers can be assigned to each object created in a domain.

roaming profile—A Windows user account profile stored on a network server and copied locally at login, so user-specific settings follow a user around the network.

round robin—A method of answering DNS queries where a query for a record that has multiple-associated values will sequentially return each value first in the list. This provides a primitive form of load balancing.

SACL—System Access Control List. The part of an object's security descriptor that defines which events are audited per user/group.

schema—The definition of attributes and classes that determines exactly what data can be stored in the Active Directory. An Active Directory forest shares a common schema.

schema master—A per-forest Windows 2000 operations master role. The schema master is the only server that can change the forest-wide Active Directory schema.

search base—The DN of an object beneath which an LDAP search takes places.

search filter—An LDAP construct that specifies a pattern to match for an LDAP search. For example, (**objectClass=***) would match everything and (**objectClass =user**) would match only user objects.

search scope—A parameter for LDAP search operations that specifies whether only a single object, a single level, or an entire subtree of the directory should be searched.

secondary zone—In DNS, a secondary zone is a copy of another DNS server's primary zone. Secondary zone can provide authoritative answers to queries but can't be updated locally and must be refreshed by replicating changes in.

Glossary

Security Accounts Manager (SAM)—A Windows subsystem that manages user and group information in Windows NT, on Windows 2000 computers that aren't domain controllers, and for the directory services Restore mode of a Windows 2000 domain controller. The SAM stores its data in the Registry.

security groups—Windows 2000 groups that can be security principals.

Security Identifer (SID)—A unique number assigned to a security principal to identify that security principal. SIDs are composed of the issuing domain's SID and a RID.

security principal—An object, such as a user, computer, service, or group, that has a security identifier and can have rights assigned to it through access control lists.

service (SRV) resource record—A DNS resource record used to specify a service location. In Windows 2000, SRV resource records are used as the location mechanism for domain controllers.

session ticket—A Kerberos ticket issued to clients by a Key Distribution Center (KDC) to grant access to a specific server or service.

shortcut trust—In an Active Directory forest, a shortcut trust is used to accelerate interdomain trust path evaluation by directly linking two domains and bypassing the forest root domain.

Simple Mail Transfer Protocol (SMTP)—The protocol used to send email over the Internet. In Active Directory, SMTP is used as a replication transport protocol for interdomain, intersite replication.

site—An Active Directory object used to denote an area of high network connectivity. In technical terms, it's defined in terms of a number of subnet objects, each of which specify a number of IP addresses. Sites are used by processes, such as Active Directory replication, to optimize network traffic.

site link—A site link bridge specifies that two or more Active Directory sites can communicate and specifies an arbitrary cost for doing so.

site link bridge—An object in Active Directory that represents several site links, which can all communicate with each other over a common transport protocol.

SMTP—Simple Mail Transfer Protocol. The method used to send email over the Internet. In Active Directory, SMTP is used as a replication transfer protocol for interdomain, intersite replication.

SRV (service) resource record—A DNS resource record used to specify a service location. In Windows 2000, SRV resource records are used as the location mechanism for domain controllers.

stand-alone server—A Windows 2000 server not configured as part of a domain, that is to say, neither a member server nor a domain controller.

start of authority (SOA) resource record—A DNS resource record used to show the origination of authority for a DNS zone and to set zone-wide parameters.

structural classes—An Active Directory class that can be instantiated, that is, you can create objects of structural classes.

subclass—A class derived from another (parent) class. A subclass will inherit all attributes of its parent.

subdomain—A DNS hierarchy beneath a given domain name. For example, **microsoft.com.** is a subdomain of the **com.** Domain.

subkey—In the Windows 2000 registry, a subkey is a key beneath another key.

subtree search—An LDAP search that considers all objects beneath the search base, regardless of whether they're immediate children or at lower levels.

synchronous processing—Sequential processing, that is, the default Group Policy processing method whereby one task must finish before another begins. In particular, this means that users can't log on until Group Policy has been fully applied.

Sysprep—A Windows 2000 utility, part of the System Tools deploy.cab file, used to strip unique identifiers and prepare a system for cloning with third-party utilities.

System Access Control List—The part of an object's security descriptor that defines which events are audited per user/group.

%SystemRoot%—An environment variable that refers to the installation directory of the in-use installation of Windows 2000. By default, this is **c:\winnt**.

System State—In Windows 2000 backup, the System State comprises vital data to a system, such as the Registry, startup files, and in the case of domain controllers, Active Directory data.

sysvol—The shared system volume. A directory share on a Windows 2000 domain controller that contains directory information, such as Group Policy Templates (the file portions of Group Policy Objects [GPOs], including items such as logon scripts).

TCP/IP—Transmission Control Protocol/Internet Protocol. The network protocol used by the Internet and one that's required for Windows 2000 Active Directory domains.

Telnet—A network service providing a text interface to a remote computer. Although typically associated with Unix, Windows 2000 includes a Telnet server that can be used to provide remote command-prompt functionality.

ticket granting ticket—A Kerberos ticket issued by a Key Distribution Center at logon.

tombstone—When an object is deleted in Active Directory, it isn't initially deleted but is, instead, tombstoned, so the fact of its deletion can be replicated throughout the domain.

tombstone lifetime—The time until a directory object's tombstone expires. After this time, the fact that the object has been deleted will no longer be replicated. Therefore, Active Directory backups older than the tombstone lifetime are useless, and you should ensure that your network will converge in less than the tombstone lifetime.

transitive trust relationship—A trust relationship which flows through, so domains that transitively trust Domain A will automatically trust any other domains which are transitively trusted by Domain A.

tree-root trust relationship—A trust relationship between the root domain of an Active Directory tree and the root domain of a forest.

trust relationship—A relationship between two domains that allows pass-through authentication from the trusted domain to the trusting domain, This means that permissions can be granted in the trusting domain to the trusted domain's security principals.

two-way trust relationship—A relationship between Windows domains where resources from each are available to users in the other (according to permissions).

unallocated space—A portion of a hard disk drive not assigned to a particular partition of a hard disk. At least 1MB of unallocated space is required to convert a disk from basic to dynamic storage.

UNC—Uniform Naming Convention. A method of addressing servers and network shares of the form **\\server\share**.

unique sequence number (USN)—A 64-bit number specific to a particular domain controller used to uniquely identify a change to the directory made on that server. Sequential USNs are given to successive changes.

Universal Group—A Windows 2000 group scope that's only available for Security Groups in Native mode. Universal Security Groups can contain User, Global, and Universal Groups from all domains in a tree and be added to access control lists in all domains of a forest.

Glossary

up-to-dateness vector—A vector consisting of a domain controller's Globally Unique Identifier (GUID) and the highest originating unique sequence number (USN) received. The up-to-dateness vector is used to determine whether a particular piece of replication data has already been committed to the directory.

user ticket—Another name for a Kerberos ticket granting ticket obtained at logon and used to obtain session tickets from a KDC without needing to reauthenticate.

virtual memory—Space used on hard disks as additional memory. This is transparent to applications, and virtual memory is used to extend physical RAM. Portions of memory, known as pages, are swapped between physical and virtual memory according to usage.

wide area network (WAN)—A network of geographically separate computers. The term *WAN link* is used to refer to the network infrastructure, such as a leased line of modem connection between two local area networks (LANs).

Windows Installer (.msi files)—The Windows Installer service used to manage software installation and removal.

Windows Internet Name Service (WINS)—A service that maps IP addresses to NetBIOS hostnames.

Windows Management Instrumentation (WMI)—Microsoft implementation/extension of the Web-Based Enterprise Management (WBEM) initiative. It provides programmatical access to and control of Windows components.

WINS—Windows Internet Name Service. A service that maps IP addresses to NetBIOS hostnames.

ZAP (.zap) file—A script file that takes Windows INI file format used to deploy legacy application with Group Policy.

zone—A DNS zone is a contiguous portion of the DNS namespace that forms an administrative unit.

zone file—A text file stored on a DNS server that holds the resource records for a particular zone. In Windows 2000, zone files are stored, by default, in %SystemRoot%\system32\dns. Active Directory-integrated zones don't have zone files because their data is stored in the domain partition of the directory itself.

zone transfer—The process where one portion of the DNS space (a zone) is replicated from one DNS server to another. This process can either be incremental (IXFR) or complete (AXFR) and could be the result of a notification or a period refresh.

Glossary

Index

Symbols

(comment sign), 415
:: (double colon separator), 430
/ (forward slash), 277
_ (underscore), 55, 138
%# token, 364
%First token, 364
%Last token, 364
%MAC token, 364
%Username token, 364
-i switch, 429
-k switch, 429
-y switch, 429
_msdcs protocol, 138
_tcp prefix, 137
/dsdel parameters, 96
/SAFEBOOT:DSREPAIR switch, 411

A

A records, 72
Abstract class objects, 221
Access control entry. *See* ACE.
Account Lockout Policy, 319, 482
Account Policies, 318
ACE, 244
ACL Diagnostics tool, 40
    discretionary, 245
    system-audit, 245
acldiag.exe utility, 40
Active Desktop, 345
Active Directory
    Address Book queries, 522
    administration features, 4–5
    authentication during installation, 109
    authoritative restoration, 426
    automated removal of, 463
    benefits of, 4
    component relocation, 414

    data exports, 414–415
    data imports, 414–415
    file imports, 429
    installing, 21, 108–115, 460
    as LDAP server, 4
    log file relocation, 428
    logical structure, 7
    manual removal of, 116
    minimum requirements, 106–107
    physical structure, 7
    pre-installation planning, 474
    removing, 115–116, 123–124
    resource kit tools, 43–44
    restoring, 413, 425
    schema, 4
    scripted installation, 460–463
    searching, 273–274
    security architecture, 244–245
    subnet objects, 22
    Support Tools, 40–43
    test networks, 26
    user benefits of, 5–6
Active Directory Administration Tool, 40, 133, 147–149
Active Directory Connector. *See* ADC.
Active Directory Diagnostic Tool, 40
Active Directory Domains and Trusts, 29, 166, 168
Active Directory Global Catalog, 274
Active Directory Installation Wizard, 108, 118–119, 498
Active Directory Management Tool, 275, 285–286
Active Directory Migration Tool. *See* ADMT.
Active Directory Object Manager, 40
Active Directory Replication Monitor, 41, 213–214
Active Directory Schema Snap-in, 231
Active Directory Search Tool, 41
Active Directory Service Interface. *See* ADSI.
Active Directory Sites and Services, 29–30, 176–177
Active Directory Size tool, 410–411
Active Directory Users and Computers, 29, 274–275

Related Coriolis Technology Press Titles

Active Server Pages Solutions

By Al Williams, Kim Barber, and Paul Newkirk
ISBN: 1-57610-608-X
Price: $49.99 US • $74.99 CAN
Media: CD-ROM • Available Now

Explores all the components that work with Active Server Pages, such as HTML (including Dynamic HTML), scripting, Java applets, Internet Information Server, Internet Explorer and server-side scripting for VBScript, Jscript, and ActiveX controls. Offers practical examples using commonly used tools.

Windows® 2000 TCP/IP Black Book

By Jan McLean
ISBN: 1-57610-687-X
Price: $49.99 US • $74.99 CAN
Media: CD-ROM • Available Now

Covers the TCP/IP Protocol Suite and tools, utilities, and client services. Takes you through configuration and implementation step by step. Explores Active Directory/TCP/IP integration, new Dynamic Domain Name Services, the latest version of Internet Protocol, Internet Protocol Security, and more.

Windows® 2000 Professional Upgrade Little Black Book

By Nathan Wallace
ISBN: 1-57610-748-5
Price: $29.99 US • $44.99 CAN
Media: None • Available Now

This book includes complete guidance on newly introduced technologies to help administrators upgrade or migrate users of Windows 9x, NT 4, Unix, and Macintosh. Covers advanced features of Windows 2000 Professional using a concise task-oriented approach for quickly accessing solutions.

Windows® Admin Scripting Little Black Book

By Natanya Pitts-Moultis and Cheryl Kirk
ISBN: 1-57610-284-X
Price: $49.99 US • $73.99 CAN
Media: CD-ROM • Available Now

This book takes the reader through the basics of scripting all to advanced topics such as debugging and integrating with other applications and scripting languages. Teaches the Windows administrator to quickly write complex logon scripts without requiring any expertise in programming.

Visual Basic 6 Black Book

By Steven Holzner
ISBN: 1-57610-283-1
Price: $49.99 US • $69.99 CAN
Media: CD-ROM • Available Now

Completely explains the crucial Visual Basic tool set in detail. Jam-packed with insight, programming tips and techniques, and real-world solutions. Covers everything from graphics and image processing, to ActiveX controls, database development and data-bound controls, multimedia, OLE automation, Registry handling, error handling and debugging, Windows API, and more.

Visual Basic 6 Core Language Little Black Book

By Steven Holzner
ISBN: 1-57610-390-0
Price: $24.99 US • $36.99 CAN
Media: None • Available Now

Provides a detailed reference on all Basic control structures, data types, and other code mechanisms. Includes step-by-step instructions on how to build common code structures in VB, from simple if statements to objects and ActiveX components. Not merely a syntax summary, but a detailed reference on creating code structures with VB6 code and data elements.

THE CORIOLIS GROUP, LLC   Telephone: 800.410.0192 • www.coriolis.com
Coriolis books are also available at bookstores and computer stores nationwide.

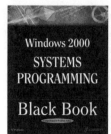
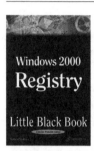